Working in America
A Humanities Reader

Working in America
A Humanities Reader

Edited by
ROBERT SESSIONS
and JACK WORTMAN

UNIVERSITY OF NOTRE DAME PRESS
NOTRE DAME

Library of Congress Cataloging-in-Publication Data

Working in America : a humanities reader / edited by Robert Sessions,
   Jack Wortman.
      p.   cm.
   ISBN 0-268-01947-9
   1. Working class writings, American.   2. Work — Literary
collections.   3. American literature.   4. Work.   I. Sessions,
Robert, 1945- .   II. Wortman, Jack.
PS508.W73W67   1992
808.8'0355 — dc20   91-50579
                                                              CIP
                                                               AC

Contents

To
Lori Erickson
and
Deanne Wortman

Robert Frost

Two Tramps in Mud Time
Or, A Full-Time Interest

Out of the mud two strangers came
And caught me splitting wood in the yard.
And one of them put me off my aim
By hailing cheerily "Hit them hard!"
I knew pretty well why he dropped behind
And let the other go on a way.
I knew pretty well what he had in mind:
He wanted to take my job for pay.

Good blocks of beech it was I split,
As large around as the chopping block;
And every piece I squarely hit
Fell splinterless as a cloven rock.
The blows that a life of self-control
Spares to strike for the common good
That day, giving a loose to my soul,
I spent on the unimportant wood.

The sun was warm but the wind was chill.
You know how it is with an April day
When the sun is out and the wind is still,
You're one month on in the middle of May.
But if you so much as dare to speak,
A cloud comes over the sunlit arch,
A wind comes off a frozen peak,
And you're two months back in the middle of March.

A bluebird comes tenderly up to alight
And fronts the wind to unruffle a plume,
His song so pitched as not to excite
A single flower as yet to bloom.
It is snowing a flake: and he half knew

Winter was only playing possum.
Except in color he isn't blue,
But he wouldn't advise a thing to blossom.

The water for which we may have to look
In summertime with a witching-wand,
In every wheelrut's now a brook,
In every print of a hoof a pond.
Be glad of water, but don't forget
The lurking frost in the earth beneath
That will steal forth after the sun is set
And show on the water its crystal teeth.

The time when most I loved my task
These two must make me love it more
By coming with what they came to ask.
You'd think I never had felt before
The weight of an axe-head poised aloft,
The grip on earth of outspread feet,
The life of muscles rocking soft
And smooth and moist in vernal heat.

Out of the woods two hulking tramps
(From sleeping God knows where last night,
But not long since in the lumber camps).
They thought all chopping was theirs of right.
Men of the woods and lumberjacks,
They judged me by their appropriate tool.
Except as a fellow handled an axe,
They had no way of knowing a fool.

Nothing on either side was said.
They knew they had but to stay their stay
And all their logic would fill my head:
As that I had no right to play
With what was another man's work for gain.
My right might be love but theirs was need.
And where the two exist in twain
Theirs was the better right — agreed.

But yield who will to their separation,
My object in living is to unite
My avocation and my vocation
As my two eyes make one in sight.
Only where love and need are one,
And the work is play for mortal stakes,
Is the deed ever really done
For Heaven and the future's sakes.

Introduction

Work and the Humanities

Although to understand an historical period until long after it has passed is notoriously difficult, many people today speculate that we are experiencing a dramatic historical transformation. While science and technology have made us more capable of predicting and controlling nearly every aspect of our world, from the weather to our own genetic make-ups, many people increasingly feel powerless in the face of the profound changes occurring in their lives. Just as we are coming to grips with population problems, we are faced with questions of genetic screening and test-tube babies; and just as we become proficient in one occupation, it becomes obsolete and we must be retrained. Our living patterns, our methods of education, our attitudes toward other countries, and our personal identities all seem to be as much a matter of taste and fad as changes in diets or clothes—the rapidity as well as the amounts and kinds of change leave us standing culturally on volcanic ground.

Most people feel these historic tremors most strongly in the workplace. Jobs and their rewards form the center around which most of our lives revolve. Jobs provide us with more than income to meet our basic needs—we derive much of our identities, values, social respectability, attitudes, beliefs, habits, and social relations from our work and work environments. To be without a job in our society is to be nearly invisible. We do work, but work also does us—it makes us much of what we are. If work is fundamentally transformed, more than our paychecks or job security will be altered—we will also change, we will become different people. And if work is the center of our lives, then there is no better place to begin looking for a glimpse of "the great transformation" that is happening to and in us.

Karl Polanyi's classic study of the change from preindustrial to industrial society bore the title *The Great Transformation*. In Europe that profound alteration in the fabric of society and of human nature has taken several hundred years, and in America the aftershocks of the Industrial Revolution are still being felt nearly 200 years after the beginning of in-

3

dustrialization of the textile industry in 1807.* The pace of change has quickened dramatically. In the 1980s more than 90 percent of the new jobs created in America were in the so-called service sector, a dramatic shift from the expansion of industrial jobs in evidence as recently as the 1960s. Nearly overnight we have changed from an industrial to a post-industrial society, from an international economy of manufacture where American products were symbolic of quality and Japanese goods represented inferiority, to an economy where the Japanese (and others) produce the goods and we provide services and purchase their goods. New threats to our prominence and material abundance occur almost daily, whether from the emergence of a powerful united Europe, the entry of yet more Asian nations such as South Korea or Taiwan into industrial competition, or the loss of cheap oil from the Mideast. The golden age of American industrialism appears to have ended abruptly, and we are scrambling to find our way in a deindustrializing landscape.

For working Americans the effects are profound. Gone are the days when a high-school graduate (or dropout) working on the assembly line could earn enough to secure a suburban home, two cars, an expensive RV, and an annual monthlong vacation. Gone are the days when unions secured contracts that brought their members wages of 20 dollars per hour plus benefit packages which nearly doubled this income. Gone, too, is the security that comes with continuity, with a company or plant that produces basically the same products in the same way at the same location over a worker's lifetime. Gone in equal measure is the security that follows from knowing that if your company changes its production line, your acquired skills will serve you well on the next job; in contrast, welding joints on an auto chassis and operating a robot that welds are alike in name only—one requires the ability to weld, the other the skills of a computer operator. Finally, we must accept the changing landscape of *jobs.* While there is plenty of work to be done, good jobs are becoming increasingly scarce. In our society (and world) we face a future where fewer and fewer people will have access to the increasing wealth in our society through jobs—technology is replacing more and more human labor, whether in manufacture, service work, or white-collar jobs.

For those who manage to find new jobs, the need for rapid and frequent changes of skills is only the surface of what workers face. Learning a new trade or technical skill often creates significant displacement in a worker's life. Often people have to return to school and interrupt their

---

*Raymond Williams' excellent book on the Industrial Revolution is called *The Long Revolution,* wherein he sees this sweeping historical movement continuing and in fact speeding up rather than being a past event.

life patterns and styles. Having to become a different kind of person, though, poses more difficult challenges. When a worker changes from industrial to service work, s/he not only usually loses half of her/his income, but the new work calls for an entirely different personal orientation—away from products and toward people. Even industrial workers who manage to keep their manufacturing jobs cannot escape this profound transition. Leading industries, mainly in response to the low productivity and quality of American workmanship and products, are now toying with modes of production that require workers to have good communication skills, imagination, leadership, and creativity. While these forays into "workplace democracy" (quality circles and other team approaches that are "worker oriented") may ultimately make the workplace a more desirable and humane place to be, the human characteristics that industry is looking for are far different from what many workers possess, and they are not as easy to come by as changes in technical skills. Dramatic changes in people's understanding of work, in their educations, and often in personality will be required before this new age of working can come about.

Few people would deny that our economy and our lives are changing rapidly. Since the 1970s women have rejoined the workforce in large numbers, and estimates are that nearly a million more women would join the paid work force tomorrow if jobs were available and if they could find adequate child care. The feminization of work has profoundly altered the workplace and has simultaneously brought about dramatic changes in family life, child rearing, poverty statistics, and politics. Just as we can view automation through the lens of lost jobs and a diminishment of human work, we can likewise view the massive reentry of women into the paid work force as a threat to men and their employment. Certainly in the experiences of many individuals automation and other workplace innovations have meant the loss of employment, and many men have lost their jobs to women. Nevertheless, these and other dimensions of the contemporary work revolution need not be viewed as negative.

Some people see the diminishment of menial jobs in a positive light. They believe that we have reached the point in our productivity where we can begin to realize fully the promises of the Industrial Revolution— the elimination of menial, meaningless, degrading work and the universal enjoyment of a level of wealth and free time which allows people to devote much of their best energies to human enrichment. The economic enfranchisement of women, seen through this lens, is part of the fulfillment of this promise. Obviously many workers (e.g., displaced and frustrated workers and most unemployed workers) have yet to experience the full effects of this great new transformation, and in fact only a small percentage of the work force has any experience with the wonders of this promise. The majority experience upheaval, disappointment, diminishment, and insecurity.

How could anyone realistically believe that working will be transformed for the better? Much of this book is aimed at answering this question. Or perhaps more accurately, this book is meant to help you think about work in such a way that you come to understand that the future of working need not resemble the past, that a very different and much happier human work experience is possible *if* you and others imagine and bring it into existence.

Like any humans, our first reaction to dramatic and threatening changes is to focus on survival: what can we do to survive this postindustrial revolution? We do what humans always have done, of course — we adapt. Just as our mothers and fathers, our grandparents and greatgrandparents, coming off farms learned to live in cities and submerge themselves in buildings where they barely saw the light of day or felt the changing of the seasons so crucial in their rural pasts, we too will change our sleeping patterns, our knowledge and skills, our diets, our goals and interests, and our very personalities to meet the demands of the new workplaces. We will become different human beings, different from any preceding generation, different from what we once were. What choice do we have? Can we change history? Can we do more than make adjustments in ourselves which accommodate the changes our society and world create and require?

This description makes our situation seem utterly hopeless. Our lives appear to be shaped by forces beyond our control: we are left without a say in what happens to us or what we become. Like lemmings or trees, humans adapt. But this generalization masks a world of options and values. We will adapt, but how? And why?

The 35-year-old former machinist who earned $30,000/year and now works at a fast-food restaurant for minimum wage to support himself and his family has a host of choices which neither he nor we should ignore, because which choices he makes and how he makes them will affect what he becomes, what his children become, and the many subtle features which determine the fabric of his life. He could decide to return to school in a variety of retraining programs; he could join a workers' collective where he would share jobs, tools, and skills; he could move to a different part of the country where his machinist skills are still in demand (for the moment); or he could continue with his fast-food job, asking his wife and children to work part-time and hoping he will soon move up the occupational ladder. Few people in our society are without substantial options. How he makes his decisions and the attitudes and perspective with which he approaches his new life will determine his happiness, his sense of himself, his health, the continuation of his family, the values his children learn from him, his community involvements, and ultimately the shape of his entire community. It is no wonder that some philosophers claim that to make a choice as seemingly simple and innocent as whether or not to continue cooking hamburgers is nothing less than to choose a world . . . and one's self.

But do we actually make such choices? Or are we more like the mere biological creatures implied by the word 'adapt'? Whether or not we are self-conscious in our choices, we still make them; and whether or not we realize how far-reaching are the implications of our decisions, the effects occur. The issue is not whether we will make such crucial decisions or if the choices we make will determine significant features of our lives; rather the issues have to do with the quality of our decisions and our measure of control over the results. Our knowledge of the forces involved in our situations, in bringing us to this historic moment, in shaping our economy and our labor markets, our knowledge of ourselves, of our desires, needs, values, and character, and our understanding of the forces working toward the future can have a great impact on the meaning of our decisions and the subsequent contours of our lives.

We learn these things from many sources and in many situations, of course, but one major source of insight about work and how it shapes us which too often gets ignored is the *humanities*. The art, literature, history, and philosophy that constitute the humanities often is viewed by humanists and the general public alike as irrelevant to practical matters like work; and indeed much of the literature which comprises the body of the humanities does not speak clearly or directly to work or other everyday concerns. Nevertheless, humanists can speak and have spoken about work in ways which can make a significant difference to our machinist trying to decide how to make a living.

Consider our example once again. The self-understanding which our worker might get from reading a short story on the plight of workers in an imaginary factory, the insights which a study of the history of wage labor might yield, or the imagination which could be stimulated from studying how people in another culture have dealt with similar issues of living might very well have profound impact on how our machinist approaches the reconstruction of his own work life. If he understands the historical, philosophical, and literary ideas offered by the humanities, the machinist will attempt more than an individualistic change of his habits or attitudes. He will realize that he must understand the social structures and forces which produced his habits, and that an intelligent attempt to change the sources of his condition will require him to work with others to improve his community.

To make this aspect more concrete, consider a fairly recent moment in history, the beginning of the Industrial Revolution. Two hundred years ago most people did not go to work; instead, they worked at home on the farm. In 1800 over 90 percent of Americans were farmers. Most people who lived in towns (there were no real cities) did not work in factories. The few factories that existed were small operations, with relatively few workers, no assembly lines, and fairly primitive machinery. For most people there was no clock, and workers moved in time with the sun and the seasons. Most of the living people made was based on growing and making their own or on trading, instead of basing their "home economies" on wages and money. In that not-so-distant past before their worlds were turned upside down, most production took place in people's homes.

The forces of industrialization hit people like a tidal wave. Within a century 95 percent of the farmers were driven off the land and into towns and cities where they became part of the industrial wage system. Nearly every part of their lives — their languages, self-conceptions, and child-rearing practices as well as obvious material and workplace changes — was altered. Yet by cooperating to affect the new contours of life, workers had an impact on their new worlds: labor unions helped to curtail the hours in a working day from sixteen to twelve to eight, concerned workers joined together to force improvements in safety and health conditions on the job, and in countless ways people were successful in making improvements in their work environments and in their lives in general.

While the forces bringing the global changes of the Industrial Revolution were mostly beyond the control of any given individual worker, a careful reading of history shows that workers had a great deal to do with shaping the changes that occurred; and to a significant extent the abilities of people to affect their own lives involved the kinds of feelings, knowledge, and perspective which are central to the humanities.

At the heart of the humanities are questions, questions which stir the imagination, generate reflection and understanding, and which ultimately can motivate as well as inform action. Studying work from a humanities perspective helps us unfold the multiple meanings, values, and effects of work so that workers can more fully appreciate the power of work to create us and our capacities to shape work. Without understanding how work has been done at other times and places we are less likely to be intelligent about our own work. Without comprehending how work can mold our personalities, determine our feelings and values, and affect every aspect of our social patterns, we will be unable to comprehend how work can be liberating as well as confining, or how we might turn bad work into good. The great transformation we are witnessing only obliquely will evoke less humane results if we fail to imagine the many futures of work which might have been.

This book is organized into three sections. After a thought-provoking essay by philosopher Frithjof Bergmann on the future of work in which he explores in more detail many of the issues we have just previewed, Section I will help you examine further dimensions of the world that underlie our experiences of work. We often are ambivalent about our work: part of us wants to stop working, while another part feels an urge to continue working. Why do we experience this conflict? What can we do about it? We also often have mixed feelings about the rewards for which we work: we would love to be rich and have the many luxuries and toys wealth affords, and yet a part of us feels uneasy about ignoring spiritual, community, and moral needs in order to achieve material abundance. Further conflicts of feelings and values characterize our experiences of work: most of us live in towns and cities, and yet many Americans still harbor a deep love for the simple rural life combined with a distaste for urban living. We are also torn between a desire to fit in and a deep urge to rebel, to be our own person despite powerful forces to conform. Finally, we perhaps experience the greatest conflicts when we undergo the forces that tend to pull us apart, to dis-integrate us, to make us at odds in our work and home lives, with our fellow workers, with our natural surroundings, and with our selves . . . in a word, modern workers often are alienated.

These and other complex features make work a place where we act out many major issues of our lives. The central purpose of Section I is to help you imagine, conceptualize, and deal with these and other issues concerning work. Through the selections by poets, philosophers, literary artists, and others from our own and other cultures we hope you will learn more about your own work and begin to imagine a future of work that is as fulfilling as Robert Frost hopes in his poem "Two Tramps at Mud Time": "My object in living is to unite / My avocation and my vocation / As my two eyes make one in sight."

While Section I will focus on personal and immediate experiences of work, Section II is concerned with broader social and historical questions. The humanities can help us become more aware of and reflective on the subtle contours of our experience, but they can also help us stand back and view ourselves as players in larger historical and cultural stories. In the first part of this section you are offered a brief look at some of the historical foundations of contemporary work from the worlds of ancient Greece and medieval Europe. You will see that our world of work is both vastly different from, and in certain ways very much like, work in those past times. The Greek and the Medieval people have given us many of our values, attitudes, and habits of work, but we have transformed them in crucial ways to create modern work.

The second part of Section II is devoted to an exploration of the foundations of modern work. By examining works by philosophers, poets, literary writers, and historians we will not only try to show you the conceptual and institutional foundations of modern work, but we will also ask you to reflect on the meanings and values that underlie our unique views and practices of work. Our historically new ways of working have brought unimagined material results, but they have also changed nearly everything about how we live and what kinds of beings we are. We believe the future of work will be a happy one for you and your children only if we understand the nature of modern work and can evaluate it objectively. Section II is meant to contribute to that understanding.

With the background provided by the questioning insights in the first two sections, you should be prepared for perspectives on the revisioning of work that is at the heart of Section III. While the humanities do not offer predictions or prognostications, they do provide images and visions. Which, if any, of these visions come to pass will depend on how powerful they are . . . and on which ones you choose to embody.

In the first part of Section III we offer you images of working from other cultures. Just as history can tell us a great deal about whom we are and where we are headed, viewing ourselves from the vantage of another culture can often give us a powerful perspective on ourselves. At the very least we expect that you will learn that work need not be as we know it, but it is also possible that you will learn, from the non-Western traditions we have selected, very different approaches to work that are quite applicable to your own situation.

The final part of the book centers around the question Why work? Asked in a serious way, this question could change our work and our entire lives for the better. As a nation and a world we possess today the capacity to meet the material needs of most people with less and less human labor. One farmer today, with the most advanced technologies available, can produce as much food as 200 farmers could 100 years ago. The same relative improvement in productive capacity exists in nearly every basic area: one trucker today can do the work of hundreds a century ago, one assembler can outperform his or her predecessors, and so on. Why work? Or at least, why work so hard? The visionaries in the final part of this book take this question very seriously, and in doing so are leading us to a new world. You will be surprised (and hopefully enlightened and motivated) by their answers. Work need not be drudgery, it need not be tied to jobs, it need not be contrary to the highest human accomplishments, and it need not require environmental devastation. In fact, work of the right sort may be necessary for human flourishing as well as be contrary to these undesirable characteristics.

Introduction
Frithjof Bergmann, "The Future of Work"

Philosopher Frithjof Bergmann raises the question and the challenge which will haunt and guide us through this book. He asks, "What will work be like in the future?" and he shows how this question is tantamount to a more fundamental question—"What will *we* be like in the future?" Bergmann believes, as do many other people represented in this book, that a major (and inevitable) product of our labors is our selves. Thus the challenge: in shaping the future of work we shape the selves we and our children will become; what shall we do? What begins as a question that seems answerable by social scientists and other predictors of trends has become a deep moral or religious question; Bergmann has shifted us from being observers to being participants.

Bergmann begins, like many other critics of contemporary life, by observing that although relative to most humans in most of human history we have much greater material abundance than anyone has ever had, people continue to work very hard. Furthermore, as we get more, the relative value of ever more hard work diminishes in comparison with our actual material needs and with the value of what we might do if we had more nonwork time. Why do we work so hard?

Unlike many critics of our contemporary way of life, Bergmann does not conclude that people should quit working or at least work much less. Instead, he takes seriously what people get from their work besides money —social status, a sense of self and self worth, social life, enjoyment, relief from unhappy aspects of their personal lives, and so on. Rather than recommending a reduction or elimination of work, Bergmann argues for its improvement.

Although modern industrial societies have enriched our lives in many ways (especially materially), Bergmann believes that much of human potential cannot be fulfilled given the nature of most people's work. In order to enrich our lives and communities, he thinks we must take seriously the question of what work is for. His answer is that work fundamentally is where human creation and creativity occur: to be human is to be a doer, to be a maker; thus, only through productive activity can we become fully human.

At this point Bergmann's challenge (enhance yourself and your community) becomes an invitation: while perhaps in the early stages of industrial society we had to do machine-like work, today we have perfected actual machines to such an extent that increasing amounts of our time can be spent doing more truly human work. Automation, that invention of the devil from the workers' point of view, need not be contrary to our deepest values — we can eliminate the dehumanizing effects of traditional factory work or other jobs where humans act like cogs in a giant machine, *and* we can also avoid the elimination of human work. Bergmann contends that at this historic moment we can have jobs to meet our material needs, and we can also have meaningful work to meet our spiritual (uniquely human) needs.

This vision, what Bergmann calls "good work," is a basic thread which runs through this book. While we have much to do to actualize this ideal for most workers, you might be surprised to discover how far we have come. As you read this essay, personalize your response to this philosopher's ideas — ask yourself what it would take for your job to become good work.

Frithjof Bergmann does not spend all his time speculating on work. When not teaching philosophy and anthropology at the University of Michigan or writing numerous articles and books (he currently is working on a book on the philosophy of work), Bergmann works with auto workers in Flint, Michigan. He helped establish the Center for New Work in Flint, which is dedicated to solving the many problems that layoffs and unemployment have created in that community.

Frithjof Bergmann

The Future of Work

At the moment we have no picture of a future — certainly we do not have an image of a more attractive, better, maybe even nobler social order that we could aim for, for which it would make sense to exert ourselves, let alone to struggle. One by one, like lights, the visions have gone out.

———————

Consider then, simply as an opening proposition, the idea that half of the sum-total of the now existing jobs could be soon eliminated; and do not take this primarily as a prediction, but think of it instead as the

From *Praxis International*, 3:4, 1983, 308–323. Reprinted with permission of Basil Blackwell.

summation of a technological capacity which we already possess now, though we, for social reasons, might use it in very different ways. Our first reaction is apt to be a panic. If this were the case, then the kind of unemployment we have had so far might only be a hint at the severity of what is still to come, and unemployment on such a scale evokes the image of a downward spiral on which we might turn at an ever faster pace.

Nonetheless, it should be possible to see this also from a very different perspective: If we could really cut in half the clock-punching and spirit-breaking grind-work that many must still do, does this not also represent a quite astonishing achievement? Do not even the first pages of the Bible describe laboring "in the sweat of one's brow" as a penalty that was incurred for a transgression? Why then is this not the long-awaited commuting of that sentence? Why do we not experience the fact that we can produce as much as or more than we did in the past, but now with only half the effort, as a liberation? Why can we not celebrate this triumph with months-long public festivals, as they would have in Athens?

To associate this capacity mainly with the advent of robots would be a mistake. . . . The technological innovations and devices which really possess the prodigious capacity to reduce by half the still required labor are by comparison with robots very ordinary and bland and inconspicuous and understated. Here are a few examples:

(1) Among the seemingly most innocuous is the electronic deciphering and adding mechanism that with a little beeping noise helps to check out our groceries at supermarkets. Though no fuss accompanied its introduction it all the same has roughly *doubled* the output of every clerk.

(2) The Office is for most Americans a synonym for the place in which they work. Yet that environment is currently in a most powerful transition: a configuration of several interlocking new machines — of which the word-processor is only the most publicized — has reduced Office work in perhaps the same fashion as, earlier, a more numerous set of linked devices compressed housework down to perhaps 1/10 of what it was before. (Remember that doing the laundry took close to two days by itself.)

(3) In many stores — especially in book-stores — a magnetic screening device rings a buzzer if one moves with an unpaid-for piece of merchandise past a magnetic screen. It would be very easy to combine this instrument with the just mentioned electronic check-out mechanism, and to combine these two once more with the technology of automatic banking: the result would be a huge reduction in all the different kinds of sales clerk jobs, for stores of every kind in effect could be converted into large walk-in Vending Automats.

(4) In a number of thinly populated areas the public schools have been permanently closed. All of the teaching is done via cable-television, since

this is incomparably cheaper than doing it 'live' in schools. This is one of numerous examples, which cast doubt on the pacifying notion that only unskilled jobs will be eliminated.

(5) It might sound a little silly, but microwave ovens may soon eliminate jobs by the ten-and-hundred-thousands. Stores that sell sandwiches which one can heat oneself have already sprung up in every state, and "self-cook restaurants" are the logical next step — in some locations one can eat in them already. (In this context it is important that the Mac-Donald Corporation has a larger number of employees in the U.S. than General Motors; and also that a considerable portion of them are people who formerly worked in other jobs — e.g. as real estate agents — so that they now would be unemployed if it were not for fast-food chains.)

This is not even a beginning. One could continue, and go on almost indefinitely. The building and construction industry has just started to make the turn towards "factory-built units." (This term is an attempt to break the associations with mobile or pre-fabricated homes.) If one has ever been a close witness to the fashion in which a bathroom is built now, where all manner of different regulations and territories — the plumber's, the electrician's, the carpenter's, the tile-setter's and so forth — conflict and intersect, then one can easily appreciate how significant the saving in the cost of labor might here be. But there is also transportation: Consider what the spread of containerization is doing just to merchant seamen alone? Or, overlook the still persisting flaws and some of the justified folk-humor, and assess the labor-related implications of a fully automated system of mass-transportation — like that of the BART in the Bay area. And so far we have hardly touched on what is surely the largest single factor: that of computers. They introduce a whole additional dimension. Judging by the great speed with which home-use computers have spread in the two or three years since their introduction a kind of circular pattern is quite likely: Clearly only a small minority will have them. Still, most of the people who do a great deal of flying will not be long without them, and if air-line schedules can be viewed on one's computer, and if the tickets can be bought by it, then the meaning for Travel Agents is all too clear. And the same kind of thinking applies equally to a considerable range of other categories: we have reached the point where a relatively small elite provides large portions of the remaining population with mostly service-related jobs. Yet computers will cut across an extended range of precisely these service jobs, and the range will be considerable, for it might extend from the repairmen (soon one will be able to view the service diagram of one's Dishwasher Timer of or Carburetor of one's car on one's computer screen) to stockbrokers and investment counsellors, but of course also to real estate agents, certainly to every kind of publishing, and the selling and distributing connected with that, but no less to lawyers and physicians, and even to Executives whose activities at the moment are still limited by the time it takes to travel: using a combination of the computer and of T.V., one executive may soon do the job that five or ten do now. So the ratio at which executives might be laid off could be even greater than that for typists or for waiters or for sales-clerks and the rest.

Certainly we cannot simply say that enough jobs will of course be found just because this has always been the case, and why should it be different now? The large, and panoramic picture is more nearly that up until about two hundred years ago ninety percent of the total population lived on farms and therefore did not have jobs at all in our sense. From that perspective one could say that the very notion that everyone could or should have a job came into being only with the Industrial Revolution, and that the brief span in which that idea had any viability may now be past. The last 200 years represented perhaps only a transition or rather a tooling-up period — which are notoriously wasteful and cumbersome — but now that full-grown technology has finally arrived there is no presumption whatsoever that 40 hours of every week for 45 years of everybody's life should be filled by a job. On the contrary: the basic purpose of technology from its first beginnings was the elimination of human labor. This is the common denominator that extends all the way back to the first wheel and from there forwards to the loom and the steam-engine and now to the computer. If there will not be enough jobs in the future it will only mean that we at long last have succeeded!

Agriculture is one enormously large example that illustrates the extent of our great achievement. We have turned the situation on its head: up until as recently as 180 years ago approximately 80 to 90% of the population was required to grow sufficient surplus for the remaining 10 or 20. Now, a mere 5% grows all of our food, and in addition the large quantities which we export. So machines really can make human labor obsolete! Still, the other side of this coin is of course that somewhere between 75 and 85% of the entire workforce was displaced. On one level this bears on the much-repeated mindless adage that it will take as many people to run the computers, and to keep them in repair as these computers will displace. In response to this one can only ask: how many people does it take to maintain and to repair the whole array of our farm-machines? The ratio of the jobs "created" by the maintaining of these machines, relative to those that were displaced may well be 1:10,000, and with computers the proportion could easily be in that same range.

On another level, this fact about agriculture evokes more than any other a comprehensive image of the larger epic in which we are perhaps involved: Starting out with between 80 and 90% of the entire population living and working on farms, we evacuated all but 5% of these. It was machines that made their presence on the land no longer necessary and that drove them off the land. Ever since then this great mass has looked for a new place to settle—like refugees after a war—and for a time they did find a space in manufacturing; but as it turned out that phase was short-lived. Technology developed further and encroached progressively into the area of manufacturing. So people moved again: this time from manufacturing into service. (The standard definition of the much-used word "post-industrial" is that more than 50% of the workforce is in service jobs.) And this brings the drama to its head, for the question is: *What comes after service?* Given the three categories of agriculture, manufacturing and service, it is not at all obvious that there is yet another, fourth such category—let alone one that could have the required breadth. And that makes very vivid one interpretation of the situation we have reached: It is like a Dunkirk with no place to go. And here it is important that progress is still in full swing. New forms of mechanization and labor-saving are still constantly being introduced even into agriculture, and it is of course the same with factories. More overwhelming still, however, is the fact that the service sector may be the area that is under greatest pressure: virtually all of the examples from which we began, from the checking out of groceries, to working as a waiter, right across to being a rental or a travel agent would be classified as "service": so the large new wave of just arriving technological innovations runs precisely into this last and already overcrowded space.

One could add that those who hope that the "Third World" will provide us with jobs by being the great market for which we can boundlessly produce are fearfully deluded. Everything moves and points in exactly the opposite direction: the "Third World" has itself millions of workers looking for jobs—much of the time they are in straits which make them ready to labor for a fraction of our customary wages. So, if anything, the "Third World" represents yet another loss in jobs. For in the same way in which whole blocks of jobs are lost to technology, they are also lost to other, still poorer regions of the world, and not just because parts of the still remaining manufacturing are moved to areas where labor is less costly, but also because these areas are rapidly acquiring technological capacities of their own, so that the tables are gradually being turned: it is not they who are our market, but the reverse: it is we who import what their labor makes.

And this brings yet one further factor on the scene: the steadily increasing and tightening international competition. The fashion in which this affects the availability of jobs involves in some instances strange turns

that give it an odd indirectness, but that in no way diminishes the seriousness or the quantity of the result. That we lose jobs because many prefer
Japanese cars to Fords has been emphasized quite enough. But a less
apparent aspect has to do with the much improved quality of *our* goods.
We are *forced* to manufacture products that will need much less repair
and that will be far more durable—that in short will no longer have all
the attributes of the once notorious built-in obsolescence—and though
this is naturally to the good from a point of view that has regard for the
scarcity of raw materials, it all the same is from the point of view of labor
yet another threat.

This is connected to still another element which also has its origin in
the escalated international competition. There are a great number of technological devices and new materials and machines that we do *not* use-often,
but by no means always, because unions have fought against them to protect their jobs. Similarly, there are hundreds of thousands of jobs that are
protected mainly by hard-won regulations, of which those that regulate
the speed of work are only the most obvious surface example. Under the
impact of intensified international competition much of this is already
in the process of a softening and contraction, if not in a full-scale retreat.

It would be extremely difficult to estimate the implications of just this
one development, even if it could be isolated. For if the union movement,
together with the very conceptions which underlie it, is seriously damaged and crushed or circumvented (and the sheer magnitude and diversity and particularly the internationality of many corporations is apt to
have this effect) then a whole series of cautiously erected channels and
safeguards is bound to collapse. This will bring on, among many other
things, an intensification of the competition for each job to a degree that
is now quite unimagined. With one hand one will be clinging to one's
job, while one will use the other to fend others off and this would bring
about not just a great compression of the number of those who work,
but it would also wholly change the ethos that now still surrounds work.

With all this said one could nonetheless still add an entire second level
to this perspective: many will lose their jobs just because others have lost
theirs. One could call this "domino unemployment" since the falling of
one single job can trigger a longish chain where each in succession brings
down the next. To this it is once more relevant that the preponderance
of jobs are already involved in the rendering of service. Many people
are likely to forego many services soon after they lose their jobs, some
from poverty, but many also because they now have the time to perform
these services themselves. So this factor, like the other general shifts which
we have just enumerated will have effects so large that our normal instruments of quantitative measure can no longer comprehend them.

If we now step away from the array of factors which we have just re-hearsed and try to gain an overview, to what more general outlook are we led? It should be put down firmly that no simplistic and oracular pre-dictions either can or should be made. Certainly it would be foolish and pretentious to say anything about what exactly will happen exactly where and when. But with that set aside there nonetheless are some assertions which can be made, and these even with considerable force. For we can know a good deal about what will *not* occur and what will *not* work and that may be very much more useful than at first appears.

Nothing, for instance, indicates, that merely the invention and the selling of new products could possibly reverse the general trend that we so far defined. Without any question new goods will naturally be invented, maybe even at a sharply accelerating rate, but there is first the considera-tion that many of these new products or services will advance the process we have been describing and will themselves still further eliminate the need for human labor. So the fact that we will of course continue to in-vent may not resolve, but could on the contrary still further aggravate the situation.

But apart from that there is the even more basic matter of the sheer magnitude or size. Nothing at all, as far as we can see, would justify the expectation that even the wildest outburst of the engineering imagi-nation or of a newly rising productivity could hope to outweigh or even just to balance the *combined* might of the factors that we have just de-tailed. It goes without saying that new jobs will be constantly created, but the simple question is, How many? So far there is not a shred of evidence that the two could be balanced, and much suggests that the ratio could be one new job for every 80 or 100 that are lost.

A closely analogous kind of thinking applies to the notion that a sim-ple upturn of the economy will somehow set everything to rights again. An upturn will of course occur, but there, too, one could first point out that no significant upswing could conceivably materialize unless a higher technology (one competitive with the Germans and the Japanese) were put into place. But if so, then that technology would itself cancel out whatever increase in employment any putative up-swing might have made. For individual industries estimates along these lines have been variously made, and one telling instance came to the conclusion that the work-force of the automobile industry would be cut in half even if five years from now car sales exceeded the previous high point of '76 and '77. But the major consideration would again be from the magnitudes involved: as with products before, it seems inconceivable that an up-swing in eco-

nomic activity could balance, let alone reverse, the technologically produced decline in the quantity of needed labor.

(Throughout — and it is crucial that this is not misunderstood — we are
of course not discussing "work". "Work" will naturally always exist in
limitless abundance; there is no end of things that any of us can always
do. But that is not the issue: we are considering *Jobs;* and that means
work which someone else is *willing* but also *able* to pay for.)

The political implications of this are intensely serious. Everybody knows
that a very large number concurred with the two most basic Reagan
measures, of reducing the programs for the poor, and of increasing the
money that would go to the rich, only because they considered these bitter medicines that despite their awful side-effects were the only way to
regain health. In essence, people were willing to give money to the rich
because they had been persuaded that this would eventually lead to an
increase in jobs. But the key-link in this calculation may no longer hold:
the hope is that putting the rich in the position to buy will ultimately
help, because it will give work to those who make the things which the
rich will acquire. But that nostrum leaves technology totally out of the
picture. In some isolated village in the Middle Ages this might have been
true, but it should have been put into a museum after the invention of
the first machine, for this already created the very plain alternative that
the rich with their money would buy *machines* — which would make them
even less dependent on all others than they were before.

The progress of technology has slowly brought about a condition where
a conjunction of machines can turn out finished products with a bare
minimum of human help. This self-sufficiency of the technological apparatus created the situation where the rich can put their money into
a set of machines and can eventually receive much more money in return,
but now they no longer need to include anyone else in this small cycle:
it is all between them and their machines and themselves. Thereby technology has among many other things also changed our most basic political equations: it is now eminently possible that money given to the rich
will benefit them and them alone. And it is possible with the same ease
for the economy to swing up high, and to improve while the number
of those that this still effects progressively decreases.

Analogous implications hold on still a different level. Not just the
cooked-up pablum of supply side economics turns pivotally on the fiction
of these jobs, the same is true for the tradition of respected conservative
economic thought all the way back to Adam Smith. For, in one way or
another the notion of wealth or benefits "trickling down" was the main
claim on which its appeal to a rational and disinterested public rested;
more than that: its very status as a genuine "theory" of economics or as

a "doctrine" stands and falls with this. And mere technology may well have brought it to its fall. For the "trickling down" is surely just a metaphor. Mere gravity alone will certainly not bring about the wider distribution. If anything is able to put substance behind this veil then it is only work and jobs. But it seems that this one avenue has now been blocked. Thanks to technology, wealth can now produce goods and beget more wealth—without labor. This has a side which is truly marvelous but it also flattens much of the carefully constructed architecture of previous thought, and forces us to grasp the quite new situation which we ourselves have managed to create.

The consequences of persisting in our current infatuation with the antiquated are neither unimaginable nor unthinkable. A somewhat realistic picture of the degree and of the magnitude that unemployment could soon reach, and of the destitution that it would entail, is fairly close at hand. A number of South American countries have endured unemployment of 50 or 60 or even 70 percent over extended periods of time. In most of these countries multitudes of peasants left the land for many reasons, and no one, as far as anyone can tell, ever assumed that all of them would find full employment in the developing economies. Each city is half-surrounded with a shanty-town that holds perhaps five times the population of the city which we know by name. Yet that version of the "South Americanization" of the United States is probably too picturesque. We know the deterioration that we should expect from almost any city close to us. There are the blocks or streets that can be easily identified by the windows which have neither glass nor frames, and in which "bums" or "drifters" or "down-and-outs" live. Nothing guarantees that this will stay localized. We already know that whole districts and quarters can easily become like that. And there are many towns in Mexico, for instance, that have their three or four very fashionable, very modern, very expensive-looking streets, but where the three or six or ten remaining *miles* of town are like a camp after a natural disaster or in a war—so crowded are the side-walks with the drunken and the sleeping and the dying and the sick. If we cannot invent a social order and an economy and above all a way to work that reckons with the technology and takes advantage of it, then St. Louis, and Chicago and San Francisco may become like this.

Our most central problem is ambivalent to a degree that is downright comic: our greatest shortage seems to be a shortage of slow, mechanical, hard labor. It is easy to imagine how much sympathy coolies and water-carriers and peasant women from previous generations might have felt for us. But that it is laughable from one side in no way detracts from the terror that it presents from the other side. The fact is that our social order and our individual lives are quite obviously organized around the spine of work. But it seems that technology can undercut and decimate and crush out of existence large quantities of this one commodity on which we utterly depend. The conflict therefore is as basic as that between our need for work—and this need is economical and social and psychological—and the whole arsenal of forces which together constitute technology whose basic purpose is the elimination of the need for human work.

The depth of this problem requires a thoroughgoing and maybe radical rethinking, and first on the agenda must perhaps be the revision of what for many is a kind of first and axiomatic premise: the notion that "less work inevitably means less money." Some portion of most of us seems conditioned in an almost Pavlovian way to assent to this patently mistaken proposition. Major shortages of labor invoke in our minds at once images of long lines of people waiting for soup, or bread, or jobs; even the idea of shorter hours evokes in most people at once a corresponding inward calculation, that cuts the paycheck in the same proportion as the hours. This association is so false and so paralyzing that we cannot hope to advance any further unless that crude reflex is somehow interrupted.

The image of factories producing with a minimum of human labor should be a help. For better or worse we have reached the point where it is not totally misleading to think of a factory as analogous to a large mill, into which we pour fifteen or twenty different kinds of raw materials at one end, while the finished product drops out at the other. The quantity and the diversity and the sheer wealth of things has almost no relationship at all to quantities of labor. Like it or not, the secret of grinding out infinite quantities of *things*—till they shove up against each other and rise up in heaps—*that* we have found. No one would have to be deprived of any of our recently developed comfort-giving niceties just because we collectively did less work. The exact opposite seems to be our problem: namely, that we seem unable to invent contraptions that would be complex enough to require the expense of our multiplying energies.

In a different, for us more authoritative and reassuring language: we do not have a problem of production, but only one of distribution. This much is clear enough; technology does not spell poverty or destitution to us as a whole or as a culture. From that point of view precisely the reverse is far more true. (Think of the proverbial agrarian republics!)

In the past two centuries work functioned as our main instrument of exchange. Not all, but many, could give foundations to the claim that they receive their share only in and through their work. What we are witnessing, therefore, is the collapse of our main means of distribution.

But as with other currencies—and this is what work was for us—a revision in the measure, or a *re-valuation* might be enough to rectify the situation.

————————

One possible procedure through which we could adjust to the sudden drop in the need and the demand for labor is simply to let things take their course. This was the method of the Reagan administration, and in our view this is the worst course *both* for the 30 or 40% who might manage to defend their jobs and for the 60 to 70% who might eventually be unemployed. An alternative approach would basically move in the direction of cutting the working hours of every present job roughly in half; which might mean that one would go through a progression, from the four day work-week, to three days, and perhaps from there down to two. What would be some of the advantages of this different course?

In the present context we shall set the moral superiority of this approach deliberately to the side. That it would be fairer and more equitable and more humane is so blatantly evident that embellishing this with many words would only weaken that categorical consideration. That it would be more just is however far from the only claim that it could make. It may in addition have very practical and material benefits and some of these it is important to rehearse. For one, there probably would be very much less of the resistance to technology which we have just discussed, and one could argue that this by itself is very major; that this country cannot possibly regain its pre-eminence unless advanced technology can be moved in more quickly than has so far been the case, and that this reduction is therefore the only hope we have to regain our former place. But there also is the need for buyers and for markets. If the rich are not by any means the most reliable and fertile buyers, since high technology has brought extreme wealth closer to a barren self-enclosement, then the thought that halving people's jobs might provide us with twice as many persistent buyers than we would have otherwise cannot be ignored.

A third consideration is not entirely economical, but it also is not mainly moral. A continuing and escalating struggle over the shrinking quantity of jobs would not just soon pass the point of diminishing returns—it would be worse: more like the cliché of the exit from a theater through which all could safely pass if they were only calm, which, however, instead is blocked shut by a mad onrush in which people die. To work only half as much would *not* hurt us; it would not even mean that we would have to live a much more frugal life. It would make room for a more effective and efficient technology that in all likelihood would more than compensate us for the loss—and there would be no unemployed. But if we cannot move intelligently and quietly through the transition period, then we may gradually work our way up into a frenzied and ferocious and yet wholly pointless struggle.

Despite these advantages there is one respect in which this second course would still be senseless and clumsy and debilitating, and though this one respect at first seems minor it is actually decisive, like the short span of a railroad switch that in itself seems brief and that yet makes the difference between our ending up in Canada if it is set in one way, or our arriving in Mexico if it points to the other. This crucial difference concerns the timing. To work on a schedule where one would have three and one half days work and then three and one half days off would be flagrantly wasteful and demoralizing for those who do the work. One would be perpetually in a state of transition, just finding one's stride when one again would be interrupted, and again barely adjusting to one's work-free time when one would again be going back to work. But the worst absurdity involved in giving to one's life this structure is that it makes it virtually impossible to undertake anything either purposeful or productive in these short bits of work-free time.

Most people's work takes place in a powerful and established external order which gives at once content and structure to that portion of their lives. The work-free time, however, has been gradually drained and emptied as we became more modern and more atomized, and everything that gave content to traditional life, from the rituals and ceremonies of religion down to the larger and more coherent family was slowly undermined and weakened.

This is a large part of the problem that our way of dealing with the sudden implosion of the quantity of labor seeks to address. We should turn away sharply from the parcelling out of both work and free-time in small crouton-sized bits. Instead we should compress and pull together the chips of each until life would be structured into larger and more satisfying blocks. One could work intensely and concentratedly for six months for example and then have six months of work-free time; and for many it might be better to divide the time by years, or even into stretches of two or three or still more years.

On the surface this might seem like a marginal and not far-reaching difference. But that is seriously deceptive. How very large a change this rearranging of a schedule, of the bare slots of time would actually bring about is hard to imagine or to convey. One way of doing it might be to propose that we now face a vastly more complex and deeper problem than the one which we addressed so far. The current antiquated mode of parcelling work out managed to paper this second problem over, but now that cover has been torn. As long as people's work-free time came in small frustrating bits, the uselessness of it, the fact that it was for many people not much more than a morose and sullen waiting, a stretch of "quiet desperation," could be hidden. But if one pictures a life in which the sum-total of job-time is reduced from forty or forty-five to twenty years and where these twenty years come perhaps in two or three or four concentrated blocks, then one is forced to ask: and what will people do in their work-free time? How will it be filled and used, what meaning will we give to it, and what ends will it be made to serve?

On one interpretation of the last 200 years we made progressively more room for work. Step by step we subordinated other spheres and other matters to it. But we at the same time also systematically dessicated work till it became an unappealing uniform cold gruel. Seeing that we first sacrificed a great deal, and that we then degraded the one thing we received in exchange, it is not surprising that we feel deprived. Still this frames the issue, for the transformation we have been considering amounts to a taking back of what we gave away, or to a turning something right side up that had been standing on its head: work might again become a means. More than that: job-time might again be marginal compared to the rest of life. This gives us a different conception of the *magnitudes* involved: we are asking what people should be doing with ⅔ of their life, with the part of it that life is all about — for the rest is only preparation.

If the question is what people will do in the large stretches of work-free time, one could as part of a preliminary short-hand answer say:

1) That it is of course true that many people now spend their leisure time in sad and silly ways, but that this may in considerable part be the *result* of the kind of work they do (or rather, of what their work does to them) — and crucially may be the effect of the timing and scheduling that we arrange. Many people would probably do much better — if they had a whole year instead of many three-day weekends, and importantly also if they had stretches of job-free time earlier in life and not only after they are 65.

2) Giving people empty time is no different from surrounding them with empty space — one can suffocate in both. Yet there also is no reason why this would have to occur. If one seriously wanted to create a culture that fostered individuality one would have to devise a gamut of institutions which encourage and support people in the enterprises and endeavors that they would pursue in their job-free times. These institutions might

give information, and counsel, and help organize, and much more. More broadly and more basically, one certainly would need a wholly different system of education. (One of the grossest absurdities of our present course is that we tailor education more and more to jobs, just at the point at which jobs occupy an ever smaller portion of our lives.) But these would only be first steps. So much more beyond this could be done that one in effect would be creating a new culture: Culture after the Elimination of Labor.

3) There should be no confusion: we are in the beginning of a great scarcity of jobs — but not of work. If people had rotating jobs they perhaps at last would have time to do some of the work that has not been gotten done: maybe they would have time to rebuild the cities and the roads, time to care for the old and to raise children, and time to make a saner world.

If the question is what actions we can take to bring about the transition to rotating work-schedules, then one could perhaps suggest:

1) The notion of rotating work-schedules is not new and not untried. In the last ten years many companies in many different countries (in Sweden, Germany, and Yugoslavia, for example, but also in the United States) have experimented with alternatives to the rote 8 hour day and 40 hour week. By now there exists a large literature on the subject. Many have pointed out that some of the various rotating work-schedules have in addition to the large societal advantages which we surveyed, a good number of diverse, more fine-grained "operational" benefits. These include: increased productivity, better morale, the capacity to attract a more qualified work-force, reduced absenteeism, fewer burn-outs, greater flexibility in relation to one's personnel during high and low work-seasons, and more of the like. This means that many companies may make the transition to rotating work-schedules with much less resistance than one might expect, and that the providing of information and of explanations in the transition is quite particularly important. (In a few cases that by itself may be sufficient.)

2) No discussion with either union members or union leaders should pretend that everyone is sitting calmly in their studies — the unions are fighting for their lives, and there are many kinds of conversations for which they now have, understandably, neither the time nor the inclination. But with that understanding one could nonetheless propose that the current situation will almost certainly become much worse, and that therefore deep and serious reconsiderations are entirely practical and needed. Unions might conduct new kinds of negotiations for new and different contracts. These contracts could provide that there are no further lay-offs; that the job-time from here on in will be divided equitably

among union members, and that a transition will be made to rotating work-schedules. (One could think in terms of 3 or 4 shifts where one shift is "rotated out" for 3 or 6 or 12 months.) Crucial to these contracts would be that reliable provision would be made for the job-free times. Most obviously these could of course be used for re-training, but as one would grow more accustomed to rotating work-schedules one could include "Community Service Projects." (In cooperation with other unions one could work on hospitals, roads, recreation parks, and much else.) In a city like Detroit or a town like Flint the automobile companies must improve their public relations, and the companies might therefore be receptive to such a proposal. In addition one could make provisions that would encourage and allow the workers to be economically productive in their job-free times. (Included in this would be a variety of projects that would make life more economical: one could undertake to reduce the cost of heat (in one's own house), or the cost of one's housing, or of one's food and the like.)

An individual worker would derive his or her income during a job-free period from at least five different sources: a) The profits of the company might be higher, since higher technology could be introduced with less resistance. Some of these profits might be shared. b) The companies might contribute—as they do now to health insurance and the like. c) Workers might pay contributions—as they do now to Social Security. d) Various levels of government should pay since funds otherwise needed to support the unemployed, and to cover the costs which they create, would be freed. e) Quite significantly: indirect income might be derived from the activities engaged in during job-free times.

3) At the present moment the idea of a rotating work-schedule is still strange, but conceivably that could change rather quickly. (In principle it is no different from rationing gasoline or food.) If it were possible to familiarize people with the justification for, and the reasoning behind this innovation then political candidates could include rotating work-schedules into the measures which they advocate. All candidates will be asked with increasing insistence for their answer to unemployment, and rotating work-schedules might be part of the answer that some candidates could soon give. The more particular and specific ways in which either the city, or the state, or the federal government could promote the institution of rotating work-schedules can be easily imagined. (A program involving "model companies" that had such schedules would be one example.)

4) There could and should be a major effort to "organize the unemployed." The difficulties that stand in the way of this are evident, but as the number of the unemployed increases the need to give them political

voice and force will of course grow commensurately—and with that also the possibilities of achieving this. An organization of the unemployed could demand and exercise pressure for the institution of rotating work-schedules.

The transition will be gradual even under the best of circumstances. But the fact that one could work towards the realization of this goal in so many forms and also in so many places makes it more likely that it can be reached.

Voices from the Workplace: Our Complex Relations to Work

The central purpose of this section is to help you begin thinking about what work means to us as individuals and as a society. We have selected poems, short stories, interviews, and essays that express a wide variety of ideas, feelings, attitudes, and perspectives about labor. Work may bore us, oppress or alienate us, and ruin our health, but it is also usually the primary source of our identities, our sense of community, and our sense of leading a useful and productive life. We believe something this influential deserves careful consideration and thought. Thus one of the basic assumptions in this book is that because work plays such an important role in making us what we are, we had better be careful about what we make of work.

Because our main intent in this section is to "jump start" your imaginations, we have tried to pick works that will reveal to you and challenge your preconceived notions about the world of work. The selections in this section do not represent a coherent and unquestionable truth; instead, they are the thoughts and opinions of intelligent and imaginative people. Try not to accept them uncritically, but also try not to dismiss them without thinking.

Besides helping you question and confront your own views, these works contain much information and some powerful images that should help you begin to construct a thoughtful and informed perspective about work. For example, you will understand something important about your own work if you are aware of the Biblical roots of much of our own thinking about work. Or you will find it quite helpful to confront the strong prejudices against the city which are endemic in Western culture, and to examine the accompanying nostalgia for the countryside that is part of our heritage, for these inherited biases color our views of different kinds of work. Most of us have also inherited certain attitudes toward materialism, and unless we gain some perspective we will be unable to analyse and evaluate the relative merits of the *several* ways we might be "materialistic."

While most people have heard the word 'alienation' used in connection with work and modern life generally, few really understand its nature, sources, and effects. Several of the writers in this section will help you understand this idea in concrete and personal ways. Finally, it is crucial that we confront the injustices connected to work: our workplaces are a major locus of the sexism, racism, and class biases that blight our society. Some of the selections in this section should help you focus on some of the dimensions of these complex issues.

Remember as you read these pieces that the purpose of the humanities is to help us see, that is, to help us experience the world in a new way. Allow yourself to see through the vision provided by the poem or story or essay that you are reading, while still maintaining your ability to think critically. We have provided introductions to the major ideas, issues, and images in each subsection and each individual work. We hope these introductions will help you understand the rich ideas and feelings in the various selections, but try to experience the works on your own and formulate your own interpretations. You should expect that since your experiences and perceptions of work differ from anyone else's, your interpretations of these pieces will at least differ slightly from any other.

Finally, we want you to understand that the humanities deal with those areas of human experience that are surrounded by mystery. While science and technology have given us unprecedented control over and knowledge about our world, they have not necessarily brought us closer to understanding the great mysteries of life. Why do we exist? Is there purpose in life, or is our existence an accident, a mere random event in a universe driven by chaos? How should we act: is it merely up to us, or are there laws or principles that come from outside ourselves to which we should conform? While the humanities do not give definitive answers to such questions, in the asking of them we have learned a great deal that is important. Part of what it means to be human is to exercise our "rage for order," to give form to the seeming chaos of our origins and ends. We begin this section with a brief excerpt from the Old Testament book of Ecclesiastes that sets the tone for our attempt to make sense of working and living.

Ecclesiastes 1:2–5, 2 and 3

The emptiness of all endeavor

Emptiness, emptiness, says the Speaker, emptiness, all is empty. What does man gain from all his labour and his toil here under the sun? Generations come and generations go, while the earth endures for ever.

The sun rises and the sun goes down; back it returns to its place and rises there again.

I said to myself, 'Come, I will plunge into pleasures and enjoy myself'; but this too was emptiness. Of laughter I said, 'It is madness!' And of pleasure, 'What is the good of that?' So I sought to stimulate myself with wine, in the hope of finding out what was good for men to do under heaven throughout the brief span of their lives. But my mind was guided by wisdom, not blinded by folly.

I undertook great works; I built myself houses and planted vineyards; I made myself gardens and parks and planted all kinds of fruit-trees in them; I made myself pools of water to irrigate a grove of growing trees; I bought slaves, male and female, and I had my home-born slaves as well; I had possessions, more cattle and flocks than any of my predecessors in Jerusalem; I amassed silver and gold also, the treasure of kings and provinces; I acquired singers, men and women, and all that man delights in. I was great, greater than all my predecessors in Jerusalem; and my wisdom stood me in good stead. Whatever my eyes coveted, I refused them nothing, nor did I deny myself any pleasure. Yes indeed, I got pleasure from all my labour, and for all my labour this was my reward. Then I turned and reviewed all my handiwork, all my labour and toil, and I saw that everything was emptiness and chasing the wind, of no profit under the sun.

I set myself to look at wisdom and at madness and folly. Then I perceived that wisdom is more profitable than folly, as light is more profitable than darkness: the wise man has eyes in his head, but the fool walks in the dark. Yet I saw also that one and the same fate overtakes them both. So I said to myself, 'I too shall suffer the fate of the fool. To what purpose have I been wise? What is the profit of it? Even this', I said to myself, 'is emptiness. The wise man is remembered no longer than the fool, for, as the passing days multiply, all will be forgotten. Alas, wise man and fool die the same death!' So I came to hate life, since everything that was done here under the sun was a trouble to me; for all is emptiness and chasing the wind. So I came to hate all my labour and toil here under the sun, since I should have to leave its fruits to my successor. What sort of a man will he be who succeeds me, who inherits what others have acquired? Who knows whether he will be a wise man or a fool? Yet he will be master of all the fruits of my labour and skill here under the sun. This too is emptiness.

Then I turned and gave myself up to despair, reflecting upon all my labour and toil here under the sun. For anyone who toils with wisdom, knowledge, and skill must leave it all to a man who has spent no labour on it. This too is emptiness and utterly wrong. What reward has a man for all his labour, his scheming, and his toil here under the sun? All his life long his business is pain and vexation to him; even at night his mind knows no rest. This too is emptiness. There is nothing better for a man to do than to eat and drink and enjoy himself in return for his labours. And yet I saw that this comes from the hand of God. For without him who can enjoy his food, or who can be anxious? God gives wisdom and knowledge and joy to the man who pleases him, while to the sinner is given the trouble of gathering and amassing wealth only to hand it over to someone else who pleases God. This too is emptiness and chasing the wind.

For everything its season, and for every activity under heaven its time:

> a time to be born and a time to die;
> a time to plant and a time to uproot;
> a time to kill and a time to heal;
> a time to pull down and a time to build up;
> a time to weep and a time to laugh;
> a time for mourning and a time for dancing;
> a time to scatter stones and a time to gather them;
> a time to embrace and a time to refrain from embracing;
> a time to seek and a time to lose;
> a time to keep and a time to throw away;
> a time to tear and a time to mend;
> a time for silence and a time for speech;
> a time to love and a time to hate;
> a time for war and a time for peace.

What profit does one who works get from all his labour? I have seen the business that God has given men to keep them busy. He has made everything to suit its time; moreover he has given men a sense of time past and future, but no comprehension of God's work from beginning to end. I know that there is nothing good for man except to be happy and live the best life he can while he is alive. Moreover, that a man should eat and drink and enjoy himself, in return for all his labours, is a gift of God. I know that whatever God does lasts for ever; to add to it or subtract from it is impossible. And he has done it all in such a way that men must feel awe in his presence. Whatever is has been already, and whatever is to come has been already, and God summons each event back in its turn. Moreover I saw here under the sun that, where justice ought to be, there was wickedness, and where righteousness ought to be, there was wickedness. I said to myself, 'God will judge the just man and the wicked equally; every activity and every purpose has its proper time.' I said to myself, 'In dealing with men it is God's purpose to test them and to see what they truly are. For man is a creature of chance and the beasts are creatures of chance, and one mischance awaits them all: death comes to both alike. They all draw the same breath. Men have no advantage over beasts; for everything is emptiness. All go to the same place: all came from the dust, and to the dust all return. Who knows whether the spirit of man goes upward or whether the spirit of the beast goes downward to the earth?' So I saw that there is nothing better than that a man should enjoy his work, since that is his lot. For who can bring him through to see what will happen next?

IA. The Yin and Yang of Work

Our Ambivalent Feelings about Work

Anyone who has worked long can tell you that work has many moods —as many, perhaps, as there are human emotions. We not only can love or hate our work, but we can find it amusing, perplexing, tasteless, sad, curious, mystifying, empowering, draining, delightful, depressing, or frightening. Often we can feel several of these emotions simultaneously as we work: our feelings about work can be mixed, and work can as easily confuse us as any human relationship.

We should not be surprised that as astute an observer of the human psyche as Freud should consider work, along with love, to be one of the two most fundamental human needs beyond survival needs such as food. Our everyday speech reflects not only that love and work are equally important but also that they are intimately related. We imbue our work with human characteristics (work can be cruel, sweet, like a stern father, etc.), and whether or not our love life goes well depends, in large measure, on our relationship to our work. Like the proverbial spouse, we often cannot seem to get along with work, and we cannot get along without it.

This brief introductory section on the Yin/Yang of work is meant to show you some of the many emotions people can and do experience in relation to their work, and to stir your imaginations to begin understanding how fundamental, diverse, and widespread work is. Yin and Yang are the basic opposites in Oriental thought. Or better, they represent all opposition: winter and summer, black and white, hot and cold, male and female are manifestations of Yin and Yang. Humans tend to think in pairs and in contrasts —we learn as much about something by examining what it is not as by looking at what it is. And often we talk of having a "love/hate relationship" with someone (or with our work) when referring to our mixed emotions (ambivalence). Our feelings about work pull us in many directions. As you examine the following brief selections, try to think of other ways you and others have experienced work. And while you are at it, you might begin to wonder what work is that it could be so important for being human.

In the West we have a long tradition of viewing work as a curse, at best as the lesser half of life. In the book of Genesis from the Old Testament, when humans "fall" from grace with God by eating of the sacred fruit of the knowledge of good and evil, women are condemned to pain in childbirth (those who have experienced it know why it is called *labor*), and men to work to earn a living. This crucial passage from one of the founding texts of the Western tradition is not unambiguous about work and childbirth, though. For while labor has its down side (pain and sweat), it can also be seen as crucial to becoming an adult. To be in Eden can be viewed as being in childhood—a place of innocence where we are taken care of. To be an adult, where we make our own decisions for good or bad ("eating" of the fruit) and thereby stand between animals and God, is also to be responsible, which includes having to use our efforts to make decisions and to provide for ourselves and our fellow humans. With freedom comes responsibility, with the joys and wonders of adulthood come pain and toil . . . with Yin comes Yang.

The fiery and rather scornful abuse heaped upon Mr. Stephen Duck by an anonymous eighteenth-century British farm woman reflects this Yin/Yang of work. While her acid irony leaves no doubt about her contempt for Mr. Duck's sexist complaints about how hard he works, this hardworking woman does not simply hate work. Rather, what she desires is recognition—for her effort, for her accomplishments, for her person—and equality. She sees that Mr. Duck, while complaining about his burden of work, also gets his sense of value from working; and she, too, wants to be valued for what she does.

Mike Lefevre, a contemporary steelworker, also realizes that work is a mixed blessing, and that recognition is crucial. But he moves us one step further and distinguishes between kinds of work: work can be ennobling or a curse (or anything in between), but not all work is equal. While factory work is a way to make a living, he does not see how it can provide the kinds of status, time, and truly human benefits his son could get if he goes to college. Lefevre carries deep ambivalence toward "intellectuals" (college-educated people), toward blacks, toward women, and toward his fellow workers. He wants to be recognized for his work and for himself, but he sees that he is *not* equal because his work has de-humanized him. He deals with the deep resentments generated by his mixed emotions in a number of ways: his mind realizes blacks and his fellow workers are his equals, yet he knows he cannot hit the boss, so he brawls with his peers; he hates intellectuals and communists for their superior attitudes and lack of understanding of the plight of the worker, yet he wants his son to become an "effete snob" (college educated); and he wants to be fully human but feels he can only realize his desire through his children. The Yin/Yang of work is very complex indeed.

People have realized for a long time that we work for our *selves* as well as for our daily bread. Work provides us with much of our identities:

notice how people most often introduce themselves by talking about their work, and we associate with some people rather than others to a great extent because of our work status (our identities). In the short selections in Part 2 of this subsection you will find expression of various dimensions of the link between personal identity and work. In Jesus' parable from Matthew the servants (workers) are praised for their working rather than merely for the results of their efforts. The frugal servant who plays it safe and does not risk development of his personhood is criticized because he misunderstood the game — he thought the only goal was to save, to rest on his laurels, while the more important purpose of working is who we become. In the set of brief selections from history, writers as diverse as Hesiod (ancient Greece), St. Benedict (Middle Ages), and Lao Tsu (ancient China) record a common understanding from most traditions that among the most important products of work is the human character. Dolores Dante, a contemporary worker (waitress), reflects this understanding and talks about how, even as a waitress, she goes about making her work creative of a better self.

Contemporary poet Paul Zimmer echoes the sentiment of the writers in this part, but he also introduces new ambiguities. In Zimmer's experience work sometimes seems to engulf as well as reflect and create him — he always seems to be "working, working, working." He has good work, mind you, and he does grow with and gain recognition for his work, but sometimes he seems to become lost in his work. We work for our pay and we work for ourselves, but do *we* always direct and do the work? Just as Mike Lefevre helped us see that not all work is equally productive, Zimmer asks us to reflect about whether *always* working is good for us. In the ensuing subsections we will pursue related questions about how our work keeps us from other crucial human activities.

Finally, we have included a voice of dissent that rejects the value of work completely as it celebrates the joys of laziness. Drawing from the Appalachian tradition of tall tales, we have included two products of Old Southwest humor: the folk song "The Arkansas Traveler" and an excerpt from Mark Twain's *The Adventures of Huckleberry Finn*. Both express the sheer joy of living for the moment in nature without a care for the future.

1. Work as a Curse

Genesis 3:14-24

And the Lord God said unto the serpent, Because thou hast done this, thou *art* cursed above all cattle, and above every beast of the field; upon thy belly shalt thou go, and dust shalt thou eat all the days of thy life:

And I will put enmity between thee and the woman, and between thy seed and her seed; it shall bruise thy head, and thou shalt bruise his heel.

Unto the woman he said, I will greatly multiply thy sorrow and thy conception; in sorrow thou shalt bring forth children; and thy desire *shall be* to thy husband, and he shall rule over thee.

And unto Adam he said Because thou hast hearkened unto the voice of thy wife, and hast eaten of the tree, of which I commanded thee, saying, Thou shalt not eat of it: cursed is the ground for thy sake; in sorrow shalt thou eat *of* it all the days of thy life;

Thorns also and thistles shall it bring forth to thee: and thou shalt eat the herb of the field;

In the sweat of thy face shalt thou eat bread, till thou return unto the ground; for out of it wast thou taken: for dust thou *art*, and unto dust shalt thou return.

And Adam called his wife's name Eve; because she was the mother of all living.

Unto Adam also and to his wife did the Lord God make coats of skins, and clothed them.

And the Lord God said, Behold, the man is become as one of us, to know good and evil: and now, lest he put forth his hand and take also of the tree of life, and eat, and live for ever:

Therefore the Lord God sent him forth from the garden of Eden, to till the ground from whence he was taken.

So he drove out the man; and he placed at the east of the garden of Eden Cherubims, and a flaming sword which turned every way, to keep the way of the tree of life.

Introduction
An Anonymous Eighteenth-Century Woman Poet

Industrialization did not create the exploitation of women. Patriarchy and its various forms of gender inequality and control of women by men is widespread in human history. Industrialization fragmented the family and gave women only the lowliest slots in the industrial process but was only refining or altering an already existing pattern. As Rosemary Radford Ruether explains in Section III, women began losing their place in society at least as early as ancient Greece.

In the following folk poem an anonymous woman responds to a poem by Stephen Duck in which he complains of the heavy work load for men while slighting the efforts of women. Her lament about the double work load of eighteenth-century women should sound familiar to working women today, as should her fiery criticisms of Duck's chauvinism.

The Woman's Labour:
To Mr. Stephen Duck

Immortal Bard! thou Fav'rite of the Nine!
Enrich'd by Peers, advanc'd by Caroline!
Deign to look down on One that's poor and low,
Remembering you yourself was lately so;
Accept these Lines: Alas! what can you have
From her, who ever was, and's still a Slave?
No Learning ever was bestow'd on me;
My Life was always spent in Drudgery:
And not alone; alas! with Grief I find,
It is the Portion of poor Woman-kind.
Oft have I thought as on my Bed I lay,
Eas'd from the tiresome Labours of the Day,
Our first Extraction from a Mass refin'd,
Could never be for Slavery design'd;
Till Time and Custom by degrees destroy'd
That happy State our Sex at first enjoy'd.
When Men had us'd their utmost Care and Toil,
Their Recompence was but a Female Smile;
When they by Arts or Arms were render'd Great,

They laid their Trophies at a Woman's Feet;
They, in those Days, unto our Sex did bring
Their Hearts, their All, a Free-will Offering;
And as from us their Being they derive,
They back again should all due Homage give.

―――――――――

In your late *Poem* boldly did declare
Alcides' Labours can't with your's compare;
And of your annual Task have much to say,
Of Threshing, Reaping, Mowing Corn and Hay;
Boasting your daily Toil, and nightly Dream,
But can't conclude your never-dying Theme,
And let our hapless Sex in Silence lie
Forgotten, and in dark Oblivion die;
But on our abject State you throw your Scorn,
And Women wrong, your Verses to adorn.
You of Hay-making speak a Word or two,
As if our Sex but little Work could do:
This makes the honest Farmer smiling say,
He'll seek for Women still to make his Hay;
For if his Back be turn'd, their Work they mind
As well as Men, as far as he can find.
For my own Part, I many a *Summer's* Day
Have spent in throwing, turning, making Hay;
But ne'er could see, what you have lately found,
Our Wages paid for sitting on the Ground.
'Tis true, that when our Morning's Work is done,
And all our Grass expos'd unto the Sun,
While that his scorching Beams do on it shine,
As well as you, we have a Time to dine:
I hope, that since we freely toil and sweat
To earn our Bread, you'll give us Time to eat.

―――――――――

When Ev'ning does approach, we homeward hie,
And our domestic Toils incessant ply:
Against your coming Home prepare to get
Our Work all done, our House in order sets
Bacon and *Dumpling* in the Pot we boil,
Our Beds we make, our Swine we feed the while;
Then wait at Door to see you coming Home,
And set the Table out against you come:
Early next Morning we on you attend;
Our Children dress and feed, their Cloaths we mend;

And in the Field our daily Task renew,
Soon as the rising Sun has dry'd the Dew.

When Harvest comes, into the Field we go,
And help to reap the Wheat as well as you;
Or else we go the Ears of Corn to glean;
No Labour scorning, be it e'er so mean;
But in the Work we freely bear a Part,
And what we can, perform with all our Heart.
To get a Living we so willing are,
Our tender Babes into the Field we bear,
And wrap them in our Cloaths to keep them warm,
While round about we gather up the Corn;
And often unto them our Course do bend,
To keep them safe, that nothing them offend:
Our Children that are able, bear a Share
In gleaning Corn, such is our frugal Care.
When Night comes on, unto our Home we go,
Our Corn we carry, and our Infant too;
Wary, alas! but 'tis not worth our while
Once to complain, or *rest at ev'ry Stile;*
We must make haste, for when we Home are come,
Alas! we find our Work but just begun;
So many Things for our Attendance call,
Had we ten Hands, we could employ them all.
Our Children put to Bed, with greatest Care
We all Things for your coming Home prepare:
You sup, and go to Bed without delay,
And rest yourselves till the ensuing Day;
While we, alas! but little Sleep can have,
Because our froward Children cry and rave;
Yet, without fail, soon as Day-light doth spring,
We in the Field again our Work begin,
And there, with all our Strength, our Toil renew,
Till *Titan's* golden Rays have dry'd the Dew;
Then home we go unto our Children dear,
Dress, feed, and bring them to the Field with care.
Were this your Case, you justly might complain
That Day nor Night you are secure from Pain;
Those mighty Troubles which perplex your Mind,
(*Thistles* before, and *Females* come behind)
Would vanish soon, and quickly disappear, . . .

Now Night comes on, from whence you have Relief,
But that, alas! does but increase our grief;

With heavy Hearts we often view the Sun,
Fearing he'll set before our Work is done;
For either in the Morning, or at Night,
We piece the *Summer*'s Day with Candle-light.
Tho' we all Day with Care our Work attend,
Such is our Fate, we know not when 'twill end:
When Ev'ning's come, you Homeward take your Way,
We, till our Work is done, are forc'd to stay;
And after all our Toil and Labour past,
Six-pence or Eight-pence pays us off at last;
For all our Pains, no Prospect can we see
Attend us, but *Old Age* and *Poverty.*

The *Washing* is not all we have to do:
We oft change Work for Work as well as you.
Our Mistress of her Pewter doth complain,
And 'tis our Part to make it clean again.
This Work, tho' very hard and tiresome too,
Is not the worst we hapless Females do:
When Night comes on, and we quite weary are,
We scarce can count what falls unto our Share;
Pots, Kettles, Sauce-pans, Skillets, we may see,
Skimmers and Ladles, and such Trumpery,
Brought in to make complete our Slavery.
Tho' early in the Morning 'tis begun,
'Tis often very late before we've done;
Alas! our Labours never know an End;
On Brass and Iron we our Strength must spend; . . .

But to rehearse all Labour is in vain,
Of which we very justly might complain:
For us, you see, but little Rest is found;
Our Toil increases as the Year runs round.
While you to *Sysiphus* yourselves compare,
With *Danaus' Daughters* we may claim a Share;
For while *he* labours hard against the Hill,
Bottomless Tubs of Water *they* must fill.

So the industrious Bees do hourly strive
To bring their Loads of Honey to the Hive;
Their sordid Owners always reap the Gains,
And poorly recompense their Toil and Pains.

Introduction
Studs Terkel, *Working*

Studs Terkel is a well-known Chicago-based writer, public radio personality, and gadfly. His book *Working,* from which the steelworker and waitress interviews are taken, was an immediate bestseller when published in 1974.

Terkel has interviewed people from all areas of employment—from movie stars and executives to waitresses and assembly-line operators. You will see that he has a unique knack for getting people to talk freely about significant personal issues. In both of these interviews we get a vivid sense of their work and their feelings about that work. Notice that both Mike Lefevre and Dolores Dante want more from their work than a paycheck— like most of us they see work as creating and reflecting themselves. We have chosen these representative interviews of ordinary workers in part to help you see that what makes the poems, short stories, and other selections by humanities writers so striking is that they take up the most basic human concerns felt by all workers.

Mike Lefevre

Who Built the Pyramids?

Who built the seven towers of Thebes?
The books are filled with the names of kings.
Was it kings who hauled the craggy blocks of stone? . . .
In the evening when the Chinese wall was finished
Where did the masons go? . . .

— Bertolt Brecht

It is a two-flat dwelling, somewhere in Cicero, on the outskirts of Chicago. He is thirty-seven. He works in a steel mill. On occasion, his wife Carol works as a wait-

ress in a neighborhood restaurant; otherwise, she is at home, caring for their two small children, a girl and a boy.

At the time of my first visit, a sculpted statuette of Mother and Child was on the floor, head severed from body. He laughed softly as he indicated his three-year-old daughter: "She Doctor Spock'd it."

I'm a dying breed. A laborer. Strictly muscle work . . . pick it up, put it down, pick it up, put it down. We handle between forty and fifty thousand pounds of steel a day. (Laughs) I know this is hard to believe—from four hundred pounds to three- and four-pound pieces. It's dying.

You can't take pride any more. You remember when a guy could point to a house he built, how many logs he stacked. He built it and he was proud of it. I don't really think I could be proud if a contractor built a home for me. I would be tempted to get in there and kick the carpenter in the ass (laughs), and take the saw away from him. 'Cause I would have to be part of it, you know.

It's hard to take pride in a bridge you're never gonna cross, in a door you're never gonna open. You're mass-producing things and you never see the end result of it. (Muses) I worked for a trucker one time. And I got this tiny satisfaction when I loaded a truck. At least I could see the truck depart loaded. In a steel mill, forget it. You don't see where nothing goes.

I got chewed out by my foreman once. He said, "Mike, you're a good worker but you have a bad attitude." My attitude is that I don't get excited about my job. I do my work but I don't say whoopee-doo. The day I get excited about my job is the day I go to a head shrinker. How are you gonna get excited about pullin' steel? How are you gonna get excited when you're tired and want to sit down?

It's not just the work. Somebody built the pyramids. Somebody's going to build something. Pyramids, Empire State Building—these things just don't happen. There's hard work behind it. I would like to see a building, say, the Empire State, I would like to see on one side of it a foot-wide strip from top to bottom with the name of every bricklayer, the name of every electrician, with all the names. So when a guy walked by, he could take his son and say, "See, that's me over there on the forty-fifth floor. I put the steel beam in." Picasso can point to a painting. What can I point to? A writer can point to a book. Everybody should have something to point to.

It's the not-recognition by other people. To say a woman is *just* a housewife is degrading, right? Okay. *Just* a housewife. It's also degrading to say *just* a laborer. The difference is that a man goes out and maybe gets smashed.

A mule, an old mule, that's the way I feel. Oh yeah. See. (Shows black and blue marks on arms and legs, burns.) You know what I heard from more than one guy at work? "If my kid wants to work in a factory, I am going to kick the hell out of him." I want my kid to be an effete snob. Yeah, mm-hmm. (Laughs.) I want him to be able to quote Walt Whitman, to be proud of it.

If you can't improve yourself, you improve your posterity. Otherwise life isn't worth nothing. You might as well go back to the cave and stay there. I'm sure the first caveman who went over the hill to see what was on the other side—I don't think he went there wholly out of curiosity. He went there because he wanted to get his son out of the cave. Just the same way I want to send my kid to college.

You're doing this manual labor and you know that technology can do it. (Laughs.) Let's face it, a machine can do the work of a man; otherwise they wouldn't have space probes. Why can we send a rocket ship that's unmanned and yet send a man in a steel mill to do a mule's work?

Automation? Depends how it's applied. It frightens me if it puts me out on the street. It doesn't frighten me if it shortens my work week. You read that little thing: what are you going to do when this computer replaces you? Blow up computers. (Laughs.) Really. Blow up computers. I'll be goddamned if a computer is gonna eat before I do! I want milk for my kids and beer for me. Machines can either liberate man or enslave 'im, because they're pretty neutral. It's man who has the bias to put the thing one place or another.

. . . I'm just like the colored people. Potential Einsteins don't have to be white. They could be in cotton fields, they could be in factories.

The twenty-hour week is a possibility today. The intellectuals, they always say there are potential Lord Byrons, Walt Whitmans, Roosevelts, Picassos working in construction or steel mills or factories. But I don't think they believe it. I think what they're afraid of is the potential Hitlers and Stalins that are there too. The people in power fear the leisure man. Not just the United States. Russia's the same way.

What do you think would happen in this country if, for one year, they experimented and gave everybody a twenty-hour week? How do they know that the guy who digs Wallace today doesn't try to resurrect Hitler tomorrow? Or the guy who is mildly disturbed at pollution doesn't decide to go to General Motors and shit on the guy's desk? You can become a fanatic if you had the time. The whole thing is time. That is, I think, one reason rich kids tend to be fanatic about politics: they have time. Time, that's the important thing.

I know a guy fifty-seven years old. Know what he tells me? "Mike, I'm old and tired *all* the time." The first thing happens at work: When the arms start moving, the brain stops. I punch in about ten minutes to seven in the morning. I say hello to a couple of guys I like, I kid around with them. One guy says good morning to you and you say good morning. To another guy you say fuck you. The guy you say fuck you to is your friend.

Why is it that the communists always say they're for the workingman, and as soon as they set up a country, you got guys singing to tractors? They're singing about how they love the factory. That's where I couldn't buy communism. It's the intellectuals' utopia, not mine. I cannot picture myself singing to a tractor, I just can't. (Laughs.) Or singing to steel. (Singsongs.) Oh whoop-dee-doo, I'm at the bonderizer, oh how I love this heavy steel. No thanks. Never hoppen.

Somebody has to do this work. If my kid ever goes to college, I just want him to have a little respect, to realize that his dad is one of those somebodies. This is why even on — (muses) yeah. I guess, sure — on the black thing . . . (Sighs heavily.) I can't really hate the colored fella that's working with me all day. The black intellectual I got no respect for. The white intellectual I got no use for. I got no use for the black militant who's gonna scream three hundred years of slavery to me while I'm busting my ass. You know what I mean? (Laughs.) I have one answer for that guy: go see Rockefeller. See Harriman. Don't bother me. We're in the same cotton field. So just don't bug me. (Laughs).

He saw a book in my back pocket one time and he was amazed. He walked up to me and he said, "You read?" I said, "What do you mean, I read?" He said, "All these dummies read the sports pages around here. What are you doing with a book?" I got pissed off at the kid right away. I said, "What do you mean, all these dummies? Don't knock a man who's paying somebody else's way through college." He was a nineteen-year-old effete snob.

Yet you want your kid to be an effete snob?

Yes. I want my kid to look at me and say, "Dad, you're a nice guy, but you're a fuckin' dummy." Hell yes, I want my kid to tell me that he's not gonna be like me . . .

———————

I'd like to run a combination bookstore and tavern. (Laughs.) I would like to have a place where college kids came and a steelworker could sit down and talk. Where a workingman could not be ashamed of Walt Whitman and where a college professor could not be ashamed that he painted his house over the weekend.

———————

Way back, you spoke of the guys who built the pyramids, not the pharaohs, the unknowns. You put yourself in their category?

Yes. I want my signature on 'em, too. Sometimes, out of pure meanness, when I make something, I put a little dent in it. I like to do something to make it really unique. Hit it with a hammer. I deliberately fuck it up to see if it'll get by, just so I can say I did it. It could be anything. Let me put it this way: I think God invented the dodo bird so when we get up there we could tell Him, "Don't you ever make mistakes?" and He'd say, "Sure, look." (Laughs.) I'd like to make my imprint. My dodo bird. A mistake, *mine*. Let's say the whole building is nothing but red bricks. I'd like to have just the black one or the white one or the purple one. Deliberately fuck up.

This is gonna sound square, but my kid is my imprint. He's my freedom. There's a line in one of Hemingway's books. I think it's from *For Whom the Bell Tolls*. They're behind the enemy lines, somewhere in Spain, and she's pregnant. She wants to stay with him. He tells her no. He says, "if you die, I die," knowing he's gonna die. But if you go, I go. Know what I mean? The mystics call it the brass bowl. Continuum. You know what I mean? This is why I work. Every time I see a young guy walk by with a shirt and tie and dressed up real sharp, I'm lookin' at my kid, you know? That's it.

2. Finding Our Identities through Work

Matthew 25:14-30

For it will be as when a man going on a journey called his servants and entrusted to them his property;

to one he gave five talents, to another two, to another one, to each according to his ability. Then he went away.

He who had received the five talents went at once and traded with them; and he made five talents more.

So also, he who had the two talents made two talents more.

But he who had received the one talent went and dug in the ground and hid his master's money.

Now after a long time the master of those servants came and settled accounts with them.

And he who had received the five talents came forward, bringing five talents more, saying, "Master, you delivered to me five talents; here I have made five talents more."

His master said to him, "Well done, good and faithful servant; you have been faithful over a little, I will set you over much, enter into the joy of your master."

And he also who had the two talents came forward, saying, "Master, you delivered to me two talents; here I have made two talents more."

His master said to him, "Well done, good and faithful servant; you have been faithful over a little, I will set you over much; enter into the joy of your master."

He also who had received the one talent came forward, saying, "Master, I knew you to be a hard man, reaping where you did not sow, and gathering where you did not winnow,

so I was afraid, and I went and hid your talent in the ground. Here you have what is yours."

But his master answered him, "You wicked and slothful servant! You knew that I reap where I have not sowed, and gather where I have not winnowed?

Then you ought to have invested my money with the bankers, and at my coming should have received what was my own with interest.

So take the talent from him, and give it to him who has the ten talents. For to every one who has will more be given, and he will have abundance; but from him who has not, even what he has will be taken away.

And cast the worthless servant into the outer darkness; there men will weep and gnash their teeth."

Dolores Dante

Waitress from Working

She has been a waitress in the same restaurant for twenty-three years. Many of its patrons are credit card carriers on an expense account — conventioneers, politicians, labor leaders, agency people. Her hours are from 5:00 P.M. to 2:00 A.M. six days a week. She arrives earlier "to get things ready, the silverware, the butter. When people come in and ask for you, you would like to be in a position to handle them all, because that means more money for you.

"I became a waitress because I needed money fast and you don't get it in an office. My husband and I broke up and he left me with debts and three children. My baby was six months. The fast buck, your tips. The first ten-dollar bill that I got as a tip, a Viking guy gave to me. He was a very robust, terrific atheist. Made very good conversation for us, 'cause I am too.

"Everyone says all waitresses have broken homes. What they don't realize is when people have broken homes they need to make money fast, and do this work. They don't have broken homes because they're waitresses."

I have to be a waitress. How else can I learn about people? How else does the world come to me? I can't go to everyone. So they have to come to me. Everyone wants to eat, everyone has hunger. And I serve them. If they've had a bad day, I nurse them, cajole them. Maybe with coffee I give them a little philosophy. They have cocktails, I give them political science.

———

People imagine a waitress couldn't possibly think or have any kind of aspiration other than to serve food. When somebody says to me, "You're great, how come you're *just* a waitress?" *Just* a waitress. I'd say, "Why, don't you think you deserve to be served by me?" It's implying that he's not worthy, not that I'm not worthy. It makes me irate. I don't feel lowly at all. I myself feel sure. I don't want to change the job. I love it.

I'd get intoxicated with giving service. People would ask for me and I didn't have enough tables. Some of the girls are standing and don't have customers. There is resentment. I feel self-conscious. I feel a sense of guilt. It cramps my style. I would like to say to the customer, "Go to so-and-so." But you can't do that, because you feel a sense of loyalty. So you would rush, get to your customers quickly. Some don't care to drink and still they wait for you. That's a compliment.

Some don't care. When the plate is down you can hear the sound. I try not to have that sound. I want my hands to be right when I serve. I pick up a glass, I want it to be just right. I get to be almost Oriental in the serving. I like it to look nice all the way. To be a waitress, it's an art. I feel like a ballerina, too. I have to go between those tables, between those chairs . . . Maybe that's the reason I always stayed slim. It is a certain way I can go through a chair no one else can do. I do it with an air. If I drop a fork, there is a certain way I pick it up. I know they can see how delicately I do it. I'm on stage.

I tell everyone I'm a waitress and I'm proud. If a nurse gives service, I say, "You're a professional." Whatever you do, be professional. I always compliment people.

I like to have my station looking nice. I like to see there's enough ash trays when they're having their coffee and cigarettes. I don't like ash trays so loaded that people are not enjoying the moment. It offends me. I don't do it because I think that's gonna make a better tip. It offends me as a person.

People say, "No one does good work any more." I don't believe it. You know who's saying that? The man at the top, who says the people beneath him are not doing a good job. He's the one who always said, "You're nothing." The housewife who has all the money, she believed housework was demeaning, 'cause she hired someone else to do it. If it weren't so demeaning, why didn't *she* do it? So anyone who did her housework was a person to be demeaned. The maid who did all the housework said, "Well, hell, if this is the way you feel about it, I won't do your housework. You tell me I'm no good, I'm nobody. Well, maybe I'll go out and be somebody." They're only mad because they can't find someone to do it now. The fault is not in the people who did the—quote—lowly work.

Introduction
Paul Zimmer, "Work"

Paul Zimmer is a University of Iowa administrator whose work includes the avocation of writing poetry. In the following poem, "Work," Zimmer expresses a version of the view that work is crucial for being human.

Sigmund Freud is famous for his study of sexual instincts, but he is less well known for his insistence on the work instinct. Like Zimmer and Freud, the editors of this volume believe that for humans work is a psychologically necessary activity, that humans must engage in it not only to survive materially but to fully realize their humanity. Those who talk about work in America inevitably bring up the work ethic, the belief, often associated with Puritanism, that work is a moral duty (see Introduction, Section IIB2). This ethic is the opposite of the work instinct, for if work is instinctive, then there should be no need to make it into a duty. Thus the dominance of the work ethic in America, even in the entire industrial world, suggests to us that there is something wrong with the way in which we approach work and/or with the work we do.

In Zimmer's poem the narrator is always working, whatever his activity might be. He is searching, he tells us, for perfect work, work that "will last as long / As words will last." As you contemplate this poem, ask yourself if the work you do contributes in a positive way to your sense of yourself. What work that you do on your job brings this benefit? What role does craftsmanship play in making work attractive to you? Do you agree with Zimmer's implication that *all* work is good? Why? What are the essential characteristics of good work if not all work is good?

Paul Zimmer

Work

To have done it thirty years
Without question! Yet I tell myself
I am grateful for all work;
At noon in my air-conditioned office
With a sandwich and a poem,
I try to recollect nature;
But a clerk comes in with papers
To be signed. I tell myself
The disruption does not matter;
It is all work: computer runs,
Contracts, invoices, poems; the same
As breaking shells, hunting woods,
Making pots or gathering grain.
Jazzmen even refer to sex as work.
Some primitive people believe
That death is work. When my wife asks
What I am doing, I always answer,
I am working, working, working.

Now I know I will spend the rest
Of my life trying for perfect work,
A work as rare as aurora borealis,
So fine it will make all other work
Seem true, that will last as long
As words will last. At home
In my room, I mumble to myself
Over my poems; over supper I talk
To myself; as I carpenter or paint
Or carry the groceries up the steps,
I am speaking words to myself.
"What are you doing?" my children ask.
I am working, working, working.

Reprinted from *Family Reunion: Selected and New Poems* by Paul Zimmer by permission of the University of Pittsburgh Press. © 1983 by Paul Zimmer.

3. An Alternative American View of Work

You can't eat for eight hours a day nor drink for eight hours
a day nor make love for eight hours a day—all you can do
for eight hours is work. Which is the reason why man makes
himself and everybody else so miserable and unhappy.

William Faulkner

Although we think of America as a land governed by the Puritan work
ethic, it is important to remember that a rich dissenting tradition is
associated with the Southern yeoman farmer and is reflected in the folk-
tales and folk music of the old Southwest. Growing out of the nineteenth-
century Romantic tradition, it rejected the Northern faith in progress
and the Yankee obsession with busy-ness for a more laid-back tradition
that valued popular music, tall tales, hunting, fishing, boozing, and just
plain laying around. First given written expression in the works of Southern humorists such as G.W. Harris and Thomas Thorpe, this tradition
reached its literary heights in the works of Samuel Clemens and William
Faulkner.

We have included two excerpts that reflect the view that we should
live playfully for today in nature rather than worrying about tomorrow
or escaping from nature. As you read "The Arkansas Traveler" and the
excerpts from Mark Twain's *The Adventures of Huckleberry Finn* consider
the following questions. Do you believe people can be happy without
elaborate plans for the future? How would America be different if we
paid less attention to the work ethic? Does the idea of escaping into nature expressed in *The Adventures of Huckleberry Finn* have a place in modern American values?

The Arkansas Traveler

O once upon a time in Arkansas
An old man sat in his little cabin door,
And fiddled at a tune that he liked to hear,
A jolly old tune that he played by ear.
It was raining hard, but the fiddler didn't care,

He sawed away at the popular air,
Tho' his roof tree leaked like a water fall,
That didn't seem to bother the man at all.

A traveler was riding by that day,
And stopped to hear him a practicing away;
The cabin was afloat and his feet were wet,
But still the old man didn't seem to fret.
So the stranger said: "Now the way it seems to me,
You'd better mend your roof," said he.
But the old man said, as he played away:
"I couldn't mend it now, it's a rainy day."

The traveler replied: "That's all quite true,
But this, I think, is the thing for you to do;
Get busy on a day that is fair and bright,
Then patch the old roof till it's good and tight."
But the old man kept on a-playing at his reel,
And tapped the ground with his leathery heel:
"Get along," said he, "for you give me a pain;
My cabin never leakes when it doesn't rain."

Mark Twain

The Adventures of Huckleberry Finn

Two or three days and nights went by; I reckon I might say they swum by, they slid along so quiet and smooth and lovely. Here is the way we put in the time. It was a monstrous big river down there — sometimes a mile and a half wide; we run nights, and laid up and hid day-times; soon as night was most gone, we stopped navigating and tied up — nearly always in the dead water under a tow-head; and then cut young cottonwoods and willows and hid the raft with them. Then we set out the lines. Next we slid into the river and had a swim, so as to freshen up and cool off; then we set down on the sandy bottom where the water was about knee deep, and watched the daylight come. Not a sound, anywheres — perfectly still — just like the whole world was asleep, only sometimes the bull-frogs a-cluttering, maybe. The first thing to see, looking away over the water, was a kind of dull line — that was the woods on t'other side — you couldn't make nothing else out; then a pale place in the sky;

then more paleness, spreading around; then the river softened up, away off, and warn't black any more, but gray; you could see little dark spots drifting along, ever so far away — trading scows, and such things; and long black streaks — rafts; sometimes you could hear a sweep screaking; or jumbled up voices, it was so still, and sounds come so far; and by-and-by you could see a streak on the water which you know by the look of the streak that there's a snag there in a swift current which breaks on it and makes that streak look that way; and you see the mist curl up off of the water, and the east reddens up, and the river, and you make out a log cabin in the edge of the woods, away on the bank on t'other side of the river, being a wood-yard, likely, and piled by them cheats so you can throw a dog through it anywheres; then the nice breeze springs up, and comes fanning you from over there, so cool and fresh, and sweet to smell, on account of the woods and the flowers; but sometimes not that way, because they've left dead fish laying around, gars, and such, and they do get pretty rank; and next you've got the full day, and every-thing smiling in the sun, and the song-birds just going it!

Soon as it was night, out we shoved; when we got her out to about the middle, we let her alone, and let her float wherever the current wanted her to; then we lit the pipes, and dangled our legs in the water and talked about all kinds of things — we was always naked, day and night, when-ever the mosquitoes would let us — the new clothes Buck's folks made for me was too good to be comfortable, and besides I didn't go much on clothes, nohow.

IB. Materialism and Spiritual Values

The word 'materialism' usually conjures up images of wealth, greed, and conspicuous consumption. When we call someone materialistic, we most often mean that they are overly concerned with material things. But there are other meanings of this term, meanings that do not carry such negative judgments. A human person, like any animal, is material, a physical being. 'Materialistic' can refer to the simple fact of our physical existence. And by extension from this simple but solid base, 'materialism' refers to a philosophy of life that emphasizes the essential material nature of living things in opposition to views that distinguish the physical and the mental or the spiritual. Some religious and philosophical perspectives are based on a distinction between the physical and the spiritual: thus in orthodox Catholicism, for example, the spirit (soul) exists in union with the body and yet continues to exist after death. On the other hand some religious traditions espouse a kind of love affair with the world: Taoism, for example, says that humans will be most fulfilled when they become wide open to the intricacies and splendors of the material world. Thus materialism in our first sense (greediness, conspicuous consumption) is undesirable because it blocks this openness, this alternative materialism.

Materialism, then, like most "big words" can have many meanings. In this subsection we explore seminal expressions of some of the most important versions of materialism in our cultural tradition, especially as they relate to work. Work, after all, is a basic way we are materialistic — it is how humans affect the world through their efforts.

Benjamin Franklin speaks for a predominant view of materialism within the American tradition. As we will discuss in detail in Section II B, Franklin penned a secular version of the famous "Protestant work ethic." He believes that hard work and the material rewards it brings can and should be the heart of human existence. Franklin advises a young tradesman to "Remember that time is money. He that can earn ten shillings a day by his labour, and goes abroad, or sits idle one hour of that day, though he spends but sixpence during his diversion of idleness, ought not to reckon *that* the only expense; he has really spent, or rather thrown away, five shillings besides." Franklin further admonishes the young man: "Remember that *credit* is money." And, further, "Money can beget money . . . the more there is of it, the more it produces every turning, so that profits rise quicker and quicker." Franklin sums up his advice with the following famous quote: "In short, the way to wealth, if you desire it, is as plain as the way to market. It depends chiefly on two words, *industry* and *frugality*; that is, waste neither *time* nor *money,* but make the best use of both. Without industry and frugality nothing will do, and with them every thing."

Franklin clearly believes that thrift and hard work are virtuous. But why? Is it merely that "idle hands are the devil's tools"? Is he only concerned that humans need to be occupied lest they stray from the straight and narrow? Not entirely. Franklin had a positive motivation as well. He believed that economy and unremitting hard work are hard on the body but pleasant to the *heart* and the *purse:* "Deny self, for self's sake," he advised in 1735, and "If you know how to spend less than you get, you have the philosopher's stone." Hard work will result in this-worldly benefits—a person's pocketbook *and* self-development will thrive.

James Tate, a contemporary poet, raises some serious doubts about Franklin's faith. He has worked hard *and* he has been successful, but at what cost? Franklin's formula for *material* success *might* be true, but will the desirable self-development occur? Tate's reference to the loss of the "child" in himself as the surest sign that he has buried something important on his road to success is not incidental: many thinkers believe that full humanity must include the retention and development of our vital childlike characteristics.

In the next selection of this subsection William Wordsworth continues Tate's concerns and rejects one version of Franklin's ethic: he issues a chilling reminder of what can happen when we become too "materialistic" in the common sense of being overly concerned with material success. This great English Romantic poet says that when we spend our energies (work) "getting and spending . . . we lay waste our powers," we give "our hearts away." In a few words Wordsworth condenses our deepest fears about being too materialistic—much of what being human is about will be lost from our living if we are not careful. And this staunch Christian tells how horrible a fate such materialism would be—he would rather be a Pagan if that would get him back in touch with what really matters.

Vladimir Kirillov, a Russian poet, captures yet another strain of materialism that runs through the modern world. While he is a socialist rather than a capitalist, Kirillov simply yet powerfully sees that a major promise of modernism lies with technology, with the promises of material power and abundance our machines will deliver. So wonderful is the genie loosened by modern rationality that Kirillov likens it to the hoped-for miraculous saviors of the past. Our true salvation, so goes the modernist litany, lies in applying our rationality to material solutions, not to otherworldly supplications. If you read Kirillov's poem carefully, however (especially the last stanza), you will see that while he is not a Romantic like Wordsworth, Kirillov is a poet at heart — the cost of (materialistic) salvation may be to lose our souls.

Much of the material success of America and the Industrial Revolution more generally is based on a combination of Franklin's ethic and the technological materialism Kirillov praises. Perhaps their views too often have been used as a callous whip against the unfortunates whose poverty is viewed as proof of their poor moral character, but surely their faiths have been justified — through diligence, frugality, optimism, hard work, and technological ingenuity moderns have built an unprecedented empire wherein a greater percentage and range of humans thrive materially than ever before. Perhaps along the way we have had to ignore some of the romantic pleasures Wordsworth treasures; but surely it has been (and still is) worth it, has it not?

Henry David Thoreau, writing fully a century after Franklin, answers this question with a resounding No. Thoreau's prophetic analysis anticipates that more than a century later, in our own lives, employers will express serious concern for the physical, psychological, and social health of their most diligent and loyal employees, who so thoroughly accept the work ethic as their own that they work harder than their bosses would dare ask them to work.

Thoreau is concerned, most centrally, that most work and human development are incompatible. He, like most sages preceding or antedating him, believes that "man's capacities have never been measured; nor are we to judge of what he can do by any precedents, so little has been tried." The grand experiment of being human has just begun, Thoreau believes, and much of our work can be a dangerous sidetrack from that more important human "work," our own flourishing. Thoreau warns us that "As for work, we haven't any of consequence" . . . if human development is what is most important. It remains to our imaginations and invention whether we can create work which allows for, indeed enhances, this growth.

As you read these excerpts from Thoreau's classic essay on the art of living, ask yourself not only about the pitfalls like workaholism which come from pursuing the good life as we have come to define both its goals and processes. Also begin to ask if we could make working compatible with Thoreau's goal of living *concretely, simply,* and *fully:* "If we are really dying, let us hear the rattle in our throats and full cold in the extremities; if we are alive, let us go about our business."

Franklin's materialism seems a stark contrast to the aesthetic simplicity of Thoreau. Yet they share at least part of a vision. For both, but especially for Thoreau, democracy is a generous community, a place where people engage in material activities with joy and where they and their communities simultaneously prosper. Just how to translate this vision into reality is a crucial and difficult problem. As you sort through these contrasting views of materialism, work, and economy, ask yourself two questions: What are the purposes of our materialistic activities? and What are the best ways to attain those purposes? These questions will guide us throughout our exploration of working in America.

A Worker's Voice

A San Francisco Dockworker

One thing that has not changed over the years on the San Francisco waterfront is that if you do not want to work you do not have to work. I can still tell a Walking Boss to go to hell, and nothing much will happen. I can call the night Business Agent for a replacement, and that is the end of it. Except that I'll lose a night's pay. On the way back to the ship from the meal break last night all four of us in the car expressed a desire to call it quits. But none of us did. The undeniable fact of automation is that there are fewer jobs, which in turn means that there is more competition for the jobs that remain. On nights, we are all working an average of about three shifts a week. Neither I nor any of the other men lashing containers last night could afford to lose the work. Nevertheless, when we returned from the meal break last night, I and the man working with me on the dock chose to slow-down the operation. Very soon the crane was waiting on us, the carriage hanging over our heads as we slowly walked down the side of the container, flipping latches. Soon after that the Walking Boss was beside me, standing on first one leg and then the other.

"Hey! For Christ's sake, hurry up!" he shouted in my ear.

"What did you say?" I demanded, turning on him. He knows the rules as well as I. The night, like every other night, had started off fast. Then it had accelerated. The trucks were tearing-ass up and down the pier faster than ever. The crane was going beep-beep, and twenty tons of shit was zooming-off over our heads.

"What did you say?" I demanded again.

He immediately became defensive. "Jesus Christ," he almost pleaded, "let's hurry up. Let's hurry up so we can get the hell out of here!"

(Reg Theriault; from *Longshoring: On the San Francisco Waterfront*)

1. Finding Meaning in the Material World

Introduction
Benjamin Franklin, "Advice to a Young Tradesman"

Probably no other figure in American history better exemplifies American commercial values than Ben Franklin. Franklin's migration, as a young man, from Puritan New England to the thriving city of Philadelphia symbolizes the transformation of America from a religious to an essentially commercial land. Philadelphia was, by mideighteenth century, the most booming commercial center among the colonies.

Yet this journey was not so long as it may seem, for it was no accident that the Puritan community was also a prosperous business community. While the Puritan migrants of the early seventeenth century were driven by great spiritual energy, they saw nothing sinful in the accumulation of material goods and wealth. The Puritans believed that we serve God through careful attention to worldly affairs, and their idea of vocation, the notion of a secular calling, was a major contributor to the American work ethic.

While Franklin had adopted the scientific doctrines of the eighteenth-century Enlightenment, he also carried with him the religious mind-set of his New England roots. He rejected the overt Puritan religious beliefs, but there is a Puritan zeal about the way in which he pursues wealth. As you read Franklin's advice to a young tradesman, ask yourself *why* they (or we) should work so hard and be so frugal.

Benjamin Franklin

Advice to a Young Tradesman

Written in 1748, as Franklin was retiring from active business life to devote himself to science and public service.

To My Friend, A.B.:

As you have desired it of me, I write the following hints, which have been of service to me, and may, if observed, be so to you.

Remember, that *time* is money. He that can earn ten shillings a day by his labour, and goes abroad, or sits idle, one half of that day, though he spends but sixpence during his diversion or idleness, ought not to reckon *that* the only expense; he has really spent, or rather thrown away, five shillings besides.

Remember, that *credit* is money. If a man lets his money lie in my hands after it is due, he gives me the interest, or so much as I can make of it during that time. This amounts to a considerable sum where a man has good and large credit, and makes good use of it.

Remember, that money is of the prolific, generating nature. Money can beget money, and its offspring can beget more, and so on. Five shillings turned is six, turned again it is seven and three-pence, and so on till it becomes an hundred pounds. The more there is of it, the more it produces every turning, so that the profits rise quicker and quicker. He that kills a breeding sow, destroys all her offspring to the thousandth generation. He that murders a crown, destroys all that it might have produced, even scores of pounds.

Remember, that six pounds a year is but a groat a day. For this little sum (which may be daily wasted either in time or expense unperceived) a man of credit may, on his own security, have the constant possession and use of an hundred pounds. So much in stock, briskly turned by an industrious man, produces great advantage.

Remember this saying, *The good paymaster is lord of another man's purse.* He that is known to pay punctually and exactly to the time he promises, may at any time, and on any occasion, raise all the money his friends can spare. This is sometimes of great use. After industry and frugality, nothing contributes more to the raising of a young man in the world than punctuality and justice in all his dealings; therefore never keep borrowed money an hour beyond the time you promised, lest a disappointment shut up your friend's purse for ever.

The most trifling actions that affect a man's credit are to be regarded. The sound of your hammer at five in the morning, or nine at night, heard by a creditor, makes him easy six months longer; but, if he see you at a billiard table, or hears your voice at a tavern, when you should be at work, he sends for his money the next day; demands it, before he can receive it, in a lump.

It shows, besides, that you are mindful of what you owe; it makes you appear a careful as well as an honest man, and that still increases your credit.

Beware of thinking all your own that you possess, and of living accordingly. It is a mistake that many people who have credit fall into. To prevent this, keep an exact account for some time, both of your expenses and your income. If you take the pains at first to mention particulars, it will have this good effect: you will discover how wonderfully small, trifling expenses mount up to large sums, and will discern what might have been, and may for the future be saved, without occasioning any great inconvenience.

In short, the way to wealth, if you desire it, is as plain as the way to market. It depends chiefly on two words, *industry* and *frugality;* that is, waste neither *time* nor *money,* but make the best use of both. Without industry and frugality nothing will do, and with them every thing. He that gets all he can honestly, and saves all he gets (necessary expenses excepted), will certainly become *rich,* if that Being who governs the world, to whom all should look for a blessing on their honest endeavors, doth not, in his wise providence, otherwise determine.

An Old Tradesman

Introduction
James Tate, "The Professor Waking"

Poet James Tate was born in Kansas City, Missouri, in 1943. A graduate of Kansas State College with a Master of Fine Arts degree from The University of Iowa's writer's workshop, Tate has taught at a number of colleges and universities, including The University of Iowa, The University of California, Berkeley, and Boston College. Besides his work as a teacher and an editor, Tate's favorite work is writing poetry, and both the quantity and quality of his work have been impressive.

Tate's poem "The Professor Waking" is about finding meaning in the modern materialistic world. The professor "wakes" one day to the seeming hollowness of his existence; he wonders what happened to the playful child that he once was. This is a common postmodern theme, with its roots in the Romantic Movement. The child represents the natural, the innocent and uncontrived. As the narrator tells us, it is "opportunity, the position, the money that destroys the child." The professor finds in ambition the antidote for his depression, and the poem ends on a seemingly happy note. If you think about the ending, however, you might decide that the professor chose success as a compensation for something much more precious that he had lost.

James Tate

The Professor Waking

I am surprised to find today
I am no longer a child.
Waking a moment ago,
I expected to see my small
blue trousers waiting for me

on the hamper, to hear the voices
of Susan and Johnny outside
urging me to hurry. Where
have I been these fifty years?
I am not a proud keeper

of bees with a wealth of honey.
I have had no time to think,
to learn, to grow: the wild yearning
forward, without real laughter
or tears. It is always the great
opportunity, the position,
the money that destroys the child
left in us and creates adult

fears. So now I have a decent
name and two months in sunny
Italy—then it's back to the blue
books and cold winds of Blabber-
mouth University. Whatever

happened to the mild boy named
Tommy, whom all the school loved?
Too many beers would have been
a better ending, a bulbous
red runny nose giving off

a bit of light for the bums
and queers as I wander home

Printed from *Fire Frenzy*, edited by Robert Baylor and Brenda Stokes. Published by McGraw-Hill. Copyright © 1972. Reprinted with permission of James Tate.

at 5 A.M. through the Bowery.
Or I could have died in Veracruz
of syphilis, beguiled by

a fourteen-year-old prostitute.
It is almost funny: Chairman
of the Department, a Deacon.
Next, the City Council! I am
Dean of Crime and Cultural Trends!

I can get you a good job in Zagreb
or South Bend. So who the hell
was Tommy? What was so real
about him! If they ask me to run
for President, I might give in!

2. Worlds to Choose From

Introduction
William Wordsworth,
"The World Is Too Much with Us"

While Benjamin Franklin and other thinkers of the Enlightenment, not to mention a booming business community, embraced the materialism and entrepreneurship of industrialization, another group in England began to react against the ready acceptance of the new values. The English Romantic poets saw in industrialization a submergence of traditional spiritual values beneath the tide of materialism. William Wordsworth (1770–1850) was one of the first to give voice to this concern. In "The World Is Too Much with Us, Late and Soon" he rejects the "busyness" that Franklin urges upon the young tradesman. For Wordsworth and the other Romantic poets nature was a source of God-derived spiritual values. They believed that the intent of God could be seen in the patterns of nature: that the rush to transform the natural world not only deprives us of nature but leaves humankind little time to contemplate the magic to be found in the world as God made it.

The values in the poem are almost directly opposed to those in Franklin's "Tradesman." While Franklin urges us not to waste time when we could be accumulating wealth, Wordsworth sees work in pursuit of the material world as the great waste, depriving us of time to be in nature. While Franklin urges accumulation of money, even saying that time is money, Wordsworth laments the hurry that has cost us our identity with nature. He ends by saying that he would rather "be suckled in a creed outworn" than lose the magic of nature, suggesting that the loss of nature is as serious as the loss of God.

This classic disagreement is often mirrored in contemporary America. The conflict in the Pacific Northwest between loggers who want jobs and conservationists who want to save the old growth forests is an example. Why should we care about the snowy owl or the Douglas fir in which the owls live? Why should we care about coastal wetlands when the cost of caring is a loss of the oil that will keep some Americans working? Those who, like Wordsworth, would defend nature find in nature more than mere "resources" to fuel our economy: they see in "undeveloped" nature the source of what is best in humanity as well as a reflection of God's creation. Like Wordsworth, contemporary conservationists are not antijobs or against material comforts, but they believe that we cannot avoid alienation from the deepest sources of our being if we live entirely in human-made worlds.

William Wordsworth

The World Is Too Much with Us

The world is too much with us; late and soon,
Getting and spending, we lay waste our powers;
Little we see in Nature that is ours;
We have given our hearts away, a sordid boon!
This Sea that bares her bosom to the moon;
The winds that will be howling at all hours,
And are up-gathered now like sleeping flowers;
For this, for everything, we are out of tune;
It moves us not.—Great God! I'd rather be
A Pagan suckled in a creed outworn;
So might I, standing on this pleasant lea,
Have glimpses that would make me less forlorn:
Have sight of Proteus rising from the sea;
Or hear old Triton blow his wreathéd horn.

Introduction
Vladimir Timofeevich Kirillov, "The Iron Messiah"

As we try to understand our world, often we find it useful to try to stand outside our own culture. The Industrial Revolution and the new work it created have not been limited to capitalist economies; thus in the following poem by the Russian poet Vladimir Kirillov we see that others have shared our concern with the curses that have accompanied the blessings of industrialization.

Vladimir Timofeevich Kirillov is a maker as well as a recorder of history. The son of a bookstore manager, he was born in 1890 in a small village outside of Smolensk. At thirteen he went to sea as a cabin boy, and by fifteen he was an active revolutionary. He began publishing poetry as early as 1913, but his career as a poet was cut short by World War I. During the 1917 revolution he led an insurgent regiment, and after the Bolshevik victory he served as party secretary in one of the Moscow districts. As early as 1920 Kirillov came in conflict with the party over the principle of an independent proletarian poetry, free of party regimentation. In 1921 he began criticizing the party for betraying the Revolution and shortly thereafter resigned his party membership. Kirillov fell victim to the Stalinist purges in 1937 and died in a concentration camp in 1943.

When "The Iron Messiah" was written in 1918, Kirillov still believed that the Bolshevik Revolution would solve the major problems of society, although as the poem shows, he does not allow his art to become simple propaganda. The poem begins with the traditional Christian idea of a Messiah and gives it a Marxist twist. Salvation, he argues, will come, not from a supernatural god, but from humankind's own creation, the Industrial Revolution. This new force will accomplish all that is desirable from a Marxist perspective, destroying thrones and prisons, calling the people to eternal fraternity, and crushing the yoke of destiny. But if you read the last stanza of the poem carefully, you will see that this poem is more than Marxist propaganda. Kirillov gives us one more ironic twist when he says: "We shall conquer the *enchanting* world." Ask yourself if even Kirillov, the rational Marxist, does not have doubts about a world too enamored with reason and its resultant technologies.

Vladimir Timofeevich Kirillov

The Iron Messiah

There he is—the saviour, the lord of the earth,
The master of titanic forces—
In the roar of countless steel machinery,
In the sparkle of suns of electricity.

We thought he would appear in a starry stole,
With a nimbus of divine mystery,
But he came to us clad in black smoke
From the suburbs, foundries, factories.

We thought he would appear in glory and glitter,
Meek, blessing and gentle,
But he, like the molten lava,
Came—multifaced and turbulent. . . .

There he walks o'er the abyss of seas,
All of steel, unyielding and impetuous;
He scatters sparks of rebellious thoughts,
And the purging flames are pouring forth.

Wherever his masterful call is heard,
The world's bosom is bared,
The mountains give way before him,
The earth's poles together are brought.

Wherever he walks, he leaves a trail
Of ringing iron rail;
He brings joy and light to us,
A desert he strews with blossoms.

To the world he brings the New Sun,
He destroys the thrones and prisons.
He calls the peoples to eternal fraternity,
And wipes out boundary lines.

His crimson banner is the symbol of struggle;
For the oppressed it is the guiding beacon;
With it we shall crush the yoke of destiny,
We shall conquer the enchanting world.

Reprinted with permission of the Editors of the *Slavonic Review*.

3. Finding Meaning in Spiritual Living

Introduction
Henry David Thoreau, from *Walden*

Henry David Thoreau, writing almost a century after Franklin, has a radically different perspective from his famous predecessor. Franklin wrote as a participant and an aspirant in the American dream; Thoreau, although a Harvard graduate and a former factory manager, wrote as an observer, an outsider, a prophet who, like Melville and Hawthorne, saw the underside as well as the positive side of the American system. Like the prophets of old, Thoreau speaks from the wilderness, from a long historical viewpoint, and from concern with fundamental experiences of the human spirit. Like Old Testament prophets, Thoreau raises truly radical questions.

Thoreau's famous essay *Walden,* written in 1854, reminds us of the teaching of Jesus, who, when asked to measure true success, said "it is easier for a camel to go through the eye of a needle than for a rich man to enter the Kingdom of Heaven." Thoreau is not opposed to the material success of industrial America, but he is concerned that it will hamper the development of the human spirit. He is most concerned that the way we work will turn us into machines: "The finest qualities of our nature, like the bloom on fruits, can be preserved only by the most delicate handling. Yet we do not treat ourselves nor one another thus tenderly."

Thoreau is extremely sensitive to the potential traps of materialism. We begin, innocently enough, accepting the goals and means of our society. Like all good followers of Franklin, we seek to avoid poverty and debt by working and laying up property to guard against as many of the unforeseen calamities of life as we can. Unfortunately, Thoreau observes, too often "we make ourselves sick, that [we] may lay up something against a sick day" . . . and the circle begins.

To make things even worse, Thoreau contends, we internalize the work habits that are necessary to enslave us. Literal slavery is unnecessary: "there are so many keen and subtle masters that enslave both North and South. It is hard to have a Southern overseer; it is worse to have a Northern one; but worst of all when you are the slave-driver of yourself. Talk of the divinity of man!" Materialists can easily become workaholics, and as the comparison with alcoholics suggests, workaholics are not people who experience a deep satisfaction and serenity from living a life of excellence; rather they, as Thoreau tells us, lead "lives of quiet desperation."

One might easily gather from this that Thoreau is the advocate for a life of indolence, but as you read you will see that this is far from the case. What he attacks is work with the wrong theme. He tells us "that we inhabitants of New England live this mean life that we do because our vision does not penetrate the surface of things. We think that that *is* which *appears* to be." Thoreau believes, like Plato, that a deeper spiritual reality lies behind the material surface of things. Here is where our real work lies. This is where the art of living begins. And as we said above, ask yourself how we can make work more compatible with Thoreau's goal of living *concretely, simply,* and *fully.*

Henry David Thoreau

Walden

. . . I have traveled a good deal in Concord; and everywhere, in shops, and offices, and fields, the inhabitants have appeared to me to be doing penance in a thousand remarkable ways. What I have heard of Bramins sitting exposed to four fires and looking in the face of the sun; or hanging suspended, with their heads downward, over flames; or looking at the heavens over their shoulders "until it becomes impossible for them to resume their natural position, while from the twist of the neck nothing but liquids can pass into the stomach"; or dwelling, chained for life, at the foot of a tree; or measuring with their bodies, like caterpillars, the breadth of vast empires; or standing on one leg on the tops of pillars — even these forms of conscious penance are hardly more incredible and astonishing than the scenes which I daily witness. The twelve labors of Hercules were trifling in comparison with those which my neighbors have undertaken; for they were only twelve, and had an end; but I could never see that these men slew or captured any monster or finished any labor. They have no friend Iolaus to burn with a hot iron the root of the hydra's head, but as soon as one head is crushed, two spring up.

I see young men, my townsmen, whose misfortune it is to have inherited farms, houses, barns, cattle, and farming tools; for these are more easily acquired than got rid of. Better if they had been born in the open pasture and suckled by a wolf, that they might have seen with clearer eyes what field they were called to labor in. Who made them serfs of the soil? Why should they eat their sixty acres, when man is condemned to eat only his peck of dirt? Why should they begin digging their graves as soon as they are born? They have got to live a man's life, pushing all these things before them, and get on as well as they can. How many a poor immortal soul have I met well nigh crushed and smothered under its load, creeping down the road of life, pushing before it a barn seventy-five feet by forty, its Augean stables never cleansed, and one hundred acres of land, tillage, mowing, pasture, and wood-lot! The portionless, who struggle with no such unnecessary inherited encumbrances, find it labor enough to subdue and cultivate a few cubic feet of flesh.

But men labor under a mistake. The better part of the man is soon ploughed into the soil for compost. By a seeming fate, commonly called necessity, they are employed, as it says in an old book, laying up treasures which moth and rust will corrupt and thieves break through and steal. It is a fool's life, as they will find when they get to the end of it, if not before.

Most men, even in this comparatively free country, through mere ignorance and mistake, are so occupied with the factitious cares and superfluously coarse labors of life that its finer fruits cannot be plucked by them. Their fingers, from excessive toil, are too clumsy and tremble too much for that. Actually, the laboring man has not leisure for a true integrity day by day; he cannot afford to sustain the manliest relations to men; his labor would be depreciated in the market. He has no time to be anything but a machine. How can he remember well his ignorance — which his growth requires — who has so often to use his knowledge? We should feed and clothe him gratuitously sometimes, and recruit him with our cordials, before we judge of him. The finest qualities of our nature, like the bloom on fruits, can be preserved only by the most delicate handling. Yet we do not treat ourselves nor one another thus tenderly.

Some of you, we all know, are poor, find it hard to live, are sometimes, as it were, gasping for breath. I have no doubt that some of you who read this book are unable to pay for all the dinners which you have actually eaten, or for the coats and shoes which are fast wearing or are already worn out, and have come to this page to spend borrowed or stolen time, robbing your creditors of an hour. It is very evident what mean and sneaking lives many of you live, for my sight has been whetted by experience; always on the limits, trying to get into business and trying to get out of debt, a very ancient slough, called by the Latins *æs alienum,* another's brass, for some of their coins were made of brass; still living, and dying, and buried by this other's brass; always promising to pay, promising to pay, tomorrow, and dying today, insolvent; seeking to curry favor, to get custom, by how many modes, only not state-prison offenses; lying, flattering, voting, contracting yourselves into a nutshell of civility, or dilating into an atmosphere of thin and vaporous generosity, that you may persuade your neighbor to let you make his shoes, or his hat, or his coat, or his carriage, or import his groceries for him; making yourselves sick, that you may lay up something against a sick day, something to be tucked away in an old chest, or in a stocking behind the plastering, or, more safely, in the brick bank; no matter where, no matter how much or how little.

I sometimes wonder that we can be so frivolous, I may almost say, as to attend to the gross but somewhat foreign form of servitude called Negro Slavery, there are so many keen and subtle masters that enslave both North and South. It is hard to have a Southern overseer; it is worse to have a Northern one; but worst of all when you are the slave-driver of yourself. Talk of a divinity in man! Look at the teamster on the highway, wending to market by day or night; does any divinity stir within him? His highest duty to fodder and water his horses! What is his destiny to him compared with the shipping interests? Does not he drive for Squire Make-a-stir? How godlike, how immortal, is he? See how he cowers and sneaks, how vaguely all the day he fears, not being immortal nor divine, but the slave and prisoner of his own opinion of himself, a fame won by his own deeds. Public opinion is a weak tyrant compared with our own private opinion. What a man thinks of himself, that it is which determines, or rather indicates, his fate. Self-emancipation even in the West Indian provinces of the fancy and imagination—what Wilberforce is there to bring that about? Think, also, of the ladies of the land weaving toilet cushions against the last day, not to betray too green an interest in their fates! As if you could kill time without injuring eternity.

The mass of men lead lives of quiet desperation. What is called resignation is confirmed desperation. From the desperate city you go into the desperate country, and have to console yourself with the bravery of minks and muskrats. A stereotyped but unconscious despair is concealed even under what are called the games and amusements of mankind. There is no play in them, for this comes after work. But it is a characteristic of wisdom not to do desperate things.

When we consider what, to use the words of the catechism, is the chief end of man, and what are the true necessaries and means of life, it appears as if men had deliberately chosen the common mode of living because they preferred it to any other. Yet they honestly think there is no choice left. But alert and healthy natures remember that the sun rose clear. It is never too late to give up our prejudices. No way of thinking or doing, however ancient, can be trusted without proof. What everybody echoes or in silence passes by as true today may turn out to be falsehood tomorrow, mere smoke of opinion, which some had trusted for a cloud that would sprinkle fertilizing rain on their fields. What old people say you cannot do you try and find that you can. Old deeds for old people, and new deeds for new. Old people did not know enough once, perchance, to fetch fresh fuel to keep the fire a-going; new people put a little dry wood under a pot, and are whirled round the globe with the speed of birds, in a way to kill old people, as the phrase is. Age is no better, hardly so well, qualified for an instructor as youth, for it has not profited so much as it has lost. One may almost doubt if the wisest man has learned anything of absolute value by living. Practically, the old have no very important advice to give the young, their own experience has been so partial, and their lives have been such miserable failures, for private reasons, as they must believe; and it may be that they have some faith left which belies that experience, and they are only less young than they were. I have lived some thirty years on this planet, and I have yet to hear the first syllable of valuable or even earnest advice from my seniors. They have told me nothing, and probably cannot tell me anything to the purpose. Here is life, an experiment to a great extent untried by me; but it does not avail me that they have tried it. If I have any experience which I think valuable, I am sure to reflect that this my Mentors said nothing about.

. . . But man's capacities have never been measured; nor are we to judge of what he can do by any precedents, so little has been tried. Whatever have been thy failures hitherto, "be not afflicted, my child, for who shall assign to thee what thou hast left undone?"

I think that we may safely trust a good deal more than we do. We may waive just so much care of ourselves as we honestly bestow elsewhere. Nature is as well adapted to our weakness as to our strength. The incessant anxiety and strain of some is a well-nigh incurable form of disease. We are made to exaggerate the importance of what work we do; and yet how much is not done by us! or, what if we had been taken sick? How vigilant we are! determined not to live by faith if we can avoid it; all the day long on the alert, at night we unwillingly say our prayers and commit ourselves to uncertainties. So thoroughly and sincerely are we compelled to live, reverencing our life, and denying the possibility of change. This is the only way, we say; but there are as many ways as there can be drawn radii from one center. All change is a miracle to contemplate; but it is a miracle which is taking place every instant. Confucius said, "To know that we know what we know, and that we do not know what we do not know, that is true knowledge." When one man has reduced a fact of the imagination to be a fact to his understanding, I foresee that all men will at length establish their lives on that basis.

Why should we live with such hurry and waste of life? We are determined to be starved before we are hungry. Men say that a stitch in time saves nine, and so they take a thousand stitches today to save nine tomorrow. As for *work,* we haven't any of any consequence. We have the Saint Vitus' dance, and cannot possibly keep our heads still. If I should only give a few pulls at the parish bell-rope, as for a fire, that is, without setting the bell, there is hardly a man on his farm in the outskirts of Concord, notwithstanding that press of engagements which was his excuse so many times this morning, nor a boy, nor a woman, I might almost say, but would forsake all and follow that sound, not mainly to save property from the flames, but, if we will confess the truth, much more to see it burn, since burn it must, and we, be it known, did not set it on fire — or to see it put out, and have a hand in it, if that is done as handsomely; yes, even if it were the parish church itself. Hardly a man takes a half hour's nap after dinner, but when he wakes he holds up his head and asks, "What's the news?" as if the rest of mankind had stood his sentinels. Some give directions to be waked every half hour, doubtless for no other purpose; and then, to pay for it, they tell what they have dreamed. After a night's sleep the news is as indispensable as the breakfast. "Pray tell me anything new that has happened to a man anywhere on this globe" — and he reads it over his coffee and rolls, that a man has had his eyes gouged out this morning on the Wachito River; never dreaming the while that he lives in the dark unfathomed mammoth cave of this world, and has but the rudiment of an eye himself.

Shams and delusions are esteemed for soundest truths, while reality is fabulous. If men would steadily observe realities only, and not allow themselves to be deluded, life, to compare it with such things as we know, would be like a fairy tale and the Arabian Nights' Entertainments. If we respected only what is inevitable and has a right to be, music and poetry would resound along the streets. When we are unhurried and wise, we perceive that only great and worthy things have any permanent and absolute existence — that petty fears and petty pleasures are but the shadow of the reality. This is always exhilarating and sublime. By closing the eyes and slumbering, and consenting to be deceived by shows, men establish and confirm their daily life of routine and habit everywhere, which still is built on purely illusory foundations. Children, who play life, discern its true law and relations more clearly than men, who fail to live it worthily, but who think that they are wiser by experience, that is, by failure. I have read in a Hindu book that "there was a king's son, who, being expelled in infancy from his native city, was brought up by a forester, and, growing up to maturity in that state, imagined himself to belong to the barbarous race with which he lived. One of his father's ministers, having discovered him, revealed to him what he was, and the misconception of his character was removed, and he knew himself to be a prince. So soul," continues the Hindu philosopher, "from the circumstances in which it is placed, mistakes its own character, until the truth is revealed to it by some holy teacher, and then it knows itself to be *Brahme.*" I perceive that we inhabitants of New England live this mean life that we do because our vision does not penetrate the surface of things. We think that that *is* which *appears* to be. If a man should walk through this town and see only the reality, where, think you, would the "Mill-dam" go to? If he should give us an account of the realities he beheld there, we should not recognize the place in his description. Look at a meeting-house, or a courthouse, or a jail, or a shop, or a dwelling-house, and say what that thing really is before a true gaze, and they would all go to pieces in your account of them. Men esteem truth remote, in the outskirts of the system, behind the farthest star, before Adam and after the last man. In eternity there is indeed something true and sublime. But all these times and places and occasions are now and here. God himself culminates in the present moment, and will never be more divine in the lapse of all the ages. And we are enabled to apprehend at all what is sublime and noble only by the perpetual instilling and drenching of the reality that surrounds us. The universe constantly and obediently answers to our conceptions; whether we travel fast or slow, the track is laid for us. Let us spend our lives in conceiving then. The poet or the artist never yet had so fair and noble a design but some of his posterity at least could accomplish it.

Let us spend one day as deliberately as Nature, and not be thrown off the track by every nutshell and mosquito's wing that falls on the rails. Let us rise early and fast, or break fast, gently and without perturbation; let company come and let company go, let the bells ring and the children cry—determined to make a day of it. Why should we knock under and go with the stream? Let us not be upset and overwhelmed in that terrible rapid and whirlpool called a dinner, situated in the meridian shallows.

Weather this danger and you are safe, for the rest of the way is down hill. With unrelaxed nerves, with morning vigor, sail by it, looking another way, tied to the mast like Ulysses. If the engine whistles, let it whistle till it is hoarse for its pains. If the bell rings, why should we run? We will consider what kind of music they are like. Let us settle ourselves, and work and wedge our feet downward through the mud and slush of opinion, and prejudice, and tradition, and delusion, and appearance, that alluvion which covers the globe, through Paris and London, through New York and Boston and Concord, through church and state, through poetry and philosophy and religion, till we come to a hard bottom and rocks in place, which we can call *reality*, and say, This is, and no mistake; and then begin, having a *point d'appui*, below freshet and frost and fire, a place where you might found a wall or a state, or set a lamppost safely, or perhaps a gauge, not a Nilometer, but a Realometer, that future ages might know how deep a freshet of shams and appearances had gathered from time to time. If you stand right fronting and face to face to a fact, you will see the sun glimmer on both its surfaces, as if it were a cimeter, and feel its sweet edge dividing you through the heart and marrow, and so you will happily conclude your mortal career. Be it life or death, we crave only reality. If we are really dying, let us hear the rattle in our throats and feel cold in the extremities; if we are alive, let us go about our business.

Time is but the stream I go a-fishing in. I drink at it; but while I drink I see the sandy bottom and detect how shallow it is. Its thin current slides away, but eternity remains. I would drink deeper; fish in the sky, whose bottom is pebbly with stars. I cannot count one. I know not the first letter of the alphabet. I have always been regretting that I was not as wise as the day I was born. The intellect is a cleaver; it discerns and rifts its way into the secret of things. I do not wish to be any more busy with my hands than is necessary. My head is hands and feet. I feel all my best faculties concentrated in it. My instinct tells me that my head is an organ for burrowing, as some creatures use their snout and forepaws, and with it I would mine and burrow my way through these hills. I think that the richest vein is somewhere hereabouts; so by the divining rod and thin rising vapors I judge; and here I will begin to mine.

IC. Humans as Commodities

Conformity and Rebellion

As we will see in Section II of this book, the Industrial Revolution radically changed the lives of ordinary people. Wrenching millions out of the countryside and urbanizing them often under terribly inhumane conditions, the new economic order redefined people's entire lives according to its needs. While industrialization produced immense material wealth, the human cost was, at least in the short run, extremely high. As we saw in the subsection on materialism, the Romantics questioned the balance of benefits accompanying these great changes. To quote the New Testament, we might paraphrase their complaint thus: "What benefit it a man if he gain the whole world, but lose his immortal soul?"

People responded to the difficulties created by the new order in many ways. Some people, following the likes of Kirillov's Marxists, embraced the radical changes as progress. Others, perhaps listening more to Thoreau or Wordsworth, tried to avoid the advances of industrialization by clinging to traditional ways or by escaping to some out-of-the-way places. In this part we will examine two other possible responses. One way to think of the new world order is as a dominating parent who dictates most everything about how we are to live. Given such a parent, people typically choose one of two responses — to conform to the parent's wishes or to rebel against them, be the obedient child or resist parental control.

This scenario, of course, is too simple. Children can seem to be obedient but secretly rebel; they can conform at one point and later rebel (or vice versa); and, of course, in reality children are complex mixtures of conformity and rebellion in response to various interchanges with their parents. This too-simple dichotomy (the Yin/Yang of parent-child relationships) can be very instructive, though, for it illustrates once again that opposite reactions can derive from the same source and that these reactions are strategies based on how people feel and think.

The four poems on conformity all warn, in one way or another, of the danger of losing something crucial to our humanity if we get caught up in the "machine." None of these poets, though, is a simpleminded machine basher. They understand that humans have always been machine makers and users, and they do not believe merely eliminating "machines" will solve our problems. Instead, they are concerned with the logic (or better, psycho-logic and socio-logic) of how we can get sucked into becoming "slaves" to the "systems" we create, and how our relations to these systems can stifle our humanity.

When we think of the ill effects of working in the Industrial Revolution we usually think of the factory. And rightly so. But the psychic numbing of forced conformity can grip anyone, as each of these poets shows. W.H. Auden's unknown citizen could be an assembly-line worker, but he could as well be the proverbial white-collar worker, the "organization man" who, in Donald Hall's powerful image, can become like a dead fighter pilot whose corpse lies undiscovered for years. Our third poet, Fenton Johnson, pursues the source of this horrible death and proposes that the "grind" of the system slowly turning can (and will!) wear down anyone. And finally, Louis Untermeyer tries to understand why we place ourselves in the path of this machine, why we conform. Our usual answer might be that we are coerced, we have no choice. Untermeyer suggests that perhaps *seduction* is a better explanation: the machine runs so beautifully and promises so much that its seductive magnetism is nearly inescapable.

Yet some people escape. Or at least they rebel. The five voices in the unit on rebellion speak as and for different people, but they each speak as one who has been in the "belly of the machine," has seen what it does to people, and has finally refused to conform. As you listen to their voices try to figure out *why* these people resist the numbness and psychic death the poets in the first part describe. Are they specially gifted people? What has happened to them that helps them rebel? How do they rebel? What role do ideas and words play in their abilities to rebel effectively?

The realization that we are conforming to our detriment (is all conformity bad?) is a beginning step to preventing our decline, and rebellion is a necessary step to changing our situation; but how we rebel and toward what alternatives we might work remain to be seen. In the next subsection, and especially in Section III, we will explore these crucial issues.

A Worker's Voice

An 11-Year-Old Scottish Coal-Mining Girl

She works with her father and has done so for two years.

Father gangs at 2 in the morning: I gang with the women at 5, and come up at 5 at night; work all night on Fridays, and come away at 12 in the day. I carry the large bits of coal from the wall-face to the pit-bottom, and the small pieces called chows, in a creel; the weight is usually a hundred-weight; does not know how many pounds there are in the hundred-weight, but it is some work to carry; it takes three journeys to fill a tub of 4 cwt. . . . The roof is very low; I have to bend my back and legs, and the water comes frequently up to the calves of my legs; has no likening for the work; father makes me like it. . . . Never got hurt, but often obliged to scramble out when bad air was in the pit.

I am learning to read at the night-school; am in the twopenny book; sometimes to sabbath-school. Jesus was God; David wrote the Bible; has a slight knowledge of the first six questions in the Shorter Catechism.

(Janet Cumming, 1842. From testimonies in E. Royston Pike, *Human Documents of the Industrial Revolution in Britain*)

1. Conformity

Introduction
W.H. Auden, "The Unknown Citizen"

W.H. Auden was born in York, England, in 1907. A socialist and a Freudian, he was a second-generation modernist poet. Auden moved to the United States in 1934, and after brief periods abroad he became an American citizen. In time he became more an American than an English poet, both in his viewpoint and in his use of language.

In "The Unknown Citizen" Auden satirizes the mindless worker and the system that has turned him from an individual to become like the interchangeable parts he handles on the assembly line at "Fudge Motors."

Auden asks us to consider what it means to be human. On the assembly line uniformity, obedience, and lack of imagination lead to efficient production of products. But what happens to the people who make themselves instruments of this end? Auden implies that nonconformity, imagination, and uniqueness are the proper means and ends for humans. As you read this poem, consider this question of ends and means. Auden seems to think that we have sacrificed proper human ends to the means of production. What is your experience with "assembly lines"? Do you think Auden is just talking about assembly lines in factories, or has the idea of the assembly line had influence elsewhere . . . in education, for instance?

W.H. Auden

The Unknown Citizen

He was found by the Bureau of Statistics to be
One against whom there was no official complaint,
And all the reports on his conduct agree
That, in the modern sense of an old-fashioned word, he was a saint,
For in everything he did he served the Greater Community.
Except for the War till the day he retired
He worked in a factory and never got fired,
But satisfied his employers, Fudge Motors Inc.
Yet he wasn't a scab or odd in his views,
For his Union reports that he paid his dues,
(Our report on his Union shows it was sound)
And our Social Psychology workers found
That he was popular with his mates and liked a drink.
The Press are convinced that he bought a paper every day
And that his reactions to advertisements were normal in every way.
Policies taken out in his name prove that he was fully insured,
And his Health-card shows he was once in hospital but left it cured.
Both Producers Research and High-Grade Living declare
He was fully sensible to the advantages of the Installment Plan
And had everything necessary to the Modern Man,
A phonograph, a radio, a car and a frigidaire.

Our researchers into Public Opinion are content
That he held the proper opinions for the time of year;
When there was peace, he was for peace; when there was war, he went.
He was married and added five children to the population,
Which our Eugenist says was the right number for a parent of his
    generation,
And our teachers report that he never interfered with their education.
Was he free? Was he happy? The question is absurd:
Had anything been wrong, we would certainly have heard.

Introduction
Donald Hall, "The Man in the Dead Machine"

Donald Hall is a contemporary poet, teacher, and critic. Besides several books of poetry he has authored a best-selling composition text, *Writing Well,* and an introduction to the study of poetry, *The Pleasures of Poetry.* Mr. Hall has also been on the faculty at The University of Michigan. The following poem reflects a theme common among poets of the industrial era, the deadening conformity imposed upon the individual. The poem uses another commonplace of our age, irony.

For purposes of analysis the poem divides nicely into two parts. Part one, containing the first two stanzas, is the story of a World War II pilot who has been shot down in the New Guinea jungles, where to this day his skeleton sits strapped in the plane which is still held by the heavy vines of the jungle where it crashed. In part two, which consists of the final stanza, the narrator invites us to imagine a different and even more chilling ending. What if the shrapnel missed, he asks, and the pilot had survived the war? What if the pilot returned to civilian life and took a white-collar job?

Hall suggests that the second ending is in a way more horrifying than the first. Why? What does this last stanza have to say about the modern world of work? Is the title "The Man in the Dead Machine" about the second part of the poem as well as the first? And why is the title not "The Dead Man in the Machine"?

Donald Hall

The Man in the Dead Machine

High on a slope in New Guinea
the Grumman Hellcat
lodges among bright vines
as thick as arms. In 1942,
the clenched hand of a pilot
glided it here
where no one has ever been.

In the cockpit the helmeted
skeleton sits
upright, held
by dry sinews at neck
and shoulder, and webbing
that straps the pelvic cross
to the cracked
leather of the seat, and the breastbone
to the canvas cover
of the parachute.

Or say that the shrapnel
missed him, he flew
back to the carrier, and every
morning takes his chair, his pale
hands on the black arms, and sits
upright, held
by the firm webbing.

Introduction
Fenton Johnson, "The Daily Grind"

Fenton Johnson was born in Chicago in 1888. He attended The University of Chicago and became active in Chicago literary circles. Johnson joined the "new poetry" movement and was published in *Poetry Magazine* along with such major figures as William Carlos Williams, Wallace Stevens, and Marianne Moore.

As a black poet, Fenton Johnson is not so much a recorder of the American dream as of the American nightmare. While America offered hope for millions of Europeans who sought to build a new life through their work, slavery denied this hope to millions of blacks laboring in bondage. When the civil rights movement began breaking down legal barriers which allowed African-Americans to participate fully in the economic life of the country, many felt that the last barrier against hope had fallen. Yet, as we have come to understand, formal legal obstacles were only a part of the handicap afflicting black Americans. Those who have labored without hope for generations do not easily become hopeful. Achievement begins with dreams. We must have not only a dream of what we hope to accomplish but some reasonable belief that our dream can become an accomplishment. Otherwise, as Fenton Johnson shows us, the dreams of the night can seduce us away from the dreams of the day.

Fenton Johnson

The Daily Grind

If Nature says to you,
"I intend you for something fine,
For something to sing the song
That only my whirling stars can sing,
For something to burn in the firmament
With all the fervor of my golden sun,

Reprinted from *American Negro Poetry*, edited by Arna Bontemps and published in 1970 by Hill and Wang. We have been unable to reach the copyright holder of "The Daily Grind" and would welcome any information that would help us do so.

For something to moisten the parched souls
As only my rivulets can moisten the parched,"

What can you do?

If the System says to you,
"I intend you to grind and grind
Grains of corn beneath millstones;
I intend you to shovel and sweat
Before a furnace of Babylon;
I intend you for grist and meat
To fatten my pompous gods
As they wallow in an alcoholic nectar,"

What can you do?

Naught can you do
But watch that eternal battle
Between Nature and the System.
You cannot blame God,
You cannot blame man;
For God did not make the System,
Neither did man fashion Nature.
You can only die each morning,
And live again in the dreams of the night.
If Nature forgets you,
If the System forgets you,
God has blest you.

Introduction
Louis Untermeyer, "Portrait of a Machine"

"Portrait of a Machine" was published in 1923 by American writer
Louis Untermeyer as part of his collection *Long Feud*. The 1920s are the
beginning of a new era in American industrial history, the age of the
consumer. Consumerism was made possible by new kinds of banking
that extended credit to consumers and by a great increase in advertising
that encouraged people to fulfill themselves through possession of ever
more material goods. Consumerism was seen as the solution to overproduction and the problem of recurring recession: the logic of this new
version of industrial capitalism says that if we could consume all that
we could make, then we could maintain full employment in order to make
more. Advertising helped create desire, and credit and full employment

helped to provide the means to satisfy those desires. In this way we made the transition to a society that defined itself as much by its possessions as by its work.

A relatively new category of business people became prominent during the 1920s — public relations experts, advertisers, and salesmen. Their job was to make the system work by making sure that people continued consuming. The consumerism phase of industrial capitalism became the great age of the "booster." Boosterism teaches us that all is well so long as there is prosperity. It reduces all worth to dollars and cents, it judges people and communities by their affluence, and it sees little intrinsic worth in anything that cannot be turned to profit. During the 1920s writers like Sinclair Lewis (whose most famous novel, *Babbitt,* is about boosterism) and Untermeyer made fun of boosterism, but they did not persuade people to give it up. Today consumerism and boosterism are alive and well.

Untermeyer's poem describes the machine as an obedient and beautiful monster because while it gives us no end of wonders, in the long run we will become slaves to its processes and its products. People often talk about the machine freeing us from drudgery. How do you think Untermeyer would respond to this view? Does the consumer society of the 1920s make work better? Does it make work easier? Keep these questions in mind as you read Section II, where we will look again at this question, this time by examining a broad sweep of Western history.

Louis Untermeyer

Portrait of a Machine

What nudity is beautiful as this
Obedient monster purring at its toil;
These naked iron muscles dripping oil;
And the sure-fingered rods that never miss.
This long and shiny flank of metal is
Magic that greasy labor cannot spoil;
While this vast engine that could rend the soil
Conceals its fury with a gentle hiss.

It does not vent its loathing, does not turn
Upon its makers with destroying hate.
It bears a deeper malice; throbs to earn
Its master's bread and lives to see this great
Lord of the earth, who rules but cannot learn,
Become the slave of what his slaves create.

2. Rebellion

Introduction
Sojourner Truth, "Ain't I a Woman"

Sojourner Truth was born into slavery as Isabella Van Wagenen in 1797 in Hurley, New York. After obtaining her freedom, she rejected her slave name for the name that symbolized for her what her life was to be about. As a devout Christian and a zealous crusader for abolition and women's rights, she rebelled against the demeaning position accorded both women and blacks in Antebellum America.

The power of the following speech delivered in 1851 at a women's rights convention in Akron, Ohio, derives from the concreteness of her images and the simplicity of her language. She is responding to a group of clergymen who have charged women with inferiority because of their physical frailty and because Christ was not a woman.

Sojourner Truth

Ain't I a Woman

That man over there says that women need to be helped into carriages, and lifted over ditches and to have the best place everywhere.

Well, nobody ever helps me into carriages or over mud puddles or gives me any best place . . . ain't I a woman?

Look at me! Look at my arm! I have ploughed and planted and gathered into barns, and no man could head me. Ain't I a woman?

I could work as much and eat as much as a man (when I could get it), and bear the lash as well. Ain't I a woman?

I have born five childern and seen most all of them sold off into slavery, and when I cried out with mother's grief, none but Jesus heard me, none but Jesus heard me. Ain't I a woman?

And that man says women can't have as much rights as a man 'cause Christ wasn't a woman. Where did your Christ come from? Where did your Christ come from? From God and a woman. Man had nothing to do with him.

Introduction
Percy Bysshe Shelley, "Song to the Men of England"

Shelley, one of the greatest of English lyrical poets, was born in 1792 into a very wealthy gentry family in Sussex County in Southwest England. At a precocious age he rebelled against the English educational, social, and political systems and was expelled from University College, Oxford, before completing his first year. His rebellion extended even to God, as he was expelled for publishing an essay entitled "The Necessity of Atheism." At the age of twenty-five Shelley left England for Italy with his second wife, author Mary Shelley, soon to be famous for her novel *Franken-stein*. He never returned to England, drowning in a sailing accident shortly before his thirtieth birthday.

Although Shelley was much criticized for his opinions and actions during his lifetime, he is today recognized as one of the greatest of the Romantic poets and as perhaps the most scholarly. Careful study of his writings reveals a thoughtfulness and scholarly sophistication that is at odds with his reputation for wild recklessness. While many Romantics found refuge in adopting traditions out of the European past, Shelley rejects this manner of dealing with the fragmented order of the nineteenth century. Instead he insists upon rebellion to create a new order based upon social justice. In the following poem he calls upon the proletariat of England to overthrow "Those ungrateful drones who would / Drain your sweat — nay, drink your blood." This poem, "Song to the Men of England," is surprisingly contemporary. The argument it makes for early nineteenth-century England is revolutionary in at least two ways: first, it rejects the claims of landowners and capitalists to the fruits of others' labors and, second, it implicitly recognizes the virtues of labor. Shelley wrote this poem shortly after the Napoleonic wars at a time of great labor unrest. Intended as one of a series of songs for working men, it has become, as Shelley wished, a hymn of the British labor movement.

Percy Bysshe Shelley

Song to the Men of England

I

Men of England, wherefore plough
For the lords who lay ye low?
Wherefore weave with toil and care
The rich robes your tyrants wear?

II

Wherefore feed, and clothe, and save,
From the cradle to the grave,
Those ungrateful drones who would
Drain your sweat — nay, drink your blood?

III

Wherefore, Bees of England, forge
Many a weapon, chain, and scourge,
That these stingless drones may spoil
The forced produce of your toil?

IV

Have ye leisure, comfort, calm,
Shelter, food, love's gentle balm?
Or what is it ye buy so dear
With your pain and with your fear?

V

The seed ye sow, another reaps;
The wealth ye find, another keeps;
The robes ye weave, another wears;
The arms ye forge, another bears.

VI

Sow seed, — but let no tyrant reap;
Find wealth, — let no impost heap;

Weave robes, — let not the idle wear;
Forge arms, — in your defence to bear.

VII

Shrink to your cellars, holes, and cells;
In halls ye deck another dwells.
Why shake the chains ye wrought? Ye see
The steel ye tempered glance on ye.

VIII

With plough and spade, and hoe and loom,
Trace your grave, and build your tomb,
And weave your winding sheet, till fair
England be your sepulchre.

Introduction
Virginia Woolf, "Professions for Women"

Virginia Woolf was born in London in 1882, the daughter of an eminent literary critic, Sir Leslie Stephen. An outspoken feminist, she was one of the key members of the "Bloomsbury Group," a London-based organization devoted to the arts and sciences. As a novelist she became known for her experimentation, particularly with stream of consciousness, a technique also being tried by James Joyce.

In "Professions for Women" Woolf asks us to look beyond the formal limitations upon women in the professions to consider more complex issues of human freedom. Freedom, as she sees, is not simply a lack of legal or economic restraint. It has to do with our larger worldview and how we have been conditioned to see ourselves within that imagined universe. For her a fundamental contradiction exists between what her worldview tells her it means to be feminine and what she needs to do to be a writer. As she says, the woman who would be a professional writer must kill that part of herself that denies her freedom, and this act costs women a great deal. Rebellion against our shackles is vital, but we must pay a price.

Virginia Woolf

Professions for Women

When your secretary invited me to come here, she told me that your
Society is concerned with the employment of women and she suggested
that I might tell you something about my own professional experiences.
It is true I am a woman; it is true I am employed; but what professional
experiences have I had? It is difficult to say. My profession is literature;
and in that profession there are fewer experiences for women than in
any other, with the exception of the stage — fewer, I mean, that are peculiar
to women. For the road was cut many years ago — by Fanny Burney, by
Aphra Behn, by Harriet Martineau, by Jane Austen, by George Eliot —
many famous women, and many more unknown and forgotten, have been
before me, making the path smooth, and regulating my steps. Thus, when
I came to write, there were very few material obstacles in my way. Writing was a reputable and harmless occupation. The family peace was not
broken by the scratching of a pen. No demand was made upon the family purse. For ten and sixpence one can buy paper enough to write all
the plays of Shakespeare — if one has a mind that way. Pianos and models, Paris, Vienna and Berlin, masters and mistresses, are not needed
by a writer. The cheapness of writing paper is, of course, the reason why
women have succeeded as writers before they have succeeded in the other
professions.

But to tell you my story — it is a simple one. You have only got to figure to yourselves a girl in a bedroom with a pen in her hand. She had
only to move that pen from left to right — from ten o'clock to one. Then
it occurred to her to do what is simple and cheap enough after all — to
slip a few of those pages into an envelope, fix a penny stamp in the corner, and drop the envelope into the red box at the corner. It was thus
that I became a journalist; and my effort was rewarded on the first day
of the following month — a very glorious day it was for me — by a letter
from an editor containing a cheque for one pound ten shillings and sixpence. But to show you how little I deserve to be called a professional
woman, how little I know of the struggles and difficulties of such lives,
I have to admit that instead of spending that sum upon bread and butter,
rent, shoes and stockings, or butcher's bills, I went out and bought a
cat — a beautiful cat, a Persian cat, which very soon involved me in bitter
disputes with my neighbours.

What could be easier than to write articles and to buy Persian cats with the profits? But wait a moment. Articles have to be about something. Mine, I seem to remember, was about a novel by a famous man. And while I was writing this review, I discovered that if I were going to review books I should need to do battle with a certain phantom. And the phantom was a woman, and when I came to know her better I called her after the heroine of a famous poem, The Angel in the House. It was she who used to come between me and my paper when I was writing reviews. It was she who bothered me and wasted my time and so tormented me that at last I killed her. You who come of a younger and happier generation may not have heard of her—you may not know what I mean by the Angel in the House. I will describe her as shortly as I can. She was intensely sympathetic. She was immensely charming. She was utterly unselfish. She excelled in the difficult arts of family life. She sacrificed herself daily. If there was chicken, she took the leg; if there was a draught she sat in it—in short she was so constituted that she never had a mind or a wish of her own, but preferred to sympathize always with the minds and wishes of others. Above all—I need not say it—she was pure. Her purity was supposed to be her chief beauty—her blushes, her great grace. In those days—the last of Queen Victoria—every house had its Angel. And when I came to write I encountered her with the very first words. The shadow of her wings fell on my page; I heard the rustling of her skirts in the room. Directly, that is to say, I took my pen in hand to review that novel by a famous man, she slipped behind me and whispered: "My dear, you are a young woman. You are writing about a book that has been written by a man. Be sympathetic; be tender; flatter; deceive; use all the arts and wiles of our sex. Never let anybody guess that you have a mind of your own. Above all, be pure." And she made as if to guide my pen. I now record the one act for which I take some credit to myself, though the credit rightly belongs to some excellent ancestors of mine who left me a certain sum of money—shall we say five hundred pounds a year?—so that it was not necessary for me to depend solely on charm for my living. I turned upon her and caught her by the throat. I did my best to kill her. My excuse, if I were to be had up in a court of law, would be that I acted in self-defence. Had I not killed her she would have killed me. She would have plucked the heart out of my writing. For, as I found, directly I put pen to paper, you cannot review even a novel without having a mind of your own, without expressing what you think to be the truth about human relations, morality, sex. And all these questions, according to the Angel in the House, cannot be dealt with freely and openly by women; they must charm, they must conciliate, they must—to put it bluntly—tell lies if they are to succeed. Thus, whenever I felt the shadow of her wing or the radiance of her halo upon my page, I took up the inkpot and flung it at her. She died hard. Her fictitious nature was of great assistance to her. It is far harder to kill a phantom than a reality. She was always creeping back when I thought I had despatched her. Though I flatter myself that I killed her in the end, the struggle was severe; it took much time that had better have been spent upon learning Greek grammar; or in roaming the world in search of adventures. But it was a real experience; it was an experience that was bound to befall all women writers at that time. Killing the Angel in the House was part of the occupation of a woman writer.

But to continue my story. The Angel was dead; what then remained? You may say that what remained was a simple and common object—a young woman in a bedroom with an inkpot. In other words, now that she had rid herself of falsehood, that young woman had only to be herself. Ah, but what is "herself"? I mean, what is a woman? I assure you, I do not know. I do not believe that you know. I do not believe that anybody can know until she has expressed herself in all the arts and professions open to human skill. That indeed is one of the reasons why I have come here—out of respect for you, who are in process of showing us by your experiments what a woman is, who are in process of providing us, by your failures and successes, with that extremely important piece of information.

But to continue the story of my professional experiences. I made one pound ten and six by my first review; and I bought a Persian cat with the proceeds. Then I grew ambitious. A Persian cat is all very well, I said; but a Persian cat is not enough. I must have a motor car. And it was thus that I became a novelist—for it is a very strange thing that people will give you a motor car if you will tell them a story. It is a still stranger thing that there is nothing so delightful in the world as telling stories. It is far pleasanter than writing reviews of famous novels. And yet, if I am to obey your secretary and tell you my professional experiences as a novelist, I must tell you about a very strange experience that befell me as a novelist. And to understand it you must try first to imagine a novelist's state of mind. I hope I am not giving away professional secrets if I say that a novelist's chief desire is to be as unconscious as possible. He has to induce in himself a state of perpetual lethargy. He wants life to proceed with the utmost quiet and regularity. He wants to see the same faces, to read the same books, to do the same things day after day, month after month, while he is writing, so that nothing may break the illusion in which he is living—so that nothing may disturb or disquiet the mysterious nosings about, feelings round, darts, dashes and sudden discoveries of that very shy and illusive spirit, the imagination. I suspect that this state is the same both for men and women. Be that as it may, I want you to imagine me writing a novel in a state of trance. I want you to figure to yourselves a girl sitting with a pen in her hand, which for minutes, and indeed for hours, she never dips into the inkpot. The image that comes to my mind when I think of this girl is the image of a fisherman lying sunk in dreams on the verge of a deep lake with a rod held out over the water. She was letting her imagination sweep unchecked round every rock and cranny of the world that lies submerged in the depths of our unconscious being. Now came the experience, the experience that I believe to be far commoner with women writers than with men. The line raced through the girl's fingers. Her imagination had rushed away. It had sought the pools, the depths, the dark places where the largest fish slumber. And then there was a smash. There was an explosion. There was foam and confusion. The imagination had dashed itself against something hard. The girl was roused from her dream. She was indeed in a state of the most acute and difficult distress. To speak without figure she had thought of something, something about the body, about the passions which it was unfitting for her as a woman to say. Men, her reason told her, would be shocked. The consciousness of what men will say of a woman who speaks the truth about her passions had roused her from her artist's state of unconsciousness. She could write no more. The trance was over. Her imagination could work no longer. This I believe to be a very common experience with women writers — they are impeded by the extreme conventionality of the other sex. For though men sensibly allow themselves great freedom in these respects, I doubt that they realize or can control the extreme severity with which they condemn such freedom in women.

These then were two very genuine experiences of my own. These were two of the adventures of my professional life. The first — killing the Angel in the House — I think I solved. She died. But the second, telling the truth about my own experiences as a body, I do not think I solved. I doubt that any woman has solved it yet. The obstacles against her are still immensely powerful — and yet they are very difficult to define. Outwardly, what is simpler than to write books? Outwardly, what obstacles are there for a woman rather than for a man? Inwardly, I think, the case is very different; she has still many ghosts to fight, many prejudices to overcome. Indeed it will be a long time still, I think, before a woman can sit down to write a book without finding a phantom to be slain, a rock to be dashed against. And if this is so in literature, the freest of all professions for women, how is it in the new professions which you are now for the first time entering?

Those are the questions that I should like, had I time, to ask you. And indeed, if I have laid stress upon these professional experiences of mine, it is because I believe that they are, though in different forms, yours also. Even when the path is nominally open—when there is nothing to prevent a woman from being a doctor, a lawyer, a civil servant—there are many phantoms and obstacles, as I believe, looming in her way. To discuss and define them is I think of great value and importance; for thus only can the labour be shared, the difficulties be solved. But besides this, it is necessary also to discuss the ends and the aims for which we are fighting, for which we are doing battle with these formidable obstacles. Those aims cannot be taken for granted; they must be perpetually questioned and examined. The whole position, as I see it—here in this hall surrounded by women practising for the first time in history I know not how many different professions—is one of extraordinary interest and importance. You have won rooms of your own in the house hitherto exclusively owned by men. You are able, though not without great labour and effort, to pay the rent. You are earning your five hundred pounds a year. But this freedom is only a beginning; the room is your own, but it is still bare. It has to be furnished; it has to be decorated; it has to be shared. How are you going to furnish it, how are you going to decorate it? With whom are you going to share it, and upon what terms? These, I think are questions of the utmost importance and interest. For the first time in history you are able to ask them; for the first time you are able to decide for yourselves what the answers should be. Willingly would I stay and discuss those questions and answers—but not tonight. My time is up; and I must cease.

Introduction
Richard Wright, "I Have Seen Black Hands"

Richard Wright was born in a sharecropper's cabin in 1908 near Natchez, Mississippi. Deserted by his father, he grew up in extreme poverty and violence. At nineteen Wright moved out of the South to Chicago where he became active in the Communist Party. Communism was attractive because it addressed the issue of social justice, but in time Wright became frustrated by Communist "gospel." As a writer, Wright sought to understand the subtle psychology of racism, and he did not want his understanding limited by party dogma. Thus in 1942 the conflict between party dogma and his search for artistic truth caused him to split with the party. In the best of his writing Wright goes beyond the litany of violence and racial injustice in the South to explore the psychology of racism everywhere in America. In *Native Son* and *Black Boy* we see the best of this exploration, his deepest expression of what it means to be black in America.

In "I Have Seen Black Hands" he records the agony of African Americans struggling to survive in a brutal economy that has flourished through their exploitation. But while the poem records the history of exploited black work, it ends with the hopeful image of black and white fists clenched together in rebellion against a system that has used racial hatred to exploit all workers, black and white.

Wright understands that racism has been used to divide black and white workers throughout American history. Do you think this remains an issue today? Have you experienced racism in the workplace? Are racial stereotypes still common among workers? Why?

Richard Wright

I Have Seen Black Hands

I

I am black and I have seen black hands, millions and millions of them —
Out of millions of bundles of wool and flannel tiny black fingers have
    reached restlessly and hungrily for life.
Reached out for the black nipples at the black breasts of black mothers,
And they've held red, green, blue, yellow, orange, white, and purple toys
    in the childish grips of possession,
And chocolate drops, peppermint sticks, lollypops, wineballs, ice cream
    cones, and sugared cookies in fingers sticky and gummy,
And they've held balls and bats and gloves and marbles and jack-knives
    and sling-shots and spinning tops in the thrill of sport and play,
And pennies and nickels and dimes and quarters and sometimes on New
    Year's, Easter, Lincoln's Birthday, May Day, a brand new green
    dollar bill,

Reprinted from the *Partisan Review*, copyright 1935, with permission.

They've held pens and rulers and maps and tablets and books in palms
    spotted and smeared with ink,
And they've held dice and cards and half-pint flasks and cue sticks and
    cigars and cigarettes in the pride of new maturity . . .

II

I am black and I have seen black hands, millions and millions of them —
They were tired and awkward and calloused and grimy and covered with
    hangnails,
And they were caught in the fast-moving belts of machines and snagged
    and smashed and crushed,
And they jerked up and down at the throbbing machines massing taller
    and taller the heaps of gold in the banks of bosses,
And they piled higher and higher the steel, iron, the lumber, wheat, rye,
    the oats, corn, the cotton, the wool, the oil, the coal, the meat, the
    fruit, the glass, and the stone until there was too much to be used,
And they grabbed guns and slung them on their shoulders and marched
    and groped in trenches and fought and killed and conquered nations
    who were customers for the goods black hands had made.
And again black hands stacked goods higher and higher until there was
    too much to be used,
And then black hands trembling at the factory gates the dreaded lay-off
    slip,
And the black hands hung idle and swung empty and grew soft and got
    weak and bony from unemployment and starvation,
And they grew nervous and sweaty, and opened and shut in anguish and
    doubt and hesitation and irresolution . . .

III

I am black and I have seen black hands, millions and millions of them —
Reaching hesitantly out of days of slow death for the goods they had
    made, but the bosses warned that the goods were private and did not
    belong to them,
And the black hands struck desperately out in defense of life and there
    was blood, but the enraged bosses decreed that this too was wrong,
And the black hands felt the cold steel bars of the prison they had made,
    in despair tested their strength and found that they could neither
    bend nor break them,
And the black hands fought and scratched and held back but a thousand
    white hands took them and tied them,
And the black hands lifted palms in mute and futile supplication to the
    sodden faces of mobs wild in the revelries of sadism,
And the black hands strained and clawed and struggled in vain at the
    noose that tightened about the black throat,

And the black hands waved and beat fearfully at the tall flames that
   cooked and charred the black flesh . . .

IV

I am black and I have seen black hands
Raised in fists of revolt, side by side with the white fists of white workers,
And some day—and it is only this which sustains me—
Some day there shall be millions and millions of them,
On some red day in a burst of fists on a new horizon!

Introduction
Norman Mailer, "The White Negro"

Norman Mailer first gained fame with his publication of *The Naked
and the Dead,* one of the great American novels about World War II. He
has since pioneered a new genre that combines the art of fiction with
the craft of reporting. Mailer seems, with many others, to believe that
fiction has become outdated in the "stranger-than-fiction" world of twentieth-century America. This does not mean that he has become a mere
reporter of fantastical events. In works such as *The Executioner's Song,* the
story of murderer Gary Gilmore's execution, and *The Armies of the Night,*
his record of antiwar protest during the 1960s, Mailer interprets his
world from a clear and consistent viewpoint.

"The White Negro" is excerpted from a collection called *Advertisements
for Myself,* a title that suggests that Mailer is not a passive observer. In
this essay, written in the 1950s, he attempts to explain the phenomena
of the "hipster." The hipster has chosen rebellion from a banal and meaningless consumer world living under constant threat of extinction from
the bomb. Mailer argues that this 1950s rebel has consciously chosen
to *live* in a dangerous world rather than simply to *exist.* Appropriately,
the hipster has chosen the African American as a model for his existential life. Mailer tells us that for the African American there has only been
the choice of a life of humility or of ever-threatening danger. So, ironically, the white man who chooses to live rather than be suffocated by a
banal life can turn to those adventuresome African Americans who have
chosen to live the dangerous life of the body, where a meaningful life
of the mind has become impossible. Occupationally, the jazz musician

symbolizes the hipster's way of surviving with meaning. Existing in the night world of sensual pleasure, jazz is, as Mailer tells us, orgasm, but an orgasm that gives expression to "the character and quality of his existence, to his rage and the infinite variations of joy, lust, languor, growl, cramp, pinch, scream, and despair of his orgasm."

As Mailer predicted, this small rebellious movement of the 1950s was copied and expanded by the generation of the 1960s. The Hippie became the more popular and more tame version of the hipster, shaping the counterculture that continues to influence our own time. Do you agree with Mailer that our choice as humans is to either live dangerously or condemn ourselves to banality? Like Hemingway, Mailer believes that life is at best tragic but usually is just hackneyed. Are these our only choices, or can we change our world to include more satisfying options? For both Hemingway and Mailer the only option seems to be extreme individualism, the individual of courage adopting a lifestyle that wrings meaning from an otherwise meaningless existence. Might part of their difficulty be individualism itself? Think about this question and keep an open mind. You will soon be reading other writers who have much to say about this issue.

Norman Mailer

The White Negro
Superficial Reflections on the Hipster

Our search for the rebels of the generation led us to the hipster. The hipster is an *enfant terrible* turned inside out. In character with his time, he is trying to get back at the conformists by lying low . . . You can't interview a hipster because his main goal is to keep out of a society which, he thinks, is trying to make everyone over in its own image. He takes marijuana because it supplies him with experiences that can't be shared with "squares." He may affect a broad-brimmed hat or a zoot suit, but usually he prefers to skulk unmarked. The hipster may be a jazz musician; he is rarely an artist, almost never a writer. He may

From *Advertisements for Myself* by Norman Mailer. Reprinted by permission of the author and the author's agents, Scott Meredith Literary Agency, Inc., 845 Third Avenue, New York, New York 10022.

earn his living as a petty criminal, a hobo, a carnival roustabout or a free-lance moving man in Greenwich Village, but some hipsters have found a safe refuge in the upper income brackets as television comics or movie actors. (The late James Dean, for one, was a hipster hero.) . . . It is tempting to describe the hipster in psychiatric terms as infantile, but the style of his infantilism is a sign of the times. He does not try to enforce his will on others, Napoleon-fashion, but contents himself with a magical omnipotence never disproved because never tested. . . . As the only extreme nonconformist of his generation, he exercises a powerful if underground appeal for conformists, through newspaper accounts of his delinquencies, his structureless jazz, and his emotive grunt words.

— *"Born 1930: The Unlost Generation"*
by Caroline Bird
Harper's Bazaar, *Feb. 1957*

Probably, we will never be able to determine the psychic havoc of the concentration camps and the atom bomb upon the unconscious mind of almost everyone alive in these years. For the first time in civilized history, perhaps for the first time in all of history, we have been forced to live with the suppressed knowledge that the smallest facets of our personality or the most minor projection of our ideas, or indeed the absence of ideas and the absence of personality could mean equally well that we might still be doomed to die as a cipher in some vast statistical operation in which our teeth would be counted, and our hair would be saved, but our death itself would be unknown, unhonored, and unremarked, a death which could not follow with dignity as a possible consequence to serious actions we had chosen, but rather a death by *deus ex machina* in a gas chamber or a radioactive city; and so if in the midst of civilization — that civilization founded upon the Faustian urge to dominate nature by mastering time, mastering the links of social cause and effect — in the middle of an economic civilization founded upon the confidence that time could indeed be subjected to our will, our psyche was subjected itself to the intolerable anxiety that death being causeless, life was causeless as well, and time deprived of cause and effect had come to a stop.

The Second World War presented a mirror to the human condition which blinded anyone who looked into it. For if tens of millions were killed in concentration camps out of the inexorable agonies and contractions of super-states founded upon the always insoluble contradictions of injustice, one was then obliged also to see that no matter how crippled and perverted an image of man was the society he had created, it was nonetheless his creation, his collective creation (at least his collective creation from the past) and if society was so murderous, then who could ignore the most hideous of questions about his own nature?

Worse. One could hardly maintain the courage to be individual, to speak with one's own voice, for the years in which one could complacently accept oneself as part of an elite by being a radical were forever gone. A man knew that when he dissented, he gave a note upon his life which could be called in any year of overt crisis. No wonder then that these have been the years of conformity and depression. A stench of fear has come out of every pore of American life, and we suffer from a collective failure of nerve. The only courage, with rare exceptions, that we have been witness to, has been the isolated courage of isolated people.

2.

It is on this bleak scene that a phenomenon has appeared: the American existentialist — the hipster, the man who knows that if our collective condition is to live with instant death by atomic war, relatively quick death by the State as *l'univers concentrationnaire,* or with a slow death by conformity with every creative and rebellious instinct stifled (at what damage to the mind and the heart and the liver and the nerves no research foundation for cancer will discover in a hurry), if the fate of twentieth-century man is to live with death from adolescence to premature senescence, why then the only life-giving answer is to accept the terms of death, to live with death as immediate danger, to divorce oneself from society, to exist without roots, to set out on that uncharted journey into the rebellious imperatives of the self. In short, whether the life is criminal or not, the decision is to encourage the psychopath in oneself, to explore that domain of experience where security is boredom and therefore sickness, and one exists in the present, in that enormous present which is without past or future, memory or planned intention, the life where a man must go until he is beat, where he must gamble with his energies through all those small or large crises of courage and unforeseen situations which beset his day, where he must be with it or doomed not to swing. The unstated essence of Hip, its psychopathic brilliance, quivers with the knowledge that new kinds of victories increase one's power for new kinds of perception; and defeats, the wrong kind of defeats, attack the body and imprison one's energy until one is jailed in the prison air of other people's habits, other people's defeats, boredom, quiet desperation, and muted icy self-destroying rage. One is Hip or one is Square (the alternative which each new generation coming into American life is beginning to feel), one is a rebel or one conforms, one is a frontiersman in the Wild West of American night life, or else a Square cell, trapped in the totalitarian tissues of American society, doomed willy-nilly to conform if one is to succeed.

A totalitarian society makes enormous demands on the courage of men, and a partially totalitarian society makes even greater demands, for the general anxiety is greater. Indeed if one is to be a man, almost any kind of unconventional action often takes disproportionate courage. So it is no accident that the source of Hip is the Negro for he has been living on the margin between totalitarianism and democracy for two centuries. But the presence of Hip as a working philosophy in the sub-worlds of American life is probably due to jazz, and its knifelike entrance into culture, its subtle but so penetrating influence on an avant-garde generation — that postwar generation of adventurers who (some consciously, some by osmosis) had absorbed the lessons of disillusionment and disgust of the twenties, the depression, and the war. Sharing a collective disbelief in the words of men who had too much money and controlled too many things, they knew almost as powerful a disbelief in the socially monolithic ideas of the single mate, the solid family and the respectable love life. If the intellectual antecedents of this generation can be traced to such separate influences as D. H. Lawrence, Henry Miller, and Wilhelm Reich, the viable philosophy of Hemingway fit most of their facts: in a bad world, as he was to say over and over again (while taking time out from his parvenu snobbery and dedicated gourmandize), in a bad world there is no love nor mercy nor charity nor justice unless a man can keep his courage, and this indeed fitted some of the facts. What fitted the need of the adventurer even more precisely was Hemingway's categorical imperative that what made him feel good became therefore The Good.

So no wonder that in certain cities of America, in New York of course, and New Orleans, in Chicago and San Francisco and Los Angeles, in such American cities as Paris and Mexico, D.F., this particular part of a generation was attracted to what the Negro had to offer. In such places as Greenwich Village, a ménage-à-trois was completed — the bohemian and the juvenile delinquent came face-to-face with the Negro, and the hipster was a fact in American life. If marijuana was the wedding ring, the child was the language of Hip for its argot gave expression to abstract states of feeling which all could share, at least all who were Hip. And in this wedding of the white and the black it was the Negro who brought the cultural dowry. Any Negro who wishes to live must live with danger from his first day, and no experience can ever be casual to him, no Negro can saunter down a street with any real certainty that violence will not visit him on his walk. The cameos of security for the average white: mother and the home, job and the family, are not even a mockery to millions of Negroes; they are impossible. The Negro has the simplest of alternatives: live a life of constant humility or ever-threatening danger. In such a pass where paranoia is as vital to survival as blood, the Negro had stayed alive and begun to grow by following the need of his body where he could. Knowing in the cells of his existence that life was war, nothing but war, the Negro (all exceptions admitted) could rarely afford the sophisticated inhibitions of civilization, and so he kept for his survival the art of the primitive, he lived in the enormous present, he subsisted for his Saturday night kicks, relinquishing the pleasures of the mind for the more obligatory pleasures of the body, and in his music he gave voice to the character and quality of his existence, to his rage and the infinite variations of joy, lust, languor, growl, cramp, pinch, scream and despair of his orgasm. For jazz is orgasm, it is the music of orgasm, good orgasm and bad, and so it spoke across a nation, it had the communication of art even where it was watered, perverted, corrupted, and almost killed, it spoke in no matter what laundered popular way of instantaneous existential states to which some whites could respond, it was indeed a communication by art because it said, "I feel this, and now you do too."

So there was a new breed of adventurers, urban adventurers who drifted out at night looking for action with a black man's code to fit their facts. The hipster had absorbed the existentialist synapses of the Negro, and for practical purposes could be considered a white Negro.

To be an existentialist, one must be able to feel oneself—one must know one's desires, one's rages, one's anguish, one must be aware of the character of one's frustration and know what would satisfy it. The over-civilized man can be an existentialist only if it is chic, and deserts it quickly for the next chic. To be a real existentialist (Sartre admittedly to the contrary) one must be religious, one must have one's sense of the "purpose"—whatever the purpose may be—but a life which is directed by one's faith in the necessity of action is a life committed to the notion that the substratum of existence is the search, the end meaningful but mysterious; it is impossible to live such a life unless one's emotions provide their profound conviction. Only the French, alienated beyond alienation from their unconscious could welcome an existential philosophy without ever feeling it at all; indeed only a Frenchman by declaring that the unconscious did not exist could then proceed to explore the delicate involutions of consciousness, the microscopically sensuous and all but ineffable *frissons* of mental becoming, in order finally to create the theology of atheism and so submit that in a world of absurdities the existential absurdity is most coherent.

In the dialogue between the atheist and the mystic, the atheist is on the side of life, rational life, undialectical life—since he conceives of death as emptiness, he can, no matter how weary or despairing, wish for nothing but more life; his pride is that he does not transpose his weakness and spiritual fatigue into a romantic longing for death, for such appreciation of death is then all too capable of being elaborated by his imagination into a universe of meaningful structure and moral orchestration.

Yet this masculine argument can mean very little for the mystic. The mystic can accept the atheist's description of his weakness, he can agree that his mysticism was a response to despair. And yet . . . and yet his argument is that he, the mystic, is the one finally who has chosen to live with death, and so death is his experience and not the atheist's, and the atheist by eschewing the limitless dimensions of profound despair has rendered himself incapable to judge the experience. The real argument which the mystic must always advance is the very intensity of his private vision — his argument depends from the vision precisely because what was felt in the vision is so extraordinary that no rational argument, no hypotheses of "oceanic feelings" and certainly no skeptical reductions can explain away what has become for him the reality more real than the reality of closely reasoned logic. His inner experience of the possibilities within death is his logic. So, too, for the existentialist. And the psychopath. And the saint and the bullfighter and the lover. The common denominator for all of them is their burning consciousness of the present, exactly that incandescent consciousness which the possibilities within death has opened for them. There is a depth of desperation to the condition which enables one to remain in life only by engaging death, but the reward is their knowledge that what is happening at each instant of the electric present is good or bad for them, good or bad for their cause, their love, their action, their need.

It is this knowledge which provides the curious community of feeling in the world of the hipster, a muted cool religious revival to be sure, but the element which is exciting, disturbing, nightmarish perhaps, is that incompatibles have come to bed, the inner life and the violent life, the orgy and the dream of love, the desire to murder and the desire to create, a dialectical conception of existence with a lust for power, a dark, romantic, and yet undeniably dynamic view of existence for it sees every man and woman as moving individually through each moment of life forward into growth or backward into death.

ID. Alienation and Integration

We have seen that the new conditions ushered in by the Industrial Revolution created new experiences for and a variety of responses by people. Depending on who you were and what work you did (if any), you could experience the proverbial cup as half full or as half empty: this great revolution in human life brought unprecedented material abundance and technological prowess to some; it brought hard, boring, dangerous, or meaningless toil and misery to others; and for most it was a mixed blessing. People reacted in many ways to these changes, as we have seen, but what exactly was work in the new industrial order like for people?

We must be careful, of course, not to pretend that everyone had the same experiences, but many observers of these global changes in Western societies have felt that the changes and their impacts had at least one pattern clear enough to be labeled. "Alienation" is the general term most often used by critics to describe a widespread negative dimension of work and life in industrial societies. People become *alien* to and through their work; they are no longer *at home* in their own lives; their lives become *dis-integrated.*

The massive disorientation generated by industrialization in part is an inevitable feature of any great historical change, be it from hunting and gathering to agricultural societies, from rural to urban living, from the days of the horse to living with the automobile, or from a preindustrial to an industrial society. In this sense alienation should be expected. But the alienation of the Industrial Revolution, say the critics, is more permanent and pervasive. People moving into agricultural societies soon settled into the new life and felt at home. Industrial workers are condemned to *permanent* alienation.

Why? What is this new life and new work like that people cannot overcome their alienation? And if we grant that this undesirable dimension to modern life does exist, how can we deal with it? These are the questions we will *begin* addressing in this subsection and will continue to address throughout the remainder of the book. Our main goals in this part are to help you attain a vivid sense for what alienation means for human existence and to begin exploring what we might do to ameliorate, if not eliminate, this seemingly unique and unhappy modern experience.

The two short stories in this unit depict the alienation of two very different people. Melville's Bartleby is a lowly clerk on Wall Street in the midnineteenth century whose job is to be a human copy machine. Tillie

Olson's character in "I Stand Here Ironing" labors far away from the hub of economic power, and she lives a century later than the miserable scrivener. As far as we know, Bartleby has no family, while the housewife's life revolves around her family. She works alone, with her children, at home; he works amidst the hustle of commercial activity, alongside others. Yet these two pitiful characters seem to share a common condition. It is not simply that they are both unhappy, although they are that; nor does their commonality lie merely in their inabilities to affect their worlds. What these very different characters share, according to critics of industrial society, is something deep and pervasive, something that links them over the years and situations — alienation.

One reason alienation is both so difficult to analyze and is such an important concept is that it links the individual and the larger social-cultural world. Bartleby's condition, like Olson's unnamed ironer (note the similarity to Auden's unknown citizen), occurs as a part of a system and in particular from the interactions that occur within his particular place of work in that system. Above all Bartleby wants recognition. Not only or mainly recognition for his work but also recognition of his humanity. If all he receives is pay or other such rewards for his labor, and if the work has little of the humanity-enhancing characteristics of which Thoreau speaks, then Bartleby can only feel like a cog in a machine.

Olson's housewife suffers from a similar condition. She "irons" — she does the work of motherhood and housewifery, but she does not get the recognition she needs. Nor does she feel any more in control of the products of her work than does Bartleby. Both the making process and the products are beyond their control. Bartleby, in his attempt to find recognition, dies a rather pitiful death, while the housewife worries that her daughter (her most important *product*) will end up like herself, run over by an "iron."

As you read these powerful literary pieces try to take on the experiences of these characters. What is it like to be an alien in your work and even in your own home? What causes them to experience the world in this way? How do they respond? And what might be done to ameloriate their situations?

Olson and Melville hint at what might be needed in order for Bartleby and the housewife not to be alienated — they need recognition, and they need better work. But what, more precisely, might this different work be like in order to lessen or even eradicate worker alienation? William Morris, a nineteenth-century British social activist and thinker, and Dylan Thomas, the famous twentieth-century Welsh poet, propose that in order to be truly human we need *good work*. According to Thomas good work does not necessarily have to be the work you do for a living (your job), but you must do such work in order truly to live. For Thomas this good work happens late at night when he is most in touch with his deepest self — it is a sullen art. But it is also *craft,* the construction of something personal, something unique. Finally, Thomas addresses the question of why we need to do this work. His answer has two parts, echoing the personal and interpersonal dimensions of Bartleby's striving for recognition: he does it for his own satisfaction, but that satisfaction is tied intimately to how his poetry touches the hearts of lovers, his intended audience.

Morris' perspective is similar to Thomas' in many ways, but in none so much as his emphasis on craft. For Morris there are several criteria for work to be good: "hope of rest, hope of product, hope of pleasure in the work itself; and hope of these also in some abundance and of good quality; rest enough and good enough to be worth having; product worth having by one who is neither a fool nor an ascetic; pleasure enough for all for us to be conscious of it while we are at work." The goal of all work, Morris believes, is satisfaction, and most critical to this result is that the work come from and shape the person — it must be personal. In the crafting, in the creating, people discover, develop, and express themselves. Baldly stated, without such work we do not become persons.

Although it may sound a bit odd, one could say that Thomas agrees with Morris that work should be *useful,* for useful does not mean mere utility. Both writers stress the importance of our work meeting our most human needs and satisfying our deepest desires. Work can have no higher use.

How do we get more good work and less alienation? Thomas advocates an individual solution — seek your deepest self and express it — and that individual effort is a crucial ingredient. But alienation is more than individual feeling: it is caused by large-scale social, political, and economic conditions. Morris addresses those conditions as well, proposing an end to a class society, be it capitalist, socialist centralist, or totalitarian, wherein some people dictate to the rest. He also peers a half century into the future and sees that the cult of consumerism (what Marx calls a commodities fetish) is also socially and individually destructive. In consumer societies people spend their time, talents, and efforts pursuing material objects which have little value, leaving little of themselves for more fulfilling activities.

Morris also recommends that we take the promises of modern technology and science to task to actually save labor. Too often, he contends, the "labor saving devices" create more alienating work rather than reducing it. Finally, Morris shows his prescience by contending that peace, as well as the end of a class society, will be necessary for reducing or eliminating alienation. As with the other themes in this first section, we will return to these topics raised by this farsighted social thinker in the course of this book. For now your task is to get a feel for these issues and ideas as they are raised by these selections.

A Worker's Voice

A General Motors Autoworker

We adjusted to the heat and grew accustomed to the noise. After awhile, we even got used to the claustrophobia of the wheel wells. The idea that we were being paid handsome wages to mimic a bunch of overachieving simians suited us just dandy. In America there was nothing to accomplish as long as the numbers on your pay stub tumbled out in a sequence that served to justify your daily dread.

The one thing we couldn't escape was the monotony of our new jobs. Every minute, every hour, every truck, and every movement totaled nothing but a plodding replica of the one that had gone before. The monotony especially began to gnaw away at Roy. When the lunch horn sounded, we'd race out to his pickup and Roy would start pulling these enormous joints from a glove box. His stash was incredible. "Take one," he'd offer. Pot made me nervous, so I would stick to beer or slug a little whiskey.

1. Alienation

Introduction
Herman Melville, "Bartleby the Scrivener"

Herman Melville, author of *Moby Dick,* today is viewed as one of America's greatest writers; yet if you had been studying American literature around the turn of the twentieth century, you would not have found anything by Melville in the canon. Indeed, his last masterpiece, *Billy Budd,* was never published in his lifetime. It was not until the 1920s that Mel-

(Ben Hamper, 1986, from "I Rivethead," published in *Mother Jones,* Sept. 27, 1986)

ville was rediscovered, and perhaps this speaks to the modernity of this one time merchant seaman, who ended his days, like his character Bartleby, in the obscurity of a clerk's position.

The theme of this section is alienation and integration. In Melville's case we should perhaps reverse this order: his life was a long journey from early literary success and popularity to obscurity and almost complete alienation from his culture. As a result, probably no other American writer more clearly understood and felt the transformations taking place in American life during the nineteenth century.

In Melville's "Bartleby the Scrivener" we have one of the earliest descriptions of worker alienation in American fiction. Melville not only describes alienation; he also explores the human implications as few have since his time. In interpreting this story it is important to note that it is told from a first-person point of view. The narrator is Bartleby's employer, and it is as much his story as Bartleby's. Through the first-person point of view, Melville shows us the employer's attitudes and feelings and actually develops him as a character. A crucial aspect of this story is the challenge Bartleby issues to the employer's humanity. Be sure to pay attention to how the employer handles this challenge.

Setting is also an important element in the interpretation of fiction. The setting is the environment in which the story happens, in this case a nineteenth-century law office on Wall Street where copyists (scriveners) do the work that today would be done by xerox machines. You will notice that Melville plays with the idea of walls. The setting is Wall Street, and the setting is further developed as a place boxed in on all sides by walls, which suggests entrapment. It is also significant that the setting is not only a place of business but also the location that symbolizes the new economic order in America. As the subtitle says, this is a story of Wall Street, the epicenter of the new order.

Besides Bartleby and the narrator you should notice three other characters: the office boy Ginger Nut and the copyists Turkey and Nippers. Ginger Nut is an errand boy apprenticed by his father, who wants his son to get ahead in life, to learn the law. The father is a cartman, a small, independent businessman. His son, by becoming part of a larger business enterprise, mirrors the changes taking place in the nineteenth-century economic order. As the large corporations grew, the number of small, independent business entrepreneurs declined. One of the questions you should ask yourself is in what ways, if any, Ginger Nut's job represents progress for him.

The older of the copyists, Turkey, shows us one way of accommodating the meaninglessness of the new work. Turkey is an alcoholic. He functions well in the morning, but after "lunch," which he drinks, he is un-fit. Turkey represents one common way of coping with meaningless and boring work—blot it out by blotting out your mind.

The younger of the copyists is an ambitious young man named Nippers. Nippers' excessive ambition is stifled by the repetitive work, and this produces "nerves" that make it impossible for him to do good work in the morning, but by afternoon he has calmed down enough to be productive. As we said earlier, the work in this office is the work that today would be done by a copy machine. It represents the work created by the new industrial order, that is, work so fragmented that the worker can no longer identify with it. The mindless copying shows us what it means to be alienated from work. How can you take pride in or achieve identity from work which does not involve either your mind or your skills?

In the famous story of the ancient Greek hero Sisyphus (see Section IIIB), Sisyphus is condemned by the gods to the worst imaginable punishment—to perform meaningless labor. Sisyphus was forced to engage in an endless struggle against a giant boulder, raising it to the top of a peak, only to see it roll back to the valley below time after time. While Bartleby's labor is not without purpose, the crucial point is that his mind, his consciousness, is not engaged in that purpose: Bartleby is alienated from the purposes of his work. In similar fashion, the goods produced by the assembly-line worker may go toward producing a very useful car, but the process does not engage the consciousness of the assembly-line worker. As you will see, what is unique about Bartleby is his response to meaningless work. Unlike Turkey who escapes by deadening his mind, or Nippers who violently acts out his frustrations, Bartleby rebels. He is a passive resister. Instead of working he "prefers not to."

We should warn you that many people reading this story find it difficult to sympathize with Bartleby. Because most of us have learned to make an accommodation with bad work, we tend not to be sympathetic with those who refuse to make this accommodation. Our lack of sympathy is further reinforced by the seeming humanity of the narrator who tries hard to be sensitive to Bartleby's predicament. His rebellion does not, on the surface, appear to be reasonable. But if you read carefully, you will notice that there is a method to his resistance. Bartleby withdraws his work, but only in stages. As soon as the boss accepts his withdrawal of work, he withdraws more. Why? We would suggest that Bartleby is testing the narrator, testing his humanity. Perhaps Bartleby has decided that, unlike Turkey and Nippers, he cannot live as a machine. Therefore he issues his challenge: accept me, not for my productive capacity, but only for my humanity, he seems to say. The narrator, who wants to accept Bartleby, keeps trying to find a way around the dilemma but ultimately cannot. He is forced to choose between Bartleby and his business. Naturally he chooses his business. For Melville this is a metaphor for the choices that modern society has made. The modern economic system has created great wealth and has made our lives much easier. As you will see as you read the story, the narrator prefers a life of ease.

But what is the psychological state of Bartleby whereby he pushes the boss to deny him? This is a critical question that must be answered if the story is going to work for us. We expect characters in fiction to have believable motivations that in some way reflect life in the nonfiction world. We might begin by pointing out that apparently Bartleby's previous job was in the dead-letter office. Presumably this is meant to symbolize similar meaningless work, sending letters that have lost their purpose. We would suggest that Bartleby represents the Biblical injunction that "man cannot live by bread alone." Having met his physical needs through meaningless labor, he has become "starved" for the food of purpose. Notice that Bartleby seems to live on minimal amounts of food and ends up rejecting food altogether. We would suggest that Bartleby's martyrdom is brought on by his recognition that humans cannot remain truly human without spiritual food as well as material food. Life without a spiritual dimension must be challenged, since it makes the physical dimension irrelevant. Melville tells us that we have paid too dearly for the comfort and ease of modern life, and that in doing so we have lost sight of deeper purposes for our existences.

Herman Melville

Bartleby the Scrivener
A Story of Wall Street

I am a rather elderly man. The nature of my avocations for the last thirty years has brought me into more than ordinary contact with what would seem an interesting and somewhat singular set of men, of whom as yet nothing that I know of has ever been written: — I mean the law-copyists or scriveners. I have known very many of them, professionally and privately, and if I pleased, could relate divers histories, at which good-natured gentlemen might smile, and sentimental souls might weep. But I waive the biographies of all other scriveners for a few passages in the life of Bartleby, who was a scrivener the strangest I ever saw or heard of. While of other law-copyists I might write the complete life, of Bartleby nothing of that sort can be done. I believe that no materials exist for a full and satisfactory biography of this man. It is an irreparable loss to literature. Bartleby was one of those beings of whom nothing is ascertainable, except from the original sources, and in his case those are very small. What my own astonished eyes saw of Bartleby, *that* is all I know of him, except, indeed, one vague report which will appear in the sequel.

Ere introducing the scrivener, as he first appeared to me, it is fit I make some mention of myself, my *employées,* my business, my chambers, and general surroundings; because some such description is indispensable to an adequate understanding of the chief character about to be presented.

Imprimis: I am a man who, from his youth upwards, has been filled with a profound conviction that the easiest way of life is the best. Hence, though I belong to a profession proverbially energetic and nervous, even to turbulence, at times, yet nothing of that sort have I ever suffered to invade my peace. I am one of those unambitious lawyers who never addresses a jury, or in any way draws down public applause; but in the cool tranquillity of a snug retreat, do a snug business among rich men's bonds and mortgages and title-deeds. All who know me, consider me an eminently *safe* man. The late John Jacob Astor, a personage little given to poetic enthusiasm, had no hesitation in pronouncing my first grand point to be prudence; my next, method. I do not speak it in vanity, but simply record the fact, that I was not unemployed in my profession by the late John Jacob Astor; a name which, I admit, I love to repeat, for it hath a rounded and orbicular sound to it, and rings like unto bullion. I will freely add, that I was not insensible to the late John Jacob Astor's good opinion.

Some time prior to the period at which this little history begins, my avocations had been largely increased. The good old office, now extinct in the State of New-York, of a Master in Chancery, had been conferred upon me. It was not a very arduous office, but very pleasantly remunerative. I seldom lose my temper; much more seldom indulge in dangerous indignation at wrongs and outrages; but I must be permitted to be rash here and declare, that I consider the sudden and violent abrogation of the office of Master in Chancery, by the new Constitution, as a ——— premature act; inasmuch as I had counted upon a life-lease of the profits, whereas I only received those of a few short years. But this is by the way.

My chambers were up stairs at No. ——— Wall-street. At one end they looked upon the white wall of the interior of a spacious sky-light shaft, penetrating the building from top to bottom. This view might have been considered rather tame than otherwise, deficient in what landscape painters call "life." But if so, the view from the other end of my chambers offered, at least, a contrast, if nothing more. In that direction my windows commanded an unobstructed view of a lofty brick wall, black by age and everlasting shade; which wall required no spy-glass to bring out its lurking beauties, but for the benefit of all near-sighted spectators, was pushed up to within ten feet of my window panes. Owing to the great height of the surrounding buildings, and my chambers being on the second floor, the interval between this wall and mine not a little resembled a huge square cistern.

At the period just preceding the advent of Bartleby, I had two persons as copyists in my employment, and a promising lad as an office-boy. First, Turkey; second, Nippers; third, Ginger Nut. These may seem names, the like of which are not usually found in the Directory. In truth they were nicknames, mutually conferred upon each other by my three clerks, and were deemed expressive of their respective persons or characters. Turkey was a short, pursy Englishman of about my own age, that is, somewhere not far from sixty. In the morning, one might say, his face was of a fine florid hue, but after twelve o'clock, meridian—his dinner hour—it blazed like a grate full of Christmas coals; and continued blazing—but, as it were, with a gradual wane—till 6 o'clock, P.M. or thereabouts, after which I saw no more of the proprietor of the face, which gaining its meridian with the sun, seemed to set with it, to rise, culminate, and decline the following day, with the like regularity and undiminished glory. There are many singular coincidences I have known in the course of my life, not the least among which was the fact, that exactly when Turkey displayed his fullest beams from his red and radiant countenance, just then, too, at that critical moment, began the daily period when I considered his business capacities as seriously disturbed for the remainder of the twenty-four hours. Not that he was absolutely idle, or averse to business then; far from it. The difficulty was, he was apt to be altogether too energetic. There was a strange, inflamed, flurried, flighty recklessness of activity about him. He would be incautious in dipping his pen into his inkstand. All his blots upon my documents, were dropped there after twelve o'clock meridian. Indeed, not only would he be reckless and sadly given to making blots in the afternoon, but some days he went further, and was rather noisy. At such times, too, his face flamed with augmented blazonry, as if cannel coal had been heaped on anthracite. He made an unpleasant racket with his chair; spilled his sand-box; in mending his pens, impatiently split them all to pieces, and threw them on the floor in a sudden passion; stood up and leaned over his table, boxing his papers about in a most indecorous manner, very sad to behold in an elderly man like him. Nevertheless, as he was in many ways a most valuable person to me, and all the time before twelve o'clock, meridian, was the quickest, steadiest creature too, accomplishing a great deal of work in a style not easy to be matched — for these reasons, I was willing to overlook his eccentricities, though indeed, occasionally, I remonstrated with him. I did this very gently, however, because, though the civilest, nay, the blandest and most reverential of men in the morning, yet in the afternoon he was disposed, upon provocation, to be slightly rash with his tongue, in fact, insolent. Now, valuing his morning services as I did, and resolved not to lose them; yet, at the same time made uncomfortable by his inflamed ways after twelve o'clock; and being a man of peace, unwilling by my admonitions to call forth unseemly retorts from him; I took upon me, one Saturday noon (he was always worse on Saturdays), to hint to him, very kindly, that perhaps now that he was growing old, it might be well to abridge his labors; in short, he need not come to my chambers after twelve o'clock, but, dinner over, had best go home to his lodgings and rest himself till tea-time. But no; he insisted upon his afternoon devotions. His countenance became intolerably fervid, as he oratorically assured me — gesticulating with a long ruler at the other end of the room — that if his services in the morning were useful, how indispensable, then, in the afternoon?

"With submission, sir," said Turkey on this occasion, "I consider myself your right-hand man. In the morning I but marshal and deploy my columns; but in the afternoon I put myself at their head, and gallantly charge the foe, thus!"—and he made a violent thrust with the ruler.

"But the blots, Turkey," intimated I.

"True,—but, with submission, sir, behold these hairs! I am getting old. Surely, sir, a blot or two of a warm afternoon is not to be severely urged against gray hairs. Old age — even if it blot the page — is honorable. With submission, sir, we *both* are getting old."

This appeal to my fellow-feeling was hardly to be resisted. At all events, I saw that go he would not. So I made up my mind to let him stay, resolving, nevertheless, to see to it, that during the afternoon he had to do with my less important papers.

Nippers, the second on my list, was a whiskered, sallow, and, upon the whole, rather piratical-looking young man of about five and twenty. I always deemed him the victim of two evil powers — ambition and indigestion. The ambition was evinced by a certain impatience of the duties of a mere copyist, an unwarrantable usurpation of strictly professional affairs, such as the original drawing up of legal documents. The indigestion seemed betokened in an occasional nervous testiness and grinning irritability, causing the teeth to audibly grind together over mistakes committed in copying; unnecessary maledictions, hissed, rather than spoken, in the heat of business; and especially by a continual discontent with the height of the table where he worked. Though of a very ingenious mechanical turn, Nippers could never get this table to suit him. He put chips under it, blocks of various sorts, bits of pasteboard, and at last went so far as to attempt an exquisite adjustment by final pieces of folded blotting-paper. But no invention would answer. If, for the sake of easing his back, he brought the table lid at a sharp angle well up towards his chin, and wrote there like a man using the steep roof of a Dutch house for his desk: — then he declared that it stopped the circulation in his arms. If now he lowered the table to his waistbands and stooped over it in writing, then there was a sore aching in his back. In short, the truth of the matter was, Nippers knew not what he wanted. Or, if he wanted any thing, it was to be rid of a scrivener's table altogether. Among the manifestations of his diseased ambition was a fondness he had for receiving visits from certain ambiguous-looking fellows in seedy coats, whom he called his clients. Indeed I was aware that not only was he, at times, considerable of a ward-politician, but he occasionally did a little business at the Justices' courts, and was not unknown on the steps of the Tombs. I have good reason to believe, however, that one individual who called upon him at my chambers, and who, with a grand air, he insisted was his client, was no other than a dun, and the alleged title-deed, a bill. But with all his failings, and the annoyances he caused me, Nippers, like his compatriot Turkey, was a very useful man to me; wrote a neat, swift hand; and, when he chose, was not deficient in a gentlemanly sort of deportment. Added to this, he always dressed in a gentlemanly sort of way; and so, incidentally, reflected credit upon my chambers. Whereas with respect to Turkey, I had much ado to keep him from being a reproach to me. His clothes were apt to look oily and smell of eating-houses. He wore his pantaloons very loose and baggy in summer. His coats were execrable; his hat not to be handled. But while the hat was a thing of indifference to me, inasmuch as his natural civility and deference, as a dependent Englishman, always led him to doff it at the moment he entered the room, yet his coat was another matter. Concerning his coats, I reasoned with him; but with no effect. The truth was, I suppose, that a man with so small an income, could not afford to sport such a lustrous face and a lustrous coat at one and the same time. As Nippers once observed, Turkey's money went chiefly for red ink. One winter day I presented Turkey with a highly-respectable looking coat of my own, a padded gray coat, of a most comfortable warmth, and which buttoned straight up from the knee to the neck. I thought Turkey would appreciate the favor, and abate his rashness and obstreperousness of afternoons. But no. I verily believe that buttoning himself up in so downy and blanket-like a coat had a pernicious effect upon him; upon the same principle that too much oats are bad for horses. In fact, precisely as a rash, restive horse is said to feel his oats, so Turkey felt his coat. It made him insolent. He was a man whom prosperity harmed.

Though concerning the self-indulgent habits of Turkey I had my own private surmises, yet touching Nippers I was well persuaded that whatever might be his faults in other respects, he was, at least, a temperate young man. But indeed, nature herself seemed to have been his vintner, and at his birth charged him so thoroughly with an irritable, brandy-like disposition, that all subsequent potations were needless. When I consider how, amid the stillness of my chambers, Nippers would sometimes impatiently rise from his seat, and stooping over his table, spread his arms wide apart, seize the whole desk, and move it, and jerk it, with a grim, grinding motion on the floor, as if the table were a perverse voluntary agent, intent on thwarting and vexing him; I plainly perceive that for Nippers, brandy and water were altogether superfluous.

It was fortunate for me that, owing to its peculiar cause — indigestion — the irritability and consequent nervousness of Nippers, were mainly observable in the morning, while in the afternoon he was comparatively mild. So that Turkey's paroxysms only coming on about twelve o'clock, I never had to do with their eccentricities at one time. Their fits relieved each other like guards. When Nippers' was on, Turkey's was off; and *vice versa*. This was a good natural arrangement under the circumstances.

Ginger Nut, the third on my list, was a lad some twelve years old. His father was a carman, ambitious of seeing his son on the bench instead of a cart, before he died. So he sent him to my office as student at law, errand boy, and cleaner and sweeper, at the rate of one dollar a week. He had a little desk to himself, but he did not use it much. Upon inspection, the drawer exhibited a great array of the shells of various sorts of nuts. Indeed, to this quick-witted youth the whole noble science of the law was contained in a nut-shell. Not the least among the employments of Ginger Nut, as well as one which he discharged with the most alacrity, was his duty as cake and apple purveyor for Turkey and Nippers. Copying law papers being proverbially a dry, husky sort of business, my two scriveners were fain to moisten their mouths very often with Spitzenbergs to be had at the numerous stalls nigh the Custom House and Post Office. Also, they sent Ginger Nut very frequently for that peculiar cake — small, flat, round, and very spicy — after which he had been named by them. Of a cold morning when business was but dull, Turkey would gobble up scores of these cakes, as if they were mere wafers — indeed they sell them at the rate of six or eight for a penny — the scrape of his pen blending with the crunching of the crisp particles in his mouth.

Of all the fiery afternoon blunders and flurried rashnesses of Turkey, was his once moistening a ginger-cake between his lips, and clapping it on to a mortgage for a seal. I came within an ace of dismissing him then. But he mollified me by making an oriental bow, and saying—"With submission, sir, it was generous of me to find you in stationery on my own account."

Now my original business—that of a conveyancer and title hunter, and drawer-up of recondite documents of all sorts—was considerably increased by receiving the master's office. There was now great work for scriveners. Not only must I push the clerks already with me, but I must have additional help. In answer to my advertisement, a motionless young man one morning, stood upon my office threshold, the door being open, for it was summer. I can see that figure now—pallidly neat, pitiably respectable, incurably forlorn! It was Bartleby.

After a few words touching his qualifications, I engaged him, glad to have among my corps of copyists a man of so singularly sedate an aspect, which I thought might operate beneficially upon the flighty temper of Turkey, and the fiery one of Nippers.

I should have stated before that ground glass folding-doors divided my premises into two parts, one of which was occupied by my scriveners, the other by myself. According to my humor I threw open these doors, or closed them. I resolved to assign Bartleby a corner by the folding-doors, but on my side of them, so as to have this quiet man within easy call, in case any trifling thing was to be done. I placed his desk close up to a small side-window in that part of the room, a window which originally had afforded a lateral view of certain grimy back-yards and bricks, but which, owing to subsequent erections, commanded at present no view at all, though it gave some light. Within three feet of the panes was a wall, and the light came down from far above, between two lofty buildings, as from a very small opening in a dome. Still further to a satisfactory arrangement, I procured a high green folding screen, which might entirely isolate Bartleby from my sight, though not remove him from my voice. And thus, in a manner, privacy and society were conjoined.

At first Bartleby did an extraordinary quantity of writing. As if long famishing for something to copy, he seemed to gorge himself on my documents. There was no pause for digestion. He ran a day and night line, copying by sun-light and by candle-light. I should have been quite delighted with his application, had he been cheerfully industrious. But he wrote on silently, palely, mechanically.

It is, of course, an indispensable part of a scrivener's business to verify the accuracy of his copy, word by word. Where there are two or more scriveners in an office, they assist each other in this examination, one reading from the copy, the other holding the original. It is a very dull, wearisome, and lethargic affair. I can readily imagine that to some sanguine temperaments it would be altogether intolerable. For example, I cannot credit that the mettlesome poet Byron would have contentedly sat down with Bartleby to examine a law document of, say five hundred pages, closely written in a crimpy hand.

Now and then, in the haste of business, it had been my habit to assist in comparing some brief document myself, calling Turkey or Nippers for this purpose. One object I had in placing Bartleby so handy to me behind the screen, was to avail myself of his services on such trivial occasions. It was on the third day, I think, of his being with me, and before any necessity had arisen for having his own writing examined, that, being much hurried to complete a small affair I had in hand, I abruptly called to Bartleby. In my haste and natural expectancy of instant compliance, I sat with my head bent over the original on my desk, and my right hand sideways, and somewhat nervously extended with the copy, so that immediately upon emerging from his retreat, Bartleby might snatch it and proceed to business without the least delay.

In this very attitude did I sit when I called to him, rapidly stating what it was I wanted him to do — namely, to examine a small paper with me. Imagine my surprise, nay, my consternation, when without moving from his privacy, Bartleby in a singularly mild, firm voice, replied, "I would prefer not to."

I sat awhile in perfect silence, rallying my stunned faculties. Immediately it occurred to me that my ears had deceived me, or Bartleby had entirely misunderstood my meaning. I repeated my request in the clearest tone I could assume. But in quite as clear a one came the previous reply, "I would prefer not to."

"Prefer not to," echoed I, rising in high excitement, and crossing the room with a stride. "What do you mean? Are you moon-struck? I want you to help me compare this sheet here — take it," and I thrust it towards him.

"I would prefer not to," said he.

I looked at him steadfastly. His face was leanly composed; his gray eye dimly calm. Not a wrinkle of agitation rippled him. Had there been the least uneasiness, anger, impatience or impertinence in his manner; in other words, had there been any thing ordinarily human about him, doubtless I should have violently dismissed him from the premises. But as it was, I should have as soon thought of turning my pale plaster-of-paris bust of Cicero out of doors. I stood gazing at him awhile, as he went on with his own writing, and then reseated myself at my desk. This is very strange, thought I. What had one best do? But my business hurried me. I concluded to forget the matter for the present, reserving it for my future leisure. So calling Nippers from the other room, the paper was speedily examined.

A few days after this, Bartleby concluded four lengthy documents, being quadruplicates of a week's testimony taken before me in my High Court of Chancery. It became necessary to examine them. It was an important suit, and great accuracy was imperative. Having all things arranged I called Turkey, Nippers and Ginger Nut from the next room, meaning to place the four copies in the hands of my four clerks, while I should read from the original. Accordingly Turkey, Nippers and Ginger Nut had taken their seats in a row, each with his document in hand, when I called to Bartleby to join this interesting group.

"Bartleby! quick, I am waiting."

I heard a slow scrape of his chair legs on the uncarpeted floor, and soon he appeared standing at the entrance of his hermitage.

"What is wanted?" said he mildly.

"The copies, the copies," said I hurriedly. "We are going to examine them. There"—and I held towards him the fourth quadruplicate.

"I would prefer not to," he said, and gently disappeared behind the screen.

For a few moments I was turned into a pillar of salt, standing at the head of my seated column of clerks. Recovering myself, I advanced towards the screen, and demanded the reason for such extraordinary conduct.

"*Why* do you refuse?"

"I would prefer not to."

With any other man I should have flown outright into a dreadful passion, scorned all further words, and thrust him ignominiously from my presence. But there was something about Bartleby that not only strangely disarmed me, but in a wonderful manner touched and disconcerted me. I began to reason with him.

"These are your own copies we are about to examine. It is labor saving to you, because one examination will answer for your four papers. It is common usage. Every copyist is bound to help examine his copy. Is it not so? Will you not speak? Answer!"

"I prefer not to," he replied in a flutelike tone. It seemed to me that while I had been addressing him, he carefully revolved every statement that I made; fully comprehended the meaning; could not gainsay the irresistible conclusion; but, at the same time, some paramount consideration prevailed with him to reply as he did.

"You are decided, then, not to comply with my request—a request made according to common usage and common sense?"

He briefly gave me to understand that on that point my judgment was sound. Yes: his decision was irreversible.

It is not seldom the case that when a man is browbeaten in some unprecedented and violently unreasonable way, he begins to stagger in his own plainest faith. He begins, as it were, vaguely to surmise that, wonderful as it may be, all the justice and all the reason is on the other side. Accordingly, if any disinterested persons are present, he turns to them for some reinforcement for his own faltering mind.

"Turkey," said I, "what do you think of this? Am I not right?"

"With submission, sir," said Turkey, with his blandest tone, "I think that you are."

"Nippers," said I, "what do *you* think of it?"

"I think I should kick him out of the office."

(The reader of nice perceptions will here perceive that, it being morning, Turkey's answer is couched in polite and tranquil terms, but Nippers replies in ill-tempered ones. Or, to repeat a previous sentence, Nippers's ugly mood was on duty, and Turkey's off.)

"Ginger Nut," said I, willing to enlist the smallest suffrage in my behalf, "what do *you* think of it?"

"I think, sir, he's a little *luny*," replied Ginger Nut with a grin.

"You hear what they say," said I, turning towards the screen, "come forth and do your duty."

But he vouchsafed no reply. I pondered a moment in sore perplexity. But once more business hurried me. I determined again to postpone the consideration of this dilemma to my future leisure. With a little trouble we made out to examine the papers without Bartleby, though at every page or two, Turkey deferentially dropped his opinion that this proceeding was quite out of the common; while Nippers, twitching in his chair with a dyspeptic nervousness, ground out between his set teeth occasional hissing maledictions against the stubborn oaf behind the screen. And for his (Nippers's) part, this was the first and the last time he would do another man's business without pay.

Meanwhile Bartleby sat in his hermitage, oblivious to every thing but his own peculiar business there.

Some days passed, the scrivener being employed upon another lengthy work. His late remarkable conduct led me to regard his ways narrowly. I observed that he never went to dinner; indeed that he never went any where. As yet I had never of my personal knowledge known him to be outside of my office. He was a perpetual sentry in the corner. At about eleven o'clock though, in the morning, I noticed that Ginger Nut would advance toward the opening in Bartleby's screen, as if silently beckoned thither by a gesture invisible to me where I sat. The boy would then leave the office jingling a few pence, and reappear with a handful of ginger-nuts which he delivered in the hermitage, receiving two of the cakes for his trouble.

He lives, then, on ginger-nuts, thought I; never eats a dinner, properly speaking; he must be a vegetarian then; but no; he never eats even vegetables, he eats nothing but ginger-nuts. My mind then ran on in reveries concerning the probable effects upon the human constitution of living entirely on ginger-nuts. Ginger-nuts are so called because they contain ginger as one of their peculiar constituents, and the final flavoring one. Now what was ginger? A hot, spicy thing. Was Bartleby hot and spicy? Not at all. Ginger, then, had no effect upon Bartleby. Probably he preferred it should have none.

Nothing so aggravates an earnest person as a passive resistance. If the individual so resisted be of a not inhumane temper, and the resisting one perfectly harmless in his passivity; then, in the better moods of the former, he will endeavor charitably to construe to his imagination what proves impossible to be solved by his judgment. Even so, for the most part, I regarded Bartleby and his ways. Poor fellow! thought I, he means no mischief; it is plain he intends no insolence; his aspect sufficiently evinces that his eccentricities are involuntary. He is useful to me. I can get along with him. If I turn him away, the chances are he will fall in with some less indulgent employer, and then he will be rudely treated, and perhaps driven forth miserably to starve. Yes. Here I can cheaply purchase a delicious self-approval. To befriend Bartleby; to humor him in his strange wilfulness, will cost me little or nothing, while I lay up in my soul what will eventually prove a sweet morsel for my conscience. But this mood was not invariable with me. The passiveness of Bartleby sometimes irritated me. I felt strangely goaded on to encounter him in new opposition, to elicit some angry spark from him answerable to my own. But indeed I might as well have essayed to strike fire with my knuckles against a bit of Windsor soap. But one afternoon the evil impulse in me mastered me, and the following little scene ensued:

"Bartleby," said I, "when those papers are all copied, I will compare them with you."

"I would prefer not to."

"How? Surely you do not mean to persist in that mulish vagary?"

No answer.

I threw open the folding-doors near by, and turning upon Turkey and Nippers, exclaimed in an excited manner—

"He says, a second time, he won't examine his papers. What do you think of it, Turkey?"

It was afternoon, be it remembered. Turkey sat glowing like a brass boiler, his bald head steaming, his hands reeling among his blotted papers.

"Think of it?" roared Turkey; "I think I'll just step behind his screen, and black his eyes for him!"

So saying, Turkey rose to his feet and threw his arms into a pugilistic position. He was hurrying away to make good his promise, when I detained him, alarmed at the effect of incautiously rousing Turkey's combativeness after dinner.

"Sit down, Turkey," said I, "and hear what Nippers has to say. What do you think of it, Nippers? Would I not be justified in immediately dismissing Bartleby?"

"Excuse me, that is for you to decide, sir. I think his conduct quite unusual, and indeed unjust, as regards Turkey and myself. But it may only be a passing whim."

"Ah," exclaimed I, "you have strangely changed your mind then—you speak very gently of him now."

"All beer," cried Turkey; "gentleness is effects of beer—Nippers and I dined together to-day. You see how gentle *I* am, sir. Shall I go and black his eyes?"

"You refer to Bartleby, I suppose. No, not to-day, Turkey," I replied; "pray, put up your fists."

I closed the doors, and again advanced towards Bartleby. I felt additional incentives tempting me to my fate. I burned to be rebelled against again. I remembered that Bartleby never left the office.

"Bartleby," said I, "Ginger Nut is away; just step round to the Post Office, won't you? (it was but a three minutes walk,) and see if there is any thing for me."

"I would prefer not to."

"You *will* not?"

"I *prefer* not."

I staggered to my desk, and sat there in a deep study. My blind inveteracy returned. Was there any other thing in which I could procure myself to be ignominiously repulsed by this lean, penniless wight?—my hired clerk? What added thing is there, perfectly reasonable, that he will be sure to refuse to do?

"Bartleby!"

No answer.

"Bartleby," in a louder tone.

No answer.

"Bartleby," I roared.

Like a very ghost, agreeably to the laws of magical invocation, at the third summons, he appeared at the entrance of his hermitage.

"Go to the next room, and tell Nippers to come to me."

"I prefer not to," he respectfully and slowly said, and mildly disappeared.

"Very good, Bartleby," said I, in a quiet sort of serenely severe self-possessed tone, intimating the unalterable purpose of some terrible retribution very close at hand. At the moment I half intended something of the kind. But upon the whole, as it was drawing towards my dinner-hour, I thought it best to put on my hat and walk home for the day, suffering much from perplexity and distress of mind.

Shall I acknowledge it? The conclusion of this whole business was, that it soon became a fixed fact of my chambers, that a pale young scrivener, by the name of Bartleby, had a desk there; that he copied for me at the usual rate of four cents a folio (one hundred words); but he was permanently exempt from examining the work done by him, that duty being transferred to Turkey and Nippers, one of compliment doubtless to their superior acuteness; moreover, said Bartleby was never on any account to be dispatched on the most trivial errand of any sort; and that even if entreated to take upon him such a matter, it was generally understood that he would prefer not to — in other words, that he would refuse point-blank.

As days passed on, I became considerably reconciled to Bartleby. His steadiness, his freedom from all dissipation, his incessant industry (except when he chose to throw himself into a standing revery behind his screen), his great stillness, his unalterableness of mean demeanor under all circumstances, made him a valuable acquisition. One prime thing was this, — *he was always there;* — first in the morning, continually through the day, and the last at night. I had a singular confidence in his honesty. I felt my most precious papers perfectly safe in his hands. Sometimes to be sure I could not, for the very soul of me, avoid falling into sudden spasmodic passions with him. For it was exceeding difficult to bear in mind all the time those strange peculiarities, privileges, and unheard of exemptions, forming the tacit stipulations on Bartleby's part under which he remained in my office. Now and then, in the eagerness of dispatching pressing business, I would inadvertently summon Bartleby, in a short, rapid tone, to put his finger, say, on the incipient tie of a bit of red tape with which I was about compressing some papers. Of course, from behind the screen the usual answer, "I prefer not to," was sure to come; and then, how could a human creature with the common infirmities of our nature, refrain from bitterly exclaiming upon such perverseness — such unreasonableness. However, every added repulse of this sort which I received only tended to lessen the probability of my repeating the inadvertence.

Here it must be said, that according to the custom of most legal gentlemen occupying chambers in densely-populated law buildings, there were several keys to my door. One was kept by a woman residing in the attic, which person weekly scrubbed and daily swept and dusted my apartments. Another was kept by Turkey for convenience sake. The third I sometimes carried in my own pocket. The fourth I knew not who had.

Now, one Sunday morning I happened to go to Trinity Church, to hear a celebrated preacher, and finding myself rather early on the ground, I thought I would walk round to my chambers for a while. Luckily I had my key with me; but upon applying it to the lock, I found it resisted by something inserted from the inside. Quite surprised, I called out; when to my consternation a key was turned from within; and thrusting his lean visage at me, and holding the door ajar, the apparition of Bartleby appeared, in his shirt sleeves, and otherwise in a strangely tattered dishabille, saying quietly that he was sorry, but he was deeply engaged just then, and—preferred not admitting me at present. In a brief word or two, he moreover added, that perhaps I had better walk round the block two or three times, and by that time he would probably have concluded his affairs.

Now, the utterly unsurmised appearance of Bartleby, tenanting my law-chambers of a Sunday morning, with his cadaverously gentlemanly *nonchalance,* yet withal firm and self-possessed, had such a strange effect upon me, that incontinently I slunk away from my own door, and did as desired. But not without sundry twinges of impotent rebellion against the mild effrontery of this unaccountable scrivener. Indeed, it was his wonderful mildness chiefly, which not only disarmed me, but unmanned me, as it were. For I consider that one, for the time, is a sort of unmanned when he tranquilly permits his hired clerk to dictate to him, and order him away from his own premises. Furthermore, I was full of uneasiness as to what Bartleby could possibly be doing in my office in his shirt sleeves, and in an otherwise dismantled condition of a Sunday morning. Was any thing amiss going on? Nay, that was out of the question. It was not to be thought of for a moment that Bartleby was an immoral person. But what could he be doing there?—copying? Nay again, whatever might be his eccentricities, Bartleby was an eminently decorous person. He would be the last man to sit down to his desk in any state approaching to nudity. Besides, it was Sunday; and there was something about Bartleby that forbade the supposition that he would by any secular occupation violate the proprieties of the day.

Nevertheless, my mind was not pacified; and full of a restless curiosity, at last I returned to the door. Without hindrance I inserted my key, opened it and entered. Bartleby was not to be seen. I looked round anxiously, peeped behind his screen; but it was very plain that he was gone. Upon more closely examining the place, I surmised that for an indefinite period Bartleby must have ate, dressed, and slept in my office, and that too without plate, mirror, or bed. The cushioned seat of a ricketty old sofa in one corner bore the faint impress of a lean, reclining form. Rolled away under his desk, I found a blanket; under the empty grate, a blacking box and brush; on a chair, a tin basin, with soap and a ragged towel; in a newspaper a few crumbs of ginger-nuts and a morsel of cheese. Yes, thought I, it is evident enough that Bartleby has been making his home here, keeping bachelor's hall all by himself. Immediately then the thought came sweeping across me, What miserable friendlessness and loneliness are here revealed! His poverty is great; but his solitude, how horrible! Think of it. Of a Sunday, Wall-street is deserted as Petra; and every night of every day it is an emptiness. This building too, which of week-days hums with industry and life, at nightfall echoes with sheer vacancy, and all through Sunday is forlorn. And here Bartleby makes his home; sole spectator of a solitude which he has seen all populous—a sort of innocent and transformed Marius brooding among the ruins of Carthage!

For the first time in my life a feeling of overpowering stinging melancholy seized me. Before, I had never experienced aught but a not-unpleasing sadness. The bond of a common humanity now drew me irresistibly to gloom. A fraternal melancholy! For both I and Bartleby were sons of Adam. I remembered the bright silks and sparkling faces I had seen that day, in gala trim, swan-like sailing down the Mississippi of Broadway; and I contrasted them with the pallid copyist, and thought to myself, Ah, happiness courts the light, so we deem the world is gay; but misery hides aloof, so we deem that misery there is none. These sad fancyings—chimeras, doubtless, of a sick and silly brain—led on to other and more special thoughts, concerning the eccentricities of Bartleby. Presentiments of strange discoveries hovered round me. The scrivener's pale form appeared to me laid out, among uncaring strangers, in its shivering winding sheet.

Suddenly I was attracted by Bartleby's closed desk, the key in open sight left in the lock.

I mean no mischief, seek the gratification of no heartless curiosity, thought I; besides, the desk is mine, and its contents too, so I will make bold to look within. Everything was methodically arranged, the papers smoothly placed. The pigeon holes were deep, and removing the files of documents, I groped into their recesses. Presently I felt something there, and dragged it out. It was an old bandanna handkerchief, heavy and knotted. I opened it, and saw it was a savings' bank.

I now recalled all the quiet mysteries which I had noted in the man. I remembered that he never spoke but to answer; that though at intervals he had considerable time to himself, yet I had never seen him read-

ing—no, not even a newspaper; that for long periods he would stand
looking out, at his pale window behind the screen, upon the dead brick
wall; I was quite sure he never visited any refectory or eating house;
while his pale face clearly indicated that he never drank beer like Turkey,
or tea and coffee even, like other men; that he never went any where
in particular that I could learn; never went out for a walk, unless indeed
that was the case at present; that he had declined telling who he was,
or whence he came, or whether he had any relatives in the world; that
though so thin and pale, he never complained of ill health. And more
than all, I remembered a certain unconscious air of pallid—how shall
I call it?—of pallid haughtiness, say, or rather an austere reserve about
him, which had positively awed me into my tame compliance with his
eccentricities, when I had feared to ask him to do the slightest incidental
thing for me, even though I might know, from his long-continued mo-
tionlessness, that behind his screen he must be standing in one of those
dead-wall reveries of his.

Revolving all these things, and coupling them with the recently discovered fact that he made my office his constant abiding place and home,
and not forgetful of his morbid moodiness; revolving all these things,
a prudential feeling began to steal over me. My first emotions had been
those of pure melancholy and sincerest pity; but just in proportion as
the forlornness of Bartleby grew and grew to my imagination, did that
same melancholy merge into fear, that pity into repulsion. So true it is,
and so terrible too, that up to a certain point the thought or sight of misery enlists our best affections; but, in certain special cases, beyond that
point it does not. They err who would assert that invariably this is owing
to the inherent selfishness of the human heart. It rather proceeds from
a certain hopelessness of remedying excessive and organic ill. To a sensitive being, pity is not seldom pain. And when at last it is perceived
that such pity cannot lead to effectual succor, common sense bids the
soul be rid of it. What I saw that morning persuaded me that the scrivener was the victim of innate and incurable disorder. I might give alms
to his body; but his body did not pain him; it was his soul that suffered,
and his soul I could not reach.

I did not accomplish the purpose of going to Trinity Church that morning. Somehow, the things I had seen disqualified me for the time from
church-going. I walked homeward, thinking what I would do with Bartleby.
Finally, I resolved upon this;—I would put certain calm questions to him
the next morning, touching his history, &c., and if he declined to answer
them openly and unreservedly (and I supposed he would prefer not), then
to give him a twenty dollar bill over and above whatever I might owe
him, and tell him his services were no longer required; but that if in any

other way I could assist him, I would be happy to do so, especially if he desired to return to his native place, wherever that might be, I would willingly help to defray the expenses. Moreover, if, after reaching home, he found himself at any time in want of aid, a letter from him would be sure of a reply.

The next morning came.

"Bartleby," said I, gently calling to him behind his screen.

No reply.

"Bartleby," said I, in a still gentler tone, "come here; I am not going to ask you to do any thing you would prefer not to do — I simply wish to speak to you."

Upon this he noiselessly slid into view.

"Will you tell me, Bartleby, where you were born?"

"I would prefer not to."

"Will you tell me *any thing* about yourself?"

"I would prefer not to."

"But what reasonable objection can you have to speak to me? I feel friendly towards you."

He did not look at me while I spoke, but kept his glance fixed upon my bust of Cicero, which as I then sat, was directly behind me, some six inches above my head.

"What is your answer, Bartleby?" said I, after waiting a considerable time for a reply, during which his countenance remained immovable, only there was the faintest conceivable tremor of the white attenuated mouth.

"At present I prefer to give no answer," he said, and retired into his hermitage.

It was rather weak in me I confess, but his manner on this occasion nettled me. Not only did there seem to lurk in it a certain calm disdain, but his perverseness seemed ungrateful, considering the undeniable good usage and indulgence he had received from me.

Again I sat ruminating what I should do. Mortified as I was at his behavior, and resolved as I had been to dismiss him when I entered my office, nevertheless I strangely felt something superstitious knocking at my heart, and forbidding me to carry out my purpose, and denouncing me for a villain if I dared to breathe one bitter word against this forlornest of mankind. At last, familiarly drawing my chair behind his screen, I sat down and said: "Bartleby, never mind then about revealing your history; but let me entreat you, as a friend, to comply as far as may be with the usages of this office. Say now you will help to examine papers tomorrow or next day: in short, say now that in a day or two you will begin to be a little reasonable: — say so, Bartleby."

"At present I would prefer not to be a little reasonable," was his mildly cadaverous reply.

Just then the folding-doors opened, and Nippers approached. He seemed suffering from an unusually bad night's rest, induced by severer indigestion than common. He overheard those final words of Bartleby.

"*Prefer not,* eh?" gritted Nippers—"I'd *prefer* him, if I were you, sir," addressing me—"I'd *prefer* him; I'd give him preferences, the stubborn mule! What is it, sir, pray, that he *prefers* not to do now?"

Bartleby moved not a limb.

"Mr. Nippers," said I, "I'd prefer that you would withdraw for the present."

Somehow, of late I had got into the way of involuntarily using this word "prefer" upon all sorts of not exactly suitable occasions. And I trembled to think that my contact with the scrivener had already and seriously affected me in a mental way. And what further and deeper aberration might it not yet produce? This apprehension had not been without efficacy in determining me to summary means.

As Nippers, looking very sour and sulky, was departing, Turkey blandly and deferentially approached.

"With submission, sir," said he, "yesterday I was thinking about Bartleby here, and I think that if he would but prefer to take a quart of good ale every day, it would do much towards mending him, and enabling him to assist in examining his papers."

"So you have got the word too," said I, slightly excited.

"With submission, what word, sir," asked Turkey, respectfully crowding himself into the contracted space behind the screen, and by so doing, making me jostle the scrivener. "What word, sir?"

"I would prefer to be left alone here," said Bartleby, as if offended at being mobbed in his privacy.

"*That's* the word, Turkey," said I—"*that's* it."

"Oh, *prefer?* oh yes—queer word. I never use it myself. But, sir, as I was saying, if he would but prefer—"

"Turkey," interrupted I, "you will please withdraw."

"Oh certainly, sir, if you prefer that I should."

As he opened the folding-door to retire, Nippers at his desk caught a glimpse of me, and asked whether I would prefer to have a certain paper copied on blue paper or white. He did not in the least roguishly accent the word prefer. It was plain that it involuntarily rolled from his tongue. I thought to myself, surely I must get rid of a demented man, who already has in some degree turned the tongues, if not the heads of myself and clerks. But I thought it prudent not to break the dismission at once.

The next day I noticed that Bartleby did nothing but stand at his window in his dead-wall revery. Upon asking him why he did not write, he said that he had decided upon doing no more writing.

"Why, how now? what next?" exclaimed I, "do no more writing?"

"No more."

"And what is the reason?"

"Do you not see the reason for yourself," he indifferently replied.

I looked steadfastly at him, and perceived that his eyes looked dull and glazed. Instantly it occurred to me, that his unexampled diligence in copying by his dim window for the first few weeks of his stay with me might have temporarily impaired his vision.

I was touched. I said something in condolence with him. I hinted that of course he did wisely in abstaining from writing for a while; and urged him to embrace that opportunity of taking wholesome exercise in the open air. This, however, he did not do. A few days after this, my other clerks being absent, and being in a great hurry to dispatch certain letters by the mail, I thought that, having nothing else earthly to do, Bartleby would surely be less inflexible than usual, and carry these letters to the post-office. But he blankly declined. So, much to my inconvenience, I went myself.

Still added days went by. Whether Bartleby's eyes improved or not, I could not say. To all appearance, I thought they did. But when I asked him if they did, he vouchsafed no answer. At all events, he would do no copying. At last, in reply to my urgings, he informed me that he had permanently given up copying.

"What!" exclaimed I; "suppose your eyes should get entirely well—better than ever before—would you not copy then?"

"I have given up copying," he answered, and slid aside.

He remained as ever, a fixture in my chamber. Nay—if that were possible—he became still more of a fixture than before. What was to be done? He would do nothing in the office: why should he stay there? In plain fact, he had now become a millstone to me, not only useless as a necklace, but afflictive to bear. Yet I was sorry for him. I speak less than truth when I say that, on his own account, he occasioned me uneasiness. If he would but have named a single relative or friend, I would instantly have written, and urged their taking the poor fellow away to some convenient retreat. But he seemed alone, absolutely alone in the universe. A bit of wreck in the mid Atlantic. At length, necessities connected with my business tyrannized over all other considerations. Decently as I could, I told Bartleby that in six days' time he must unconditionally leave the office. I warned him to take measures, in the interval, for procuring some other abode. I offered to assist him in this endeavor, if he himself would but take the first step towards a removal. "And when you finally quit me, Bartleby," added I, "I shall see that you go not away entirely unprovided. Six days from this hour, remember."

At the expiration of that period, I peeped behind the screen, and lo! Bartleby was there.

I buttoned up my coat, balanced myself; advanced slowly towards him, touched his shoulder, and said, "The time has come; you must quit this place; I am sorry for you; here is money; but you must go."

"I would prefer not," he replied, with his back still towards me.

"You *must*."

He remained silent.

Now I had an unbounded confidence in this man's common honesty. He had frequently restored to me sixpences and shillings carelessly dropped upon the floor, for I am apt to be very reckless in such shirt-button affairs. The proceeding then which followed will not be deemed extraordinary.

"Bartleby," said I, "I owe you twelve dollars on account; here are thirty-two; the odd twenty are yours.—Will you take it?" and I handed the bills towards him.

But he made no motion.

"I will leave them here then," putting them under a weight on the table. Then taking my hat and cane and going to the door I tranquilly turned and added—"After you have removed your things from these offices, Bartleby, you will of course lock the door—since every one is now gone for the day but you—and if you please, slip your key underneath the mat, so that I may have it in the morning. I shall not see you again; so good-bye to you. If hereafter in your new place of abode I can be of any service to you, do not fail to advise me by letter. Good-bye, Bartleby, and fare you well."

But he answered not a word; like the last column of some ruined temple, he remained standing mute and solitary in the middle of the otherwise deserted room.

As I walked home in a pensive mood, my vanity got the better of my pity. I could not but highly plume myself on my masterly management in getting rid of Bartleby. Masterly I call it, and such it must appear to any dispassionate thinker. The beauty of my procedure seemed to consist in its perfect quietness. There was no vulgar bullying, no bravado of any sort, no choleric hectoring, and striding to and fro across the apartment, jerking out vehement commands for Bartleby to bundle himself off with his beggarly traps. Nothing of the kind. Without loudly bidding Bartleby depart—as an inferior genius might have done—I *assumed* the ground that depart he must; and upon that assumption built all I had to say. The more I thought over my procedure, the more I was charmed

with it. Nevertheless, next morning, upon awakening, I had my doubts,—
I had somehow slept off the fumes of vanity. One of the coolest and wisest hours a man has, is just after he awakes in the morning. My procedure seemed as sagacious as ever,—but only in theory. How it would
prove in practice—there was the rub. It was truly a beautiful thought
to have assumed Bartleby's departure; but, after all, that assumption was
simply my own, and none of Bartleby's. The great point was, not whether
I had assumed that he would quit me, but whether he would prefer so
to do. He was more a man of preferences than assumptions.

After breakfast, I walked down town, arguing the probabilities *pro* and
con. One moment I thought it would prove a miserable failure, and Bartleby would be found all alive at my office as usual; the next moment
it seemed certain that I should see his chair empty. And so I kept veering
about. At the corner of Broadway and Canal-street, I saw quite an excited group of people standing in earnest conversation.

"I'll take odds he doesn't," said a voice as I passed.

"Doesn't go?—done!" said I, "put up your money."

I was instinctively putting my hand in my pocket to produce my own,
when I remembered that this was an election day. The words I had
overheard bore no reference to Bartleby, but to the success or non-success
of some candidate for the mayoralty. In my intent frame of mind, I had,
as it were, imagined that all Broadway shared in my excitement, and
were debating the same question with me. I passed on, very thankful
that the uproar of the street screened my momentary absent-mindedness.

As I had intended, I was earlier than usual at my office door. I stood
listening for a moment. All was still. He must be gone. I tried the knob.
The door was locked. Yes, my procedure had worked to a charm; he indeed must be vanished. Yet a certain melancholy mixed with this: I was
almost sorry for my brilliant success. I was fumbling under the door mat
for the key, which Bartleby was to have left there for me, when acciden-
tally my knee knocked against a panel, producing a summoning sound,
and in response a voice came to me from within—"Not yet; I am occupied."

It was Bartleby.

I was thunderstruck. For an instant I stood like the man who, pipe
in mouth, was killed one cloudless afternoon long ago in Virginia, by
summer lightning; at his own warm open window he was killed, and remained leaning out there upon the dreamy afternoon, till some one touched
him, when he fell.

"Not gone!" I murmured at last. But again obeying that wondrous
ascendancy which the inscrutable scrivener had over me, and from which
ascendancy, for all my chafing, I could not completely escape, I slowly
went down stairs and out into the street, and while walking round the

block, considered what I should next do in this unheard-of perplexity. Turn the man out by an actual thrusting I could not; to drive him away by calling him hard names would not do; calling in the police was an unpleasant idea; and yet, permit him to enjoy his cadaverous triumph over me,—this too I could not think of. What was to be done? or, if nothing could be done, was there any thing further that I could *assume* in the matter? Yes, as before I had prospectively assumed that Bartleby would depart, so now I might retrospectively assume that departed he was. In the legitimate carrying out of this assumption, I might enter my office in a great hurry, and pretending not to see Bartleby at all, walk straight against him as if he were air. Such a proceeding would in a singular degree have the appearance of a home-thrust. It was hardly possible that Bartleby could withstand such an application of the doctrine of assumptions. But upon second thoughts the success of the plan seemed rather dubious. I resolved to argue the matter over with him again.

"Bartleby," said I, entering the office, with a quietly severe expression. "I am seriously displeased. I am pained, Bartleby. I had thought better of you. I had imagined you of such a gentlemanly organization, that in any delicate dilemma a slight hint would suffice—in short, an assumption. But it appears I am deceived. Why," I added, unaffectedly starting, "you have not even touched that money yet," pointing to it, just where I had left it the evening previous.

He answered nothing.

"Will you, or will you not, quit me?" I now demanded in a sudden passion, advancing close to him.

"I would prefer *not* to quit you," he replied, gently emphasizing the *not.*

"What earthly right have you to stay here? Do you pay any rent? Do you pay my taxes? Or is this property yours?"

He answered nothing.

"Are you ready to go on and write now? Are your eyes recovered? Could you copy a small paper for me this morning? or help examine a few lines? or step round to the post-office? In a word, will you do any thing at all, to give a coloring to your refusal to depart the premises?"

He silently retired into his hermitage.

I was now in such a state of nervous resentment that I thought it but prudent to check myself at present from further demonstrations. Bartleby and I were alone. I remembered the tragedy of the unfortunate Adams and the still more unfortunate Colt in the solitary office of the latter; and how poor Colt, being dreadfully incensed by Adams, and imprudently permitting himself to get wildly excited, was at unawares hurried into his fatal act—an act which certainly no man could possibly deplore more than the actor himself. Often it had occurred to me in my ponderings upon the subject, that had that altercation taken place in the public street, or at a private residence, it would not have terminated as it did. It was the circumstance of being alone in a solitary office, up stairs, of a building entirely unhallowed by humanizing domestic associations — an uncarpeted office, doubtless, of a dusty, haggard sort of appearance; — this it must have been, which greatly helped to enhance the irritable desperation of the hapless Colt.

But when this old Adam of resentment rose in me and tempted me concerning Bartleby, I grappled him and threw him. How? Why, simply by recalling the divine injunction: "A new commandment give I unto you, that ye love one another." Yes, this it was that saved me. Aside from higher considerations, charity often operates as a vastly wise and prudent principle — a great safeguard to its possessor. Men have committed murder for jealousy's sake, and anger's sake, and hatred's sake, and selfishness' sake, and spiritual pride's sake; but no man that ever I heard of, ever committed a diabolical murder for sweet charity's sake. Mere self-interest, then, if no better motive can be enlisted, should, especially with high-tempered men, prompt all beings to charity and philanthropy. At any rate, upon the occasion in question, I strove to drown my exasperated feelings towards the scrivener by benevolently construing his conduct. Poor fellow, poor fellow! thought I, he don't mean any thing; and besides, he has seen hard times, and ought to be indulged.

I endeavored also immediately to occupy myself, and at the same time to comfort my despondency. I tried to fancy that in the course of the morning, at such time as might prove agreeable to him, Bartleby, of his own free accord, would emerge from his hermitage, and take up some decided line of march in the direction of the door. But no. Half-past twelve o'clock came; Turkey began to glow in the face, overturn his inkstand, and become generally obstreperous; Nippers abated down into quietude and courtesy; Ginger Nut munched his noon apple; and Bartleby remained standing at his window in one of his profoundest dead-wall reveries. Will it be credited? Ought I to acknowledge it? That afternoon I left the office without saying one further word to him.

Some days now passed, during which, at leisure intervals I looked a little into "Edwards on the Will," and "Priestley on Necessity." Under the circumstances, those books induced a salutary feeling. Gradually I slid into the persuasion that these troubles of mine touching the scrivener, had been all predestinated from eternity, and Bartleby was billeted upon me for some mysterious purpose of an all-wise Providence, which it was not for a mere mortal like me to fathom. Yes, Bartleby, stay there behind your screen, thought I; I shall persecute you no more; you are harmless and noiseless as any of these old chairs; in short, I never feel so private as when I know you are here. At least I see it, I feel it; I penetrate to the predestinated purpose of my life. I am content. Others may have loftier parts to enact; but my mission in this world, Bartleby, is to furnish you with office-room for such period as you may see fit to remain.

I believe that this wise and blessed frame of mind would have continued with me, had it not been for the unsolicited and uncharitable remarks obtruded upon me by my professional friends who visited the rooms. But thus it often is, that the constant friction of illiberal minds wears out at last the best resolves of the more generous. Though to be sure, when I reflected upon it, it was not strange that people entering my office should be struck by the peculiar aspect of the unaccountable Bartleby, and so be tempted to throw out some sinister observations concerning him. Sometimes an attorney having business with me, and calling at my office, and finding no one but the scrivener there, would undertake to obtain some sort of precise information from him touching my whereabouts; but without heeding his idle talk, Bartleby would remain standing immovable in the middle of the room. So after contemplating him in that position for a time, the attorney would depart, no wiser than he came.

Also, when a Reference was going on, and the room full of lawyers and witnesses and business was driving fast; some deeply occupied legal gentleman present, seeing Bartleby wholly unemployed, would request him to run round to his (the legal gentleman's) office and fetch some papers for him. Thereupon, Bartleby would tranquilly decline, and yet remain idle as before. Then the lawyer would give a great stare, and turn to me. And what could I say? At last I was made aware that all through the circle of my professional acquaintance, a whisper of wonder was running round, having reference to the strange creature I kept at my office. This worried me very much. And as the idea came upon me of his possibly turning out a long-lived man, and keep occupying my chambers, and denying my authority; and perplexing my visitors; and scandalizing my professional reputation; and casting a general gloom over the premises; keeping soul and body together to the last upon his savings (for doubtless he spent but half a dime a day), and in the end perhaps outlive me, and claim possession of my office by right of his perpetual occupancy: as all these dark anticipations crowded upon me more and more, and my friends continually intruded their relentless remarks upon the apparition in my room; a great change was wrought in me. I resolved to gather all my faculties together, and for ever rid me of this intolerable incubus.

Ere revolving any complicated project, however, adapted to this end, I first simply suggested to Bartleby the propriety of his permanent departure. In a calm and serious tone, I commended the idea to his careful and mature consideration. But having taken three days to meditate upon it, he apprised me that his original determination remained the same; in short, that he still preferred to abide with me.

What shall I do? I now said to myself, buttoning up my coat to the last button. What shall I do? what ought I to do? what does conscience say I *should* do with this man, or rather ghost. Rid myself of him, I must; go, he shall. But how? You will not thrust him, the poor, pale, passive mortal, — you will not thrust such a helpless creature out of your door? you will not dishonor yourself by such cruelty? No, I will not, I cannot do that. Rather would I let him live and die here, and then mason up his remains in the wall. What then will you do? For all your coaxing, he will not budge. Bribes he leaves under your own paperweight on your table; in short, it is quite plain that he prefers to cling to you.

Then something severe, something unusual must be done. What! surely you will not have him collared by a constable, and commit his innocent pallor to the common jail? And upon what ground could you procure such a thing to be done?—a vagrant, is he? What! he a vagrant, a wanderer, who refuses to budge? It is because he will *not* be a vagrant, then, that you seek to count him *as* a vagrant. That is too absurd. No visible means of support: there I have him. Wrong again: for indubitably he *does* support himself, and that is the only unanswerable proof that any man can show of his possessing the means so to do. No more then. Since he will not quit me, I must quit him. I will change my offices; I will move elsewhere; and give him fair notice, that if I find him on my new premises I will then proceed against him as a common trespasser.

Acting accordingly, next day I thus addressed him: "I find these chambers too far from the City Hall; the air is unwholesome. In a word, I propose to remove my offices next week, and shall no longer require your services. I tell you this now, in order that you may seek another place."

He made no reply, and nothing more was said.

On the appointed day I engaged carts and men, proceeded to my chambers, and having but little furniture, every thing was removed in a few hours. Throughout, the scrivener remained standing behind the screen, which I directed to be removed the last thing. It was withdrawn; and being folded up like a huge folio, left him the motionless occupant of a naked room. I stood in the entry watching him a moment, while something from within me upbraided me.

I re-entered, with my hand in my pocket—and—and my heart in my mouth.

"Good-bye, Bartleby; I am going—good-bye, and God some way bless you; and take that," slipping something in his hand. But it dropped upon the floor, and then, — strange to say — I tore myself from him whom I had so longed to be rid of.

Established in my new quarters, for a day or two I kept the door locked, and started at every footfall in the passages. When I returned to my rooms after any little absence, I would pause at the threshold for an instant, and attentively listen, ere applying my key. But these fears were needless. Bartleby never came nigh me.

I thought all was going well, when a perturbed looking stranger visited me, inquiring whether I was the person who had recently occupied rooms at No. — Wall-street.

Full of forebodings, I replied that I was.

"Then sir," said the stranger, who proved a lawyer, "you are responsible for the man you left there. He refuses to do any copying; he refuses to do any thing; he says he prefers not to; and he refuses to quit the premises."

"I am very sorry, sir," said I, with assumed tranquillity, but an inward tremor, "but, really, the man you allude to is nothing to me — he is no relation or apprentice of mine, that you should hold me responsible for him."

"In mercy's name, who is he?"

"I certainly cannot inform you. I know nothing about him. Formerly I employed him as a copyist; but he has done nothing for me now for some time past."

"I shall settle him then, — good morning, sir."

Several days passed, and I heard nothing more; and though I often felt a charitable prompting to call at the place and see poor Bartleby, yet a certain squeamishness of I know not what withheld me.

All is over with him, by this time, thought I at last, when through another week no further intelligence reached me. But coming to my room the day after, I found several persons waiting at my door in a high state of nervous excitement.

"That's the man — here he comes," cried the foremost one, whom I recognized as the lawyer who had previously called upon me alone.

"You must take him away, sir, at once," cried a portly person among them, advancing upon me, and whom I knew to be the landlord of No. — Wall-street. "These gentlemen, my tenants, cannot stand it any longer; Mr. B —" pointing to the lawyer, "has turned him out of his room, and he now persists in haunting the building generally, sitting upon the banisters of the stairs by day, and sleeping in the entry by night. Every body is concerned; clients are leaving the offices; some fears are entertained of a mob; something you must do, and that without delay."

Aghast at this torrent, I fell back before it, and would fain have locked myself in my new quarters. In vain I persisted that Bartleby was nothing to me—no more than to any one else. In vain:—I was the last person known to have any thing to do with him, and they held me to the terrible account. Fearful then of being exposed in the papers (as one person present obscurely threatened) I considered the matter, and at length said, that if the lawyer would give me a confidential interview with the scrivener, in his (the lawyer's) own room, I would that afternoon strive my best to rid them of the nuisance they complained of.

Going up stairs to my old haunt, there was Bartleby silently sitting upon the banister at the landing.

"What are you doing here, Bartleby?" said I.

"Sitting upon the banister," he mildly replied.

I motioned him into the lawyer's room, who then left us.

"Bartleby," said I, "are you aware that you are the cause of great tribulation to me, by persisting in occupying the entry after being dismissed from the office?"

No answer.

"Now one of two things must take place. Either you must do something, or something must be done to you. Now what sort of business would you like to engage in? Would you like to re-engage in copying for some one?"

"No; I would prefer not to make any change."

"Would you like a clerkship in a dry-goods store?"

"There is too much confinement about that. No, I would not like a clerkship; but I am not particular."

"Too much confinement," I cried, "why you keep yourself confined all the time!"

"I would prefer not to take a clerkship," he rejoined, as if to settle that little item at once.

"How would a bar-tender's business suit you? There is no trying of the eyesight in that."

"I would not like it at all; though, as I said before, I am not particular."

His unwonted wordiness inspirited me. I returned to the charge.

"Well then, would you like to travel through the country collecting bills for the merchants? That would improve your health."

"No, I would prefer to be doing something else."

"How then would going as a companion to Europe, to entertain some young gentleman with your conversation,—how would that suit you?"

"Not at all. It does not strike me that there is any thing definite about that. I like to be stationary. But I am not particular."

"Stationary you shall be then," I cried, now losing all patience, and for the first time in all my exasperating connection with him fairly flying into a passion. "If you do not go away from these premises before night, I shall feel bound—indeed I *am* bound—to—to—to quit the premises myself!" I rather absurdly concluded, knowing not with what possible threat to try to frighten his immobility into compliance. Despairing of all further efforts, I was precipitately leaving him, when a final thought occurred to me—one which had not been wholly unindulged before.

"Bartleby," said I, in the kindest tone I could assume under such exciting circumstances, "will you go home with me now—not to my office, but my dwelling—and remain there till we can conclude upon some convenient arrangement for you at your leisure? Come, let us start now, right away."

"No: at present I would prefer not to make any change at all."

I answered nothing; but effectually dodging every one by the suddenness and rapidity of my flight, rushed from the building, ran up Wall-street towards Broadway, and jumping into the first omnibus was soon removed from pursuit. As soon as tranquillity returned I distinctly perceived that I had now done all that I possibly could, both in respect to the demands of the landlord and his tenants, and with regard to my own desire and sense of duty, to benefit Bartleby, and shield him from rude persecution. I now strove to be entirely care-free and quiescent; and my conscience justified me in the attempt; though indeed it was not so successful as I could have wished. So fearful was I of being again hunted out by the incensed landlord and his exasperated tenants, that, surrendering my business to Nippers, for a few days I drove about the upper part of the town and through the suburbs, in my rockaway; crossed over to Jersey City and Hoboken, and paid fugitive visits to Manhattanville and Astoria. In fact I almost lived in my rockaway for the time.

When again I entered my office, lo, a note from the landlord lay upon the desk. I opened it with trembling hands. It informed me that the writer had sent to the police, and had Bartleby removed to the Tombs as a vagrant. Moreover, since I knew more about him than any one else, he wished me to appear at that place, and make a suitable statement of the facts. These tidings had a conflicting effect upon me. At first I was indignant; but at last almost approved. The landlord's energetic, summary disposition, had led him to adopt a procedure which I do not think I would have decided upon myself; and yet as a last resort, under such peculiar circumstances, it seemed the only plan.

As I afterwards learned, the poor scrivener, when told that he must be conducted to the Tombs, offered not the slightest obstacle, but in his pale unmoving way, silently acquiesced.

Some of the compassionate and curious bystanders joined the party; and headed by one of the constables arm in arm with Bartleby, the silent procession filed its way through all the noise, and heat, and joy of the roaring thoroughfares at noon.

The same day I received the note I went to the Tombs, or to speak more properly, the Halls of Justice. Seeking the right officer, I stated the purpose of my call, and was informed that the individual I described was indeed within. I then assured the functionary that Bartleby was a perfectly honest man, and greatly to be compassionated, however unaccountably eccentric. I narrated all I knew, and closed by suggesting the idea of letting him remain in as indulgent confinement as possible till something less harsh might be done—though indeed I hardly knew what. At all events, if nothing else could be decided upon, the alms-house must receive him. I then begged to have an interview.

Being under no disgraceful charge, and quite serene and harmless in all his ways, they had permitted him freely to wander about the prison, and especially in the inclosed grass-platted yards thereof. And so I found him there, standing all alone in the quietest of the yards, his face towards a high wall, while all around, from the narrow slits of the jail windows, I thought I saw peering out upon him the eyes of murderers and thieves.

"Bartleby!"

"I know you," he said, without looking round,—"and I want nothing to say to you."

"It was not I that brought you here, Bartleby," said I, keenly pained at his implied suspicion. "And to you, this should not be so vile a place. Nothing reproachful attaches to you by being here. And see, it is not so sad a place as one might think. Look, there is the sky, and here is the grass."

"I know where I am," he replied, but would say nothing more, and so I left him.

As I entered the corridor again, a broad meat-like man, in an apron, accosted me, and jerking his thumb over his shoulder said—"Is that your friend?"

"Yes."

"Does he want to starve? If he does, let him live on the prison fare, that's all."

"Who are you?" asked I, not knowing what to make of such an unofficially speaking person in such a place.

"I am the grub-man. Such gentlemen as have friends here, hire me to provide them with something good to eat."

"Is this so?" said I, turning to the turnkey.

He said it was.

"Well then," said I, slipping some silver into the grub-man's hands (for so they called him). "I want you to give particular attention to my friend

there; let him have the best dinner you can get. And you must be as polite to him as possible."

"Introduce me, will you?" said the grub-man, looking at me with an
expression which seem to say he was all impatience for an opportunity
to give a specimen of his breeding.

Thinking it would prove of benefit to the scrivener, I acquiesced; and
asking the grub-man his name, went up with him to Bartleby.

"Bartleby, this is Mr. Cutlets; you will find him very useful to you."

"Your sarvant, sir, your sarvant," said the grub-man, making a low
salutation behind his apron. "Hope you find it pleasant here, sir; — spacious grounds — cool apartments, sir — hope you'll stay with us some time
— try to make it agreeable. May Mrs. Cutlets and I have the pleasure
of your company to dinner, sir, in Mrs. Cutlets' private room?"

"I prefer not to dine to-day," said Bartleby, turning away. "It would
disagree with me; I am unused to dinners." So saying he slowly moved
to the other side of the inclosure, and took up a position fronting the
dead-wall.

"How's this?" said the grub-man, addressing me with a stare of astonishment. "He's odd, aint he?"

"I think he is a little deranged," said I, sadly.

"Deranged? deranged is it? Well now, upon my word, I thought that
friend of yourn was a gentleman forger; they are always pale and genteel-
like, them forgers. I can't help pity 'em — can't help it, sir. Did you know
Monroe Edwards?" he added touchingly, and paused. Then, laying his
hand pityingly on my shoulder, sighed, "he died of consumption at Sing-
Sing. So you weren't acquainted with Monroe?"

"No, I was never socially acquainted with any forgers. But I cannot
stop longer. Look to my friend yonder. You will not lose by it. I will see
you again."

Some few days after this, I again obtained admission to the Tombs,
and went through the corridors in quest of Bartleby; but without finding him.

"I saw him coming from his cell not long ago," said a turnkey, "may
be he's gone to loiter in the yards."

So I went in that direction.

"Are you looking for the silent man?" said another turnkey passing
me. "Yonder he lies — sleeping in the yard there. 'Tis not twenty minutes
since I saw him lie down."

The yard was entirely quiet. It was not accessible to the common
prisoners. The surrounding walls, of amazing thickness, kept off all sounds
behind them. The Egyptian character of the masonry weighed upon me
with its gloom. But a soft imprisoned turf grew under foot. The heart

of the eternal pyramids, it seemed, wherein, by some strange magic, through the clefts, grass-seed, dropped by birds, had sprung.

Strangely huddled at the base of the wall, his knees drawn up, and lying on his side, his head touching the cold stones, I saw the wasted Bartleby. But nothing stirred. I paused; then went close up to him; stooped over, and saw that his dim eyes were open; otherwise he seemed profoundly sleeping. Something prompted me to touch him. I felt his hand, when a tingling shiver ran up my arm and down my spine to my feet.

The round face of the grub-man peered upon me now. "His dinner is ready. Won't he dine to-day either? Or does he live without dining?"

"Lives without dining," said I, and closed the eyes.

"Eh! — He's asleep, aint he?"

"With kings and counsellors," murmured I.

*   *   *   *

There would seem little need for proceeding further in this history. Imagination will readily supply the meagre recital of poor Bartleby's interment. But ere parting with the reader, let me say, that if this little narrative has sufficiently interested him, to awaken curiosity as to who Bartleby was, and what manner of life he led prior to the present narrator's making his acquaintance, I can only reply, that in such curiosity I fully share, but am wholly unable to gratify it. Yet here I hardly know whether I should divulge one little item of rumor, which came to my ear a few months after the scrivener's decease. Upon what basis it rested, I could never ascertain; and hence, how true it is I cannot now tell. But inasmuch as this vague report has not been without a certain strange suggestive interest to me, however sad, it may prove the same with some others; and so I will briefly mention it. The report was this: that Bartleby had been a subordinate clerk in the Dead Letter Office at Washington, from which he had been suddenly removed by a change in the administration. When I think over this rumor, I cannot adequately express the emotions which seize me. Dead letters! does it not sound like dead men? Conceive a man by nature and misfortune prone to a pallid hopelessness, can any business seem more fitted to heighten it than that of continually handling these dead letters, and assorting them for the flames? For by the cart-load they are annually burned. Sometimes from out the folded paper the pale clerk takes a ring: — the finger it was meant for, perhaps, moulders in the grave; a bank-note sent in swiftest charity: — he whom it would relieve, nor eats nor hungers any more; pardon for those who died despairing; hope for those who died unhoping; good tidings for those who died stifled by unrelieved calamities. On errands of life, these letters speed death.

Ah Bartleby! Ah humanity!

Introduction
Tillie Olsen, "I Stand Here Ironing"

Tillie Olsen was born in 1913 and spent the Great Depression as a young mother trying to raise children while coping with work in and outside the home. Her best-known stories are about the vicissitudes of women dealing with poverty while trying to raise children.

We have included this story because, although it is set in an earlier generation, we think it speaks forcefully about issues that have become part of the public debate during recent years. We have all heard the statistics about the growing feminization of poverty and about the ever-increasing percentage of children raised in poverty. Tillie Olsen helps us see the life behind the statistics.

This story is told by a mother while she stands ironing, to someone we might guess is a counselor, who says she wants to find out about Emily, the ironer's oldest daughter, so that she can help her. As the mother tells her story, we feel her pain, resentment, and near hopelessness. She has tried, against impossible odds, to be a good mother, but she feels she has failed, she feels both anguish for the daughter she loves and resentment toward her listener, who represents a system that has failed both her and her daughter. Her mother's last hope is that the woman will help Emily to know that there is hope: "that she is more than this dress on the ironing board, helpless before the iron."

Olsen asks us to feel the pain and anxiety of the mother and child who are victims of the impersonal economy we have created. This story raises important questions about our own time and the economy we live in by giving us a vivid picture of what living in the culture of poverty is like. Ask yourself how a child like Emily can realize the American dream when all of her life she has been taught to be a victim?

Tillie Olsen

I Stand Here Ironing

I stand here ironing, and what you asked me moves tormented back and forth with the iron.

"I wish you would manage the time to come in and talk with me about your daughter. I'm sure you can help me understand her. She's a youngster who needs help and whom I'm deeply interested in helping."

"Who needs help." . . . Even if I came, what good would it do? You think because I am her mother I have a key, or that in some way you could use me as a key? She has lived for nineteen years. There is all that life that has happened outside of me, beyond me.

And when is there time to remember, to sift, to weigh, to estimate, to total? I will start and there will be an interruption and I will have to gather it all together again. Or I will become engulfed with all I did or did not do, with what should have been and what cannot be helped.

She was a beautiful baby. The first and only one of our five that was beautiful at birth. You do not guess how new and uneasy her tenancy in her now-loveliness. You did not know her all those years she was thought homely, or see her poring over her baby pictures, making me tell her over and over how beautiful she had been—and would be, I would tell her—and was now, to the seeing eye. But the seeing eyes were few or nonexistent. Including mine.

I nursed her. They feel that's important nowadays. I nursed all the children, but with her, with all the fierce rigidity of first motherhood, I did like the books then said. Though her cries battered me to trembling and my breasts ached with swollenness, I waited till the clock decreed.

Why do I put that first? I do not even know if it matters, or if it explains anything.

She was a beautiful baby. She blew shining bubbles of sound. She loved motion, loved light, loved color and music and textures. She would lie on the floor in her blue overalls patting the surface so hard in ecstasy her hands and feet would blur. She was a miracle to me, but when she was eight months old I had to leave her daytimes with the woman downstairs to whom she was no miracle at all, for I worked or looked for work and for Emily's father, who "could no longer endure" (he wrote in his good-bye note) "sharing want with us."

I was nineteen. It was the pre-relief, pre-WPA world of the depression. I would start running as soon as I got off the streetcar, running up the stairs, the place smelling sour, and awake or asleep to startle awake, when she saw me she would break into a clogged weeping that could not be comforted, a weeping I can hear yet.

After a while I found a job hashing at night so I could be with her days, and it was better. But it came to where I had to bring her to his family and leave her.

It took a long time to raise the money for her fare back. Then she got chicken pox and I had to wait longer. When she finally came, I hardly knew her, walking quick and nervous like her father, looking like her father, thin, and dressed in a shoddy red that yellowed her skin and glared at the pockmarks. All the baby loveliness gone.

She was two. Old enough for nursery school they said, and I did not know then what I know now — the fatigue of the long day, and the lacerations of group life in the kinds of nurseries that are only parking places for children.

Except that it would have made no difference if I had known. It was the only place there was. It was the only way we could be together, the only way I could hold a job.

And even without knowing, I knew. I knew the teacher that was evil because all these years it has curdled into my memory, the little boy hunched in the corner, her rasp, "why aren't you outside, because Alvin hits you? that's no reason, go out, scaredy." I knew Emily hated it even if she did not clutch and implore "don't go Mommy" like the other children, mornings.

She always had a reason why we should stay home. Momma, you look sick. Momma, I feel sick. Momma, the teachers aren't there today, they're sick. Momma, we can't go, there was a fire there last night. Momma, it's a holiday today, no school, they told me.

But never a direct protest, never rebellion. I think of our others in their three-, four-year-oldness — the explosions, the tempers, the denunciations, the demands — and I feel suddenly ill. I put the iron down. What in me demanded that goodness in her? And what was the cost, the cost to her of such goodness?

The old man living in the back once said in his gentle way: "You should smile at Emily more when you look at her." What *was* in my face when I looked at her? I loved her. There were all the acts of love.

It was only with the others I remembered what he said, and it was

the face of joy, and not of care or tightness or worry I turned to them —
too late for Emily. She does not smile easily, let alone almost always as
her brothers and sisters do. Her face is closed and sombre, but when
she wants, how fluid. You must have seen it in her pantomimes, you spoke
of her rare gift for comedy on the stage that rouses a laughter out of
the audience so dear they applaud and applaud and do not want to let
her go.

Where does it come from, that comedy? There was none of it in her
when she came back to me that second time, after I had had to send
her away again. She had a new daddy now to learn to love, and I think
perhaps it was a better time.

Except when we left her alone nights, telling ourselves she was old
enough.

"Can't you go some other time, Mommy, like tomorrow?" she would
ask. "Will it be just a little while you'll be gone? Do you promise?"

The time we came back, the front door open, the clock on the floor
in the hall. She rigid awake. "It wasn't just a little while. I didn't cry. Three
times I called you, just three times, and then I ran downstairs to open
the door so you could come faster. The clock talked loud. I threw it away,
it scared me what it talked."

She said the clock talked loud again that night I went to the hospital
to have Susan. She was delirious with the fever that comes before red
measles, but she was fully conscious all the week I was gone and the week
after we were home when she could not come near the new baby or me.

She did not get well. She stayed skeleton thin, not wanting to eat, and
night after night she had nightmares. She would call for me, and I would
rouse from exhaustion to sleepily call back: "You're all right, darling, go
to sleep, it's just a dream," and if she still called, in a sterner voice, "now
go to sleep, Emily, there's nothing to hurt you." Twice, only twice, when
I had to get up for Susan anyhow, I went in to sit with her.

Now when it is too late (as if she would let me hold and comfort her
like I do the others) I get up and go to her at once at her moan or restless stirring. "Are you awake, Emily? Can I get you something?" And the
answer is always the same: "No, I'm all right, go back to sleep, Mother."

They persuaded me at the clinic to send her away to a convalescent
home in the country where "she can have the kind of food and care you
can't manage for her, and you'll be free to concentrate on the new baby."
They still send children to that place. I see pictures on the society page
of sleek young women planning affairs to raise money for it, or dancing
at the affairs, or decorating Easter eggs or filling Christmas stockings
for the children.

They never have a picture of the children so I do not know if the girls still wear those gigantic red bows and the ravaged looks on the every other Sunday when parents can come to visit "unless otherwise notified"—as we were notified the first six weeks.

Oh it is a handsome place, green lawns and tall trees and fluted flower beds. High up on the balconies of each cottage the children stand, the girls in their red bows and white dresses, the boys in white suits and giant red ties. The parents stand below shrieking up to be heard and the children shriek down to be heard and between them the invisible wall "Not To Be Contaminated by Parental Germ or Physical Affection."

There was a tiny girl who always stood hand in hand with Emily. Her parents never came. One visit she was gone. "They moved her to Rose Cottage" Emily shouted in explanation. "They don't like you to love anybody here."

She wrote once a week, the labored writing of a seven-year-old. "I am fine. How is the baby. If I write my leter nicly I will have a star. Love." There never was a star. We wrote every other day, letters she could never hold or keep but only hear read—once. "We simply do not have room for children to keep any personal possessions," they patiently explained when we pieced one Sunday shrieking together to plead how much it would mean to Emily, who loved so to keep things, to be allowed to keep her letters and cards.

Each visit she looked frailer. "She isn't eating," they told us.

·(They had runny eggs for breakfast or mush with lumps, Emily said later. I'd hold it in my mouth and not swallow. Nothing ever tasted good, just when they had chicken.)

It took us eight months to get her released home, and only the fact that she gained back so little of her seven lost pounds convinced the social worker.

I used to try to hold and love her after she came back, but her body would stay stiff, and after a while she'd push away. She ate little. Food sickened her and I think much of life too. Oh she had physical lightness and brightness, twinkling by on skates, bouncing like a ball up and down up and down over the jump rope, skimming over the hill; but these were momentary.

She fretted about her appearance, thin and dark and foreign-looking at a time when every little girl was supposed to look or thought she should look a chubby blonde replica of Shirley Temple. The doorbell sometimes rang for her, but no one seemed to come and play in the house or be a best friend. Maybe because we moved so much.

There was a boy she loved painfully through two school semesters. Months later she told me how she had taken pennies from my purse to buy him candy. "Licorice was his favorite and I brought him some every

day, but he still liked Jennifer better'n me. Why, Mommy?" The kind
of question for which there is no answer.

School was a worry to her. She was not glib or quick in a world where
glibness and quickness were easily confused with ability to learn. To her
overworked and exasperated teachers she was an overconscientious "slow
learner" who kept trying to catch up and was absent entirely too often.

I let her be absent, though sometimes the illness was imaginary. How
different from my now-strictness about attendance with the others. I wasn't
working. We had a new baby, I was home anyhow. Sometimes, after Susan
grew old enough, I would keep her home from school, too, to have them
all together.

Mostly Emily had asthma, and her breathing, harsh and labored, would
fill the house with a curiously tranquil sound. I would bring the two old
dresser mirrors and her boxes of collections to her bed. She would select
beads and single earrings, bottle tops and shells, dried flowers and pebbles, old postcards and scraps, all sorts of oddments; then she and Susan
would play Kingdom, setting up landscapes and furniture, peopling them
with action.

Those were the only times of peaceful companionship between her
and Susan. I have edged away from it, that poisonous feeling between
them, that terrible balancing of hurts and needs I had to do between
the two, and did so badly, those earlier years.

Oh there are conflicts between the others too, each one human, needing, demanding, hurting, taking—but only between Emily and Susan,
no, Emily toward Susan that corroding resentment. It seems so obvious
on the surface, yet it is not obvious. Susan, the second child, Susan, golden-
and curly-haired and chubby, quick and articulate and assured, everything in appearance and manner Emily was not; Susan, not able to resist
Emily's precious things, losing or sometimes clumsily breaking them;
Susan telling jokes and riddles to company for applause while Emily sat
silent (to say to me later: that was *my* riddle, Mother, I told it to Susan);
Susan, who for all the five years' difference in age was just a year behind
Emily in developing physically.

I am glad for that slow physical development that widened the difference between her and her contemporaries, though she suffered over it.
She was too vulnerable for that terrible world of youthful competition,
of preening and parading, of constant measuring of yourself against every
other, of envy, "If I had that copper hair," "If I had that skin. . . ." She
tormented herself enough about not looking like the others, there was
enough of the unsureness, the having to be conscious of words before
you speak, the constant caring—what are they thinking of me? without
having it all magnified by the merciless physical drives.

Ronnie is calling. He is wet and I change him. It is rare there is such a cry now. That time of motherhood is almost behind me when the ear is not one's own but must always be racked and listening for the child cry, the child call. We sit for a while and I hold him, looking out over the city spread in charcoal with its soft aisles of light. "*Shoogily,*" he breathes and curls closer. I carry him back to bed, asleep. *Shoogily.* A funny word, a family word, inherited from Emily, invented by her to say: *comfort.*

In this and other ways she leaves her seal, I say aloud. And startle at my saying it. What do I mean? What did I start to gather together, to try and make coherent? I was at the terrible, growing years. War years. I do not remember them well. I was working, there were four smaller ones now, there was not time for her. She had to help be a mother, and housekeeper, and shopper. She had to set her seal. Mornings of crisis and near hysteria trying to get lunches packed, hair combed, coats and shoes found, everyone to school or Child Care on time, the baby ready for transportation. And always the paper scribbled on by a smaller one, the book looked at by Susan then mislaid, the homework not done. Running out to that huge school where she was one, she was lost, she was a drop; suffering over the unpreparedness, stammering and unsure in her classes.

There was so little time left at night after the kids were bedded down. She would struggle over books, always eating (it was in those years she developed her enormous appetite that is legendary in our family) and I would be ironing, or preparing food for the next day, or writing V-mail to Bill, or tending the baby. Sometimes, to make me laugh, or out of her despair, she would imitate happenings or types at school.

I think I said once: "Why don't you do something like this in the school amateur show?" One morning she phoned me at work, hardly understandable through the weeping: "Mother, I did it. I won, I won; they gave me first prize; they clapped and clapped and wouldn't let me go."

Now suddenly she was Somebody, and as imprisoned in her difference as she had been in anonymity.

She began to be asked to perform at other high schools, even in colleges, then at city and statewide affairs. The first one we went to, I only recognized her that first moment when thin, shy, she almost drowned herself into the curtains. Then: Was this Emily? The control, the command, the convulsing and deadly clowning, the spell, then the roaring, stamping audience, unwilling to let this rare and precious laughter out of their lives.

Afterwards: You ought to do something about her with a gift like that — but without money or knowing how, what does one do? We have left it all to her, and the gift has as often eddied inside, clogged and clotted, as been used and growing.

She is coming. She runs up the stairs two at a time with her light graceful step, and I know she is happy tonight. Whatever it was that occasioned your call did not happen today.

"Aren't you ever going to finish the ironing, Mother? Whistler painted his mother in a rocker. I'd have to paint mine standing over an ironing board." This is one of her communicative nights and she tells me everything and nothing as she fixes herself a plate of food out of the icebox.

She is so lovely. Why did you want me to come in at all? Why were you concerned? She will find her way.

She starts up the stairs to bed. "Don't get me up with the rest in the morning." "But I thought you were having midterms." "Oh, those," she comes back in, kisses me, and says quite lightly, "in a couple of years when we'll all be atom-dead they won't matter a bit."

She has said it before. She *believes* it. But because I have been dredging the past, and all that compounds a human being is so heavy and meaningful in me, I cannot endure it tonight.

I will never total it all. I will never come in to say: She was a child seldom smiled at. Her father left me before she was a year old. I had to work her first six years when there was work, or I sent her home and to his relatives. There were years she had care she hated. She was dark and thin and foreign-looking in a world where the prestige went to blondeness and curly hair and dimples, she was slow where glibness was prized. She was a child of anxious, not proud, love. We were poor and could not afford for her the soil of easy growth. I was a young mother. I was a distracted mother. There were the other children pushing up, demanding. Her younger sister seemed all that she was not. There were years she did not want me to touch her. She kept too much in herself, her life was such she had to keep too much in herself. My wisdom came too late. She has much to her and probably little will come of it. She is a child of her age, of depression, of war, of fear.

Let her be. So all that is in her will not bloom—but in how many does it? There is still enough left to live by. Only help her to know—help make it so there is cause for her to know—that she is more than this dress on the ironing board, helpless before the iron.

2. Integration

Introduction
William Morris, "Useful Work versus Useless Toil"

William Morris was born in 1834 in the village of Walthamstow near London, an area of striking natural beauty. When Morris was six, his wealthy stockbroker father moved the family to a Georgian mansion within the nearby Epping forest. Young Morris, after a sickly infancy, took vigorously to the outdoors and developed a great love for nature. At the same time he was beginning to read the Romantic literature, particularly Sir Walter Scott's Waverly novels, that would turn him toward an interest in medieval civilization, a civilization against which he would later unfavorably judge the culture of his own day.

Like many idealistic young men at this time, Morris was influenced by Newman and the Oxford Movement within the Anglican Church. For a brief time he planned a career in the church, but in 1855, while on tour in France, he came to a sudden decision to dedicate himself to the arts, and for several years he struggled to find his metier. Although a poet of some ability, it was in the "lesser arts" that he was to find his passion. After trying architecture and painting, he settled upon household design. Morris wanted to design those ordinary things that he believed profoundly influence us through their daily presence: wallpaper, furniture, rugs, and the other artifacts of the home.

This preoccupation was critical to Morris's interpretation of English industrial society. It both influenced his viewpoint and was itself, to some degree, a product of this viewpoint. Since his early adherence to the Oxford Movement, Morris had been disturbed by the crassness of English "machine society." He came to believe that the uniformity created by the industrial revolution, with its repetitive work and mass-designed products, were destroying English culture. A partial antidote to this was to reestablish craftsmanship, and through craftsmanship design a more beautiful and exciting environment for society.

As Morris developed his theory of craftsmanship, more and more he turned away from his upper-class background and toward the working class, whom he saw both as the victims of industrial capitalism and as the hope for overcoming it. In time he would turn from his establishment roots and become a harsh critic of the system and an advocate for revolutionary socialism.

In "Useful Work versus Useless Toil" Morris attacks the exploitation of the working classes under the British system and develops the case for revitalizing craftsmanship. Like Marx, Morris embraced a healthy kind of materialism that would allow the worker to overcome his alienation and to reintegrate himself with his work through the development of his craft. Morris wants to free workers from the burden of supporting parasitic members of the upper class and to give the workers time away from work, but also time to enjoy their work. He argues that workers become alienated when they have to work too much and under too much time pressure. Unlike American industrial engineer Frederick Winslow Taylor, who wanted to speed up work, Morris wanted to slow it down. For Morris work is not simply a means to an end but is an end in itself. Like many of the writers in this book, Morris is very prowork, and his complaint is with those who have destroyed good work. Like Freud, Morris seems to believe in a work instinct rather than a work ethic. The work ethic may be necessary to force people to work who do not love work, but Morris believes that under the right circumstances we can all come to love our work.

Do you agree that work can be made interesting for all people? Can you think of a craft that you would like to learn that would make work more satisfying for you? Do you think that Morris is right that we all have an instinctual need to work?

William Morris

Useful Work versus Useless Toil

The above title may strike some of my readers as strange. It is assumed by most people nowadays that all work is useful, and by most *well-to-do* people that all work is desirable. Most people, well-to-do or not, believe that, even when a man is doing work which appears to be useless, he is earning his livelihood by it — he is "employed," as the phrase goes; and most of those who are well-to-do cheer on the happy worker with congratulations and praises, if he is only "industrious" enough and deprives himself of all pleasure and holidays in the sacred cause of labour. In short, it has become an article of the creed of modern morality that all labour is good in itself — a convenient belief to those who live on the labour of others. But as to those on whom they live, I recommend them not to take it on trust, but to look into the matter a little deeper.

Let us grant, first, that the race of man must either labour or perish. Nature does not give us our livelihood gratis; we must win it by toil of some sort or degree. Let us see, then, if she does not give us some compensation for this compulsion to labour, since certainly in other matters she takes care to make the acts necessary to the continuance of life in the individual and the race not only endurable, but even pleasurable.

You may be sure that she does so, that it is of the nature of man, when he is not diseased, to take pleasure in his work under certain conditions. And, yet, we must say in the teeth of the hypocritical praise of all labour, whatsoever it may be, of which I have made mention, that there is some labour which is so far from being a blessing that it is a curse; that it would be better for the community and for the worker if the latter were to fold his hands and refuse to work, and either die or let us pack him off to the workhouse or prison—which you will.

Here, you see, are two kinds of work—one good, the other bad; one not far removed from a blessing, a lightening of life; the other a mere curse, a burden to life.

What is the difference between them, then? This: one has hope in it, the other has not. It is manly to do the one kind of work, and manly also to refuse to do the other.

What is the nature of the hope which, when it is present in work, makes it worth doing?

It is threefold, I think—hope of rest, hope of product, hope of pleasure in the work itself; and hope of these also in some abundance and of good quality; rest enough and good enough to be worth having; product worth having by one who is neither a fool nor an ascetic; pleasure enough for all for us to be conscious of it while we are at work; not a mere habit, the loss of which we shall feel as a fidgety man feels the loss of the bit of string he fidgets with.

I have put the hope of rest first because it is the simplest and most natural part of our hope. Whatever pleasure there is in some work, there is certainly some pain in all work, the beast-like pain of stirring up our slumbering energies to action, the beast-like dread of change when things are pretty well with us; and the compensation for this animal pain in animal rest. We must feel while we are working that the time will come when we shall not have to work. Also the rest, when it comes, must be long enough to allow us to enjoy it; it must be longer than is merely necessary for us to recover the strength we have expended in working, and it must be animal rest also in this, that it must not be disturbed by anxiety, else we shall not be able to enjoy it. If we have this amount and kind of rest we shall, so far, be no worse off than the beasts.

As to the hope of product, I have said that Nature compels us to work for that. It remains for *us* to look to it that we *do* really produce something, and not nothing, or at least nothing that we want or are allowed to use. If we look to this and use our wills we shall, so far, be better than machines.

The hope of pleasure in the work itself: how strange that hope must seem to some of my readers—to most of them! Yet I think that to all living things there is a pleasure in the exercise of their energies, and that even beasts rejoice in being lithe and swift and strong. But a man at work, making something which he feels will exist because he is working at it and wills it, is exercising the energies of his mind and soul as well as of his body. Memory and imagination help him as he works. Not only his own thoughts, but the thoughts of the men of past ages guide his hands; and, as a part of the human race, he creates. If we work thus we shall be men, and our days will be happy and eventful.

Thus worthy work carries with it the hope of pleasure in rest, the hope of the pleasure in our using what it makes, and the hope of pleasure in our daily creative skill.

All other work but this is worthless; it is slaves' work—mere toiling to live, that we may live to toil.

Therefore, since we have, as it were, a pair of scales in which to weigh the work now done in the world, let us use them. Let us estimate the worthiness of the work we do, after so many thousand years of toil, so many promises of hope deferred, such boundless exultation over the progress of civilization and the gain of liberty.

Now, the first thing as to the work done in civilization and the easiest to notice is that it is portioned out very unequally amongst the different classes of society. First, there are people—not a few—who do no work, and make no pretence of doing any. Next, there are people, and very many of them, who work fairly hard, though with abundant easements and holidays, claimed and allowed; and lastly, there are people who work so hard that they may be said to do nothing else than work, and are accordingly called "the working classes," as distinguished from the middle classes and the rich, or aristocracy, whom I have mentioned above.

It is clear that this inequality presses heavily upon the "working" class, and must visibly tend to destroy their hope of rest at least, and so, in that particular, make them worse off than mere beasts of the field; but that is not the sum and end of our folly of turning useful work into useless toil, but only the beginning of it.

For first, as to the class of rich people doing no work, we all know that they consume a great deal while they produce nothing. Therefore, clearly, they have to be kept at the expense of those who do work, just as paupers have, and are a mere burden on the community. In these days there are many who have learned to see this, though they can see no further into the evils of our present system, and have formed no idea of any scheme for getting rid of this burden; though perhaps they have a vague hope that changes in the system of voting for members of the House of Commons, may, as if by magic, tend in that direction. With such hopes or superstitions we need not trouble ourselves. Moreover, this class, the aristocracy, once thought most necessary to the State, is scant of numbers, and has now no power of its own, but depends on the support of the class next below it—the middle class. In fact, it is really composed either of the most successful men of that class, or of their immediate descendants.

As to the middle class, including the trading, manufacturing, and professional people of our society, they do, as a rule, seem to work quite hard enough, and so at first sight might be thought to help the community, and not burden it. But by far the greater part of them, though they work, do not produce, and even when they do produce, as in the case of those engaged (wastefully indeed) in the distribution of goods, or doctors, or (genuine) artists and literary men, they consume out of all proportion to their due share. The commercial and manufacturing part of them, the most powerful part, spend their lives and energies in fighting amongst themselves for their respective shares of the wealth which they *force* the genuine workers to provide for them; the others are almost wholly the hangers-on of these; they do not work for the public, but a privileged class: they are the parasites of property, sometimes, as in the case of lawyers, undisguisedly so; sometimes, as the doctors and others above mentioned, professing to be useful, but too often of no use save as supporters of the system of folly, fraud, and tyranny of which they form a part. And all these we must remember have, as a rule, one aim in view; not the production of utilities, but the gaining of a position either for themselves or their children in which they will not have to work at all. It is their ambition and the end of their whole lives to gain, if not for themselves yet at least for their children, the proud position of being obvious burdens on the community. For their work itself, in spite of the sham dignity with which they surround it, they care nothing: save a few enthusiasts, men of science, art or letters, who, if they are not the salt of the earth, are at least (and oh, the pity of it!) the salt of the miserable system of which they are the slaves, which hinders and thwarts them at every turn, and even sometimes corrupts them.

Here then is another class, this time very numerous and all-powerful, which produces very little and consumes enormously, and is therefore in the main supported, as paupers are, by the real producers. The class that remains to be considered produces all that is produced, and supports both itself and the other classes, though it is placed in a position of inferiority to them; real inferiority, mind you, involving a degradation both of mind and body. But it is a necessary consequence of this tyranny and folly that again many of these workers are not producers. A vast number of them once more are merely parasites of property, some of them openly so, as the soldiers by land and sea who are kept on foot for the perpetuating of national rivalries and enmities, and for the purposes of the national struggle for the share of the product of unpaid labour. But besides this obvious burden on the producers and the scarcely less obvious one of domestic servants, there is first the army of clerks, shop-assistants, and so forth, who are engaged in the service of the private war for wealth, which, as above said, is the real occupation of the well-to-do middle class. This is a larger body of workers than might be supposed, for it includes amongst others all those engaged in what I should call competitive salesmanship, or, to use a less dignified word, the puffery of wares, which has now got to such a pitch that there are many things which cost far more to sell than they do to make.

Next there is the mass of people employed in making all those articles of folly and luxury, the demand for which is the outcome of the existence of the rich non-producing classes; things which people leading a manly and uncorrupted life would not ask for or dream of. These things, whoever may gainsay me, I will for ever refuse to call wealth: they are not wealth, but waste. Wealth is what Nature gives us and what a reasonable man can make out of the gifts of Nature for his reasonable use. The sunlight, the fresh air, the unspoiled face of the earth, food, raiment and housing necessary and decent; the storing up of knowledge of all kinds, and the power of disseminating it; means of free communication between man and man; works of art, the beauty which man creates when he is most a man, most aspiring and thoughtful—all things which serve the pleasure of people, free, manly and uncorrupted. This is wealth. Nor can I think of anything worth having which does not come under one or other of these heads. But think, I beseech you, of the product of England, the workshop of the world, and will you not be bewildered, as I am, at the thought of the mass of things which no sane man could desire, but which our useless toil makes—and sells?

Now, further, there is even a sadder industry yet, which is forced on many, very many, of our workers—the making of wares which are necessary to them and their brethren, *because they are an inferior class*. For if many men live without producing, nay, must live lives so empty and foolish that they *force* a great part of the workers to produce wares which no one needs, not even the rich, it follows that most men must be poor; and, living as they do on wages from those whom they support, cannot get for their use the *goods* which men naturally desire, but must put up with miserable makeshifts for them, with coarse food that does not nourish, with rotten raiment which does not shelter, with wretched houses which may well make a town-dweller in civilization look back with regret to the tent of the nomad tribe, or the cave of the pre-historic savage. Nay, the workers must even lend a hand to the great industrial invention of the age—adulteration, and by its help produce for their own use shams and mockeries of the luxury of the rich; for the wage-earners must always live as the wage-payers bid them, and their very habits of life are *forced* on them by their masters.

But it is waste of time to try to express in words due contempt of the productions of the much-praised cheapness of our epoch. It must be enough to say that this cheapness is necessary to the system of exploiting on which modern manufacture rests. In other words, our society includes a great mass of slaves, who must be fed, clothed, housed and amused as slaves, and that their daily necessity compels them to make the slave-wares whose use is the perpetuation of their slavery.

To sum up, then, concerning the manner of work in civilized States, these States are composed of three classes—a class which does not even pretend to work, a class which pretends to work but which produces nothing, and a class which works, but is compelled by the other two classes to do work which is often unproductive.

Thus then have the fruits of our victory over Nature been stolen from us, thus has compulsion by Nature to labour in hope of rest, gain, and pleasure been turned into compulsion by man to labour in hope—of living to labour!

What shall we do then, can we mend it?

————————

. . .All must work according to their ability, and so produce what they consume—that is, each man should work as well as he can for his own livelihood, and his livelihood should be assured to him; that is to say, all the advantages which society would provide for each and all of its members.

Thus, at last, would true Society be founded. It would rest on equality of condition. No man would be tormented for the benefit of another—

nay, no one man would be tormented for the benefit of Society. Nor, indeed, can that order be called Society which is not upheld for the benefit of every one of its members.

———————

But when revolution has made it "easy to live," when all are working harmoniously together and there is no one to rob the worker of his time, that is to say, his life; in those coming days there will be no compulsion on us to go on producing things we do not want, no compulsion on us to labour for nothing; we shall be able calmly and thoughtfully to consider what we shall do with our wealth of labour-power. Now, for my part, I think the first use we ought to make of that wealth, of that freedom, should be to make all our labour, even the commonest and most necessary, pleasant to everybody; for thinking over the matter carefully I can see that the one course which will certainly make life happy in the face of all accidents and troubles is to take a pleasurable interest in all the details of life. And lest perchance you think that an assertion too universally accepted to be worth making, let me remind you how entirely modern civilization forbids it; with what sordid, and even terrible, details it surrounds the life of the poor, what a mechanical and empty life she forces on the rich; and how rare a holiday it is for any of us to feel ourselves a part of Nature, and unhurriedly, thoughtfully, and happily to note the course of our lives amidst all the little links of events which connect them with the lives of others, and build up the great whole of humanity.

But such a holiday our whole lives might be, if we were resolute to make all our labour reasonable and pleasant. But we must be resolute indeed; for no half measures will help us here.

———————

. . . The first step towards making labour attractive is to get the means of making labour fruitful, the Capital, including the land, machinery, factories, etc., into the hands of the community, to be used for the good of all alike, so that we might all work at "supplying" the real "demands" of each and all—that is to say, work for livelihood, instead of working to supply the demand of the profit market—instead of working for profit —*i.e.,* the power of compelling other men to work against their will.

When this first step has been taken and men begin to understand that Nature wills all men either to work or starve, and when they are no longer such fools as to allow some the alternative of stealing, when this happy day is come, we shall then be relieved from the tax of waste, and consequently shall find that we have, as aforesaid, a mass of labour-power available, which will enable us to live as we please within reasonable limits. We shall no longer be hurried and driven by the fear of starvation, which at present presses no less on the greater part of men in civilized communities than it does on mere savages. The first and most obvious necessities will be so easily provided for in a community in which there is no waste of labour, that we shall have time to look round and consider what we really do want, that can be obtained without over-taxing our energies; for the often-expressed fear of mere idleness falling upon us when the force supplied by the present hierarchy of compulsion is withdrawn, is a fear which is but generated by the burden of excessive and repulsive labour, which we most of us have to bear at present.

We must begin to build up the ornamental part of life — its pleasures, bodily and mental, scientific and artistic, social and individual — on the basis of work undertaken willingly and cheerfully, with the consciousness of benefiting ourselves and our neighbours by it. Such absolutely necessary work as we should have to do would in the first place take up but a small part of each day, and so far would not be burdensome; but it would be a task of daily recurrence, and therefore would spoil our day's pleasure unless it were made at least endurable while it lasted. In other words, all labour, even the commonest, must be made attractive.

How can this be done? — is the question the answer to which will take up the rest of this paper. . . .

From all that has been said already it follows that labour, to be attractive, must be directed towards some obviously useful end, unless in cases where it is undertaken voluntarily by each individual as a pastime. This element of obvious usefulness is all the more to be counted on in sweetening tasks otherwise irksome, since social morality, the responsibility of man towards the life of man, will, in the new order of things, take the place of theological morality, or the responsibility of man to some abstract idea. Next, the day's work will be short. This need not be insisted on. It is clear that with work unwasted it *can* be short. It is clear also that much work which is now a torment, would be easily endurable if it were much shortened.

Variety of work is the next point, and a most important one. To compel a man to do day after day the same task, without any hope of escape or change, means nothing short of turning his life into a prison-torment. Nothing but the tyranny of profit-grinding makes this necessary. A man might easily learn and practise at least three crafts, varying sedentary occupation with outdoor — occupation calling for the exercise of strong bodily energy for work in which the mind had more to do. There are few men, for instance, who would not wish to spend part of their lives in the most necessary and pleasantest of all work—cultivating the earth. One thing which will make this variety of employment possible will be the form that education will take in a socially ordered community. At present all education is directed towards the end of fitting people to take their places in the hierarchy of commerce—these as masters, those as workmen. The education of the masters is more ornamental than that of the workmen, but it is commercial still; and even at the ancient universities learning is but little regarded, unless it can in the long run be made *to pay.* Due education is a totally different thing from this, and concerns itself in finding out what different people are fit for, and helping them along the road which they are inclined to take. In a duly ordered society, therefore, young people would be taught such handicrafts as they had a turn for as a part of their education, the discipline of their minds and bodies; and adults would also have opportunities of learning in the same schools, for the development of individual capacities would be of all things chiefly aimed at by education, instead, as now, the subordination of all capacities to the great end of "money-making" for oneself—or one's master. The amount of talent, and even genius, which the present system crushes, and which would be drawn out by such a system, would make our daily work easy and interesting.

Under this head of variety I will note one product of industry which has suffered so much from commercialism that it can scarcely be said to exist, and is, indeed, so foreign from our epoch that I fear there are some who will find it difficult to understand what I have to say on the subject, which I nevertheless must say, since it is really a most important one. I mean that side of art which is, or ought to be, done by the ordinary workman while he is about his ordinary work, and which has got to be called, very properly, Popular Art. This art, I repeat, no longer exists now, having been killed by commercialism. But from the beginning of man's contest with Nature till the rise of the present capitalistic system, it was alive, and generally flourished. While it lasted, everything that was made by man was adorned by man, just as everything made by Nature is adorned by her. The craftsman, as he fashioned the thing he had under his hand, ornamented it so naturally and so entirely without conscious effort, that it is often difficult to distinguish where the mere utilitarian part of his work ended and the ornamental began. Now the origin of this art was the necessity that the workman felt for variety in his work, and though the beauty produced by this desire was a great gift to the world, yet the obtaining variety and pleasure in the work by the workman was a matter of more importance still, for it stamped all labour with the impress of pleasure. All this has now quite disappeared from the work of civilization. If you wish to have ornament, you must pay specially for it, and the workman is compelled to produce ornament, as he is to produce other wares. He is compelled to pretend happiness in his work, so that the beauty produced by man's hand, which was once a solace to his labour, has now become an extra burden to him, and ornament is now but one of the follies of useless toil, and perhaps not the least irksome of its fetters.

Besides the short duration of labour, its conscious usefulness, and the variety which should go with it, there is another thing needed to make it attractive, and that is pleasant surroundings. The misery and squalor which we people of civilization bear with so much complacency as a necessary part of the manufacturing system, is just as necessary to the community at large as a proportionate amount of filth would be in the house of a private rich man.

As to that part of labour which must be associated on a large scale, this very factory system, under a reasonable order of things (though to my mind there might still be drawbacks to it), would at least offer opportunities for a full and eager social life surrounded by many pleasures. The factories might be centres of intellectual activity also, and work in them might well be varied very much: the tending of the necessary machinery might to each individual be but a short part of the day's work. The other work might vary from raising food from the surrounding country to the study and practice of art and science. It is a matter of course that people engaged in such work, and being the masters of their own lives, would not allow any hurry or want of foresight to force them into enduring dirt, disorder, or want of room. Science duly applied would enable them to get rid of refuse, to minimize, if not wholly to destroy, all the inconveniences which at present attend the use of elaborate machinery, such as smoke, stench and noise; nor would they endure that the buildings in which they worked or lived should be ugly blots on the fair face of the earth. Beginning by making their factories, buildings, and sheds decent and convenient like their homes, they would infallibly go on to make them not merely negatively good, inoffensive merely, but even beautiful, so that the glorious art of architecture, now for some time slain by commercial greed, would be born again and flourish.

So, you see, I claim that work in a duly ordered community should be made attractive by the consciousness of usefulness, by its being carried on with intelligent interest, by variety, and by its being exercised amidst pleasurable surroundings. But I have also claimed, as we all do, that the day's work should not be wearisomely long. It may be said, "How can you make this last claim square with the others? If the work is to be so refined, will not the goods made be very expensive?"

Meantime, in any case, the refinement, thoughtfulness, and deliberation of labour must indeed be paid for, but not by compulsion to labour long hours. Our epoch has invented machines which would have appeared wild dreams to the men of past ages, and of those machines we have as yet *made no use*.

They are called "labour-saving" machines—a commonly used phrase which implies what we expect of them; but we do not get what we expect. What they really do is to reduce the skilled labourer to the ranks of the unskilled, to increase the number of the "reserve army of labour"—that is, to increase the precariousness of life among the workers and to intensify the labour of those who serve the machines (as slaves their masters). All this they do by the way, while they pile up the profits of the employers of labour, or force them to expend those profits in bitter commercial war with each other. In a true society these miracles of ingenuity would be for the first time used for minimizing the amount of time spent in unattractive labour, which by their means might be so reduced as to be but a very light burden on each individual. All the more as these machines would most certainly be very much improved when it was no longer a question as to whether their improvement would "pay" the individual, but rather whether it would benefit the community.

Again, as people freed from the daily terror of starvation find out what they really wanted, being no longer compelled by anything but their own needs, they would refuse to produce the mere inanities which are now called luxuries, or the poison and trash now called cheap wares. No one would make plush breeches when there were no flunkies to wear them, nor would anybody waste his time over making oleomargarine when no one was *compelled* to abstain from real butter. Adulteration laws are only needed in a society of thieves—and in such a society they are a dead letter.

And yet if there be any work which cannot be made other than repulsive, either by the shortness of its duration or the intermittency of its recurrence, or by the sense of special and peculiar usefulness (and therefore honour) in the mind of the man who performs it freely,—if there be any work which cannot be but a torment to the worker, what then?

Well, then, let us see if the heavens will fall on us if we leave it undone, for it were better that they should. The produce of such work cannot be worth the price of it.

Now we have seen that the semi-theological dogma that all labour, under any circumstances, is a blessing to the labourer, is hypocritical and false; that, on the other hand, labour is good when due hope of rest and pleasure accompanies it. We have weighed the work of civilization in the balance and found it wanting, since hope is mostly lacking to it, and therefore we see that civilization has bred a dire curse for men. But we have seen also that the work of the world might be carried on in hope and with pleasure if it were not wasted by folly and tyranny, by the perpetual strife of opposing classes.

It is Peace, therefore, which we need in order that we may live and work in hope and with pleasure. Peace so much desired, if we may trust men's words, but which has been so continually and steadily rejected by them in deeds. But for us, let us set our hearts on it and win it at whatever cost.

What the cost may be, who can tell? Will it be possible to win peace peaceably? Alas, how can it be? We are so hemmed in by wrong and folly, that in one way or other we must always be fighting against them: our own lives may see no end to the struggle, perhaps no obvious hope of the end. It may be that the best we can hope to see is that struggle getting sharper and bitterer day by day, until it breaks out openly at last into the slaughter of men by actual warfare instead of by the slower and crueller methods of "peaceful" commerce. If we live to see that, we shall live to see much; for it will mean the rich classes grown conscious of their own wrong and robbery, and consciously defending them by open violence; and then the end will be drawing near.

But in any case, and whatever the nature of our strife for peace may be, if we only aim at it steadily and with singleness of heart, and ever keep it in view, a reflection from that peace of the future will illumine the turmoil and trouble of our lives, whether the trouble be seemingly petty, or obviously tragic; and we shall, in our hopes at least, live the lives of men: nor can the present times give us any reward greater than that.

Introduction
Dylan Thomas, "In My Craft or Sullen Art"

Dylan Thomas was born in Wales in 1914 and died less than forty years later in 1953. His life was an intense, inebriated dance of life that produced some of the twentieth century's finest English verse.

In "In My Craft or Sullen Art" Thomas tries to tell us why he does the hard work of poetry, which he refers to as his craft or sullen art. The poet, or artist, represents a very special category of worker. Unless we are talking about hackwriters of murder mysteries or potboiler Westerns, we are talking about people who choose to pursue a lonely vocation which offers very little chance of material reward. While a few are successful (the Hemingways and Fitzgeralds) and gain immense fame and wealth, Thomas tells us that he does not write for these reasons. Instead he writes at night, when the moon rages, suggesting that poetry is for him a non-rational (not irrational) activity, perhaps akin to love, that comes from a deeper source than the intellect. He says he does it for the lovers, for wages of the heart.

We have included this poem under the heading alienation and integration because we believe that modern poetry such as Thomas' can help us face our alienation and perhaps, through an act of language, help us become reintegrated into a meaningful existence. As you read, ask yourself some questions about Thomas' poetry and his worldview. Why, for instance, does he refer to his poetry as a "sullen" art? Why does he write for lovers, "their arms / Round the griefs of the ages, / Who pay no praise or wages / Nor heed my craft or art"? Finally, ask what is perhaps the most confusing of all questions for modern humanity, why does he choose to labor for other than monetary profit?

Dylan Thomas

In My Craft or Sullen Art

In my craft or sullen art
Exercised in the still night
When only the moon rages
And the lovers lie abed
With all their griefs in their arms,
I labour by singing light
Not for ambition or bread
Or the strut and trade of charms
On the ivory stages
But for the common wages
Of their most secret heart.
Not for the proud man apart
From the raging moon I write
On these spindrift pages
Nor for the towering dead
With their nightingales and psalms
But for the lovers, their arms
Round the griefs of the ages,
Who pay no praise or wages
Nor heed my craft or art.

The History of Work in the Western World

In the previous section we confronted a variety of issues that color the way we work, how work is arranged, the value work has for us, and our relative happiness with work. To better understand these issues, the next step is to trace the origins of the institutions, practices, and values that have given form to the modern economy and the modern workplace.

An historical perspective can help us in at least two ways. First, it can show us the logic of change. History can shed light on why we have the particular kinds of government, economies, habits, and values that are characteristic of our society. It can help us understand the reasons for the evolution of social structures, changes in government, and the triumph of new ideas. In other words, it can show us how we got to be what we are.

A second use of history is to give us perspective. By showing us that in the past people have lived and worked very differently from the ways we live and work today, history can help us understand what is unique and valuable in the world around us, as well as in what we may have lost. As we look at our own pasts, we will see that many things are very different today, and yet much is the same. Most importantly, we will see that the way things are today is not permanent and that we can have some influence in shaping the way the world will change tomorrow.

In Part A we begin with classical Greece. Greece is the birthplace of many of our most important ideas about ourselves: it is where much of our civilization began. We take its stories and institutions as our own, and we see it as the source of Western philosophy, drama, government, and science. In countless ways — in our language, our categories of thought, our images and stories — the world of classical Greece is an essential part of our consciousnesses. In this subsection you will find that the stories and ideas of both Hesiod and Plato seem familiar. They are familiar because they are our own source for much of what we believe to be true and right and good.

The second part of Part A is devoted to the medieval world from which the modern West evolved. In many ways the Middle Ages will seem less

161

familiar than ancient Greece, even though it is only 500 years in our past. This is because unlike our emulation of ancient Greece, much of modernism is a rebellion against medieval values and practices. Yet we have a great deal to learn from the Middle Ages both because it is such a rich and diverse era and because we carry so much of it with us today.

In Part B of this section we trace the growth and adoption of new ideas that become the basis for the modern state and the modern economy. This section is at the heart of this book, for it is here that you will see the elements that form you and the work that you do. We begin with the "founding story" of modernism by John Locke in which he gives his vision of what it means to be a human being and how we should order our societies. Then we turn to Adam Smith's attempt to flesh out the skeleton Locke had pictured by describing the details of how the everyday activities of production, distribution, and consumption should be arranged. Combined, these two "practical philosophies" continue to define for modern people who we are, how we should relate to each other, and what our place is in the world at large.

If we and you have done our work up to this point, you should not only find Locke and Smith familiar, but you should see their stories in new ways. You should have a better understanding for why they offer us new stories, and from your work in Section I you should see that there are some problems in the "garden" they describe. The remainder of Section II is devoted to understanding in more detail the strengths and weaknesses of Locke's and Smith's story and to examining the historical consequences of our living by this rather than the medieval or classical Greek stories we have just studied.

Quotes about work from Western history

Millwork ain't easy / Millwork ain't hard
Millwork ain't nothing but an awful borin' job

James Taylor

I think there is a work instinct; it's what developed human civilization, and I think that this instinct in itself can be disturbed, affected and pathological. . . . Like love and sex, work can have its pathologies. . . . That link between work and money is precisely what makes us feel like slaves. . . . If we could just loosen that linkage, work could be returned to instinct and it could be reimagined as a psychological phenomenon, a soul activity, not an economic activity, merely. . . . Money pay is a substitute for [work that meets our] soul needs.

James Hillman

Now in myth and ritual the great instinctive forces of civilized life have their origin: law and order, commerce and profit, craft and art, poetry, wisdom and science. All are rooted in the primaeval soil of play.

Johan Huizinga

But men labor under a mistake. The better part of the man is soon ploughed into the soil for compost. By a seeming fate, commonly called necessity, they are employed, as it says in an old book, laying up treasures which moth and rust will corrupt and thieves break through and steal. It is a fools life. . . . He has no time to be anything but a machine. . . . [For] the finest qualities of our nature, like the bloom on fruits, can be preserved only by the most delicate handling. Yet we do not treat ourselves nor one another thus tenderly. [We] make ourselves sick, that we may lay up something against a sick day. . . . The mass of men lead lives of quiet desperation.

Thoreau

Neither famine nor inward disaster comes the way of those people who are straight and just; they do their work as if work were a holiday; the earth gives them livelihood. . . . but when men like harsh violence and cruel acts, Zeus . . . ordains their punishment.

Hesiod

Gods and men alike resent that man who, without work himself, lives the life of the stingless drones, who without working eat away the substance of the honeybees' hard work. . . . It is from work that men grow rich and own flocks and herds; by work, too, they become better friends of the immortals. . . . Work is no disgrace; the disgrace is in not working. . . . It is best to work at whatever you have talent for doing, without turning your greedy thought toward what some other man possesses, but take care of your own livelihood.

Hesiod

Idleness is the enemy of the soul. . . . If the needs of the place demand that the Brothers gather in the harvest let them not be disheartened, for they are truly monks when they live from the work of their hands.

Rules of St. Benedict

Some people in the world don't have to do [religious] prostrations because they do them day by day in work with their hands and bodies. All over the world are people who are doing their [religious practices] while they fix the machinery, while they plant the grain, or while they tend the horses.

Gary Snyder

Lots of Americans work hard and play hard. But some just work, either from the unquenchable love of it or from a compulsion beyond their control. Work lovers—the unquenchables—provide society with many leaders in business, politics, science and the arts. Those who overwork out of compulsion—the work addicts, or workaholics, of this world—are in trouble. Their addiction can lead to dead-end careers, to poor health, even to early death. They are so emotionally dependent on work that without it they start coming unglued. Though the purebred workaholic is rare, there is a little of him in almost everyone. It is well to know the warning signals and how to cope with them.

Warren Boroson

"No one can serve two masters; for either he will hate the one and love the other, or he will be devoted to the one and despise the other. You cannot serve God and mammon.

"Therefore I tell you, do not be anxious about your life, what you shall eat or what you shall drink, nor about your body, what you shall put on. Is not life more than food, and the body more than clothing? Look at the birds of the air: they neither sow nor reap nor gather into barns, and yet your heavenly Father feeds them. Are you not of more value than they? And which of you by being anxious can add one cubit to his span of life? And why are you anxious about clothing? Consider the lilies of the field, how they grow; they neither toil nor spin; yet I tell you, even Solomon in all his glory was not arrayed like one of these. But if God so clothes the grass of the field, which today is alive and tomorrow is thrown into the oven, will he not much more clothe you, O men of little faith? Therefore do not be anxious, saying, 'What shall we eat?' or 'What shall we drink?' or 'What shall we wear?' For the Gentiles seek all these things; and your heavenly Father knows that you need them all. But seek first his kingdom and his righteousness, and all these things shall be yours as well.

"Therefore do not be anxious about tomorrow, for tomorrow will be anxious for itself. Let the day's own trouble be sufficient for the day."

Matthew 6:24–34

It may be true that work on the assembly line dulls the faculties and empties the mind, the cure only being fewer hours of work at higher pay. But during fifty years as a workingman, I have found dull routine compatible with an active mind. I can still savor the joy I used to derive from the fact that while doing dull, repetitive work on the waterfront, I could talk with my partners and compose sentences in the back of my mind, at the same time. Life seemed glorious. Chances are that had my work been of absorbing interest I could not have done any thinking and composing on the company's time or even on my own time after returning from work.

People who find dull jobs unendurable are often dull people who do not know what to do with themselves when at leisure. Children and mature people thrive on dull routine, while the adolescent, who has lost the child's capacity for concentration and is without the inner resources of the mature, needs excitement and novelty to stave off boredom.

Eric Hoffer

IIA. Western Ways of Working before the Industrial Revolution

As human societies became larger and more complex, people had to work more. Thus in every corner of the earth when societies changed from small-scale hunting and gathering patterns to the more settled strategies of farming and centers of trade (towns and cities), most people felt the need to justify increased toil. One interpretation of the Genesis story about Eden, as we have seen, was to tell people that God ordained hard work as a result of human choice: if you want to have lives wherein you choose the conditions of your existence, you will have to work for it. We are all familiar with the modern motivation: if you do not work, others will succeed where you fail. But other strategies for justifying human labor have been offered in Western history.

The strategies used by the two writers we have selected from classical Greece differ from both of the familiar rationalizations just mentioned. While disagreeing with each other in crucial ways, both Hesiod and Plato share a view of human life and community. Neither thinker accepts the explanations of the "fall of man" or competitive individualism that provide the underpinnings of most modern views of work. Instead, they, like people from a host of other societies, believe in the relative commonness of good work and in the importance of community for the existence of such work. As you read these selections, try to find the underpinnings of this justification of work. According to Hesiod and Plato how can work be good for us? Why is community important for good work to occur? What must people do to avoid falling into the traps whereby others have come to view work as onerous or a necessary evil?

The medieval world, like the modern, looked to classical Greece for inspiration and direction in establishing the contours of society. Ideas from Plato and Aristotle were transformed to fit the conditions of a Christian and Roman world order. Plato's two-tier metaphysics was transformed into a hierarchy of being with heaven at the top and material reality on the bottom, and human labor was the main determinant for whether and how far people moved up this "great chain of being." Work thus became the major mechanism for spiritual growth and redemption.

Both of the selections from this period illustrate certain dimensions and implications of this theory. John of Salisbury emphasizes the importance of work for spiritual growth while downplaying its material results.

William Langland's "Piers Ploughman" is also based on the great chain idea, but mainly to justify to humans the miserable conditions under which they toiled and the seeming uselessness of that toil. For Piers the physical world is a kind of proving ground—even the misery of an economic and social 1000-year dark age comes to have a purpose with this powerful conceptual tool. Thus the work people do while physically alive may seem to accomplish little except to wear people down, but if the fabric of heaven and earth can be stitched together with the great chain, not only misery but also seemingly useless toil is given the highest dignity.

As you read the selections from this section try to avoid simply dismissing the ideas and beliefs you find; instead, try to appreciate both their beauty and power. For we too live in a world dominated by beliefs and ideas that justify the world to us and us to the world. Ideas and beliefs may be as thin and immaterial as the morning mist, but they are also as strong as the invisible forces of the atom we believe hold the universe together.

1. Classical Greece

Introduction
Hesiod, from "Works and Days"

The ancient Greeks, like the Hebrews of the Old Testament, provided us with many of our enduring stories. Tales about Odysseus, Zeus, Pandora, Oedipus, and Athena are as familiar to people today as are the legends of Noah, Abraham, and Rebecca, and we still have much to learn from these great Greek myths. Hesiod, an eighth century BCE contemporary of the legendary poet Homer, was the poet of the common folk. While Homer spun tales of nobility, of kings, queens, heroes, and their wars, Hesiod used his stock of stories and symbols to tell of life for more ordinary humans. His major poem "Works and Days" begins with a series of creation myths that provide alternative views of the human condition. We are first told the story of the "fall," when humans were displaced from their original cohabitation with the gods and goddesses to a life of mortality and struggle. A second story describes the devolution of humans from more to less magnificent cultures, ending with the dismal prediction that even from this lowly life human misery will increase.

Like the ancient Hebrews, the Greeks were trying to come to grips with a life in which humans no longer had the privilege (or bliss) of living like animals or children. The glory days were over (if they ever existed!). Furthermore, humans are cursed with a variety of limitations, not the least of which is to not know what the gods will do next (whom or where the plague or lightning or drought will strike). In at least one of these early myths work is viewed much as we saw in Genesis 3 — as a curse, and Hesiod adds the paradigmatic sexist version of Pandora's box, the view of woman as a curse. Humans, it would seem, are condemned to quite miserable existences. To this point Hesiod would seem to be even more pessimistic than Homer. While Homer's heroic characters find no end of suffering, at least their lives are partially redeemed by their heroic actions and characters. What is there for common folk? Hesiod's third story not only answers this question in a way with which we can identify today, but the perceptive reader might see that he is poking fun at the Homeric legends in the process.

The grandiose tales of the deities and of previous generations of larger-than-life heroes are fine, Hesiod seems to be saying, but perhaps some down-to-earth talk would be more helpful. Hesiod talks to Perses (his listener) of *justice*. This is not the abstract justice of some philosopher's tower; Hesiod's justice is about doing one's work in an intelligent way — justice is founded on good work. Listen to his opening summary of the just society: "Neither famine nor inward disaster comes the way of those people who are straight and just; they do their work as if work were a holiday; the earth gives them great livelihood." Life does not have to be miserable . . . if one lives justly. Work *can* be seen as a curse, but if done well, "Work is no disgrace"; in fact "the disgrace is in not working."

Hesiod is turning tables on Homer's heroic order and the elitist views it contains. For the aristocrats of Homer's society work is for the *common* people — the peasant, the craftsperson, the slave. "Others" work so that the heroes can heed their "higher callings" to adventure and high culture. This kind of hierarchical system requires some good stories to justify and maintain it. Hesiod is suggesting that the first two standard creation myths we just described are perfect for this task: in those stories the glory days are associated with the past and with aristocrats, and ordinary people in the present are condemned to work hard with no promise of much except eking out a living.

Hesiod's view of working is in sharp contrast to Homer's. In fact, it seems much like Franklin's. Hesiod says life is not easy, but the world is not ungenerous either. If humans apply themselves, they not only can survive, but they can thrive. What they must do is to develop the proper habits, the proper relations with nature, and the right relations with their fellow humans. But note the subtle differences between Hesiod's and Franklin's views. While both emphasize the virtuousness of hard work and thrift, Hesiod's view seems broader. Franklin's concern is with individual success, which means becoming increasingly wealthy. Hesiod encourages individual wisdom and effort, but he also emphasizes the integral ties with the community and with nature a person must have in order to be successful. In a word, Franklin is concerned with *righteousness,* while Hesiod speaks of *justice.* Both men address the individual, but Franklin is concerned with a version of the Protestant's individual salvation, while Hesiod focuses on relationships with others and with nature (and thus to the gods) that constitute justice (good living).

As you read these excerpts from "The Works and Days," examine carefully the elements in this ethic. Hesiod is not moralistic—he does not take a holier-than-thou attitude toward those who lack his ethic, and he does not threaten hellfire and brimstone to those who "fall from the way." Instead, his view is highly *practical:* if you work hard (but not addictively), if you work closely with nature, and if you develop the proper communities, you will lead a comfortable life. The dangers, too, are straightforward: beware of greed, poor business deals, untrustworthy people, and so on. Hesiod's is an ethic cut from rugged cloth meant for the hard wear of everyday use.

Hesiod

Works and Days

As for those who give straight judgments to visitors and to their own people and do not deviate from what is just, their community flourishes, and the people blooms in it. Peace is about the land, fostering the young, and wide-seeing Zeus never marks out grievous war as their portion. Neither does Famine attend straight-judging men, nor Blight, and they feast on the crops they tend. For them Earth bears plentiful food, and on the mountains the oak carries acorns at its surface and bees at its centre. The fleecy sheep are laden down with wool; the womenfolk bear children that resemble their parents; they enjoy a continual sufficiency of good things. Nor do they ply on ships, but the grain-giving ploughland bears them fruit.

But for those who occupy themselves with violence and wickedness and brutal deeds, Kronos' son, wide-seeing Zeus, marks out retribution.

Often a whole community together suffers in consequence of a bad man who does wrong and contrives evil. From heaven Kronos' son brings disaster upon them, famine and with it plague, and the people waste away. The womenfolk do not give birth, and households decline, by Olympian Zeus' design. At other times again he either destroys those men's broad army or city wall, or punishes their ships at sea.

Best of all is the man who perceives everything himself, taking account of what will be better in the long run and in the end. Good is he, too, who follows good advice. But he who neither perceives by himself nor takes in a lesson from another, he on the other hand is a worthless man. But you, ever bearing my instruction in mind, must work, Perses, you who are of Zeus' stock, so that Hunger may shun you and august fair-crowned Demeter favour you and fill your granary with substance; for Hunger goes always with a workshy man. Gods and men disapprove of that man who lives without working, like in temper to the blunt-tailed drones who wear away the toil of the bees, eating it in idleness. You should embrace work-tasks in their due order, so that your granaries may be full of substance in its season. It is from work that men are rich in flocks and wealthy, and a working man is much dearer to the immortals. Work is no reproach, but not working is a reproach; and if you work, it will readily come about that a workshy man will envy you as you become wealthy. Wealth brings worth and prestige. But whatever your fortune, work is preferable, that is, if you turn your blight-witted heart from others' possessions towards work and show concern for livelihood as I tell you.

> Inhibition is no good provider for a needy man,
> Inhibition, which does men great harm and great good.
> Inhibition attaches to poverty, boldness to wealth.

Property is not for seizing: far better God-given. For if a man does seize wealth by force of his hands, or appropriates it by means of words— the sort of thing that often happens when profit deludes men's minds, and Shamelessness drives away Shame—the gods easily bring him low, and diminish that man's house, and it is but a short time that prosperity attends him. It is the same if a man does wrong by a suppliant or a visitor; or if he mounts his own brother's bed in secret union with his wife in breach of all propriety; or if in his folly he wrongs someone's orphan children, or if he rails at his old father on the ugly threshold of age, assaulting him with harsh words. With that man Zeus himself is indignant, and in the end he imposes a harsh return for his unrighteous actions.

For if you lay down even a little on a little, and do this often, even that may well grow big. He who adds to what is there, wards off burning hunger. What is stored up at home is not a source of worry; better for things to be in the house, for what is outside is at risk. It is good to take from what is available, but sorrow to the heart to be wanting what is not available. I suggest you reflect on this.

No, I suggest you reflect on the clearing of your debts and the avoidance of famine. First, a household, a woman, and a ploughing ox—a chattel woman, not wedded, one who could follow the herds. The utilities in the house must all be got ready, lest you ask another, and he refuse, and you be lacking, and the right time go past, and your cultivation suffer. Do not put things off till tomorrow and the next day. A man of ineffectual labour, a postponer, does not fill his granary: it is application that promotes your cultivation, whereas a postponer of labour is constantly wrestling with Blights.

When the keen sun's strength stops scorching and sweltering, after mighty Zeus begins the autumn rain, and human skin feels the change with relief—for then the star Sirius goes but briefly by day above the heads of men who are born to die, having a larger share of the night—then timber is freest from the worm when hewn by the iron, when it sheds its leaves to the ground and stops putting out shoots. Then do your woodcutting, do not neglect it, a job in season. Cut a mortar to three feet, a pestle to three cubits, an axle to seven feet, that will do very well; or if to eight feet, you may cut a mallet off it too. Cut a three-span wheel for a ten-palm cart. Many timbers are bent: take a plough-tree home when you find one, searching on the mountain or on the ploughland—one of holm-oak, for that is the firmest for ploughing with oxen when Athene's servant has fixed it in the stock with dowels and brought it up and fastened it to the pole. Take the trouble to provide yourself with two ploughs at home, a self-treed one and a joined one, for it is much better so: if you should break one, you can set the other to the oxen. Bay or elm make the most worm-free poles, oak the stock, and holm-oak the plough-tree.

Introduction
Plato, from *The Republic*

Alfred North Whitehead, a twentieth-century Anglo-American philosopher, said that all Western philosophy is a footnote to Plato. Whether
or not that is literally true, no one doubts the powerful influence Plato
has had on philosophy and on Western civilization more broadly. Plato
was born in Athens, probably in 428 B.C., and died at the age of eighty
or eighty-one in 348 B.C. On both sides of his family he was descended
from a distinguished aristocratic lineage that had been active in the affairs
of Athens. Plato's childhood and youth were spent under the shadow of
the Peloponnesian War, and perhaps it was the insecurity of this world
that started Plato on the road, through philosophy, to discovering a more
permanent reality than he found in his own physical environment. As
a young man Plato became a follower of Socrates, who was asking the
most probing questions about the nature of truth and the ethical life.
The execution of Socrates by the Athenian democracy probably finally
turned the young Plato completely toward the contemplative life.

Having withdrawn from the corrupt world of active public life, Plato
set out to discover the fundamental nature of reality and then to build
upon it a just state. The case for Plato's ideal state is contained in *The
Republic,* perhaps the greatest work of political philosophy ever written.
In *The Republic* Plato divides the world into two parts, the physical world
and the world of forms or ideas. He sees the material world as the lesser
part of reality because it is imperfect and impermanent, and he finds
the permanence he is seeking in the world of forms, or the ideal world.
For him the material world is only a shadow of the ideal and permanent
reality. Happily, he believes, we can come to know the ideal truth, beauty,
and goodness if we go through the proper process. And only then can
we have the blueprints we need for our actions in the material world.
In particular this process is philosophy as practiced by Socrates, and what
this process reveals is that by doing as well as we can (the Greek word
is 'arete,' meaning, roughly, excellence) at what proper assessment reveals we are cut out for, we and society will thrive.

In the following excerpt from *The Republic,* Plato's spokesman, Socrates, advances his notion of how the ideal community should be organized.
Critical to this notion is the idea of society as an organic whole. Plato
draws an analogy between society and an organism. The whole organism
is healthy (just) if each part is healthy and does its job well. The role
that the heart should play is not up to the heart to choose—the heart

is born to its job—and anyone who tries to think with his heart or digest with her hand is in trouble. A successful organism is based on specialization, which results in the most efficient and highest quality products. While he does not believe in democracy, Plato believes that each organ (person) in the organism is important. Thus, society should not neglect the well-being of any member. Each citizen needs to be educated for her role, and everyone should be respected and protected and have her needs met if she does her part.

Does this mean that people are confined to the position to which they are born? No. Although he does argue for rule by an elite (the "head," not the "stomach" or some other part), by the person or persons most qualified to govern, Plato's is a meritocracy rather than a traditional or inherited aristocracy. For Plato the son or daughter of a commoner could be born with the characteristics of a ruler, and the offspring of a noble-man could be best suited for farming.

Plato gives work a very high status. Not only is the individual enhanced through work, but everyone's work is critical for the well-being of the whole society. Work brings not only a sense of identity, but Plato sees that it is the means whereby each person contributes to, and becomes a member of, the whole community. Furthermore, we are born to a certain task (I am most fulfilled when I am teaching; he while fixing an electrical circuit; she while practicing law), to work is the fulfillment of a sacred trust. The corollary of this last point is that if one does not work, does not work at one's calling, or does not work well, then the world (society) is out of harmony.

Even though Plato dismisses democracy and probably some other values that you hold dear, you should resonate with many of his ideas about work. We have inherited his world. Our world is not the same as Plato's, but he helped to make ours what it is. Perhaps there are features of his views on work that we have ignored or altered that we would be well advised to reconsider.

Plato

The Republic

I will tell you, I said. There is, we say, the justice of one man, and also the justice of a whole city? — Certainly.

And a city is larger than one man? — It is.

Perhaps there is more justice in the larger unit, and it may be easier to grasp. So, if you are willing, let us first investigate what justice is in the cities, and afterwards let us look for it in the individual, observing the similarities to the larger in the smaller. — Your proposal seems sound.

Well then, I said, if we observed the birth of a city in theory, we would also see its justice and injustice beginning to exist. — Probably.

I think a city comes to be, I said, because not one of us is self-sufficient, but needs many things. Do you think a city is founded on any other principle? — On no other.

As they need many things, people make use of one another for various purposes. They gather many associates and helpers to live in one place, and to this settlement we give the name of city. Is that not so? — It is.

And they share with one another, both giving and taking, in so far as they do, because they think this better for themselves? — Quite so.

Come then, I said, let us create a city from the beginning in our discussion. And it is our needs, it seems, that will create it. — Of course.

Surely our first and greatest need is to provide food to sustain life. — It certainly is.

Our second need is for shelter, our third for clothes and such things. — Quite so.

Consider then, said I, how the city will adequately provide for all this. One man obviously must be a farmer, another a builder, and another a weaver. Or should we add a cobbler and some other craftsman to look after our physical needs? — All right.

So the essential minimum for the city is four or five men. — Apparently.

A further point: must each of them perform his own work as common for them all, for example the one farmer provide food for them all, and spend four times as much time and labour to provide food which is shared by the others, or will he not care for this but provide for himself a quarter of such food in a quarter of the time and spend the other three quarters, one in building a house, one in the production of clothes, and one to make shoes, and not trouble to associate with the others but for and by himself mind his own business?

Perhaps, Socrates, Adeimantus replied, the way you suggested first would be easier than the other.

By Zeus, said I, there is nothing surprising in this, for even as you were speaking I was thinking that, in the first place, each one of us is born somewhat different from the others, one more apt for one task, one for another. Don't you think so? — I do.

Further, does a man do better if he practises many crafts, or if, being one man, he restricts himself to one craft. — When he restricts himself to one.

This at any rate is clear, I think, that if one misses the proper time to do something, the opportunity to do it has gone. — Clear enough.

For I do not think that the thing to be done awaits the leisure of the doer, but the doer must of necessity adjust himself to the requirements of his task, and not consider this of secondary importance. — He must.

Both production and quality are improved in each case, and easier, if each man does one thing which is congenial to him, does it at the right time, and is free of other pursuits. — Most certainly.

We shall then need more than four citizens, Adeimantus, to provide the things we have mentioned. It is likely that the farmer will not make his own plough if it is to be a good one, nor his mattock, nor other agricultural implements. Neither will the builder, for he too needs many things; and the same is true of the weaver and the cobbler, is it not? — True.

Carpenters, metal workers, and many such craftsmen will share our little city and make it bigger. — Quite so.

Yet it will not be a very big settlement if we add cowherds, shepherds, and other herdsmen in order that our farmers have oxen to do their ploughing, and the builders will join the farmers in the use of them as beasts of burden to transport their materials, while the weavers and cobblers will use their wool and hides.

Neither will it be a small city, said he, if it has to hold all these things.

And further, it is almost impossible to establish the city in the kind of place that will need no imports. — Impossible.

So we shall still need other people to bring what is needed from other cities. — We shall.

Now if one who serves in this way goes to the other city without a cargo of the things needed by those from whom he is to bring what his own people need, he will come away empty-handed, will he not? — I think so.

Therefore our citizens must not only produce enough for themselves at home, but also the things these others require, of the right quality and in the right quantity. — They must.

So we need more farmers and other craftsmen in our city. — We do.

Then again we need more people to service imports and exports. These are merchants, are they not? — Yes.

So we shall need merchants too. — Quite so.

And if the trade is by sea, we shall need a number of others who know how to sail the seas. — A good many, certainly.

A further point: how are they going to share the things that each group produces within the city itself? This association with each other was the very purpose for which we established the city.

Clearly, he said, they must do this by buying and selling.

It follows that we must have a market place and a currency for this exchange. — Certainly.

If the farmer brings some of his produce to market, or any other craftsman, and he does not arrive at the same time as those who want to exchange things with him, will he be sitting idly in the market place, away from his own work?

Not at all, he said. There will be people who realize this and engage in this service. In well-organized cities this will be pretty well those of feeble physique who are not fit for other work. They must stay around the market, buying for money from those who have something to sell, and then again selling at a price to those who want to buy.

To fill this need there will be retailers in our city. Do we not call retailers those who establish themselves in the market place for this service of buying and selling, while those who travel between cities are called merchants? — Quite so.

There are some others to serve, as I think, who are not worth admitting into our society for their intelligence, but they have sufficient physical strength for heavy labour. These sell the use of their strength; their reward for this is a wage and they are, I think, called wage-earners. Is that not so? — Certainly.

So the wage-earners complete our city. — I think so.

Well, Adeimantus, has our city now grown to its full size? — Perhaps.

Where then would justice and injustice be in it? With which of the parts we have examined have they come to be?

I do not notice them, Socrates, he said, unless it is in the relations of these very people to one another.

You may be right, I said, but we must look into it and not grow weary. First then let us see what kind of life our citizens will lead when they have thus been provided for. Obviously they will produce grain and wine and clothes and shoes. They will build their houses. In the summer they will strip for their work and go without shoes, though they will be adequately clothed and shod in the winter. For food they will make flour from wheat and meal from barley; they will bake the former and knead the latter; they will put their excellent cakes and loaves upon reeds or clean leaves; then, reclining upon a bed of strewn bryony and myrtle leaves, they will feast together with their children, drinking of their wine. Crowned with wreaths they will hymn the gods and enjoy each other, bearing no more children than their means allow, cautious to avoid poverty and war.

Glaucon interrupted and said: You make your people feast, it seems, without cooked dishes or seasoning.

True enough, I said, I was forgetting that they will need these, salt obviously and olives and cheese; they will boil roots and vegetables such as are found in the fields. We shall put sweetmeats before them consisting of figs and chickpeas and beans, and they will bake myrtles and acorns before the fire, drinking moderately. So they will live at peace and in good health, and when they die at a ripe age they will bequeath a similar life to their offspring.

Very well, I said, I understand. We should examine not only the birth of a city, but of a luxurious city. This may not be a bad idea, for in examining such a one we might very well see how justice and injustice grow in the cities. Yet to me the true city is that which we described, like a healthy individual. However, if you wish, let us also observe the feverish city. There is nothing to prevent us. The things I mentioned would not, it seems, satisfy some people, nor would that kind of life. There will be couches, then, and tables and the other kinds of furniture. They must have cooked dishes and unguents and perfumes, and courtesans and pastries — various kinds of all these. We must no longer provide them only with the necessities we mentioned at first, houses and clothes and shoes, but we must call in painting and embroidery; we must acquire gold and ivory and all such things. Is that not so? — Yes.

We must then again enlarge our city. That healthy community is no longer adequate, but it must be swollen in bulk and filled with a multitude of things which are no longer necessities, as, for example, all kinds of hunters and artists, many of them concerned with shapes and colours, many with music; poets and their auxiliaries, actors, choral dancers, and contractors; and makers of all kinds of instruments, including those needed for the beautification of women. And further we shall require more services in the city, or do you not think we shall need tutors, wet nurses, dry nurses, beauty parlours, barbers, and again chefs and cooks, also swineherds? These were not needed in our earlier city, but in this one there is need of them, as there will be for many other fatted beasts, once one eats them. Is that not so? — Of course.

And if we live like this we shall have far greater need of physicians than before. — Much greater.

So fine speech, fine music, gracefulness, and fine rhythm are all adapted to a simplicity of character, and I do not mean simplicity in the sense we use it as a euphemism for foolishness, but where the mind has established a truly good and fine character. — Most certainly.

And should our young men not aim at this everywhere, if they are to fulfill the task that is theirs? — They must indeed.

Painting is full of these qualities, and all such artistic works; so is weaving and embroidery and architecture and the making of furniture; so is our bodily nature and that of other growing things; in all these there is seemliness and unseemliness. Unseemliness, poor rhythm, and discord are closely akin to poor language and poor character, while their opposites are closely akin to, and imitations of, the opposite, a good and moderate character. — This is altogether true.

Is it then the poets only whom we shall command and compel to represent the image of good character in their poems or else not practise among us, or are we to give orders also to other craftsmen, and forbid them to represent, whether in pictures or in buildings or in any other works, character that is vicious, mean, unrestrained, or graceless? We must not allow one who cannot do this to work among us, that our guardians may not, bred among images of evil as in an evil meadow, culling and grazing much every day from many sources, little by little collect all unawares a great evil in their own soul. We must seek out such artists as have the talent to pursue the beautiful and the graceful in their work, in order that our young men shall be benefited from all sides like those who live in a healthy place, whence something from these beautiful works will strike their eyes and ears like a breeze that brings health from salubrious places, and lead them unawares from childhood to love of, resemblance to, and harmony with, the beauty of reason. — This, he said, would be by far the best nurture for them.

Are these not the reasons, Glaucon, I said, why nurture in the arts is most important, because their rhythm and harmony permeate the inner part of the soul, bring graciousness to it, and make the strongest impression, making a man gracious if he has the right kind of upbringing; if he has not, the opposite is true. The man who has been properly nurtured in this area will be keenly aware of things which are neglected, things not beautifully made by art or nature. He will rightly resent them, he will praise beautiful things, rejoice in them, receive them into his soul, be nurtured by them and become both good and beautiful in character. He will rightly object to what is ugly and hate it while still young before he can grasp the reason, and when reason comes he who has been reared thus will welcome it and easily recognize it because of its kinship with himself. — Yes, he said, I agree those are the reasons for education in the arts.

When a man's soul has a beautiful character, and his body matches it in beauty and is thus in harmony with it, that harmonizing combination, sharing the same mould, is the most beautiful spectacle for anyone who has eyes to see. — It certainly is.

And that which is most beautiful is most lovable. — Of course.

A cultured man would love such people, but would not love one lacking in such harmony.

Not, he said, if he had some defect in the soul, yet a physical defect he might overlook and be fond of him.

Do you agree that we have now completed our discussion of education in the arts, I said, and that it has ended as it should? For a discussion of the arts must end in the love of the beautiful. — I agree.

After education in the arts, our young men must have physical training. — Quite so.

In this too they must have careful training from childhood throughout life. The matter stands, it seems to me, something like this. You too consider the point. It seems to me that a fit body does not by its own excellence ensure a good soul, but on the contrary it is a good soul which by its own excellence ensures that the body shall be as fit as possible. What do you think? — I think as you do.

I get the point, he said. You mean that those who devote themselves exclusively to physical culture turn out to be harsher than they should be, while those who devote themselves to the arts become softer than is good for them.

What if a man labours much at physical exercises and lives well but is quite out of touch with the arts and philosophy? Is he not in good physical condition at first, full of resolution and spirit, and becomes braver than he was before? — Certainly.

But if he does nothing else and never associates with the Muse? He never has a taste of any learning or any investigation; he has no share in any reasoned discussion or any other form of culture; even if he had some love of learning in his soul it soon becomes enfeebled, deaf, and blind as it is not aroused or nurtured; and even his senses are not sharpened. — That is so, he said.

We should then quite correctly call the man who achieves the most beautiful blend of physical and artistic culture, and in due measure impresses this upon his soul, the completely Muse-inspired and harmonious man, far more so than the musician who harmonizes the strings of his instrument. — That is very likely, Socrates.

Therefore in our city too, Glaucon, we shall always need this kind of man as an overseer, if our community is to be preserved? — We shall certainly have the greatest need of him.

Adeimantus took up the argument and said: What defence, Socrates, would you offer against the charge that you are not making your guardians very happy, and that through their own fault? The city is really in their power, yet they derive no good from this. Others own land, build grand and beautiful houses, acquire furnishings appropriate to them, make their own private sacrifices to the gods, entertain, also, as you mentioned just now, have gold and silver and all the possessions which are thought to belong to people who will be happy. One might well say that your guardians are simply settled in the city like paid mercenaries, with nothing to do but to watch over it.

Yes, said I. Moreover, they work for their keep and get no extra wages as the others do, so that if they want to leave the city privately they cannot do so; they have nothing to give their mistresses, nothing to spend in whatever other way they wish, as men do who are considered happy. You have omitted these and other such things from the charge. — Let these accusations be added, he said.

Now you ask what defence we shall offer? — Yes.

I think we shall discover what to say if we follow the same path as before, I said. We shall say that it would not be at all surprising if these men too were very happy. In any case, in establishing our city, we are not aiming to make any one group outstandingly happy, but to make the whole city so, as far as possible. We thought that in such a city we would most easily find justice, find injustice in a badly governed one, and then decide what we have been looking for all the time. Now we think we are fashioning the happy city not by separating a few people in it and making them happy, but by making the whole city so. We shall look at the opposite kind of city presently. If someone came to us while we were painting a statue and objected because we did not apply the finest colours to the finest parts of the body, for the eyes are the most beautiful part, and they are not made purple but black, we should appear to offer a reasonable defence if we said: "My good sir, do not think that we must make the eyes so beautiful that they no longer appear to be eyes at all, and so with the other parts, but look to see whether by dealing with each part appropriately we are making the whole statue beautiful." And so now, do not force us to give our guardians the kind of happiness which would make them anything but guardians.

We know how to clothe our farmers too in purple robes, surround them with gold and tell them to work the land at their pleasure, and how to settle our potters on couches by the fire, feasting and passing the wine, put their wheel by them and tell them to make pots as much as they want; we know how to make all the others also happy in the same way, so that the whole city is happy. Do not exhort us to do this, however. If we do, the farmer will not be a farmer, nor the potter a potter; nor would anyone else fulfill any of the functions which make up the state. For the others this is less important: if shoemakers become inferior and corrupt, and claim to be what they are not, the state is not in peril, but, if the guardians of our laws and city only appear to be guardians and are not, you surely see that they destroy the city utterly, as they alone have the opportunity to govern it well and to make it happy.

If then we are making true guardians who are least likely to work wickedness upon the city, whereas our accuser makes some farmers into banqueters, happy as at some festival but not in a city, he would be talking about something else than a city. We should examine then, with this in mind, whether our aim in establishing our guardians should be to give them the greatest happiness, or whether we should in this matter look to the whole city and see how its greatest happiness can be secured. We must compel and persuade the auxiliaries and the guardians to be excellent performers of their own task, and so with all the others. As the whole city grows and is well governed, we must leave it to nature to provide each group with its share of happiness.

I think, he said, that you put that very well.

Will you also, said I, think that I speak reasonably when I make the next point which is closely akin to this? — What is that?

Consider whether these factors corrupt the other workers also, so that they become bad at their job? — What factors?

Wealth, I said, and poverty. — How do you mean?

Like this. Do you think that a potter who has become wealthy will still be willing to pay attention to his craft? — Not in any way.

He will become more idle and careless than he was? — Much.

And therefore become a worse potter? — Far worse.

And surely if poverty prevents him having the tools or anything else his craft needs, he will produce poorer work, and his sons or any others he may teach will not be as good workers. — Of course.

So both poverty and wealth make the products of the crafts worse, and the craftsmen too. — Apparently.

We have, it seems, found other dangers against which our guardians must guard most carefully, lest these should penetrate the city unnoticed. — What are these?

Both wealth and poverty, I said. The former makes for luxury, idleness, and political change, the latter for meanness, bad work, and change as well.

This then would be the best limitation which our guardians should put upon the size of the city; they should then mark off the amount of land required for its size, and let the rest go. — What is this limitation?

I think, I said, that it is this: to let the city grow as long as it is willing to retain its unity, but not beyond that point. — Quite right.

This then is another order we shall give our guardians: to watch most carefully that the city should not appear either small or big, but sufficient, and remain one. — This, he said, is indeed an easy order we shall give them!

Even easier than that, I said, is the one we mentioned before when we said that, if an offspring of the guardians is inferior, he must be sent off to join the other citizens, and if the others have an able offspring, he must be taken into the guardian group. This was meant to make clear that the other citizens must each be directed to the one task for which each is naturally fitted, so that he should pursue that one task which is his own and be himself one person and not many, and the city itself be a unity and not a plurality. — That is an even easier order than the other!

These orders we give them, my good Adeimantus, I said, are not, as one might think, either numerous or important; they are all secondary, provided that they guard the one great thing, as people say, though rather than great I would call it sufficient. — What is that?

Their education and their upbringing, I said. If they become cultured, moderate men, they will easily see these things for themselves, and other things too which we are now omitting, the acquiring of wives and children which must all accord with the old proverb, that the possessions of friends must be held in common. — That would be the best way.

Surely, I said, once our city gets a good start, it would go on growing in a circle. Good education and upbringing, if preserved, will lead to men of a better nature, and these in turn, if they cling to their education, will improve with each generation both in other respects and also in their children, just like other animals. — Quite likely.

Further, we have heard many people say, and have often said ourselves, that justice is to perform one's own task and not to meddle with that of others. — We have said that.

This then, my friend, I said, when it happens, is in some way justice, to do one's own job. And do you know what I take to be a proof of this? — No, tell me.

I think what is left over of those things we have been investigating, after moderation and courage and wisdom have been found, was that which made it possible for those three qualities to appear in the city and to continue as long as it is present. We also said that what remained after we found the other three was justice. — It had to be.

And surely, I said, if we had to decide which of the four will make the city good by its presence, it would be hard to judge whether it is a common belief among the rulers and the ruled, or the preservation among the soldiers of a law-inspired belief as to the nature of what is, and what is not, to be feared, or the knowledge and guardianship of the rulers, or whether it is, above all, the presence of this fourth in child and woman, slave and free, artisan, ruler and subject, namely that each man, a unity in himself, performed his own task and was not meddling with that of others. — How could this not be hard to judge?

It seems then that the capacity for each in the city to perform his own task rivals wisdom, moderation, and courage as a source of excellence for the city. — It certainly does.

You would then describe justice as a rival to them for excellence in the city? — Most certainly.

Look at it this way and see whether you agree: you will order your rulers to act as judges in the courts of the city? — Surely.

And will their exclusive aim in delivering judgment not be that no citizen should have what belongs to another or be deprived of what is his own? — That would be their aim.

That being just? — Yes.

In some way then possession of one's own and the performance of one's own task could be agreed to be justice. — That is so.

Consider then whether you agree with me in this: if a carpenter attempts to do the work of a cobbler, or a cobbler that of a carpenter, and they exchange their tools and the esteem that goes with the job, or the same man tries to do both, and all the other exchanges are made, do you think that this does any great harm to the city? — No.

But I think that when one who is by nature a worker or some other kind of moneymaker is puffed up by wealth, or by the mob, or by his own strength, or some other such thing, and attempts to enter the warrior class, or one of the soldiers tries to enter the group of counsellors and guardians, though he is unworthy of it, and these exchange their tools and the public esteem, or when the same man tries to perform all these jobs together, then I think you will agree that these exchanges and this meddling bring the city to ruin. — They certainly do.

The meddling and exchange between the three established orders does very great harm to the city and would most correctly be called wickedness. — Very definitely.

And you would call the greatest wickedness worked against one's own city injustice? — Of course.

That then is injustice. And let us repeat that the doing of one's own job by the moneymaking, auxiliary, and guardian groups, when each group is performing its own task in the city, is the opposite, it is justice and makes the city just. — I agree with you that this is so.

Do not let us, I said, take this as quite final yet. If we find that this quality, when existing in each individual man, is agreed there too to be justice, then we can assent to this — for what can we say? — but if not, we must look for something else. For the present, let us complete that examination which we thought we should make, that if we tried to observe justice in something larger which contains it, this would make it easier to observe it in the individual. We thought that this larger thing was a city, and so we established the best city we could, knowing well that justice would be present in the good city. It has now appeared to us there, so let us now transfer it to the individual and, if it corresponds, all will be well. But if it is seen to be something different in the individual, then we must go back to the city and examine this new notion of justice. By thus comparing and testing the two, we might make justice light up like fire from the rubbing of firesticks, and when it has become clear, we shall fix it firmly in our own minds. — You are following the path we set, and we must do so.

Well now, when you apply the same name to a thing whether it is big or small, are these two instances of it like or unlike with regard to that to which the same name applies? — They are alike in that, he said.

So the just man and the just city will be no different but alike as regards the very form of justice. — Yes, they will be.

Now the city was thought to be just when the three kinds of men within it each performed their own task, and it was moderate and brave and wise because of some other qualities and attitudes of the same groups. — True.

2. The Medieval World

Introduction
John of Salisbury, "The Feet of the Commonwealth"

Considered by many historians to be the most typical pre-Thomistic medieval political philosopher, John of Salisbury was known for his advocacy of the supremacy of the spiritual power of the church over the temporal powers of the monarchy. An Englishman, he defended Archbishop Thomas Beckett in his struggle with the British king, Henry II. He was believed to have been present when Beckett was murdered in Canterbury Cathedral by Henry's henchmen.

John was educated in France at the University of Paris and at Chartres, the leading center for the study of the humanities in twelfth-century Europe. In the *Statesman's Handbook* (*Policraticus*), from which the following excerpt was taken, he is the first Englishman (writing five hundred years before Locke) to argue for strict limits on the powers of the king.

The rhetorical power of this brief exhortation by John of Salisbury to the peasants to accept their lots and carry out their obligations rests on the power of the metaphor of the great chain of being. In his *The Heavenly City of God*, written in 426, St. Augustine of Hippo put words to this crucial organizing idea that helped shape and stabilize a way of life which held sway for a millennium. For the Middle Ages this idea was as important as the ideas of freedom and democracy are for our own form of social organization today.

In the picture of the world outlined in the great chain of being, the top layer of the three-part hierarchy is filled with heavenly beings, beginning with God at the top, with good angels and other good heavenly beings above bad angels (including the devil, of course), and finally with the spirits of humans who have made it to the spiritual realm. The bottom layer is the totally material realm of nonhuman nature, and that realm, too, is hierarchical. Today we might think (wrongly, of course) of the theory of evolution telling us which creatures are *most* evolved, and the medievalists had something like that in mind, placing rocks above mud, trees above rocks, worms above trees, cats above worms, and so on. The center tier in this hierarchy is occupied by humans. We are neither fully divine nor fully material. This theory rests on Plato's two-worlds philosophy according to which humans have the unique ability and opportunity to bridge the gap between these realms. The Catholic version of Plato's doctrine turns this opportunity into a threat—if you do not behave properly while embodied, you will not make it to the higher realm.

Contrary to Plato it is probably safe to say that ideas come and go. Those that last do so because they somehow move from conceptualization into application. Through this excerpt from Salisbury's political treatise we can begin to imagine how this idea of the chain of being became implanted simultaneously in social forms and in people's heads. Between the time Augustine penned his (a Catholic) version of the great chain and John of Salisbury used it there was a period of life so miserable we often refer to it as the Dark Ages. The idea of the great chain justified this existence to people, making them content with material misery because "that is the order of things" and because people can move up the chain (go to heaven) if they accept their miserable lot with equanimity (faith). The great chain of being, then, was a powerful tool the ruling class could employ to influence people to accept the status quo.

John of Salisbury

The Feet of the Commonwealth

Those are called the feet who discharge the humbler offices, and by whose services the members of the whole commonwealth walk upon solid earth. Among these are to be counted the husbandmen, who always cleave to the soil, busied about their plough-lands or vineyards or pastures or flower-gardens. To these must be added the many species of cloth-making, and the mechanic arts, which work in wood, iron, bronze, and the different metals; also the menial occupations, and the manifold forms of getting a livelihood and sustaining life, or increasing household property, all of which, while they do not pertain to the authority of the governing power, are yet in the highest degree useful and profitable to the corporate whole of the commonwealth. All these different occupations are so numerous that the commonwealth in the number of its feet exceeds not only the eight-footed crab but even the centipede, and because of their very multitude they cannot be enumerated; for while they are not infinite by nature, they are yet of so many different varieties that no writer on the subject of offices or duties has ever laid down particular precepts

From *Policraticus,* trans. J. Dickinson.

for each special variety. But it applies generally to each and all of them that in their exercise they should not transgress the limits of the law, and should in all things observe constant reference to the public utility. For inferiors owe it to their superiors to provide them with service, just as the superiors in their turn owe it to their inferiors to provide them with all things needful for their protection and succour.

Introduction
William Langland, from *Piers Ploughman*

We know very little about William Langland. In fact we are not sure that Langland is only one person. Since three versions of the epic poem *Piers Ploughman* exist, there could be two or three authors. Whoever the writer, we are sure that the poem reflects the ideals and the harsh realities of the late fourteenth century in England. We have included the poem because we think it will give you a more concrete picture of our medieval past. We say "our" because whatever your lineage, we all share in the heritage from the medieval world of Piers Ploughman.

The poem deals with the greatest of themes: the meaning of our life on earth in relation to our ultimate destiny. Like Dante's *Divine Comedy* and Milton's *Paradise Lost, Piers Plowman* develops a Christian worldview that explains and justifies the ways of God to mortals. It does this through allegory, a common medieval literary technique. In allegory characters come to stand for basic concepts, and often, as in this poem, they are named accordingly. Piers Ploughman represents the common man, a kind of "everyman." He is appropriately named in a society where most people earn their bread through tilling the soil. Other characters also personify important realities and values such as the characters Truth or Hunger, or Piers' wife, Dame Work-While-You've-A-Chance.

As you read, again note the extent to which the medieval worldview borrowed heavily from Plato. There are two worlds: the world of a harsh physical reality and the sought-after spiritual world. Piers and his compatriots struggle in a cruel world of limited material abundance and hard labor, with Hunger always standing by. This is the world of suffering that humankind was condemned to in the book of Genesis. In this hard world tough laws of nature are enforced by Hunger, and there are also rules and obligations enforced by a social order.

Piers lived in an agricultural society which was organized into a social order known as feudalism. Feudalism bound people into an organic whole through a hierarchical set of personal relationships that allowed the local community to function as one body. At the bottom of the hierarchy were the peasants who tilled the soil and pledged to their own lords services and a portion of their crops. The overlords, represented in *Piers Plough-man* by the knight, pledged to their peasants both protection against the outside world and a system of justice within the community. Feudal society fragmented Europe into thousands of small, local centers of power and was economically stagnant. By the sixteenth century it was being superseded by the increasing power of the new urban bourgeoisie and by the growing power of a centralized authority, the king.

Piers' organic society, like Plato's *Republic,* strives toward a higher ideal. The higher ideal is symbolized by the pilgrimage. After he is old and gray and has met the challenge of physical survival, Piers prepares to leave on pilgrimage. This represents the spiritual journey that medieval people believed life to be about. Hope is not to be found in the material world of pain and suffering. Hope is otherworldly. Our time within the material world will pass, and if we spend our time well, we can hope for an eternity in the enduring spiritual world.

It should be obvious that this view of the world does not lead to dramatic change. It teaches us to accept the material world as it is and to look to heaven for progress. As you will see, it is not until new ideas begin to challenge the values expressed here by Langland that the modern world will be born.

William Langland

Piers Sets the World to Work

The story. *Piers offers to go with the pilgrims himself, on condition that they first help him to sow his field. They agree to do so, and after setting them all to work, Piers makes his will in preparation for the pilgrimage. The work in the field goes well until Piers finds some of the men shirking. He tries to make them work, but they defy him, and he is forced to call up Hunger to punish them. Hunger chastises them soundly, they all return to work eagerly, and at last produce enough food to put Hunger to sleep. Then the men relapse into idleness.*

Then the people complained to Piers and said, 'This is a grim way you've described to us. We should need a guide for every step of the road.'

'Now look,' said Piers the Ploughman, 'I have half an acre of land here by the highway. Once I can get it ploughed and sown, I will go with you and show you the way myself.'

'We should have a long time to wait,' said a veiled lady. 'What work could we women be doing to pass the time?'

'Why, some of you can sew up the sacks,' said Piers, 'to keep the seed from spilling. And you fair ladies with slender fingers — you have plenty of silks and fine stuffs to sew. Make some vestments for priests, while you've got the time, and lend a hand in beautifying the churches. And those of you who are married or widows can spin flax and make some cloth, and teach your daughters to do it too. For Truth commands us to take care of the needy and clothe the naked. I'll give them food myself, so long as the harvest doesn't fail. For I don't mind working all my life for the love of God, to provide meat and bread for rich and poor.

'So come along now, all you men who live by food and drink — lend a hand to the man who provides you with it, and we will finish the job quickly.'

'By Heavens!' said a knight, 'this fellow knows what's good for us! But to tell the truth, I've never handled a team of oxen. Give me a lesson, Piers, and I'll do my best, by God!'

'That's a fair offer,' said Piers. 'And for my part, I'll sweat and toil for us both as long as I live, and gladly do any job you want. But you must promise in return to guard over Holy Church, and protect me from the thieves and wasters who ruin the world. And you'll have to hunt down all the hares and foxes and boars and badgers that break down my hedges, and tame falcons to kill the wild birds that crop my wheat.'

Then the knight answered courteously and said, 'I give you my word, Piers, as I am a true knight; and I'll keep this promise through thick and thin and protect you to the end of my days.'

'Ah, but there's one thing more I must ask you,' said Piers. 'Never ill-treat your tenants, and see that you punish them only when Truth compels you to — even then, let Mercy assess the fine, and be ruled by Meekness, and at all costs have no truck with Fee. And if poor men offer you gifts, don't ever accept them — it may be that you do not deserve them, and will have to pay them all back at the year's end, in a perilous place called Purgatory!

'And take care also that you never ill-use your serfs. It will be better for you in the long run, for though they are your underlings here on earth, they may be above you in Heaven, in greater happiness, unless you lead a better life than they do. For Our Lord said: "When thou art bidden, go and sit down in the lowest room; that when he that bade thee cometh, he may say unto thee, Friend, go up higher." And it is very hard to tell a knight from a serf when he comes to lie in the church-vaults — so lay that to heart.

'And you must always speak the truth, and show contempt for all tales that are told you, except such as are wise, and apt for rebuking your workmen. Have nothing to do with jesters and don't listen to their tattle, least of all when you sit at meals in your hall. For believe me, they are the Devil's minstrels!'

'Now, by St James,' the knight answered, 'I'll abide by your words for ever.'

'Then I will dress as a pilgrim,' said Piers, 'and go with you till we find Truth. I will put on my working clothes, all darned and patched, my leggings, and my old gloves to keep my fingers warm; and I'll hang my hopper around my neck for a scrip, with a bushel of rye inside. And then, when I have sown my seed, I will turn palmer, and go on a pilgrim-age to gain a pardon.

'And those who help me to plough and sow before I set out, shall have leave to glean here in harvest-time, and make merry with what they can get, no matter what people say. And I will provide food for men of all trades, so long as they are faithful and honest. — But there'll be none for Jack the juggler or Janet from the stews, none for Daniel the dice-player or Doll the Whore, nor Friar Rogue nor any of his Order, nor Robin the ribald with his bawdy jokes. For Truth once told me to have no deal-ings with such men — "Let them be blotted out of the book of the living" — and so He bade me tell others. Holy Church is forbidden so much as to take tithes from them, for the Scripture says: "Let them not be writ-ten with the righteous." And they get off lightly at that, God help them!'

Now Piers' wife was called Dame *Work-while-you've-got-a-chance,* his daugh-ter was called *Do-as-you're-told-or-you'll-get-a-good-hiding,* and his son's name was *Always-give-way-to-your-elders-and-don't-contradict-or-maybe-you'll-wish-you-hadn't.*

Then Piers turned to his wife and children, saying, 'May God be with you all, as His word teaches. For now that I am old and grey, and have enough to live on, I am going away with these folk on a pilgrimage, to do penance. So before I go, I will have my will written: —

Piers' Will. 'In the name of God, Amen. I, Piers, make this will myself. My soul shall go to Him who has best deserved it, and He shall, I trust, defend it from the Devil till I come to the day of reckoning, as my Creed tells me. And then I shall have a release and a remission from all the rent I owe on it.

'The Church shall have my flesh and shall keep my bones. For the parish priest took his tithe of my corn and earnings, and for my soul's sake I always paid it promptly; so he is bound, I hope, to remember me in his Mass, when he prays for all Christians.

'My wife shall have what I've earned by honest toil alone; and she shall share it among my daughters and my dear children. For though I should die this very day, my debts are all paid, and I've always returned what I've borrowed, before going to bed.

'And now I swear by the Holy Rood of Lucca to devote all that is left to the worship of Truth, and to serve Him for the rest of my life. And I will be His pilgrim, following the plough for poor men's sake; and my plough-shoe shall be my pike-staff, to cleave through the roots, and help my coulter to cut and cleanse the furrows.'

And now Piers and his pilgrims have gone to the plough, and many folk are helping him to till his half acre. Ditchers and diggers are turning up the headlands, and others, to please Peter, are hoeing up the weeds, while he is delighted with their labours and quick to praise them. They are all eager to work, and every man finds something useful to do.

Then at nine o'clock in the morning Piers left his plough in order to see how things were going, and pick out the best workers to hire again at harvest-time. At this, some of them sat down to drink their ale and sing songs — thinking to plough his field with a *'Hey-nonny-nonny'*!

'By the Lord!' said Piers, bursting with rage, 'Get up and go back to your work at once — or you'll get no bread to sing about when famine comes. You can starve to death, and to hell with the lot of you!'

Then the shirkers were scared, and pretended to be blind, or twisted their legs askew, as these beggars can, moaning and whining to Piers to have pity on them. — 'We're sorry, master, but we've no limbs to work with. But we'll pray for you, Piers — God bless you, sir, and may God in His goodness multiply your grain, and reward you for the charity you give us here. For we're so racked with pain, we can't lift a finger.'

'I shall soon see if what you say is true,' said Piers. 'But I know quite well you are shirking — you can't get away from Truth. I'm an old servant of His, and I've promised to keep an eye open for folk in the world who wrong His workmen, and warn Him about them. You are the men who waste the food that others sweat for. Still, Truth will soon teach you to drive His oxen — or you'll be eating barley-bread and drinking from the stream!

'If anyone is really blind or crippled, or has his limbs bolted with irons, he shall eat wheaten bread and drink at my table, till God in His goodness sends him better days. But as for you, you could work for Truth well enough if you wanted: you could earn your food and wages by herding cattle or keeping the beasts from the corn, or ditch or dig or thresh away at the sheaves; or you could help mix mortar or cart muck to the field. The fact is you would rather have a life of lechery, lying, and sloth, and it is only through God's mercy that you go unpunished.

'No, I would rather give my earnings to hermits and anchorites, who eat nothing from one noon to the next; and those who have cloisters and churches to maintain—I'm quite willing to keep them in clothes. But Robert Runabout will get nothing from me, nor the wandering preachers, unless they know how to preach, and have the Bishop's licence. And if that is so, they can make themselves at home, and I'll give them bread and soup—for even an Apostle can't live on air!'

Then one of the vagabonds lost his temper with Piers, flung out a challenge and squared up for a fight. And a blustering Frenchman shouted out, 'Go and stuff your plough, you stingy old scoundrel! We'll do as we please—you can take it or leave it. We shall fetch as much of your flour and meat as we want, and make a feast with it—so you go and hang yourself!'

Then Piers the Ploughman begged the knight to keep his promise, and protect him from these damned villains, the wolves who rob the world of its food. 'For while they devour it all,' he said, 'and produce nothing themselves, there will never be plenty for the people. And meanwhile my plough lies idle.'

So the knight, who was courteous by nature, spoke kindly to Waster, and warned him to mend his ways—'or, by my Order of Knighthood,' he said, 'I shall bring you to justice.'

'I have never worked yet,' said Waster, 'and I don't intend to start now' —and he began to jeer at the Law and rail at the knight, and told Piers to go and piddle with his plough, for he'd beat him up if ever they met again.

'By God!' said Piers, 'I'll teach you all a lesson!' And with that he holloed out for Hunger; and Hunger heard him at once and started up. 'Avenge me on these wretches who eat up the world,' cried Piers.

Then Hunger leapt at Waster and seized him by the belly, wringing his guts till the water ran from his eyes. And he gave the Frenchman such a drubbing that he looked as lean as a rake for the rest of his life. He pasted them so soundly that he almost broke their ribs; and if Piers hadn't offered Hunger a pease-loaf and besought him to leave off, by now they'd both be pushing up the daisies! 'Spare their lives,' said Piers, 'and let them eat with the hogs and have bean and bran swill, or milk and thin ale.'

Then these rogues fled in terror to the barns, and threshed away with their flails from morning till night; and Hunger did not dare to molest them, because Piers had made them a pot of pease-pudding. And a crowd of hermits, cutting their cloaks to make jerkins and seizing some tools, went to work with spades and shovels, and dug and ditched like mad to stave off Hunger. Then thousands of blind and bed-ridden folk suddenly recovered, and men who used to sit begging for silver were miraculously cured! And the starving people appeased their hunger with bran-mash, and beggars and poor men worked gladly with peas for wages, pouncing like sparrowhawks on any work that Piers gave them. And Piers was proud of his success, and he set them all to work, giving them a fair wage and as much food as he could spare.

Then Piers took pity on the people, and begged Hunger to go home and stay in his own country. 'For thanks to you,' he said, 'I am well avenged on these wastrels.—But before you go, there's one thing I would like to ask you. What is the best thing to do with beggars and loafers? Once you've gone, I know quite well they will start slacking again. It is only their misery that makes them so submissive, and famine which has put them in my power. Yet they are truly my blood-brothers,' said Piers, 'for Christ redeemed us all, and Truth once taught me to love all men alike and give freely to everyone in need. So I should like you to tell me what would be best, and advise me as to how to control them and make them work.'

'Listen then,' said Hunger, 'and mark my words. The big tough beggars who are capable of hard work, you can keep alive with horse-bread and dog-biscuits, and bring their weight down with a diet of beans—that will flatten their bellies! And if they grumble, tell them to go and work, and they'll get tastier suppers when they've earned them.

'But if you find a man who has fallen on evil days or been ruined by swindlers, for the love of Christ do your best to relieve him. You must seek out such folk and give them alms, and love them, as the law of God teaches—"Bear ye one another's burdens, and so ye shall fulfil the law of Christ." So give all you can spare to those who are penniless—show them charity and do not reproach them; leave God to punish them if they have done wrong—"Vengeance is mine; I will repay, said the Lord." For if you wish to find favour with God, you must obey the Gospel, and make yourself beloved among humble folk—"Make to yourselves friends of the mammon of unrighteousness"—and then God will reward you.'

'I would not offend God for all the world,' said Piers. 'Are you sure I can treat the shirkers as you say, without committing a sin?'

'Yes, I assure you,' said Hunger, 'or else the Bible is wrong. Ask the giant Genesis, the begetter of all men: "In the sweat of thy brow," he says, "shalt thou eat bread"—that is God's command. It says the same in the Book of Proverbs—

"The sluggard will not plow by reason of the cold:
therefore shall he beg in harvest, and have nothing."

And St Matthew, whose sign has a man's face, tells this parable: —There
was a worthless servant who had only one talent; and because he would
not work and trade with it, he lost his master's favour for evermore. And
his master took his talent away from him, and gave it to the one who
had ten, saying: "He that hath shall receive, and find help when he needs
it; but he that hath not shall receive nothing, and no one shall help him;
and I shall take away from him even that which he thinks he hath."

'It is common sense that every man must work, either by ditching and
digging, or by travailing in prayer — the active or the contemplative life —
for such is God's will. And according to Psalm 128, a man who lives by
his own honest labour is blessed in body and soul —

"For thou shalt eat the labours of thine hands:
O well is thee, and happy shalt thou be."'

'Thank you,' said Piers, 'and now, friend Hunger, if you have any
knowledge of medicine, I pray you, teach me it, for the love of God. For
I and a number of my servants have got such a belly-ache, that we've
been off work now for a whole week.'

'Ah! I know what's wrong with you,' said Hunger; 'you've been eating
too much — no wonder you are in such agonies. If you want to get better,
follow these instructions: never drink on an empty stomach, and never
eat till hunger pinches you and sends you some of his sharp sauce to whet
your appetite. And don't sit too long over dinner and spoil your supper;
always get up before you've eaten your fill. What is more, never allow
Sir Surfeit at your table — don't trust him, he's a great gourmand and
his guts are always crying out for more dishes.

'If you follow these instructions, I'll bet you the doctors will soon be
selling their ermine hoods and their fine cloaks of Calabrian fur with
gold tassels, to get themselves a square meal; and you'll see them gladly
giving up their medicine for farmwork to avoid starvation. For these doctors are mostly murderers, God help them! — their medicines kill thousands before their time.'

'By heaven!' said Piers. 'This is the best advice I've heard. And now,
Hunger, I know you must be anxious to go — so the best of luck, and
God reward you for all you have done for me.'

'Good gracious!' said Hunger, 'I'm not going yet — not until I've had
a square meal and something to drink.'

'I haven't a penny left,' said Piers, 'so I can't buy you pullets or geese or pigs. All I've got is a couple of fresh cheeses, a little curds and cream, an oat-cake, and two loaves of beans and bran which I baked for my children. Upon my soul, I haven't a scrap of bacon, and I haven't a cook to fry you steak and onions. But I've some parsley and shallots and plenty of cabbages, and a cow and a calf, and a mare to cart my dung, till the drought is over. And with these few things we must live till Lammas time, when I hope to reap a harvest in my fields. Then I can spread you a feast, as I'd really like to.'

Then all the poor folk came with peas-cods, and brought beans and baked apples by the lapful, and spring onions and chervils and hundreds of ripe cherries, and offered these gifts to Piers, to satisfy Hunger.

Hunger soon gobbled it all up and asked for more. So the poor folk were afraid, and quickly brought up supplies of green leeks and peas, and would gladly have poisoned him. But by that time the harvest was approaching, and new corn came to market. So the people took comfort, and fed Hunger royally — Glutton himself couldn't wish for better ale. And so they put him to sleep.

And then Waster would not work any more, but set out as a tramp. And the beggars refused the bread that had beans in it, demanding milk loaves and fine white wheaten bread. And they would not drink cheap beer at any price, but only the best brown ale that is sold in the towns.

And the day-labourers, who have no land to live on but their shovels, would not deign to eat yesterday's vegetables. And draught-ale was not good enough for them, nor a hunk of bacon, but they must have fresh meat or fish, fried or baked and *chaud* or *plus chaud* at that, lest they catch a chill on their stomachs!

And so it is nowadays — the labourer is angry unless he gets high wages, and he curses the day that he was ever born a workman. And he won't listen to wise Cato's advice — 'Bear the burden of poverty patiently.' But he blames God, and murmurs against Reason, and curses the king and his Council for making Statutes on purpose to plague the workmen! — Yet none of them ever complained while Hunger was their master, nor quarrelled with *his* Statutes, he had such a fierce look about him.

But I warn you labourers, work while you have the chance, for Hunger is coming fast, and shall awake with the floods to deal justice on wastrels. And before five years have passed, a famine shall arise, and floods and tempests shall destroy the fruits of the earth. For so Saturn had predicted, and has sent you this warning: *When you see the sun awry and two monks' heads in the Heavens — when a Maiden has magical power, then multiply by eight — the Black Death shall withdraw, and Famine shall judge the world, and Davy the ditcher shall die of hunger — unless God, in His mercy, grants us all a truce.*

IIB. The Conceptual Foundations of Modern Work

Every age has its story, its worldview, a paradigm which guides the lives of the people who embody a given culture at a given time. There are, of course, many versions of the founding story of an age, as we have just seen in our brief glimpse of the medieval period. Furthermore, as we saw in the discrepancies between official Catholic doctrine and actual economic life, a perfect match never exists between the stories people tell and what actually occurs. Such stories, after all, are more moral ideals than they are historical descriptions. Nevertheless, one of the best ways to comprehend the contours and tenor of an age is to examine its basic myths.

We turn now to look at the story that guides modern life — the founding paradigm of modernism. One way to determine the extent to which this 350-year-old myth is still with us is to ask yourself if and when you have heard versions of it. Probably you have never heard the story told in the articulate or thorough fashion you are about to hear it (that is the job of great thinkers like those you are about to read), but you probably have heard shortened versions of it in history books, in the speeches of politicians, in arguments about important issues, in music, and perhaps most of all in talk about modern material achievements.

Although he was an Englishman writing fully a century and a half before the founding of the American Republic, probably no thinker had as profound an impact on the minds of the late eighteenth-century architects of the American system as John Locke. In his 1689 essay *The Second Treatise of Government* Locke brilliantly put to paper the myth which both described and sanctified the transition from the old, medieval order to liberal, capitalist societies.

Like any philosophical writing, *The Second Treatise* was created to solve a problem. As we saw in the preceding subsection, the values and rules inherent in the medieval system prohibited many of the kinds of activities which are crucial to begin and operate a modern market system. Locke's genius was to propose a rationale for circumventing these limitations while seeming to respect and maintain the very values he undermined. His main tool was a story, a myth, which continues to live in and justify contemporary liberal democracies.

Locke's familiar tale goes like this: humans once lived without rules and laws, in an idyllic world of plenty. In this "state of nature" (Locke's phrase for this paradise) people did what they pleased without the need of governance, *and* they were blessed with the natural (God-given) rights to life, liberty, and property. No one could infringe on another's natural rights unless that person first abrogated her (or his) right. At first "frontier justice" was a satisfactory way to resolve disputes and redress wrongdoing when someone infringed on another's basic right. But as the population increased and more altercations occurred, people were faced with the grave dangers that come with escalating conflicts — Locke's "state of war." To avoid this awful disintegration of the state of nature, Locke's story says that humans decided to construct a compromise, a latter-day halfway house between his Eden (state of nature) and the ultimate hell of the fall (state of war): humans chose (should choose) to build limited governments which prevent the state of war while simultaneously preserving the fundamental rights which no society should transgress. Limited democracy which preserves the peace while respecting natural rights is not only *ideal* (that is, the best we can do under the circumstances), but it is the *only* justifiable form of government.

Like many seminal myths, this tale has an element of factual plausibility: it is likely that people once lived with few conflicts or at least without real warfare and that as human numbers increased, the conflicts between people worsened. Warfare is a civilized activity, after all. Notice the central feature of the myth to this point — paradise is living without government, without rules and regulations, and in relative isolation. *Any* community structures are going to be worse than none at all *except* insofar as they prevent a decline into chaos. This story nicely captures a vein running through our thinking about governmental and other regulations — in America we distrust any authority and only tolerate someone telling us what to do as the lesser of two evils.

The second feature of the state of nature is as important as the first — we are not only best off when totally unbridled, but we also have presocial rights which no one has any right to harm unless we first do something wrong to them. Thus, no governmental structure is justifiable except one which guarantees that no other person, *or the government itself,* will infringe on our God-given rights. People who live out this myth, as we do, never fully trust government; however, at the same time we need a strong government to protect our rights. We believe that "the government which governs least is the government which governs best"; and we also believe government should have a strong criminal justice system and a strong military.

The next crucial step in Locke's story is to establish the nearly absolute right to private property. Basic to all human rights is the sanctity of the person: our rights are justified and recognized because without them something central to personhood is demeaned. Locke agrees with the medieval tradition in judging that personhood is so precious that even we have no right to end our own lives or to sell ourselves into slavery. But we must distinguish, he says, suicide and enslavement from working and producing, and from selling our labor and its products. When we *work* we are doing what God desires (remember, in the Christian tradition our talents are to be developed and exercised), and, furthermore, while we cannot alienate our selves (sell or even kill our selves), we can alienate our labor (sell our labor for *wages*). Wage labor, in fact, not only is allowable in Locke's system: it becomes a highest value. Whereas in the medieval world wage labor was a second-rate way of making a living, for moderns working for wages is necessary and quite virtuous because only through human labor does value come into the world (his famous "labor theory of value").

Locke's view is that the natural world is not worth much until people do something with it ("develop" it, transform it into something *useful*). (Notice the contrast with the medieval world, where nature is holy because God made it.) In a system of wage labor we not only can avoid the medieval problem of spoilage (money does not spoil like grain or meat), but we can produce much more overall value (wealth) if we allow for capital accumulation in the hands of a few and let them return some of the value back to the laborers in the form of wages. In this system both capitalists and workers are better off, and this well-being is based on *private ownership of property*.

The rest of Locke's system flows naturally from this seemingly innocuous beginning. Some people, through luck, talent, and/or hard work, will accumulate more than others, but they should be allowed (in fact, encouraged) to become rich because then everyone is better off . . . provided no one is left with nothing. Beginning with a radical equality of rights, Locke concludes by justifying a dramatic inequality of wealth, power, and political enfranchisement based on differences in "natural endowment" (women and people of color are like children in lacking *full rationality*, the crucial ability necessary to handle the responsibilities of ownership) or *character* (poor white men do not deserve wealth or full citizenship because they lack the proper desire to work).

Obviously Locke's little story is a tremendously powerful myth; you should be beginning to see that it provides many of the background values and assumptions to much of modern life. Even Marxism, which supposedly is contrary to capitalism, accepts many basic features of Locke's myth: for example, Marx's justification for the proletariat (worker's) revolution is based on his belief in the labor theory of value; he simply believes that the capitalist robs the workers of the true value their labor has created, and he wants the system to be just. This entire subsection revolves around the central images of Locke's story. The interplay between ideas and economic and social reality is complex and is very controversial among students of history. For us at the moment the value of this story is to expose the contours of our modern worldview. In the remainder of this subsection we will explore the parts in greater detail and then hold them up to critical scrutiny. Only by knowing from where we have come, how our world is put together, and critically examining it can we hope to think intelligently about our own current and future work.

Writing nearly a hundred years after Locke, Adam Smith in his *Wealth of Nations* spells out in great detail how Locke's story might operate in concrete economic life. While Locke was concerned mainly with political rights and governmental organization, Smith's focus was on the economic conditions of ordinary people. In the England of his day the promises of industrialization had not yet brought improved material conditions for most people. If anything, the eradication of most of the remnants of the feudal system increased human misery. Rather than decry the new order, though, Smith argued that only if industrialization is accompanied by true market capitalism will the promise of dramatically increased wealth be realized. For Smith this meant eradicating most limitations (except for outright theft and other clear crimes) on production and competition: it meant, in short, a free-market economic system.

The combination of Locke's social and political story with Smith's economic prescriptions helped transform the lives of workers from where most industry was done in the home to where most work was industrial, from a focus on social, ritual, and spiritual concerns where work is what you must do to survive to where work often became the center of spiritual as well as material existence, and from country life to life in the city. It is small wonder that Karl Polanyi, in his controversial book about the Industrial Revolution written in the 1930s, calls it "the great transformation"; for modern people, as well as the systems they inhabit, are very different from their medieval predecessors. Once you achieve an initial understanding of the "founding story" by studying Locke and Smith, we hope to enrich your understanding by exploring further dimensions and criticisms of this story.

We begin this task of elaboration in Part 2 of this subsection with the role of religion. In the Middle Ages there is little separation of church and state: religious concerns, and the church itself, permeate nearly every dimension of medieval life. Modern liberal societies, in contrast, are founded on the separation of church and state. Yet modernism could not be as it is without the central role played by religion. The waning of the Catholic Church did not signal the disappearance of religion. Instead, religion, like the society itself, was transformed. Beginning with Martin Luther's Protestant Reformation in 1517, over several centuries the Christian church and its doctrines were reformed in such a way that they became amenable to the conceptual and moral alterations of Catholic doctrine necessary for Locke's story to be acceptable. The two selections in Part B attempt to describe this radical transformation in belief and in human character that helped bring about the "great transformation" of the entire culture.

R.H. Tawney, like his more famous predecessor Max Weber (*The Protestant Ethic and the Spirit of Capitalism*), sought to show that Protestantism, and in particular one version of Puritanism, is compatible with a world where material accumulation is not only tolerated but becomes a major virtue, and also that this new religion is a wellspring of this new order. In his *Religion and the Rise of Capitalism* Tawney shows that a distortion of Puritanism was necessary and that the marriage of spiritual salvation with material success was never an easy one. Nevertheless, through some twists of logic the Puritan's original focus on spiritual salvation becomes an emphasis on material success.

Tawney shares with Weber a belief that Calvinism (Puritanism) was a major promoter of the work ethic which was essential to the rise of modern market economies. He sees the essence of this Puritanism to be a fanatical single-mindedness. The Puritan stands at the opposite end of the spectrum from the classical Greeks who believed in proportion and who believed that nothing should be pursued to excess. The hallmark of Calvinism, on the other hand, is narrow obsession.

Why is this true, and what does it have to do with the rise of capitalism? As Tawney explains, their belief in predestination causes Puritans to reject any role for church or society in helping the individual attain salvation. Because God simply chooses or rejects us, all we can do is await His call. For most people He will never come. Even if He chooses us, we must endure a lonely wait, focused on only one event, the moment of salvation. The hallmark of Calvinist theology, according to Tawney, is the focus on a slender chain of logical events and fanatical adherence to this chain. The Puritan's job is to prepare for the moment of salvation; how is s/he to do this?

Tawney explains it this way:

> since conduct and action, though availing nothing to attain the free gift of salvation, are proof that the gift has been accorded, what is rejected as a means is resumed as a consequence, and the Puritan flings himself into practical activities with the daemonic energy of one who, all doubts

allayed, is conscious that he is a sealed and chosen vessel. In other words, the logic of his situation leads him to prove his salvation by displaying those single-minded work virtues that are a sign of grace.

Our second selection in this part explores the psychologic of this world-view to its lonely, bitter end. Nathaniel Hawthorne was not only one of America's greatest early writers, but he was also among the most insightful students of the American psyche. In his "Young Goodman Brown" Hawthorne creates an allegory about what it is like to live on the inside of the perspective Tawney is describing from the outside. You will be captivated and probably appalled by Brown's character, but do not lose sight of Hawthorne's and Tawney's points: this Puritan character is part of the American character, and it often lives in how many of us work.

While Tawney's and Hawthorne's descriptions of one version of the Protestant (Puritan) work ethic contain implicit criticisms of the lives and psyches of the characters they illuminate, we come, finally, in Part 3 to two outright critiques of modern liberal societies. Karl Marx's criticism is telling partly because he accepts certain key elements of the modernist philosophy, and thus he writes as an insider, often taking key ideas from Locke or Smith and following their logic where good capitalists or liberal democrats do not want to go. As we mentioned earlier, Marx accepts Locke's labor theory of value and then rejects capitalism because in capitalism much of the value workers produce remains in the pockets of the employers rather than being fairly distributed to those who created it. To Marx this is just plain theft.

Marx's famous chapter on alienated labor included in this section builds on his critique of the literal theft of wealth in capitalism to illuminate deeper and more crippling ways industrial capitalism steals from workers. 'Alienation' is his word to sum up and point to a complex personal/social/cultural phenomenon of modern life wherein what workers have stolen from them are their opportunities to thrive as persons and to live in healthy communities.

In the second selection in Part 3 literary artist Flannery O'Connor takes a different, but brutally honest, look at the flaws in Locke and Smith's world. Her concern is, not so much with the material hypocrisy Marx finds between the initial mythical equality and the actual dramatic inequalities of wealth, power, and meaning of life people in capitalist industrial societies experience, but with the spiritual hypocrisy of modern life. For her modernism is a godless world with no ultimate purposes; instead, it is based on competition, greed, and accumulation. She would prefer a moral universe such as the medieval world wherein her favored Catholicism flourished, but if people are going to choose the modern world, she believes they should do so honestly. Throughout her writings O'Connor complains that most modern people are unwilling to accept the world they have chosen. Instead, they operate according to the logic of cut-throat materialism while simultaneously espousing higher moral purposes — such as Smith's hidden hand, the trickle-down theory of economic justice, manifest destiny, Social Darwinism, or many other hypocritical theories that pretend a moral universe — and practicing the amoral world of business as usual.

This section begins with clear and powerful statements of the modern myth and ends with some equally powerful critiques of that myth and its results. What are we to make of this contrast? Who is right? You do not have to, and indeed you should not yet, decide anything at this rather lofty level of abstraction. The next subsection is meant to provide you with much more of the story, this time with an emphasis on the concrete history of working in modern America. As you examine these new pieces of evidence bear in mind, though, that the issues raised in Part B are fundamental to our lives as workers and as humans. We cannot escape them, but we cannot resolve them without the careful historical analysis of Part C and the hard debate and imaginative thinking you will find in Section III.

1. The Founding Story: A New Paradigm

Introduction
John Locke, from *Second Treatise of Government*

John Locke was born into a middle-class Puritan family in 1632. He was to live through one of the most exciting and politically important periods in English history, and as a political activist, but even more as a writer and thinker, he would greatly influence the long-term outcome of events.

Locke was a child during the English civil war, and his father fought against the king. Later Locke would champion the rebellion against the ruling monarchy during the "Glorious Revolution" of 1688. Ostensibly the war was a religious struggle between proto-Catholics and Puritans, but there was a deeper issue that became more overt in the aftermath of the war — a class struggle. The Puritans were drawn from the new business class, while the king and aristocracy represented the feudal system.

Locke's initial interests were in philosophy, although he later developed an equally strong fascination with science. He became a skilled physician and also made important contributions to scientific theory and psychology. Our concern is with Locke the political and social philosopher, however, for his great legacy is his story about how we should reform society.

Like any of us, Locke was a creature of the times in which he lived. As a child of a partisan of the parliamentary party, and later as an aide to the leader of the Whig party, it is not surprising that Locke would be committed to the new middle class and the antimonarchical party. But while he is a creature of this world, he is also to considerable degree a creator. Locke sets out to defend and justify the "Glorious Revolution," and in so doing he lays the foundation for the modern Western system of government and way of life. More than any theoretician, Locke helps invent liberal democracies.

The medieval world was dying. A new world, led by the entrepreneurial middle class, was being born. Locke fashioned the new mythology to support the new order. His story sanctions one particular kind of government (and, as we shall see, a certain kind of economy as well) to the exclusion of others. In his *First Treatise of Government* Locke argued for the rejection of monarchy: essentially he argued that kings have no divine right to their thrones. The *Second Treatise* shows that they have no right of any kind to rule. In premodern European monarchies kings and queens made the rules and determined who would benefit and in what ways. They ruled over hierarchical systems wherein some people had far more rights and privileges than others, and many people had few rights at all. Basic human dignity and equality were not essential to medieval monarchies. For Locke, at least initially, equality of human rights *is* fundamental; thus monarchies are not justifiable.

Feudalism as an economic system went hand in hand with medieval monarchies. In feudalism, while commoners had no right to private property as we know it, they did have the inherited right to the use of land in exchange for rents and services-in-kind to their feudal overlords. While they had the right to use, they did not have the right to misuse or abuse the land or to waste resources. Built into the system were limitations on human greed and wealth: medieval economic life was a moral as well as a social and political system. Locke's story argues that the old order is unjustifiable from the point of view of human rights that are built into the nature of things. Yet he also maintains that we must adhere to the moral limits of the medieval worldview. How is this juggling act possible?

Humans have not only a natural right to life and to liberty, but according to this story their right to private property is also fundamental. From the first two rights we see that in themselves humans are valuable;

thus it is wrong to kill humans unjustifiably, and, further, it is wrong to limit most human activities without some very good reasons. But property is something distinct from us. How can it deserve the same valuation as life or liberty? Essentially Locke's argument is that property is an extension of humans. Private property is created when a person mixes her or his labor with it. This is Locke's famous Labor Theory of Value: if someone produces something, then it is his because he has put some part of himself into it.

Thus labor is the critical element in making property into a third basic right. However, there is a difference with labor. While you do not have the right to give up your life or your liberty, you do, according to Locke, have the right to "alienate" your labor and the products of your labor: both can be sold. Wage labor is a critical feature of Locke's system and of the capitalist system that is its outgrowth.

As you read the rest of Locke's story, you will see that he is able to use this beginning to justify actions that were considered unethical in the medieval system, such as the massive accumulation of wealth and the rejection of charity as a social responsibility. Obviously Locke's story is a powerful myth; as we shall see, it helps provide the background assumptions to much of modern life. Even Marxism, which supposedly is contrary to capitalism, accepts many of the basic features of Locke's story, such as the labor theory of value. This entire subsection revolves around the central images to which Locke gave words 350 years ago. Locke's story is truly *the founding story* of the modern world.

John Locke

Of Property

25. Whether we consider natural reason, which tells us that men, being once born, have a right to their preservation, and consequently to meat and drink and such other things as nature affords for their subsistence; or revelation, which gives us an account of those grants God made of the world to Adam, and to Noah and his sons; it is very clear that God, as King David says (Psalm cxv. 16), "has given the earth to the children of men," given it to mankind in common. But this being supposed, it seems to some a very great difficulty how any one should ever come to have a property in anything. I will not content myself to answer

that if it be difficult to make out property upon a supposition that God gave the world to Adam and his posterity in common, it is impossible that any man but one universal monarch should have any property upon a supposition that God gave the world to Adam and his heirs in succession, exclusive of all the rest of his posterity. But I shall endeavor to show how men might come to have a property in several parts of that which God gave to mankind in common, and that without any express compact of all the commoners.

26. God, who has given the world to men in common, has also given them reason to make use of it to the best advantage of life and convenience. The earth and all that is therein is given to men for the support and comfort of their being. And though all the fruits it naturally produces and beasts it feeds belong to mankind in common, as they are produced by the spontaneous hand of nature; and nobody has originally a private dominion exclusive of the rest of mankind in any of them, as they are thus in their natural state; yet, being given for the use of men, there must of necessity be a means to appropriate them some way or other before they can be of any use or at all beneficial to any particular man. The fruit or venison which nourishes the wild Indian, who knows no enclosure and is still a tenant in common, must be his, and so his, i.e., a part of him, that another can no longer have any right to it before it can do him any good for the support of his life.

27. Though the earth and all inferior creatures be common to all men, yet every man has a property in his own person; this nobody has any right to but himself. The labor of his body and the work of his hands, we may say, are properly his. Whatsoever then he removes out of the state that nature has provided and left it in, he has mixed his labor with, and joined to it something that is his own, and thereby makes it his property. It being by him removed from the common state nature has placed it in, it has by this labor something annexed to it that excludes the common right of other men. For this labor being the unquestionable property of the laborer, no man but he can have a right to what that is once joined to, at least where there is enough and as good left in common for others.

28. He that is nourished by the acorns he picked up under an oak, or the apples he gathered from the trees in the wood, has certainly appropriated them to himself. Nobody can deny but the nourishment is his. I ask, then, When did they begin to be his? When he digested or when he ate or when he boiled or when he brought them home? Or when he picked them up? And it is plain, if the first gathering made them not his, nothing else could. That labor put a distinction between them and common; that added something to them more than nature, the common

mother of all, had done; and so they became his private right. And will anyone say he had no right to those acorns or apples he thus appropriated because he had not the consent of all mankind to make them his? Was it a robbery thus to assume to himself what belonged to all in common? If such a consent as that was necessary, man had starved, notwithstanding the plenty God had given him. We see in commons, which remain so by compact, that it is the taking any part of what is common and removing it out of the state nature leaves it in which begins the property, without which the common is of no use. And the taking of this or that part does not depend on the express consent of all the commoners. Thus the grass my horse has bit, the turfs my servant has cut, and the ore I have digged in any place where I have a right to them in common with others, become my property without the assignation or consent of anybody. The labor that was mine, removing them out of that common state they were in, has fixed my property in them.

29. By making an explicit consent of every commoner necessary to any one's appropriating to himself any part of what is given in common, children or servants could not cut the meat which their father or master had provided for them in common without assigning to every one his peculiar part. Though the water running in the fountain be every one's, yet who can doubt but that in the pitcher is his only who drew it out? His labor has taken it out of the hands of nature where it was common and belonged equally to all her children, and has thereby appropriated it to himself.

30. Thus this law of reason makes the deer that Indian's who has killed it; it is allowed to be his goods who has bestowed his labor upon it, though before it was the common right of every one. And amongst those who are counted the civilized part of mankind, who have made and multiplied positive laws to determine property, this original law of nature, for the beginning of property in what was before common, still takes place; and by virtue thereof what fish any one catches in the ocean, that great and still remaining common of mankind, or what ambergris any one takes up here, is, by the labor that removes it out of that common state nature left it in, made his property who takes that pains about it. And even amongst us, the hare that anyone is hunting is thought his who pursues her during the chase; for, being a beast that is still looked upon as common and no man's private possession, whoever has employed so much labor about any of that kind as to find and pursue her has thereby removed her from the state of nature wherein she was common, and has begun a property.

31. It will perhaps be objected to this that "if gathering the acorns, or other fruits of the earth, etc., makes a right to them, then any one

may engross as much as he will." To which I answer: not so. The same law of nature that does by this means give us property does also bound that property, too. "God has given us all things richly" (I Tim. vi. 17), is the voice of reason confirmed by inspiration. But how far has he given it us? To enjoy. As much as any one can make use of to any advantage of life before it spoils, so much he may by his labor fix a property in; whatever is beyond this is more than his share and belongs to others. Nothing was made by God for man to spoil or destroy. And thus considering the plenty of natural provisions there was a long time in the world, and the few spenders, and to how small a part of that provision the industry of one man could extend itself and engross it to the prejudice of others, especially keeping within the bounds set by reason of what might serve for his use, there could be then little room for quarrels or contentions about property so established.

32. But the chief matter of property being now not the fruits of the earth and the beasts that subsist on it, but the earth itself, as that which takes in and carries with it all the rest, I think it is plain that property in that, too, is acquired as the former. As much land as a man tills, plants, improves, cultivates, and can use the product of, so much is his property. He by his labor does, as it were, enclose it from the common. Nor will it invalidate his right to say everybody else has an equal title to it, and therefore he cannot appropriate, he cannot enclose, without the consent of all his fellow commoners—all mankind. God, when he gave the world in common to all mankind, commanded man also to labor, and the penury of his condition required it of him. God and his reason commanded him to subdue the earth, i.e., improve it for the benefit of life, and therein lay out something upon it that was his own, his labor. He that in obedience to this command of God subdued, tilled, and sowed any part of it, thereby annexed to it something that was his property, which another had no title to, nor could without injury take from him.

33. Nor was this appropriation of any parcel of land by improving it any prejudice to any other man, since there was still enough and as good left, and more than the yet unprovided could use. So that, in effect, there was never the less left for others because of his enclosure for himself; for he that leaves as much as another can make use of does as good as take nothing at all. Nobody could think himself injured by the drinking of another man, though he took a good draught, who had a whole river of the same water left him to quench his thirst; and the case of land and water, where there is enough for both, is perfectly the same.

34. God gave the world to men in common; but since he gave it them for their benefit and the greatest conveniences of life they were capable to draw from it, it cannot be supposed he meant it should always remain

common and uncultivated. He gave it to the use of the industrious and rational — and labor was to be his title to it — not to the fancy or covetousness of the quarrelsome and contentious. He that had as good left for his improvement as was already taken up needed not complain, ought not to meddle with what was already improved by another's labor; if he did, it is plain he desired the benefit of another's pains which he had no right to, and not the ground which God had given him in common with others to labor on, and whereof there was as good left as that already possessed, and more than he knew what to do with, or his industry could reach to.

35. It is true, in land that is common in England or any other country where there are plenty of people under government who have money and commerce, no one can enclose or appropriate any part without the consent of all his fellow commoners; because this is left common by compact, i.e., by the law of the land, which is not to be violated. And though it be common in respect of some men, it is not so to all mankind, but is the joint property of this country or this parish. Besides, the remainder after such enclosure would not be as good to the rest of the commoners as the whole was when they could all make use of the whole; whereas in the beginning and first peopling of the great common of the world it was quite otherwise. The law man was under was rather for appropriating. God commanded, and his wants forced, him to labor. That was his property which could not be taken from him wherever he had fixed it. And hence subduing or cultivating the earth and having dominion, we see, are joined together. The one gave title to the other. So that God, by commanding to subdue, gave authority so far to appropriate; and the condition of human life which requires labor and material to work on necessarily introduces private possessions.

36. The measure of property nature has well set by the extent of men's labor and the conveniences of life. No man's labor could subdue or appropriate all, nor could his enjoyment consume more than a small part, so that it was impossible for any man, this way, to entrench upon the right of another, or acquire to himself a property to the prejudice of his neighbor, who would still have room for as good and as large a possession — after the other had taken out his — as before it was appropriated. This measure did confine every man's possession to a very moderate proportion, and such as he might appropriate to himself without injury to anybody, in the first ages of the world, when men were more in danger to be lost by wandering from their company in the then vast wilderness of the earth than to be straitened for want of room to plant in. And the same measure may be allowed still without prejudice to anybody, as full as the world seems; for supposing a man or family in the state they were

at first peopling of the world by the children of Adam or Noah, let him plant in some inland, vacant places of America; we shall find that the possessions he could make himself, upon the measures we have given, would not be very large, nor, even to this day, prejudice the rest of mankind, or give them reason to complain or think themselves injured by this man's encroachment, though the race of men have now spread themselves to all the corners of the world and do infinitely exceed the small number which was at the beginning. Nay, the extent of ground is of so little value without labor that I have heard it affirmed that in Spain itself a man may be permitted to plough, sow, and reap, without being disturbed, upon land he has no other title to but only his making use of it. But, on the contrary, the inhabitants think themselves beholden to him who by his industry on neglected and consequently waste land has increased the stock of corn which they wanted. But be this as it will, which I lay no stress on, this I dare boldly affirm — that the same rule of property, viz., that very man should have as much as he could make use of, would hold still in the world without straitening anybody, since there is land enough in the world to suffice double the inhabitants, had not the invention of money and the tacit agreement of men to put a value on it introduced — by consent — larger possessions and a right to them; which, how it has done, I shall by-and-by show more at large.

37. This is certain, that in the beginning, before the desire of having more than man needed had altered the intrinsic value of things which depends only on their usefulness to the life of man, or had agreed that a little piece of yellow metal which would keep without wasting or decay should be worth a great piece of flesh or a whole heap of corn, though men had a right to appropriate, by their labor, each one to himself as much of the things of nature as he could use, yet this could not be much, nor to the prejudice of others, where the same plenty was still left to those who would use the same industry. To which let me add that he who appropriates land to himself by his labor does not lessen but increase the common stock of mankind; for the provisions serving to the support of human life produced by one acre of enclosed and cultivated land are — to speak much within compass — ten times more than those which are yielded by an acre of land of an equal richness lying waste in common. And therefore he that encloses land, and has a greater plenty of the conveniences of life from ten acres than he could have from a hundred left to nature, may truly be said to give ninety acres to mankind; for his labor now supplies him with provisions out of ten acres which were by the product of a hundred lying in common. I have here rated the improved land very low in making its product but as ten to one, when it is much nearer a hundred to one; for I ask whether in the wild woods and uncultivated

waste of America, left to nature, without any improvement, tillage, or husbandry, a thousand acres yield the needy and wretched inhabitants as many conveniences of life as ten acres of equally fertile land do in Devonshire, where they are well cultivated.

Before the appropriation of land, he who gathered as much of the wild fruit, killed, caught, or tamed as many of the beasts as he could; he that so employed his pains about any of the spontaneous products of nature as any way to alter them from the state which nature put them in, by placing any of his labor on them, did thereby acquire a propriety in them; but, if they perished in his possession without their due use, if the fruits rotted or the venison putrified before he could spend it, he offended against the common law of nature and was liable to be punished; he invaded his neighbor's share, for he had no right further than his use called for any of them and they might serve to afford him conveniences of life.

38. The same measures governed the possession of land, too: whatsoever he tilled and reaped, laid up and made use of before it spoiled, that was his peculiar right; whatsoever he enclosed and could feed and make use of, the cattle and product was also his. But if either the grass of his enclosure rotted on the ground, or the fruit of his planting perished without gathering and laying up, this part of the earth, notwithstanding his enclosure, was still to be looked on as waste and might be the possession of any other. Thus, at the beginning, Cain might take as much ground as he could till and make it his own land, and yet leave enough to Abel's sheep to feed on; a few acres would serve for both their possessions. But as families increased and industry enlarged their stocks, their possessions enlarged with the need of them; but yet it was commonly without any fixed property in the ground they made use of till they incorporated, settled themselves together, and built cities; and then, by consent, they came in time to set out the bounds of their distinct territories, and agree on limits between them and their neighbors, and by laws within themselves settled the properties of those of the same society; for we see that in that part of the world which was first inhabited, and therefore like to be best peopled, even as low down as Abraham's time they wandered with their flocks and their herds, which was their substance, freely up and down; and this Abraham did in a country where he was a stranger. Whence it is plain that at least a great part of the land lay in common, that the inhabitants valued it not, nor claimed property in any more than they made use of. But when there was not room enough in the same place for their herds to feed together, they, by consent, as Abraham and Lot did (Gen. xiii. 5), separated and enlarged their pasture where it best liked them. And for the same reason Esau went from his father and his brother and planted in Mount Seir (Gen. xxxvi. 6).

39. And thus, without supposing any private dominion and property in Adam over all the world exclusive of all other men, which can in no way be proven, nor any one's property be made out from it; but supposing the world given, as it was, to the children of men in common, we see how labor could make men distinct titles to several parcels of it for their private uses, wherein there could be no doubt of right, no room for quarrel.

40. Nor is it so strange, as perhaps before consideration it may appear, that the property of labor should be able to overbalance the community of land; for it is labor indeed that put the difference of value on everything; and let anyone consider what the difference is between an acre of land planted with tobacco or sugar, sown with wheat or barley, and an acre of the same land lying in common without any husbandry upon it, and he will find that the improvement of labor makes the far greater part of the value. I think it will be but a very modest computation to say that, of the products of the earth useful to the life of man, nine-tenths are the effects of labor; nay, if we will rightly estimate things as they come to our use and cast up the several expenses about them, what in them is purely owing to nature, and what to labor, we shall find that in most of them ninety-nine hundredths are wholly to be put on the account of labor.

41. There cannot be a clearer demonstration of anything than several nations of the Americans are of this, who are rich in land and poor in all the comforts of life; whom nature having furnished as liberally as any other people with the materials of plenty, i.e., a fruitful soil, apt to produce in abundance what might serve for food, raiment, and delight, yet for want of improving it by labor have not one-hundredth part of the conveniences we enjoy. And a king of a large and fruitful territory there feeds, lodges, and is clad worse than a day-laborer in England.

42. To make this a little clear, let us but trace some of the ordinary provisions of life through their several progresses before they come to our use and see how much of their value they receive from human industry. Bread, wine, and cloth are things of daily use and great plenty; yet, notwithstanding, acorns, water, and leaves, or skins must be our bread, drink, and clothing, did not labor furnish us with these more useful commodities; for whatever bread is more worth than acorns, wine than water, and cloth or silk than leaves, skins, or moss, that is wholly owing to labor and industry: the one of these being the food and raiment which unassisted nature furnishes us with; the other, provisions which our industry and pains prepare for us, which how much they exceed the other in value when anyone has computed, he will then see how much labor makes the far greatest part of the value of things we enjoy in this world. And the

ground which produces the materials is scarce to be reckoned in as any, or at most but a very small, part of it; so little that even amongst us land that is left wholly to nature, that has no improvement of pasturage, tillage, or planting, is called, as indeed it is, 'waste'; and we shall find the benefit of it amount to little more than nothing.

This shows how much numbers of men are to be preferred to largeness of dominions; and that the increase of lands and the right employing of them is the great art of government; and that prince who shall be so wise and godlike as by established laws of liberty to secure protection and encouragement to the honest industry of mankind, against the oppression of power and narrowness of party, will quickly be too hard for his neighbors; but this by the bye.

To return to the argument in hand.

43. An acre of land that bears here twenty bushels of wheat, and another in America which with the same husbandry would do the like, are, without doubt, of the same natural intrinsic value; but yet the benefit mankind receives from the one in a year is worth £5, and from the other possibly not worth a penny if all the profit an Indian received from it were to be valued and sold here; at least, I may truly say, not one-thousandth. It is labor, then, which puts the greatest part of the value upon land, without which it would scarcely be worth anything; it is to that we owe the greatest part of all its useful products; for all that the straw, bran, bread of that acre of wheat is more worth than the product of an acre of as good land which lies waste is all the effect of labor. For it is not barely the ploughman's pains, the reaper's and thresher's toil, and the baker's sweat [that] is to be counted into the bread we eat; the labor of those who broke the oxen, who digged and wrought the iron and stones, who felled and framed the timber employed about the plough, mill, oven, or any other utensils, which are a vast number requisite to this corn, from its being seed to be sown to its being made bread, must all be charged on the account of labor, and received as an effect of that; nature and the earth furnished only the almost worthless materials as in themselves. It would be a strange "catalogue of things that industry provided and made use of, about every loaf of bread" before it came to our use, if we could trace them: iron, wood, leather, bark, timber, stone, bricks, coals, lime, cloth, dyeing drugs, pitch, tar, masts, ropes, and all the materials made use of in the ship that brought any of the commodities used by any of the workmen to any part of the work; all which it would be almost impossible, at least too long, to reckon up.

44. From all which it is evident that, though the things of nature are given in common, yet man, by being master of himself and proprietor of his own person and the actions or labor of it, had still in himself the

great foundation of property; and that which made up the greater part of what he applied to the support or comfort of his being, when invention and arts had improved the conveniences of life, was perfectly his own and did not belong in common to others.

45. Thus labor, in the beginning, gave a right of property wherever anyone was pleased to employ it upon what was common, which remained a long while the far greater part and is yet more than mankind makes use of. Men, at first, for the most part contented themselves with what unassisted nature offered to their necessities; and though afterwards, in some parts of the world—where the increase of people and stock, with the use of money, had made land scarce and so of some value—the several communities settled the bounds of their distinct territories and, by laws within themselves, regulated the properties of the private men of their society, and so, by compact and agreement, settled the property which labor and industry began. And the leagues that have been made between several states and kingdoms either expressly or tacitly disowning all claim and right to the land in the others' possession have, by common consent, given up their pretenses to their natural common right which originally they had to those countries, and so have, by positive agreement, settled a property amongst themselves in distinct parts and parcels of the earth; yet there are still great tracts of ground to be found which—the inhabitants thereof not having joined with the rest of mankind in the consent of the use of their common money—lie waste, and are more than the people who dwell on it do or can make use of, and so still lie in common; though this can scarce happen amongst that part of mankind that have consented to the use of money.

46. The greatest part of things really useful to the life of man, and such as the necessity of subsisting made the first commoners of the world look after, as it does the Americans now, are generally things of short duration, such as, if they are not consumed by use, will decay and perish of themselves; gold, silver, and diamonds are things that fancy or agreement has put the value on, more than real use and the necessary support of life. Now of those good things which nature has provided in common, every one had a right, as has been said, to as much as he could use, and property in all that he could effect with his labor; all that his industry could extend to, to alter from the state nature had put it in, was his. He that gathered a hundred bushels of acorns or apples had thereby a property in them; they were his goods as soon as gathered. He was only to look that he used them before they spoiled, else he took more than his share and robbed others. And indeed it was a foolish thing, as well as dishonest, to hoard up more than he could make use of. If he gave away a part to anybody else so that it perished not uselessly in his posses-

sion, these he also made use of. And if he also bartered away plums that would have rotted in a week for nuts that would last good for his eating a whole year, he did no injury; he wasted not the common stock, destroyed no part of the portion of the goods that belonged to others, so long as nothing perished uselessly in his hands. Again, if he would give his nuts for a piece of metal, pleased with its color, or exchange his sheep for shells, or wool for a sparkling pebble or a diamond, and keep those by him all his life, he invaded not the right of others; he might heap as much of these durable things as he pleased; the exceeding of the bounds of his just property not lying in the largeness of his possession, but the perishing of anything uselessly in it.

47. And thus came in the use of money—some lasting thing that men might keep without spoiling, and that by mutual consent men would take in exchange for the truly useful but perishable supports of life.

48. And as different degrees of industry were apt to give men possessions in different proportions, so this invention of money gave them the opportunity to continue and enlarge them; for supposing an island, separate from all possible commerce with the rest of the world, wherein there were but a hundred families, but there were sheep, horses, and cows, with other useful animals, wholesome fruits, and land enough for corn for a hundred thousand times as many, but nothing in the island, either because of its commonness or perishableness, fit to supply the place of money; what reason could anyone have there to enlarge his possessions beyond the use of his family and a plentiful supply to its consumption, either in what their own industry produced or they could barter for like perishable, useful commodities with others? Where there is not something both lasting and scarce, and so valuable to be hoarded up, there men will not be apt to enlarge their possessions of land were it ever so rich, ever so free for them to take. For, I ask, what would a man value ten thousand or a hundred thousand acres of excellent land, ready cultivated and well stocked, too, with cattle, in the middle of the inland parts of America where he had no hopes of commerce with other parts of the world to draw money to him by the sale of the product? It would not be worth the enclosing, and we should see him give up again to the wild common of nature whatever was more than would supply the conveniences of life to be had there for him and his family.

49. Thus in the beginning all the world was America, and more so than that is now; for no such thing as money was anywhere known. Find out something that has the use and value of money amongst his neighbors, you shall see the same man will begin presently to enlarge his possessions.

50. But since gold and silver, being little useful to the life of man in

proportion to food, raiment, and carriage, has its value only from the consent of men, whereof labor yet makes, in great part, the measure, it is plain that men have agreed to a disproportionate and unequal possession of the earth, they having, by a tacit and voluntary consent, found out a way how a man may fairly possess more land than he himself can use the product of, by receiving in exchange for the overplus gold and silver which may be hoarded up without injury to anyone, these metals not spoiling or decaying in the hands of the possessor. This partage of things in an inequality of private possessions men have made practicable out of the bounds of society and without compact, only by putting a value on gold and silver, and tacitly agreeing in the use of money; for, in governments, the laws regulate the right of property, and the possession of land is determined by positive constitutions.

51. And thus, I think, it is very easy to conceive how labor could at first begin a title of property in the common things of nature, and how the spending it upon our uses bounded it. So that there could then be no reason of quarreling about title, nor any doubt about the largeness of possession it gave. Right and convenience went together; for as a man had a right to all he could employ his labor upon, so he had no temptation to labor for more than he could make use of. This left no room for controversy about the title, nor for encroachment on the right of others; what portion a man carved to himself was easily seen, and it was useless, as well as dishonest, to carve himself too much or take more than he needed.

Introduction

Adam Smith, from *Wealth of Nations*

While Locke created the myth which helped prepare for modern society, his story contained little practical advice about how this new society was to be established and operated. Adam Smith's *Wealth of Nations,* published the same year as the American Declaration of Independence, provided these more concrete descriptions and recommendations. His masterpiece of "worldly philosophy" has for two centuries given moderns a blueprint and a vocabulary for how to think about and run market economies.

The founder of capitalistic economics was born in 1723 in Kirkcaldy, Scotland. As a child he was kidnapped by a band of roving gypsies, who later abandoned him when they were pursued by Smith's uncle. Whether from this traumatic incident, or for some other reason, Smith became in his adult life a man of marked eccentricities. He was known to fall into reveries of thought that would last for hours, during which times strange and often embarrassing things happened to him. Nevertheless, Smith became an outstanding scholar and one of the favorite teachers at the University of Edinburgh, where he held the chair in moral philosophy. Perhaps nothing more would have been heard of Smith had it not been that he was selected to tutor to a wealthy young nobleman on tour of the Continent. On this tour Smith met Quesnay, the brilliant French economist, and was stimulated to improve upon Quesnay's ideas and wrote *Wealth of Nations*.

Smith was a keen and encyclopedic observer of his society and of history. Where others might have seen chaos or decline in the long transition from medieval to modern societies and in the diversity of economic activities of his eighteenth-century England, he saw an underlying pattern at work. Medievalists could refer to their staunch faith in the divine order God built into the social and natural worlds. Smith and his Enlightenment contemporaries put the divine source of the moral order of the universe into the background, but they found an order in the universe nevertheless. Writing at the beginning of the Industrial Revolution, Smith's perspective on the new economic order was a wonderful mixture of description and prescription.

His central concern was with production. Looking around him at mid-eighteenth-century England, Smith saw great poverty and misery and sought to understand how an economy could meet its most basic charge — to provide for the material well-being of the populace. His answer was simple, and to us quite familiar: produce more wealth, and in the process create jobs for everyone so that through wage labor they can share in that wealth. Wealth, for Smith, is all the goods and services people consume. Note his democratic orientation: the more everyone is able to consume, the wealthier will be the nation be. The best way to produce a maximum of wealth, according to Smith, is to allow individuals free rein to pursue their own self-interests. While this will create conflict (competition), in the long run this apparently disintegrative process will produce the most and highest quality products that people desire (and need?).

Somehow this seemingly chaotic process of everyone working hard for their own self-interests will be orderly rather than disorderly. How? Smith seems to rely on two answers to this question which actually amount to the same idea. The first is a kind of backdoor reintroduction of divinity: he says an "invisible hand" is at work bringing overall harmony out of local and temporary chaos. His second response is an organismic metaphor of society: just as the parts of the body go about their own business in apparent oblivion to the good of the other parts or of the whole, so individuals in society should serve their own self-interest; for just as the body is best served by the parts doing their business well, in the same way society (seen as a kind of organism) will be best served by individuals pursuing their own wealth.

For Smith the open, competitive market is central. With the opportunity to pursue and attain their own wealth people will be motivated to work hard. At the same time the competition itself will regulate individual activity both in terms of quality (someone else might do it better than you) and producing what people need (you can only sell what someone wants). Public demand, another crucial ingredient in Smith's market economy, naturally regulates prices, the number of goods, and the profits which will be extracted. The market will give us these benefits, however, only if we allow it to be self-regulating.

Smith's description of (prescription for) a "free-market economy" is so familiar to us that we usually take it as gospel and often treat it as cliche. We must remember that like Locke's myth of the founding of society, this was a revolutionary doctrine that was contrary to traditional wisdom and took some time to become accepted. The central role for business activity in Smith's story overturns a world order dominated by the church and the landed aristocracy, and his story played no minor role in sanctifying a new order. Our world today is largely Adam Smith's world. Most American economists accept most of the basic tenets of Smith's system, and most disputes between economic thinkers today have to do with fine-tuning his precepts.

However, we should also be careful not to overlook serious difficulties with unquestioning acceptance of Adam Smith's worldview. In the early industrial societies that Smith observed perhaps competition existed between relatively small and equal actors. In today's complex economy, with businesses ranging from multinational corporations to small individual enterprises, combined with a variety of governmental regulatory devices, to describe what we have as free-market economies in Smith's sense is questionable. This ignoring of economic realities is the focus of much criticism of Smithian societies, and ironically many critics echo a concern Smith himself had when he championed market societies in the first place — the plight of the poor. Smith believed societies could not flourish unless all parts flourished; many critics of market societies say these economies require an underclass of poor and unemployed.

In a similar way Smith believed that division of labor is crucial for progress and will bring "universal opulence." Many of his critics, as we shall see, contend that this opulence (by no means universal) comes at a dear cost. As you read Smith's description of the market economy, try to step outside his system and raise questions about the results of two hundred years of capitalism and about the differences between the promise and the actualities of this new way of life.

Adam Smith

Wealth of Nations

CHAPTER I

Of the Division of Labour

The greatest improvement in the productive powers of labour, and the greater part of the skill, dexterity, and judgment with which it is any where directed, or applied, seem to have been the effects of the division of labour.

The effects of the division of labour, in the general business of society, will be more easily understood, by considering in what manner it operates in some particular manufactures. It is commonly supposed to be carried furthest in some very trifling ones; not perhaps that it really is carried further in them than in others of more importance: but in those trifling manufactures which are destined to supply the small wants of but a small number of people, the whole number of workmen must necessarily be small; and those employed in every different branch of the work can often be collected into the same workhouse, and placed at once under the view of the spectator. In those great manufactures, on the contrary, which are destined to supply the great wants of the great body of the people, every different branch of the work employs so great a number of workmen, that it is impossible to collect them all into the same workhouse. We can seldom see more, at one time, than those employed in one single branch. Though in such manufactures, therefore, the work may really be divided into a much greater number of parts, than in those of a more trifling nature, the division is not near so obvious, and has accordingly been much less observed.

To take an example, therefore, from a very trifling manufacture; but one in which the division of labour has been very often taken notice of, the trade of the pin-maker; a workman not educated to this business (which the division of labour has rendered a distinct trade), nor acquainted with the use of the machinery employed in it (to the invention of which the same division of labour has probably given occasion), could scarce, perhaps, with his utmost industry, make one pin in a day, and certainly could not make twenty. But in the way in which this business is now carried on, not only the whole work is a peculiar trade, but it is divided into a number of branches, of which the greater part are likewise peculiar trades. One man draws out the wire, another straights it, a third cuts it, a fourth points it, a fifth grinds it at the top for receiving the head; to make the head requires two or three distinct operations; to put it on, is a peculiar business, to whiten the pins is another; it is even a trade by itself to put them into the paper; and the important business of making a pin is, in this manner, divided into about eighteen distinct operations, which, in some manufactories, are all performed by distinct hands, though in others the same man will sometimes perform two or three of them. I have seen a small manufactory of this kind where ten men only were employed, and where some of them consequently performed two or three distinct operations. But though they were very poor, and therefore but indifferently accommodated with the necessary machinery, they could, when they exerted themselves, make among them about twelve pounds of pins in a day. There are in a pound upwards of four thousand pins of a middling size. Those ten persons, therefore, could make among them upwards of forty-eight thousand pins in a day. Each person, therefore, making a tenth part of forty-eight thousand pins, might be considered as making four thousand eight hundred pins in a day. But if they had all wrought separately and independently, and without any of them having been educated to this peculiar business, they certainly could not each of them have made twenty, perhaps not one pin in a day; that is, certainly, not the two hundred and fortieth, perhaps not the four thousand eight hundredth part of what they are at present capable of performing, in consequence of a proper division and combination of their different operations.

In every other art and manufacture, the effects of the division of labour are similar to what they are in this very trifling one; though, in many of them, the labour can neither be so much subdivided, nor reduced to so great a simplicity of operation. The division of labour, however, so far as it can be introduced, occasions, in every art, a proportionable increase of the productive powers of labour. The separation of different trades and employments from one another, seems to have taken place, in consequence of this advantage. This separation too is generally carried furthest in those countries which enjoy the highest degree of industry and improvement; what is the work of one man in a rude state of society, being generally that of several in an improved one. In every improved society, the farmer is generally nothing but a farmer; the manufacturer, nothing but a manufacturer. The labour too which is necessary to produce any one complete manufacture, is almost always divided among a great number of hands. How many different trades are employed in each branch of the linen and woollen manufactures, from the growers of the flax and the wool, to the bleachers and smoothers of the linen, or to the dyers and dressers of the cloth! The nature of agriculture, indeed, does not admit of so many subdivisions of labour, nor of so complete a separation of one business from another, as manufactures. It is impossible to separate so entirely, the business of the grazier from that of the corn-farmer, as the trade of the carpenter is commonly separated from that of the smith. The spinner is almost always a distinct person from the weaver; but the ploughman, the harrower, the sower of the seed, and the reaper of the corn, are often the same. The occasions for those different sorts of labour returning with the different seasons of the year, it is impossible that one man should be constantly employed in any one of them. This impossibility of making so complete and entire a separation of all the different branches of labour employed in agriculture, is perhaps the reason why the improvement of the productive powers of labour in this art, does not always keep pace with their improvement in manufactures. The most opulent nations, indeed, generally excel all their neighbours in agriculture as well as in manufactures; but they are commonly more distinguished by their superiority in the latter than in the former. Their lands are in general better cultivated, and having more labour and expence bestowed upon them, produce more in proportion to the extent and natural fertility of the ground. But this superiority of produce is seldom much more than in proportion to the superiority of labour and expence. In agriculture, the labour of the rich country is not always much more productive than that of the poor; or, at least, it is never so much more productive, as it commonly is in manufactures. The corn of the rich country, therefore, will not always, in the same degree of goodness, come cheaper to market than that of the poor. The corn of Poland, in the same degree of goodness, is as cheap as that of France, notwithstanding the superior opulence and improvement of the latter country. The corn of France is, in the corn provinces, fully as good, and in most years nearly about the same price with the corn of England, though, in opulence and improvement, France is perhaps inferior to England. The corn-lands of England, however, are better cultivated than those of France, and the corn-lands of France are said to be much better cultivated than those of Poland. But though the poor country, notwithstanding the inferiority of its cultivation, can, in some measure, rival the rich in the cheapness and goodness of its corn, it can pretend to no such competition in its manufactures; at least if those manufactures suit the soil, climate, and situation of the rich country. The silks of France are better and cheaper than those of England, because the silk manufacture, at least under the present high duties upon the importation of raw silk, does not so well suit the climate of England as that of France. But the hard-ware and the coarse woollens of England are beyond all comparison superior to those of France, and much cheaper too in the same degree of goodness. In Poland there are said to be scarce any manufactures of any kind, a few of those coarser household manufactures excepted, without which no country can well subsist.

This great increase of the quantity of work, which, in consequence of the division of labour, the same number of people are capable of performing, is owing to three different circumstances; first, to the increase of dexterity in every particular workman; secondly, to the saving of the time which is commonly lost in passing from one species of work to another; and lastly, to the invention of a great number of machines which facilitate and abridge labour, and enable one man to do the work of many.

It is the great multiplication of the productions of all the different arts, in consequence of the division of labour, which occasions, in a well-governed society, that universal opulence which extends itself to the lowest ranks of the people. Every workman has a great quantity of his own work to dispose of beyond what he himself has occasion for; and every other workman being exactly in the same situation, he is enabled to exchange a great quantity of his own goods for a great quantity, or, what comes to the same thing, for the price of a great quantity of theirs. He supplies them abundantly with what they have occasion for, and they accommodate him as amply with what he has occasion for, and a general plenty diffuses itself through all the different ranks of the society.

Observe the accommodation of the most common artificer or day-labourer in a civilized and thriving country, and you will perceive that the number of people of whose industry a part, though but a small part, has been employed in procuring him this accommodation, exceeds all computation. The woollen coat, for example, which covers the day-labourer, as coarse and rough as it may appear, is the produce of the joint labour of a great multitude of workmen. The shepherd, the sorter of the wool, the wool-comber or carder, the dyer, the scribbler, the spinner, the weaver, the fuller, the dresser, with many others, must all join their different arts in order to complete even this homely production. How many merchants and carriers, besides, must have been employed in transporting the materials from some of those workmen to others who often live in a very distant part of the country! How much commerce and navigation in particular, how many ship-builders, sailors, sail-makers, rope-makers, must have been employed in order to bring together the different drugs made use of by the dyer, which often come from the remotest corners of the world! What a variety of labour too is necessary in order to produce the tools of the meanest of those workmen! To say nothing of such complicated machines as the ship of the sailor, the mill of the fuller, or even the loom of the weaver, let us consider only what a variety of labour is requisite in order to form that very simple machine, the shears with which the shepherd clips the wool. The miner, the builder of the furnace for smelting the ore, the feller of the timber, the burner of the charcoal to be made use of in the smelting-house, the brick-maker, the brick-layer, the workmen who attend the furnace, the mill-wright, the forger, the smith, must all of them join their different arts in order to produce them. Were we to examine, in the same manner, all the different parts of his dress and household furniture, the coarse linen shirt which he wears next his skin, the shoes which cover his feet, the bed which he lies on, and all the different parts which compose it, the kitchen-grate at which he prepares his victuals, the coals which he makes use of for that purpose, dug from the bowels of the earth, and brought to him perhaps by a long sea and a long land carriage, all the other utensils of his kitchen, all the furniture of his table, the knives and forks, the earthen or pewter plates upon which he serves up and divides his victuals, the different hands employed in preparing his bread and his beer, the glass window which lets in the heat and the light, and keeps out the wind and the rain, with all the knowledge and art requisite for preparing that beautiful and happy invention, without which these northern parts of the world could scarce have afforded a very comfortable habitation, together with the tools of all the different workmen employed in producing those different conveniencies; if we examine, I say, all these things, and consider what a variety of labour is employed about each of them, we shall be sensible that without the assistance and co-operation of many thousands, the very meanest person in a civilized country could not be provided, even according to, what we very falsely imagine, the easy and simple manner in which he is commonly accommodated. Compared, indeed, with the more extravagant luxury of the great, his accommodation must no doubt appear extremely simple and easy; and yet it may be true, perhaps, that the accommodation of an European prince does not always so much exceed that of an industrious and frugal peasant, as the accommodation of the latter exceeds that of many an African king, the absolute master of the lives and liberties of ten thousand naked savages.

CHAPTER II

Of the Principle Which Gives Occasion
to the Division of Labor

This division of labour, from which so many advantages are derived, is not originally the effect of any human wisdom, which foresees and intends that general opulence to which it gives occasion. It is the necessary, though very slow and gradual, consequence of a certain propensity in human nature which has in view no such extensive utility; the propensity to truck, barter, and exchange one thing for another.

Whether this propensity be one of those original principles in human nature, of which no further account can be given; or whether, as seems more probable, it be the necessary consequence of the faculties of reason and speech, it belongs not to our present subject to enquire. It is common to all men, and to be found in no other race of animals, which seem to know neither this nor any other species of contracts. Two greyhounds, in running down the same hare, have sometimes the appearance of acting in some sort of concert. Each turns her towards his companion, or endeavours to intercept her when his companion turns her towards himself. This, however, is not the effect of any contract, but of the accidental concurrence of their passions in the same object at that particular time. Nobody ever saw a dog make a fair and deliberate exchange of one bone for another with another dog. Nobody ever saw one animal by its gestures and natural cries signify to another, this is mine, that yours; I am willing to give this for that. When an animal wants to obtain something either of a man or of another animal, it has no other means of persuasion but to gain the favour of those whose service it requires. A puppy fawns upon its dam, and a spaniel endeavours by a thousand attractions to engage the attention of its master who is at dinner, when it wants to be fed by him. Man sometimes uses the same arts with his brethren, and when he has no other means of engaging them to act according to his inclinations, endeavours by every servile and fawning attention to obtain their good will. He has not time, however, to do this upon every occasion. In civilized society he stands at all times in need of the co-operation and assistance of great multitudes, while his whole life is scarce sufficient to gain the friendship of a few persons. In almost every other race of animals each individual, when it is grown up to maturity, is entirely independent, and in its natural state has occasion for the assistance of no other living creature. But man has almost constant occasion for the help of his brethren, and it is in vain for him to expect it from their benevolence only. He will be more likely to prevail if he can interest their self-love in his favour, and show them that it is for their own advantage to do for him what he requires of them. Whoever offers to another a bargain of any kind, proposes to do this. Give me that which I want, and you shall have this which you want, is the meaning of every such offer; and it is in this manner that we obtain from one another the far greater part of those good offices which we stand in need of. It is not from the benevolence of the butcher, the brewer, or the baker, that we expect our dinner, but from their regard to their own interest. We address ourselves, not to their humanity but to their self-love, and never talk to them of our own necessities but of their advantages. Nobody but a beggar chuses to depend chiefly upon the benevolence of his fellow-citizens. Even a beggar does not depend upon it entirely. The charity of well-disposed people, indeed, supplies him with the whole fund of his subsistence. But though this principle ultimately provides him with all the necessaries of life which he has occasion for, it neither does nor can provide him with them as he has occasion for them. The greater part of his occasional wants are supplied in the same manner as those of other people, by treaty, by barter, and by purchase. With the money which one man gives him he purchases food. The old cloaths which another bestows upon him he exchanges for other old cloaths which suit him better, or for lodging, or for food, or for money, with which he can buy either food, cloaths, or lodging, as he has occasion.

As it is by treaty, by barter, and by purchase, that we obtain from one another the greater part of those mutual good offices which we stand in need of, so it is this same trucking disposition which originally gives occasion to the division of labour. In a tribe of hunters or shepherds a particular person makes bows and arrows, for example, with more readiness and dexterity than any other. He frequently exchanges them for cattle or for venison with his companions; and he finds at last that he can in this manner get more cattle and venison, than if he himself went to the field to catch them. From a regard to his own interest, therefore, the making of bows and arrows grows to be his chief business, and he becomes a sort of armourer. Another excels in making the frames and covers of their little huts or moveable houses. He is accustomed to be of use in this way to his neighbours, who reward him in the same manner with cattle and with venison, till at last he finds it his interest to dedicate himself entirely to this employment, and to become a sort of house-carpenter. In the same manner a third becomes a smith or a brazier; a fourth a tanner or dresser of hides or skins, the principal part of the clothing of savages. And thus the certainty of being able to exchange all that surplus part of the produce of his own labour, which is over and above his own consumption, for such parts of the produce of other men's labour as he may have occasion for, encourages every man to apply himself to a particular occupation, and to cultivate and bring to perfection whatever talent or genius he may possess for that particular species of business.

The difference of natural talents in different men is, in reality, much less than we are aware of; and the very different genius which appears to distinguish men of different professions, when grown up to maturity, is not upon many occasions so much the cause, as the effect of the division of labour. The difference between the most dissimilar characters, between a philosopher and a common street porter, for example, seems to arise not so much from nature, as from habit, custom, and education. When they came into the world, and for the first six or eight years of their existence, they were perhaps, very much alike, and neither their parents nor playfellows could perceive any remarkable difference. About that age, or soon after, they come to be employed in very different occupations. The difference of talents comes then to be taken notice of, and widens by degrees, till at last the vanity of the philosopher is willing to acknowledge scarce any resemblance. But without the disposition to truck, barter, and exchange, every man must have procured to himself every necessary and conveniency of life which he wanted. All must have had the same duties to perform, and the same work to do, and there could have been no such difference of employment as could alone give occasion to any great difference of talents.

As it is this disposition which forms that difference of talents, so remarkable among men of different professions, so it is this same disposition which renders that difference useful. Many tribes of animals acknowledged to be all of the same species, derive from nature a much more remarkable distinction of genius, than what, antecedent to custom and education, appears to take place among men. By nature a philosopher is not in genius and disposition half so different from a street porter, as a mastiff is from a greyhound, or a greyhound from a spaniel, or this last from a shepherd's dog. Those different tribes of animals, however, though all of the same species, are of scarce any use to one another. The strength of the mastiff is not in the least supported either by the swiftness of the greyhound, or by the sagacity of the spaniel, or by the docility of the shepherd's dog. The effects of those different geniuses and talents, for want of the power or disposition to barter and exchange, cannot be brought into a common stock, and do not in the least contribute to the better accommodation and conveniency of the species. Each animal is still obliged to support and defend itself, separately and independently, and derives no sort of advantage from that variety of talents with which nature has distinguished its fellows. Among men, on the contrary, the most dissimilar geniuses are of use to one another; the different produces of their respective talents, by the general disposition to truck, barter, and exchange, being brought, as it were, into a common stock, where every man may purchase whatever part of the produce of other men's talents he has occasion for.

2. Salvation, Work, and the New Paradigm

Introduction

R.H. Tawney, from *Religion and the Rise of Capitalism*

R.H. Tawney (1880–1962), son of an eminent Sanskrit scholar, was a radical English social and economic historian. He was educated at Rugby, where he was grounded in the classics and the Old Testament, and at Balliol College, Oxford. In spite of his privileged educational background Tawney throughout all his life was a champion of common people. This identification with working people brought him to refuse an officer's commission in World War I and to serve in the ranks, where he was severely wounded in 1918; and as an historian he wrote from a radical left perspective.

In the following excerpt from *Religion and the Rise of Capitalism* Tawney analyzes the relationship between the growth of capitalism and Calvinist religious beliefs. It had long been noticed that those areas in Europe where Calvinism flourished—Britain, Holland, and Huguenot France—were also areas where capitalism became earliest and most successfully entrenched. German sociologist Max Weber in his famous study *The Protestant Ethic and the Spirit of Capitalism* argued that the values of Calvinism—hard work coming from a sense of vocation and the regard of wealth as a sign of grace—contributed to create a spirit of capitalism. Tawney looks critically at this thesis and modifies it, but he agrees that capitalism "found in certain aspects of later Puritanism a tonic which braced its energies and fortified its already vigorous temper."

The problem that both Weber and Tawney address is: How do we proceed from the medieval Christian worldview that considers material accumulation as sinful and poverty as blessed to the modern view that sees the accumulation of wealth as blessed and poverty as sinful? The key, as Tawney sees it, is the great emphasis Calvin places upon human sinfulness. For Calvin the fall of Adam and Eve is a more serious matter than most anyone had understood. Beginning with Luther, Protestants saw original sin as more serious than Catholics did. Luther rejected the idea that people could help with their own salvations through their "works" and substituted the method of faith: Luther believed that our sin was so great that only by throwing ourselves at the mercy of God could we achieve redemption.

Calvin went one step further according to Tawney: for Calvin our sin is so bad that only God could act to redeem it. Humans, for Calvin, are predestined to either rot in hell or be saved, and no amount of works or faith could possibly make any difference. All we can do is prepare ourselves to receive God's gift and wait. The suspense, of course, was awful: Tawney pictures the English Puritans as living in a lonely, despairing world surrounded by people God despises. Community, for such people, is not much happier than spiritual activity. What are these guilt-ridden believers to do? In short, Weber and Tawney believe that they threw themselves into work, for they came to believe that although you cannot do any works to earn your way into heaven, you might (a thin hope, this) take material wealth as a sign of God's favor. In their spiritual desperation a mutated version of Protestantism brought some Puritans to turn the Biblical edict about wealth on its head: now material wealth is a sign of God's favor rather than an impediment to salvation.

How we got to the Protestant work ethic is a long story, involving many important thinkers, including both Locke and Smith whom we have discussed (both from Calvinist backgrounds). Still, Tawney's excerpt will add a crucial chapter to this epic tale. America has a powerful Puritan heritage, and Tawney's account will tell you much about a mind-set that persists here even as modern America has become secularized.

Tawney will also contribute to your understanding of several short stories that appear later in the book, especially "Young Goodman Brown" by Nathaniel Hawthorne and "The Rockinghorse Winner" by D.H. Lawrence. Both stories are about the influence of Puritanism on different aspects of our lives. Central to Tawney's thesis is that Puritanism has destroyed our natural need for community and substituted a "wintry" individualism in its place. As you read, consider the costs as well as the benefits of "progress." Do you think that Puritanism is still an influence in American life? If so, in what ways?

R. H. Tawney

The Puritan Movement

"The capitalist spirit" is as old as history, and was not, as has sometimes been said, the offspring of Puritanism. But it found in certain aspects of later Puritanism a tonic which braced its energies and fortified its already vigorous temper. At first sight, no contrast could be more violent than that between the iron collectivism, the almost military discipline, the remorseless and violent rigors practiced in Calvin's Geneva, and preached elsewhere, if in a milder form, by his disciples, and the impatient rejection of all traditional restrictions on economic enterprise which was the temper of the English business world after the Civil War. In reality, the same ingredients were present throughout, but they were mixed in changing proportions, and exposed to different temperatures at different times. Like traits of individual character which are suppressed till the approach of maturity releases them, the tendencies in Puritanism, which were to make it later a potent ally of the movement against the control of economic relations in the name either of social morality or of the public interest, did not reveal themselves till political and economic changes had prepared a congenial environment for their growth. Nor, once those conditions were created, was it only England which witnessed the transformation. In all countries alike, in Holland, in America, in Scotland, in Geneva itself, the social theory of Calvinism went through the same process of development. It had begun by being the very soul of authoritarian regimentation. It ended by being the vehicle of an almost Utilitarian individualism. While social reformers in the sixteenth century could praise Calvin for his economic rigor, their successors in Restoration England, if of one persuasion, denounced him as the parent of economic license, if of another, applauded Calvinist communities for their commercial enterprise and for their freedom from antiquated prejudices on the subject of economic morality. So little do those who shoot the arrows of the spirit know where they will light.

III. The Triumph of the Economic Virtues

. . . While the revelation of God to the individual soul is the center of all religion, the essence of Puritan theology was that it made it, not only the center, but the whole circumference and substance, dismissing as dross and vanity all else but this secret and solitary communion. Grace alone can save, and this grace is the direct gift of God, unmediated by any earthly institution. The elect cannot by any act of their own evoke it; but they can prepare their hearts to receive it, and cherish it when received. They will prepare them best, if they empty them of all that may disturb the intentness of their lonely vigil. . . . the Puritan attunes his heart to the voice from Heaven by an immense effort of concentration and abnegation. To win all, he renounces all. When earthly props have been cast down, the soul stands erect in the presence of God. Infinity is attained by a process of subtraction.

To a vision thus absorbed in a single intense experience, not only religious and ecclesiastical systems, but the entire world of human relations, the whole fabric of social institutions, witnessing in all the wealth of their idealism and their greed to the infinite creativeness of man, reveal themselves in a new and wintry light. The fire of the spirit burns brightly on the hearth; but through the windows of his soul the Puritan, unless a poet or a saint, looks on a landscape touched by no breath of spring. What he sees is a forbidding and frost-bound wilderness, rolling its snow-clad leagues towards the grave — a wilderness to be subdued with aching limbs beneath solitary stars. Through it he must take his way, alone. No aid can avail him: no preacher, for only the elect can apprehend with the spirit the word of God; no Church, for to the visible Church even reprobates belong; no sacrament, for sacraments are ordained to increase the glory of God, not to minister spiritual nourishment to man; hardly God himself, for Christ died for the elect, and it may well be that the majesty of the Creator is revealed by the eternal damnation of all but a remnant of the created.

Those who seek God in isolation from their fellowmen, unless trebly armed for the perils of the quest, are apt to find, not God, but a devil, whose countenance bears an embarrassing resemblance to their own. The moral self-sufficiency of the Puritan nerved his will, but it corroded his sense of social solidarity. For, if each individual's destiny hangs on a private transaction between himself and his Maker, what room is left for human intervention? A servant of Jehovah more than of Christ, he revered God as a Judge rather than loved him as a Father, and was moved less by compassion for his erring brethren than by impatient indignation at the blindness of vessels of wrath who "sinned their mercies." A spiritual aristocrat, who sacrificed fraternity to liberty, he drew from his idealization of personal responsibility a theory of individual rights, which, secularized and generalized, was to be among the most potent explosives that the world has known. He drew from it also a scale of ethical values, in which the traditional scheme of Christian virtues was almost exactly reversed, and which, since he was above all things practical, he carried as a dynamic into the routine of business and political life.

For, since conduct and action, though availing nothing to attain the free gift of salvation, are a proof that the gift has been accorded, what is rejected as a means is resumed as a consequence, and the Puritan flings himself into practical activities with the dæmonic energy of one who, all doubts allayed, is conscious that he is a sealed and chosen vessel. Once engaged in affairs, he brings to them both the qualities and limitations of his creed in all their remorseless logic. Called by God to labor in his vineyard, he has within himself a principle at once of energy and of order, which makes him irresistible both in war and in the struggles of commerce. Convinced that character is all and circumstances nothing, he sees in the poverty of those who fall by the way, not a misfortune to be pitied and relieved, but a moral failing to be condemned, and in riches, not an object of suspicion — though like other gifts they may be abused — but the blessing which rewards the triumph of energy and will. Tempered by self-examination, self-discipline, self-control, he is the practical ascetic, whose victories are won not in the cloister, but on the battlefield, in the counting-house, and in the market.

The England of Shakespeare and Bacon was still largely medieval in its economic organization and social outlook, more interested in maintaining customary standards of consumption than in accumulating capital for future production, with an aristocracy contemptuous of the economic virtues, a peasantry farming for subsistence amid the organized confusion of the open-field village, and a small, if growing, body of jealously conservative craftsmen. In such a society Puritanism worked like the yeast which sets the whole mass fermenting. It went through its slack and loosely knit texture like a troop of Cromwell's Ironsides through the disorderly cavalry of Rupert. Where, as in Ireland, the elements were so alien that assimilation was out of the question, the result was a wound that festered for three centuries. In England the effect was that at once of an irritant and of a tonic. Puritanism had its own standards of social conduct, derived partly from the obvious interests of the commercial classes, partly from its conception of the nature of God and the destiny of man. These standards were in sharp antithesis, both to the considerable surviving elements of feudalism in English society, and to the policy of the authoritarian State, with its ideal of an ordered and graded society, whose different members were to be maintained in their traditional

status by the pressure and protection of a paternal monarchy. Sapping
the former by its influence and overthrowing the latter by direct attack,
Puritanism became a potent force in preparing the way for the commercial civilization which finally triumphed at the Revolution.

―――――――

From the very beginning, Calvinism had comprised two elements,
which Calvin himself had fused, but which contained the seeds of future
discord. It had at once given a whole-hearted *imprimatur* to the life of
business enterprise, which most earlier moralists had regarded with suspicion, and had laid upon it the restraining hand of an inquisitorial discipline. At Geneva, where Calvinism was the creed of a small and homo-
geneous city, the second aspect had predominated; in the many-sided
life of England, where there were numerous conflicting interests to balance it, and where it was long politically weak, the first. Then, in the
late sixteenth and early seventeenth centuries, had come the wave of
commercial and financial expansion — companies, colonies, capitalism
in textiles, capitalism in mining, capitalism in finance — on the crest of
which the English commercial classes, in Calvin's day still held in leading-
strings by conservative statesmen, had climbed to a position of dignity
and affluence.

Naturally, as the Puritan movement came to its own, these two elements flew apart. The collectivist, half-communistic aspect, which had
never been acclimatized in England, quietly dropped out of notice, to
crop up once more, and for the last time, to the disgust and terror of
merchant and landowner, in the popular agitation under the Commonwealth. The individualism congenial to the world of business became the
distinctive characteristic of a Puritanism which had arrived, and which,
in becoming a political force, was at once secularized and committed
to a career of compromise. Its note was not the attempt to establish on
earth a "Kingdom of Christ," but an ideal of personal character and conduct, to be realized by the punctual discharge both of public and private
duties. Its theory had been discipline; its practical result was liberty.

―――――――

. . . What in Calvin had been a qualified concession to practical exigencies appeared in some of his later followers as a frank idealization of the
life of the trader, as the service of God and the training-ground of the
soul. Discarding the suspicion of economic motives, which had been as
characteristic of the reformers as of medieval theologians, Puritanism
in its later phases added a halo of ethical sanctification to the appeal of
economic expediency, and offered a moral creed, in which the duties of

religion and the calls of business ended their long estrangement in an
unanticipated reconciliation. Its spokesmen pointed out, it is true, the
peril to the soul involved in a single-minded concentration on economic
interests. The enemy, however, was not riches, but the bad habits sometimes associated with them, and its warnings against an excessive preoccupation with the pursuit of gain wore more and more the air of after-
thoughts, appended to teaching the main tendency and emphasis of which
were little affected by these incidental qualifications. It insisted, in short,
that money-making, if not free from spiritual dangers, was not a danger
and nothing else, but that it could be, and ought to be, carried on for
the greater glory of God.

The conception to which it appealed to bridge the gulf sprang from the
very heart of Puritan theology. It was that expressed in the characteristic
and oft-used phrase, "a Calling." The rational order of the universe is the
work of God, and its plan requires that the individual should labor for
God's glory. There is a spiritual calling, and a temporal calling. It is the
first duty of the Christian to know and believe in God; it is by faith that he
will be saved. But faith is not a mere profession, such as that of Talkative
of Prating Row, whose "religion is to make a noise." The only genuine
faith is the faith which produces works. "At the day of Doom men shall
be judged according to their fruits. It will not be said then, Did you believe? but, Were you doers, or talkers only?" The second duty of the Christian is to labor in the affairs of practical life, and this second duty is subordinate only to the first. "God," wrote a Puritan divine, "doth call every man
and woman . . . to serve him in some peculiar employment in this world,
both for their own and the common good. . . . The Great Governour of
the world hath appointed to every man his proper post and province,
and let him be never so active out of his sphere, he will be at a great
loss, if he do not keep his own vineyard and mind his own business."

From this reiterated insistence on secular obligations as imposed by
the divine will, it follows that, not withdrawal from the world, but the
conscientious discharge of the duties of business, is among the loftiest
of religious and moral virtues.

The idea was not a new one. Luther had advanced it as a weapon against
monasticism. But for Luther, with his patriarchal outlook on economic
affairs, the calling means normally that state of life in which the individual has been set by Heaven, and against which it is impiety to rebel.
On the lips of Puritan divines, it is not an invitation to resignation, but
the bugle-call which summons the elect to the long battle which will end
only with their death. "The world is all before them." They are to hammer

out their salvation, not merely *in vocatione,* but *per vocationem.* The calling is not a condition in which the individual is born, but a strenuous and exacting enterprise, to be undertaken, indeed, under the guidance of Providence, but to be chosen by each man for himself, with a deep sense of his solemn responsibilities. "God hath given to man reason for this use, that he should first consider, then choose, then put in execution; and it is a preposterous and brutish thing to fix or fall upon any weighty business, such as a calling or condition of life, without a careful pondering it in the balance of sound reason."

Laborare est orare. By the Puritan moralist the ancient maxim is repeated with a new and intenser significance. The labor which he idealizes is not simply a requirement imposed by nature, or a punishment for the sin of Adam. It is itself a kind of ascetic discipline, more rigorous than that demanded of any order of mendicants—a discipline imposed by the will of God, and to be undergone, not in solitude, but in the punctual discharge of secular duties. It is not merely an economic means, to be laid aside when physical needs have been satisfied. It is a spiritual end, for in it alone can the soul find health, and it must be continued as an ethical duty long after it has ceased to be a material necessity. Work thus conceived stands at the very opposite pole from "good works," as they were understood, or misunderstood, by Protestants. They, it was thought, had been a series of single transactions, performed as compensation for particular sins, or out of anxiety to acquire merit. What is required of the Puritan is not individual meritorious acts, but a holy life—a system in which every element is grouped round a central idea, the service of God, from which all disturbing irrelevances have been pruned, and to which all minor interests are subordinated.

His conception of that life was expressed in the words, "Be wholly taken up in diligent business of your lawful callings, when you are not exercised in the more immediate service of God." In order to deepen his spiritual life, the Christian must be prepared to narrow it. He "is blind in no man's cause, but best sighted in his own. He confines himself to the circle of his own affairs and thrusts not his fingers in needless fires. . . . He sees the falseness of it [the world] and therefore learns to trust himself ever, others so far as not to be damaged by their disappointment." There must be no idle leisure: "those that are prodigal of their time despise their own souls." Religion must be active, not merely contemplative. Contemplation is, indeed, a kind of self-indulgence. "To neglect this [i.e., bodily employment and mental labor] and say, 'I will pray and meditate,' is as if your servant should refuse your greatest work, and tye himself to some lesser, easie part. . . . God hath commanded you some way or other to labour for your daily bread." The rich are no more excused from work than the poor, though they may rightly use their riches to select some occupation specially serviceable to others. Covetousness is a danger to the soul, but it is not so grave a danger as sloth. "The standing pool is prone to putrefaction: and it were better to beat down the body and to keep it in subjection by a laborious calling, than through luxury to become a cast-away." So far from poverty being meritorious, it is a duty to choose the more profitable occupation. "If God show you a way in which you may lawfully get more than in another way (without wrong to your soul or to any other), if you refuse this, and choose the less gainful way, you cross one of the ends of your Calling, and you refuse to be God's steward." Luxury, unrestrained pleasure, personal extravagance, can have no place in a Christian's conduct, for "every penny which is laid out . . . must be done as by God's own appointment." Even excessive devotion to friends and relations is to be avoided. "It is an irrational act, and therefore not fit for a rational creature, to love any one farther than reason will allow us. . . . It very often taketh up men's minds so as to hinder their love to God." The Christian life, in short, must be systematic and organized, the work of an iron will and a cool intelligence.

The springs of economic conduct lie in regions rarely penetrated by moralists, and to suggest a direct reaction of theory on practice would be paradoxical. But, if the circumstances which determine that certain kinds of conduct shall be profitable are economic, those which decide that they shall be the object of general approval are primarily moral and intellectual. For conventions to be adopted with wholehearted enthusiasm, to be not merely tolerated, but applauded, to become the habit of a nation and the admiration of its philosophers, the second condition must be present as well as the first. The insistence among men of pecuniary motives, the strength of economic egotism, the appetite for gain — these are the commonplaces of every age and need no emphasis. What is significant is the change of standards which converted a natural frailty into a resounding virtue. After all, it appears, a man can serve two masters, for — so happily is the world disposed — he may be paid by one, while he works for the other. Between the old-fashioned denunciation of uncharitable covetousness and the new-fashioned applause of economic enterprise, a bridge is thrown by the argument which urges that enterprise itself is the discharge of a duty imposed by God.

The transition from the anabaptist to the company promoter was less abrupt than might at first sight be supposed. It had been prepared, however unintentionally, by Puritan moralists. In their emphasis on the moral duty of untiring activity, on work as an end in itself, on the evils of luxury and extravagance, on foresight and thrift, on moderation and self-discipline and rational calculation, they had created an ideal of Christian conduct, which canonized as an ethical principle the efficiency which economic theorists were preaching as a specific for social disorders. It was as captivating as it was novel. To countless generations of religious thinkers, the fundamental maxim of Christian social ethics had seemed to be expressed in the words of St. Paul to Timothy: "Having food and raiment, let us be therewith content. For the love of money is the root of all evil." Now, while, as always, the world battered at the gate, a new standard was raised within the citadel by its own defenders. The garrison had discovered that the invading host of economic appetites was, not an enemy, but an ally. Not sufficiency to the needs of daily life, but limitless increase and expansion, became the goal of the Christian's efforts. Not consumption, on which the eyes of earlier sages had been turned, but production, became the pivot of his argument. Not an easy-going and open-handed charity, but a systematic and methodical accumulation, won the meed of praise that belongs to the good and faithful servant. The shrewd, calculating commercialism which tries all human relations by pecuniary standards, the acquisitiveness which cannot rest while there are competitors to be conquered or profits to be won, the love of social power and hunger for economic gain — these irrepressible appetites had evoked from time immemorial the warnings and denunciations of saints and sages. Plunged in the cleansing waters of later Puritanism, the qualities which less enlightened ages had denounced as social vices emerged as economic virtues. They emerged as moral virtues as well. For the world exists not to be enjoyed, but to be conquered. Only its conqueror deserves the name of Christian. For such a philosophy the question "What shall it profit a man?" carries no sting. In winning the world, he wins the salvation of his own soul as well.

The idea of economic progress as an end to be consciously sought, while ever receding, had been unfamiliar to most earlier generations of Englishmen, in which the theme of moralists had been the danger of unbridled cupidity, and the main aim of public policy had been the stability of traditional relationships. It found a new sanction in the identification of labor and enterprise with the service of God. The magnificent energy which changed in a century the face of material civilization was to draw nourishment from that temper. The worship of production and ever greater production — the slavish drudgery of the millionaire and his unhappy servants — was to be hallowed by the precepts of the same compelling creed.

To such a generation, a creed which transformed the acquisition of wealth from a drudgery or a temptation into a moral duty was the milk of lions. It was not that religion was expelled from practical life, but that religion itself gave it a foundation of granite. In that keen atmosphere of economic enterprise, the ethics of the Puritan bore some resemblance to those associated later with the name of Smiles. The good Christian was not wholly dissimilar from the economic man.

Introduction
Nathaniel Hawthorne, "Young Goodman Brown"

In the excerpt from Tawney's *Religion and the Rise of Capitalism* you read about the Puritan influence in shaping the habits and ethics of Western capitalism. He claims that a by-product of Puritanism is an isolation and loneliness perhaps without parallel in Western history. In the following story Hawthorne illustrates for us this mutation from the Puritan character that was to become the basis for the work ethic so critical to the success of capitalism.

Hawthorne was himself a nineteenth-century Puritan descended from Judge John Hawthorne, who presided over the Salem witch trials. Growing up in Massachusetts among the ruins of New England Puritanism, he was uniquely situated to observe those residual Calvinist traits still found in New England Yankees. Perhaps with the exception of his friend Melville, no American writer has seen more deeply into the modern American psyche and its early Puritan roots.

In "Young Goodman Brown" we are taken on an archetypal adventure, from the world of childhood innocence into the dark world of adulthood. The story is told as an allegory. Thus, for example, Salem Village in daylight represents innocence, the world of things as they seem; the dark forest at night, on the other hand, represents the more complex world within the human psyche, or, as English novelist D.H. Lawrence put it, "the dark forest of the human soul." All of us are doomed to journey into this dark forest, for it is the world of adult desires and sin. But not all are doomed to be destroyed by this journey. Brown, the young and would-be good man, represents the innocent youth journeying into the world of adult knowledge for the first time. Will he survive this experience and develop into a full human being, or will he be destroyed?

Destruction in this case is not a physical matter. It is Brown's soul that we should be concerned with rather than his physical well-being. When Brown finds that humans and the world are flawed, what is his reaction? Is he able to accept human imperfection and continue to live as part of the community? What does Hawthorne mean by the following sentence: "they carved no hopeful verse upon his tomb, for his dying hour was gloom"? New England Puritans were concerned that all of their members should live together as part of a community. What does this story have to say about the failure of true community among the Puritans and among modern Americans? Is there more to community than living in the same town?

Nathaniel Hawthorne

Young Goodman Brown[1]

Young goodman[2] Brown came forth, at sunset, into the street of Salem village, but put his head back, after crossing the threshold, to exchange a parting kiss with his young wife. And Faith, as the wife was aptly named, thrust her own pretty head into the street, letting the wind play with the pink ribbons of her cap, while she called to goodman Brown.

'Dearest heart,' whispered she, softly and rather sadly, when her lips were close to his ear, 'pr'y thee, put off your journey until sunrise, and sleep in your own bed to-night. A lone woman is troubled with such dreams and such thoughts, that she's afeard of herself, sometimes. Pray, tarry with me this night, dear husband, of all nights in the year!'

'My love and my Faith,' replied young goodman Brown, 'of all nights in the year, this one night must I tarry away from thee. My journey, as thou callest it, forth and back again, must needs be done 'twixt now and sunrise. What, my sweet, pretty wife, dost thou doubt me already, and we but three months married!'

---

1. The text followed here is that of the first publication, in the *New-England Magazine* (April, 1935); the story was ascribed to "the author of 'The Gray Champion,'" which had appeared in the same magazine three months earlier.

2. Hawthorne puns on the title used to address a man of humble birth and the moral implications of "good man"; what with "Brown" as a surname, the hero is equivalent to Young Mister Anybody.

'Then, God bless you!' said Faith, with the pink ribbons, 'and may you find all well, when you come back.'

'Amen!' cried goodman Brown. 'Say thy prayers, dear Faith, and go to bed at dusk, and no harm will come to thee.'

So they parted; and the young man pursued his way, until, being about to turn the corner by the meeting-house, he looked back, and saw the head of Faith still peeping after him, with a melancholy air, in spite of her pink ribbons.

'Poor little Faith!' thought he, for his heart smote him. 'What a wretch am I, to leave her on such an errand! She talks of dreams, too. Methought, as she spoke, there was trouble in her face, as if a dream had warned her what work is to be done to-night. But, no, no! 't would kill her to think it. Well; she's a blessed angel on earth; and after this one night, I'll cling to her skirts and follow her to Heaven.'

With this excellent resolve for the future, goodman Brown felt himself justified in making more haste on his present evil purpose. He had taken a dreary road, darkened by all the gloomiest trees of the forest, which barely stood aside to let the narrow path creep through, and closed immediately behind. It was all as lonely as could be; and there is this peculiarity in such a solitude, that the traveler knows not who may be concealed by the innumerable trunks and the thick boughs overhead; so that, with lonely footsteps, he may yet be passing through an unseen multitude.

'There may be a devilish Indian behind every tree,' said goodman Brown, to himself; and he glanced fearfully behind him, as he added, 'What if the devil himself should be at my very elbow!'

His head being turned back, he passed a crook of the road, and looking forward again, beheld the figure of a man, in grave and decent attire, seated at the foot of an old tree. He arose, at goodman Brown's approach, and walked onward, side by side with him.

'You are late, goodman Brown,' said he. 'The clock of the Old South was striking as I came through Boston; and that is full fifteen minutes agone.'[3]

'Faith kept me back awhile,' replied the young man, with a tremor in his voice, caused by the sudden appearance of his companion, though not wholly unexpected.

It was now deep dusk in the forest, and deepest in that part of it where these two were journeying. As nearly as could be discerned, the second traveler was about fifty years old, apparently in the same rank of life as goodman Brown, and bearing a considerable resemblance to him, though

---

3. This speed could only be supernatural.

perhaps more in expression than features. Still, they might have been taken for father and son. And yet, though the elder person was as simply clad as the younger, and as simple in manner too, he had an indescribable air of one who knew the world, and would not have felt abashed at the governor's dinner-table, or in king William's[4] court, were it possible that his affairs should call him thither. But the only thing about him, that could be fixed upon as remarkable, was his staff, which bore the likeness of a great black snake, so curiously wrought, that it might almost be seen to twist and wriggle itself, like a living serpent. This, of course, must have been an ocular deception, assisted by the uncertain light.

'Come, goodman Brown!' cried his fellow-traveler, 'this is a dull pace for the beginning of a journey. Take my staff, if you are so soon weary.'

'Friend,' said the other, exchanging his slow pace for a full stop, 'having kept covenant by meeting thee here, it is my purpose now to return whence I came. I have scruples, touching the matter thou wot'st of.'

'Sayest thou so?' replied he of the serpent, smiling apart. 'Let us walk on, nevertheless, reasoning as we go, and if I convince thee not, thou shalt turn back. We are but a little way in the forest, yet.'

'Too far, too far!' exclaimed the goodman, unconsciously resuming his walk. 'My father never went into the woods on such an errand, nor his father before him. We have been a race of honest men and good Christians, since the days of the martyrs.[5] And shall I be the first of the name of Brown, that ever took this path, and kept'—

'Such company, thou wouldst say,' observed the elder person, interpreting his pause. 'Good, goodman Brown! I have been as well acquainted with your family as with ever a one among the Puritans; and that's no trifle to say. I helped your grandfather, the constable, when he lashed the Quaker woman so smartly through the streets of Salem. And it was I that brought your father a pitch-pine knot, kindled at my own hearth, to set fire to an Indian village, in king Philip's[6] war. They were my good friends, both; and many a pleasant walk have we had along this path, and returned merrily after midnight. I would fain be friends with you, for their sake.'

---

4. William of Orange, first cousin and husband of Queen Mary II, with whom he jointly ruled England, 1689–1702.

5. I.e., during the reign of the Catholic Mary Tudor of England (1553–58), called "Bloody Mary" for her persecution of Protestants. Common reading in New England was John Foxe's *Acts and Monuments* (1563), soon known as the *Book of Martyrs;* it concluded with horrifically detailed accounts of martyrdoms under Mary.

6. Indian leader of the Wampanoags who waged war (1675–76) against the New England colonists.

'If it be as thou sayest,' replied goodman Brown, 'I marvel they never spoke of these matters. Or, verily, I marvel not, seeing that the least rumor of the sort would have driven them from New-England. We are a people of prayer, and good works, to boot, and abide no such wickedness.'

'Wickedness or not,' said the traveler with the twisted staff, 'I have a very general acquaintance here in New-England. The deacons of many a church have drunk the communion wine with me; the selectmen, of divers towns, make me their chairman; and a majority of the Great and General Court[7] are firm supporters of my interest. The governor and I, too—but these are state-secrets.'

'Can this be so!' cried goodman Brown, with a stare of amazement at his undisturbed companion. 'Howbeit, I have nothing to do with the governor and council; they have their own ways, and are no rule for a simple husbandman,[8] like me. But, were I to go on with thee, how should I meet the eye of that good old man, our minister, at Salem village? Oh, his voice would make me tremble, both Sabbath-day and lecture day!'[9]

Thus far, the elder traveler had listened with due gravity, but now burst into a fit of irrepressible mirth, shaking himself so violently, that his snake-like staff actually seemed to wriggle in sympathy.

'Ha! ha! ha!' shouted he, again and again; then composing himself, 'Well, go on, goodman Brown, go on; but, pr'y thee, don't kill me with laughing!'

'Well, then, to end the matter at once,' said goodman Brown, considerably nettled, 'there is my wife, Faith. It would break her dear little heart; and I'd rather break my own!'

'Nay, if that be the case,' answered the other, 'e'en go thy ways, goodman Brown. I would not, for twenty old women like the one hobbling before us, that Faith should come to any harm.'

As he spoke, he pointed his staff at a female figure on the path, in whom goodman Brown recognized a very pious and exemplary dame, who had taught him his catechism, in youth, and was still his moral and spiritual adviser, jointly with the minister and deacon Gookin.

'A marvel, truly, that goody Cloyse[10] should be so far in the wilderness, at night-fall!' said he. 'But, with your leave, friend, I shall take a cut through the woods, until we have left this Christian woman behind.

---

7. The legislature.
8. Usually, farmer; here, man of ordinary status.
9. Midweek sermon day, Wednesday or Thursday.
10. Hawthorne uses historical names of people involved in the Salem witchcraft trials. "Goody" means "goodwife" and was a polite title for a married woman of humble rank.

Being a stranger to you, she might ask whom I was consorting with, and whither I was going.'

'Be it so,' said his fellow-traveler. 'Betake you to the woods, and let me keep the path.'

Accordingly, the young man turned aside, but took care to watch his companion, who advanced softly along the road, until he had come within a staff's length of the old dame. She, meanwhile, was making the best of her way, with singular speed for so aged a woman, and mumbling some indistinct words, a prayer, doubtless, as she went. The traveler put forth his staff, and touched her withered neck with what seemed the serpent's tail.

'The devil!' screamed the pious old lady.

'Then goody Cloyse knows her old friend?' observed the traveler, confronting her, and leaning on his writhing stick.

'Ah, forsooth, and is it your worship, indeed?' cried the good dame. 'Yea, truly is it, and in the very image of my old gossip, goodman Brown, the grandfather of the silly fellow that now is. But, would your worship believe it? my broomstick hath strangely disappeared, stolen, as I suspect, by that unhanged witch, goody Cory, and that, too, when I was all anointed with the juice of smallage and cinque-foil and wolf's-bane'— [11]

'Mingled with fine wheat and the fat of a new-born babe,' said the shape of old goodman Brown.

'Ah, your worship knows the receipt,' cried the old lady, cackling aloud. 'So, as I was saying, being all ready for the meeting, and no horse to ride on, I made up my mind to foot it; for they tell me, there is a nice young man to be taken into communion to-night. But now your good worship will lend me your arm, and we shall be there in a twinkling.'

'That can hardly be,' answered her friend. 'I may not spare you my arm, goody Cloyse, but here is my staff, if you will.'

So saying, he threw it down at her feet, where, perhaps, it assumed life, being one of the rods which its owner had formerly lent to the Egyptian Magi. [12] Of this fact, however, goodman Brown could not take cognizance. He had cast up his eyes in astonishment, and looking down again, beheld neither goody Cloyse nor the serpentine staff, but his fellow-traveler alone, who waited for him as calmly as if nothing had happened.

---

11. Plants associated with witchcraft: wild celery or parsley; a five-lobed plant of the rose family (from the Latin for "five fingers"); hooded, poisonous plant known as monkshood ("bane" means "poison").

12. See Exodus 7.11 for the magicians of Egypt who duplicated Aaron's feat of casting down his rod before Pharaoh and making it turn into a serpent.

'That old woman taught me my catechism!' said the young man; and there was a world of meaning in this simple comment.

They continued to walk onward, while the elder traveler exhorted his companion to make good speed and persevere in the path, discoursing so aptly, that his arguments seemed rather to spring up in the bosom of his auditor, than to be suggested by himself. As they went, he plucked a branch of maple, to serve for a walking-stick, and began to strip it of the twigs and little boughs, which were wet with evening dew. The moment his fingers touched them, they became strangely withered and dried up, as with a week's sunshine. Thus the pair proceeded, at a good free pace, until suddenly, in a gloomy hollow of the road, goodman Brown sat himself down on the stump of a tree, and refused to go any farther.

'Friend,' said he, stubbornly, 'my mind is made up. Not another step will I budge on this errand. What if a wretched old woman do choose to go to the devil, when I thought she was going to Heaven! Is that any reason why I should quit my dear Faith, and go after her?'

'You will think better of this, by-and-by,' said his acquaintance, composedly. 'Sit here and rest yourself awhile; and when you feel like moving again, there is my staff to help you along.'

Without more words, he threw his companion the maple stick, and was as speedily out of sight, as if he had vanished into the deepening gloom. The young man sat a few moments, by the roadside, applauding himself greatly, and thinking with how clear a conscience he should meet the minister, in his morning-walk, nor shrink from the eye of good old deacon Gookin. And what calm sleep would be his, that very night, which was to have been spent so wickedly, but purely and sweetly now, in the arms of Faith! Amidst these pleasant and praiseworthy meditations, goodman Brown heard the tramp of horses along the road, and deemed it advisable to conceal himself within the verge of the forest, conscious of the guilty purpose that had brought him thither, though now so happily turned from it.

On came the hoof-tramps and the voices of the riders, two grave old voices, conversing soberly as they drew near. These mingled sounds appeared to pass along the road, within a few yards of the young man's hiding-place; but owing, doubtless, to the depth of the gloom, at that particular spot, neither the travelers nor their steeds were visible. Though their figures brushed the small boughs by the way-side, it could not be seen that they intercepted, even for a moment, the faint gleam from the strip of bright sky, athwart which they must have passed. Goodman Brown alternately crouched and stood on tip-toe, pulling aside the branches, and thrusting forth his head as far as he durst, without discerning so much as a shadow. It vexed him the more, because he could have sworn, were such a thing possible, that he recognized the voices of the minister and deacon Gookin, jogging along quietly, as they were wont to do, when bound to some ordination or ecclesiastical council. While yet within hearing, one of the riders stopped to pluck a switch.

'Of the two, reverend Sir,' said the voice like the deacon's, 'I had rather miss an ordination-dinner than to-night's meeting. They tell me that some of our community are to be here from Falmouth[13] and beyond, and others from Connecticut and Rhode-Island; besides several of the Indian powows,[14] who, after their fashion, know almost as much deviltry as the best of us. Moreover, there is a goodly young woman to be taken into communion.'

'Mighty well, deacon Gookin!' replied the solemn old tones of the minister. 'Spur up, or we shall be late. Nothing can be done, you know, until I get on the ground.'

The hoofs clattered again, and the voices, talking so strangely in the empty air, passed on through the forest, where no church had ever been gathered, nor solitary Christian prayed. Whither, then, could these holy men be journeying, so deep into the heathen wilderness? Young goodman Brown caught hold of a tree, for support, being ready to sink down on the ground, faint and overburthened with the heavy sickness of his heart. He looked up to the sky, doubting whether there really was a Heaven above him. Yet, there was the blue arch, and the stars brightening in it.

'With Heaven above, and Faith below, I will yet stand firm against the devil!' cried goodman Brown.

While he still gazed upward, into the deep arch of the firmament, and had lifted his hands to pray, a cloud, though no wind was stirring, hurried across the zenith, and hid the brightening stars. The blue sky was still visible, except directly overhead, where this black mass of cloud was sweeping swiftly northward. Aloft in the air, as if from the depths of the cloud, came a confused and doubtful sound of voices. Once, the listener fancied that he could distinguish the accents of town's-people of his own, men and women, both pious and ungodly, many of whom he had met at the communion-table, and had seen others rioting at the tavern. The next moment, so indistinct were the sounds, he doubted whether he had heard aught but the murmur of the old forest, whispering without a wind. Then came a stronger swell of those familiar tones, heard daily in the sunshine, at Salem village, but never, until now, from a cloud of night. There was one voice, of a young woman, uttering lamentations, yet with

---

13. Town on Cape Cod, about 70 miles from Salem.

14. Medicine men. Usually spelled "pow-wow" and later used to refer to any conference or gathering.

an uncertain sorrow, and entreating for some favor, which, perhaps, it would grieve her to obtain. And all the unseen multitude, both saints and sinners, seemed to encourage her onward.

'Faith!' shouted goodman Brown, in a voice of agony and desperation; and the echoes of the forest mocked him, crying—'Faith! Faith!' as if bewildered wretches were seeking her, all through the wilderness.

The cry of grief, rage, and terror, was yet piercing the night, when the unhappy husband held his breath for a response. There was a scream, drowned immediately in a louder murmur of voices, fading into far-off laughter, as the dark cloud swept away, leaving the clear and silent sky above goodman Brown. But something fluttered lightly down through the air, and caught on the branch of a tree. The young man seized it, and beheld a pink ribbon.

'My Faith is gone!' cried he, after one stupefied moment. 'There is no good on earth; and sin is but a name. Come, devil! for to thee is this world given.'

And maddened with despair, so that he laughed loud and long, did goodman Brown grasp his staff and set forth again, at such a rate, that he seemed to fly along the forest-path, rather than to walk or run. The road grew wilder and drearier, and more faintly traced, and vanished at length, leaving him in the heart of the dark wilderness, still rushing onward, with the instinct that guides mortal man to evil. The whole forest was peopled with frightful sounds; the creaking of the trees, the howling of wild beasts, and the yell of Indians; while, sometimes, the wind tolled like a distant church-bell, and sometimes gave a broad roar around the traveler, as if all Nature were laughing him to scorn. But he was himself the chief horror of the scene, and shrank not from its other horrors.

'Ha! ha! ha!' roared goodman Brown, when the wind laughed at him. 'Let us hear which will laugh loudest! Think not to frighten me with your deviltry! Come witch, come wizard, come Indian powow, come devil himself! and here comes goodman Brown. You may as well fear him as he fear you!'

In truth, all through the haunted forest, there could be nothing more frightful than the figure of goodman Brown. On he flew, among the black pines, brandishing his staff with frenzied gestures, now giving vent to an inspiration of horrid blasphemy, and now shouting forth such laughter, as set all the echoes of the forest laughing like demons around him. The fiend in his own shape is less hideous, than when he rages in the breast of man. Thus sped the demoniac on his course, until, quivering among the trees, he saw a red light before him, as when the felled trunks and branches of a clearing have been set on fire, and throw up their lurid blaze against the sky, at the hour of midnight. He paused, in a lull of the tempest that had driven him onward, and heard the swell of what seemed a hymn, rolling solemnly from a distance, with the weight of many voices. He knew the tune; it was a familiar one in the choir of the village meeting-house. The verse died heavily away, and was lengthened by a chorus, not of human voices, but of all the sounds of the benighted wilderness, pealing in awful harmony together. Goodman Brown cried out; and his cry was lost to his own ear, by its unison with the cry of the desert.

In the interval of silence, he stole forward, until the light glared full upon his eyes. At one extremity of an open space, hemmed in by the dark wall of the forest, arose a rock, bearing some rude, natural resemblance either to an altar or a pulpit, and surrounded by four blazing pines, their tops a flame, their stems untouched, like candles at an evening meeting. The mass of foliage, that had overgrown the summit of the rock, was all on fire, blazing high into the night, and fitfully illuminating the whole field. Each pendent twig and leafy festoon was in a blaze. As the red light arose and fell, a numerous congregation alternately shone forth, then disappeared in shadow, and again grew, as it were, out of the darkness, peopling the heart of the solitary woods at once.

'A grave and dark-clad company!' quoth goodman Brown.

In truth, they were such. Among them, quivering to-and-fro, between gloom and splendor, appeared faces that would be seen, next day, at the council-board of the province, and others which, Sabbath after Sabbath, looked devoutly heavenward, and benignantly over the crowded pews, from the holiest pulpits in the land. Some affirm, that the lady of the governor was there. At least, there were high dames well known to her, and wives of honored husbands, and widows, a great multitude, and ancient maidens, all of excellent repute, and fair young girls, who trembled, lest their mothers should espy them. Either the sudden gleams of light, flashing over the obscure field, bedazzled goodman Brown, or he recognized a score of the church-members of Salem village, famous for their especial sanctity. Good old deacon Gookin had arrived, and waited at the skirts of that venerable saint, his revered pastor. But, irreverently consorting with these grave, reputable, and pious people, these elders of the church, these chaste dames and dewy virgins, there were men of dissolute lives and women of spotted fame, wretches given over to all mean and filthy vice, and suspected even of horrid crimes. It was strange to see, that the good shrank not from the wicked, nor were the sinners abashed by the saints. Scattered, also, among their pale-faced enemies, were the Indian priests, or powows, who had often scared their native forest with more hideous incantations than any known to English witchcraft.

'But, where is Faith?' thought goodman Brown; and, as hope came into his heart, he trembled.

Another verse of the hymn arose, a slow and solemn strain, such as the pious love, but joined to words which expressed all that our nature can conceive of sin, and darkly hinted at far more. Unfathomable to mere mortals is the lore of fiends. Verse after verse was sung, and still the chorus of the desert swelled between, like the deepest tone of a mighty organ. And, with the final peal of that dreadful anthem, there came a sound, as if the roaring wind, the rushing streams, the howling beasts, and every other voice of the unconverted wilderness, were mingling and according with the voice of guilty man, in homage to the prince of all. The four blazing pines threw up a loftier flame, and obscurely discovered shapes and visages of horror on the smoke-wreaths, above the impious assembly. At the same moment, the fire on the rock shot redly forth, and formed a glowing arch above its base, where now appeared a figure. With reverence be it spoken, the apparition bore no slight similitude, both in garb and manner, to some grave divine of the New-England churches.

'Bring forth the converts!' cried a voice, that echoed through the field and rolled into the forest.

At the word, goodman Brown stept forth from the shadow of the trees, and approached the congregation, with whom he felt a loathful brotherhood, by the sympathy of all that was wicked in his heart. He could have well nigh sworn, that the shape of his own dead father beckoned him to advance, looking downward from a smoke-wreath, while a woman with dim features of despair, threw out her hand to warn him back. Was it his mother? But he had no power to retreat one step, nor to resist, even in thought, when the minister and good old deacon Gookin, seized his arms, and led him to the blazing rock. Thither came also the slender form of a veiled female, led between Goody Cloyse, that pious teacher of the catechism, and Martha Carrier, who had received the devil's promise to be queen of hell. A rampant hag was she! And there stood the proselytes, beneath the canopy of fire.

'Welcome, my children,' said the dark figure, 'to the communion of your race![15] Ye have found, thus young, your nature and your destiny. My children, look behind you!'

They turned; and flashing forth, as it were, in a sheet of flame, the fiend-worshippers were seen; the smile of welcome gleamed darkly on every visage.

'There,' resumed the sable form, 'are all whom ye have reverenced from

---

15. The *New-England Magazine* erroneously printed "grave," corrected to "race" in *Mosses from an Old Manse* (1846).

youth. Ye deemed them holier than yourselves, and shrank from your own sin, contrasting it with their lives of righteousness, and prayerful aspirations heavenward. Yet, here are they all, in my worshipping assembly! This night it shall be granted you to know their secret deeds; how hoary-bearded elders of the church have whispered wanton words to the young maids of their households; how many a woman, eager for widow's weeds, has given her husband a drink at bed-time, and let him sleep his last sleep in her bosom; how beardless youths have made haste to inherit their fathers' wealth; and how fair damsels — blush not, sweet ones! — have dug little graves in the garden, and bidden me, the sole guest, to an infant's funeral. By the sympathy of your human hearts for sin, ye shall scent out all the places — whether in church, bed-chamber, street, field, or forest — where crime has been committed, and shall exult to behold the whole earth one stain of guilt, one mighty blood-spot. Far more than this! It shall be your's to penetrate, in every bosom, the deep mystery of sin, the fountain of all wicked arts, and which, inexhaustibly supplies more evil impulses than human power — than my power, at its utmost! — can make manifest in deeds. And now, my children, look upon each other.'

They did so; and, by the blaze of the hell-kindled torches, the wretched man beheld his Faith, and the wife her husband, trembling before that unhallowed altar.

'Lo! there ye stand, my children,' said the figure, in a deep and solemn tone, almost sad, with its despairing awfulness, as if his once angelic nature could yet mourn for our miserable race. 'Depending upon one another's hearts, ye had still hoped, that virtue were not all a dream. Now are ye undeceived! Evil is the nature of mankind. Evil must be your only happiness. Welcome, again, my children, to the communion of your race!'

'Welcome!' repeated the fiend-worshippers, in one cry of despair and triumph.

And there they stood, the only pair, as it seemed, who were yet hesitating on the verge of wickedness, in this dark world. A basin was hollowed, naturally, in the rock. Did it contain water, reddened by the lurid light? or was it blood? or, perchance, a liquid flame? Herein did the Shape of Evil dip his hand, and prepare to lay the mark of baptism upon their foreheads, that they might be partakers of the mystery of sin, more conscious of the secret guilt of others, both in deed and thought, than they could now be of their own. The husband cast one look at his pale wife, and Faith at him. What polluted wretches would the next glance shew them to each other, shuddering alike at what they disclosed and what they saw!

'Faith! Faith!' cried the husband. 'Look up to Heaven, and resist the Wicked One!'

Whether Faith obeyed, he knew not. Hardly had he spoken, when he found himself amid calm night and solitude, listening to a roar of the wind, which died heavily away through the forest. He staggered against the rock and felt it chill and damp, while a hanging twig, that had been all on fire, besprinkled his cheek with the coldest dew.

The next morning, young goodman Brown came slowly into the street of Salem village, staring around him like a bewildered man. The good old minister was taking a walk along the graveyard, to get an appetite for breakfast and meditate his sermon, and bestowed a blessing, as he passed, on goodman Brown. He shrank from the venerable saint, as if to avoid an anathema. Old deacon Gookin was at domestic worship, and the holy words of his prayer were heard through the open window. 'What God doth the wizard pray to?' quoth goodman Brown. Goody Cloyse, that excellent old Christian, stood in the early sunshine, at her own lattice, catechising a little girl, who had brought her a pint of morning's milk. Goodman Brown snatched away the child, as from the grasp of the fiend himself. Turning the corner by the meeting-house, he spied the head of Faith, with the pink ribbons, gazing anxiously forth, and bursting into such joy at sight of him, that she skipt along the street, and almost kissed her husband before the whole village. But, goodman Brown looked sternly and sadly into her face, and passed on without a greeting.

Had goodman Brown fallen asleep in the forest, and only dreamed a wild dream of a witch-meeting?

Be it so, if you will. But alas! it was a dream of evil omen for young goodman Brown. A stern, a sad, a darkly meditative, a distrustful, if not a desperate man, did he become, from the night of that fearful dream. On the Sabbath-day, when the congregation were singing a holy psalm, he could not listen, because an anthem of sin rushed loudly upon his ear, and drowned all the blessed strain. When the minister spoke from the pulpit, with power and fervid eloquence, and, with his hand on the open bible, of the sacred truths of our religion, and of saint-like lives and triumphant deaths, and of future bliss or misery unutterable, then did goodman Brown turn pale, dreading, lest the roof should thunder down upon the gray blasphemer and his hearers. Often, awakening suddenly at midnight, he shrank from the bosom of Faith, and at morning or eventide, when the family knelt down at prayer, he scowled, and muttered to himself, and gazed sternly at his wife, and turned away. And when he had lived long, and was borne to his grave, a hoary corpse, followed by Faith, an aged woman, and children and grandchildren, a goodly procession, besides neighbors, not a few, they carved no hopeful verse upon his tomb-stone; for his dying hour was gloom.

3. Moral and Religious Concerns with the New Paradigm

Introduction
Karl Marx, "Alienated Labour"

Karl Marx is the most famous and influential critic of the system Locke's myth helped create. While Eastern Europe and the Soviet Union are undergoing dramatic changes, apparently in the direction of a free-market economy, Marx's influence goes beyond those societies that view him as a guiding thinker. His influence is inescapable even in the staunchest centers of capitalism — he is the opponent who must be defeated. Yet in the United States Marx is seldom read, and more rarely is he understood.

Few people know, for example, that Marx, like Locke or Smith before him, was a humanist first and an economist second: as the following selection from his early writings shows, Marx's basic concern was the well-being of ordinary humans. While ultimately an opponent of capitalism because he felt it was a system which allowed a few people to thrive on the efforts of the majority (who are cheated from most of the bounties of their efforts), Marx believed that capitalism was a necessary and important phase in human history. Like his Enlightenment predecessors, Marx was a firm believer in progress — he was a utopian thinker who envisioned a glorious future ushered in by industrialization. His utopia, however, was one where wealth and power were to be distributed equitably among all citizens.

For most Westerners, though, Marx is best known for his systematic and sustained criticism of capitalism. Words like 'alienation' and 'proletariat' have become part of our vocabulary, and it is through his critique that we can best comprehend his ideas. Like Locke, Marx begins with a story, with a version of history and prehistory which permeates his entire work. The major contours of his myth are taken from Hegel.

Marx (and Hegel) believed that humans become whatever they become only through interaction with others: if we become selves at all (or better, whatever selves we become), social interactions are the key. Furthermore, conflicts not only are inevitable (as Locke decried), but they are essential for human growth and development. Human development requires effort and struggle with others. Finally, Marx believed that whole societies, like individuals, are more or less developed depending on the social histories they have had.

Contrary to Locke's vision of human history being a fall from the ideal (his paradise: "the state of nature"), for Marx, while humans did lose their animal-like innocence through evolution, more sophisticated societies and individuals have steadily been evolving. His central disagreement with Locke's vision, though, is his insistence that humans cannot become human without civilization, without rules and authority, without organization and government of some kind, or without conflict. Locke's myth is extremely misleading, Marx contends, when it instills the image that we are best off in isolation, that individuals are mainly weakened by society. For Marx strong individuals are born of and sustained by society. To be fully human is to be social, not pre-social.

Marx's contribution through this essay is not only to call our attention to the ways in which the capitalist system creates alienation but most centrally to argue that it is an inevitable result of this system.

With this background we will be able to understand Marx's concerns in our selection. While the relationship between capitalists and workers is not at all unique in being based on conflict, it is a tremendously unfair conflict which the worker can only lose. Perhaps ultimately the workers will become so desperate that they will overthrow the capitalists (perhaps even in an organized and successful transformation of the entire edifice of capitalism — a revolution), but under the existing system workers inevitably will be exploited, and their alienation will be immense.

Marx believes that this exploitation benefits mainly the owners *and* that it is built into the system. Capital, according to Marx, is accumulated labor (this is part of Marx's version of Locke's labor theory of value). People who control capital (capitalists) are in essence controlling the labor that workers have performed, while the workers themselves have little access to this accumulated labor (wealth and power). For Marx capitalism is a grand form of theft which is sanctified by myths like Locke's. Workers are prevented from owning money-making property, and they are kept from becoming wealthy enough to join the capitalists (who, after all, want to win the race by minimizing competition) through the system of *wages*. The good of the individual employer is to minimize production costs; thus wages should be kept as low as possible. Capitalists want a ready supply of labor, and therefore they pay workers enough to live on. But they also keep workers coming back for more by making it impossible for them to make a living in any other way and by keeping a certain number of people unemployed so that workers compete with each other for scarce jobs.

Marx's logic is quite simple. The system of wage labor is a rationalized but not especially sophisticated form of theft. Marx wants people to see that wage labor is one of the neatest hat tricks in history: the capitalists steal the workers' wealth, pretend it is their own, and then act magnanimous in "allowing" people to work for a small share of the wealth which was theirs in the first place. In the process not only do workers get cheated out of the full fruits of their labor, but they become mere cogs in a machine. In this system workers are valued only as one more unit in the cost of production, only as commodities. *Alienation* inevitably results.

What does Marx mean by alienation? Humans become alienated, they become *as aliens,* in the process of working as mere commodities. When people work on objects (nature), they put themselves into their working and the products of their work. If workers control the selection and use of these objects, they will not become alienated—they will be *at home* in their working, and the selves as well as the other products they produce will be theirs to use as they wish. When someone else controls the means of production (nature, the tools, and processes of production) and the products, then the worker cannot relate to the entire process and its results except as an alien.

For Marx labor (*at least* for factory workers in early industrial societies) in a capitalist system erodes 1) craftsmanship, 2) human harmony with nature, 3) the integration of the self, and 4) human community.

1) Craftsmanship declines because workers cannot identify with the process of production. Recent innovations in factory work such as quality circles or flexible hours recognize this connection between the worker's sense of involvement with what is produced (and how it is produced) and the quality of craftsmanship. Someone who mindlessly acts like a cog in a machine loses the desire for quality. This results from what Marx calls "forced labor"—in order to survive a person must sell (alienate) one's labor, sell it to someone who then takes away from the worker's decision-making in the productive process.

2) If when I work I only relate to the world around me through the terms set by someone else, then I do not choose what aspects of the world to work with or how I will do so. Nature itself becomes alien to me: it becomes a mere object to overcome, to modify into someone else's product. This estrangement, of course, also adds to the degeneration of craftsmanship. Excellent craftspeople are those who have an intimate and caring relation with the materials on which they work.

3) Marx believes that by lacking control over the productive (creative) process, a person also becomes alienated from himself. Any work we do, whether paid or not, whether forced or not, involves self-creation. When we work we literally make ourselves: through the process of working we

learn, we grow, we change, we become much of what we are. If someone else owns our laboring, then we lose control over much of what *we* are made in the process. Marx believes that if our creative, working time and energies are spent becoming an automaton, then our only opportunity for truly being human is when we are not working—when we are "eating, sleeping, and procreating." Marx finds this ironic as well as sad and outrageous: "the worker feels himself to be freely active only in his animal functions [eating, etc.], while in his human functions [productive, creative work] he is reduced to an animal."

4) Marx believes, finally, that when we sell our labor and compete with others for the scarce commodities (wages) offered up by the capitalist system, we irrupt the bonds of community. When this happens we lose our ties to what Marx calls our "species nature," our basic source of humanity. Recall that for Marx (and Hegel) we become human through community; thus to erode community through competition is to erode our links to the ground of our being human. To cease being community-centered is to cease being human.

While various aspects of the system he criticized have changed in ways Marx did not anticipate, thus mitigating parts of his critique, his analysis is a brilliant and humanistic attack on the nature and results of the capitalist system. He, like Locke and Smith, turns our attention to economic systems as a fundamental dimension of human existence around which much of life revolves, and he, like his capitalist as well as socialist predecessors and contemporaries, is most concerned with human flourishing. There are great differences in perspective between Marx and his foes, but those differences probably would not be very threatening to the capitalist order if Marx did not share fundamental values with the worldview he wishes to dethrone.

"Alienated Labour" is the central part of the young Marx's *Economic and Philosophical Manuscript of 1844*. While incomplete and in need of revision, these *Manuscripts* provide us with the philosophical and moral underpinnings of Marx's entire corpus.

Karl Marx

Alienated Labour

[XXII] We have begun from the presuppositions of political economy. We have accepted its terminology and its laws. . . . From political economy itself, in its own words, we have shown that the worker sinks to the level of a commodity, and to a most miserable commodity; that the misery of the worker increases with the power and volume of his production; that the necessary result of competition is the accumulation of capital in a few hands, and thus a restoration of monopoly in a more terrible form; and finally that the distinction between capitalist and landlord, and between agricultural labourer and industrial worker, must disappear, and the whole of society divide into the two classes of property *owners* and *propertyless* workers.

Political economy begins with the fact of private property; it does not explain it. It conceives the *material* process of private property, as this occurs in reality, in general and abstract formulas which then serve it as laws. It does not *comprehend* these laws; that is, it does not show how they arise out of the nature of private property. Political economy provides no explanation of the basis for the distinction of labour from capital, or capital from land. When, for example, the relation of wages to profits is defined, this is explained in terms of the interests of capitalists; in other words, what should be explained is assumed. Similarly, competition is referred to at every point and is explained in terms of external conditions. Political economy tells us nothing about the extent to which these external and apparently accidental conditions are simply the expression of a necessary development. We have seen how exchange itself seems an accidental fact. The only motive forces which political economy recognizes are *avarice* and the *war between the avaricious, competition.*

Just because political economy fails to understand the interconnexions within this movement it was possible to oppose the doctrine of competition to that of monopoly, the doctrine of freedom of the crafts to that of the guilds, the doctrine of the division of landed property to that of the great estates; for competition, freedom of crafts, and the division of

From *Economic and Philosophical Manuscripts of 1844*, translated by Martin Milligan, International Publishing Company, © 1964, pages 65–72. Reprinted by permission of the publisher.

landed property were conceived only as accidental consequences brought about by will and force, rather than as necessary, inevitable and natural consequences of monopoly, the guild system and feudal property.

Thus we have now to grasp the real connexion between this whole system of alienation — private property, acquisitiveness, the separation of labour, capital and land, exchange and competition, value and the devaluation of man, monopoly and competition — and the system of *money*.

Let us not begin our explanation, as does the economist, from a legendary primordial condition. Such a primordial condition does not explain anything; it merely removes the question into a grey and nebulous distance. It asserts as a fact or event what it should deduce, namely, the necessary relation between two things; for example, between the division of labour and exchange. In the same way theology explains the origin of evil by the fall of man; that is, it asserts as a historical fact what it should explain.

We shall begin from a *contemporary* economic fact. The worker becomes poorer the more wealth he produces and the more his production increases in power and extent. The worker becomes an ever cheaper commodity the more goods he creates. The *devaluation* of the human world increases in direct relation with the *increase in value* of the world of things. Labour does not only create goods; it also produces itself and the worker as a *commodity,* and indeed in the same proportion as it produces goods.

This fact simply implies that the object produced by labour, its product, now stands opposed to it as an *alien being,* as a *power independent* of the producer. The product of labour is labour which has been embodied in an object and turned into a physical thing; this product is an *objectification* of labour. The performance of work is at the same time its objectification. The performance of work appears in the sphere of political economy as a *vitiation* of the worker, objectification as a *loss* and as *servitude to the object,* and appropriation as *alienation.*

So much does the performance of work appear as vitiation that the worker is vitiated to the point of starvation. So much does objectification appear as loss of the object that the worker is deprived of the most essential things not only of life but also of work. Labour itself becomes an object which he can acquire only by the greatest effort and with unpredictable interruptions. So much does the appropriation of the object appear as alienation that the more objects the worker produces the fewer he can possess and the more he falls under the domination of his product, of capital.

All these consequences follow from the fact that the worker is related to the *product of his labour* as to an *alien* object. For it is clear on this presupposition that the more the worker expends himself in work the more powerful becomes the world of objects which he creates in face of himself, the poorer he becomes in his inner life, and the less he belongs to himself. It is just the same as in religion. The more of himself man attributes to God the less he has left in himself. The worker puts his life into the object, and his life then belongs no longer to himself but to the object. The greater his activity, therefore, the less he possesses. What is embodied in the product of his labour is no longer his own. The greater this product is, therefore, the more he is diminished. The *alienation* of the worker in his product means not only that his labour becomes an object, assumes an *external* existence, but that it exists independently, *outside himself,* and alien to him, and that it stands opposed to him as an autonomous power. The life which he has given to the object sets itself against him as an alien and hostile force.

[XXIII] Let us now examine more closely the phenomenon of *objectification;* the worker's production and the *alienation* and *loss* of the object it produces, which is involved in it. The worker can create nothing without *nature,* without the *sensuous external world.* The latter is the material in which his labour is realized, in which it is active, out of which and through which it produces things.

But just as nature affords the *means of existence* of labour, in the sense that labour cannot *live* without objects upon which it can be exercised, so also it provides the *means of existence* in a narrower sense; namely the means of physical existence for the *worker* himself. Thus, the more the worker *appropriates* the external world of sensuous nature by his labour the more he deprives himself of *means of existence,* in two respects: first, that the sensuous external world becomes progressively less an object belonging to his labour or a means of existence of his labour, and secondly, that it becomes progressively less a means of existence in the direct sense, a means for the physical subsistence of the worker.

In both respects, therefore, the worker becomes a slave of the object; first, in that he receives an *object of work,* i.e. receives *work,* and secondly, in that he receives *means of subsistence.* Thus the object enables him to exist, first as a *worker* and secondly, as a *physical subject.* The culmination of this enslavement is that he can only maintain himself as a *physical subject* so far as he is a *worker,* and that it is only as a *physical subject* that he is a worker.

(The alienation of the worker in his object is expressed as follows in the laws of political economy: the more the worker produces the less he has to consume; the more value he creates the more worthless he becomes; the more refined his product the more crude and misshapen the worker; the more civilized the product the more barbarous the worker; the more powerful the work the more feeble the worker; the more the work manifests intelligence the more the worker declines in intelligence and becomes a slave of nature.)

Political economy conceals the alienation in the nature of labour in so far as it does not examine the direct relationship between the worker (work) and production. Labour certainly produces marvels for the rich but it produces privation for the worker. It produces palaces, but hovels for the worker. It produces beauty, but deformity for the worker. It replaces labour by machinery, but it casts some of the workers back into a barbarous kind of work and turns the others into machines. It produces intelligence, but also stupidity and cretinism for the workers.

The direct relationship of labour to its products is the relationship of the worker to the objects of his production. The relationship of property owners to the objects of production and to production itself is merely a *consequence* of this first relationship and confirms it. We shall consider this second aspect later.

Thus, when we ask what is the important relationship of labour, we are concerned with the relationship of the *worker* to production.

So far we have considered the alienation of the worker only from one aspect; namely, *his relationship with the products of his labour.* However, alienation appears not merely in the result but also in the *process* of *production,* within *productive activity* itself. How could the worker stand in an alien relationship to the product of his activity if he did not alienate himself in the act of production itself? The product is indeed only the *résumé* of activity, of production. Consequently, if the product of labour is alienation, production itself must be active alienation — the alienation of activity and the activity of alienation. The alienation of the object of labour merely summarizes the alienation in the work activity itself.

What constitutes the alienation of labour? First, that the work is *external* to the worker, that it is not part of his nature; and that, consequently, he does not fulfil himself in his work but denies himself, has a feeling of misery rather than well-being, does not develop freely his mental and physical energies but is physically exhausted and mentally debased. The worker, therefore, feels himself at home only during his leisure time, whereas at work he feels homeless. His work is not voluntary but imposed, *forced labour.* It is not the satisfaction of a need, but only a *means* for satisfying other needs. Its alien character is clearly shown by the fact that as soon as there is no physical or other compulsion it is avoided like the plague. External labour, labour in which man alienates himself, is a labour of self-sacrifice, of mortification. Finally, the external character of work for the worker is shown by the fact that it is not his own work but work for someone else, that in work he does not belong to himself but to another person.

Just as in religion the spontaneous activity of human fantasy, of the human brain and heart, reacts independently as an alien activity of gods or devils upon the individual, so the activity of the worker is not his own spontaneous activity. It is another's activity and a loss of his own spontaneity.

We arrive at the result that man (the worker) feels himself to be freely active only in his animal functions — eating, drinking and procreating, or at most also in his dwelling and in personal adornment — while in his human functions he is reduced to an animal. The animal becomes human and the human becomes animal.

Eating, drinking and procreating are of course also genuine human functions. But abstractly considered, apart from the environment of human activities, and turned into final and sole ends, they are animal functions.

[XXIV] We have now to infer a third characteristic of *alienated labour* from the two we have considered.

Man is a species-being not only in the sense that he makes the community (his own as well as those of other things) his object both practically and theoretically, but also (and this is simply another expression for the same thing) in the sense that he treats himself as the present, living species, as a *universal* and consequently free being.[1]

Species-life, for man as for animals, has its physical basis in the fact that man (like animals) lives from inorganic nature, and since man is more universal than an animal so the range of inorganic nature from which he lives is more universal. Plants, animals, minerals, air, light, etc. constitute, from the theoretical aspect, a part of human consciousness as objects of natural science and art; they are man's spiritual inorganic nature, his intellectual means of life, which he must first prepare for enjoyment and perpetuation. So also, from the practical aspect, they form a part of human life and activity. In practice man lives only from these natural products, whether in the form of food, heating, clothing, housing, etc. The universality of man appears in practice in the universality which makes the whole of nature into his inorganic body: (1) as a direct means of life; and equally (2) as the material object and instrument of his life activity. Nature is the inorganic body of man; that is to say nature, excluding the human body itself. To say that man *lives* from nature means that nature is his *body* with which he must remain in a continuous interchange in order not to die. The statement that the physical and mental life of man, and nature, are interdependent means simply that nature is interdependent with itself, for man is a part of nature.

Since alienated labour: (1) alienates nature from man; and (2) alienates man from himself, from his own active function, his life activity; so it alienates him from the species. It makes *species-life* into a means of individual life. In the first place it alienates species-life and individual life, and secondly, it turns the latter, as an abstraction, into the purpose of the former, also in its abstract and alienated form.

For labour, *life activity, productive life,* now appear to man only as *means* for the satisfaction of a need, the need to maintain his physical existence. Productive life is, however, species-life. It is life creating life. In the type of life activity resides the whole character of a species, its species-character; and free, conscious activity is the species-character of human beings. Life itself appears only as a *means of life.*

The animal is one with its life activity. It does not distinguish the activity from itself. It is *its activity.* But man makes his life activity itself an object of his will and consciousness. He has a conscious life activity. It is not a determination with which he is completely identified. Conscious life activity distinguishes man from the life activity of animals. Only for this reason is he a species-being. Or rather, he is only a self-conscious being, i.e. his own life is an object for him, because he is a species-being. Only for this reason is his activity free activity. Alienated labour reverses the relationship, in that man because he is a self-conscious being makes his life activity, his *being,* only a means for his *existence.*

The practical construction of an *objective world,* the *manipulation* of inorganic nature, is the confirmation of man as a conscious species-being, i.e. a being who treats the species as his own being or himself as a species-being. Of course, animals also produce. They construct nests, dwellings, as in the case of bees, beavers, ants, etc. But they only produce what is strictly necessary for themselves or their young. They produce only in a single direction, while man produces universally. They produce only under the compulsion of direct physical needs, while man produces when he is free from physical need and only truly produces in freedom from such need. Animals produce only themselves, while man reproduces the whole of nature. The products of animal production belong directly to their physical bodies, while man is free in face of his product. Animals construct only in accordance with the standards and needs of the species to which they belong, while man knows how to produce in accordance with the standards of every species and knows how to apply the appropriate standard to the object. Thus man constructs also in accordance with the laws of beauty.

It is just in his work upon the objective world that man really proves himself as a *species-being.* This production is his active species-life. By means of it nature appears as *his* work and his reality. The object of labour is, therefore, the *objectification of man's species-life;* for he no longer reproduces himself merely intellectually, as in consciousness, but actively and in a real sense, and he sees his own reflection in a world which he has constructed. While, therefore, alienated labour takes away the object of production from man, it also takes away his *species-life,* his real objectivity as a species-being, and changes his advantage over animals into a disadvantage in so far as his inorganic body, nature, is taken from him.

Just as alienated labour transforms free and self-directed activity into a means, so it transforms the species-life of man into a means of physical existence.

Consciousness, which man has from his species, is transformed through alienation so that species-life becomes only a means for him. (3) Thus alienated labour turns the *species-life of man,* and also nature as his mental species-property, into an *alien* being and into a *means* for his *individual existence.* It alienates from man his own body, external nature, his mental life and his *human* life. (4) A direct consequence of the alienation of man from the product of his labour, from his life activity and from his species-life, is that *man is alienated* from other *men.* When man confronts himself he also confronts *other* men. What is true of man's relationship to his work, to the product of his work and to himself, is also true of his relationship to other men, to their labour and to the objects of their labour.

In general, the statement that man is alienated from his species-life means that each man is alienated from others, and that each of the others is likewise alienated from human life.

Human alienation, and above all the relation of man to himself, is first realized and expressed in the relationship between each man and other men. Thus in the relationship of alienated labour every man regards other men according to the standards and relationships in which he finds himself placed as a worker.

Introduction
Flannery O'Connor, "Good Country People"

Like another great American twentieth-century writer, T.S. Eliot, Flannery O'Connor rejected the values of the Enlightenment and found inspiration in traditional Western religious beliefs. Born in rural Georgia in 1925, she received her Master of Fine Arts degree from the University of Iowa's writer's workshop in 1946 and returned to Georgia to live with her mother and write until her premature death in 1964. A committed Roman Catholic, she defended traditional spiritual values and opposed compromises that were designed to make the church more palatable to a secularized world. The following excerpt from one of her letters discussing the church's prohibition of birth control is typical:

> I wish various [church] fathers would quit trying to defend it [ban on contraceptives] by saying the world can support 40 billion. I will rejoice the day they say: this is right, whether we all rot on top of one another or not, dear children, as we certainly may.

O'Connor is not impressed by the scientific and technological progress of modern society. Like Mathew Arnold, she understands that it has alienated us from the eternal in favor of a more abundant temporal existence. And like another earlier Christian existentialist, Soren Kierkegaard, she chooses to leap the chasm of temporal nihilism and grasp the rock of faith. As a Christian existentialist she insists upon completing the act of faith by rigorously following the moral standards of her belief. As you will see, she holds her fictional characters to the same high standards, believing that only through living our faith are we protected from the chaos of the industrial world.

In "Good Country People" she creates a world where people are held strictly accountable for their actions. As you read, pay particular attention to the mother, Mrs. Hopewell, and to her daughter, Joy-Hulga. You will see that Mrs. Hopewell is very good at coping with the flawed and limited temporal world. She accepts the limitations of her existence and makes the best of things. She negotiates her world with the aid of cliches that categorize and neutralize the problems she faces ("good country people, nothing's perfect"). While we might find her coping skills admirable, in O'Connor's cosmos she is not one of the saved. She is guilty of accepting the small Lockean vision rather than aspiring to a truly spiritual realm. She may represent the best we can be without God, but for Flannery O'Connor that is not enough.

Mrs. Hopewell's daughter, whom she has named Joy, has a doctorate in philosophy, but because of her physical disabilities she has chosen to live at home rather than seek an academic position. Joy has legally changed her name to Hulga, suggesting the cynicism she feels toward her mother's approach to life. She has assumed the posture of a free-thinking nihilist, with utter contempt for the small world her circumstances force her to inhabit. She has committed the classic Christian sin: she has chosen to live by terms dictated by her finite and flawed body rather than use her rich intellectual gifts. She has chosen the body over the soul. By not making the leap of faith, she has created her own hell, but as you will see, her hypocrisy creates for her an even greater hell.

A third character, Manley Pointer, is a con artist and Bible salesman. A complete cynic, he becomes a vehicle for showing Hulga that believing in nothing is an easy, but fatal, choice.

O'Connor's rejection of modern materialistic values has enormous implications for our world of work. O'Connor is not inhumane or in favor of suffering; rather, her philosophy leads her to focus less on temporal issues. She would have agreed with the French Catholic philosopher Pascal that the world of finite earthly concerns pales next to our proper concern with eternity. What would you expect her to say about the ideal of progress, for instance? Would you expect sympathy for the demands of labor unions? Great concern about child labor? How would she respond to the consumer economy? Her approach to faith seems very tough-minded; would you expect her ideas to be attractive to many contemporaries? Do you find it attractive?

Flannery O'Connor

Good Country People

Besides the neutral expression that she wore when she was alone, Mrs. Freeman had two others, forward and reverse, that she used for all her human dealings. Her forward expression was steady and driving like the advance of a heavy truck. Her eyes never swerved to left or right but turned as the story turned as if they followed a yellow line down the center of it. She seldom used the other expression because it was not often necessary for her to retract a statement, but when she did, her face came to a complete stop, there was an almost imperceptible movement of her black eyes, during which they seemed to be receding, and then the observer would see that Mrs. Freeman, though she might stand there as real as several grain sacks thrown on top of each other, was no longer there in spirit. As for getting anything across to her when this was the case, Mrs. Hopewell had given it up. She might talk her head off. Mrs. Freeman could never be brought to admit herself wrong on any point. She would stand there and if she could be brought to say anything, it was something like, "Well, I wouldn't of said it was and I wouldn't of said it wasn't," or letting her gaze range over the top kitchen shelf where there was an assortment of dusty bottles, she might remark, "I see you ain't ate many of them figs you put up last summer."

They carried on their most important business in the kitchen at breakfast. Every morning Mrs. Hopewell got up at seven o'clock and lit her gas heater and Joy's. Joy was her daughter, a large blonde girl who had an artificial leg. Mrs. Hopewell thought of her as a child though she was thirty-two years old and highly educated. Joy would get up while her mother was eating and lumber into the bathroom and slam the door, and before long, Mrs. Freeman would arrive at the back door. Joy would hear her mother call, "Come on in," and then they would talk for a while in low voices that were indistinguishable in the bathroom. By the time Joy came in, they had usually finished the weather report and were on one or the other of Mrs. Freeman's daughters, Glynese or Carramae. Joy called them Glycerin and Caramel. Glynese, a redhead, was eighteen and had many admirers; Carramae, a blonde, was only fifteen but already married and pregnant. She could not keep anything on her stomach. Every morning Mrs. Freeman told Mrs. Hopewell how many times she had vomited since the last report.

Mrs. Hopewell liked to tell people that Glynese and Carramae were two of the finest girls she knew and that Mrs. Freeman was a *lady* and that she was never ashamed to take her anywhere or introduce her to anybody they might meet. Then she would tell how she had happened to hire the Freemans in the first place and how they were a godsend to her and how she had had them four years. The reason for her keeping them so long was that they were not trash. They were good country people. She had telephoned the man whose name they had given as a reference and he had told her that Mr. Freeman was a good farmer but that his wife was the nosiest woman ever to walk the earth. "She's got to be into everything," the man said. "If she don't get there before the dust settles, you can bet she's dead, that's all. She'll want to know all your business. I can stand him real good," he had said, "but me nor my wife neither could have stood that woman one more minute on this place." That had put Mrs. Hopewell off for a few days.

She had hired them in the end because there were no other applicants but she had made up her mind beforehand exactly how she would handle the woman. Since she was the type who had to be into everything, then, Mrs. Hopewell had decided, she would not only let her be into everything, she would *see to it* that she was into everything—she would give her the responsibility of everything, she would put her in charge. Mrs. Hopewell had no bad qualities of her own but she was able to use other people's in such a constructive way that she never felt the lack. She had hired the Freemans and she had kept them four years.

Nothing is perfect. This was one of Mrs. Hopewell's favorite sayings. Another was: that is life! And still another, the most important, was: well, other people have their opinions too. She would make these statements, usually at the table, in a tone of gentle insistence as if no one held them but her, and the large hulking Joy, whose constant outrage had obliterated every expression from her face, would stare just a little to the side of her, her eyes icy blue, with the look of someone who has achieved blindness by an act of will and means to keep it.

When Mrs. Hopewell said to Mrs. Freeman that life was like that, Mrs. Freeman would say, "I always said so myself." Nothing had been arrived at by anyone that had not first been arrived at by her. She was quicker than Mr. Freeman. When Mrs. Hopewell said to her after they had been on the place a while, "You know, you're the wheel behind the wheel," and winked, Mrs. Freeman had said, "I know it. I've always been quick. It's some that are quicker than others."

"Everybody is different," Mrs. Hopewell said.

"Yes, most people is," Mrs. Freeman said.

"It takes all kinds to make the world."

"I always said it did myself."

The girl was used to this kind of dialogue for breakfast and more of it for dinner; sometimes they had it for supper too. When they had no guest they ate in the kitchen because that was easier. Mrs. Freeman always managed to arrive at some point during the meal and to watch them finish it. She would stand in the doorway if it were summer but in the winter she would stand with one elbow on top of the refrigerator and look down on them, or she would stand by the gas heater, lifting the back of her skirt slightly. Occasionally she would stand against the wall and roll her head from side to side. At no time was she in any hurry to leave. All this was very trying on Mrs. Hopewell but she was a woman of great patience. She realized that nothing is perfect and that in the Freemans she had good country people and that if, in this day and age, you get good country people, you had better hang onto them.

She had had plenty of experience with trash. Before the Freemans she had averaged one tenant family a year. The wives of these farmers were not the kind you would want to be around you for very long. Mrs. Hopewell, who had divorced her husband long ago, needed someone to walk over the fields with her; and when Joy had to be impressed for these services, her remarks were usually so ugly and her face so glum that Mrs. Hopewell would say, "If you can't come pleasantly, I don't want you at all," to which the girl, standing square and rigid-shouldered with her

neck thrust slightly forward, would reply, "If you want me, here I am —
like I am."

Mrs. Hopewell excused this attitude because of the leg (which had
been shot off in a hunting accident when Joy was ten). It was hard for
Mrs. Hopewell to realize that her child was thirty-two now and that for
more than twenty years she had had only one leg. She thought of her
still as a child because it tore her heart to think instead of the poor stout
girl in her thirties who had never danced a step or had any *normal* good
times. Her name was really Joy but as soon as she was twenty-one and
away from home, she had had it legally changed. Mrs. Hopewell was
certain that she had thought and thought until she had hit upon the ugli-
est name in any language. Then she had gone and had the beautiful
name, Joy, changed without telling her mother until after she had done
it. Her legal name was Hulga.

When Mrs. Hopewell thought the name, Hulga, she thought of the
broad blank hull of a battleship. She would not use it. She continued
to call her Joy to which the girl responded but in a purely mechanical way.

Hulga had learned to tolerate Mrs. Freeman who saved her from taking walks with her mother. Even Glynese and Carramae were useful when
they occupied attention that might otherwise have been directed at her.
At first she had thought she could not stand Mrs. Freeman for she had
found that it was not possible to be rude to her. Mrs. Freeman would
take on strange resentments and for days together she would be sullen
but the source of her displeasure was always obscure; a direct attack, a
positive leer, blatant ugliness to her face — these never touched her. And
without warning one day, she began calling her Hulga.

She did not call her that in front of Mrs. Hopewell who would have
been incensed but when she and the girl happened to be out of the house
together, she would say something and add the name Hulga to the end
of it, and the big spectacled Joy-Hulga would scowl and redden as if her
privacy had been intruded upon. She considered the name her personal
affair. She had arrived at it first purely on the basis of its ugly sound
and then the full genius of its fitness had struck her. She had a vision
of the name working like the ugly sweating Vulcan who stayed in the
furnace and to whom, presumably, the goddess had to come when called.
She saw it as the name of her highest creative act. One of her major
triumphs was that her mother had not been able to turn her dust into
Joy, but the greater one was that she had been able to turn it herself into
Hulga. However, Mrs. Freeman's relish for using the name only irritated
her. It was as if Mrs. Freeman's beady steel-pointed eyes had penetrated
far enough behind her face to reach some secret fact. Something about
her seemed to fascinate Mrs. Freeman and then one day Hulga realized

that it was the artificial leg. Mrs. Freeman had a special fondness for the details of secret infections, hidden deformities, assaults upon children. Of diseases, she preferred the lingering or incurable. Hulga had heard Mrs. Hopewell give her the details of the hunting accident, how the leg had been literally blasted off, how she had never lost consciousness. Mrs. Freeman could listen to it any time as if it had happened an hour ago.

When Hulga stumped into the kitchen in the morning (she could walk without making the awful noise but she made it — Mrs. Hopewell was certain — because it was ugly-sounding), she glanced at them and did not speak. Mrs. Hopewell would be in her red kimono with her hair tied around her head in rags. She would be sitting at the table, finishing her breakfast and Mrs. Freeman would be hanging by her elbow outward from the refrigerator, looking down at the table. Hulga always put her eggs on the stove to boil and then stood over them with her arms folded, and Mrs. Hopewell would look at her — a kind of indirect gaze divided between her and Mrs. Freeman — and would think that if she would only keep herself up a little, she wouldn't be so bad looking. There was nothing wrong with her face that a pleasant expression wouldn't help. Mrs. Hopewell said that people who looked on the bright side of things would be beautiful even if they were not.

Whenever she looked at Joy this way, she could not help but feel that it would have been better if the child had not taken the Ph.D. It had certainly not brought her out any and now that she had it, there was no more excuse for her to go to school again. Mrs. Hopewell thought it was nice for girls to go to school to have a good time but Joy had "gone through." Anyhow, she would not have been strong enough to go again. The doctors had told Mrs. Hopewell that with the best of care, Joy might see forty-five. She had a weak heart. Joy had made it plain that if it had not been for this condition, she would be far from these red hills and good country people. She would be in a university lecturing to people who knew what she was talking about. And Mrs. Hopewell could very well picture her there, looking like a scarecrow and lecturing to more of the same. Here she went about all day in a six-year-old skirt and a yellow sweat shirt with a faded cowboy on a horse embossed on it. She thought this was funny; Mrs. Hopewell thought it was idiotic and showed simply that she was still a child. She was brilliant but she didn't have a grain of sense. It seemed to Mrs. Hopewell that every year she grew less like other people and more like herself — bloated, rude, and squint-eyed. And she said such strange things! To her own mother she had said — without warning, without excuse, standing up in the middle of a meal with her face purple and her mouth half full — "Woman! do you ever look inside? Do you ever look inside and see what you are *not?* God!" she had cried sinking down again and staring at her plate, "Malebranche was right: we are not our own light. We are not our own light!" Mrs. Hopewell had no idea to this day what brought that on. She had only made the remark, hoping Joy would take it in, that a smile never hurt anyone.

The girl had taken the Ph.D. in philosophy and this left Mrs. Hopewell at a complete loss. You could say, "My daughter is a nurse," or "My daughter is a school teacher," or even, "My daughter is a chemical engineer." You could not say, "My daughter is a philosopher." That was something that had ended with the Greeks and Romans. All day Joy sat on her neck in a deep chair, reading. Sometimes she went for walks but she didn't like dogs or cats or birds or flowers or nature or nice young men. She looked at nice young men as if she could smell their stupidity.

One day Mrs. Hopewell had picked up one of the books the girl had just put down and opening it at random, she read, "Science, on the other hand, has to assert its soberness and seriousness afresh and declare that it is concerned solely with what-is. Nothing—how can it be for science anything but a horror and a phantasm? If science is right, then one thing stands firm: science wishes to know nothing of nothing. Such is after all the strictly scientific approach to Nothing. We know it by wishing to know nothing of Nothing." These words had been underlined with a blue pencil and they worked on Mrs. Hopewell like some evil incantation in gibberish. She shut the book quickly and went out of the room as if she were having a chill.

This morning when the girl came in, Mrs. Freeman was on Carramae. "She thrown up four times after supper," she said, "and was up twict in the night after three o'clock. Yesterday she didn't do nothing but ramble in the bureau drawer. All she did. Stand up there and see what she could run up on."

"She's got to eat," Mrs. Hopewell muttered, sipping her coffee, while she watched Joy's back at the stove. She was wondering what the child had said to the Bible salesman. She could not imagine what kind of a conversation she could possibly have had with him.

He was a tall gaunt hatless youth who had called yesterday to sell them a Bible. He had appeared at the door, carrying a large black suitcase that weighted him so heavily on one side that he had to brace himself against the door facing. He seemed on the point of collapse but he said in a cheerful voice, "Good morning, Mrs. Cedars!" and set the suitcase down on the mat. He was not a bad-looking young man though he had on a bright blue suit and yellow socks that were not pulled up far enough.

He had prominent face bones and a streak of sticky-looking brown hair falling across his forehead.

"I'm Mrs. Hopewell," she said.

"Oh!" he said, pretending to look puzzled but with his eyes sparkling, "I saw it said 'The Cedars,' on the mailbox so I thought you was Mrs. Cedars!" and he burst out in a pleasant laugh. He picked up the satchel and under cover of a pant, he fell forward into her hall. It was rather as if the suitcase had moved first, jerking him after it. "Mrs. Hopewell!" he said and grabbed her hand. "I hope you are well!" and he laughed again and then all at once his face sobered completely. He paused and gave her a straight earnest look and said, "Lady, I've come to speak of serious things."

"Well, come in," she muttered, none too pleased because her dinner was almost ready. He came into the parlor and sat down on the edge of a straight chair and put the suitcase between his feet and glanced around the room as if he were sizing her up by it. Her silver gleamed on the two sideboards; she decided he had never been in a room as elegant as this.

"Mrs. Hopewell," he began, using her name in a way that sounded almost intimate, "I know you believe in Chrustian service."

"Well yes," she murmured.

"I know," he said and paused, looking very wise with his head cocked on one side, "that you're a good woman. Friends have told me."

Mrs. Hopewell never liked to be taken for a fool. "What are you selling?" she asked.

"Bibles," the young man said and his eye raced around the room before he added, "I see you have no family Bible in your parlor, I see that is the one lack you got!"

Mrs. Hopewell could not say, "My daughter is an atheist and won't let me keep the Bible in the parlor." She said, stiffening slightly, "I keep my Bible by my bedside." This was not the truth. It was in the attic somewhere.

"Lady," he said, "the word of God ought to be in the parlor."

"Well, I think that's a matter of taste," she began. "I think . . ."

"Lady," he said, "for a Chrustian, the word of God ought to be in every room in the house besides in his heart. I know you're a Chrustian because I can see it in every line of your face."

She stood up and said, "Well, young man, I don't want to buy a Bible and I smell my dinner burning."

He didn't get up. He began to twist his hands and looking down at them, he said softly, "Well lady, I'll tell you the truth—not many people want to buy one nowadays and besides, I know I'm real simple. I don't know how to say a thing but to say it. I'm just a country boy." He glanced up into her unfriendly face. "People like you don't like to fool with country people like me!"

"Why!" she cried, "good country people are the salt of the earth! Besides, we all have different ways of doing, it takes all kinds to make the world go 'round. That's life!"

"You said a mouthful," he said.

"Why, I think there aren't enough good country people in the world!" she said, stirred. "I think that's what's wrong with it!"

His face had brightened. "I didn't inraduce myself," he said. "I'm Manley Pointer from out in the country around Willohobie, not even from a place, just from near a place."

"You wait a minute," she said. "I have to see about my dinner." She went out to the kitchen and found Joy standing near the door where she had been listening.

"Get rid of the salt of the earth," she said, "and let's eat."

Mrs. Hopewell gave her a pained look and turned the heat down under the vegetables. "I can't be rude to anybody," she murmured and went back into the parlor.

He had opened the suitcase and was sitting with a Bible on each knee. "You might as well put those up," she told him. "I don't want one."

"I appreciate your honesty," he said. "You don't see any more real honest people unless you go way out in the country."

"I know," she said, "real genuine folks!" Through the crack in the door she heard a groan.

"I guess a lot of boys come telling you they're working their way through college," he said, "but I'm not going to tell you that. Somehow," he said, "I don't want to go to college. I want to devote my life to Chrustian service. See," he said, lowering his voice, "I got this heart condition. I may not live long. When you know it's something wrong with you and you may not live long, well then, lady . . ." He paused, with his mouth open, and stared at her.

He and Joy had the same condition! She knew that her eyes were filling with tears but she collected herself quickly and murmured, "Won't you stay for dinner? We'd love to have you!" and was sorry the instant she heard herself say it.

"Yes mam," he said in an abashed voice, "I would sher love to do that!"

Joy had given him one look on being introduced to him and then throughout the meal had not glanced at him again. He had addressed several remarks to her, which she had pretended not to hear. Mrs. Hopewell could not understand deliberate rudeness, although she lived with it, and she felt she had always to overflow with hospitality to make up for Joy's lack of courtesy. She urged him to talk about himself and he did. He said he was the seventh child of twelve and that his father had been crushed under a tree when he himself was eight year old. He had been crushed very badly, in fact, almost cut in two and was practically not recognizable. His mother had got along the best she could by hard working and she had always seen that her children went to Sunday School and that they read the Bible every evening. He was now nineteen year old and he had been selling Bibles for four months. In that time he had sold seventy-seven Bibles and had the promise of two more sales. He wanted to become a missionary because he thought that was the way you could do most for people. "He who losest his life shall find it," he said simply and he was so sincere, so genuine and earnest that Mrs. Hopewell would not for the world have smiled. He prevented his peas from sliding onto the table by blocking them with a piece of bread which he later cleaned his plate with. She could see Joy observing sidewise how he handled his knife and fork and she saw too that every few minutes, the boy would dart a keen appraising glance at the girl as if he were trying to attract her attention.

After dinner Joy cleared the dishes off the table and disappeared and Mrs. Hopewell was left to talk with him. He told her again about his childhood and his father's accident and about various things that had happened to him. Every five minutes or so she would stifle a yawn. He sat for two hours until finally she told him she must go because she had an appointment in town. He packed his Bibles and thanked her and prepared to leave, but in the doorway he stopped and wrung her hand and said that not on any of his trips had he met a lady as nice as her and he asked if he could come again. She had said she would always be happy to see him.

Joy had been standing in the road, apparently looking at something in the distance, when he came down the steps toward her, bent to the side with his heavy valise. He stopped where she was standing and confronted her directly. Mrs. Hopewell could not hear what he said but she trembled to think what Joy would say to him. She could see that after a minute Joy said something and that then the boy began to speak again, making an excited gesture with his free hand. After a minute Joy said something else at which the boy began to speak once more. Then to her amazement, Mrs. Hopewell saw the two of them walk off together, toward the gate. Joy had walked all the way to the gate with him and Mrs. Hopewell could not imagine what they had said to each other, and she had not yet dared to ask.

Mrs. Freeman was insisting upon her attention. She had moved from the refrigerator to the heater so that Mrs. Hopewell had to turn and face her in order to seem to be listening. "Glynese gone out with Harvey Hill again last night," she said. "She had this sty."

"Hill," Mrs. Hopewell said absently, "is that the one who works in the garage?"

"Nome, he's the one that goes to chiropracter school," Mrs. Freeman said. "She had this sty. Been had it two days. So she says when he brought her in the other night he says, 'Lemme get rid of that sty for you,' and she says, 'How?' and he says, 'You just lay yourself down acrost the seat of that car and I'll show you.' So she done it and he popped her neck. Kept on a-popping it several times until she made him quit. This morning," Mrs. Freeman said, "she ain't got no sty. She ain't got no traces of a sty."

"I never heard of that before," Mrs. Hopewell said.

"He ast her to marry him before the Ordinary," Mrs. Freeman went on, "and she told him she wasn't going to be married in no *office*."

"Well, Glynese is a fine girl," Mrs. Hopewell said. "Glynese and Carramae are both fine girls."

"Carramae said when her and Lyman was married Lyman said it sure felt sacred to him. She said he said he wouldn't take five hundred dollars for being married by a preacher."

"How much would he take?" the girl asked from the stove.

"He said he wouldn't take five hundred dollars," Mrs. Freeman repeated.

"Well we all have work to do," Mrs. Hopewell said.

"Lyman said it just felt more sacred to him," Mrs. Freeman said. "The doctor wants Carramae to eat prunes. Says instead of medicine. Says them cramps is coming from pressure. You know where I think it is?"

"She'll be better in a few weeks," Mrs. Hopewell said.

"In the tube," Mrs. Freeman said. "Else she wouldn't be as sick as she is."

Hulga had cracked her two eggs into a saucer and was bringing them to the table along with a cup of coffee that she had filled too full. She sat down carefully and began to eat, meaning to keep Mrs. Freeman there by questions if for any reason she showed an inclination to leave. She could perceive her mother's eye on her. The first roundabout question would be about the Bible salesman and she did not wish to bring it on. "How did he pop her neck?" she asked.

Mrs. Freeman went into a description of how he had popped her neck. She said he owned a '55 Mercury but that Glynese said she would rather marry a man with only a '36 Plymouth who would be married by a preacher. The girl asked what if he had a '32 Plymouth and Mrs. Freeman said what Glynese had said was a '36 Plymouth.

Mrs. Hopewell said there were not many girls with Glynese's common sense. She said what she admired in those girls was their common sense. She said that reminded her that they had had a nice visitor yesterday, a young man selling Bibles. "Lord," she said, "he bored me to death but he was so sincere and genuine I couldn't be rude to him. He was just good country people, you know," she said, "—just the salt of the earth."

"I seen him walk up," Mrs. Freeman said, "and then later—I seen him walk off," and Hulga could feel the slight shift in her voice, the slight insinuation, that he had not walked off alone, had he? Her face remained expressionless but the color rose into her neck and she seemed to swallow it down with the next spoonful of egg. Mrs. Freeman was looking at her as if they had a secret together.

"Well, it takes all kinds of people to make the world go 'round," Mrs. Hopewell said. "It's very good we aren't all alike."

"Some people are more alike than others," Mrs. Freeman said.

Hulga got up and stumped, with about twice the noise that was necessary, into her room and locked the door. She was to meet the Bible salesman at ten o'clock at the gate. She had thought about it half the night. She had started thinking of it as a great joke and then she had begun to see profound implications in it. She had lain in bed imagining dialogues for them that were insane on the surface but that reached below to depths that no Bible salesman would be aware of. Their conversation yesterday had been of this kind.

He had stopped in front of her and had simply stood there. His face was bony and sweaty and bright, with a little pointed nose in the center of it, and his look was different from what it had been at the dinner table. He was gazing at her with open curiosity, with fascination, like a child watching a new fantastic animal at the zoo, and he was breathing as if he had run a great distance to reach her. His gaze seemed somehow familiar but she could not think where she had been regarded with it before. For almost a minute he didn't say anything. Then on what seemed an insuck of breath, he whispered, "You ever ate a chicken that was two days old?"

The girl looked at him stonily. He might have just put this question up for consideration at the meeting of a philosophical association. "Yes," she presently replied as if she had considered it from all angles.

"It must have been mighty small!" he said triumphantly and shook all over with little nervous giggles, getting very red in the face, and subsiding finally into his gaze of complete admiration, while the girl's expression remained exactly the same.

"How old are you?" he asked softly.

She waited some time before she answered. Then in a flat voice she said, "Seventeen."

His smiles came in succession like waves breaking on the surface of a little lake. "I see you got a wooden leg," he said. "I think you're real brave. I think you're real sweet."

The girl stood blank and solid and silent.

"Walk to the gate with me," he said. "You're a brave sweet little thing and I liked you the minute I seen you walk in the door."

Hulga began to move forward.

"What's your name?" he asked, smiling down on the top of her head.

"Hulga," she said.

"Hulga," he murmured, "Hulga. Hulga. I never heard of anybody name Hulga before. You're shy, aren't you, Hulga?" he asked.

She nodded, watching his large red hand on the handle of the giant valise.

"I like girls that wear glasses," he said. "I think a lot. I'm not like these people that a serious thought don't ever enter their heads. It's because I may die."

"I may die too," she said suddenly and looked up at him. His eyes were very small and brown, glittering feverishly.

"Listen," he said, "don't you think some people was meant to meet on account of what all they got in common and all? Like they both think serious thoughts and all?" He shifted the valise to his other hand so that the hand nearest her was free. He caught hold of her elbow and shook it a little. "I don't work on Saturday," he said. "I like to walk in the woods and see what Mother Nature is wearing. O'er the hills and far away. Picnics and things. Couldn't we go on a pic-nic tomorrow? Say yes, Hulga," he said and gave her a dying look as if he felt his insides about to drop out of him. He had even seemed to sway slightly toward her.

During the night she had imagined that she seduced him. She imagined that the two of them walked on the place until they came to the storage barn beyond the two back fields and there, she imagined, that things came to such a pass that she very easily seduced him and that then, of course, she had to reckon with his remorse. True genius can get an idea across even to an inferior mind. She imagined that she took his remorse in hand and changed it into a deeper understanding of life. She took all his shame away and turned it into something useful.

She set off for the gate at exactly ten o'clock, escaping without drawing Mrs. Hopewell's attention. She didn't take anything to eat, forgetting that food is usually taken on a picnic. She wore a pair of slacks and a dirty white shirt, and as an afterthought, she had put some Vapex on the collar of it since she did not own any perfume. When she reached the gate no one was there.

She looked up and down the empty highway and had the furious feeling that she had been tricked, that he had only meant to make her walk to the gate after the idea of him. Then suddenly he stood up, very tall, from behind a bush on the opposite embankment. Smiling, he lifted his hat which was new and wide-brimmed. He had not worn it yesterday and she wondered if he had bought it for the occasion. It was toast-colored with a red and white band around it and was slightly too large for him. He stepped from behind the bush still carrying the black valise. He had on the same suit and the same yellow socks sucked down in his shoes from walking. He crossed the highway and said, "I knew you'd come!"

The girl wondered acidly how he had known this. She pointed to the valise and asked, "Why did you bring your Bibles?"

He took her elbow, smiling down on her as if he could not stop. "You can never tell when you'll need the word of God, Hulga," he said. She had a moment in which she doubted that this was actually happening and then they began to climb the embankment. They went down into the pasture toward the woods. The boy walked lightly by her side, bouncing on his toes. The valise did not seem to be heavy today; he even swung it. They crossed half the pasture without saying anything and then, putting his hand easily on the small of her back, he asked softly, "Where does your wooden leg join on?"

She turned an ugly red and glared at him and for an instant the boy looked abashed. "I didn't mean you no harm," he said. "I only meant you're so brave and all. I guess God takes care of you."

"No," she said, looking forward and walking fast, "I don't even believe in God."

At this he stopped and whistled. "No!" he exclaimed as if he were too astonished to say anything else.

She walked on and in a second he was bouncing at her side, fanning with his hat. "That's very unusual for a girl," he remarked, watching her out of the corner of his eye. When they reached the edge of the wood, he put his hand on her back again and drew her against him without a word and kissed her heavily.

The kiss, which had more pressure than feeling behind it, produced that extra surge of adrenalin in the girl that enables one to carry a packed trunk out of a burning house, but in her, the power went at once to the brain. Even before he released her, her mind, clear and detached and ironic anyway, was regarding him from a great distance, with amusement but with pity. She had never been kissed before and she was pleased to discover that it was an unexceptional experience and all a matter of the mind's control. Some people might enjoy drain water if they were told it was vodka. When the boy, looking expectant but uncertain, pushed her gently away, she turned and walked on, saying nothing as if such business, for her, were common enough.

He came along panting at her side, trying to help her when he saw a root that she might trip over. He caught and held back the long swaying blades of thorn vine until she had passed beyond them. She led the way and he came breathing heavily behind her. Then they came out on a sunlit hillside, sloping softly into another one a little smaller. Beyond, they could see the rusted top of the old barn where the extra hay was stored.

The hill was sprinkled with small pink weeds. "Then you ain't saved?" he asked suddenly, stopping.

The girl smiled. It was the first time she had smiled at him at all. "In my economy," she said, "I'm saved and you are damned but I told you I didn't believe in God."

Nothing seemed to destroy the boy's look of admiration. He gazed at her now as if the fantastic animal at the zoo had put its paw through the bars and given him a loving poke. She thought he looked as if he wanted to kiss her again and she walked on before he had the chance.

"Ain't there somewheres we can sit down sometime?" he murmured, his voice softening toward the end of the sentence.

"In that barn," she said.

They made for it rapidly as if it might slide away like a train. It was a large two-story barn, cool and dark inside. The boy pointed up the ladder that led into the loft and said, "It's too bad we can't go up there."

"Why can't we?" she asked.

"Yer leg," he said reverently.

The girl gave him a contemptuous look and putting both hands on the ladder, she climbed it while he stood below, apparently awestruck. She pulled herself expertly through the opening and then looked down at him and said, "Well, come on if you're coming," and he began to climb the ladder, awkwardly bringing the suitcase with him.

"We won't need the Bible," she observed.

"You never can tell," he said, panting. After he had got into the loft, he was a few seconds catching his breath. She had sat down in a pile of straw. A wide sheath of sunlight, filled with dust particles, slanted over her. She lay back against a bale, her face turned away, looking out the front opening of the barn where hay was thrown from a wagon into the loft. The two pink-speckled hillsides lay back against a dark ridge of woods. The sky was cloudless and cold blue. The boy dropped down by her side and put one arm under her and the other over her and began methodically kissing her face, making little noises like a fish. He did not remove his hat but it was pushed far enough back not to interfere. When her glasses got in his way, he took them off of her and slipped them into his pocket.

The girl at first did not return any of the kisses but presently she began to and after she had put several on his cheek, she reached his lips and remained there, kissing him again and again as if she were trying to draw all the breath out of him. His breath was clear and sweet like a child's and the kisses were sticky like a child's. He mumbled about loving her and about knowing when he first seen her that he loved her, but the mumbling was like the sleepy fretting of a child being put to sleep by his mother. Her mind, throughout this, never stopped or lost itself for a second to her feelings. "You ain't said you loved me none," he whispered finally, pulling back from her. "You got to say that."

She looked away from him off into the hollow sky and then down at a black ridge and then down farther into what appeared to be two green swelling lakes. She didn't realize he had taken her glasses but this landscape could not seem exceptional to her for she seldom paid any close attention to her surroundings.

"You got to say it," he repeated. "You got to say you love me."

She was always careful how she committed herself. "In a sense," she began, "if you use the word loosely, you might say that. But it's not a word I use. I don't have illusions. I'm one of those people who see *through* to nothing."

The boy was frowning. "You got to say it. I said it and you got to say it," he said.

The girl looked at him almost tenderly. "You poor baby," she murmured. "It's just as well you don't understand," and she pulled him by the neck, face-down, against her. "We are all damned," she said, "but some of us have taken off our blindfolds and see that there's nothing to see. It's a kind of salvation."

The boy's astonished eyes looked blankly through the ends of her hair. "Okay," he almost whined, "but do you love me or don'tcher?"

"Yes," she said and added, "in a sense. But I must tell you something. there mustn't be anything dishonest between us." She lifted his head and looked him in the eye. "I am thirty years old," she said. "I have a number of degrees."

The boy's look was irritated but dogged. "I don't care," he said. "I don't care a thing about what all you done. I just want to know if you love me or don'tcher?" and he caught her to him and wildly planted her face with kisses until she said, "Yes, yes."

"Okay then," he said, letting her go. "Prove it."

She smiled, looking dreamily out on the shifty landscape. She had seduced him without even making up her mind to try. "How?" she asked, feeling that he should be delayed a little.

He leaned over and put his lips to her ear. "Show me where your wooden leg joins on," he whispered.

The girl uttered a sharp little cry and her face instantly drained of color. The obscenity of the suggestion was not what shocked her. As a child she had sometimes been subject to feelings of shame but education had removed the last traces of that as a good surgeon scrapes for cancer; she would no more have felt it over what he was asking than she would have believed in his Bible. But she was as sensitive about the artificial leg as a peacock about his tail. No one ever touched it but her. She took care of it as someone else would his soul, in private and almost with her own eyes turned away. "No," she said.

"I known it," he muttered, sitting up. "You're just playing me for a sucker."

"Oh no no!" she cried. "It joins on at the knee. Only at the knee. Why do you want to see it?"

The boy gave her a long penetrating look. "Because," he said, "it's what makes you different. You ain't like anybody else."

She sat staring at him. There was nothing about her face or her round freezing-blue eyes to indicate that this had moved her; but she felt as if her heart had stopped and left her mind to pump her blood. She decided that for the first time in her life she was face to face with real innocence. This boy, with an instinct that came from beyond wisdom, had touched the truth about her. When after a minute, she said in a hoarse high voice, "All right," it was like surrendering to him completely. It was like losing her own life and finding it again, miraculously, in his.

Very gently he began to roll the slack leg up. The artificial limb, in a white sock and brown flat shoe, was bound in a heavy material like canvas and ended in an ugly jointure where it was attached to the stump. The boy's face and his voice were entirely reverent as he uncovered it and said, "Now show me how to take it off and on."

She took it off for him and put it back on again and then he took it off himself, handling it as tenderly as if it were a real one. "See!" he said with a delighted child's face. "Now I can do it myself!"

"Put it back on," she said. She was thinking that she would run away with him and that every night he would take the leg off and every morning put it back on again. "Put it back on," she said.

"Not yet," he murmured, setting it on its foot out of her reach. "Leave it off for a while. You got me instead."

She gave a little cry of alarm but he pushed her down and began to kiss her again. Without the leg she felt entirely dependent on him. Her brain seemed to have stopped thinking altogether and to be about some other function that it was not very good at. Different expressions raced back and forth over her face. Every now and then the boy, his eyes like two steel spikes, would glance behind him where the leg stood. Finally she pushed him off and said, "Put it back on me now."

"Wait," he said. He leaned the other way and pulled the valise toward him and opened it. It had a pale blue spotted lining and there were only two Bibles in it. He took one of these out and opened the cover of it. It was hollow and contained a pocket flask of whiskey, a pack of cards, and a small blue box with printing on it. He laid these out in front of her one at a time in an evenly-spaced row, like one presenting offerings at the shrine of a goddess. He put the blue box in her hand. THIS PRODUCT TO BE USED ONLY FOR THE PREVENTION OF DISEASE, she read, and dropped it. The boy was unscrewing the top of the flask. He stopped and pointed, with a smile, to the deck of cards. It was not an ordinary deck but one with an obscene picture on the back of each card. "Take a swig," he said, offering her the bottle first. He held it in front of her, but like one mesmerized, she did not move.

Her voice when she spoke had an almost pleading sound. "Aren't you," she murmured, "aren't you just good country people?"

The boy cocked his head. He looked as if he were just beginning to understand that she might be trying to insult him. "Yeah," he said, curling his lip slightly, "but it ain't held me back none. I'm as good as you any day in the week."

"Give me my leg," she said.

He pushed it farther away with his foot. "Come on now, let's begin to have us a good time," he said coaxingly. "We ain't got to know one another good yet."

"Give me my leg!" she screamed and tried to lunge for it but he pushed her down easily.

"What's the matter with you all of a sudden?" he asked, frowning as he screwed the top on the flask and put it quickly back inside the Bible. "You just a while ago said you didn't believe in nothing. I thought you was some girl!"

Her face was almost purple. "You're a Christian!" she hissed. "You're a fine Christian! You're just like them all — say one thing and do another. You're a perfect Christian, you're . . ."

The boy's mouth was set angrily. "I hope you don't think," he said in a lofty indignant tone, "that I believe in that crap! I may sell Bibles but I know which end is up and I wasn't born yesterday and I know where I'm going!"

"Give me my leg!" she screeched. He jumped up so quickly that she barely saw him sweep the cards and the blue box back into the Bible and throw the Bible into the valise. She saw him grab the leg and then she saw it for an instant slanted forlornly across the inside of the suitcase with a Bible at either side of its opposite ends. He slammed the lid shut and snatched up the valise and swung it down the hole and then stepped through himself.

When all of him had passed but his head, he turned and regarded her with a look that no longer had any admiration in it. "I've gotten a lot of interesting things," he said. "One time I got a woman's glass eye this way. And you needn't to think you'll catch me because Pointer ain't really my name. I use a different name at every house I call at and don't stay nowhere long. And I'll tell you another thing, Hulga," he said, using the name as if he didn't think much of it, "you ain't so smart. I been believing in nothing ever since I was born!" and then the toast-colored hat disappeared down the hole and the girl was left, sitting on the straw in the dusty sunlight. When she turned her churning face toward the opening, she saw his blue figure struggling successfully over the green speckled lake.

Mrs. Hopewell and Mrs. Freeman, who were in the back pasture, digging up onions, saw him emerge a little later from the woods and head across the meadow toward the highway. "Why, that looks like that nice dull young man that tried to sell me a Bible yesterday," Mrs. Hopewell said, squinting. "He must have been selling them to the Negroes back in there. He was so simple," she said, "but I guess the world would be better off if we were all that simple."

Mrs. Freeman's gaze drove forward and just touched him before he disappeared under the hill. Then she returned her attention to the evil-smelling onion shoot she was lifting from the ground. "Some can't be that simple," she said. "I know I never could."

IIC. The Promises and Problems of Modernism

No description of or story about the kinds of changes Americans experienced during the Industrial Revolution in the nineteenth century can very satisfactorily capture the dramatic and multifaceted alterations that occurred in American life. Nevertheless, we believe that the kinds of selections from the humanities we have included in this part of Section II give as good an impression of the contours and colors of human experience during our great transformation as are available. Early Americans had been succored on a Franklinesque and Jeffersonian diet of self-sufficiency, small government, rural living, and a semimarket/semiself-sufficient economy. The Industrial Revolution changed most of the material conditions of American life, but in important ways American language and professed values did not change with the times. Even today, nearly 200 years after our version of the Industrial Revolution began, we often hear people (especially politicians seeking reelection) talk about multinational corporations as if they were "mom-and-pop" grocery stores or about the nation's economy in general as if it adhered to the logic and rules of home economics. It is small wonder that people are confused about work when they are taught the virtues of diligence, self-sacrifice, honesty, and having a community spirit when what so often count are values and behaviors quite contrary to these virtues.

To make this transformation and its subsequent conflicts more vivid, recall our comparison of the situation of a typical American family in the early nineteenth century with a family living 100 years later. In the earlier period most white male Americans headed households that lived on the land and were relatively independent producers of agricultural goods. Some things were produced for the market, but much of what they made met their own needs directly. While a depression year such as 1819 might damage some overextended landowners, it was generally true that the fate of the average farmer mainly had to do with their own hard work and shrewdness. You could make a good case for Franklin's or Jefferson's perspectives that a person's success or failure depended primarily upon adhering to the virtues of hard work and sobriety. Something similar could be said for most town and city dwellers who usually owned their small businesses or at least their own work tools. If they failed to prosper, one could assign responsibility to personal failings, that is, to failure to follow the Protestant work ethic.

By late in the century the economic system had been revolutionized. Suppose you were a Kansas wheat farmer in the 1880s. You worked hard, remained sober, and followed the traditional values of rugged individualism. But some crucial things happen that are beyond your control. First, you are now tied totally to a market economy, and that economy is already worldwide. Because of massive overproduction, the price of wheat drops below the cost of production. To add to your problems, because Kansas does not have water transport, you are totally dependent upon the railroads both for shipping your wheat to market and for shipping goods back to you. Because the railroad is what is called a "natural monopoly" (there is little or no competition from other railroads), the cost of shipping is set very high. Thus, in spite of your adherence to the work ethic, you go broke, and as happened to many farmers in the latter half of the nineteenth century, you find yourself on the way to the city to work in one of the new industrial factories. Once there, you realize, if your farming experiences had not taught you before, that you have lost control of your life and that following traditional values brought you little success in this new economic order.

Meanwhile a commensurate loss of independence has occurred among the traditional skilled workers who also have lost their self-sustaining occupations and work along side you in the factories. You all now use tools owned by the corporation, you must conform to their working conditions and schedules, and, perhaps most devastating to skilled craftspeople, whether rural or urban, is the incipient de-skilling process that happens as industrial engineers analyze the production process into easier steps, so that eventually lower-paid unskilled workers will replace more highly skilled ones. This process, of course, will reach its zenith when Ford introduces the assembly line in the early years of the twentieth century. When the smoke of the start-up of the Industrial Revolution clears, in a period of about 75 years America has undergone a wrenching transformation from a nation of small independent producers to corporate America.

This part of Section II will help you explore a diversity of features of and responses to this revolution. Let us begin with the most striking fact of this great transformation, the fact that is most often used to justify the continuance of Locke and Smith's system: the enormous increase in the amount of wealth. By 1860, with the revolution well underway, the amount of production was already vastly greater than merely twenty years earlier. In 1860 American manufacturing was producing nearly two billion dollars worth of manufactured goods. But by 1900 this value had catapulted to eleven and a half billion dollars, a sixfold increase. We cannot ignore this enormous wealth-producing capacity. Clearly it held and still holds great hope for humankind: the great masses of humanity who live on (or beyond) the edge of survival can be freed from material want, and in most places where a Smithian version of industrialization has occurred the most unfortunate have been "brought up from poverty." But once you move beyond basic survival, poverty is a relative concept, and with the new order came what today is a familiar litany of difficulties: environmental pollution and destruction, alienation, violence, vandalism, new forms of discrimination and hatred, a class system based on wealth, and so on. In this subsection we will examine the Yin and Yang of the American Industrial Revolution in some detail.

We have broken Part C into four units, with the first and longest one mainly focusing on the promises and desirable results of industrialization and the other three examining specific problems. Remember, though, that few blessings or curses are unmixed or are experienced by everyone in the same ways. Progress and development, for example, are positive values in the eyes of most real-estate agents, construction workers, or economists, but to people concerned with the quality of the environment or with preserving tradition they can be anathema. In the same way, what seems like senseless waste when farmers are forced from their lands and migrate to the cities is from another perspective a hard but important step in the increased efficiency and productivity of American agriculture. We invite you to examine the plethora of issues raised here with an open yet critical mind. None of them is simple, yet we can and must render some evaluation of them if we are to make sense of our own current and future work.

The enormous increase in wealth we just described was not equally distributed. Much of it did find its way to the pockets of workers, but much more of it quickly became concentrated in the hands of a relatively few corporations and individuals. If Smith's free-market system, wherein anyone with a little capital and initiative can enter, ever existed in industrializing America, very quickly the game became played by a few powerful people who wielded their power to amass great personal fortunes. A major chord in Smith's theory, *entrepreneurship* (which says any individual, through hard work, can be successful), soon is replaced by what was at best for Smith a minor chord, the *trickle-down theory* (which establishes a more modest sign of economic justice—that at least the worst off will be relatively better off). From the start, progress and success were shared unequally.

We begin with a discussion of progress. Without the notion that change will be for the better, it would have been very difficult to convince people to accept industrialization. Today we have a difficult time thinking of progress (and development, its handmaiden) as anything but good because it has had a golden throne in our pantheon of values for so long. But many people, such as Matthew Arnold, have had some reservations about the costs of progress. You will see, as we move through this part of the book, that as people got a clearer picture of the changes ushered in by industrialization, they began to question ever more strongly whether all change is progress and what ends the progress was to serve.

The two historical pieces in subpart 1 tell you more about the great benefits of modernization and about the costs. Peter Laslett describes some of the poor working conditions industrialism supplanted, but he also asks us to reflect on the insecurities and loss of community that accompanied the new order with its emphasis on individualism and competition. Thomas Cochran and William Miller show that the "triumph of American enterprise" (the title of their book from which our selection is taken) included a great deal of greed, corruption, inefficiency, and poor workmanship as well as impressive accomplishments like the transcontinental railroad or Rockefeller's oil empire.

We have included in this subpart a brief excerpt from the nineteenth-century Scottish essayist Thomas Carlyle because he, as eloquently as anyone during the great transformation, captures the most positive features to be found in any work ethic. He believes that labor, *when done properly,* is a spiritual activity parallel with prayer; but he also sees that the work ethic can be subverted by self-serving employers or by overzealous workers.

Andrew Carnegie, one of the great economic barons of the late nineteenth century, is an employer Carlyle would have criticized. Carnegie chose an alternative to Locke's and Smith's stories to justify his extreme wealth and ruthless business practices: in his "Gospel of Wealth" he gives us his version of a theory still popular today called Social Darwinism. From Smith's concern with the wealth of *nations* to Carnegie's individualistic gospel of wealth we descend from a moral philosopher concerned with the well-being of the populace and the health of the community to the attempts by a rich man to justify his excessive and exclusive wealth.

We begin, then, with the promises and achievements of nineteenth-century industrial America. What follows, in subparts 2–4, are questions, concerns, and criticisms about this new world. Social Darwinism is an attractive theory . . . until you think about it. Not only is it bad science (it rests on a false understanding of Darwin's theory of evolution), but the implications are downright antisocial and quite undesirable for the vast majority of people. In his poem "The Trees in the Garden" Stephen Crane criticizes Carnegie's doctrine by saying that even if society runs according to the "red in tooth and claw" principle, we should not glorify and assist this reality. Crane, a muckraking journalist/poet, believes that Social Darwinism is a theory coined by and for the rich who want to get ordinary people to accept their robber baron activities.

A number of other selections raise similar complaints about the desirability of the new order. American workers had to struggle long and hard to win more humane working conditions in factories, mines, shops, farms, and the home, and just as the "long revolution" continues, so do conflicts between the wealthy and powerful owners and their much less powerful and well-off employees. And, of course, industrial America has long had an underclass of under- and unemployed citizens who sometimes, to some extent, are aided by social or private charities but who remain painfully disenfranchised from the spoils of American success. Selections by David Montgomery, Charles Dickens, John Steinbeck, Arna Bontemps, Charlotte Perkins Gilman, and D.H. Lawrence, amplifying many of the themes we developed in Section I, speak to various instances and dimensions of how industrial workplaces affect people.

Thomas Jefferson and Alexis de Tocqueville are observers of early industrialism in America who raise concerns about how many of the changes will affect democracy based on what it does to people and their communities. They wonder if a populace of deskilled, overworked, and dependent workers who are alienated from their communities, homes, and each other will be capable of active participation in a democracy, and they raise further concerns about the tyranny the powerful and the majority can have on any individual but especially on the underclass.

Those who owned the major workplaces of early industrial society were concerned with how they would find the cheap and disciplined workers they needed. A new work ethic and time discipline would be needed to change preindustrial folk into urban industrial workers. We have already discussed several elements that were necessary—the Protestant work ethic, massive migration to the cities from rural areas and from overseas, high unemployment, and a promise of wealth to come—but we would be ignoring a crucial ingredient if we did not mention schools. It was no accident that mass public education grew up with industrialization: schools were intentionally created to be the "factories" where industrial workers were produced. (Many observers have commented, for example, on the striking similarities between factory, school, and prison architecture.) In our selection from *The Hidden Injuries of Class* Richard Sennett and Jonathan Cobb give their version of how workers are "made" in schools. In particular this selection shows how working-class children take on social attitudes and behaviors that virtually guarantee they will remain working class. The authors argue that schools, rather than being institutions of hope and social mobility, are places where our class structures and barriers are firmed up.

As it is with individual human development, much of what has occurred since the early years of the Industrial Revolution has been elaboration and modification of the "system" as it was during its "childhood." Working conditions and material benefits have improved in many ways as industrialization and technological innovation have replaced much human labor with machine work, as people have brought new technologies into their workplaces and homes, and as overall wealth has increased. Yet women still make less than 65 cents for every dollar that men make doing the same jobs—a figure that has not changed throughout this century. Under- and unemployment have grown steadily as America has moved away from its post–World War II manufacturing heyday to become a "service economy" with its lower-paying jobs. American workers have only managed to stay even with inflation since 1970, and for the first time in American history growing numbers of people do not expect to be better off than their parents. After a decade of deregulation and massive transfer of wealth from the middle to the upper classes in the 1980s, most Americans have not seen the increase in wealth that this "priming of the economic pump" promised, but they are finally becoming aware of some of the great costs of this most recent amplification of the unbridled economic activity that the modern story glorifies: the awful deterioration of the environment, the simultaneous decline of rural and urban life, and signs of increased social alienation and disintegration such as increased drug use, growing racism, and the feminization of poverty. Why has it taken so many people so long to discover (or face) these "troubles in the garden"?

Our final set of readings in this section are meant to address this question. During the first 75 years of industrialization in America most of our economic energies and resources went into building the "infrastructure" (roads, dams, factories, power facilities, etc.) vital to any industrial society. Much of this was accomplished by the end of World War I, and yet to thrive our market economy needed to grow. It would do no good to produce yet one more factory, make one more automobile, or lay one more road if only a few rich people could afford to buy a car. Thus, however reluctantly, the captains of industry gave their workers more money and produced more and more goods for people to consume. Then, with increasing fervor, they began to try to convince people, mainly through advertising, to leave behind their preindustrial values of frugality, modesty, and material conservation to become avid consumers. The age of *consumerism* was born, and a second phase of the Industrial Revolution, which we still inhabit today, ushered in a new kind of person with new values, desires, and habits . . . and with new reasons for working. In sub-part 4 poet E.E. Cummings and theologian Harvey Cox address concerns for what happens to people when they are defined by their things and their images rather than by their characters and their accomplishments. Doris Lessing adds to these concerns by showing how the sense of inadequacy created by the consumer economy and its workplaces manifests itself in gender relations on and off the job. These writers suggest, then, that we have ignored the problems modernism creates because we have been lulled by consumerism with its pretense to real satisfaction in the possessions offered as a substitute for real love, community, and good work.

In this subsection we have focused most of our attention on the great transformation and on consumerism. While there is much more that we might explore concerning living and working in twentieth-century America, because the major features of and problems with contemporary work were there from the beginning of the new order, and because we have but become more skilled at (and perhaps cynical about) consumerism, you should now be fairly well equipped to think seriously about work now and into the next century. We hope that Section III will provide you with a healthy dose of a characteristic which is at the heart of the humanities—imagination. For whether or not our work will be better in the future depends, at least in part, on our understandings and imaginations about working in the past and in the present.

1. Progress, Wealth, and New Images of Individuals and Society

Introduction
Matthew Arnold, "Dover Beach"

We begin this discussion of modern workers and their workplace with a poem that is not about workers but is about the psychological landscape within which work takes place. The revolution in scientific thought and in technology has done more than create a richer material existence—it has also swept away an old and familiar world, a world based largely on faith and personal relationships.

Matthew Arnold, who had strong affinities with the earlier Romantic

Age, lived during the Victorian period in England and was witness to the triumph of the Industrial Revolution. Arnold saw about him the wreckage of a lost world. Villages lay forgotten, coal slag choked streams, soot blackened new cities erupting in the midlands, and a social fabric was coming apart. His poem is about the loss of certitude that comes with the destruction of faith by reason and science.

The poem begins peacefully and hopefully enough with the moon overlooking a calm sea and a tranquil bay. The narrator invites his love to the window to witness the full tide in this apparently enchanting scene. But suddenly our attention is called to the "grating roar of pebbles," as the tide rolls back. Arnold goes on to tell us that the sea of faith once safely girdled the land, but it too, like the tide, has ebbed. The poem ends with the narrator desperately calling for devotion between him and his loved one as the only hope in a world given over to chaos.

Because the postindustrial world is all that we have known, it may be hard for us to imagine Arnold's fear. Still, most of us at one time or another have known the feeling of uncertainty he is talking about. What has been lost? Do we need the certitude Arnold is talking about to be happy? Is a world based upon reason contrary to our human needs? As you read on, you will see that some accept Arnold's concerns, but others, notably French philosopher and novelist Albert Camus, reject his solution if not his fears. Camus (see Section IIIB) urges us to abandon the world of certitude and to push ahead to create a world of our own, abandoning God and faith.

Matthew Arnold

Dover Beach

The sea is calm tonight.
The tide is full, the moon lies fair
Upon the straits; on the French coast the light
Gleams and is gone; the cliffs of England stand,
Glimmering and vast, out in the tranquil bay.
Come to the window, sweet is the night-air!
Only, from the long line of spray
Where the sea meets the moon-blanched land,
Listen! you hear the grating roar
Of pebbles which the waves draw back and fling,

At their return, up the high strand,
Begin, and cease, and then again begin,
With tremulous cadence slow, and bring
The eternal note of sadness in.

Sophocles long ago
Heard it on the Ægean, and it brought
Into his mind the turbid ebb and flow
Of human misery; we
Find also in the sound a thought,
Hearing it by this distant northern sea.

The Sea of Faith
Was once, too, at the full, and round earth's shore
Lay like the folds of a bright girdle furled.
But now I only hear
Its melancholy, long, withdrawing roar,
Retreating, to the breath
Of the night-wind, down the vast edges drear
And naked shingles of the world.

Ah, love, let us be true
To one another! for the world, which seems
To lie before us like a land of dreams,
So various, so beautiful, so new,
Hath really neither joy, nor love, nor light,
Nor certitude, nor peace, nor help for pain;
And we are here as on a darkling plain
Swept with confused alarms of struggle and flight,
Where ignorant armies clash by night.

Introduction

Peter Laslett, from *The World We Have Lost*

Peter Laslett has been director of a Cambridge group for the history of population and social structure since 1964 and a fellow of Trinity College, Cambridge, since 1953. *The World We Have Lost* is his best-known social history. Written in 1964, this book provides a balanced analysis and makes an important contribution to our understanding of the social changes caused by industrialization.

Laslett makes it clear that industrialization is not unique in creating economic oppression and exploitation. These abuses already existed when industrialization began, and they had existed throughout recorded history. His discussion of London bakeries creates a vivid picture of one part of preindustrial life, and you are likely to think that life was rather constricted and harsh. Still, Laslett makes the case that its loss brought at least two potentially traumatizing changes. First, in the preindustrial world there was a certain sense of permanence and stability. Stability, of course, is a two-edged sword. If you do not like your situation, you may not value stability. Nevertheless, in "the world we have lost" there is not the sense of aimlessness and of restlessness that so characterizes our own world.

The second change is from a personal scale to an impersonal scale. As you will see, Laslett shows us how the family in preindustrial societies functions as the primary social, economic, and even political unit. Work is part of family life and is done within the home. Only rarely do preindustrial Englishmen have to cope with large-scale impersonal institutions.

As you read this essay, consider the role of the family and of work in modern industrial society. We think you will find that the institutions essential to our survival are now much more impersonal and are located outside the shrunken modern family. Also look at work, education, the marketplace, and the role of government: precisely in what ways is this a better world? Certainly most of us appreciate the greater material advantages it bestows, but we must also take serious note of the costs.

Peter Laslett

English Society before and after the coming of industry

In the year 1619 the bakers of London applied to the authorities for an increase in the price of bread. They sent in support of their claim a complete description of a bakery and an account of its weekly costs. There were thirteen or fourteen people in such an establishment: the baker and his wife, four paid employees who were called journeymen, two apprentices, two maidservants and the three or four children of the master baker himself. Six pounds ten shillings a week was reckoned to be the outgoings of this establishment of which only eleven shillings and eightpence went for wages: half a crown a week for each of the journeymen and tenpence for each of the maids. Far and away the greatest cost was for food: two pounds nine shillings out of the six pounds ten shillings, at five shillings a head for the baker and his wife, four shillings a head for their helpers and two shillings for their children. It cost much more in food to keep a journeyman than it cost in money; four times as much to keep a maid. Clothing was charged up too, not only for the man, wife and children, but for the apprentices as well. Even school fees were claimed as a justifiable charge on the price of bread for sale, and it cost sixpence a week for the teaching and clothing of a baker's child.

A London bakery was undoubtedly what we should call a commercial or even an industrial undertaking, turning out loaves by the thousand. Yet the business was carried on in the house of the baker himself. There was probably a *shop* as part of the house, *shop* as in *workshop* and not as meaning a retail establishment. Loaves were not ordinarily sold over the counter: they had to be carried to the open-air market and displayed on stalls. There was a garner behind the house, for which the baker paid two shillings a week in rent, and where he kept his wheat, his *sea-coal* for the fire and his store of salt. The house itself was one of those high, half-timbered overhanging structures on the narrow London street which we always think of when we remember the scene in which Shakespeare, Pepys or even Christopher Wren lived. Most of it was taken up with the living-quarters of the dozen people who worked there.

It is obvious that all these people ate in the house since the cost of their food helped to determine the production cost of the bread. Except for the journeymen they were all obliged to sleep in the house at night and live together as a family.

The only word used at that time to describe such a group of people was 'family'. The man at the head of the group, the entrepreneur, the employer, or the manager, was then known as the master or head of the family. He was father to some of its members and in place of father to the rest. There was no sharp distinction between his domestic and his economic functions. His wife was both his partner and his subordinate, a partner because she ran the family, took charge of the food and man-aged the women-servants, a subordinate because she was woman and wife, mother and in place of mother to the rest.

The paid servants of both sexes had their specified and familiar po-sition in the family, as much part of it as the children but not quite in the same position. At that time the family was not one society only but three societies fused together; the society of man and wife, of parents and children and of master and servant. But when they were young, and servants were, for the most part, young, unmarried people, they were very close to children in their status and their function. Here is the agreement made between the parents of a boy about to become an apprentice and his future master. The boy covenants to dwell as an apprentice with his master for seven years, to keep his secrets and to obey his commandments.

Taverns and alehouses he shall not haunt, dice, cards or any other unlawful games he shall not use, fornication with any woman he shall not commit, matrimony with any woman he shall not contract. He shall not absent himself by night or by day without his master's leave but be a true and faithful servant.

On his side, the master undertakes to teach his apprentice his '*art, science or occupation with moderate correction*'.

Finding and allowing unto his said servant meat, drink, apparel, washing, lodging and all other things during the said term of seven years, and to give unto his said apprentice at the end of the said term double apparel, to wit, one suit for holydays and one suit for worken days.

Apprentices, therefore, were workers who were also children, extra sons or extra daughters (for girls could be apprenticed too), clothed and educated as well as fed, obliged to obedience and forbidden to marry, unpaid and absolutely dependent until the age of twenty-one. If apprentices were workers in the position of sons and daughters, the sons and daughters of the house were workers too. John Locke laid it down in 1697 that the children of the poor must work for some part of the day when they reached the age of three. The sons and daughters of a London baker were not free to go to school for many years of their young lives, or even to play as they wished when they came back home. Soon they would find themselves doing what they could in *bolting*, that is sieving flour, or in helping the maidservant with her panniers of loaves on the way to the market stall, or in playing their small parts in preparing the never-ending succession of meals for the whole household.

We may see at once, therefore, that the world we have lost, as I have chosen to call it, was no paradise or golden age of equality, tolerance or loving kindness. It is so important that I should not be misunderstood on this point that I will say at once that the coming of industry cannot be shown to have brought economic oppression and exploitation along with it. It was there already. The patriarchal arrangements which we have begun to explore were not new in the England of Shakespeare and Elizabeth. They were as old as the Greeks, as old as European history, and not confined to Europe. And it may well be that they abused and enslaved people quite as remorselessly as the economic arrangements which had replaced them in the England of Blake and Victoria. When people could expect to live for only thirty years in all, how must a man have felt when he realized that so much of his adult life, perhaps all, must go in working for his keep and very little more in someone else's family?

But people do not recognize facts of this sort, and no one is content to expect to live as long as the majority in fact will live. Every servant in the old social world was probably quite confident that he or she would some day get married and be at the head of a new family, keeping others in subordination. If it is legitimate to use the words exploitation and oppression in thinking of the economic arrangements of the pre-industrial world, there were nevertheless differences in the manner of oppressing and exploiting. The ancient order of society was felt to be eternal and unchangeable by those who supported, enjoyed and endured it. There was no expectation of reform. How could there be when economic organization was domestic organization, and relationships were rigidly regulated by the social system, by the content of Christianity itself?

Here is a vivid contrast with social expectation in Victorian England, or in industrial countries everywhere today. Every relationship in our world which can be seen to affect our economic life is open to change, is expected indeed to change of itself, or if it does not, to *be* changed, made better, by an omnicompetent authority. This makes for a less stable social world, though it is only one of the features of our society which impels us all in that direction. All industrial societies, we may suppose, are far less stable than their predecessors. The lack the extraordinarily cohesive influence which familial relationships carry with them, that power of reconciling the frustrated and the discontented by emotional means. Social revolution, meaning an irreversible changing of the pattern of social relationships, never happened in traditional, patriarchal, pre-industrial human society. It was almost impossible to contemplate.

Almost, but not quite. Sir Thomas More, in the reign of Henry VIII, could follow Plato in imagining a life without privacy and money, even if he stopped short of imagining a life where children would not know their parents and where promiscuity could be a political institution. Sir William Petty, 150 years later, one of the very first of the political sociologists, could speculate about polygamy; and the England of the Tudors and the Stuarts already knew of social structures and sexual arrangements, existing in the newly discovered world, which were alarmingly different from their own. But it must have been an impossible effort of the imagination to suppose that they were anything like as satisfactory.

It will be noticed that the roles we have allotted to all the members of the capacious family of the master-baker of London in the year 1619 are, emotionally, all highly symbolic and highly satisfactory. We may feel that in a whole society organized like this, in spite of all the subordination, the exploitation and the obliteration of those who were young, or feminine, or in service, everyone belonged in a group, a family group. Everyone had his circle of affection: every relationship could be seen as a love-relationship.

Not so with us. Who could love the name of a limited company or of a government department as an apprentice could love his superbly satisfactory father-figure master, even if he were a bully and a beater, a usurer and a hypocrite? But if a family is a circle of affection, it can also be the scene of hatred. The worst tyrants among human beings, the murderers and the villains, are jealous husbands and resentful wives, possessive parents and deprived children. In the traditional, patriarchal society of Europe, where practically everyone lived out his whole life within the family, often within one family only, tension like this must have been incessant and unrelieved, incapable of release except in crisis. Men, women and children have to be very close together for a very long time to generate the emotional power which can give rise to a tragedy of Sophocles, or Shakespeare, or Racine. Conflict in such a society was between individual people, on the personal scale. Except when the Christians fought with the infidels, or Protestants fought with Catholics, clashes between masses of persons did not often arise. There could never be a situation such as that which makes our own time, as some men say, the scene of perpetual revolution.

We have hinted that a fundamental characteristic of the world we have lost was the scene of labour, which was universally supposed to be the home. It has been implied in the case of industry and in towns, that the hired man who came in to work during the day and went home to his meals and at night was looked on as exceptional. Apart from the provisions about journeymen, who were, in fact, the focus of whatever difficulty in 'labour relations' was experienced at this time in the towns, no standard arrangement has been found which contemplated any permanent division of place of living and place of employment. That such divisions existed, and may even have been commonplace in town and in country, cannot be in doubt. There is evidence that a clothmaker in a big way, in the city of Beauvais in France at any rate, would have machinery in his house for more men than could possibly have lived there. It is thought that men walked in from the villages to Beauvais to do their day's work, just as men used to walk from the villages to the towns to work on the building sites in Victorian England. In those areas of England which first became industrial, there are signs that, like those in Beauvais, they too must have contained economic units which had to be supplied by daily wage labour. It came also, maybe, from the surrounding country, but certainly from the grown sons of families living in the town as well, young men, perhaps, even older men and married men, who cannot have been working where they lived. But when all this is said, the division of dwelling place and working place was no recognized feature of the social structure of the towns which our ancestors inhabited. The journey to work, the lonely lodger paying his rent out of a factory wage, are the distinguishing marks of our society, not of theirs. We are forced to suppose that in industrial and commercial matters the working family was assumed to be self-sufficient in its labour, in spite of the vicissitudes of the market.

Industry at this time was carried on not only by individual productive units, like the bakery in London, but by the *putting-out* system, in which several households were set on work by one middleman, the clothier-capitalist we have referred to. Much of it was done in the spare time of the farming population, not simply by the labourers, but by the farmers and their families as well, the simpler operations, that is to say, the sorting and carding and spinning of the wool. But the weaving, the dyeing and dressing of the cloth was usually the work of families of weavers, shearmen or dyers which did nothing else for nine months of the year. They worked on the land of the villages where they lived only in harvest-time, from late June, when the haymaking began, till late September when the last of the wheat or the barley would be brought home.

Hence it came about that the English village contained not simply the husbandmen, the labourers and their families, with the smith, the ploughwright, the miller and the men who plied the agricultural trade, but textile workers too. In the Midlands there were nailers and miners, and everywhere everyone was also a worker on the land, during the crisis of harvest-time. Such are the rough outlines of the system whereby the independent household was preserved, yet made to collaborate with other independent households in the working of the land, and in the production of cloth. Capitalism, we must notice, was a feature of the system, that store of wealth and raw materials in the hands of the clothier which made it possible for him to give work to the villagers and yet not move them from the village. In the world we have lost, then, industry and agriculture lived together in some sort of symmetry, and the unity of the family was in no way in jeopardy.

The bourgeoisie, wherever it has got the upper hand, has put an end to all feudal, patriarchal, idyllic relations. It has pitilessly torn asunder the motley feudal ties that bound man to his natural superiors, *and has left remaining no other nexus between man and man than naked self-interest, than callous* cash-payment. *It has drowned the most heavenly ecstasies of religious fervour, of chivalrous enthusiasm, of philistine sentimentalism, in the icy water of egotistical calculation. It has resolved personal worth into exchange value, and in place of the numberless indefeasible chartered freedoms, has set up that single, unconscionable freedom — Free Trade. In one word, for exploitation veiled by religious and political illusions, it has substituted naked, shameless, direct, brutal exploitation.*

The bourgeoisie has stripped of its halo every occupation hitherto honoured and looked up to with reverent awe. It has converted the physician, the lawyer, the priest, the poet, the man of science, into its paid wage-labourers.

The bourgeoisie has torn away from the family its sentimental veil, and has reduced the family relation to a mere money-relation.

These were the fervent words used by the most penetrating of all observers of the world we have lost when they came to pronounce on its passing. The idyllic patriarchalism and the exploitation which Marx and Engels had in mind in this passage from the *Communist Manifesto* written in 1848 is recognizable in the arrangements we have been discussing in this introductory chapter. The ending of the system which ensured that however he was paid, however little he owned, or close he was to the point of starvation, a man usually lived and worked within the family, the circle of affection, released enough dissatisfaction to account for all the restlessness which has marked the progress of the industrial world.

The factory won its victory by outproducing the working family, taking away the market for the products of hand-labour and cutting prices to the point where the craftsman had either to starve or take a job under factory discipline himself. It was no sudden, complete and final triumph, for the seamstresses were working in the garrets right up to the twentieth century, and the horrors of sweated labour which so alarmed our grandfathers took place amongst the out-workers, not on the factory floor. It was not a transformation which affected only commerce, industry and the towns, for the handwork of the cottages disappeared entirely, till, by the year 1920, rural England was an agrarian remnant, an almost lifeless shell. The process was not English alone, at any point in its development, and its effects on the Continent of Europe were in some ways more obviously devastating than ever they were amongst our people. But ours was the society which first ventured into the industrial era, and English men and women were the first who had to try to find a home for themselves in a world where family and household seemed to have no place.

But Marx and the historians who have followed him were surely wrong to call this process by the simple name of the triumph of capitalism, the rise and victory of the bourgeoisie. The presence of capital, we have seen, was the very circumstance which made it possible in earlier times for the working family to preserve its independence both on the land and in the cities, linking together the scattered households of the workers in such a way that no one had to make the daily double journey from home to workshop, from suburb to office and factory. Capitalism, however defined, did not begin at the time when the working household was endangered by the beginnings of the factory system, and economic inequality was not the product of the social transformation which so quickly followed after. Though the enormous, insolent wealth of the new commercial and industrial fortunes emphasized the iniquity of the division between rich and poor, it is doubtful whether Victorian England was any worse in this respect than the England of the Tudors and the Stuarts. It was not the fact of capitalism alone, not simply the concentration of the means of production in the hands of the few and the reduction of the rest to a position of dependence, which opened wide the social gulf, though the writers of the eighteenth and nineteenth centuries give us ample evidence that this was observed and was resented—by the dispossessed peasantry in England especially. More important, it is suggested, far more likely a source for the feeling that there is a world which once we all possessed, a world now passed away, is the fact of the transformation of the family life of everyone which industrialism brought with it.

In the vague and difficult verbiage of our own generation, we can say that the removal of the economic functions from the patriarchal family at the point of industrialization created a mass society. It turned the people who worked into a mass of undifferentiated equals, working in a factory or scattered between the factories and mines, bereft for ever of the feeling that work, a family affair, carried with it. The Marxist historical sociology presents this as the growth of class consciousness amongst the proletariat, and this is an important hisotrical truth. But because it belongs with the large-scale class model for all social change it can also be misleading, as we shall hope to show. Moreover it has tended to divert attention from the structural function of the family in the preindustrial world, and made impossible up till now a proper, informed contrast between our world and the lost world we have to analyse.

European society is of the patriarchal type, and with some variations, of which the feudal went the furthest, it remained patriarchal in its institutions right up to the coming of the factories, the offices and the rest. European patriarchalism, we may notice, was of a rather surprising kind, for it was marked by the independence of the nuclear family, man, wife and children, not by the extended family of relatives living together in a group of several generations under the same patriarchal head. Yet society was patriarchal, nevertheless, right up to the time of industrial transformation: it can now no longer be said to be patriarchal at all, except vestigially and in its emotional predisposition. The time has now come to divide our European past in a simpler way with industrialization as the point of critical change.

The word alienation is part of the cant of the mid-twentieth century and it began as an attempt to describe the separation of the worker from his world of work. We need not accept all that this expression has come to convey in order to recognize that it does point to something vital to us all in relation to our past. Time was when the whole of life went forward in the family, in a circle of loved, familiar faces, known and fondled objects, all to human size. That time has gone for ever. It makes us very different from our ancestors.

Introduction
Thomas Carlyle, "Labour"

Thomas Carlyle was born in 1795, the son of a poor Scottish stonemason and farmer. From poverty and from his devout Calvinist parents he developed a reverence for labor that remained even after his religious faith had failed. Carlyle was educated at Edinburgh University and supported himself as a teacher after graduation. During this period he read David Hume's writings, which precipitated the great intellectual and emotional crisis of his life. His faith shattered, he sank into a despair that threatened both his sanity and his health. His anguish came to a crisis in 1822, at which time he was able to overcome his sense of the world as a meaningless machine and once again conceive of it as a spiritual entity with an implicit and discernable purpose.

Embarked upon a literary career, in 1843 he published his study of English social and political life, *Past and Present,* which included the following selection, "Labour." This essay is an attack on social injustice in English society, on English materialism, and on devotion to laissez-faire economics.

Critical in this attack is Carlyle's insistence not only upon the dignity of labor but also upon the essential role it must play in giving meaning to human existence. In adopting this position Carlyle confronted the traditional Western view that work is a curse and unworthy of a true gentleman. He believed that the appalling treatment of workers was a consequence of upper-class contempt for work, a point of view which Carlyle, with his Calvinist work-ethic background, opposed vigorously. As you read this brief excerpt from Carlyle's essay, notice the religious tone of the language. Clearly, Carlyle sees in work not merely a means of production but even nothing less than a means to the salvation of the human spirit.

Thomas Carlyle

Labour

For there is a perennial nobleness, and even sacredness, in Work. Were he never so benighted, forgetful of his high calling, there is always hope in a man that actually and earnestly works: in Idleness alone is there perpetual despair. Work, never so Mammonish, mean, *is* in communication with Nature; the real desire to get Work done will itself lead one more and more to truth, to Nature's appointments and regulations, which are truth.

The latest Gospel in this world is, Know thy work and do it. 'Know thyself': long enough has that poor 'self' of thine tormented thee; thou wilt never get to 'know' it, I believe! Think it not thy business, this of knowing thyself; thou art an unknowable individual: know what thou canst work at; and work at it, like a Hercules! That will be thy better plan.

It has been written, 'an endless significance lies in Work'; a man perfects himself by working. Foul jungles are cleared away, fair seedfields rise instead, and stately cities; and withal the man himself first ceases to be a jungle and foul unwholesome desert thereby. Consider how, even in the meanest sorts of Labour, the whole soul of a man is composed into a kind of real harmony, the instant he sets himself to work! Doubt, Desire, Sorrow, Remorse, Indignation, Despair itself, all these like hell-dogs lie beleaguering the soul of the poor day-worker, as of every man: but he bends himself with free valour against his task, and all these are stilled, all these shrink murmuring far off into their caves. The man is now a man. The blessed glow of Labour in him, is it not as purifying fire, wherein all poison is burnt up, and of sour smoke itself there is made bright blessed flame!

Destiny, on the whole, has no other way of cultivating us. A formless Chaos, once set it *revolving*, grows round and ever rounder; ranges itself, by mere force of gravity, into strata, spherical courses; is no longer a Chaos, but a round compacted World. What would become of the Earth, did she cease to revolve? In the poor old Earth, so long as she revolves, all inequalities, irregularities disperse themselves; all irregularities are incessantly becoming regular. Hast thou looked on the Potter's wheel,— one of the venerablest objects; old as the Prophet Ezekiel and far older? Rude lumps of clay, how they spin themselves up, by mere quick whirling, into beautiful circular dishes. And fancy the most assiduous Potter, but without his wheel; reduced to make dishes, or rather amorphous botches, by mere kneading and baking! Even such a Potter were Destiny, with a human soul that would rest and lie at ease, that would not work and spin! Of an idle unrevolving man the kindest Destiny, like the most assiduous Potter without wheel, can bake and knead nothing other than a botch; let her spend on him what expensive colouring, what gilding and enamelling she will, he is but a botch. Not a dish; no, a bulging, kneaded, crooked, shambling, squint-cornered, amorphous botch,—a mere enamelled vessel of dishonour! Let the idle think of this.

Blessed is he who has found his work; let him ask no other blessedness. He has a work, a life-purpose; he has found it, and will follow it! How, as a free-flowing channel, dug and torn by noble force through the sour mud-swamp of one's existence, like an ever-deepening river there, it runs and flows:—draining-off the sour festering water, gradually from the root of the remotest grass-blade; making, instead of pestilential swamp, a green fruitful meadow with its clear-flowing stream. How blessed for the meadow itself, let the stream and *its* value be great or small! Labour is Life: from the inmost heart of the Worker rises his god-given Force, the sacred celestial Life-essence breathed into him by Almighty God; from his inmost heart awakens him to all nobleness,—to all knowledge, 'self-knowledge' and much else, so soon as Work fitly begins. Knowledge? The knowledge that will hold good in working, cleave thou to that; for Nature herself accredits that, says Yea to that. Properly thou hast no other knowledge but what thou hast got by working: the rest is yet all a hypothesis of knowledge; a thing to be argued of in schools, a thing floating in the clouds, in endless logic-vortices, till we try it and fix it. 'Doubt, of whatever kind, can be ended by Action alone.'

And again, hast thou valued Patience, Courage, Perseverance, Openness to light; readiness to own thyself mistaken, to do better next time?

All these, all virtues, in wrestling with the dim brute Powers of Fact, in ordering of thy fellows in such wrestle, there and elsewhere not at all, thou wilt continually learn. Set down a brave Sir Christopher in the middle of black ruined Stoneheaps, of foolish unarchitectural Bishops, red-tape Officials, idle Nell-Gwyn Defenders of the Faith; and see whether he will ever raise a Paul's Cathedral out of all that, yea or no! Rough, rude, contradictory are all things and persons, from the mutinous masons and Irish hodmen, up to the idle Nell-Gwyn Defenders, to blustering redtape Officials, foolish unarchitectural Bishops. All these things and persons are there not for Christopher's sake and his Cathedral's; they are there for their own sake mainly! Christopher will have to conquer and constrain all these, — if he be able. All these are against him. Equitable Nature herself, who carries her mathematics and architectonics not on the face of her, but deep in the hidden heart of her, — Nature herself is but partially for him; will be wholly against him, if he constrain her not! His very money, where is it to come from? The pious munificence of England lies far-scattered, distant, unable to speak, and say, 'I am here'; — must be spoken to before it can speak. Pious munificence, and all help, is so silent, invisible like the gods; impediment, contradictions manifold are so loud and near! O brave Sir Christopher, trust thou in those notwithstanding, and front all these; understand all these; by valiant patience, noble effort, insight, by man's strength, vanquish and compel all these, — and, on the whole, strike down victoriously the last topstone of that Paul's Edifice; thy monument for certain centuries, the stamp 'Great Man' impressed very legibly on Portland-stone there! —

Yes, all manner of help, and pious response from Men or Nature, is always what we call silent; cannot speak or come to light, till it be seen, till it be spoken to. Every noble work is at first 'impossible.' In very truth, for every noble work the possibilities will lie diffused through Immensity; inarticulate, undiscoverable except to faith. Like Gideon thou shalt spread out thy fleece at the door of thy tent; see whether under the wide arch of Heaven there be any bounteous moisture, or none. Thy heart and life-purpose shall be as a miraculous Gideon's fleece, spread out in silent appeal to Heaven: and from the kind Immensities, what from the poor unkind Localities and town and country Parishes there never could, blessed dew-moisture to suffice thee shall have fallen!

Work is of a religious nature: — work is of a *brave* nature; which it is the aim of all religion to be. All work of man is as the swimmer's: a waste ocean threatens to devour him; if he front it not bravely, it will keep its word. By incessant wise defiance of it, lusty rebuke and buffet of it, behold how it loyally supports him, bears him as its conqueror along. 'It is so,' says Goethe, 'with all things that man undertakes in this world.'

Brave Sea-captain, Norse Sea-King—Columbus, my hero, royalest Sea-king of all! it is no friendly environment this of thine, in the waste deep waters; around thee mutinous discouraged souls, behind thee disgrace and ruin, before thee the unpenetrated veil of Night. Brother, these wild water-mountains, bounding from their deep bases (ten miles deep, I am told), are not entirely there on thy behalf! Meseems *they* have other work than floating thee forward:—and the huge Winds, that sweep from Ursa Major to the Tropics and Equators, dancing their giant-waltz through the kingdoms of Chaos and Immensity, they care little about filling rightly or filling wrongly the small shoulder-of-mutton sails in this cockle-skiff of thine! Thou art not among articulate-speaking friends, my brother; thou art among immeasurable dumb monsters, tumbling, howling wide as the world here. Secret, far off, invisible to all hearts but thine, there lies a help in them: see how thou wilt get at that. Patiently thou wilt wait till the mad Southwester spend itself, saving thyself by dextrous science of defence, the while: valiantly, with swift decision, wilt thou strike in, when the favouring East, the Possible, springs up. Mutiny of men thou wilt sternly repress; weakness, despondency, thou wilt cheerily encourage: thou wilt swallow down complaint, unreason, weariness, weakness of others and thyself;—how much wilt thou swallow down! There shall be a depth of Silence in thee, deeper than this Sea, which is but ten miles deep: a Silence unsoundable; known to God only. Thou shalt be a Great man. Yes, my World-Soldier, thou of the World Marine-service,—thou wilt have to be *greater* than this tumultuous unmeasured World here round thee is: thou, in thy strong soul, as with wrestler's arms, shalt embrace it, haress it down; and make it bear thee on,—to new Americas, or whither God wills!

———

All true Work is sacred; in all true Work, were it but true hand-labour, there is something of divineness. Labour, wide as the Earth, has its summit in Heaven. Sweat of the brow; and up from that to sweat of the brain, sweat of the heart; which includes all Kepler calculations, Newton meditations, all Sciences, all spoken Epics, all acted Heroisms, Martyrdoms,—up to that 'Agony of bloody sweat,' which all men have called divine! O brother, if this is not 'worship,' then I say, the more pity for worship; for this is the noblest thing yet discovered under God's sky. Who art thou that complainest of thy life of toil? Complain not. Look up, my wearied brother; see thy fellow Workmen there, in God's Eternity; surviving there, they alone surviving: sacred Band of the Immortals, celestial Bodyguard of the Empire of Mankind. Even in the weak Human Memory they survive so long, as saints, as heroes, as gods; they alone surviving; peopling, they alone, the unmeasured solitudes of Time! To thee Heaven, though severe, is *not* unkind; Heaven is kind, — as a noble Mother; as that Spartan Mother, saying while she gave her son his shield, 'With it, my son, or upon it!' Thou too shalt return *home* in honour; to thy far-distant Home, in honour; doubt it not, — if in the battle thou keep thy shield! Thou, in the Eternities and deepest Death-kingdoms, art not an alien; thou everywhere art a denizen! Complain not; the very Spartans did not *complain.*

———————

As to the Wages of Work there might innumerable things be said; there will and must yet innumerable things be said and spoken, in St. Stephen's and out of St. Stephen's; and gradually not a few things be ascertained and written, on Law-parchment, concerning this very matter: — 'Fair day's-wages for a fair day's-work' is the most unrefusable demand! Money-wages 'to the extent of keeping your worker alive that he may work more'; these, unless you mean to dismiss him straightway out of this world, are indispensable alike to the noblest Worker and to the least noble!

One thing only I will say here, in special reference to the former class, the noble and noblest; but throwing light on all the other classes and their arrangements of this difficult matter: The 'wages' of every noble Work do yet lie in Heaven or else Nowhere. Not in Bank-of-England bills, in Owen's Labour-bank, or any the most improved establishment of banking and money-changing, needest thou, heroic soul, present thy account of earnings. Human banks and labour-banks know thee not; or know thee after generations and centuries have passed away, and thou art clean gone from 'rewarding,' — all manner of bank-drafts, shop-tills, and Downing-street Exchequers lying very invisible, so far from thee! Nay, at bottom, dost thou need any reward? Was it thy aim and life-purpose to be filled with good things for thy heroism; to have a life of pomp and ease, and be what men call 'happy,' in this world, or in any other world? I answer for thee deliberately, No. The whole spiritual secret of the new epoch lies in this, that thou canst answer for thyself, with thy whole clearness of head and heart, deliberately, No!

Introduction
Thomas C. Cochran and William Miller,
The Triumph of Industrial Enterprise

Cochran and Miller are American historians who specialize in nine-teenth-century economic history. This excerpt from their book *The Age of Enterprise* summarizes the major aspects of late nineteenth-century economic expansion. Noting the brutal competitive struggle, and the often-times dubious ethics of those who triumphed, they record for us one of the most dramatic transformations in world history.

We would like you to read this essay with Adam Smith's model of competition in mind. Recall that Smith justified unleashing human greed (enlightened self-interest as he called it) because competition would channel human acquisitiveness into socially useful purposes. It would distribute wealth to all of society and generally help avoid extremes of wealth and poverty. Yet, as you will see, the powerful industrialists of this era are very selective about what parts of Smith's philosophy they buy into. Like Smith, they are opposed to government interference with their actions. On the other hand, they are not at all reluctant to seek special help from government, as in the case of the railroads seeking and gaining massive land grants and government loans. Nor are they opposed to arrangements among themselves that reduce or eliminate competition, such as forming pools or trusts.

The result is an efficient manufacturing and distribution system that produces a vastly wealthier society. But the result is also a world with extremes of wealth and poverty, new class distinctions, and more restricted entry into the marketplace for would-be entrepreneurs. The gaps between theory and practice, between the stories of Locke and Smith in contrast to historical reality, are many and great.

Thomas C. Cochran and William Miller

The Triumph of Industrial Enterprise

For half a century before 1860, American industrialists had been altering the course of American history. Their corporations had affected property relations, their machines had revolutionized conditions of labor, their locomotives and telegraphs had speeded the pace of American life, their railroads had begun to draw outlying rural areas into the orbits of great cities. At every stage these changes had been resisted by sovereign planters and their commercial allies, until, at last, on the battlefield, their ranks were broken, their influence destroyed. Times had changed in America and in the world since 1800, mainly because of the impact of *industrial enterprise*. It was not strange, therefore, when the revolution came that industrialists should carry the mace of authority.

Traditional language had no words to describe the business activities of the new leaders after the Civil War, no words to define the functions of their institutions. Traditional politics could not cope with their demands, nor could traditional law harness them to social welfare. In place of the old canons, they imposed the rule of the jungle upon a willing people who worshiped at the altar of "Progress." Remorselessly they exploited precious resources, stripping incomparable forests, leaving gaping holes in mountain sides to mark exhausted mines, dotting with abandoned derricks oil fields drained of petroleum and natural gas. In reckless haste, they constructed railroads through the wilderness, and immense factories to supply the needs of millions yet unborn. They promoted many similar projects simply to mulct a nation of speculators for the private benefit of the "Fittest."

With magnificent optimism these industrial leaders plunged forward for thirty years in Olympian combat among themselves for the spoils of the land and the people. Gradually, however, a new order began to emerge out of the chaos of brutal competition. Entrepreneurs were learning the profitable lessons of specialized and standardized production, of geo-

Reprinted with permission of Macmillan Publishing Company from *The Age of Enterprise* by Thomas C. Cochran and William Miller. Copyright 1942 (Authors).

graphical concentration of plants, of centralized management. Corporations at war were learning that combination was a surer way to wealth and power. Above all, a small number of investment bankers were acquiring interests in great properties against which they had loaned large fortunes only to see them dissipated by wildcat managements, or to which they had extended liberal credit on condition that they participate in control. The nerve centers of the proliferating system, by the early 1890's, thus were becoming fewer and more complex, the instruments of control more centralized, the managers a select class of professional corporation directors. In the struggle for survival, competition had yielded to cooperation, individualism to combination. Corporations, in an age of gigantic personalities, had become super-persons, as incorporeal as angels and as little amenable to punishment, in mysterious ways directing the life of the new society, but seemingly outside its laws.

Railroad Imperialism

As industrial capitalism spread over Europe in the late nineteenth century and even across the world to Japan, Frenchmen, Germans, Belgians, Dutch, Italians, Russians, and Orientals joined the English who had preceded them in seeking raw materials, cheap labor, free markets in Asia, Africa, and the uncharted islands of the seas. American industrialists, however, blessed with a fabulously rich continent of their own, a political system fashioned to their order, a legend irresistibly attractive to impoverished aliens eager to work for the meanest subsistence only to breathe the free air of the United States, did not have to venture so far afield. In America, obstacles were fewer, opportunities infinitely greater, than elsewhere in the world. Need we seek other explanations for the extraordinary vitality of our industrialism?

First to operate on a grand scale in the new atmosphere of business enterprise were American railroad men, and they made the greatest fortunes. Vigorous, violent, and corrupt, they showed by their accumulations of wealth that their business methods were best suited to the conditions of their time and place. Their contributions to the Gilded Age, however, were not limited to techniques of exploitation. Though they chased the Indian from western valleys and fertile plateaus, they peopled his territories with Europeans, Orientals, and emigrants from eastern states, with farmers and cattlemen who improved the land and laborers who helped them in their tasks. To eastern imperialists they opened mines in Colorado, Nevada, Idaho, Montana, timberlands in Minnesota, Washington, Oregon, and California where nature for countless millennia had stored prodigious wealth. On river shores and crossroads in the wilderness, they laid the cornerstones of future cities. From the Missouri, the Mississippi, and the Great Lakes, over the Rockies, Sierras, and Cascades, they joined in indissoluble union with older commonwealths the Pacific tier of states, ending the threat of other powers to our "continental destiny."

Between 1867 and 1873, more than 30,000 miles of new track were opened to traffic in the United States; and by 1893, though more than eight years of depression intervened, 150,000 miles had been laid since the war. Capital invested in American railroads jumped in this period from two to nearly ten billion dollars. Though most of this mileage and most of this capital went to complete old trunk lines and their links to new centers in the valleys of the Ohio, Mississippi, and Missouri, the most spectacular of all the roads and perhaps the most important were the transcontinentals. These really blazed the trail of American industry in the Gilded Age, gave great impetus to lesser western railroad building, set the fashion in methods of construction and finance. These gave the nation its heroes, its Stanfords, Huntingtons, Hills, and Cookes, as well as its villains in the Crédit Mobilier and other construction companies. These were the governments within governments, the owners of executives, legislators, and judges, the leviers of taxes, the arbiters of the destiny of cities, counties, states, industries, and farms.

We need seek no further for the key to the power of American railroad men when we realize that in an age of corruption they knew best how to use their opportunities; that in a country of tremendous distances they were gaining a monopoly of long-haul transportation; that in regions where wealth was mainly land they were cornering the best of it. The promoters of the transcontinentals as well as lesser railroads spent millions in Washington, state capitals, county seats, and city halls to get land grants, loans and subsidies, and then spent millions more to maintain their grants inviolate. The Union Pacific, for instance, between 1866 and 1872 handed out $400,000 in graft; the Central Pacific, as late as the decade between 1875 and 1885, distributed $500,000 annually. Part of this went to fight water competition, to win rich mail contracts, to riddle with restrictions and objections bills for river and harbor improvements. Most of it, however, went to make private capital out of the public domain. When the fury of competitive building had run its course in the West and depression shrouded the countryside after 1893, it was found that railroads had been granted one-fourth of the whole area of Minnesota and Washington; one-fifth of Wisconsin, Iowa, Kansas, North Dakota, and Montana, one-seventh of Nebraska, one-eighth of California, one-ninth of Louisiana. It was found that in 1872, to meet the demands of the Southern Pacific, Los Angeles County had donated the equivalent of a $100 tax on each of its six thousand inhabitants; that Superior, Minnesota, in 1880, had granted one-third of its "lands, premises and real estate" as well as a right of way to get the Northern Pacific to run through it; that between 1867 and 1892 forty-three sparsely settled Nebraska counties had voted almost $5,000,000 to railroad companies, some of which never built a mile of track.

All told, Congress, in twenty-one grants between 1862 and 1872, chartered to the railroads 200,000,000 acres of land, of which, for one reason or another, slightly more than half actually came into their possession. In addition, federal loans to railroads totaled $64,623,512, the bulk of which went to the Union and Central Pacific. The aggregate of state land grants and state loans was also great and certain cities and counties which had not repudiated their liabilities remained in debt even in the twentieth century for railroad bonds issued in the seventies and eighties. These subsidies and loans supplied hardly enough capital to build the roads to which they were granted and to yield as well an acceptable profit to the promoters. By using such grants to guarantee private loans, however, the promoters were able to supplement public gifts with private capital. Even so, they had their difficulties in raising money. Americans enriched by the war were finding other investments more attractive than transcontinentals that took seven to sixteen years to build, more attractive than shorter lines that traversed as yet untenanted western deserts. On the other hand, foreign rentiers who were eager to invest in booming America demanded higher interest rates than promoters generally cared to offer. Thus even with the support of public grants, the promoters were forced to sell their securities well below par, the Union Pacific, for instance, issuing $111,000,000 worth of bonds for $74,000,000 in cash.

Such practices burdened the roads with excessive capitalizations, forced them to charge high rates to service their debts, left them vulnerable to complaints of shippers at monopoly points and to cutthroat competition in shared territories from lines less speculative in conception and more economically constructed.

Though they encounted many difficulties in raising capital, *promoters* of the transcontinentals and other land-grant railroads, once having accumulated it, had little difficulty in making money. Many great American fortunes have been accumulated not by producing goods or supplying services but by manipulating securities and diverting to personal uses the *capital* these securities nominally represent. We have seen how Drew milked into his own bucket the construction funds of the Erie. Of that company's stock, Jay Gould testified before a court in 1869:

> There is no intrinsic value to it, probably; it has speculative value; people buy and sell it, and sometimes they get a little too much.

———————

If the promoters of the land-grant roads were corrupt or crooked according to the moralists of their age, it was mainly because, in an age of private enterprise and the competitive pursuit of profit, they could not otherwise have completed their tasks. If private corporations had to build the western railroads, they could hardly have been expected to do so without making a profit. Since there was little traffic while the roads were being built, profits had to be found from other sources. Through the construction companies, they were taken out of capital. Because that capital had been supplied by public agencies, or by private investors only with public grants as collateral, a hue and cry was raised when this practice was revealed. The crime of the railroad profiteers, however — if crime it may be called — was not that they, as great speculators, milked an army of little speculators either directly or through venal politicians. Their crime was that they built poor roads. It was not so much that their construction work sometimes cost 100 per cent more than was warranted by expenses for labor, materials, and reasonable dividends; it was that for all this expense the nation got a very extensive but very shaky railroad system.

The Industrial Scene

Though the new railroads were attracting swarms of cheap labor to the United States, opening up vast markets and incredible resources in mines and forests, they were also causing competitive havoc in other industries by their policies of rebates, "midnight tariffs," drawbacks, and special concessions. Such favoritism and secrecy, said the Cullom Senate committee in 1886, "introduce an element of uncertainty into legitimate business that greatly retards the development of our industries and commerce." And speaking of the period before 1887, Carnegie himself declared: "Railway officials, free from restrictions, could make or unmake mining and manufacturing concerns in those days."

Despite their subjection to such practices, however, American industrialists soon outstripped all rivals. By 1893, New England alone was producing manufactured goods more valuable per capita than those of any country in the world. In the manufacture of timber and steel, the refinement of crude oil, the packing of meat, the extraction of gold, silver, coal, and iron, the United States surpassed all competitors. America had more telephones, more incandescent lighting and electric traction, more miles of telegraphy wires than any other nation. In specialties like hardware, machine tools, arms, and ammunition, she retained the leadership assumed before the Civil War, while her pianos as well as her locomotives had become the best in the world.

In any age, this would have been a towering performance; in an age wedded to "bigness," it made an impression so profound that, even in the doldrums of the middle seventies, few cared to question the right of the industrial businessmen to leadership. Americans had much to complain of in this early age of industrial enterprise, and their most frequent complaint was of hard times. Yet there was no questioning of the "system," no lessening of faith in entrepreneurial leadership. This was an age of consistently falling prices, a period shaken by three financial panics and a severe depression of seven lean years. It closed on the precipice of another. Yet industrialists were certain that Civilization was safe in their hands, that their methods were those of God and Nature and were in the end as infallible. With their record of physical achievement to boast of and the unassailable authority of Spencer to support them, they had little difficulty convincing the nation they were right.

For all its tremendous records of physical growth and technical innovations, however, for all its magnetic attractiveness to capital and eager receptivity to new ideas, this iron age of American culture was marked from the start by gross inefficiency and waste. Its catalogue of great inventions fails to disclose any social Bessemer system to blow out the impurities of competition or any blue print for scientific management to harness the potentialities of monopoly. To contemporaries, these deficiencies seemed but the results of partial adaptation to the new industrial environment. It is clear now that the costliness of competitive *laissez faire* was a defect of its qualities, and not simply the result of temporary conditions that would ultimately disappear.

Pools, Trusts, and Corporations

Far from being "the life of trade," competition by the last decades of the nineteenth century had reduced efficiency in business, had encouraged colossal waste of natural resources, plant capacity, capital. It had not only destroyed many companies but had decimated the incomes even of those powerful enough to weather from time to time the periodic unbalancing of freely competitive markets. As conditions for such firms in any industry went from bad to worse and even the most liquid among them came to be threatened with destruction, their managers naturally sought some escape from the perils of cutthroat competition. Somehow, order had to be maintained among the anarchists of industry or imposed upon them from outside. Since businessmen feared government regulation even more than they had come to fear competition, their lobbyists, in the popular name of *laissez faire,* neatly eliminated the state as a possible peacemaker. Left to themselves, however, industrialists managed only to devise new schemes to devour one another. It was not until the 1890's, when large corporations had become as prominent in manufacturing as they had been for half a century in railroading, and private bankers thus could impose order in exchange for essential credit, that umpires of adequate stature were found to regulate industrial strife. Until that time, trade agreements, associations, and pools were made and remade only in the end to be broken.

Pools, or pooling agreements administered by trade associations, attempted to limit competition in many ways — controlling output, by dividing the market among member firms, by establishing consolidated selling agencies, and later by controlling patents. Their object was artificially to keep prices at a profitable level. Their ultimate effect, because of constant breakdowns and reorganizations, was to increase the severity of price movements, thus dislocating business more than stabilizing it.

The trust was a device through which the stock of many competing corporations was assigned to a group of trustees in exchange for trustee certificates, ownership remaining in the same hands as before, management now being concentrated in a single board of directors. Trusts could appear only in a society in which the corporation had become the dominant type of business organization, in which property rights were represented not by land or other physical assets, but by negotiable paper easily convertible into other types of negotiable paper. As a business organization the trust was really identical with a large corporation though it was created by different legal contrivances and functioned under somewhat different laws. The Standard Oil Company set the trust pattern in 1879, and so effectively did it operate under this new type of business enterprise that in the next decade appeared the Cottonseed Oil Trust, the Linseed Oil Trust, the Salt Trust, the Lead Trust, the Leather Trust, the Cordage Trust, the Sugar Trust, until by the 1890's the term "trust" was applied invidiously to every seeming monopoly.

John D. Rockefeller was easily the most outstanding among these leaders. Of the trend toward consolidation he said:

> This movement was the origin of the whole system of modern economic administration. It has revolutionized the way of doing business all over the world. The time was ripe for it. It had to come, though all we saw at the moment was the need to save ourselves from wasteful conditions. . . . The day of combination is here to stay. Individualism has gone, never to return.

Rockefeller had little use for half measures. When he went into oil, he gave up his other interests. When he set out to organize Cleveland refiners, he tackled "the largest concerns first." When dependence upon railroads became too troublesome and expensive, he built his own pipe lines. When producers of crude oil combined against him, they found that he had cornered transportation facilities. When he embarked upon retail distribution, he undersold great wholesalers and little grocers until they either became his agents or collapsed. When he extended his empire beyond the borders of the United States, he employed in competition with alien companies the same rigorous price policies that had proved so profitable at home.

Rockefeller abhorred waste. Having first eliminated it from every nook and cranny of his own business, mainly by vertical integration and complete utilization of by-products, he was ready to attack it in the entire oil refining industry and thus give scope to his imperial ambitions. Aided by the panic of 1873 and the ensuing long depression, by 1879 he had accomplished his objective.

Expansion meant economy, said Rockefeller, and in pursuit of economy he was relentless. He was hated by his contemporaries for his methods, but it was chiefly because he was more adept than they at using means that lay to his hand. By 1879, he said,

> we had taken steps of progress that our rivals could not take. They had not the means to build pipe lines, bulk ships, tank wagons; they couldn't have their agents all over the country; couldn't manufacture their own acid, bungs, wicks, lamps, do their own cooperage — so many other things; it ramified indefinitely. They couldn't have their own purchasing agents as we did, taking advantage of large buying.

In a society which strove to apply the laws of individualism to the activities of corporations, Rockefeller found plenty of company among the successful seekers after loopholes and evasions. As always, business conditions in the Gilded Age were changing faster than the legal system;

and, being ever in the van among businessmen, Rockefeller was generally more than two jumps ahead of the law. Testifying about him and
his colleagues before the Hepburn Committee in 1879, William Vander-
bilt expressed the popular opinion of his time:

> Yes, they are very shrewd men. I don't believe that by any
> legislative enactment or anything else, through any of the States
> or all of the States, you can keep such men down. You can't do
> it! They will be on top all the time. You see if they are not.

Much more ebullient than Rockefeller was Andrew Carnegie, and it
was quite in character that while the oil nabob's genius was management
Carnegie's was salesmanship. Nevertheless, they often used similar methods to achieve like results. Both were wonderfully astute in selecting the
right men for the right jobs and pushing them to the limit of their capacities. Both abhorred pools, being the best competitors in their lines and
needing no protection. And both believed in the justice of monopoly.
"Pullman monopolized everything," wrote Carnegie after he had successfully merged the Woodruff and Pullman sleeping-car companies in 1869.
"It was well that it should be so. The man had arisen who could manage
and the tools belonged to him." In pressing their pursuit of order and
organization both scrupled little over methods, making the ends justify
rebates, drawbacks, and, if occasion required, violence. And in achieving their ends, both were materially aided by the panic of 1873. In the
depression that followed, Carnegie said afterward,

> so many of my friends needed money, that they begged me to
> repay them. I did so and bought out five or six of them. That
> was what gave me my leading interest in this steel business.

Besides the Carnegie Company, by 1892 three other great corporations had organized regional monopolies in the steel industry, preparing
the stage for the gigantic consolidations of the twentieth century. In the
South was the Tennessee Coal & Iron Company, which in 1892 absorbed
its largest competitor and emerged with a capitalization of $18,000,000.
In the mountain region was the Colorado Fuel & Iron Company, capital-
ized at $13,000,000. In the Middle West was the Illinois Steel Company,
formed in 1889, a giant equal in capitalization to Carnegie's firm and
"believed to have a larger output than any other steel company in the world."
Outside steel and oil, similar combinations were being pushed to com-
pletion by Armour and Swift in meat packing, Pillsbury in flour milling,

Havemeyer in sugar, Weyerhaeuser in lumber. By 1893 all had become leaders of great corporations composed in part of shoestring competitors that had fallen in every financial storm.

Industrial Society

Just as modern industrialism in the western world profoundly affected such distant places as China, India, and South Africa in the nineteenth century, so industrial leaders in the great cities of America affected life in every distant hamlet in the land. They controlled the railroads that brought the farmer's produce to market, the flour mills that ground his wheat, the slaughterhouses that purchased his pigs, the machine shops that supplied his tools, the shoe factories that made his shoes, the salt and sugar refineries that supplied his table with these necessities, and the oil refineries that gave him kerosene by which to read. There was in America no miner who did not depend upon machine-made tools, no lonely cultivator who did not strive in vain to keep his sons on the farm, his daughters from some wicked metropolis.

The growth of the railroads, the perfection of the telephone and Atlantic cable, the development of the telegraph, the improvement of postal and express services in the decades after the Civil War, all gave businessmen almost instantaneous communication with every department of their far-flung economic empires — with their lieutenants at the sources of raw materials, their managers at fabrication centers, their salesmen in the markets of the nation and the world. Often they had but to sit in their offices in great cities and press the proper buttons, call the proper clerks, dictate the pertinent letters, and their wishes would be transmitted to the proper subordinates and carried out a hundred, a thousand, three thousand miles away. No village was too distant to escape the influence of New York, Chicago, St. Louis, or San Francisco. No region was too secluded to escape the net cast by the imperialists of every great center to catch the labor, capital, and natural resources of the ever more accessible hinterlands.

While business expansion and business competition were drawing millions to the cities of America, technological inventions and improvements were encouraging city life. Refrigerator cars on the railroads after 1875 helped to feed large landless populations. Structural steel, introduced in the late seventies, helped to house them in their work. Urban rapid transit, beginning in 1869 with the Ninth Avenue Elevated in New

York, helped them to move quickly and cheaply to and from their offices and factories.

It is impossible to exaggerate the role of business in developing great cities in America, and it is impossible to exaggerate the role of the cities in creating our business culture. The cities subjected hundreds of thousands of people to identical pressures, at the same time exporting to every rural river valley, plain, and plateau uniform factory products. Creating a national market for standardized goods, they also created a national model of the successful man: the thrifty, shrewd, and practical clerk or mechanic who rose from the ranks to leadership. "The millionaires who are in active control," wrote Carnegie, "started as poor boys and were trained in the sternest but most efficient of all schools — poverty." And he held up as examples, besides himself, McCormick, Pullman, Westinghouse, and Rockefeller in manufacturing; Stanford, Huntington, Gould, Sage, and Dillon, in finance; Wanamaker, Stewart, Claflin, Marshall Field, Phelps, and Dodge in merchandising.[35] Boys in the cities saw the stately mansions of these great men, saw their princely carriages, their gigantic offices and stores. Boys on the farms heard of them or studied their photographs in newspapers and magazines that were achieving national circulation. They read how these leaders of business society had acquired their rewards, and the ambitious set out to emulate them. Thus the ideals of our business leaders became the ideals of the great majority of the people, though only a few were themselves endowed with talent for leadership.

Introduction
Andrew Carnegie, "The Gospel of Wealth"

Andrew Carnegie was born in Scotland in 1835 and immigrated to the United States as a young man. After training himself as a telegraph operator, he secured a job as an aide to Thomas Scott, the assistant secretary of war in charge of all government railroads and transportation lines during the Civil War. From this vantage point Carnegie was able to anticipate the postwar expansion and invest his savings in the expanding railroads. Investing the fortune he made on railroads in steel production, by the end of the century he was able to dominate that industry.

Carnegie is clearly not entirely typical of the so-called "robber barons" of the late nineteenth century. While he shared their ruthlessness in building his empire, leaving behind a record of brutal working conditions and broken unions, upon retirement he also set out to give away the vast fortune he had accumulated. Most of the wealth went to provide free public libraries throughout the country. This generous gesture met Carnegie's own standard of responsible charity as outlined in the following essay. A public library, as Carnegie saw it, was a place where those with ability and energy could help themselves and, in helping themselves, improve all of society.

While Carnegie was unlike most of the new millionaires of late nineteenth-century America in his generosity, he was typical in the economic values he espoused. In the following essay, "The Gospel of Wealth," he spells out the principles and habits that he believed would build and maintain a just and prosperous society. Central to Carnegie's concerns are the autonomy of the individual and competition. If we look at this essay in the proper context of the late nineteenth century—what Mark Twain labeled "the Gilded Age"—it is hard not to feel that this tough, self-made man is really quite innocent in his own way. Carnegie championed the virtues and social responsibilities of the wealthy at a time when most of them were displaying very little of either. While Carnegie was encouraging society to trust the new wealth, Leland Stanford was buying the entire California legislature, and as David Graham Phillips showed in his book *The Treason of the Senate,* monied interests were corrupting the United States Senate. Most wealthy people, rather than giving money for libraries, were indulging in an orgy of conspicuous consumption.

Carnegie is an advocate of a variation on Adam Smith's economics called Social Darwinism. This late nineteenth-century theory carries the case for Adam Smith's economic individualism to its greatest extreme, arguing that poverty and misery among the mass of the people are inevitable and acceptable costs we must pay for progress. Notice that this contradicts the view of Smith himself who argued that a good free-market system was one that lessened poverty. As a Social Darwinist, Carnegie draws less on Smith than on British thinker Herbert Spencer. Spencer took Darwin's ideas about natural selection in nature and applied them to the economic marketplace. The lesson drawn by Spencer and Carnegie was that government should not intervene in the economy to save the small producers and consumers from the big producers because this would disrupt the "natural workings" of the marketplace "jungle" and in the long run retard progress.

Other writers will respond to Carnegie and his Social Darwinist argument, but before going on, notice how Carnegie plays into the older American values. His advocacy of entrepreneurship rang true to a nation of people most of whom had themselves been small, independent entrepreneurs, usually farmers. Carnegie appealed to the natural-law tradition which had long been respected in America, and he also appealed to individualism (ironically in the name of the corporation). Finally, unlike most of those who espoused Social Darwinism, Carnegie's actions were consistent with his beliefs. Rather than found a family dynasty with his money, as for instance the Mellons and Rockefellers, he endowed the greatest of all self-help institutions, the public libraries of America.

Andrew Carnegie

The Gospel of Wealth

The problem of our age is the proper administration of wealth, that the ties of brotherhood may still bind together the rich and poor in harmonious relationship. The conditions of human life have not only been changed, but revolutionized, within the past few hundred years. In former days there was little difference between the dwelling, dress, food, and environment of the chief and those of his retainers. . . . The contrast between the palace of the millionaire and the cottage of the laborer with us to-day measures the change which has come with civilization. This change, however, is not to be deplored, but welcomed as highly beneficial. It is well, nay, essential for the progress of the race that the houses of some should be homes for all that is highest and best in literature and the arts, and for all the refinements of civilization, rather than that none should be so. Much better this great irregularity than universal squalor. Without wealth there can be no Maecenas. The "good old times" were not good old times. Neither master nor servant was as well situated then as to-day. A relapse to old conditions would be disastrous to both — not the least so to him who serves — and would sweep away civilization with it. But whether the change be for good or ill, it is upon us, beyond our power to alter, and therefore, to be accepted and made the best of. It is a waste of time to criticize the inevitable. . . .

The price we pay for this salutary change is, no doubt, great. We assemble thousands of operatives in the factory, and in the mine, of whom the employer can know little or nothing, and to whom he is little better than a myth. All intercourse between them is at an end. Rigid castes are formed, and, as usual, mutual ignorance breeds mutual distrust. Each caste is without sympathy with the other, and ready to credit anything disparaging in regard to it. Under the law of competition, the employer of thousands is forced into the strictest economies, among which the rates paid to labor figure prominently, and often there is friction between the employer and the employed, between capital and labor, between rich and poor. Human society loses homogeneity.

The price which society pays for the law of competition, like the price it pays for cheap comforts and luxuries, is also great; but the advantages of this law are also greater still than its cost — for it is to this law that we owe our wonderful material development, which brings improved conditions in its train. But, whether the law be benign or not, we must say of it, as we say of the change in the conditions of men to which we have referred: It is here; we cannot evade it, no substitutes for it have been found; and while the law may be sometimes hard for the individual, it is best for the race, because it insures the survival of the fittest in every department. We accept and welcome, therefore, as conditions to which we must accommodate ourselves, great inequality of environment; the concentration of business, industrial and commercial, in the hands of a few; and the law of competition between these, as being not only beneficial, but essential to the future progress of the race. . . . Nor is there any middle ground which such men can occupy, because the great manufacturing or commercial concern which does not earn at least interest upon its capital soon becomes bankrupt. It must either go forward or fall behind; to stand still is impossible. It is a condition essential to its successful operation that it should be thus far profitable, and even that, in addition to interest on capital, it should make profit. It is a law, as certain as any of the others named that men possessed of this peculiar talent for affairs, under the free play of economic forces must, of necessity, soon be in receipt of more revenue than can be judiciously expended upon themselves; and this law is as beneficial for the race as the others.

Objections to the foundations upon which society is based are not in order, because the condition of the race is better with these than it has been with any other which has been tried. Of the effect of any new substitutes proposed we cannot be sure. The Socialist or Anarchist who seeks to overturn present conditions is to be regarded as attacking the foundation upon which civilization itself rests, for civilization took its start from the day when the capable, industrious workman said to his incompetent and lazy fellow, "If thou dost not sow, thou shalt not reap," and thus ended primitive Communism by separating the drones from the bees. One who studies this subject will soon be brought face to face with the conclusion that upon the sacredness of property civilization itself depends — the right of the laborer to his hundred dollars in the savings-bank, and equally the legal right of the millionaire to his millions. . . . To those who propose to substitute Communism for this intense Individualism, the answer therefore is: The race has tried that. All progress from that barbarous day to the present time has resulted from its displacement. Not evil, but good, has come to the race from the accumulation of wealth by those who have had the ability and energy to produce it. But even if we admit for a moment that it might be better for the race to discard its present foundation, Individualism — that it is a nobler ideal that man should labor, not for himself alone, but in and for a brotherhood of his fellows, and share with them all in common, . . . — even admit all this, and a sufficient answer is, This is not evolution, but revolution. It necessitates the changing of human nature itself — a work of eons, even if it were good to change it, which we cannot know.

It is not practicable in our day or in our age. Even if desirable theoretically, it belongs to another and long-succeeding sociological stratum. Our duty is with what is practicable now — with the next step possible in our day and generation. It is criminal to waste our energies in endeavoring to uproot, when all we can profitably accomplish is to bend the universal tree of humanity a little in the direction most favorable to the production of good fruit under existing circumstances. We might as well urge the destruction of the highest existing type of man because he failed to reach our ideal as to favor the destruction of Individualism, Private Property, the Law of Accumulation of Wealth, and the Law of Competition; for these are the highest result of human experience, the soil in which society, so far, has produced the best fruit. Unequally or unjustly, perhaps, as these laws sometimes operate, and imperfect as they appear to the Idealist, they are, nevertheless, like the highest type of man, the best and most valuable of all that humanity has yet accomplished. . . .

Poor and restricted are our opportunities in this life, narrow our horizon, our best work most imperfect; but rich men should be thankful for one inestimable boon. They have it in their power during their lives to busy themselves in organizing benefactions from which the masses of their fellows will derive lasting advantage, and thus dignify their own lives. The highest life is probably to be reached, not by such imitation of the life of Christ as Count Tolstoi gives us, but, while animated by Christ's spirit, by recognizing the changed conditions of this age, and adopting modes of expressing this spirit suitable to the changed conditions under which we live, still laboring for the good of our fellows, which was the essence of his life and teaching, but laboring in a different manner.

This, then, is held to be the duty of the man of wealth: To set an example of modest, unostentatious living, shunning display or extravagance; to provide moderately for the legitimate wants of those dependent upon him; and, after doing so, to consider all surplus revenues which come to him simply as trust funds, which he is called upon to administer, and strictly bound as a matter of duty to administer in the manner which, in his judgment, is best calculated to produce the most beneficial result for the community—the man of wealth thus becoming the mere trustee and agent for his poorer brethren, bringing to their service his superior wisdom, experience, and ability to administer, doing for them better than they would or could do for themselves. . . .

One of the serious obstacles to the improvement of our race is indiscriminate charity. It were better for mankind that the millions of the rich were thrown into the sea than so spent as to encourage the slothful, the drunken, the unworthy. Of every thousand dollars spent in so-called charity today, it is probable that nine hundred and fifty dollars is unwisely spent—so spent, indeed, as to produce the very evils which it hopes to mitigate or cure. A well-known writer of philosophic books admitted the other day that he had given a quarter of a dollar to a man who approached him as he was coming to visit the house of his friend. He knew nothing of the habits of this beggar, knew not the use that would be made of this money, although he had every reason to suspect that it would be spent improperly. This man professed to be a disciple of Herbert Spencer; yet the quarter-dollar given that night will probably work more injury than all the money will do good which its thoughtless donor will ever be able to give in true charity. He only gratified his own feelings, saved himself from annoyance—and this was probably one of the most selfish and very worst actions of his life, for in all respects he is most worthy.

In bestowing charity, the main consideration should be to help those who will help themselves; to provide part of the means by which those who desire to improve may do so; to give those who desire to rise the aids by which they may rise; to assist, but rarely or never to do all. Neither the individual nor the race is improved by almsgiving. Those worthy of assistance, except in rare cases, seldom require assistance. The really valuable men of the race never do, except in case of accident or sudden change. Every one has, of course, cases of individuals brought to his own knowledge where temporary assistance can do genuine good, and these he will not overlook. But the amount which can be wisely given by the individual for individuals is necessarily limited by his lack of knowledge of the circumstances connected with each. He is the only true reformer who is as careful and as anxious not to aid the unworthy as he is to aid the worthy, and, perhaps, even more so, for in almsgiving more injury is probably done by rewarding vice than by relieving virtue. . . .

Thus is the problem of rich and poor to be solved. The laws of accumulation will be left free, the laws of distribution free. Individualism will continue, but the millionaire will be but a trustee for the poor, intrusted for a season with a great part of the increased wealth of the com-

munity, but administering it for the community far better than it could
or would have done for itself. The best minds will thus have reached a
stage in the development of the race in which it is clearly seen that there
is no mode of disposing of surplus wealth creditable to thoughful and
earnest men into whose hands it flows, save by using it year by year for
the general good. This day already dawns.

Introduction
Stephen Crane, "The Trees in the Garden"

Stephen Crane was born in Newark, New Jersey, in 1871, the son of a
Methodist minister. His mother, the daughter of a minister, was a prominent leader of the Women's Christian Temperance Union. Crane grew
up in a strict, but loving, Christian home. In spite of this he early adopted
the *fatalistic* and *naturalistic* view of the world that would be the central
theme of all of his writing. As a naturalist, Crane believed that human
fate was formed by large, impersonal forces beyond human control. For
naturalists there is no destiny, only the chance happenings humans seem
to need to interpret as meaningful.

Within one year after leaving home, Crane managed to flunk out of
two separate colleges and discover the sordid life of slums, bars, and prostitutes that would make up much of the content of his earliest work. After
college Crane worked as a reporter, joining the muckraking ranks of late
nineteenth-century journalism. Reporting not only influenced his style
as a writer but also gave him important material. His first novel, *Maggie,
a Girl of the Streets,* came partially out of this experience.

Although Crane is best known for his fiction, especially *The Red Badge
of Courage,* his poetry is worth examining for its intense irony and its
naturalistic depiction of late nineteenth-century America. "The Trees in
the Garden" is Crane's response to Social Darwinism. Using irony to the
point of sarcasm, he gives us a sense of his impotent outrage at a world
devoid of moral order and dominated by forces beyond human control.

Stephen Crane

The Trees in the Garden

The trees in the garden rained flowers.
Children ran there joyously.
They gathered the flowers
Each to himself.
Now there were some
Who gathered great heaps—
Having opportunity and skill—
Until, behold, only chance blossoms
Remained for the feeble.
Then a little spindling tutor
Ran importantly to the father, crying:
"Pray, come hither!
"See this unjust thing in your garden!"
But when the father had surveyed
He admonished the tutor:
"Not so, small sage!
"This thing is just.
"For, look you,
"Are not they who possess the flowers
"Stronger, bolder, shrewder
"Than they who have none?
"Why should the strong—
"The beautiful strong—
"Why should they not have the flowers?"
Upon reflection, the tutor bowed to the ground.
"My lord," he said,
"The stars are displaced
"By this towering wisdom."

2. *Problems in the Workplace*

Anonymous

Hard Times in the Mill

Every morning at half-past four
You hear the cook's hop on the floor.

Refrain:

It's hard times in the mill, my love,
Hard times in the mill.

Every morning just at five,
You gotta get up dead or alive.

Every morning right at six,
Don't that old bell just make you sick?

The pulley got hot, the belt jumped off,
Knocked Mr. Guyon's derby off.

Old Pat Goble thinks he's a hon
He puts me in mind of a doodle in the sun.

The section hand thinks he's a man,
And he ain't got sense to pay off his hands.

They steal his rings, they steal his knife,
They steal everything but his big fat wife.

My mobbin's all out, my ends all down
The doffer's in my alley and I can't get around.

The section hand's standing at the door
Ordering the sweepers to sweep up the floor.

Every night when I go home,
A piece of cornbread and an old jaw bone.

Ain't it enough to break your heart?
Hafta work all day and at night it's dark.

Introduction
Thomas Jefferson, "On Manufacturers"

It is doubtful that anyone has influenced American political thought more than Thomas Jefferson, author of the Declaration of Independence and third president of the United States. In the following brief essay on manufacturers Jefferson makes his case against the industrial revolution and in favor of a nation of small independent farmers.

His fear of industry is tied to his vision of what a democratic society should be like. True democracy, he believed, must be based upon an independent citizenry with a genuine economic stake in society. The farmer, owning his own land and having a responsible interest in keeping government small, best met this need. Jefferson realized that manufacturing would threaten democracy in two ways. First, it would create a working class of wage earners who would lack property and therefore would lack an economic stake in society and be dependent upon employers. Second, it would create a class of owners who would control great concentrations of wealth. This concentrated wealth and its accompanying political power would be used to influence government on behalf of their special interests, and democracy would be corrupted. One of history's ironies was that Jefferson's own actions in embargoing British manufactured goods during the Napoleonic wars was a major influence in stimulating the American Industrial Revolution.

The relevance of Jefferson's essay to the late nineteenth century is easy to see. Certainly democracy was seriously threatened by the powerful industrial interests of that time. In the early twentieth century Progressive reformers attempted to correct the problems of concentrated wealth and the influence that accompanied it. It is not clear to what degree they succeeded. Have we solved the problem of special interests? Can we make democracy and industrial capitalism work together?

Thomas Jefferson

On Manufacturers

The political economists of Europe have established it as a principle that every state should endeavour to manufacture for itself; and this principle, like many others, we transfer to America, without calculating the difference of circumstance which should often produce a difference of result. In Europe the lands are either cultivated or locked up against the cultivator. Manufacture must therefore be resorted to of necessity not of choice, to support the surplus of their people. But we have an immensity of land courting the industry of the husbandman. Is it best then that all our citizens should be employed in its improvement, or that one half should be called off from that to exercise manufactures and handicraft arts for the other? Those who labour in the earth are the chosen people of God, if ever he had a chosen people, whose breasts he has made his peculiar deposit for substantial and genuine virtue. It is the focus in which he keeps alive that sacred fire, which otherwise might escape from the face of the earth. Corruption of morals in the mass of cultivators is a phenomenon of which no age nor nation has furnished an example. It is the mark set on those, who not looking up to heaven, to their own soil and industry, as does the husbandman, for their subsistance, depend for it on the casualties and caprice of customers. Dependence begets subservience and venality, suffocates the germ of virtue, and prepares fit tools for the designs of ambition. This, the natural progress and consequence of the arts, has sometimes perhaps been retarded by accidental circumstances: but, generally speaking, the proportion which the aggregate of the other classes of citizens bears in any state to that of its husbandmen, is the proportion of its unsound to its healthy parts, and is a good-enough barometer whereby to measure its degree of corruption. While we have land to labour then, let us never wish to see our citizens occupied at a work-bench, or twirling a distaff. Carpenters, masons, smiths, are wanting in husbandry; but, for the general operations of manufacture, let our work-shops remain in Europe. It is better to carry provisions and materials to workmen there, than bring them to the provisions and materials, and with them their manners and principles. The loss by the transportation of commodities across the Atlantic will be made up in happiness and permanence of government. The mobs of great cities add just so much to the support of pure government, as sores do to the strength of the human body. It is the manners and spirit of a people which preserve a republic in vigour. A degeneracy in these is a canker which soon eats to the heart of its laws and constitution.

Introduction
Alexis de Tocqueville, "That Aristocracy May Be Engendered by Manufactures"

Many contemporary observers comment on the decline of public discourse. Public Television's Bill Moyers suggests, for example, that we speak more of consumers than of citizens. Increasingly our politics is performed by interest groups rather than by "public man" (see Richard Sennett's *The Fall of Public Man*). For those who know Alexis de Tocqueville, one of the shrewdest ever to comment on American life, it should come as no surprise that he addressed this issue as a possible danger to democratic society in America over one hundred and fifty years ago.

De Tocqueville was a French aristocrat, but of liberal views and sympathetic with democracy. He toured America during the 1830s when the new democracy was coming into being under President Andrew Jackson and viewed firsthand the phenomena he would write about in *Democracy in America*. While de Tocqueville is prodemocratic, this does not keep him from seeing possible problems in its development. For instance, he comments on the dangers of the "tyranny of the majority": if the majority rules, what is to prevent them from imposing their values upon various minorities in society? De Tocqueville is also concerned about the way in which industrialization will influence democratic society. In some ways his concerns are similar to Jefferson's, although he is not so troubled as to reject industrial society.

In the following excerpt from *Democracy in America* de Tocqueville calls on us to consider what happens to the humanity of those who become the instruments of industrial efficiency. Echoing a central concern of this book he says, "when a workman is unceasingly and exclusively engaged in the fabrication of one thing, he ultimately does his work with singular dexterity; but at the same time he loses the general faculty of applying his mind to the direction of the work. He every day becomes more adroit and less industrious; so that it may be said of him, that in proportion as the workman improves, the man is degraded." De Tocqueville ends by saying that we should keep our eyes on this problem.

As you read, ask yourself if his warning has merit today. Can we enjoy a truly democratic society if citizens are not interested and actively involved in public life? Does specialization rob us of our capacities to understand public life and even our own interests? Are we as a people doomed to control by special-interest groups through means such as thirty-second sound bites on television as some critics argue? These questions are probably even more essential for citizens in democratic societies to answer today than when de Tocqueville raised these issues in the early nineteenth century.

Alexis de Tocqueville

That Aristocracy May Be
Engendered by Manufactures

I have shown that democracy is favourable to the growth of manufactures, and that it increases without limit the numbers of the manufacturing classes: we shall now see by what side-road manufacturers may possibly in their turn bring men back to aristocracy. It is acknowledged that when a workman is engaged every day upon the same detail, the whole commodity is produced with greater ease, promptitude, and economy. It is likewise acknowledged that the cost of the production of manufactured goods is diminished by the extent of the establishment in which they are made, and by the amount of capital employed or of credit. These truths had long been imperfectly discerned, but in our time they have been demonstrated. They have been already applied to many very important kinds of manufactures, and the humblest will gradually be governed by them. I know of nothing in politics which deserves to fix the attention of the legislator more closely than these two new axioms of the science of manufactures.

When a workman is unceasingly and exclusively engaged in the fabrication of one thing, he ultimately does his work with singular dexterity; but at the same time he loses the general faculty of applying his mind to the direction of the work. He every day becomes more adroit and less industrious; so that it may be said of him, that in proportion as the workman improves the man is degraded. What can be expected of a man who has spent twenty years of his life in making heads for pins? and to what can that mighty human intelligence, which has so often stirred the world, be applied in him, except it be to investigate the best method of making pins' heads? When a workman has spent a considerable portion of his existence in this manner, his thoughts are for ever set upon the object of his daily toil; his body has contracted certain fixed habits, which it can never shake off: in a word, he no longer belongs to himself, but to the calling which he has chosen. It is in vain that laws and manners have been at the pains to level all barriers round such a man, and to open to him on every side a thousand different paths to fortune; a theory of manufactures more powerful than manners and laws binds him to a craft, and frequently to a spot, which he cannot leave: it assigns to him a certain place in society, beyond which he cannot go: in the midst of universal movement it has rendered him stationary.

In proportion as the principle of the division of labour is more extensively applied, the workman becomes more weak, more narrow-minded, and more dependent. The art advances, the artisan recedes. On the other hand, in proportion as it becomes more manifest that the productions of manufactures are by so much the cheaper and better as the manufacture is larger and the amount of capital employed more considerable, wealthy and educated men come forward to embark in manufactures which were heretofore abandoned to poor or ignorant handicraftsmen. The magnitude of the efforts required, and the importance of the results to be obtained, attract them. Thus at the very time at which the science of manufactures lowers the class of workmen, it raises the class of masters.

Whereas the workman concentrates his faculties more and more upon the study of a single detail, the master surveys a more extensive whole, and the mind of the latter is enlarged in proportion as that of the former is narrowed. In a short time the one will require nothing but physical strength without intelligence; the other stands in need of science, and almost of genius, to ensure success. This man resembles more and more the administrator of a vast empire — that man, a brute. The master and the workman have then here no similarity, and their differences increase every day. They are only connected as the two rings at the extremities of a long chain. Each of them fills the station which is made for him, and out of which he does not get: the one is continually, closely, and necessarily dependent upon the other, and seems as much born to obey as that other is to command. What is this but aristocracy?

As the conditions of men constituting the nation become more and more equal, the demand for manufactured commodities becomes more general and more extensive; and the cheapness which places these objects within the reach of slender fortunes becomes a great element of success. Hence there are every day more men of great opulence and education who devote their wealth and knowledge to manufactures; and who seek, by opening large establishments, and by strict division of labour, to meet the fresh demands which are made on all sides. Thus, in proportion as the mass of the nation turns to democracy, that particular class which is engaged in manufactures becomes more aristocratic. Men grow more alike in the one—more different in the other; and inequality increases in the less numerous class in the same ratio in which it decreases in the community. Hence it would appear, on searching to the bottom, that aristocracy should naturally spring out of the bosom of democracy.

But this kind of aristocracy by no means resembles those kinds which preceded it. It will be observed at once, that as it applies exclusively to manufactures and to some manufacturing callings, it is a monstrous exception in the general aspect of society. The small aristocratic societies which are formed by some manufacturers in the midst of the immense democracy of our age, contain, like the great aristocratic societies of former ages, some men who are very opulent, and a multitude who are wretchedly poor. The poor have few means of escaping from their condition and becoming rich; but the rich are constantly becoming poor, or they give up business when they have realised a fortune. Thus the elements of which the class of the poor is composed are fixed; but the elements of which the class of the rich is composed are not so. To say the truth, though there are rich men, the class of rich men does not exist; for these rich individuals have no feelings or purposes in common, no mutual traditions or mutual hopes; there are therefore members, but no body.

Not only are the rich not compactly united amongst themselves, but there is no real bond between them and the poor. Their relative position is not a permanent one; they are constantly drawn together or separated by their interests. The workman is generally dependent on the master, but not on any particular master; these two men meet in the factory, but know not each other elsewhere; and whilst they come into contact on one point, they stand very wide apart on all others. The manufacturer asks nothing of the workman but his labour; the workman expects nothing from him but his wages. The one contracts no obligation to protect, nor the other to defend; and they are not permanently connected either by habit or by duty. The aristocracy created by business rarely settles in the midst of the manufacturing population which it directs: the object is not to govern that population, but to use it. An aristocracy thus constituted can have no great hold upon these whom it employs; and even if it succeed in retaining them at one moment, they escape the next: it knows not how to will, and it cannot act. The territorial aristocracy of former ages was either bound by law, or thought itself bound by usage, to come to the relief of its serving-men, and to succour their distresses. But the manufacturing aristocracy of our age first impoverishes and debases the men who serve it, and then abandons them to be supported by the charity of the public. This is a natural consequence of what has been said before. Between the workman and the master there are frequent relations, but no real partnership.

I am of opinion, upon the whole, that the manufacturing aristocracy which is growing up under our eyes, is one of the harshest which ever existed in the world; but at the same time it is one of the most confined and least dangerous. Nevertheless the friends of democracy should keep their eyes anxiously fixed in this direction; for if ever a permanent inequality of conditions and aristocracy again penetrate into the world, it may be predicted that this is the channel by which they will enter.

Introduction
David Montgomery,
"Workers and the Reorganization of Production"

David Montgomery is a contemporary American historian who specializes in American labor history. In the following study he looks at the transformation taking place in labor practices during the early decades of the twentieth century, tracing the mania for efficiency, organization, and standardization that swept through American business after 1900 and that presented the final challenge to the independence of the skilled American worker.

Leading the challenge for American business interests was Frederick Winslow Taylor. It was Taylor's task to wrest control of the work enterprise from workers and to subject them to efficient control through standardization of tasks and through time and motion studies. Taylor strove to give more control to managers and to transform the worker into the efficient "hands" of the industrial engineers. Taylor sincerely believed that the efficiency gained would benefit the worker as well as the corporation.

While skilled workers were able to resist many of these encroachments during the war years, by the mid-1920s it was clear that the new scientific management would prevail. As you read this account of the triumph of Taylorism and Fordism, consider what is lost by workers as well as what is gained in efficiency.

David Montgomery

Workers and the
Reorganization of Production

During the first two decades of the twentieth century both managers and workers in America's large-scale factories sought to reorganize the human relationships involved in industrial production. The authority of foremen and the autonomy which skilled craftsmen had customarily exercised in the direction of their own work and that of their helpers came under attack from two directions at once, as the scale and complexity of industrial enterprises grew. From one side, the craftsmen themselves developed increasingly collective and formal practices for the regulation of their trades, both openly through union work rules and covertly through group-enforced codes of ethical behavior on the job. The rapid growth of trade union strength in most sectors of the economy between 1898 and 1903, the eagerness of workers to undertake massive strikes to obtain or preserve union recognition, such as the coal strike of 1897, the steel and machinists' strikes of 1901, and the meat packing strike of 1904, and the revival of sympathetic strikes all increased the ability of skilled workers to impose their union work rules and standard rates (minimum wages) on their employers.

From the other side, the owners and managers of large enterprises developed more direct and systematic controls over the production side of their firms. By the end of the 1890s many metallurgical, textile, and machinery-making companies had erected new plants, which were well adapted to the unencumbered flow of materials through successive operations, introduced large numbers of specialized machines, developed careful methods of cost accounting, and experimented widely with systems of incentive pay, which, the managers hoped, would entice their workers to greater exertion. After 1900 a veritable mania for efficiency, organization, and standardization swept through American business and literary circles.

The scientific management movement of Frederick Winslow Taylor and his disciples was the articulate and self-conscious vanguard of the businessmen's reform effort. Although fewer than thirty factories had been thoroughly reorganized by Taylor and his colleagues before 1917, the essential elements of their proposals had found favor in almost every industry by the mid-1920s. Those basic elements were as simple as they were profound: (1) centralized planning and routing of the successive phases in fabrication, (2) systematic analysis of each distinct operation, (3) detailed instruction and supervision of each worker in the performance of his discrete task, and (4) wage payments carefully designed to induce the worker to do as he was told. All of these points undermined the traditional autonomy of the craftsmen, and the last three were incompatible with the wage scales and work rules of trade unions. As its impact spread, therefore, the scientific management movement not only clashed frontally with the growing power of trade unionism, but also exposed basic weaknesses in the craft-based structure of American unionism and inspired many workers to experiment with new forms of struggle.

Three aspects of the battle to reshape work relations at the beginning of this century will be examined: management's standardization of tasks, the conversion of laborers into machine tenders, and the controversy over incentive pay schemes and job classifications. Special attention will be devoted to the metal-working industries, where these issues appeared first. The struggles of munitions workers in Bridgeport, Connecticut, will be used to illustrate the innovations which appeared during these years at the initiative of workers.

Standardization of tasks

"It is only through *enforced* standardization of methods, *enforced* adoption of the best implements and working conditions, *enforced* cooperation that this faster work can be assured," wrote Taylor. "And the duty of enforcing the adoption of standards and enforcing this cooperation rests with the *management* alone." The quest for systematic control by the management of all aspects of the production process, which Taylor described, arose in part from its needs for more thorough cost accounting, interchangeable parts, and integration of the various departments of large-scale manufacturing. On the other hand, it also involved the destruction of work practices which had grown up over the last half of the nineteenth century, and through which skilled workmen had exercised considerable discretion in the direction of their own work and that of their helpers. Iron molders, iron rollers and heaters, glass blowers, bricklayers, coal miners, machinists, jiggermen in potteries, stitching-machine operators and lasters in shoe factories, mule spinners, and other craftsmen not only enjoyed broad autonomy in their own work, but also defended that autonomy by their own codes of ethical work behavior. The operation of more than one machine by one man, undermining a fellow worker's position, employing more than one helper at a time, suffering any supervisor to watch one work, turning out more production than the stint set by the group, and, among carpenters, machinists, and others, accepting any piecework form of payment, were all seen as "hoggish" and "unmanly" forms of conduct, unbecoming a true craftsman.

Taylor denounced the craftsmen's code as "soldiering" (restriction of output), but, as he was keenly aware, skilled workers were able to direct their portions of any production process and to defend work patterns which they considered honorable and rational, because their knowledge of their own tasks was superior to that of their employers. The first step in reform, said Taylor, was "the deliberate gathering in on the part of those on the management's side of all of the great mass of traditional knowledge, which in the past has been in the heads of the workmen, and in the physical skill and knack of the workman, which he has acquired through years of experience." The best technique for "gathering" the craftsmen's knowledge into the engineer's head was time and motion study, which Taylorites called "the basis of all modern management."

To the craftsman, therefore, time study symbolized simultaneously the theft of his knowledge by his employers and an outrage against his sense of honorable behavior at work. Hugo Lueders, a machinist at the Watertown arsenal, spoke for thousands of his colleagues, when he said that he had no objection to improved planning of production. "The men would welcome any system," he said. "They want it bad." But, he added quickly and emphatically, "as far as having a man stand back of you and taking all the various operations you go through, that is one thing they do not care for." The molders where he worked agreed among themselves that none would work under the clock. A machinist at the Rock Island arsenal, who was seen measuring the bed of a planer for standardized bolts and clamps, was ostracised by his workmates. Time-study men at Pittsburgh's American Locomotive Company were attacked and beaten by workers in 1911, despite the fact that they had been introduced into the plant with the consent of the unions. The appearance of time clocks and work tickets at the Norfolk Navy Yard in 1915 led to a mass walkout and a union rally "in emphatic protest." Five years earlier machinists at Starrett Tool had resolved to treat such clocks "as part of the furniture." The mere suspicion that time study was to be introduced into the repair shops of the Illinois Central Railroad was enough to forge a united front of all the shop crafts and precipitate a strike in 1911, which lasted four bloody years.

Time study, like incentive pay, was introduced most easily in non-union shops, where each worker could be induced to accept the new ways separately. When the National Metal Trades Association launched its open-shop drive against the machinists' union in 1901, it demanded "full discretion" for employers "to designate the men we consider competent to perform the work and to determine the conditions under which that work shall be prosecuted." Its declaration of principles added: "We will not permit employees to place any restriction on the management, methods, or production of our shop, and will require a fair day's work for a fair day's pay."

Where unions were effectively excluded from the plant, many craftsmen acquiesced in time study and learned to grasp at incentive pay, as the only means available to improve their incomes. In remarkable contrast to the machinists of American Locomotive in Pittsburgh, who threw their premium pay envelopes into trash bins to demonstrate their contempt for the new system, those of United Shoe Machinery in Beverly, Massachusetts, lined up to volunteer for premium pay contracts and crossed streets to avoid meeting union members. In the machine shops of Bethlehem Steel, Taylor's disciple Henry Gantt observed to his satisfaction that the lathe operators, in ardent pursuit of bonuses, lost their scruples against hurrying the helpers and crane men, not to speak of themselves.

In such factories, the stint, by which craftsmen had openly and deliberately regulated output in former times, had been abolished. But extensive studies of nonunion factories in the 1920s revealed that it had survived in a new form. Everywhere Stanley B. Mathewson looked in that decade he found that the restriction of output which "Taylor discovered [still] obtains today," while "payment plans, designed as incentives to increase production . . . turn out to be incentives to restriction." In fact, he observed, "the mere intimation that the time-study man is to make his appearance will often slow up a worker, a group or a whole department." This is not to say, however, that scientific management had changed nothing. The customary craftsman's stint had been an overt and deliberate act of collective regulation by workers who directed their own productive operations. The group regulation which replaced it was a covert act of disruption of management's direction of production. The stint had become sabotage.

The scientifically managed factory appeared to employers to be under rational engineering control. But to craftsmen of the prewar generation that plant resembled a bedlam: arbitrary and pretentious men in white shirts shouted orders, crept up behind workers with stopwatches, had them running incessantly back and forth to time clocks, and posted silly notices on bulletin boards. Incentive pay in any form impressed machinists as a "vile, insidious disease," which "encourages greed, is immoral in its tendencies, and does more to create discord and make a perfect hell of a harmonious shop or factory of our craft, than all the evils that escaped from Pandora's box." Taylor's famous paper *Shop Management* was widely read by union machinists. In fact, it was their main source of information on their employers' intentions. Their response to it was angrily summed up by Nels Alifas, a machinist from Davenport, Iowa:

> Now we object to being reduced to a scientific formula, and we do not want to have the world run on that kind of a basis at all. We would a good deal rather have the world run on the basis that everybody should enjoy some of the good things in it, and if the people of the United States do not want to spend all of their time working, they have a right to say so, even though the scientific engineers claim that they can do five times as much as they are doing now. If they don't want to do it, why should they be compelled to do it?

Laborers and machine tenders

By the end of the First World War the most numerous group of workers in the major metal-working industries (auto, electrical equipment, farm machinery, and machine tools) was made up not of craftsmen, but of specialized machine tenders. A survey of the automobile industry in 1923 found that only 9 percent of the workers were in skilled trades, such as machinists or die sinkers, and less than 9 percent were common laborers. On the other hand, almost 18 percent worked on assembly lines and 47 percent were machine tenders. "The ability to meet ('to hit') and maintain a constant pace," noted a contemporary observer, "to be able to eliminate all waste and false motions; to follow without wavering printed instructions emanating from an unseen source lodged in some far off planning department — these constitute the requirements of a successful machine tender."

The "dilution" of skilled trades (to borrow the splendid British expression) involved both placing men and women with little prior training at the controls of machine tools and creating a large supervisory force to direct their work. In Taylor's view this innovation provided promotions for both the skilled workers who became foremen and the laborers who operated the machines. In fact, there were workers who experienced improvements in their status and earnings as a result of the dilution of crafts, and such workers were unlikely to battle for restoration of the old ways. The new art of welding with oxyacetylene torches, for example, had been part of the general skill which a machinist acquired during his apprenticeship, but during the war many women were trained exclusively as welders in railroad car shops and other metal works. To the women involved, most of whom had previously been garment and textile workers, the welder's job represented a considerable improvement in their economic status, which they were prepared to defend. The machinists, however, saw the women's presence as an intolerable erosion of their trade and an unwelcome intrusion by women into shops which had previously been male preserves. They reacted furiously, and often violently, against the women welders in their midst.

It was the rapid expansion of the metal-working industries, however, which accounted for both the widespread conversion of unskilled laborers into machine tenders and the improvement in earnings which the new positions often represented for them before 1920. During the war decade the number of journeymen and apprentice machinists listed in the U.S. census actually grew by 8 percent annually, from 460 thousand to 841 thousand. In the next decade, however, that growth turned to a decline of 2 percent per year (to 656 thousand in 1930). On the other hand, the number of machine operatives in the auto and farm equipment industries alone swelled by almost 40 percent each year between 1910 and 1920 (from 26 thousand to 129 thousand) and continued to grow, though at a much slower rate, through the twenties. This change was not the result of the introduction of new machine tools. Although there was extensive retooling by American industry after the crisis of 1907–9, the new lathes, boring mills, milling machines, and radial drills were no simpler to operate than the old. The simplification resulted from prefabricated jigs and fixtures and from the detailed instruction and supervision given to those who repeated the same standardized operations again and again on those machines.

Ironically the same dilution also created a new skilled trade, that of tool and die maker. "Cheap men need expensive jigs," said Taylor's associate Sterling Bunnell, while "highly skilled men need little outside of their tool chests." Nowhere was the truth of this observation more evident than in the wartime production of artillery shells, where tens of thousands of inexperienced men and women manipulated form tools, jigs, dies, and taper fixtures, which had been fabricated in the tool room. In 1900 the category "tool and die maker" had not existed in the national census of occupations. In 1910 there were nine thousand of them listed, and by 1920 there were 55 thousand, a growth of more than 50 percent per year during the war decade. In many wartime strikes the practitioners of this new skill proved to be the most militant and the most innovative of the workers involved.

The process of converting skilled workers into tool makers or supervisors, so that production itself could be assigned to untrained operatives, performing minutely subdivided tasks, was carried to its ultimate development in Ford's Highland Park plant. Ford's circumstances were unique. So great was the demand for the company's Model T's that 90 percent of the one thousand or more cars which came off its final assembly lines each day were shipped immediately to dealers. Consequently, it was possible to commit fifteen thousand men and women to fabricating a single product in a plant which was characterized not only by large and small chain-driven assembly lines, but also by thousands of machine tools especially designed for making a single cut on a single part (and capable of nothing else).

To perform such jobs, the company had "no use for experience." In the words of one engineer: "It desires and prefers machine-tool operators who have nothing to unlearn, who have no theories of correct surface speeds for metal finishing, and will simply do what they are told, over and over again, from bell-time to bell-time." On the other hand, outfitting the machine tools which those novices could operate required a staff of 240 tool makers, 50 tool-fixture draftsmen, and 105 pattern makers, for whom nothing was "scamped and hurried." No fewer than 255 overseers in the machine shops alone watched over the machine tenders, with absolute authority to fire any of them at will.

Such conditions obviated the need for incentive-pay schemes, so everyone in the plant was on hourly rates. They also produced staggering rates of labor turnover. Company officials had discovered that to maintain an average force of thirteen thousand during the prosperous times between October, 1912 and October, 1913, they had to hire 54 thousand men (an annual turnover rate of 416 percent). They introduced elaborate personnel checks and a system of periodic wage increases based upon the recommendations of foremen, and later a personnel department to which a worker might appeal his discharge, in order to reduce this separation rate. The campaign of the Industrial Workers of the World at the gates of Detroit's auto plants and the strikes which that organization led in the tire industry and at smaller auto plants added to the company's anxiety. Consequently, in January, 1914, the company proclaimed an 8-hour day and five-dollars-a-day pay for all those employees who were over twenty-two years of age, contributed to the support of others, and were pronounced "acceptable." A staff of 100 "sociologists" examined the habits, home lives, and attitudes of workers to discover who was "acceptable," and by the end of March, 1914, 57 percent of them were receiving the magical five dollars. Later in the year Ford introduced classes in the English language, which foreign-born employees were required to attend, and subsequently it celebrated the graduation of the first such group with an "Americanization Day" festival, featuring a parade of more than six thousand Ford workers.

Small wonder there was always a crowd outside the gates of the Highland Park plant looking for work, and a riot had broken out among job-seekers the day after the five-dollar day had been announced to the press. The fact remains, however, that Ford's policies were unique, even within the automobile industry. No other firms could undertake mass production of a single item on so lavish a scale. On the other hand, there is no doubt that unskilled workers throughout the land did enjoy substantial improvements in their incomes between 1909 and 1920, even if they did not rush off to Detroit. Those gains were the consequences of rapid economic growth, which enabled laborers to move from job to job incessantly in search of better incomes, and to undertake wage strikes with increasing frequency and effectiveness. They were not benefits which flowed from managerial reform.

In fact, during the war years, when workers in munitions and other industries most often struck and won the most significant advances in their earnings (relative to those of more skilled workers, as well as in absolute terms), they also challenged management's efforts to systematize and intensify their work. The experience of the Brighton Mills of Passaic, one of the very few textile mills to be reformed by Taylor's colleagues before the war, illustrates this development. Henry Gantt boasted in 1914 that his introduction of functional foremanship and the task-and-bonus plan had stimulated new "habits of industry" among the weavers and accomplished miracles of production. All of the weavers he studied had either conformed to the new output standards or quit. In April 1916, however, the weavers struck the Brighton Mills, demanding an end to Gantt's innovations.

Conflict over the pace of work raged with special intensity in shell turning. As early as 1910 a preview of the wartime disputes in that line of work had been offered by the workers of Bethlehem Steel. The operatives in Machine Shop No. 4, where the strike began, complained that the premiums paid to lathe operators and their foremen had created unbearable chaos. The eagerness of foremen to maximize their own bonuses had led them to monopolize the crane men and other laborers for the use of the shell-turning lathes, charge work on which there was no bonus up to shell-turning time, and, worst of all, to order the shell turners into work one Sunday after another. The strike began when one lathe operator feigned illness on a Saturday in order to avoid being told to come in on Sunday. He was caught in the act and fired. All the machine shop's workers then went on strike.

The frenzied atmosphere of the war years reproduced this type of situation time and time again. At the Westinghouse works of East Pittsburgh the workers' demands in the strikes of 1914 and 1916 and in the acrimonious negotiations of 1915 and 1917 consistently involved efforts to abolish premium pay and to ease the pace of work. Workers could stay home from work more safely as jobs became more plentiful, and at Bethlehem Steel an average of 20 percent of the force was missing each day by the fall of 1918. After those workers had struck several times, the National War Labor Board ordered Gantt's task-and-bonus system abolished, on the grounds that it had had a "serious detrimental effect upon the production of war materials."

To the eyes of leading figures in American business, output per hour was declining during the war years at the very same time that the number of hours regularly worked each week was falling. This trend not only injured the war effort, they claimed, it also threatened their plans for the postwar world. The 1916 convention of the National Metal Trades Association was warned by its president, James A. Emery, that the current war of arms would be followed swiftly by a war of economic competition. Only by resisting union interference and efforts to reduce working hours could American business prepare itself for the "world contest of peace succeeding that of war." "It is no hour for watered capital or watered labor," Emery declared, "but for management trained to the moment and operatives conscious that harmonious co-operation and intelligent self-interest can alone insure the joint industrial success of employer and employee."

In short, the war crisis itself intensified the struggle for power within the factory, increased labor's ability to impose its standards and resist those of the employer, and greatly increased the appeal of scientific management to industrialists. It also forced the apostles of scientific management to wrestle with the problems of industrial psychology, personnel management, and "Americanization" of immigrants, in addition to the more familiar questions of standardizing tasks and wage systems. Although the transformation of immigrant laborers into machine tenders and the rapid increase in the number of supervisors and tool and die makers had initially weakened the position of craft unions in the metalworking industries, the unskilled operatives came to assert themselves with increasing militancy, and sometimes undid the once-successful work of efficiency experts. The day of reckoning came, of course, in the postwar depression of 1920–2. Then union strength in basic industries toppled like a house of cards, and the wages of all workers plummeted downward (especially those of the unskilled). Weekly hours of work were lengthened again, and productivity per worker rose rapidly. Only then did the standards of scientific management, now in harness with the new concerns of personnel management, carry the day.

Introduction
Charlotte Perkins Gilman, "Making a Change"

As Peter Laslett told us earlier, before industrialization most people worked in the home. Husbands and wives were partners who shared the labor necessary to run the economies of their households. Early industrialization changed all that, sending women and children, as well as men, into the factories. Later, however, as industrial economies brought increased wealth, the living and working patterns changed to where middle-class households became the ideal in America. Increasingly American households saw men leaving home alone to go to their workplaces, and one sign of a man's status was that he could leave his wife behind to maintain the home and to minister to his off-work needs and comforts. In middle-class culture women's jobs and careers were bypassed in favor of those of their husbands.

Charlotte Perkins Gilman was born into a prominent middle-class family, but she, her mother, and an older brother were soon abandoned to a life of poverty. After much hardship she was able to attend the Rhode Island School of Design, which allowed her to earn a living as an art teacher. Gilman's first marriage resulted in divorce, and this trauma, combined with her childhood experience of sliding into poverty, radicalized her for the rest of her life. She did not become dogmatic or strident and in fact insisted she was not a feminist (she said she was merely trying to deal with a world that was "masculinist"), but Gilman became devoted to freeing women from the tyranny of the patriarchal industrial order.

A committed socialist, she focused on practical solutions for freeing women from the drudgery of the home. "Making a Change," for example, contains a down-to-earth solution to some very real problems of everyday life. Gilman is not a great artist (her fiction, with a few exceptions, is didactic, more a vehicle for her politics than good art), but hers is a strong voice for women at the turn of the twentieth century. She was an advocate for day care, flextime, equal pay for equal work, maternity leave, and work-sharing at home. She is a voice from early in America's bourgeois period reminding us that housework is real work and also that women, like men, need good work in the community that brings recognition.

Charlotte Perkins Gilman

Making a Change

"Wa-a-a-a-a! Waa-a-a-aaa!"

Frank Gordins set down his coffee cup so hard that it spilled over into the saucer.

"Is there no way to stop that child crying?" he demanded.

"I do not know of any," said his wife, so definitely and politely that the words seemed cut off by machinery.

"*I do,*" said his mother with even more definiteness, but less politeness.

Young Mrs. Gordins looked at her mother-in-law from under her delicate level brows, and said nothing. But the weary lines about her eyes deepened; she had been kept awake nearly all night, and for many nights.

So had he. So, as a matter of fact, had his mother. She had not the care of the baby—but lay awake wishing she had.

"There's no use talking about it," said Julia, "If Frank is not satisfied with the child's mother, he must say so—perhaps we can make a change."

This was ominously gentle. Julia's nerves were at the breaking point. Upon her tired ears, her sensitive mother's heart, the grating wail from the next room fell like a lash—burnt in like fire. Her ears were hypersensitive, always. She had been an ardent musician before her marriage, and had taught quite successfully on both piano and violin. To any mother a child's cry is painful; to a musical mother it is torment.

But if her ears were sensitive, so was her conscience. If her nerves were weak, her pride was strong. The child was her child, it was her duty to take care of it, and take care of it she would. She spent her days in unremitting devotion to its needs and to the care of her neat flat; and her nights had long since ceased to refresh her.

Again the weary cry rose to a wail.

"It does seem to be time for a change of treatment," suggested the older woman acidly.

"Or a change of residence," offered the younger, in a deadly quiet voice.

"Well, by Jupiter! There'll be a change of some kind, and p.d.q.!" said the son and husband, rising to his feet.

His mother rose also, and left the room, holding her head high and refusing to show any effects of that last thrust.

Frank Gordins glared at his wife. His nerves were raw, too. It does not benefit anyone in health or character to be continuously deprived of sleep. Some enlightened persons use that deprivation as a form of torture.

She stirred her coffee with mechanical calm, her eyes sullenly bent on her plate.

"I will not stand having Mother spoken to like that," he stated with decision.

"I will not stand having her interfere with my methods of bringing up children."

"Your methods! Why, Julia, my mother knows more about taking care of babies than you'll ever learn! She has the real love of it—and the practical experience. Why can't you *let* her take care of the kid—and we'll all have some peace!"

She lifted her eyes and looked at him; deep inscrutable wells of angry light. He had not the faintest appreciation of her state of mind. When people say they are "nearly crazy" from weariness, they state a practical fact. The old phrase which describes reason as "tottering on her throne" is also a clear one.

Julia was more near the verge of complete disaster than the family dreamed. The conditions were so simple, so usual, so inevitable.

Here was Frank Gordins, well brought up, the only son of a very capable and idolatrously affectionate mother. He had fallen deeply and desperately in love with the exalted beauty and fine mind of the young music teacher, and his mother had approved. She too loved music and admired beauty.

Her tiny store in the savings bank did not allow of a separate home, and Julia had cordially welcomed her to share in their household.

Here was affection, propriety, and peace. Here was a noble devotion on the part of the young wife, who so worshipped her husband that she used to wish she had been the greatest musician on earth—that she might give it up for him! She had given up her music, perforce, for many months, and missed it more than she knew.

She bent her mind to the decoration and artistic management of their little apartment, finding her standards difficult to maintain by the ever-changing inefficiency of her help. The musical temperament does not always include patience, nor, necessarily, the power of management.

When the baby came, her heart overflowed with utter devotion and thankfulness; she was his wife—the mother of his child. Her happiness lifted and pushed within till she longed more than ever for her music, for the free-pouring current of expression, to give forth her love and pride and happiness. She had not the gift of words.

So now she looked at her husband, dumbly, while wild visions of separation, of secret flight—even of self-destruction—swung dizzily across her mental vision. All she said was, "All right, Frank. We'll make a change. And you shall have—some peace."

"Thank goodness for that, Jule! You do look tired, girlie—let Mother see to His Nibs, and try to get a nap, can't you?"

"Yes," she said. "Yes . . . I think I will." Her voice had a peculiar note in it. If Frank had been an alienist, or even a general physician, he would have noticed it. But his work lay in electric coils, in dynamos and copper wiring—not in women's nerves—and he did not notice it.

He kissed her and went out, throwing back his shoulders and drawing a long breath of relief as he left the house behind him and entered his own world.

"This being married—and bringing up children—is not what it's cracked up to be." That was the feeling in the back of his mind. But it did not find full admission, much less expression.

When a friend asked him, "All well at home?" he said, "Yes, thank you—pretty fair. Kid cries a good deal—but that's natural, I suppose."

He dismissed the whole matter from his mind and bent his faculties to a man's task—how he can earn enough to support a wife, a mother, and a son.

At home his mother sat in her small room, looking out of the window at the ground-glass one just across the "well," and thinking hard.

By the disorderly little breakfast table his wife remained motionless, her chin in her hands, her big eyes staring at nothing, trying to formulate in her weary mind some reliable reason why she should not do what she was thinking of doing. But her mind was too exhausted to serve her properly.

Sleep—sleep—sleep—that was the one thing she wanted. Then his mother could take care of the baby all she wanted to, and Frank could have some peace. . . . Oh, dear! It was time for the child's bath.

She gave it to him mechanically. On the stroke of the hour, she prepared the sterilized milk and arranged the little one comfortably with his bottle. He snuggled down, enjoying it, while she stood watching him.

She emptied the tub, put the bath apron to dry, picked up all the towels and sponges and varied appurtenances of the elaborate performance of bathing the first-born, and then sat staring straight before her, more weary than ever, but growing inwardly determined.

Greta had cleared the table, with heavy heels and hands, and was now rattling dishes in the kitchen. At every slam, the young mother winced, and when the girl's high voice began a sort of doleful chant over her work, young Mrs. Gordins rose to her feet with a shiver and made her decision.

She carefully picked up the child and his bottle, and carried him to his grandmother's room.

"Would you mind looking after Albert?" she asked in a flat, quiet voice. "I think I'll try to get some sleep."

"Oh, I shall be delighted," replied her mother-in-law. She said it in a tone of cold politeness, but Julia did not notice. She laid the child on the bed and stood looking at him in the same dull way for a little while, then went out without another word.

Mrs. Gordins, senior, sat watching the baby for some long moments. "He's a perfectly lovely child!" she said softly, gloating over his rosy beauty. "There's not a *thing* the matter with him! It's just her absurd ideas. She's so irregular with him! To think of letting that child cry for an hour! He is nervous because she is. And of course she couldn't feed him till after his bath — of course not!"

She continued in these sarcastic meditations for some time, taking the empty bottle away from the small wet mouth, that sucked on for a few moments aimlessly and then was quiet in sleep.

"I could take care of him so that he'd *never* cry!" she continued to herself, rocking slowly back and forth. "And I could take care of twenty like him — and enjoy it! I believe I'll go off somewhere and do it. Give Julia a rest. Change of residence, indeed!"

She rocked and planned, pleased to have her grandson with her, even while asleep.

Greta had gone out on some errand of her own. The rooms were very quiet. Suddenly the old lady held up her head and sniffed. She rose swiftly to her feet and sprang to the gas jet — no, it was shut off tightly. She went back to the dining-room — all right there.

"That foolish girl has left the range going and it's blown out!" she thought, and went to the kitchen. No, the little room was fresh and clean, every burner turned off.

"Funny! It must come in from the hall." She opened the door. No, the hall gave only its usual odor of diffused basement. Then the parlor — nothing there. The little alcove called by the renting agent "the music room" where Julia's closed piano and violin case stood dumb and dusty — nothing there.

"It's in her room — and she's asleep!" said Mrs. Gordins, senior; and she tried to open the door. It was locked. She knocked — there was no answer; knocked louder — shook it — rattled the knob. No answer.

Then Mrs. Gordins thought quickly. "It may be an accident, and nobody must know. Frank mustn't know. I'm glad Greta's out. I *must* get in somehow!" She looked at the transom, and the stout rod Frank had himself put up for the portieres Julia loved.

"I believe I can do it, at a pinch."

She was a remarkable active woman of her years, but no memory of earlier gymnastic feats could quite cover the exercise. She hastily brought the step-ladder. From its top she could see in, and what she saw made her determine recklessly.

Grabbing the pole with small strong hands, she thrust her light frame bravely through the opening, turning clumsily but successfully, and dropping breathlessly and somewhat bruised to the floor, she flew to open the windows and doors.

When Julia opened her eyes she found loving arms around her, and wise, tender words to soothe and reassure.

"Don't say a thing, dearie—I understand. I *understand*, I tell you! Oh, my dear girl—my precious daughter! We haven't been half good enough to you, Frank and I! But cheer up now—I've got the *loveliest* plan to tell you about! We *are* going to make a change! Listen now!"

And while the pale young mother lay quiet, petted and waited on to her heart's content, great plans were discussed and decided on.

Frank Gordins was pleased when the baby "outgrew his crying spells." He spoke of it to his wife.

"Yes," she said sweetly. "He has better care."

"I knew you'd learn," said he, proudly.

"I have!" she agreed. "I've learned—ever so much!"

He was pleased, too, vastly pleased, to have her health improve rapidly and steadily, the delicate pink come back to her cheeks, the soft light to her eyes; and when she made music for him in the evening, soft music, with shut doors—not to waken Albert—he felt as if his days of courtship had come again.

Greta the hammer-footed had gone, and an amazing French matron who came in by the day had taken her place. He asked no questions as to this person's peculiarities, and did not know that she did the purchasing and planned the meals, meals of such new delicacy and careful variance as gave him much delight. Neither did he know that her wages were greater than her predecessor's. He turned over the same sum weekly, and did not pursue details.

He was pleased also that his mother seemed to have taken a new lease of life. She was so cheerful and brisk, so full of little jokes and stories— as he had known her in his boyhood; and above all she was so free and affectionate with Julia, that he was more than pleased.

"I tell you what it is!" he said to a bachelor friend. "You fellows don't know what you're missing!" And he brought one of them home to dinner —just to show him.

"Do you do all that on thirty-five a week?" his friend demanded.

"That's about it," he answered proudly.

"Well, your wife's a wonderful manager — that's all I can say. And you've got the best cook I ever saw, or heard of, or ate of — I suppose I might say — for five dollars."

Mrs. Gordins was pleased and proud. But he was neither pleased nor proud when someone said to him, with displeasing frankness, "I shouldn't think you'd want your wife to be giving music lessons, Frank!"

He did not show surprise nor anger to his friend, but saved it for his wife. So surprised and so angry was he that he did a most unusual thing — he left his business and went home early in the afternoon. He opened the door of his flat. There was no one in it. He went through every room. No wife; no child; no mother; no servant.

The elevator boy heard him banging about, opening and shutting doors, and grinned happily. When Mr. Gordins came out, Charles volunteered some information.

"Young Mrs. Gordins is out, sir; but old Mrs. Gordins and the baby — they're upstairs. On the roof, I think."

Mr. Gordins went to the roof. There he found his mother, a smiling, cheerful nursemaid, and fifteen happy babies.

Mrs. Gordins, senior, rose to the occasion promptly.

"Welcome to my baby-garden, Frank," she said cheerfully. "I'm so glad you could get off in time to see it."

She took his arm and led him about, proudly exhibiting her sunny roof-garden, her sand-pile and big, shallow, zinc-lined pool, her flowers and vines, her seesaws, swings, and floor mattresses.

"You see how happy they are," she said. "Celia can manage very well for a few moments." And then she exhibited to him the whole upper flat, turned into a convenient place for many little ones to take their naps or to play in if the weather was bad.

"Where's Julia?" he demanded first.

"Julia will be in presently," she told him, "by five o'clock anyway. And the mothers come for the babies by then, too. I have them from nine or ten to five."

He was silent, both angry and hurt.

"We didn't tell you at first, my dear boy, because we knew you wouldn't like it, and we wanted to make sure it would go well. I rent the upper flat, you see — it is forty dollars a month, same as ours — and pay Celia five dollars a week, and pay Dr. Holbrook downstairs the same for looking over my little ones every day. She helped me to get them, too. The mothers pay me three dollars a week each, and don't have to keep a nursemaid. And I pay ten dollars a week board to Julia, and still have about ten of my own."

"And she gives music lessons?"

"Yes, she gives music lessons, just as she used to. She loves it, you know. You must have noticed how happy and well she is now—haven't you? And so am I. And so is Albert. You can't feel very badly about a thing that makes us all happy, can you?"

Just then Julia came in, radiant from a brisk walk, fresh and cheery, a big bunch of violets at her breast

"Oh, Mother," she cried, "I've got tickets and we'll all go to hear Melba —if we can get Celia to come in for the evening."

She saw her husband, and a guilty flush rose to her brow as she met his reproachful eyes.

"Oh, Frank!" she begged, her arms around his neck. "Please don't mind! Please get used to it! Please be proud of us! Just think, we're all so happy, and we earn about a hundred dollars a week—all of us together. You see, I have Mother's ten to add to the house money, and twenty or more of my own!"

They had a long talk together than evening, just the two of them. She told him, at last, what a danger had hung over them—how near it came.

"And Mother showed me the way out, Frank. The way to have my mind again—and not lose you! She is a different woman herself now that she has her heart and hands full of babies. Albert does enjoy it so! And *you've* enjoyed it—till you found it out!

"And dear—my own love—I don't mind it now at all! I love my home, I love my work, I love my mother, I love you. And as to children—I wish I had six!"

He looked at her flushed, eager, lovely face, and drew her close to him.

"If it makes all of you as happy as that," he said, "I guess I can stand it."

And in after years he was heard to remark, "this being married and bringing up children is as easy as can be—when you learn how!"

3. Problems for Workers

Introduction
Richard Sennett and Jonathan Cobb,
from *The Hidden Injuries of Class*

Richard Sennet received his PhD in sociology from Harvard University and is on the faculty at New York University and serves as director of the Center for Humanistic Studies. Besides his many scholarly publications he was politically active as a speech writer for Eugene McCarthy. Coauthor Jonathan Cobb is a Columbia University graduate and has worked as a free-lance writer and in urban family studies.

One of the great promises of Western life since Locke, and especially since the founding of the American Republic, has been the creation of a meritocracy that would allow the best people, from whatever background, to rise to positions of influence and leadership. Indeed, the Horatio Alger rags-to-riches story is the prototypical American tale, and as Locke and Smith asserted, this is how we can best achieve the most abundant world for all of society. In the following study Sennett and Cobb look at certain features of the American educational system and how it has affected this sacred American ideal. What they find has to be disturbing to all who share in this ideal.

Their analysis shows why, in spite of a legally open system, we have created a largely permanent working class in American society. As you will see, at the heart of this problem is the normal human need to have an identity as part of a community. Because we are a society that prides itself on individualism, we often fail to look at those forces that shape the individual. Yet if we have produced institutions that cripple competitors before they reach the starting line, open access to the race does not have much meaning. Remember, if Sennett and Cobb are right, the implications are not simply about justice for the individual. If the potentially best people are not able to achieve, the consequences will be bad for all of us.

Richard Sennett
and Jonathan Cobb

The Hidden Injuries of Class

Josiah Watson Grammar School is an old red-brick building with a simple but well-kept playground. It is a large school, in the midst of an urban neighborhood of mostly three-decker houses. In Watson School, teachers restrict the freedom of the children because these figures of authority have a peculiar fear of the children. It is the mass who seem to the teachers to threaten classroom order, by naughty or unruly behavior; only a few are seen as having "good habits" or the right attitude. As one teacher explained, "These children come from simple laborers' homes where the parents don't understand the value of education." Yet in the early grades the observer noticed few examples of disruptive behavior. He sensed among the six- and seven-year-olds a real desire to please, to accept the teacher's control and be accepted by her. One pathetic incident, although extreme, stands out. In the middle of a reading-preparedness class, a child wet his pants because he was absorbed in his lesson. "What can you do with children like that?," the teacher later remarked in a tone of disgust.

What happens is that the teachers act on their expectations of the children in such a way as to *make* the expectations become reality. Here is how the process worked in one second-grade class at Watson School — unusual in that it was taught by a young man. In this class there were two children, Fred and Vincent, whose appearance was somewhat different from that of the others: their clothes were no fancier than the other children's, but they were pressed and seemed better kept; in a class of mostly dark Italian children, these were the fairest-skinned. From the outset the teacher singled out these two children, implying that they most closely approached his own standards for classroom performance. To them he spoke with a special warmth in his voice. He never praised them openly by comparison to the other children, but a message that they were different, were better, was spontaneously conveyed. As the observer watched the children play and work over the course of the school year, he noticed these two boys becoming more serious, more solemn, as the months passed. Obedient and never unruly from the first, by the end of the year they were left alone by the other children.

By then they were also doing the best work in the class. The other children had picked up the teacher's hidden cues that their performance would not be greeted with as much enthusiasm as the work of these two little boys. "It's not true of the other children that they generally have less potential," the teacher remarked. "It's a question of not developing their ability like Fred and Vincent. I know you're right, I tend to encourage them more despite myself, but I—it's obvious to me these little boys are going to make something of themselves."

In the Watson School, by the time the children are ten or eleven the split between the many and the few who are expected to "make something of themselves" is out in the open; the aloofness developing in the second grade has become open hostility by the sixth. Among the boys, this hostility is expressed by images which fuse sex and status. Boys like Fred and Vincent are described by the "ordinary" students as effeminate and weak, as "suck-ups." The kids mean by this both that the Freds and Vincents are getting somewhere in school because they are so docile.

There is a counterculture of dignity that springs up among these ordinary working-class boys, a culture that seeks in male solidarity what cannot be found in the suspended time that comprises classroom experience. This solidarity also sets them off from the "suck-ups." Hanging around together, the boys share their incipient sexual exploits, real and imagined; sex becomes a way to compete within the group. What most cements them as a group, however, is the breaking of rules—smoking, drinking, or taking drugs together, cutting classes. Breaking the rules is an act "nobodies" can share with each other. This counterculture does not come to grips with the labels their teachers have imposed on these kids; it is rather an attempt to create among themselves badges of dignity that those in authority can't destroy.

A full circle: outside observers—parents, teachers, and others—who see only the external aspects of this counterculture, are confirmed in their view that "hanging around" is destructive to a child's self-development. Dignity in these terms exacts a toll by the standards of the outer world.

The division of children, in schools like Watson, into groups with a shared sense of loyalty and individuals alone but "getting somewhere," characterizes many levels of education; it is not something unique to, say, college-bound youth as opposed to vocational school boys. Studies of trade schools show the same phenomenon occurring: boys who are good at car mechanics in school start to feel cut off from others, even though the possession of those skills might make them admired by their less-skilled peers outside of school. It is an institutional process that makes the difference, a question of mere toleration versus active approval from those in power.

The drama played out in the Watson School has as its script the assigning and the wearing of badges of ability like those described earlier, worn by adults. The teachers cast the Freds and Vincents into the role of Andrew Carnegie's virtuous man. Ability will make these children into individuals, and as individuals they will rise in social class. The mass find themselves in a role similar to that which Lipset assigns to adult workers: their class background allegedly limits their self-development, and the counterculture of compensatory respect they create reinforces, in a vicious circle, the judgments of the teachers.

The teacher has the *power* to limit the freedom of development of his or her students through this drama. But why is he or she moved to act in this repressive way? This question is really two questions: it is first a matter of a teacher legitimizing in his own mind the power he holds, and second, a matter of the students taking that power as legitimate.

The teachers are in a terrible existential dilemma. It is true that they are "prejudiced" against most of their students; it is also true that they, like all human beings, want to believe in the dignity of their own work, no matter how difficult the circumstances in which they have to work seem to them. If a teacher believed that every single student would perpetually resist him, he would have no reason to go on teaching—his power in the classroom would be empty. A teacher needs at least a responsive few in order to feel he has a *reason* to possess power. The few will confirm to him that his power to affect other people is real, that he can truly do good. To sort out two classes of ability, then, in fear of the "lower" class of students, is to create a meaningful image of himself as an authority rather than simply a boss.

The child can try to win respect from a figure in power, alienating his peers but confirming to the judge that here is an individual who is going to make something of himself in life, i.e., move up socially. The child can try to win respect from his peers, but in that case he feels that he has not developed the abilities within himself that would earn him the respect of a powerful person in a higher class.

The situation seems clearly self-defeating. But why, then, don't those caught up in it rebel? It is true that the teacher is usually the first adult outside the family to give the children new experience. Indeed, the teachers at Watson School receive the accolades of the parents as a very important figure in the children's lives. In homes where the parents have limited education, the stress on the teacher's role is especially strong: the teacher can open the gateway to opportunities the parents never had.

The child's own experience in school, however, is most important. Since the teacher appears to him as passive, is it not his own fault if he fails to catch the teacher's attention? The system must work, for the child can see that a few are chosen—but not he. Could he have paid more attention, worked harder? He wants and needs friends; since he cannot read the teacher's mind, how can he know that forming friendships based on "hanging around," mutual defense, and breaking small rules, reinforces the teacher's belief that he hasn't much intellectual ability? Before the passive judge, some people make it, while the teacher tolerates *him* impersonally—that is what he knows. All the burden of the situation seems on him; indeed, since the teacher does tolerate him, there is nothing in this passive, judgmental authority that he feels he can fight.

To put this school situation in general terms, we may say that this is an instance of how a superior "gets away with" restricting the freedom of someone in his charge by replacing the problem of limited freedom with the problem of the inferior person asserting his own dignity—the superior will not control, he will impassively judge. This is a game of disguising power, but it is not a game in which the powerful consciously tries to "get away with" duping people in his charge or deceiving them. The game works because, in a school like this, *all the actors genuinely believe they are engaged in problems of self and in morally meaningful personal actions that transcend power;* in this drama of class and age, power becomes legitimate to those it wounds through the very means by which the powerful seek to convince themselves that, faced with inferior people, they can at least do some good.

Weber despaired of people ever breaking the bonds of legitimized power in a class society, except in very special cases. The situation in the Watson School shows an instance of how power is legitimized and maintained, not by rigidly tyrannical measures, but rather by a subtle and delicate balance. The children have a great deal of resentment against the aspersions on their dignity the teacher's power ultimately causes; but they don't know what to do about that anger, or even, because they see the teacher as passive, who is to blame. So they turn on the few who are approved, leveling at the Freds and Vincents all the accusations of weakness and inability to command respect that the authority figures implicitly level against *them*—though Max and Vinny do not blame the "suck-ups" for their own position in the classroom. The legitimization of power is like a cloak of secrecy over the origins of one's anxiety. It is this cloak of secrecy that makes these children feel responsible for a situation they did not create.

Introduction
D.H. Lawrence, "The Rocking-Horse Winner"

D.H. Lawrence was born in 1885 in Northern England, the son of a middle-class mother and a working class, coal-mining father. The inevitable tension created by this class conflict within his family became a major formative influence on Lawrence and his writing.

A second influence came from the writings of Sigmund Freud. As you have seen in John Locke, Western thinkers have long sought a basis in natural law to help them determine how we do and should act as humans. Lawrence believed that Freud had discovered the natural in his description of human instincts, and in particular in what Freud called the id: Freud believed it is most natural to seek pleasure and love. Lawrence was a kind of Neoromantic, and like the Romantics he believed we should follow our instincts. He believed that the tyranny of an overzealous and overrigid superego is the enemy. The superego is that part of our psyche that embodies the learned values of society, which inevitably forces us to limit and control our pleasure-seeking id. The superego demands that we put the work of society before the pleasures of the self. For a traditional society one might argue that this is a reasonable requirement (as Freud himself does), a necessary price for civilization. But Lawrence believed that the attack on instincts by modern middle-class society had been devastating, that it had gone too far. The superego of modern societies had gone beyond the necessary disciplining of the instinctual self to crush the fragile ego.

The result, according to Lawrence, is an impotent, joyless race of people who find meaning not in life, but in defeating life; who find meaning not in the satisfaction of a job well done, but in success for its own sake; and who find meaning most of all in keeping up appearances. Life becomes for modern humanity a means to a sterile and pointless end rather than an end in its own right. Conforming to an inhuman external ideal at the expense of inner feelings is the awful cost exacted in Lawrence's and our own middle-class society, and his story contends that the cost is too great.

In "The Rocking Horse Winner" we have the paradox of the picture-book middle-class family: a beautiful mother, with attractive children, an elegant home—all the necessities of life; yet the mother is miserably unhappy. The putative source of her misery is explained early in the story: she doesn't have enough money. Her desire for money would seem to be a vindication of the classical economists, who tell us that humans are naturally insatiable in their desire for wealth. But is it possible that money is not the real problem? Is it possible that her desire for money is a false value, and that it is really the pursuit of this false value that has made her unhappy? Has this obsession crowded out other, more natural inclinations, the loss of which is the source of much of her pain?

We see, for instance, that she cannot love her children. The children sense this loss of love, although they are compensated for it by many toys and other goods. The mother realizes that she should love her children and she tries, but she ends up only fussing over them.

Her value system has taught her that to love brings status. We are told that she feels superior to the neighbors, that she is extremely concerned with keeping up appearances. Perhaps status is a way of keeping score in a sterile world that has no intrinsic meaning. In any case she cannot get enough money to keep up appearances, and the reader soon realizes that no amount would be sufficient.

As you read this story, consider why her son Paul is driven to acquire money in such a strange way. Don't be bothered by the supernatural element in the story—this is just an unrealistic ploy by the author to help us see more realistically. Notice that the horse that Paul rides to gain wealth for his mother is a "mechanical" horse rather than a flesh-and-blood animal. Consider further that horses, physical animals with erotic overtones, are turned into instruments for making money. What does this tell us about modern work and what it does to the worker? Does this suggest a parallel in the story with the theme of the distortion of the natural for the sake of wealth? Consider the outcome of Paul's riding of the mechanical horse and what it says about the values that his mother has unwittingly encouraged him to pursue. Does the final cost of those values to Paul and his mother suggest a warning to us and to our society?

Studies by child psychologists of upper-middle-class children have shown that they prefer the attention and love of their parents to high-priced toys and trips to expensive summer camps. But the studies also show that in the absence of love they will generally attempt to work within the system as it exists and gain the approval of their parents even if they cannot gain their love. Is it too much to say that this decision on the part of the child to opt for approval rather than love involves a kind of spiritual death? Consider this as you read the story and see if it helps you understand more fully this poignant protest against the middle-class world of twentieth-century industrial society.

D.H. Lawrence

The Rocking-Horse Winner

There was a woman who was beautiful, who started with all the advantages, yet she had no luck. She married for love, and the love turned to dust. She had bonny children, yet she felt they had been thrust upon her, and she could not love them. They looked at her coldly, as if they were finding fault with her. And hurriedly she felt she must cover up some fault in herself. Yet what it was that she must cover up she never knew. Nevertheless, when her children were present, she always felt the centre of her heart go hard. This troubled her, and in her manner she was all the more gentle and anxious for her children, as if she loved them very much. Only she herself knew that at the centre of her heart was a hard little place that could not feel love, no, not for anybody. Everybody else said of her: "She is such a good mother. She adores her children." Only she herself, and her children themselves, knew it was not so. They read it in each other's eyes.

There were a boy and two little girls. They lived in a pleasant house, with a garden, and they had discreet servants, and felt themselves superior to anyone in the neighbourhood.

Although they lived in style, they felt always an anxiety in the house. There was never enough money. The mother had a small income, and the father had a small income, but not nearly enough for the social position which they had to keep up. The father went in to town to some office. But though he had good prospects, these prospects never materialized. There was always the grinding sense of the shortage of money, though the style was always kept up.

At last the mother said: "I will see if *I* can't make something." But she did not know where to begin. She racked her brains, and tried this thing and the other, but could not find anything successful. The failure made deep lines come into her face. Her children were growing up, they would have to go to school. There must be more money, there must be more money. The father, who was always very handsome and expensive in his tastes, seemed as if he never *would* be able to do anything worth doing. And the mother, who had a great belief in herself, did not succeed any better, and her tastes were just as expensive.

And so the house came to be haunted by the unspoken phrase: *There must be more money! There must be more money!* The children could hear it all the time, though nobody said it aloud. They heard it at Christmas, when the expensive and splendid toys filled the nursery. Behind the shining modern rocking-horse, behind the small doll's-house, a voice would start whispering: "There *must* be more money! There *must* be more money!" And the children would stop playing, to listen for a moment. They would look into each other's eyes, to see if they had all heard. And each one saw in the eyes of the other two that they too had heard. "There *must* be more money! There *must* be more money!"

It came whispering from the springs of the still-swaying rocking horse, and even the horse, bending his wooden, champing head, heard it. The big doll, sitting so pink and smirking in her new pram, could hear it quite plainly, and seemed to be smirking all the more self-consciously because of it. The foolish puppy, too, that took the place of the teddy bear, he was looking so extraordinarily foolish for no other reason but that he heard the secret whisper all over the house: "There *must* be more money!"

Yet nobody ever said it aloud. The whisper was everywhere, and therefore no one spoke it. Just as no one ever says: "We are breathing!" in spite of the fact that breath is coming and going all the time.

"Mother," said the boy Paul one day, "why don't we keep a car of our own? Why do we always use uncle's, or else a taxi?"

"Because we're the poor members of the family," said the mother.

"But why *are* we, mother?"

"Well—I suppose," she said slowly and bitterly, "it's because your father has no luck."

The boy was silent for some time.

"Is luck money, mother?" he asked rather timidly.

"No, Paul. Not quite. It's what causes you to have money."

"Oh!" said Paul vaguely. "I thought when Uncle Oscar said *filthy lucker,* it meant money."

"*Filthy lucre* does mean money," said the mother. "But it's lucre, not luck."

"Oh!" said the boy. "Then what *is* luck, mother?"

"It's what causes you to have money. If you're lucky you have money. That's why it's better to be born lucky than rich. If you're rich, you may lose your money. But if you're lucky, you will always get more money."

"Oh! Will you? And is father not lucky?"

"Very unlucky, I should say," she said bitterly.

The boy watched her with unsure eyes.

"Why?" he asked.

"I don't know. Nobody ever knows why one person is lucky and another unlucky."

"Don't they? Nobody at all? Does *nobody* know?"

"Perhaps God. But He never tells."

"He ought to, then. And aren't you lucky either, mother?"

"I can't be, if I married an unlucky husband."

"But by yourself, aren't you?"

"I used to think I was, before I married. Now I think I am very unlucky indeed."

"Why?"

"Well—never mind! Perhaps I'm not really," she said.

The child looked at her, to see if she meant it. But he saw, by the lines of her mouth, that she was only trying to hide something from him.

"Well, anyhow," he said stoutly, "I'm a lucky person."

"Why?" said his mother, with a sudden laugh.

He stared at her. He didn't even know why he had said it.

"God told me," he asserted, brazening it out.

"I hope He did, dear!" she said, again with a laugh, but rather bitter.

"He did, mother!"

"Excellent!" said the mother, using one of her husband's exclamations.

The boy saw she did not believe him; or, rather, that she paid no attention to his assertion. This angered him somewhat, and made him want to compel her attention.

He went off by himself, vaguely, in a childish way, seeking for the clue to "luck." Absorbed, taking no heed of other people, he went about with a sort of stealth, seeking inwardly for luck. He wanted luck, he wanted it, he wanted it. When the two girls were playing dolls in the nursery, he would sit on his big rocking-horse, charging madly into space, with a frenzy that made the little girls peer at him uneasily. Wildly the horse careered, the waving dark hair of the boy tossed, his eyes had a strange glare in them. The little girls dared not speak to him.

When he had ridden to the end of his mad little journey, he climbed down and stood in front of his rocking-horse, staring fixedly into its lowered face. Its red mouth was slightly open, its big eye was wide and glassy-bright.

"Now!" he would silently command the snorting steed. "Now, take me to where there is luck! Now take me!"

And he would slash the horse on the neck with the little whip he had asked Uncle Oscar for. He *knew* the horse could take him to where there

was luck, if only he forced it. So he would mount again, and start on
his furious ride, hoping at last to get there. He knew he could get there.

"You'll break your horse, Paul!" said the nurse.

"He's always riding like that! I wish he'd leave off!" said his elder sister
Joan.

But he only glared down on them in silence. Nurse gave him up. She
could make nothing of him. Anyhow he was growing beyond her.

One day his mother and his Uncle Oscar came in when he was on
one of his furious rides. He did not speak to them.

"Hallo, you young jockey! Riding a winner?" said his uncle.

"Aren't you growing too big for a rocking-horse? You're not a very little boy any longer, you know," said his mother.

But Paul only gave a blue glare from his big, rather close-set eyes.
He would speak to nobody when he was in full tilt. His mother watched
him with an anxious expression on her face.

At last he suddenly stopped forcing his horse into the mechanical gal-
lop, and slid down.

"Well, I got there!" he announced fiercely, his blue eyes still flaring,
and his sturdy long legs straddling apart.

"Where did you get to?" asked his mother.

"Where I wanted to go," he flared back at her.

"That's right, son!" said Uncle Oscar. "Don't you stop till you get there.
What's the horse's name?"

"He doesn't have a name," said the boy.

"Gets on without all right?" asked the uncle.

"Well, he has different names. He was called Sansovino last week."

"Sansovino, eh? Won the Ascot. How did you know his name?"

"He always talks about horse-races with Bassett," said Joan.

The uncle was delighted to find that his small nephew was posted with
all the racing news. Bassett, the young gardener, who had been wounded
in the left foot in the war and had got his present job through Oscar
Cresswell, whose batman he had been, was a perfect blade of the "turf."
He lived in the racing events, and the small boy lived with him.

Oscar Cresswell got it all from Bassett.

"Master Paul comes and asks me, so I can't do more than tell him,
sir," said Bassett, his face terribly serious, as if he were speaking of religious matters.

"And does he ever put anything on a horse he fancies?"

"Well — I don't want to give him away — he's a young sport, a fine sport,
sir. Would you mind asking him himself? He sort of takes a pleasure in
it, and perhaps he'd feel I was giving him away, sir, if you don't mind."

Bassett was serious as a church.

The uncle went back to his nephew and took him off for a ride in the car.

"Say, Paul, old man, do you ever put anything on a horse?" the uncle asked.

The boy watched the handsome man closely.

"Why, do you think I oughtn't to?" he parried.

"Not a bit of it! I thought perhaps you might give me a tip for the Lincoln."

The car sped on into the country, going down to Uncle Oscar's place in Hampshire.

"Honour bright?" said the nephew.

"Honour bright, son!" said the uncle.

"Well, then, Daffodil."

"Daffodil! I doubt it, sonny. What about Mirza?"

"I only know the winner," said the boy. "That's Daffodil."

"Daffodil, eh?"

There was a pause. Daffodil was an obscure horse comparatively.

"Uncle!"

"Yes, son?"

"You won't let it go any further, will you? I promised Bassett."

"Bassett be damned, old man! What's he got to do with it?"

"We're partners. We've been partners from the first. Uncle, he lent me my first five shillings, which I lost. I promised him, honour bright, it was only between me and him; only you gave me that ten-shilling note I started winning with, so I thought you were lucky. You won't let it go any further, will you?"

The boy gazed at his uncle from those big, hot, blue eyes, set rather close together. The uncle stirred and laughed uneasily.

"Right you are, son! I'll keep your tip private. Daffodil, eh? How much are you putting on him?"

"All except twenty pounds," said the boy. "I keep that in reserve."

The uncle thought it a good joke.

"You keep twenty pounds in reserve, do you, you young romancer? What are you betting, then?"

"I'm betting three hundred," said the boy gravely. "But it's between you and me, Uncle Oscar! Honour bright?"

The uncle burst into a roar of laughter.

"It's between you and me all right, you young Nat Gould," he said, laughing. "But where's your three hundred?"

"Bassett keeps it for me. We're partners."

"You are, are you! And what is Bassett putting on Daffodil?"

"He won't go quite as high as I do, I expect. Perhaps he'll go a hundred and fifty."

"What, pennies?" laughed the uncle.

"Pounds," said the child, with a surprised look at his uncle. "Bassett keeps a bigger reserve than I do."

Between wonder and amusement Uncle Oscar was silent. He pursued the matter no further, but he determined to take his nephew with him to the Lincoln races.

"Now, son," he said. "I'm putting twenty on Mirza, and I'll put five for you on any horse you fancy. What's your pick?"

"Daffodil, uncle."

"No, not the fiver on Daffodil!"

"I should if it was my own fiver," said the child.

"Good! Good! Right you are! A fiver for me and a fiver for you on Daffodil."

The child had never been to a race-meeting before, and his eyes were blue fire. He pursed his mouth tight, and watched. A Frenchman just in front had put his money on Lancelot. Wild with excitement, he flayed his arms up and down, yelling *"Lancelot! Lancelot!"* in his French accent.

Daffodil came in first, Lancelot second, Mirza third. The child, flushed and with eyes blazing, was curiously serene. His uncle brought him four five-pound notes, four to one.

"What am I to do with these?" he cried, waving them before the boy's eyes.

"I suppose we'll talk to Bassett," said the boy. "I expect I have fifteen hundred now; and twenty in reserve; and this twenty."

His uncle studied him for some moments.

"Look here, son!" he said. "You're not serious about Bassett and that fifteen hundred, are you?"

"Yes, I am. But it's between you and me, uncle. Honour bright!"

"Honour bright all right, son! But I must talk to Bassett."

"If you'd like to be a partner, uncle, with Bassett and me, we could all be partners. Only, you'd have to promise, honour bright, uncle, not to let it go beyond us three. Bassett and I are lucky, and you must be lucky, because it was your ten shillings I started winning with. . . ."

Uncle Oscar took both Bassett and Paul into Richmond Park for an afternoon, and there they talked.

"It's like this, you see, sir," Bassett said. "Master Paul would get me talking about racing events, spinning yarns, you know, sir. And he was always keen on knowing if I'd made or if I'd lost. It's about a year since, now, that I put five shilling on Blush of Dawn for him — and we lost. Then the luck turned, with that ten shillings he had from you, that we put on Singhalese. And since that time, it's been pretty steady, all things considering. What do you say, Master Paul?"

"We're all right when we're sure," said Paul. "It's when we're not quite sure that we go down."

"Oh, but we're careful then," said Bassett.

"But when are you *sure*?" smiled Uncle Oscar.

"It's Master Paul, sir," said Bassett, in a secret, religious voice. "It's as if he had it from heaven. Like Daffodil, now, for the Lincoln. That was as sure as eggs."

"Did you put anything on Daffodil?" asked Oscar Cresswell.

"Yes, sir. I made my bit."

"And my nephew?"

Bassett was obstinately silent, looking at Paul.

"I made twelve hundred, didn't I, Bassett? I told uncle I was putting three hundred on Daffodil."

"That's right," said Bassett, nodding.

"But where's the money?" asked the uncle.

"I keep it safe locked up, sir. Master Paul he can have it any minute he likes to ask for it."

"What, fifteen hundred pounds?"

"And twenty! And *forty,* that is, with the twenty he made on the course."

"It's amazing!" said the uncle.

"If Master Paul offers you to be partners, sir, I would, if I were you; if you'll excuse me," said Bassett.

Oscar Cresswell thought about it.

"I'll see the money," he said.

They drove home again, and sure enough, Bassett came round to the garden-house with fifteen hundred pounds in notes. The twenty pounds reserve was left with Joe Glee, in the Turf Commission deposit.

"You see, it's all right, uncle, when I'm *sure!* Then we go strong, for all we're worth. Don't we, Bassett?"

"We do that, Master Paul."

"And when are you sure?" said the uncle, laughing.

"Oh, well, sometimes I'm *absolutely* sure, like about Daffodil," said the boy; "and sometimes I have an idea; and sometimes I haven't even an idea, have I, Bassett? Then we're careful, because we mostly go down."

"You do, do you! And when you're sure, like about Daffodil, what makes you sure, sonny?"

"Oh, well, I don't know," said the boy uneasily. "I'm sure, you know, uncle; that's all."

"It's as if he had it from heaven, sir," Bassett reiterated.

"I should say so!" said the uncle.

But he became a partner. And when the Leger was coming on, Paul was "sure" about Lively Spark, which was a quite inconsiderable horse. The boy insisted on putting a thousand on the horse, Bassett went for five hundred, and Oscar Cresswell two hundred. Lively Spark came in first, and the betting had been ten to one against him. Paul had made ten thousand.

"You see," he said, "I was absolutely sure of him."

Even Oscar Cresswell had cleared two thousand.

"Look here, son," he said, "this sort of thing makes me nervous."

"It needn't, uncle! Perhaps I shan't be sure again for a long time."

"But what are you going to do with your money?" asked the uncle.

"Of course," said the boy, "I started it for mother. She said she had no luck, because father is unlucky, so I thought if *I* was lucky, it might stop whispering."

"What might stop whispering?"

"Our house. I *hate* our house for whispering."

"What does it whisper?"

"Why—why"—the boy fidgeted—"why, I don't know. But it's always short of money, you know, uncle."

"I know it, son, I know it."

"You know people send mother writs, don't you, uncle?"

"I'm afraid I do," said the uncle.

"And then the house whispers, like people laughing at you behind your back. It's awful, that is! I thought if I was lucky . . ."

"You might stop it," added the uncle.

The boy watched him with big blue eyes, that had an uncanny cold fire in them, and he said never a word.

"Well, then!" said the uncle. "What are we doing?"

"I shouldn't like mother to know I was lucky," said the boy.

"Why not, son?"

"She'd stop me."

"I don't think she would."

"Oh!"—and the boy writhed in an odd way—"I *don't* want her to know, uncle."

"All right, son! We'll manage it without her knowing."

They managed it very easily. Paul, at the other's suggestion, handed over five thousand pounds to his uncle, who deposited it with the family lawyer, who was then to inform Paul's mother that a relative had put five thousand pounds into his hands, which sum was to be paid out a thousand pounds at a time, on the mother's birthday, for the next five years.

"So she'll have a birthday present of a thousand pounds for five successive years," said Uncle Oscar. "I hope it won't make it all the harder for her later."

Paul's mother had her birthday in November. The house had been "whispering" worse than ever lately, and, even in spite of his luck, Paul could not bear up against it. He was very anxious to see the effect of the birthday letter, telling his mother about the thousand pounds.

When there were no visitors, Paul now took his meals with his parents, as he was beyond the nursery control. His mother went into town nearly every day. She had discovered that she had an odd knack of sketching furs and dress materials, so she worked secretly in the studio of a friend who was the chief "artist" for the leading drapers. She drew the figures of ladies in furs and ladies in silk and sequins for the newspaper advertisements. This young woman artist earned several thousand pounds a year, but Paul's mother only made several hundreds, and she was again dissatisfied. She so wanted to be first in something, and she did not succeed, even in making sketches for drapery advertisements.

She was down to breakfast on the morning of her birthday. Paul watched her face as she read her letters. He knew the lawyer's letter. As his mother read it, her face hardened and became more expressionless. Then a cold, determined look came on her mouth. She hid the letter under the pile of others, and said not a word about it.

"Didn't you have anything nice in the post for your birthday, mother?" said Paul.

"Quite moderately nice," she said, her voice cold and absent.

She went away to town without saying more.

But in the afternoon Uncle Oscar appeared. He said Paul's mother had had a long interview with the lawyer, asking if the whole five thousand could not be advanced at once, as she was in debt.

"What do you think, uncle?" said the boy.

"I leave it to you, son."

"Oh, let her have it, then! We can get some more with the other," said the boy.

"A bird in the hand is worth two in the bush, laddie!" said Uncle Oscar.

"But I'm sure to *know* for the Grand National; or the Lincolnshire; or else the Derby. I'm sure to know for *one* of them," said Paul.

So Uncle Oscar signed the agreement, and Paul's mother touched the whole five thousand. Then something very curious happened. The voices in the house suddenly went mad, like a chorus of frogs on a spring evening. There were certain new furnishings, and Paul had a tutor. He was *really* going to Eton, his father's school, in the following autumn. There were flowers in the winter, and a blossoming of the luxury Paul's mother had been used to. And yet the voices in the house, behind the sprays of mimosa and almond blossom, and from under the piles of iridescent cushions, simply trilled and screamed in a sort of ecstasy: "There *must* be more money! Oh-h-h; there *must* be more money. Oh, now, now-w! Now-w-w!—there *must* be more money!—more than ever! More than ever!"

It frightened Paul terribly. He studied away at his Latin and Greek with his tutors. But his intense hours were spent with Bassett. The Grand National had gone by: he had not "known," and had lost a hundred pounds. Summer was at hand. He was in agony for the Lincoln. But even for the Lincoln he didn't "know," and he lost fifty pounds. He became wild-eyed and strange, as if something were going to explode in him.

"Let it alone, son! Don't you bother about it!" urged Uncle Oscar. But it was as if the boy couldn't really hear what his uncle was saying.

"I've got to know for the Derby! I've got to know for the Derby!" the child reiterated, his big blue eyes blazing with a sort of madness.

His mother noticed how overwrought he was.

"You'd better go to the seaside. Wouldn't you like to go now to the seaside, instead of waiting? I think you'd better," she said, looking down at him anxiously, her heart curiously heavy because of him.

But the child lifted his uncanny blue eyes.

"I couldn't possibly go before the Derby, mother!" he said. "I couldn't possibly!"

"Why not?" she said, her voice becoming heavy when she was opposed. "Why what you wish. No need for you to wait here. Besides, I think you care too much about these races. It's a bad sign. My family has been a gambling family, and you won't know till you grow up how much damage it has done. But it has done damage. I shall have to send Bassett away, and ask Uncle Oscar not to talk racing to you, unless you promise to be reasonable about it; go away to the seaside and forget it. You're all nerves!"

"I'll do what you like, mother, so long as you don't send me away till after the Derby," the boy said.

"Send you away from where? Just from this house?"

"Yes," he said, gazing at her.

"Why, you curious child, what makes you care about this house so much, suddenly? I never knew you loved it."

He gazed at her without speaking. He had a secret within a secret, something he had not divulged, even to Bassett or to his Uncle Oscar.

But his mother, after standing undecided and a little bit sullen for some moments, said:

"Very well, then! Don't go to the seaside till after the Derby, if you don't wish it. But promise me you won't let your nerves go to pieces. Promise you won't think so much about horse-racing and *events*, as you call them!"

"Oh, no," said the boy casually. "I won't think much about them, mother. You needn't worry. I wouldn't worry, mother, if I were you."

"If you were me and I were you," said his mother, "I wonder what we *should* do!"

"But you know you needn't worry, mother, don't you?" the boy repeated.

"I should be awfully glad to know it," she said wearily.

"Oh, well, you *can*, you know. I mean, you *ought* to know you needn't worry," he insisted.

"Ought I? Then I'll see about it," she said.

Paul's secret of secrets was his wooden horse, that which had no name. Since he was emancipated from a nurse and a nursery-governess, he had had his rocking-horse removed to his own bedroom at the top of the house.

"Surely, you're too big for a rocking-horse!" his mother had remonstrated.

"Well, you see, mother, till I can have a *real* horse, I like to have *some* sort of animal about," had been his quaint answer.

"Do you feel he keeps you company?" she laughed.

"Oh, yes! He's very good, he always keeps me company, when I'm there," said Paul.

So the horse, rather shabby, stood in an arrested prance in the boy's bedroom.

The Derby was drawing near, and the boy grew more and more tense. He hardly heard what was spoken to him, he was very frail, and his eyes were really uncanny. His mother had sudden strange seizures of uneasiness about him. Sometimes, for half-an-hour, she would feel a sudden anxiety about him that was almost anguish. She wanted to rush to him at once, and know he was safe.

Two nights before the Derby, she was at a big party in town, when one of her rushes of anxiety about her boy, her first-born, gripped her heart till she could hardly speak. She fought with the feeling, might and main, for she believed in common-sense. But it was too strong. She had to leave the dance and go downstairs to telephone to the country. The children's nursery-governess was terribly surprised and startled at being rung up in the night.

"Are the children all right, Miss Wilmot?"

"Oh, yes, they are quite all right."

"Master Paul? Is he all right?"

"He went to bed as right as a trivet. Shall I run up and look at him?"

"No," said Paul's mother reluctantly. "No! Don't trouble. It's all right. Don't sit up. We shall be home fairly soon." She did not want her son's privacy intruded upon.

"Very good," said the governess.

It was about one o'clock when Paul's mother and father drove up to their house. All was still. Paul's mother went to her room and slipped off her white fur cloak. She had told her maid not to wait up for her. She heard her husband downstairs, mixing a whisky-and-soda.

And then, because of the strange anxiety at her heart, she stole upstairs to her son's room. Noiselessly she went along the upper corridor. Was there a faint noise? What was it?

She stood, with arrested muscles, outside his door, listening. There was a strange, heavy, and yet not loud noise. Her heart stood still. It was a soundless noise, yet rushing and powerful. Something huge, in violent, hushed motion. What was it? What in God's name was it? She ought to know. She felt that she knew the noise. She knew what it was.

Yet she could not place it. She couldn't say what it was. And on and on it went, like a madness.

Softly, frozen with anxiety and fear, she turned the door-handle.

The room was dark. Yet in the space near the window, she heard and saw something plunging to and fro. She gazed in fear and amazement.

Then suddenly she switched on the light, and saw her son, in his green pyjamas, madly surging on the rocking-horse. The blaze of light suddenly lit him up, as he urged the wooden horse, and lit her up, as she stood, blonde, in her dress of pale green and crystal, in the doorway.

"Paul!" she cried. "Whatever are you doing?"

"It's Malabar!" he screamed, in a powerful, strange voice. "It's Malabar!"

His eyes blazed at her for one strange and senseless second, as he ceased urging his wooden horse. Then he fell with a crash to the ground, and she, all her tormented motherhood flooding upon her, rushed to gather him up.

But he was unconscious, and unconscious he remained, with some brain-fever. He talked and tossed, and his mother sat stonily by his side.

"Malabar! It's Malabar! Bassett, Bassett, I *know!* It's Malabar!"

So the child cried, trying to get up and urge the rocking-horse that gave him his inspriation.

"What does he mean by Malabar?" asked the heart-frozen mother.

"I don't know," said the father stonily.

"What does he mean by Malabar?" she asked her brother Oscar.

"It's one of the horses running for the Derby," was the answer.

And, in spite of himself, Oscar Cresswell spoke to Bassett, and himself put a thousand on Malabar: at fourteen to one.

The third day of the illness was critical: they were waiting for a change. The boy, with his rather long, curly hair, was tossing ceaselessly on the pillow. He neither slept nor regained consciousness, and his eyes were like blue stones. His mother sat, feeling her heart had gone, turned actually into a stone.

In the evening Oscar Cresswell did not come, but Bassett sent a message, saying could he come up for one moment, just one moment? Paul's mother was very angry at the intrusion, but on second thought she agreed. The boy was the same. Perhaps Bassett might bring him to consciousness.

The gardener, a shortish fellow with a little brown moustache, and sharp little brown eyes, tip-toed into the room, touched his imaginary cap to Paul's mother, and stole to the bedside, staring with glittering, smallish eyes, at the tossing, dying child.

"Master Paul!" he whispered. "Master Paul! Malabar came in first all right, a clean win. I did as you told me. You've made over seventy thousand pounds, you have; you've got over eighty thousand. Malabar came in all right, Master Paul."

"Malabar! Malabar! Did I say Malabar, mother? Did I say Malabar? Do you think I'm lucky, mother? I knew Malabar, didn't I? Over eighty thousand pounds! I call that lucky, don't you, mother? Over eighty thousand pounds! I knew, didn't I know I knew? Malabar came in all right. If I ride my horse till I'm sure, then I tell you, Bassett, you can go as high as you like. Did you go for all you were worth, Bassett?"

"I went a thousand on it, Master Paul."

"I never told you, mother, that if I can ride my horse, and *get there*, then I'm absolutely sure — oh, absolutely! Mother, did I ever tell you? I *am* lucky!"

"No, you never did," said the mother.

But the boy died in the night.

And even as he lay dead, his mother heard her brother's voice saying to her: "My God, Hester, you're eighty-odd thousand to the good, and a poor devil of a son to the bad. But, poor devil, poor devil, he's best gone out of a life where he rides his rockinghorse to find a winner."

Introduction
Arna Bontemps, "A Black Man Talks of Reaping"

Arna Bontemps is important for his contributions as a novelist, poet, critic, playwright, librarian, educator, and author of short stories. Born in Louisiana in 1902, he grew up in California but came to Harlem at the beginning of the Harlem Renaissance in 1924 to become one of its best-known writers. Later he received an M.A. from the University of Chicago in library science and served for twenty-two years as the Fiske University librarian. Bontemps is important not only as a writer but as a promoter and teacher of Afro-American literature.

In "A Black Man Talks of Reaping" Bontemps laments the disparity between what blacks ("my children") have sown and what they reap. The poem is a lyrical statement about the harvest of bitterness that has come from the exploitation of black labor in America.

Arna Bontemps

A Black Man Talks Of Reaping

I have sown beside all waters in my day.
I planted deep, within my heart the fear
that wind or fowl would take the grain away.
I planted safe against this stark, lean year.

I scattered seed enough to plant the land
in rows from Canada to Mexico
but for my reaping only what the hand
can hold at once is all that I can show.

Yet what I sowed and what the orchard yields
my brother's sons are gathering stalk and root;
small wonder then my children glean in fields
they have not sown, and feed on bitter fruit.

Introduction
Charles Dickens, "Murdering the Innocents"

While it may be dangerous to speculate about what is natural to humans, since we always exist in and are shaped by a particular society with its own codes and values, it is safe to say that Western humans did not take easily to the transformation to factory work. The confinement, long hours, and tedious tasks caused such a great turnover in labor during the early years of the English Industrial Revolution that factory superintendents often found it easiest to employ young orphans who had no option other than the factory. To most, factory work seemed unnatural. Industrialists realized that if the Industrial Revolution was to flourish, it would be necessary to resocialize large parts of society.

In the following excerpt from *Hard Times* English novelist Charles Dickens (1812–1870) satirizes the new education that is devoted to ridding the child of irrelevancies such as imagination, sentiment, and fancy. Dickens himself was no stranger to the horrors of industrial society. The second of eight children, he grew up in a debt-plagued family where hunger was a companion, debtor's prison a constant threat, and harsh child labor a constant reality.

Behind the humorous characterizations of "Murdering the Innocents" are some serious questions. While the children's chief tormenter, Thomas Gradgrind, would like to reduce all life to an efficient process by getting rid of what he considers frivolous human characteristics, one might ask what is left when these individuating traits are gone? Is this not what caused the unknown citizen of Auden's poem? What should be the role of education in industrial society? If the role of progress is to make a better life for people, is a system that crushes the joyful part of the human soul really bringing progress? At what point do we stop worrying about creating efficient processes and worry about humans as an end product? These are questions you should ask about your own education. Has education made you more curious, more excited about knowing the secrets of the world? Has it stimulated your imagination as well as your intellect? Do you want to read more because of what you have read? In other words, has your education been about you as a human being or about you as part of the productive process?

Charles Dickens

Murdering the Innocents

Thomas Gradgrind, sir. A man of realities. A man of facts and calculations. A man who proceeds upon the principle that two and two are four, and nothing over, and who is not to be talked into allowing for anything over. Thomas Gradgrind, sir—peremptorily Thomas—Thomas Gradgrind. With a rule and a pair of scales, and the multiplication table always in his pocket, sir, ready to weigh and measure any parcel of human nature, and tell you exactly what it comes to. It is a mere question of figures, a case of simple arithmetic. You might hope to get some other nonsensical belief into the head of George Gradgrind, or Augustus Gradgrind, or John Gradgrind, or Joseph Gradgrind (all supposititious, non-existent persons), but into the head of Thomas Gradgrind—no sir!

In such terms Mr. Gradgrind always mentally introduced himself, whether to his private circle of acquaintance, or to the public in general. In such terms, no doubt, substituting the words "boys and girls," for "sir," Thomas Gradgrind now presented Thomas Gradgrind to the little pitchers before him, who were to be filled so full of facts.

Indeed, as he eagerly sparkled at them from the cellarage before mentioned, he seemed a kind of cannon loaded to the muzzle with facts, and prepared to blow them clean out of the regions of childhood at one discharge. He seemed a galvanizing apparatus, too, charged with a grim mechanical substitute for the tender young imaginations that were to be stormed away.

"Girl number twenty," said Mr. Gradgrind, squarely pointing with his square forefinger, "I don't know that girl. Who is that girl?"

"Sissy Jupe, sir," explained number twenty, blushing, standing up, and curtseying.

"Sissy is not a name," said Mr. Gradgrind. "Don't call yourself Sissy. Call yourself Cecilia."

"It's father as calls me Sissy, sir," returned the young girl in a trembling voice, and with another curtsey.

"Then he has no business to do it," said Mr. Gradgrind. "Tell him he mustn't. Cecilia Jupe. Let me see. What is your father?"

"He belongs to the horse-riding, if you please, sir."

Mr. Gradgrind frowned, and waved off the objectionable calling with his hand.

"We don't want to know anything about that, here. You mustn't tell us about that, here. Your father breaks horses, don't he?"

"If you please, sir, when they can get any to break, they do break horses in the ring, sir."

"You mustn't tell us about the ring, here. Very well, then. Describe your father as a horsebreaker. He doctors sick horses, I dare say?"

"Oh yes, sir."

"Very well, then. He is a veterinary surgeon, a farrier, and horsebreaker. Give me your definition of a horse."

(Sissy Jupe thrown into the greatest alarm by this demand.)

"Girl number twenty unable to define a horse!" said Mr. Grandgrind, for the general behoof of all the little pitchers. "Girl number twenty possessed of no facts, in reference to one of the commonest of animals! Some boy's definition of a horse. Bitzer, yours."

The square finger, moving here and there, lighted suddenly on Bitzer, perhaps because he chanced to sit in the same ray of sunlight which, darting in at one of the bare windows of the intensely whitewashed room, irradiated Sissy. For the boys and girls sat on the face of the inclined plane in two compact bodies, divided up the centre by a narrow interval; and Sissy, being at the corner of a row on the sunny side, came in for the beginning of a sunbeam, of which Bitzer, being at the corner of a row on the other side, a few rows in advance, caught the end. But whereas the girl was so dark-eyed and dark-haired that she seemed to receive a deeper and more lustrous colour from the sun when it shone upon her, the boy was so light-eyed and light-haired that the selfsame rays appeared to draw out of him what little colour he ever possessed. His cold eyes would hardly have been eyes but for the short ends of lashes which, by bringing them into immediate contrast with something paler than themselves, expressed their form. His short-cropped hair might have been a mere continuation of the sandy freckles on his forehead and face. His skin was so unwholesomely deficient in the natural tinge, that he looked as though, if he were cut, he would bleed white.

"Bitzer," said Thomas Gradgrind. "Your definition of a horse."

"Quadruped. Graminivorous. Forty teeth, namely, twenty-four grinders, four eye-teeth, and twelve incisive. Sheds coat in the spring; in marshy countries, sheds hoofs, too. Hoofs hard, but requiring to be shod with iron. Age known by marks in mouth." Thus (and much more) Bitzer.

"Now girl number twenty," said Mr. Gradgrind. "You know what a horse is."

She curtseyed again, and would have blushed deeper if she could have blushed deeper than she had blushed all this time. Bitzer, after rapidly blinking at Thomas Gradgrind with both eyes at once, and so catching the light upon his quivering ends of lashes that they looked like the antennae of busy insects, put his knuckles to his freckled forehead and sat down again.

The third gentleman now stepped forth. A mighty man at cutting and drying he was; a government officer; in his way (and in most other people's too), a professed pugilist; always in training, always with a system to force down the general throat like a bolus, always to be heard of at the bar of his little public-office, ready to fight all England. To continue in fistic phraseology, he had a genius for coming up to the scratch, wherever and whatever it was, and proving himself an ugly customer. He would go in and damage any subject whatever with his right, follow up with his left, stop, exchange, counter, bore his opponent (he always fought All England) to the ropes, and fall upon him neatly. He was certain to knock the wind out of common sense, and render that unlucky adversary deaf to the call of time. And he had it in charge from high authority to bring about the great public-office Millennium, when Commissioners should reign upon earth.

"Very well," said this gentleman, briskly smiling, and folding his arms. "That's a horse. Now, let me ask you girls and boys: Would you paper a room with representations of horses?"

After a pause, one half of the children cried in chorus, "Yes, sir!" Upon which the other half, seeing in the gentleman's face that Yes was wrong, cried out in chorus, "No, sir!"—as the custom is in these examinations.

"Of course, No. Why wouldn't you?"

A pause. One corpulent slow boy, with a wheezy manner of breathing, ventured the answer, Because he wouldn't paper a room at all, but would paint it.

"You *must* paper it," said the gentleman, rather warmly.

"You must paper it," said Thomas Gradgrind, "whether you like it or not. Don't tell *us* you wouldn't paper it. What do you mean, boy?"

"I'll explain to you, then," said the gentleman, after another and a dismal pause, "why you wouldn't paper a room with representations of horses. Do you ever see horses walking up and down the sides of rooms in reality —in fact? Do you?"

"Yes, sir!" from one half. "No, sir!" from the other.

"Of course, No," said the gentleman, with an indignant look at the wrong half. "Why, then, you are not to see anywhere what you don't see in fact; you are not to have anywhere what you don't have in fact. What is called Taste is only another name for Fact."

Thomas Gradgrind nodded his approbation.

"This is a new principle, a discovery, a great discovery," said the gentleman. "Now, I'll try you again. Suppose you were going to carpet a room. Would you use a carpet having a representation of flowers upon it?"

There being a general conviction by this time that "No, sir!" was always the right answer to this gentleman, the chorus of No was very strong. Only a few feeble stragglers said Yes: among them Sissy Jupe.

"Girl number twenty," said the gentleman, smiling in the calm strength of knowledge.

Sissy blushed, and stood up.

"So you would carpet your room — or your husband's room, if you were a grown woman, and had a husband — with representations of flowers, would you?" said the gentleman. "Why would you?"

"If you please, sir, I am very fond of flowers," returned the girl.

"And is that why you would put tables and chairs upon them, and have people walking over them with heavy boots?"

"It wouldn't hurt them, sir. They wouldn't crush and wither, if you please, sir. They would be the pictures of what was very pretty and pleasant, and I would fancy—"

"Aye, aye, aye! But you mustn't fancy," cried the gentleman, quite elated by coming so happily to his point. "That's it! You are never to fancy."

"You are not, Cecilia Jupe," Thomas Gradgrind solemnly repeated, "to do anything of that kind."

"Fact, fact, fact!" said the gentleman. And "Fact, fact, fact!" repeated Thomas Gradgrind.

"You are to be in all things regulated and governed," said the gentleman, "by fact. We hope to have, before long, a board of fact, composed of commissioners of fact, who will force the people to be a people of fact, and of nothing but fact. You must discard the word Fancy altogether. You have nothing to do with it. You are not to have, in any object of use or ornament, what would be a contradiction in fact. You don't walk upon flowers in fact; you cannot be allowed to walk upon flowers in carpets. You don't find that foreign birds and butterflies come and perch upon your crockery; you cannot be permitted to paint foreign birds and butterflies upon your crockery. You never meet with quadrupeds going up and down walls; you must not have quadrupeds represented upon walls. You must see," said the gentleman, "for all these purposes, combinations and modifications (in primary colours) of mathematical figures which are susceptible of proof and demonstration. This is the new discovery. This is fact. This is taste."

Introduction
John Steinbeck, from *The Grapes of Wrath*

John Steinbeck, one of America's best-known writers of serious fiction, was born in Salinas, California, in 1902. He later attended Stanford University, although he did not graduate. Even though he is famous for his novels of the 1930s, the formative period in Steinbeck's life was the 1920s. He reacted strongly against what he saw as the brutal individualism of that period. A characteristic of Steinbeck's fiction is that he finds hope in the group, not in the individual. Indeed, he has been heavily criticized for his inability to create complex individual characters. For Steinbeck the human heart is essentially good, but it has been led astray by bad political organizations or social arrangements. Much of his early fiction, *In Dubious Battle* being a prime example, is sympathetic with a Marxist viewpoint. Although he later turned in a more conservative direction, even supporting the war in Viet Nam, his early work is often classified as proletarian fiction.

The following excerpt from *The Grapes of Wrath* is typical of Steinbeck's viewpoint. In this novel about the dust bowl during the 1930s in Oklahoma the land dries up, and those who own the land drive the tenant farmers from their homes. Steinbeck's literary voice claims it is the bank, an impersonal "monster," that is to blame for this calamity.

> We're sorry, it's not us. It's the monster, the bank isn't like a man."
> "Yes, but the bank is only made of men."
> "No, you're wrong there — quite wrong there. The bank is something else than men. It happens that every man in a bank hates what the bank does, and yet the bank does it. The bank is something more than men, I tell you. It's the monster. Men made it, but they can't control it."

As you read, consider the various ways in which we have become prisoners of systems. Is this trade-off necessary in order to enjoy the material benefits of an industrial system? Have we gained better control of our system since the 1930s? Do our institutions serve more humane ends? Or are events like the Savings and Loan failures indications that the monster still affects the lives of the American people?

John Steinbeck

From The Grapes of Wrath

The owners of the land came onto the land, or more often a spokes-man for the owners came. They came in closed cars, and they felt the dry earth with their fingers, and sometimes they drove big earth augers into the ground for soil tests. The tenants, from their sun-beaten door-yards, watched uneasily when the closed cars drove along the fields. And at last the owner men drove into the dooryards and sat in their cars to talk out of the windows. The tenant men stood beside the cars for a while, and then squatted on their hams and found sticks with which to mark the dust.

In the open doors the women stood looking out, and behind them the children—corn-headed children, with wide eyes, one bare foot on top of the other bare foot, and the toes working. The women and the children watched their men talking to the owner men. They were silent.

Some of the owner men were kind because they hated what they had to do, and some of them were angry because they hated to be cruel, and some of them were cold because they had long ago found that one could not be an owner unless one were cold. And all of them were caught in something larger than themselves. Some of them hated the mathematics that drove them, and some were afraid, and some worshiped the mathe-matics because it provided a refuge from thought and from feeling. If a bank or a finance company owned the land, the owner man said, the Bank—or the Company—needs—wants—insists—must have—as though the Bank or the Company were a monster, with thought and feeling, which had ensnared them. These last would take no responsibility for the banks or the companies because they were men and slaves, while the banks were machines and masters all at the same time. Some of the owner men were a little proud to be slaves to such cold and powerful masters. The owner men sat in the cars and explained. You know the land is poor. You've scrabbled at it long enough, God knows.

The squatting tenant men nodded and wondered and drew figures in the dust, and yes, they knew, God knows. If the dust only wouldn't fly. If the top would only stay on the soil, it might not be so bad.

The owner men went on leading to their point: You know the land's getting poorer. You know what cotton does to the land; robs it, sucks all the blood out of it.

The squatters nodded—they knew, God knew. If they could only rotate the crops they might pump blood back into the land.

Well, it's too late. And the owner men explained the workings and the thinkings of the monster that was stronger than they were. A man can hold land if he can just eat and pay taxes; he can do that.

Yes, he can do that until his crops fail one day and he has to borrow money from the bank.

But—you see, a bank or a company can't do that, because those creatures don't breathe air, don't eat side-meat. They breathe profits; they eat the interest on money. If they don't get it, they die the way you die without air, without side-meat. It is a sad thing, but it is so. It is just so.

The squatting men raised their eyes to understand. Can't we just hang on? Maybe the next year will be a good year. God knows how much cotton next year. And with all the wars—God knows what price cotton will bring. Don't they make explosives out of cotton? And uniforms? Get enough wars and cotton'll hit the ceiling. Next year, maybe. They looked up questioningly.

We can't depend on it. The bank—the monster has to have profits all the time. It can't wait. It'll die. No, taxes go on. When the monster stops growing, it dies. It can't stay one size.

Soft fingers began to tap the sill of the car window, and hard fingers tightened on the restless drawing sticks. In the doorways of the sun-beaten tenant houses, women sighed and then shifted feet so that the one that had been down was now on top, and the toes working. Dogs came sniffing near the owner cars and wetted on all four tires one after another. And chickens lay in the sunny dust and fluffed their feathers to get the cleansing dust down to the skin. In the little sties the pigs grunted inquiringly over the muddy remnants of the slops.

The squatting men looked down again. What do you want us to do? We can't take less share of the crop—we're half starved now. The kids are hungry all the time. We got no clothes, torn an' ragged. If all the neighbors weren't the same, we'd be ashamed to go to meeting.

And at last the owner men came to the point. The tenant system won't work any more. One man on a tractor can take the place of twelve or fourteen families. Pay him a wage and take all the crop. We have to do it. We don't like to do it. But the monster's sick. Something's happened to the monster.

But you'll kill the land with cotton.

We know. We've got to take cotton quick before the land dies. Then we'll sell the land. Lots of families in the East would like to own a piece of land.

The tenant men looked up alarmed. But what'll happen to us? How'll we eat?

You'll have to get off the land. The plows'll go through the dooryard.

And now the squatting men stood up angrily. Grampa took up the land, and he had to kill the Indians and drive them away. And Pa was born here, and he killed weeds and snakes. Then a bad year came and he had to borrow a little money. An' we was born here. There in the door — our children born here. And Pa had to borrow money. The bank owned the land then, but we stayed and we got a little bit of what we raised.

We know that — all that. It's not us, it's the bank. A bank isn't like a man. Or an owner with fifty thousand acres, he isn't like a man either. That's the monster.

Sure, cried the tenant men, but it's our land. We measured it and broke it up. We were born on it, and we got killed on it, died on it. Even if it's no good, it's still ours. That's what makes it ours — being born on it, working it, dying on it. That makes ownership, not a paper with numbers on it.

We're sorry. It's not us. It's the monster. The bank isn't like a man.

Yes, but the bank is only made of men.

No, you're wrong there — quite wrong there. The bank is something else than men. It happens that every man in a bank hates what the bank does, and yet the bank does it. The bank is something more than men, I tell you. It's the monster. Men made it, but they can't control it.

The tenants cried, Grampa killed Indians, Pa killed snakes for the land. Maybe we can kill banks — they're worse than Indians and snakes. Maybe we got to fight to keep our land, like Pa and Grampa did.

And now the owner men grew angry. You'll have to go.

But it's ours, the tenant men cried. We —

No. The bank, the monster owns it. You'll have to go.

We'll get our guns, like Grampa when the Indians came. What then?

Well — first the sheriff, and then the troops. You'll be stealing if you try to stay, you'll be murderers if you kill to stay. The monster isn't men, but it can make men do what it wants.

But if we go, where'll we go? How'll we go? We got no money.

We're sorry, said the owner man. The bank, the fifty-thousand-acre owner can't be responsible. You're on land that isn't yours. Once over the line maybe you can pick cotton in the fall. Maybe you can go on relief. Why don't you go on west to California? There's work there, and it never gets cold. Why, you can reach out anywhere and pick an orange. Why, there's always some kind of crop to work in. Why don't you go there? And the owner men started their cars and rolled away.

The tenant men squatted down on their hams again to mark the dust with a stick, to figure, to wonder. Their sunburned faces were dark, and their sun-whipped eyes were light. The women moved cautiously out of the doorways toward their men, and the children crept behind the women, cautiously, ready to run. The bigger boys squatted beside their fathers, because that made them men. After a time the women asked, What did he want?

And the men looked up for a second, and the smolder of pain was in their eyes. We got to get off. A tractor and a superintendent. Like factories.

Where'll we go? the women asked.

We don't know. We don't know.

And the women went quickly, quietly back into the houses and herded the children ahead of them. They knew that a man so hurt and so perplexed may turn in anger, even on people he loves. They left the men alone to figure and to wonder in the dust.

After a time perhaps the tenant man looked about — at the pump put in ten years ago, with a goose-neck handle and iron flowers on the spout, at the chopping block where a thousand chickens had been killed, at the hand plow lying in the shed, and the patent crib hanging in the rafters over it.

The children crowded about the women in the houses. What we going to do, Ma? Where we going to go?

The women said, We don't know, yet. Go out and play. But don't go near your father. He might whale you if you go near him. And the women went on with the work, but all the time they watched the men squatting in the dust — perplexed and figuring.

The tractors came over the roads and into the fields, great crawlers moving like insects, having the incredible strength of insects. They crawled over the ground, laying the track and rolling on it and picking it up. Diesel tractors, puttering while they stood idle; they thundered when they moved, and then settled down to a droning roar. Snubnosed monsters, raising the dust and sticking their snouts into it, straight down the country, across the country, through fences, through dooryards, in and out of gullies in straight lines. They did not run on the ground, but on their own roadbeds. They ignored hills and gulches, water courses, fences, houses.

The man sitting in the iron seat did not look like a man; gloved, goggled, rubber dust mask over nose and mouth, he was a part of the monster, a robot in the seat. The thunder of the cylinders sounded through the country, became one with the air and the earth, so that earth and air muttered in sympathetic vibration. The driver could not control it— straight across country it went, cutting through a dozen farms and straight back. A twitch at the controls could swerve the cat', but the driver's hands could not twitch because the monster that built the tractors, the monster that sent the tractor out, had somehow got into the driver's hands, into his brain and muscle, had goggled him and muzzled him—goggled his mind, muzzled his speech, goggled his perception, muzzled his protest. He could not see the land as it was, he could not smell the land as it smelled; his feet did not stamp the clods or feel the warmth and power of the earth. He sat in an iron seat and stepped on iron pedals. He could not cheer or beat or curse or encourage the extension of his power, and because of this he could not cheer or whip or curse or encourage himself. He did not know or own or trust or beseech the land. If a seed dropped did not germinate, it was nothing. If the young thrusting plant withered in drought or drowned in a flood of rain, it was no more to the driver than to the tractor.

He loved the land no more than the bank loved the land. He could admire the tractor—its machined surfaces, its surge of power, the roar of its detonating cylinders; but it was not his tractor. Behind the tractor rolled the shining disks, cutting the earth with blades—now plowing but surgery, pushing the cut earth to the right where the second row of disks cut it and pushed it to the left; slicing blades shining, polished by the cut earth. And pulled behind the disks, the harrows combing with iron teeth so that the little clods broke up and the earth lay smooth. Behind the harrows the long seeders—twelve curved iron penes erected in the foundry, orgasms set by gears, raping methodically, raping without passion. The driver sat in his iron seat and he was proud of the straight lines he did not will, proud of the tractor he did not own or love, proud of the power he could not control. And when that crop grew, and was harvested, no man had crumbled a hot clod in his fingers and let the earth sift past his fingertips. No man had touched the seed, or lusted for the growth. Men ate what they had not raised, had no connection with the bread. The land bore under iron, and under iron gradually died; for it was not loved or hated, it had no prayers or curses.

At noon the tractor driver stopped sometimes near a tenant house and opened his lunch: sandwiches wrapped in waxed paper, white bread, pickle, cheese, Spam, a piece of pie branded like an engine part. He ate without relish. And tenants not yet moved away came out to see him, looked curiously while the goggles were taken off, and the rubber dust mask, leaving white circles around the eyes and a large white circle around nose and mouth. The exhaust of the tractor puttered on, for fuel is so cheap it is more efficient to leave the engine running than to heat the Diesel nose for a new start. Curious children crowded close, ragged children who ate their fried dough as they watched. They watched hungrily the unwrapping of the sandwiches, and their hunger-sharpened noses smelled the pickle, cheese, and Spam. They didn't speak to the driver. They watched his hand as it carried food to his mouth. They did not watch him chewing; their eyes followed the hand that held the sandwich. After a while the tenant who could not leave the place came out and squatted in the shade beside the tractor.

"Why, you're Joe Davis's boy!"

"Sure," the driver said.

"Well, what you doing this kind of work for—against your own people?"

"Three dollars a day. I got damn sick of creeping for my dinner—and not getting it. I got a wife and kids. We got to eat. Three dollars a day, and it comes every day."

"That's right," the tenant said. "But for your three dollars a day fifteen or twenty families can't eat at all. Nearly a hundred people have to go out and wander on the roads for your three dollars a day. Is that right?"

And the driver said, "Can't think of that. Got to think of my own kids. Three dollars a day, and it comes every day. Times are changing, mister, don't you know? Can't make a living on the land unless you've got two, five, ten thousand acres and a tractor. Crop land isn't for little guys like us any more. You don't kick up a howl because you can't make Fords, or because you're not the telephone company. Well, crops are like that now. Nothing to do about it. You try to get three dollars a day someplace. That's the only way."

The tenant pondered. "Funny thing how it is. If a man owns a little property, that property is him, it's part of him, and it's like him. If he owns property only so he can walk on it and handle it and be sad when it isn't doing well, and feel fine when the rain falls on it, that property is him, and some way he's bigger because he owns it. Even if he isn't successful he's big with his property. That is so."

And the tenant pondered more. "But let a man get property he doesn't see, or can't take time to get his fingers in, or can't be there to walk on it—why, then the property is the man. He can't do what he wants, he can't think what he wants. The property is the man, stronger than he is. And he is small, not big. Only his possessions are big—and he's the servant of his property. That is so, too."

The driver munched the branded pie and threw the crust away. "Times are changed, don't you know? Thinking about stuff like that don't feed the kids. Get your three dollars a day, feed your kids. You got no call to worry about anybody's kids but your own. You get a reputation for talking like that, and you'll never get three dollars a day. Big shots won't give you three dollars a day if you worry about anything but your three dollars a day."

"Nearly a hundred people on the road for your three dollars. Where will we go?"

"And that reminds me," the driver said, "you better get out soon. I'm going through the dooryard after dinner."

"You filled in the well this morning."

"I know. Had to keep the line straight. But I'm going through the dooryard after dinner. Got to keep the lines straight. And—well, you know Joe Davis, my old man, so I'll tell you this. I got orders wherever there's a family not moved out—if I have an accident—you know, get too close and cave the house in a little—well, I might get a couple of dollars. And my youngest kid never had no shoes yet."

"I built it with my hands. Straightened old nails to put the sheathing on. Rafters are wired to the stringers with baling wire. It's mine. I built it. You bump it down—I'll be in the window with a rifle. You even come too close and I'll pot you like a rabbit."

"It's not me. There's nothing I can do. I'll lose my job if I don't do it. And look—suppose you kill me? They'll just hang you, but long before you're hung there'll be another guy on the tractor, and he'll bump the house down. You're not killing the right guy."

"That's so," the tenant said. "Who gave the orders? I'll go after him. He's the one to kill."

"You're wrong. He got his orders from the bank. The bank told him, 'Clear those people out or it's your job.'"

"Well, there's a president of the bank. There's a board of directors. I'll fill up the magazine of the rifle and go into the bank."

The driver said, "Fellow was telling me the bank gets orders from the East. The orders were, 'Make the land show profit or we'll close you up.'"

"But where does it stop? Who can we shoot? I don't aim to starve to death before I kill the man that's starving me."

"I don't know. Maybe there's nobody to shoot. Maybe the thing isn't men at all. Maybe like you said, the property's doing it. Anyway I told you my orders."

"I got to figure," the tenant said. "We all got to figure. There's some way to stop this. It's not like lightning or earthquakes. We've got a bad thing made by men, and by God that's something we can change." The tenant sat in his doorway, and the driver thundered his engine and started off, tracks falling and curving, harrows combing, and the phalli of the seeder slipping into the ground. Across the dooryard the tractor cut, and the hard, footbeaten ground was seeded field, and the tractor cut through again; the uncut space was ten feet wide. And back he came. The iron guard bit into the housecorner, crumbled the wall, and wrenched the little house from its foundation so that it fell sideways, crushed like a bug. And the driver was goggled and a rubber mask covered his nose and mouth. The tractor cut a straight line on, and the air and the ground vibrated with its thunder. The tenant man stared after it, his rifle in his hand. His wife was beside him, and the quiet children behind. And all of them stared after the tractor.

4. Consumerism:
Salvaging the Promises of Modernism?

Introduction
E.E. Cummings, "pity this busy monster,manunkind"

E.E. Cummings was a true iconoclast, as you will see from the way he rejects poetic conventions and even the conventions of English grammar. His poetry strips conventions bare and reveals them for what they are . . . or are not. For Cummings the enemy is anything that seems false or phoney. He hates pretence and hypocrisy. Like Steinbeck, Cummings was a young man during the 1920s and witnessed the birth of the consumer society with its boosters, public relations experts, and advertisers. In "pity this busy monster,manunkind" Cummings unleashes the full acidic fury of his hatred for this new commercial world that justifies every kind of dishonesty in the name of progress. One of the reasons this poem is so effective in satirizing commercialism is that Cummings has such a fine ear for the rhythms of speech. The poem picks up and parodies the meter of 1920s advertising very effectively.

As you read the poem here are some questions to ponder. Why is progress a "comfortable disease"? Normally we think of progess as positive, while disease is undesirable. We fight disease because we know it is bad for us, but Cummings suggests that "progress" is really a disease that we have decided we can live with, even embrace. What does he mean when he says "electrons deify one razorblade into a mountain range"?

Does this suggest that perhaps advertising makes ordinary things, like razor blades or deodorant, into too important a part of our life? Finally, the poem says pity "manunkind, not." Is he saying we should pity the victims of mankind instead?

E.E. Cummings

pity this busy monster, manunkind

pity this busy monster,manunkind,

not. Progress is a comfortable disease:
your victim (death and life safely beyond)

plays with the bigness of his littleness
— electrons deify one razorblade
into a mountainrange; lenses extend

unwish through curving wherewhen till unwish
returns on its unself.

              A world of made
is not a world of born — pity poor flesh

and trees, poor stars and stones, but never this
fine specimen of hypermagical

ultraomnipotence. We doctors know

a hopeless case if — listen: there's a hell
of a good universe next door; let's go

Introduction

Harvey Cox, "The Playboy and Miss America"

Harvey Cox is an important contemporary theologian whose concerns with the spiritual crisis in America have brought him to "preach" from "pulpits" such as *Playboy* magazine as well as the more common forums for serious thought. In the following essay he has some surprising insights into both *Playboy* and the Miss America beauty pageant.

He begins by saying that the playboy and Miss America "symbolize the pagan deities of a leisure-consumer society that is not yet ready for full maturity and freedom." He continues his critique by asserting that both are really antisexual rather than erotic, and both, as most of us probably suspect, are false models of what it is to be an adult. Their role is not to liberate us from puritanical sexuality, as *Playboy* claims, but rather to exploit our immaturity and make us into conforming consumers. They tell us that we can achieve the ideal femininity or masculinity only by buying the products that they represent rather than through individual decision-making and through cultivating our own independent taste.

As you read this article, consider how advertising influences your life. Cox suggests that men and women living in consumer societies are especially vulnerable to pitches that offer them an identity. Too often we find our identity, not through what we have made of ourselves or through our work and character, but rather through what we wear, drive, or use. In other words, we achieve a sense of self through consumption rather than through the cultivation of character. A further problem with this, as Cox also implies, is that this false road to building a self makes us vulnerable to the machinations of the consumer society and Madison Avenue. Instead of enhancing our freedom the cult of individual consumption can cost us our freedom.

Harvey Cox

The Playboy and Miss America

Let us look at the spurious sexual models conjured up for our anxious society by the sorcerers of the mass media and the advertising guild. Like all pagan deities, these come in pairs—the god and his consort. For our purposes they are best symbolized by The Playboy and Miss America, the Adonis and Aphrodite of a leisure-consumer society which still seems unready to venture into full postreligious maturity and freedom. The Playboy and Miss America represent The Boy and The Girl. They incorporate a vision of life. They function as religious phenomena and should be exorcised and exposed.

Let us begin with Miss America. In the first century B.C., Lucretius wrote this description of the pageant of Cybele:

> Adorned with emblem and crown . . . she is carried in awe-inspiring state. Tight-stretched tambourines and hollow cymbals thunder all round to the stroke of open hands, hollow pipes stir with Phrygian strain. . . . She rides in procession through great cities and mutely enriches mortals with a blessing not expressed in words. They straw all her path with brass and silver, presenting her with bounteous alms, and scatter over her a snow-shower of roses.

Now compare this with the annual twentieth-century Miss America pageant in Atlantic City, New Jersey. Spotlights probe the dimness like votive tapers, banks of flowers exude their varied aromas, the orchestra blends feminine strings and regal trumpets. There is a hushed moment of tortured suspense, a drumroll, then the climax—a young woman with carefully prescribed anatomical proportions and exemplary "personality" parades serenely with scepter and crown to her throne. At TV sets across the nation throats tighten and eyes moisten. "There she goes, Miss America—" sings the crooner. "There she goes, your ideal." A new queen in America's emerging cult of The Girl has been crowned.

This young woman—though she is no doubt totally ignorant of the fact—symbolizes something beyond herself. She symbolizes The Girl, the primal image, the one behind the many. Just as the Virgin appears in many guises — as our Lady of Lourdes or of Fatima or of Guadalupe — but is always recognizably the Virgin, so with The Girl.

The Girl is also the omnipresent icon of consumer society. Selling beer, she is folksy and jolly. Selling gems, she is chic and distant. But behind her various theophanies she remains recognizably The Girl. In Miss America's glowingly healthy smile, her openly sexual but officially virginal figure, and in the name-brand gadgets around her, she personifies the stunted aspirations and ambivalent fears of her culture. "There she goes, your ideal."

Miss America stands in a long line of queens going back to Isis, Ceres, and Aphrodite. Everything from the elaborate sexual taboos surrounding her person to the symbolic gifts at her coronation hints at her ancient ancestry. But the real proof comes when we find that the function served by The Girl in our culture is just as much a "religious" one as that served by Cybele in hers. The functions are identical — to provide a secure personal "identity" for initiates and to sanctify a particular value structure.

Let us look first at the way in which The Girl confers a kind of identity on her initiates. Simone de Beauvoir says in *The Second Sex* that "no one is *born* a woman." One is merely born a female, and *"becomes* a woman" according to the models and meanings provided by the civilization. During the classical Christian centuries, it might be argued, the Virgin Mary served in part as this model. With the Reformation and especially with the Puritans, the place of Mary within the symbol system of the Protestant countries was reduced or eliminated. There are those who claim that this excision constituted an excess of zeal that greatly impoverished Western culture, an impoverishment from which it has never recovered. Some would even claim that the alleged failure of American novelists to produce a single great heroine (we have no Phaedra, no Anna Karenina) stems from this self-imposed lack of a central feminine ideal.

Without entering into this fascinating disucssion, we can certainly be sure that, even within modern American Roman Catholicism, the Virgin Mary provides an identity image for few American girls. Where then do they look for the "model" Simone de Beauvoir convincingly contends they need? For most, the prototype of femininity seen in their mothers, their friends, and in the multitudinous images to which they are exposed on the mass media is what we have called The Girl.

To describe the mechanics of this complex psychological process by which the fledgling American girl participates in the life of The Girl and thus attains a woman's identity would require a thorough description of American adolescence. There is little doubt, however, that such an analysis would reveal certain striking parallels to the "savage" practices by which initiates in the mystery cults shared in the magical life of their god.

For those inured to the process, the tortuous nightly fetish by which the young American female pulls her hair into tight bunches secured by metal clips may bear little resemblance to the incisions made on their arms by certain African tribesmen to make them resemble their totem, the tiger. But to an anthropologist comparing two ways of attempting to resemble the holy one, the only difference might appear to be that with the Africans the torture is over after initiation, while with the American it has to be repeated every night, a luxury only a culture with abundant leisure can afford.

In turning now to an examination of the second function of The Girl — supporting and portraying a value system — a comparison with the role of the Virgin in the twelfth and thirteenth centuries may be helpful. Just as the Virgin exhibited and sustained the ideals of the age that fashioned Chartres Cathedral, as Henry Adams saw, so The Girl symbolizes the values and aspirations of a consumer society. (She is crowned not in the political capital, remember, but in Atlantic City or Miami Beach, centers associated with leisure and consumption.) And she is not entirely incapable of exploitation. If men sometimes sought to buy with gold the Virgin's blessings on their questionable causes, so The Girl now dispenses her charismatic favor on watches, refrigerators, and razor blades — for a price. Though The Girl has built no cathedrals, without her the colossal edifice of mass persuasion would crumble. Her sharply stylized face and figure beckon us from every magazine and TV channel, luring us toward the beatific vision of a consumer's paradise.

Besides sanctifying a set of phony values, The Girl compounds her noxiousness by maiming her victims in a Procrustean bed of uniformity. This is the empty "identity" she panders. Take the Miss America pageant, for example. Are these virtually indistinguishable specimens of white, middle-class postadolescence really the best we can do? Do they not mirror the ethos of a mass-production society, in which genuine individualism somehow mars the clean, precision-tooled effect? Like their sisters, the finely calibrated Rockettes, these meticulously measured and pretested "beauties" lined up on the boardwalk bear an ominous similarity to the faceless retinues of goose-steppers and the interchangeable mass exercisers of explicitly totalitarian societies. In short, *who* says this is beauty?

The caricature becomes complete in the Miss Universe contest, when Miss Rhodesia is a blonde, Miss South Africa is white, and Oriental girls with a totally different tradition of feminine beauty are forced to display their thighs and appear in spike heels and Catalina swim suits. Miss Universe is as universal as an American adman's stereotype of what beauty should be.

The truth is that The Girl can*not* bestow the identity she promises. She forces her initiates to torture themselves with starvation diets and beauty-parlor ordeals, but still cannot deliver the satisfactions she holds out. She is young, but what happens when her followers, despite added hours in the boudoir, can no longer appear young? She is happy and smiling and loved. What happens when, despite all the potions and incantations, her disciples still feel the human pangs of rejection and loneliness? Or what about all the girls whose statistics, or "personality" (or color) do not match the authoritative "ideal"?

The Playboy, illustrated by the monthly magazine of that name, does for the boys what Miss America does for the girls. Despite accusations to the contrary, the immense popularity of this magazine is not solely attributable to pinup girls. For sheer nudity its pictorial art cannot compete with such would-be competitors as *Dude* and *Escapade*. *Playboy* appeals to a highly mobile, increasingly affluent group of young readers, mostly between eighteen and thirty, who want much more from their drugstore reading than bosoms and thighs. They need a total image of what it means to be a man. And Mr. Hefner's *Playboy* has no hesitation in telling them.

Why should such a need arise? David Riesman has argued that the responsibility for character formation in our society has shifted from the family to the peer group and to the mass-media peer-group surrogates. Things are changing so rapidly that one who is equipped by his family with inflexible, highly internalized values becomes unable to deal with the accelerated pace of change and with the varying contexts in which he is called upon to function. This is especially true in the area of consumer values toward which the "other-directed person" is increasingly oriented.

Within the confusing plethora of mass media signals and peer-group values, *Playboy* fills a special need. For the insecure young man with newly acquired free time and money who still feels uncertain about his consumer skills, *Playboy* supplies a comprehensive and authoritative guidebook to this forbidding new world to which he now has access. It tells him not only who to be; it tells him *how* to be, and even provides consolation outlets for those who secretly feel that they have not quite made it.

In supplying for the other-directed consumer of leisure both the normative identity image and the means of achieving it, *Playboy* relies on a careful integration of copy and advertising material. The comic book that appeals to a younger generation with an analogous problem skillfully intersperses illustrations of incredibly muscled men and excessively mammalian women with advertisements for body-building gimmicks and foam-rubber brassière supplements. Thus the thin-chested comic-book readers of both sexes are thoughtfully supplied with both the ends and the means for attaining a spurious brand of maturity. *Playboy* merely continues the comic-book tactic for the next age group. Since within every identity crisis, whether in teens or twenties, there is usually a sexual identity problem, *Playboy* speaks to those who desperately want to know what it means to be a man, and more specifically a *male,* in today's world.

Both the image of man and the means for its attainment exhibit a remarkable consistency in *Playboy.* The skilled consumer is cool and unruffled. He savors sports cars, liquor, high fidelity, and book-club selections with a casual, unhurried aplomb. Though he must certainly *have* and *use* the latest consumption item, he must not permit himself to get too attached to it. The style will change and he must always be ready to adjust. His persistent anxiety that he may mix a drink incorrectly, enjoy a jazz group that is passé, or wear last year's necktie style is comforted by an authoritative tone in *Playboy* beside which papal encyclicals sound irresolute.

"Don't hesitate," he is told, "this assertive, self-assured weskit is what every man of taste wants for the fall season." Lingering doubts about his masculinity are extirpated by the firm assurance that "real men demand this ruggedly masculine smoke" (cigar ad). Though "the ladies will swoon for you, no matter what they promise, don't give them a puff. This cigar is for men only." A fur-lined canvas field jacket is described as "the most masculine thing since the cave man." What to be and how to be it are both made unambiguously clear.

Since being male necessitates some kind of relationship to females, *Playboy* fearlessly confronts this problem too, and solves it by the consistent application of the same formula. Sex becomes one of the items of leisure activity that the knowledgeable consumer of leisure handles with his characteristic skill and detachment. The girl becomes a desirable — indeed an indispensable — "Playboy accessory."

In a question-answer column entitled "The Playboy Adviser," queries about smoking equipment (how to break in a meerschaum pipe), cocktail preparation (how to mix a Yellow Fever), and whether or not to wear suspenders with a vest alternate with questions about what to do with girls who complicate the cardinal principle of casualness either by suggesting marriage or by some other impulsive gesture toward a permanent relationship. The infallible answer from the oracle never varies: sex must be contained, at all costs, within the entertainment-recreation area. Don't let her get "serious."

After all, the most famous feature of the magazine is its monthly fold-out photo of a *play*mate. She is the symbol par excellence of recreational sex. When playtime is over, the playmate's function ceases, so she must be made to understand the rules of the game. As the crew-cut young man in a *Playboy* cartoon says to the rumpled and disarrayed girl he is passionately embracing, "Why speak of love at a time like this?"

The magazine's fiction purveys the same kind of severely departmentalized sex. Although the editors have recently improved the *Playboy* contents with contributions by Hemingway, Bemelmans, and even a Chekhov translation, many of the stories still rely on a repetitious and predictable formula. A successful young man, either single or somewhat less than ideally married—a figure with whom readers have no difficulty identifying—encounters a gorgeous and seductive woman who makes no demands on him except sex. She is the prose duplication of the cool-eyed but hot-blooded playmate of the foldout.

Drawing heavily on the fantasy life of all young Americans, the writers utilize for their stereotyped heroines the hero's schoolteacher, his secretary, an old girl friend, or the girl who brings her car into the garage where he works. The happy issue is always a casual but satisfying sexual experience with no entangling alliances whatever. Unlike the women he knows in real life, the *Playboy* reader's fictional girl friends know their place and ask for nothing more. They present no danger of permanent involvement. Like any good accessory, they are detachable and disposable.

Many of the advertisements reinforce the sex-accessory identification in another way—by attributing female characteristics to the items they sell. Thus a full-page ad for the MG assures us that this car is not only "the smoothest pleasure machine" on the road and that having one is a "love affair," but most important, "you drive it—it doesn't drive you." The ad ends with the equivocal question "Is it a date?"

Playboy insists that its message is one of liberation. Its gospel frees us from captivity to the puritanical "hatpin brigade." It solemnly crusades for "frankness" and publishes scores of letters congratulating it for its unblushing "candor." Yet the whole phenomenon of which *Playboy* is only a part vividly illustrates the awful fact of a new kind of tyranny.

Those liberated by technology and increased prosperity to new worlds of leisure now become the anxious slaves of dictatorial taste makers. Obsequiously waiting for the latest signal on what is cool and what is awkward, they are paralyzed by the fear that they may hear pronounced on them that dread sentence occasionally intoned by "The Playboy Adviser": "You goofed!" Leisure is thus swallowed up in apprehensive competitiveness, its liberating potential tranformed into a self-destructive compulsion to consume only what is *à la mode*. *Playboy* mediates the Word of the most high into one section of the consumer world, but it is a word of bondage, not of freedom.

Nor will *Playboy's* synthetic doctrine of man stand the test of scrutiny. Psychoanalysts constantly remind us how deep-seated sexuality is in the human being. But if they didn't remind us, we would soon discover it ourselves anyway. Much as the human male might like to terminate his relationship with a woman as he would snap off the stereo, or store her for special purposes like a camel's-hair jacket, it really can't be done. And anyone with a modicum of experience with women knows it can't be done. Perhaps this is the reason *Playboy's* readership drops off so sharply after the age of thirty.

Playboy really feeds on the existence of a repressed fear of involvement with women, which for various reasons is still present in many otherwise adult Americans. So *Playboy's* version of sexuality grows increasingly irrelevant as authentic sexual maturity is achieved.

Thus any theological critique of *Playboy* that focuses on its "lewdness" will misfire completely. *Playboy* and its less successful imitators are not "sex magazines" at all. They are basically antisexual. They dilute and dissipate authentic sexuality by reducing it to an accessory, by keeping it at a safe distance.

Freedom for mature sexuality comes to man only when he is freed from the despotic powers which crowd and cower him into fixed patterns of behavior. Both Miss America and The Playboy illustrate such powers. When they determine man's sexual life, they hold him in captivity. They prevent him from achieving maturity.

Introduction
Doris Lessing, "One off the Short List"

Harvey Cox revealed in the previous essay that sex is not always what it seems to be. More often than not sex is used in the service of other needs, material and psychological. In the consumer society, where our sense of authenticity is always open to question, sex frequently serves to bolster our identity, to help us find a victory where we seem hopelessly defeated. "One Off the Short List" continues this exploration of the relationships between work, gender, and identity.

Doris Lessing is a British writer who was born in Persia, raised in what was then the British colony of Southern Rhodesia, and now lives in Britain. Her work explores gender issues and the dehumanizing effects of violence. This story is about conquest, the victory of one person at the expense of another; or perhaps we should say it is about the intent of conquest, since the story takes an interesting turn that will leave you wondering who has been defeated.

Graham Spence is a journalist whose job is to interview celebrities from the arts. When we meet him in the story, he is a man who has come to find his life lacking: his marriage is no longer exciting, and his job has become routine. At one time he had hoped to become a writer, but after two books of modest success, he becomes a man who lives on the fringes of the art world: an interviewer, a reviewer, a journalist.

The other major character in the story is Barbara Coles, a successful stage designer, who becomes Graham's intended victim. As you read, notice that Graham's interest is heightened not so much by her physical attractiveness as by her success. In fact, it is only after he comes to realize the fullness of her success and her engagement with her work that he decides he must sleep with her. By "having" the successful person it is as though Spence has affirmed his own worth.

To Graham's surprise, Barbara, who finds meaning in her work, refuses to play by the rules of his game. As the story makes clear, Barbara is a liberated woman who, although married, is not above having an affair. But what a liaison means to her is clearly different from what it means to Spence. As you consider the strange conclusion of this story, ask yourself some questions about relationships and personal identity in the post-industrial world. What does it mean that Barbara yields to Graham's persistent advances? Why do you think Graham becomes impotent? Why does Graham insist on taking Barbara to work in the morning, and how is this insistence diffused by Barbara? Finally, ask yourself about how gender politics and more generally the politics of control operate in workplaces and homes you know.

Doris Lessing

One off the Short List

When he had first seen Barbara Coles, some years before, he only noticed her because someone said: "That's Johnson's new girl." He certainly had not used of her the private erotic formula: *Yes, that one.* He even wondered what Johnson saw in her. "She won't last long," he remembered thinking, as he watched Johnson, a handsome man, but rather flushed with drink, flirting with some unknown girl while Barbara stood by a wall looking on. He thought she had a sullen expression.

She was a pale girl, not slim, for her frame was generous, but her figure could pass as good. Her straight yellow hair was parted on one side in a way that struck him as gauche. He did not notice what she wore. But her eyes were all right, he remembered: large, and solidly green, square-looking because of some trick of the flesh at their corners. Emerald-like eyes in the face of a schoolgirl, or young schoolmistress who was watching her lover flirt and would later sulk about it.

Her name sometimes cropped up in the papers. She was a stage decorator, a designer, something on those lines.

Then a Sunday newspaper had a competition for stage design and she won it. Barbara Coles was one of the "names" in the theatre, and her photograph was seen about. It was always serious. He remembered having thought her sullen.

One night he saw her across the room at a party. She was talking with a well-known actor. Her yellow hair was still done on one side, but now it looked sophisticated. She wore an emerald ring on her right hand that seemed deliberately to invite comparison with her eyes. He walked over and said: "We have met before, Graham Spence." He noted, with discomfort, that he sounded abrupt. "I'm sorry, I don't remember, but how do you do?" she said, smiling. And continued her conversation.

He hung around a bit, but soon she went off with a group of people she was inviting to her home for a drink. She did not invite Graham. There was about her an assurance, a carelessness, that he recognised as the signature of success. It was then, watching her laugh as she went off with her friends, that he used the formula: *"Yes, that one."* And he went home to his wife with enjoyable expectation, as if his date with Barbara Coles were already arranged.

His marriage was twenty years old. At first it had been stormy, painful, tragic — full of partings, betrayals and sweet reconciliations. It had taken him at least a decade to realise that there was nothing remarkable about this marriage that he had lived through with such surprise of the mind and the senses. On the contrary, the marriages of most of the people he knew, whether they were first, second or third attempts, were just the same. His had run true to form even to the serious love affair with the young girl for whose sake he had *almost* divorced his wife — yet at the last moment had changed his mind, letting the girl down so that he must have her for always (not unpleasurably) on his conscience. It was with humiliation that he had understood that this drama was not at all the unique thing he had imagined. It was nothing more than the experience of everyone in his circle. And presumably in everybody else's circle too?

Anyway, round about the tenth year of his marriage he had seen a good many things clearly, a certain kind of emotional adventure went from his life, and the marriage itself changed.

His wife had married a poor youth with a great future as a writer. Sacrifices had been made, chiefly by her, for that future. He was neither unaware of them, nor ungrateful; in fact he felt permanently guilty about it. He at last published a decently successful book, then a second which now, thank God, no one remembered. He had drifted into radio, television, book reviewing.

He understood he was not going to make it; that he had become — not a hack, no one could call him that — but a member of that army of people who live by their wits on the fringes of the arts. The moment of realisation was when he was in a pub one lunchtime near the B.B.C. where he often dropped in to meet others like himself: he understood that was why he went there — they *were* like him. Just as that melodramatic marriage had turned out to be like everyone else's — except that it had been shared with one woman instead of with two or three — so it had turned out that his unique talent, his struggles as a writer had led him here, to this pub and the half dozen pubs like it, where all the men in sight had the same history. They all had their novel, their play, their book of poems, a moment of fame, to their credit. Yet here they were, running television programmes about which they were cynical (to each other or to their wives) or writing reviews about other people's books. Yes, that's what he had become, an impresario of other people's talent. These two moments of clarity, about his marriage and about his talent, had roughly coincided: and (perhaps not by chance) had coincided with his wife's decision to leave him for a man younger than himself who had a future, she said, as a playwright. Well, he had talked her out of it. For her part she had to understand he was not going to be the T.S. Eliot or Graham Greene of our time—but after all, how many were? She must finally understand this, for he could no longer bear her awful bitterness. For his part he must stop coming home drunk at five in the morning, and starting a new romantic affair every six months which he took so seriously that he made her miserable because of her implied deficiencies. In short he was to be a good husband. (He had always been a dutiful father.) And she a good wife. And so it was: the marriage became stable, as they say.

The formula: *Yes, that one* no longer implied a necessarily sexual relationship. In its more mature form, it was far from being something he was ashamed of. On the contrary, it expressed a humorous respect for what he was, for his real talents and flair, which had turned out to be not artistic after all, but to do with emotional life, hard-earned experience. It expressed an ironical dignity, a proving to himself not only: I can be honest about myself, but also: I have earned the best in *that* field whenever I want it.

He watched the field for the women who were well known in the arts, or in politics; looked out for photographs, listened for bits of gossip. He made a point of going to see them act, or dance, or orate. He built up a not unshrewd picture of them. He would either quietly pull strings to meet her or—more often, for there was a gambler's pleasure in waiting— bide his time until he met her in the natural course of events, which was bound to happen sooner or later. He would be seen out with her a few times in public, which was in order, since his work meant he had to entertain well-known people, male and female. His wife always knew, he told her. He might have a brief affair with this woman, but more often than not it was the appearance of an affair. Not that he didn't get pleasure from other people envying him—he would make a point, for instance, of taking this woman into the pubs where his male colleagues went. It was that his real pleasure came when he saw her surprise at how well she was understood by him. He enjoyed the atmosphere he was able to set up between an intelligent woman and himself: a humorous complicity which had in it much that was unspoken, and which almost made sex irrelevant.

Onto the list of women with whom he planned to have this relationship went Barbara Coles. There was no hurry. Next week, next month, next year, they would meet at a party. The world of well-known people in London is a small one. Big and little fishes, they drift around, nose each other, flirt their fins, wriggle off again. When he bumped into Barbara Coles, it would be time to decide whether or not to sleep with her.

Meanwhile he listened. But he didn't discover much. She had a husband and children, but the husband seemed to be in the background.
The children were charming and well brought up, like everyone else's
children. She had affairs, they said; but while several men he met sounded
familiar with her, it was hard to determine whether they had slept with
her, because none directly boasted of her. She was spoken of in terms
of her friends, her work, her house, a party she had given, a job she had
found someone. She was liked, she was respected, and Graham Spence's
self-esteem was flattered because he had chosen her. He looked forward
to saying in just the same tone: "Barbara Coles asked me what I thought
about the set and I told her quite frankly. . . ."

Then by chance he met a young man who did boast about Barbara
Coles; he claimed to have had the great love affair with her, and recently
at that; and he spoke of it as something generally known. Graham realised how much he had already become involved with her in his imagination because of how perturbed he was now, on account of the character
of this youth, Jack Kennaway. He had recently become successful as a
magazine editor — one of those young men who, not as rare as one might
suppose in the big cities, are successful from sheer impertinence, effrontery. Without much talent or taste, yet he had the charm of his effrontery.
"Yes, I'm going to succeed, because I've decided to; yes, I may be stupid,
but not so stupid that I don't know my deficiencies. Yes, I'm going to
be successful because you people with integrity, etc., etc., simply don't
believe in the possibility of people like me. You are too cowardly to stop
me. Yes, I've taken your measure and I'm going to succeed because I've
got the courage, not only to be unscrupulous, but to be quite frank about
it. And besides, you admire me, you must, or otherwise you'd stop me. . . ."
Well, that was young Jack Kennaway, and he shocked Graham. He was
a tall, languishing young man, handsome in a dark melting way, and,
it was quite clear, he was either asexual or homosexual. And this youth
boasted of the favours of Barbara Coles; boasted, indeed, of her love. Either
she was a raving neurotic with a taste for neurotics; or Jack Kennaway
was a most accomplished liar; or she slept with anyone. Graham was in-
trigued. He took Jack Kennaway out to dinner in order to hear him talk
about Barbara Coles. There was no doubt the two were pretty close — all
those dinners, theatres, weekends in the country — Graham Spence felt
he had put his finger on the secret pulse of Barbara Coles; and it was
intolerable that he must wait to meet her; he decided to arrange it.

It became unnecessary. She was in the news again, with a run of luck.
She had done a successful historical play, and immediately afterwards
a modern play, and then a hit musical. In all three, the sets were remarked
on. Graham saw some interviews in newspapers and on television. These

all centered around the theme of her being able to deal easily with so many different styles of theatre; but the real point was, of course, that she was a woman, which naturally added piquancy to the thing. And now Graham Spence was asked to do a half-hour radio interview with her. He planned the questions he would ask her with care, drawing on what people had said of her, but above all on his instinct and experience with women. The interview was to be at nine-thirty at night; he was to pick her up at six from the theatre where she was currently at work, so that there would be time, as the letter from the B.B.C. had put it, "for you and Miss Coles to get to know each other."

At six he was at the stage door, but a message from Miss Coles said she was not quite ready, could he wait a little. He hung about, then went to the pub opposite for a quick one, but still no Miss Coles. So he made his way backstage, directed by voices, hammering, laughter. It was badly lit, and the group of people at work did not see him. The director, James Poynter, had his arm around Barbara's shoulders. He was newly well-known, a carelessly good-looking young man reputed to be intelligent. Barbara Coles wore a dark blue overall, and her flat hair fell over her face so that she kept pushing it back with the hand that had the emerald on it. These two stood close, side by side. Three young men, stagehands, were on the other side of a trestle which had sketches and drawings on it. They were studying some sketches. Barbara said, in a voice warm with energy: "Well, so I thought if we did *this* — do you see, James? What do you think, Steven?" "Well, love," said the young man she called Steven, "I see your idea, but I wonder if . . ." "I think you're right, Babs," said the director. "Look," said Barbara, holding one of the sketches toward Steven, "look, let me show you." They all leaned forward, the five of them, absorbed in the business.

Suddenly Graham couldn't stand it. He understood he was shaken to his depths. He went off stage, and stood with his back against a wall in the dingy passage that led to the dressing rooms. His eyes were filled with tears. He was seeing what a long way he had come from the crude, uncompromising, admirable young egomaniac he had been when he was twenty. That group of people there — working, joking, arguing, yes, that's what he hadn't known for years. What bound them was the democracy of respect for each other's work, a confidence in themselves and in each other. They looked like people banded together against a world which they — no, not despised, but which they measured, understood, would fight to the death, out of respect for what *they* stood for, for what *it* stood for. It was a long time since he felt part of that balance. And he understood that he had seen Barbara Coles when she was most herself, at ease with a group of people she worked with. It was then, with the tears drying on his eyelids, which felt old and ironic, that he decided he would sleep with Barbara Coles. It was a necessity for him. He went back through the door onto the stage, burning with this single determination.

The five were still together. Barbara had a length of blue gleaming stuff which she was draping over the shoulder of Steven, the stagehand. He was showing it off, and the others watched. "What do you think, James?" she asked the director. "We've got that sort of dirty green, and I thought . . ." "Well," said James, not sure at all, "well, Babs, well . . ."

Now Graham went forward so that he stood beside Barbara, and said: "I'm Graham Spence, we've met before." For the second time she smiled socially and said: "Oh I'm sorry, I don't remember." Graham nodded at James, whom he had known, or at least had met off and on, for years. But it was obvious James didn't remember him either.

"From the B.B.C.," said Graham to Barbara, again sounding abrupt, against his will. "Oh I'm sorry, I'm so sorry, I forgot all about it. I've got to be interviewed," she said to the group. "Mr. Spence is a journalist." Graham allowed himself a small smile ironical of the word journalist, but she was not looking at him. She was going on with her work. "We should decide tonight," she said. "Steven's right." "Yes, I am right," said the stagehand. "She's right, James, we need that blue with that sludge-green everywhere." "James," said Barbara, "James, what's wrong with it? You haven't said." She moved forward to James, passing Graham. Remembering him again, she became contrite. "I'm sorry," she said, "we can none of us agree. Well, look"—she turned to Graham—"you advise us, we've got so involved with it that . . . " At which James laughed, and so did the stagehands. "No, Babs," said James, "of course Mr. Spence can't advise. He's just this moment come in. We've got to decide. Well I'll give you till tomorrow morning. Time to go home, it must be six by now."

"It's nearly seven," said Graham, taking command.

"It isn't!" said Barbara, dramatic. "My God, how terrible, how appalling, how could I have done such a thing. . . ." She was laughing at herself. "Well, you'll have to forgive me, Mr. Spence, because you haven't got any alternative."

They began laughing again: this was clearly a group joke. And now Graham took his chance. He said firmly, as if he were her director, in fact copying James Poynter's manner with her: "No, Miss Coles, I won't forgive you, I've been kicking my heels for nearly an hour." She grimaced, then laughed and accepted it. James said: "There, Babs, that's how you ought to be treated. We spoil you." He kissed her on the cheek, she kissed him on both his, the stagehands moved off. "Have a good evening, Babs," said James, going, and nodding to Graham, who stood concealing his pleasure with difficulty. He knew, because he had had the courage to be firm, indeed, peremptory, with Barbara, that he had saved himself hours of maneuvering. Several drinks, a dinner — perhaps two or three evenings of drinks and dinners — had been saved because he was now on this footing with Barbara Coles, a man who could say: "No, I won't forgive you, you've kept me waiting."

She said: "I've just got to . . ." and went ahead of him. In the passage she hung her overall on a peg. She was thinking, it seemed, of something else, but seeing him watching her, she smiled at him, companionably: he realised with triumph it was the sort of smile she would offer one of the stagehands, or even James. She said again: "Just one second . . ." and went to the stage-door office. She and the stage doorman conferred. There was some problem. Graham said, taking another chance: "What's the trouble, can I help?" — as if he could help, as if he expected to be able to. "Well . . ." she said, frowning. Then, to the man: "No, it'll be all right. Goodnight." She came to Graham. "We've got ourselves into a bit of a fuss because half the set's in Liverpool and half's here and — but it will sort itself out." She stood, at ease, chatting to him, one colleague to another. All this was admirable, he felt; but there would be a bad moment when they emerged from the special atmosphere of the theatre into the street. He took another decision, grasped her arm firmly, and said: "We're going to have a drink before we do anything at all, it's a terrible evening out." Her arm felt resistant, but remained within his. It was raining outside, luckily. He directed her, authoritative: "No, not that pub, there's a nicer one around the corner." "Oh, but I like this pub," said Barbara, "we always use it."

"Of course you do," he said to himself. But in that pub there would be the stagehands, and probably James, and he'd lose contact with her. He'd become a *journalist* again. He took her firmly out of danger around two corners, into a pub he picked at random. A quick look around — no, they weren't there. At least, if there were people from the theatre, she showed no sign. She asked for a beer. He ordered her a double Scotch, which she accepted. Then, having won a dozen preliminary rounds already, he took time to think. Something was bothering him — what? Yes, it was what he had observed backstage, Barbara and James Poynter. Was she having an affair with him? Because if so, it would all be much more difficult. He made himself see the two of them together, and thought with a jealousy surprisingly strong: *Yes, that's it.* Meantime he sat looking at her, seeing himself look at her, *a man gazing in calm appreciation at a woman:* waiting for her to feel it and respond. She was examining the pub. Her white woollen suit was belted, and had a not unprovocative suggestion of being a uniform. Her flat yellow hair, hastily pushed back after work, was untidy. Her clear white skin, without any colour, made her look tired.

Not very exciting, at the moment, thought Graham, but maintaining his appreciative pose for when she would turn and see it. He knew what she would see: he was relying not only on the "warm kindly" beam of his gaze, for this was merely a reinforcement of the impression he knew he made. He had black hair, a little greyed. His clothes were loose and bulky—masculine. His eyes were humorous and appreciative. He was not, never had been, concerned to lessen the impression of being settled, dependable: the husband and father. On the contrary, he knew women found it reassuring.

When she at last turned she said, almost apologetic: "Would you mind if we sat down? I've been lugging great things around all day." She had spotted two empty chairs in a corner. So had he, but rejected them, because there were other people at the table. "But my dear, of course!" They took the chairs, and then Barbara said: "If you'll excuse me a moment." She had remembered she needed make-up. He watched her go off, annoyed with himself. She was tired; and he could have understood, protected, sheltered. He realised that in the other pub, with the people she had worked with all day, she would not have thought: "I must make myself up, I must be on show." That was for outsiders. She had not, until now, considered Graham an outsider, because of his taking his chance to seem one of the working group in the theatre; but now he had thrown his opportunity away. She returned armoured. Her hair was sleek, no longer defenceless. And she had made up her eyes. Her eyebrows were untouched, pale gold streaks above the brilliant green eyes whose lashes were blackened. Rather good, he thought, the contrast. Yes, but the moment had gone when he could say: Did you know you had a smudge on your cheek? Or—my dear girl!—pushing her hair back with the edge of a brotherly hand. In fact, unless he was careful, he'd be back at starting point.

He remarked: "That emerald is very cunning"—smiling into her eyes.

She smiled politely, and said: "It's not cunning, it's an accident, it was my grandmother's." She flirted her hand lightly by her face, though, smiling. But that was something she had done before, to a compliment she had had before, and often. It was all social, she had become social entirely. She remarked: "Didn't you say it was half past nine we had to record?"

"My dear Barbara, we've got two hours. We'll have another drink or two, then I'll ask you a couple of questions, then we'll drop down to the studio and get it over, and then we'll have a comfortable supper."

"I'd rather eat now, if you don't mind. I had no lunch, and I'm really hungry."

"But my dear, of course." He was angry. Just as he had been surprised by his real jealousy over James, so now he was thrown off balance by his anger: he had been counting on the long quiet dinner afterwards to establish intimacy. "Finish your drink and I'll take you to Nott's." Nott's was expensive. He glanced at her assessingly as he mentioned it. She said: "I wonder if you know Butler's? It's good and it's rather close." Butler's was good, and it was cheap, and he gave her a good mark for liking it. But Nott's it was going to be. "My dear, we'll get into a taxi and be at Nott's in a moment, don't worry."

She obediently got to her feet: the way she did it made him understand how badly he had slipped. She was saying to herself: Very well, he's like that, then all right, I'll do what he wants and get it over with. . . .

Swallowing his own drink he followed her, and took her arm in the pub doorway. It was polite within his. Outside it drizzled. No taxi. He was having bad luck now. They walked in silence to the end of the street. There Barbara glanced into a side street where a sign said: BUTLER'S. Not to remind him of it, on the contrary, she concealed the glance. And here she was, entirely at his disposal, they might never have shared the comradely moment in the theatre.

They walked half a mile to Nott's. No taxis. She made conversation: this was, he saw, to cover any embarrassment he might feel because of a half-mile walk through rain when she was tired. She was talking about some theory to do with the theatre, with designs for theatre building. He heard himself saying, and repeatedly: Yes, yes, yes. He thought about Nott's, how to get things right when they reached Nott's. There he took the headwaiter aside, gave him a pound, and instructions. They were put in a corner. Large Scotches appeared. The menus were spread. "And now, my dear," he said, "I apologise for dragging you here, but I hope you'll think it's worth it."

"Oh, it's charming, I've always liked it. It's just that . . ." She stopped herself saying: it's such a long way. She smiled at him, raising her glass, and said: "It's one of my very favourite places, and I'm glad you dragged me here." Here voice was flat with tiredness. All this was appalling; he knew it; and he sat thinking how to retrieve his position. Meanwhile she fingered the menu. The headwaiter took the order, but Graham made a gesture which said: Wait a moment. He wanted the Scotch to take effect before she ate. But she saw his silent order; and without annoyance or reproach, leaned forward to say, sounding patient: "Graham, please, I've got to eat, you don't want me drunk when you interview me, do you?"

"They are bringing it as fast as they can," he said, making it sound as if she were greedy. He looked neither at the headwaiter nor at Barbara. He noted in himself, as he slipped further and further away from contact with her, a cold determination growing in him; one apart from, apparently, any conscious act of will, that come what may, if it took all night, he'd be in her bed before morning. And now, seeing the small pale face, with the enormous green eyes, it was for the first time that he imagined her in his arms. Although he had said: *Yes, that one,* weeks ago, it was only now that he imagined her as a sensual experience. Now he did, so strongly that he could only glance at her, and then away towards the waiters who were bringing food.

"Thank the Lord," said Barbara, and all at once her voice was gay and intimate. "Thank heavens. Thank every power that is. . . ." She was making fun of her own exaggeration; and, as he saw, because she wanted to put him at his ease after his boorishness over delaying the food. (She hadn't been taken in, he saw, humiliated, disliking her.) "Thank all the gods of Nott's," she went on, "because if I hadn't eaten inside five minutes I'd have died, I tell you." With which she picked up her knife and fork and began on her steak. He poured wine, smiling with her, thinking that *this* moment of closeness he would not throw away. He watched her frank hunger as she ate, and thought: Sensual—it's strange I hadn't wondered whether she would be or not.

"Now," she said, sitting back, having taken the edge off her hunger: "Let's get to work."

He said: "I've thought it over very carefully—how to present you. The first thing seems to me, we must get away from that old chestnut: Miss Coles, how extraordinary for a woman to be so versatile in her work . . . I hope you agree?" This was his trump card. He had noted, when he had seen her on television, her polite smile when this note was struck. (The smile he had seen so often tonight.) This smile said: All right, if you *have* to be stupid, what can I do?

Now she laughed and said: "What a relief. I was afraid you were going to do the same thing."

"Good, now you eat and I'll talk."

In his carefully prepared monologue he spoke of the different styles of theatre she had shown herself mistress of, but not directly: he was flattering her on the breadth of her experience; the complexity of her character, as shown in her work. She ate, steadily, her face showing nothing. At last she asked: "And how did you plan to introduce this?"

He had meant to spring that on her as a surprise, something like: Miss Coles, a surprisingly young woman for what she has accomplished (she was thirty? thirty-two?) and a very attractive one. . . . "Perhaps I can give you an idea of what she's like if I say she could be taken for the film star Marie Carletta. . . ." The Carletta was a strong earthy blonde, known to be intellectual. He now saw he could not possibly say this: he could imagine her cool look if he did. She said: "Do you mind if we get away from all that — my manifold talents, et cetera. . . ." He felt himself stiffen with annoyance; particularly because this was not an accusation, he saw she did not think him worth one. She had assessed him: This is the kind of man who uses this kind of flattery and therefore. . . . It made him angrier that she did not even trouble to say: Why did you do exactly what you promised you wouldn't? She was being invincibly polite, trying to conceal her patience with his stupidity.

"After all," she was saying, "it is a stage designer's job to design what comes up. Would anyone take, let's say Johnnie Cranmore" (another stage designer) "onto the air or television and say: How very versatile you are because you did that musical about Java last month and a modern play about Irish labourers this?"

He battened down his anger. "My dear Barbara, I'm sorry. I didn't realise that what I said would sound just like the mixture as before. So what shall we talk about?"

"What I was saying as we walked to the restaurant: can we get away from the personal stuff?"

Now he almost panicked. Then, thank God, he laughed from nervousness, for she laughed and said: "You didn't hear one word I said."

"No, I didn't. I was frightened you were going to be furious because I made you walk so far when you were tired."

They laughed together, back to where they had been in the theatre. He leaned over, took her hand, kissed it. He said: "Tell me again." He thought: Damn, now she's going to be earnest and intellectual.

But he understood he had been stupid. He had forgotten himself at twenty — or, for that matter, at thirty; forgotten one could live inside an idea, a set of ideas, with enthusiasm. For in talking about her ideas (also the ideas of the people she worked with) for a new theatre, a new style of theatre, she was as she had been with her colleagues over the sketches or the blue material. She was easy, informal, almost chattering. This was how, he remembered, one talked about ideas that were a breath of life. The ideas, he thought, were intelligent enough; and he would agree with them, with her, if he believed it mattered a damn one way or another, if any of these enthusiasms mattered a damn. But at least he now had the key, he knew what to do. At the end of not more than half an hour, they were again two professionals, talking about ideas they shared, for he remembered caring about all this himself once. *When? How many years ago was it that he had been able to care?*

At last he said: "My dear Barbara, do you realise the impossible position you're putting me in? Margaret Ruyen who runs this programme is determined to do you personally, the poor woman hasn't got a serious thought in her head."

Barbara frowned. He put his hand on hers, teasing her for the frown: "No, wait, trust me, we'll circumvent her." She smiled. In fact Margaret Ruyen had left it all to him, had said nothing about Miss Coles.

"They aren't very bright — the brass," he said. "Well, never mind: we'll work out what we want, do it, and it'll be a *fait accompli.*"

"Thank you, what a relief. How lucky I was to be given you to interview me." She was relaxed now, because of the whisky, the food, the wine, above all because of this new complicity against Margaret Ruyen. It would all be easy. They worked out five or six questions, over coffee, and took a taxi through rain to the studios. He noted that the cold necessity to have her, to make her, to beat her down, had left him. He was even seeing himself, as the evening ended, kissing her on the cheek and going home to his wife. This comradeship was extraordinarily pleasant. It was balm to the wound he had not known he carried until that evening, when he had had to accept the justice of the word *journalist.* He felt he could talk forever about the state of the theatre, its finances, the stupidity of the government, the philistinism of . . .

At the studios he was careful to make a joke so that they walked in on the laugh. He was careful that the interview began at once, without conversation with Margaret Ruyen; and that from the moment the green light went on, his voice lost its easy familiarity. He made sure that not one personal note was struck during the interview. Afterwards, Margaret Ruyen, who was pleased, came forward to say so; but he took her aside to say that Miss Coles was tired and needed to be taken home at once: for he knew this must look to Barbara as if he were squaring a producer who had been expecting a different interview. He led Barbara off, her hand held tight in his against his side. "Well," he said, "we've done it, and I don't think she knows what hit her."

"Thank you," she said, "it was really pleasant to talk about something sensible for once."

He kissed her lightly on the mouth. She returned it, smiling. By now he felt sure that the mood need not slip again, he could hold it.

"There are two things we can do," he said. "You can come to my club and have a drink. Or I can drive you home and you can give me a drink. I have to go past you."

"Where do you live?"

"Wimbledon." He lived, in fact, at Highgate; but she lived in Fulham. He was taking another chance, but by the time she found out, they would be in a position to laugh over his ruse.

"Good," she said. "You can drop me home then. I have to get up early." He made no comment. In the taxi he took her hand; it was heavy in his, and he asked: "Does James slave-drive you?"

"I didn't realize you knew him — no, he doesn't."

"Well I don't know him intimately. What's he like to work with?"

"Wonderful," she said at once. "There's no one I enjoy working with more."

Jealousy spurted in him. He could not help himself: "Are you having an affair with him?"

She looked: what's it to do with you? but said: "No, I'm not."

"He's very attractive," he said, with a chuckle of worldly complicity. She said nothing, and he insisted: "If I were a woman I'd have an affair with James."

It seemed she might very well say nothing. But she remarked: "He's married."

His spirits rose in a swoop. It was the first stupid remark she had made. It was a remark of such staggering stupidity that . . . he let out a humoring snort of laughter, put his arm around her, kissed her, said: "My dear little Babs."

She said: "Why Babs?"

"Is that the prerogative of James. And the stagehands?" he could not prevent himself adding.

"I'm only called that at work." She was stiff inside his arm.

"My dear Barbara, then . . ." He waited for her to enlighten and explain, but she said nothing. Soon she moved out of his arm, on the pretext of lighting a cigarette. He lit it for her. He noted that his determination to lay her, and at all costs, had come back. They were outside her house. He said quickly: "And now, Barbara, you can make me a cup of coffee and give me a brandy." She hesitated; but he was out of the taxi, paying, opening the door for her. The house had no lights on, he noted. He said: "We'll be very quiet so as not to wake the children."

She turned her head slowly to look at him. She said, flat, replying to his real question: "My husband is away. As for the children, they are visiting friends tonight." She now went ahead of him to the door of the house. It was a small house, in a terrace of small and not very pretty houses. Inside a little, bright, intimate hall, she said: "I'll go and make some coffee. Then, my friend, you must go home because I'm very tired."

The *my friend* struck him deep, because he had become vulnerable during their comradeship. He said gabbling: "You're annoyed with me — oh, please don't, I'm sorry."

She smiled, from a cool distance. He saw, in the small light from the ceiling, her extraordinary eyes. "Green" eyes are hazel, are brown with green flecks, are even blue. Eyes are chequered, flawed, changing. Hers were solid green, but really, he had never seen anything like them before. They were like very deep water. They were like — well, emeralds; or the absolute clarity of green in the depths of a tree in summer. And now, as she smiled almost perpendicularly up at him, he saw a darkness come over them. Darkness swallowed the clear green. She said: "I'm not in the least annoyed." It was as if she had yawned with boredom. "And now I'll get the things . . . in there." She nodded at a white door and left him. He went into a long, very tidy white room, that had a narrow bed in one corner, a table covered with drawings, sketches, pencils. Tacked to the walls with drawing pins were swatches of coloured stuffs. Two small chairs stood near a low round table: an area of comfort in the working room. He was thinking: I wouldn't like it if my wife had a room like this. I wonder what Barbara's husband . . .? He had not thought of her till now in relation to her husband, or to her children. Hard to imagine her with a frying pan in her hand, or for that matter, cosy in the double bed.

A noise outside: he hastily arranged himself, leaning with one arm on the mantelpiece. She came in with a small tray that had cups, glasses, brandy, coffeepot. She looked abstracted. Graham was on the whole flattered by this: it probably meant she was at ease in his presence. He realised he was a little tight and rather tired. Of course, she was tired too, that was why she was vague. He remembered that earlier that evening he had lost a chance by not using her tiredness. Well now, if he were intelligent . . . She was about to pour coffee. He firmly took the coffeepot out of her hand, and nodded at a chair. Smiling, she obeyed him. "That's better," he said. He poured coffee, poured brandy, and pulled the table towards her. She watched him. Then he took her hand, kissed it, patted it, laid it down gently. Yes, he thought, I did that well.

Now, a problem. He wanted to be closer to her, but she was fitted into a damned silly little chair that had arms. If he were to sit by her on the floor . . . ? But no, for him, the big bulky reassuring man, there could be no casual gestures, no informal postures. Suppose I scoop her out of the chair onto the bed? He drank his coffee as he plotted. Yes, he'd carry her to the bed, but not yet.

"Graham," she said, setting down her cup. She was, he saw with annoyance, looking tolerant. "Graham, in about half an hour I want to be in bed and asleep."

As she said this, she offered him a smile of amusement at this situation — man and woman maneuvering, the great comic situation. And with part of himself he could have shared it. Almost, he smiled with her, laughed. (Not till days later he exclaimed to himself: Lord what a mistake I made, not to share the joke with her then: that was where I went seriously wrong.) But he could not smile. His face was frozen, with a stiff pride. Not because she had been watching him plot; the amusement she now offered him took the sting out of that; but because of his revived determination that he was going to have his own way, he was going to have her. He was not going home. But he felt that he held a bunch of keys, and did not know which one to choose.

He lifted the second small chair opposite to Barbara, moving aside the coffee table for this purpose. He sat in this chair, leaned forward, took her two hands, and said: "My dear, don't make me go home yet, don't, I beg you." The trouble was, nothing had happened all evening that could be felt to lead up to these words and his tone — simple, dignified, human being pleading with human being for surcease. He saw himself leaning forward, his big hands swallowing her small ones; he saw his face, warm with the appeal. And he realised he had meant the words he used. They were nothing more than what he felt. He wanted to stay with her because she wanted him to, because he was her colleague, a fellow worker in the arts. He needed this desperately. But she was examining him, curious rather than surprised, and from a critical distance. He heard himself saying: "If James were here, I wonder what you'd do?" His voice was aggrieved; he saw the sudden dark descend over her eyes, and she said: "Graham, would you like some more coffee before you go?"

He said: "I've been wanting to meet you for years. I know a good many people who know you."

She leaned forward, poured herself a little more brandy, sat back, holding the glass between her two palms on her chest. An odd gesture: Graham felt that this vessel she was cherishing between her hands was herself. A patient, long-suffering gesture. He thought of various men who had mentioned her. He thought of Jack Kennaway, wavered, panicked, said: "For instance, Jack Kennaway."

And now, at the name, an emotion lit her eyes — what was it? He went on, deliberately testing this emotion, adding to it: "I had dinner with him last week — oh, quite by chance! — and he was talking about you."

"Was he?"

He remembered he had thought her sullen, all those years ago. Now she seemed defensive, and she frowned. He said: "In fact he spent most of the evening talking about you."

She said in short, breathless sentences, which he realised were due to anger: "I can very well imagine what he says. But surely you can't think I enjoy being reminded that . . ." She broke off, resenting him, he saw, because he forced her down onto a level she despised. But it was not his level either: it was all her fault, all hers! He couldn't remember not being in control of a situation with a woman for years. Again he felt like a man teetering on a tightrope. He said, trying to make good use of Jack Kennaway, even at this late hour: "Of course, he's a charming boy, but not a man at all."

She looked at him, silent, guarding her brandy glass against her breasts.

"Unless appearances are totally deceptive, of course." He could not resist probing, even though he knew it was fatal.

She said nothing.

"Do you know you are supposed to have had the great affair with Jack Kennaway?" he exclaimed, making this an amused expostulation against the fools who could believe it.

"So I am told." She set down her glass. "And now," she said, standing up, dismissing him. He lost his head, took a step forward, grabbed her in his arms, and groaned: "Barbara!"

She turned her face this way and that under his kisses. He snatched a diagnostic look at her expression — it was still patient. He placed his lips against her neck, groaned "Barbara" again, and waited. She would have to do something. Fight free, respond, something. She did nothing at all. At last she said: "For the Lord's sake, Graham!" She sounded amused: he was again being offered amusement. But if he shared it with her, it would be the end of this chance to have her. He clamped his mouth over hers, silencing her. She did not fight him off so much as blow him off. Her mouth treated his attacking mouth as a woman blows and laughs in water, puffing off waves or spray with a laugh, turning aside her head. It was a gesture half annoyance, half humour. He continued to kiss her while she moved her head and face about under the kisses as if they were small attacking waves.

And so began what, when he looked back on it afterwards, was the most embarrassing experience of his life. Even at the time he hated her for his ineptitude. For he held here there for what must have been nearly half an hour. She was much shorter than he, he had to bend, and his neck ached. He held her rigid, his thighs on either side of hers, her arms clamped to her side in a bear's hug. She was unable to move, except for her head. When his mouth ground hers open and his tongue moved and writhed inside it, she still remained passive. And he could not stop himself. While with his intelligence he watched this ridiculous scene, he was determined to go on, because sooner or later her body must soften in wanting his. And he could not stop because he could not face the horror of the moment when he set her free and she looked at him. And he hated her more, every moment. Catching glimpses of her great green eyes, open and dismal beneath his, he knew he had never disliked anything more than those "jewelled" eyes. They were repulsive to him. It occurred to him at last that even if by now she wanted him, he wouldn't know it, because she was not able to move at all. He cautiously loosened his hold so that she had an inch or so leeway. She remained quite passive. As if, he thought derisively, she had read or been told that the way to incite men maddened by lust was to fight them. He found he was thinking: Stupid cow, so you imagine I find you attractive, do you? You've got the conceit to think that!

The sheer, raving insanity of this thought hit him, opened his arms, his thighs, and lifted his tongue out of her mouth. She stepped back, wiping her mouth with the back of her hand, and stood dazed with incredulity. The embarrassment that lay in wait for him nearly engulfed him, but he let anger postpone it. She said positively apologetic, even, at this moment, humorous: "You're crazy, Graham. What's the matter, are you drunk? You don't seem drunk. You don't even find me attractive."

The blood of hatred went to his head and he gripped her again. Now she had got her face firmly twisted away so that he could not reach her mouth, and she repeated steadily as he kissed the parts of her cheeks and neck that were available to him: "Graham, let me go, do let me go, Graham." She went on saying this; he went on squeezing, grinding, kissing and licking. It might go on all night: it was a sheer contest of wills, nothing else. He thought: It's only a really masculine woman who wouldn't have given in by now out of sheer decency of the flesh! One thing he knew, however: that she would be in that bed, in his arms, and very soon. He let her go, but said: "I'm going to sleep with you tonight, you know that, don't you?"

She leaned with hand on the mantelpiece to steady herself. Her face was colourless, since he had licked all the makeup off. She seemed quite different: small and defenceless with her large mouth pale now, her smudged green eyes fringed with gold. And now, for the first time, he felt what it might have been supposed (certainly by her) he felt hours ago. Seeing the small damp flesh of her face, he felt kinship, intimacy with her, he felt intimacy of the flesh, the affection and good humour of sensuality. He felt she was flesh of his flesh, his sister in the flesh. He felt desire for her, instead of the will to have her; and because of this, was ashamed of the farce he had been playing. Now he desired simply to take her into bed in the affection of his senses.

She said: "What on earth am I supposed to do? Telephone for the police, or what?" He was hurt that she still addressed the man who had ground her into sulky apathy; she was not addressing *him* at all.

She said: "Or scream for the neighbours, is that what you want?"

The gold-fringed eyes were almost black, because of the depth of the shadow of boredom over them. She was bored and weary to the point of falling to the floor, he could see that.

He said: "I'm going to sleep with you."

"But how can you possibly want to?"—a reasonable, a civilised demand addressed to a man who (he could see) she believed would respond to it. She said: "You know I don't want to, and I know you don't really give a damn one way or the other."

He was stung back into being the boor because she had not the intelligence to see that the boor no longer existed; because she could not see that this was a man who wanted her in a way which she must respond to.

There she stood, supporting herself with one hand, looking small and white and exhausted, and utterly incredulous. She was going to turn and walk off out of simple incredulity, he could see that. "Do you think I don't mean it?" he demanded, grinding this out between his teeth. She made a movement—she was on the point of going away. His hand shot out on its own volition and grasped her wrist. She frowned. His other hand grasped her other wrist. His body hove up against hers to start the pressure of a new embrace. Before it could, she said: "Oh Lord, no, I'm not going through all that again. Right, then."

"What do you mean—right, then?" he demanded.

She said: "You're going to sleep with me. O.K. Anything rather than go through that again. Shall we get it over with?"

He grinned, saying in silence: "No darling, oh no you don't, I don't care what words you use, I'm going to have you now and that's all there is to it."

She shrugged. The contempt, the weariness of it, had no effect on him, because he was now again hating her so much that wanting her was like needing to kill something or someone.

She took her clothes off, as if she were going to bed by herself: her jacket, skirt, petticoat. She stood in white bra and panties, a rather solid girl, brown-skinned still from the summer. He felt a flash of affection for the brown girl with her loose yellow hair as she stood naked. She got into bed and lay there, while the green eyes looked at him in civilised appeal: Are you really going through with this? Do you have to? Yes, his eyes said back: I do have to. She shifted her gaze aside, to the wall, saying silently: Well, if you want to take me without any desire at all on my part, then go ahead, if you're not ashamed. He was not ashamed, because he was maintaining the flame of hate for her which he knew quite well was all that stood between him and shame. He took off his clothes, and got into bed beside her. As he did so, knowing he was putting himself in the position of raping a woman who was making it elaborately clear he bored her, his flesh subsided completely, sad, and full of reproach because a few moments ago it was reaching out for his sister whom he could have made happy. He lay on his side by her, secretly at work on himself, while he supported himself across her body on his elbow, using the free hand to manipulate her breasts. He saw that she gritted her teeth against his touch. At least she could not know that after all this fuss he was not potent.

In order to incite himself, he clasped her again. She felt his smallness, writhed free of him, sat up and said: "Lie down."

While she had been lying there, she had been thinking: The only way to get this over with is to make him big again, otherwise I've got to put up with him all night. His hatred of her was giving him a clairvoyance: he knew very well what went on through her mind. She had switched on, with the determination to *get it all over with,* a sensual good humour, a patience. He lay down. She squatted beside him, the light from the ceiling blooming on her brown shoulders, her flat fair hair falling over her face. But she would not look at his face. Like a bored, skilled wife, she was: or like a prostitute. She administered to him, she was setting herself to please him. Yes, he thought, she's sensual, or she could be. Meanwhile she was succeeding in defeating the reluctance of his flesh, which was the tender token of a possible desire for her, by using a cold skill that was the result of her contempt for him. Just as he decided: Right, it's enough, now I shall have her properly, she made him come. It was not a trick, to hurry or cheat him, what defeated him was her transparent thought: Yes, that's what he's worth.

Then, having succeeded, and waited for a moment or two, she stood up, naked, the fringes of gold at her loins and in her armpits speaking to him a language quite different from that of her green, bored eyes. She looked at him and thought, showing it plainly: What sort of man is it who . . . ? He watched the slight movement of her shoulders: a just-checked shrug. She went out of the room: then the sound of running water. Soon she came back in a white dressing gown, carrying a yellow towel. She handed him the towel, looking away in politeness as he used it. "Are you going home now?" she enquired hopefully, at this point.

"No, I'm not." He believed that now he would have to start fighting her again, but she lay down beside him, not touching him (he could feel the distaste of her flesh for his) and he thought: Very well, my dear, but there's a lot of the night left yet. He said aloud: "I'm going to have you properly tonight." She said nothing, lay silent, yawned. Then she remarked consolingly, and he could have laughed outright from sheer surprise: "Those were hardly conducive circumstances for making love." She was *consoling* him. He hated her for it. A proper little slut: I force her into bed, she doesn't want me, but she still has to make me feel good, like a prostitute. But even while he hated her he responded in kind, from the habit of sexual generosity. "It's because of my admiration for you, because . . . after all, I was holding in my arms one of the thousand women."

A pause. "The thousand?" she enquired, carefully.

"The thousand especial women."

"In Britain or in the world? You choose them for their brains, their beauty—what?"

"Whatever it is that makes them outstanding," he said, offering her a compliment.

"Well," she remarked at last, inciting him to be amused again: "I hope that at least there's a short list you can say I am on, for politeness' sake."

He did not reply for he understood he was sleepy. He was still telling himself that he must stay awake when he was slowly waking and it was morning. It was about eight. Barbara was not there. He thought: My God! What on earth shall I tell my wife? Where was Barbaba? He remembered the ridiculous scenes of last night and nearly succumbed to shame. Then he thought, reviving anger: If she didn't sleep beside me here I'll never forgive her. . . . He sat up, quietly, determined to go through the house until he found her and, having found her, to possess her, when the door opened and she came in. She was fully dressed in a green suit, her hair done, her eyes made up. She carried a tray of coffee, which she set down beside the bed. He was conscious of his big loose hairy body, half uncovered. He said to himself that he was not going to lie in bed, naked, while she was dressed. He said: "Have you got a gown of some kind?" She handed him, without speaking, a towel, and said: "The bathroom's second on the left." She went out. He followed, the towel around him. Everything in this house was gay, intimate—not at all like her efficient working room. He wanted to find out where she had slept, and opened the first door. It was the kitchen, and she was in it, putting a brown earthenware dish into the oven. "The next door," said Barbara. He went hastily past the second door, and opened (he hoped quietly) the third. It was a cupboard full of linen. "This door," said Barbara, behind him.

"So all right then, where did you sleep?"

"What's it to do with you? Upstairs, in my own bed. Now, if you have everything, I'll say goodbye, I want to get to the theatre."

"I'll take you," he said at once.

He saw again the movement of her eyes, the dark swallowing the light in deadly boredom. "I'll take you," he insisted.

"I'd prefer to go by myself," she remarked. Then she smiled: "However, you'll take me. Then you'll make a point of coming right in, so that James and everyone can see—that's what you want to take me for, isn't it?"

He hated her, finally, and quite simply, for her intelligence; that not once had he got away with anything, that she had been watching, since they had met yesterday, every movement of his campaign for her. However, some fate or inner urge over which he had no control made him say sentimentally: "My dear, you must see that I'd like at least to take you to your work."

"Not at all, have it on me," she said, giving him the lie direct. She went past him to the room he had slept in. "I shall be leaving in ten minutes," she said.

He took a shower, fast. When he returned, the workroom was already tidied, the bed made, all signs of the night gone. Also, there were no signs of the coffee she had brought in for him. He did not like to ask for it, for fear of an outright refusal. Besides, she was ready, her coat on, her handbag under her arm. He went, without a word, to the front door, and she came after him, silent.

He could see that every fibre of her body signalled a simple message: Oh God, for the moment when I can be rid of this boor! She was nothing but a slut, he thought.

A taxi came. In it she sat as far away from him as she could. He thought of what he should say to his wife.

Outside the theatre she remarked: "You could drop me here, if you liked." It was not a plea, she was too proud for that. "I'll take you in," he said, and saw her thinking: Very well, I'll go through with it to shame him. He was determined to take her in and hand her over to her colleagues, he was afraid she would give him the slip. But far from playing it down, she seemed determined to play it his way. At the stage door, she said to the doorman: "This is Mr. Spence, Tom—do you remember, Mr. Spence from last night?" "Good morning, Babs," said the man, examining Graham, politely, as he had been ordered to do.

Barbara went to the door to the stage, opened it, held it open for him. He went in first, then held it open for her. Together they walked into the cavernous, littered, badly lit place and she called out: "James, James!" A man's voice called out from the front of the house: "Here, Babs, why are you so late?"

The auditorium opened before them, darkish, silent, save for an early-morning busyness of charwomen. A vacuum cleaner roared, smally, somewhere close. A couple of stagehands stood looking up at a drop which had a design of blue and green spirals. James stood with his back to the auditorium, smoking. "You're late, Babs," he said again. He saw Graham behind her, and nodded. Barbara and James kissed. Barbara said, giving allowance to every syllable: "You remember Mr. Spence from last night?" James nodded: How do you do? Barbara stood beside him, and they looked together up at the blue-and-green backdrop. Then Barbara looked again at Graham, asking silently: All right now, isn't that enough? He could see her eyes, sullen with boredom.

He said: "Bye, Babs. Bye, James, I'll ring you, Babs." No response, she ignored him. He walked off slowly, listening for what might be said. For instance: "Babs, for God's sake, what are you doing with him?" Or she might say: "Are you wondering about Graham Spence? Let me explain."

Graham passed the stagehands who, he could have sworn, didn't recognise him. Then at last he heard James's voice to Barbara: "It's no good, Babs, I know you're enamoured of that particular shade of blue, but do have another look at it, there's a good girl. . . ." Graham left the stage, went past the office where the stage doorman sat reading a newspaper. He looked up, nodded, went back to his paper. Graham went to find a taxi, thinking: I'd better think up something convincing, then I'll telephone my wife.

Luckily he had an excuse not to be at home that day, for this evening he had to interview a young man (for television) about his new novel.

Other Paradigms: Visions of the Future of Working in America

Prediction of the future is an ancient and fallible activity. Humans naturally have always been curious about tomorrow: how we live today has a great deal to do with what we believe tomorrow will bring, and often this predictive skill has been the difference between life and death. Contemporary humans are no exceptions to this concern with the future. If anything, we are obsessive in our concerns with anticipating changes in dimensions of life such as the weather, fashions, the economy, and politics. We show our insecurity about the future in the incredible investments we make in insurance, the stock market, or in military systems. To a great extent our concerns for the future reflect our central concerns in the present. Thus it is not surprising that the future of work is of fundamental importance for most people.

By now you should have a fairly clear idea of how the humanities approach the world of work. Examining the future of work will help to clarify further how the humanities differ from the sciences. Prediction and control have been the central foci of modern science since it began in the seventeenth century. Scientists try to predict what will happen based on what previously occurred: thus, central to their methodology is a concentration on regularity and causality. Humanists do not ignore causality, but they are more concerned with *vision* than with prediction, with how the world *might* be if humans made one set of choices rather than another, and with *imagining* the most desirable futures. Humanists focus on choices rather than on necessity, on bringing into play the full range of human capacities to shape the future rather than on assuming the future will or should resemble the past.

When we explored some of the founding myths of modernism as expressed by Locke and Smith or in Tawney's account of the work ethic, we discussed not only the extent to which these stories described the worlds in which they lived but also how the stories affected the imaginations of their readers and consequently helped shape history. Ideas, images, dreams, and visions certainly are not the sole forces driving the machinery of history, but it would be foolish to deny the power of such phenomena

413

in human life. In this section we will turn to visions of the future of working which could have the same kinds of powerful effects on our futures as the myths we explored earlier had in shaping current history. Like the seminal stories of Locke or Marx, these new visions are based on images of human nature and the good life. They are all concerned with human flourishing, but they differ markedly due to the scope of their concerns and their views of what kinds of creatures we humans are, what our future development should be, and how we should get to that future. As you read these selections try to discover the basic assumptions each writer makes. Without these assumptions their projections might appear random or ungrounded; with them their philosophies are coherent. Take these visions very seriously. To be human, as Martin Heidegger, a recent German philosopher, says, is to have projects and to live them. If we have no imagination, no vision, we do not make our futures; we are only subject to what happens to us.

At the same time do not leave practicality behind in a flight of fancy. We can easily stifle a new idea by asking how much it will cost or by dismissing it as impractical, but we can also engage in useless dreaming if we do not think about what will actually work. One of the most impressive features of American history is the role of "practical imagination," and if we are to succeed in our current transformation, we will be wise to call on this strong tradition.

Given our rich tradition of ingenuity, you should not be surprised that many people have been working hard to think of and implement new work arrangements. Although we will not focus on these practical solutions, since they provide a rich background of practical experimentation for most of the visions in this section, we should at least mention some proposals and attempted solutions that seem viable to us.

In the first essay of this book Frithjof Bergmann gives us a sketch of how we simultaneously might deal with the success we have had in eliminating much menial work and with the challenges of growing un- and underemployment, the need for some new ways to distribute wealth, and the question of how to make people's work and nonwork lives more meaningful. At the end of Section III Bergmann spells out more of the philosophy that undergirds his earlier proposal to create dramatically different work schedules. He is not alone in suggesting a flexible work schedule (although he may be rare in the systematic and deep connections he makes between our work and the rest of our lives): many people have proposed and implemented new versions of flextime. The variety of proposals to alter our work schedules takes seriously the criticism of the iron law of clock time that industrialization imposed on modern workers, and the fact that so many workplaces are offering new "time disciplines" indicates the extent to which Bergmann is correct in asserting that we are now ready to seriously reap the truly human benefits the Industrial Revolution promised.

Another complaint of critics from Carlyle and Marx to contemporary thinkers is that industrial work creates alienation. Many workplaces, from small businesses to large corporations, are now experimenting with ways to involve workers more fully in more dimensions of the productive process: the introduction of quality circles, workplace democracy, work teams, recreation and education facilities at the work site, and paid counseling and child care services are some indications of employers' recognition that the work they need from their employees increasingly is less machinelike and more creative, more truly human.

While there are many workplaces that are becoming less alienating, it would be a great mistake to assume that all work is headed in this more human direction. Whether or not the overall climate for workers in our society (or elsewhere in the world) improves will depend on many complex factors. Furthermore, the *why* of these changes is crucial. If employers improve working conditions merely to improve profits, these alterations could prove to be fleeting. Only if they grow out of the kinds of visions contained in the following selections will the transformation of the workplace be deep and lasting. Otherwise we will experience something like consumerism, wherein we substitute a form (purchasable item) for substance (what we more basically need). In the end, visions of good work which are based on a deep understanding of human nature and human history are eminently *practical!*

We begin this section with excerpts from Pope John Paul II's 1981 encyclical *On Human Work.* In this influential document the Pope reaffirms a modern Catholic tradition of warning people about the dangers of materialism, the concentration of economic power, and unchecked technological growth, while affirming social and economic justice for all people. John Paul II takes great pains to separate the Catholic position from both capitalism and Marxism. He does not condemn private property, but he simultaneously asserts that "the right to private property is subordinated to the right to common use, to the fact that goods are meant for everyone." In short, this document shows clearly that the Catholic Church is an institution steeped in the medieval values we studied in Section II.

We begin with the encyclical *On Human Work,* not because we believe we can or should return to the Middle Ages, but because the Pope's decree is based on an assumption which permeates all of the selections in this section: whatever economic system we invent and live within, we should always remember to subordinate that system, and the activities we do within that way of life, to deeper values. We should be sure that our ends, not our means, dictate. Furthermore, while each of the writers in this section has a different vision of the good life and how to get there, *On Human Work* voices a common value when it claims that "since work . . . is always a personal action," work is a "spiritual activity" wherein the person is made and can get in touch with the divine.

The Pope's encyclical is one way for us to learn from the wisdom of the past. Through the representatives of an old, but continuous, institution we can reinterpret the truths of that tradition for our own times. Other ways exist to learn from the past. Many ancient traditions have no living presence as the Catholic Church. Yet we can still learn from their experiences through their stories. Today, as we undergo dramatic and accelerated change, many people are looking to past cultures with intense interest for images, models, philosophies, and examples of how to live. Some people, such as those who advocate communal living or going back to the land, attempt to return to life as it was in former times. But clearly our globe cannot sustain over five billion hunters and gatherers or primitive farmers with anything approaching the contemporary standards of living in industrial societies. In Part A of this section we explore the views of two anthropologists who believe we nevertheless can learn some valuable lessons from traditional people.

Finally, in the major part of this section we introduce a variety of contemporary visionaries who address diverse dimensions of working in the future. While none of their images are pictures of how the world actually will be tomorrow, if they stir your imaginations, the crux of their offerings might well come alive through your lives.

Just as modern work is dramatically different from work in premodern societies, so work in the future most likely will be dissimilar from work as we know it today. Work has become increasingly oriented toward the production and accumulation of things, and in contrast to many earlier societies modern people spend inordinate time and effort working. Through the long revolution of industrialization we have accomplished the wildest dreams of the founders of the market system and modern materialism in general. While this material success has freed people from many of life's drudgeries, dangers, and insecurities, few people have experienced a concomitant spiritual flourishing. In fact, many people believe the two are incompatible.

While none of the thinkers in this section believes that material success and the flowering of the human spirit are mutually exclusive, none believe that all we need to do is to keep the wheels of our economy turning. We need new visions of how to live, of what we are about, and how to become the magnificent beings history has shown us we might be.

Having the possibilities and the opportunities are not enough. We have been tied to the work ethic and the psychology of scarcity for centuries; we need new images of how to play and work. It is our fondest hope that this book will contribute to that new imagination.

John Paul II

On Human Work

Through work man must earn his daily bread and contribute to the continual advance of science and technology and, above all, to elevating unceasingly the cultural and moral level of the society within which he lives in community with those who belong to the same family. And work means any activity by man, whether manual or intellectual, whatever its nature or circumstances; it means any human activity that can and must be recognized as work, in the midst of all the many activities of which man is capable and to which he is predisposed by his very nature, by virtue of humanity itself. Man is made to be in the visible universe an image and likeness of God himself, and he is placed in it in order to subdue the earth. From the beginning therefore he is called to work. Work is one of the characteristics that distinguish man from the rest of creatures, whose activity for sustaining their lives cannot be called work. Only man is capable of work, and only man works, at the same time by work occupying his existence on earth. Thus work bears a particular mark of man and of humanity, the mark of a person operating within a community of persons. And this mark decides its interior characteristics; in a sense it constitutes its very nature.

. . . Man's life is built up every day from work, from work it derives its specific dignity, but at the same time work contains the unceasing measure of human toil and suffering and also of the harm and injustice which penetrate deeply into social life within individual nations and on the international level. While it is true that man eats the bread produced by the work of his hands—and this means not only the daily bread by which his body keeps alive but also the bread of science and progress, civilization and culture—it is also a perennial truth that he eats this bread by "the sweat of his face," that is to say, not only by personal effort and toil, but also in the midst of many tensions, conflicts and crises, which in relationship with the reality of work disturb the life of individual societies and also of all humanity.

. . . the general situation of man in the modern world, studied and analyzed in its various aspects of geography, culture and civilization, calls for the discovery of the new meanings of human work. It likewise calls for the formulation of the new tasks that in this sector face each individual, the family, each country, the whole human race and finally the church herself.

This trend of development of the church's teaching and commitment in the social question exactly corresponds to the objective recognition of the state of affairs. While in the past the "class" question was especially highlighted as the center of this issue, in more recent times it is the "world" question that is emphasized. Thus, not only the sphere of class is taken into consideration, but also the world sphere of inequality and injustice and, as a consequence, not only the class dimension, but also the world dimension of the tasks involved in the path toward the achievement of justice in the modern world. A complete analysis of the situation of the world today shows in an even deeper and fuller way the meaning of the previous analysis of social injustices; and it is the meaning that must be given today to efforts to build justice on earth, not concealing thereby unjust structures, but demanding that they be examined and transformed on a more universal scale.

While it may seem that in the industrial process it is the machine that "works" and man merely supervises it, making it function and keeping it going in various ways, it is also true that for this very reason industrial development provides grounds for reproposing in new ways the question of human work. Both the original industrialization that gave rise to what is called the worker question and the subsequent industrial and post-industrial changes show in an eloquent manner that, even in the age of ever more mechanized "work," the proper subject of work continues to be man.

The development of industry and of the various sectors connected with it, even the most modern electronics technology, especially in the fields of miniaturization, communications and telecommunications and so forth, shows how vast is the role of technology, that ally of work that human thought has produced in the interaction between the subject and object of work (in the widest sense of the word). Understood in this case not as a capacity or aptitude for work, but rather as a whole set of instruments which man uses in his work, technology is undoubtedly man's ally. It facilitates his work, perfects, accelerates and augments it. It leads to an increase in the quantity of things produced by work and in many cases improves their quality. However it is also a fact that in some instances technology can cease to be man's ally and become almost his enemy, as when the mechanization of work "supplants" him, taking away all personal satisfaction and the incentive to creativity and responsibility, when it deprives many workers of their previous employment or when, through exalting the machine, it reduces man to the status of its slave.

If the biblical words "subdue the earth" addressed to man from the very beginning are understood in the context of the whole modern age, industrial and post-industrial, then they undoubtedly include also a relationship with technology, with the world of machinery which is the fruit of the work of the human intellect and a historical confirmation of man's dominion over nature.

The recent stage of human history, especially that of certain societies, brings a correct affirmation of technology as a basic coefficient of economic progress; but at the same time this affirmation has been accompanied by and continues to be accompanied by essential questions concerning human work in relationship to its subject, which is man. These questions are particularly charged with content and tension of an ethical and social character. . . .

Man has to subdue the earth and dominate it, because as the "image of God" he is a person, that is to say, a subjective being capable of acting in a planned and rational way, capable of deciding about himself and with a tendency to self-realization. As a person, man is therefore the subject of work. As a person he works, he performs various actions belonging to the work process; independently of their objective content, these actions must all serve to realize his humanity, to fulfill the calling to be a person that is his by reason of his very humanity. . . .

And so this "dominion" spoken of in the biblical text being meditated upon here refers not only to the objective dimension of work, but at the same time introduces us to an understanding of its subjective dimension. Understood as a process whereby man and the human race subdue the earth, work corresponds to this basic biblical concept only when throughout the process man manifests himself and confirms himself as the one who "dominates." This dominion, in a certain sense, refers to the subjective dimension even more than to the objective one: This dimension conditions the very ethical nature of work. In fact there is no doubt that human work has an ethical value of its own, which clearly and directly remains linked to the fact that the one who carries it out is a person, a conscious and free subject, that is to say, a subject that decides about himself.

The ancient world introduced its own typical differentiation of people into classes according to the type of work done. Work which demanded from the worker the exercise of physical strength, the work of muscles and hands, was considered unworthy of free men and was therefore given to slaves. By broadening certain aspects that already belonged to the Old Testament, Christianity brought about a fundamental change of ideas in this field, taking the whole content of the gospel message as its point of departure, especially the fact that the one who, while being God, became like us in all things devoted most of the years of his life on earth to manual work at the carpenter's bench. This circumstance constitutes in itself the most eloquent "gospel of work," showing that the basis for determining the value of human work is not primarily the kind of work being done, but the fact that the one who is doing it is a person. The sources of the dignity of work are to be sought primarily in the subjective dimension, not in the objective one.

Such a concept practically does away with the very basis of the ancient differentiation of people into classes according to the kind of work done. This does not mean that from the objective point of view human work cannot and must not be rated and qualified in any way. It only means that the primary basis of the value of work is man himself, who is its subject. This leads immediately to a very important conclusion of an ethical nature: However true it may be that man is destined for work and called to it, in the first place work is "for man" and not man "for work." Through this conclusion one rightly comes to recognize the preeminence of the subjective meaning of work over the objective one. Given this way of understanding things and presupposing that different sorts of work that people do can have greater or lesser objective value, let us try nevertheless to show that each sort is judged above all by the measure of the dignity of the subject of work, that is to say, the person, the individual who carries it out. On the other hand, independent of the work that every man does, and presupposing that this work constitutes a purpose—at times a very demanding one—of his activity, this purpose does not possess a definitive meaning in itself. In fact, in the final analysis it is always man who is the purpose of the work, whatever work it is that is done by man — even if the common scale of values rates it as the merest "service," as the most monotonous, even the most alienating work.

. . . In the modern period, from the beginning of the industrial age, the Christian truth about work had to oppose the various trends of materialistic and economistic thought.

For certain supporters of such ideas, work was understood and treated as a sort of "merchandise" that the worker — especially the industrial worker — sells to the employer, who at the same time is the possessor of the capital, that is to say, of all the working tools and means that make production possible. This way of looking at work was widespread especially in the first half of the 19th century. Since then explicit expressions of this sort have almost disappeared and have given way to more human ways of thinking about work and evaluating it. The interaction between the worker and the tools and means of production has given rise to the development of various forms of capitalism — parallel with various forms of collectivism — into which other socioeconomic elements have entered as a consequence of new concrete circumstances, of the activity of workers' associations and public authorities, and of the emergence of large transnational enterprises. Nevertheless, the danger of treating work as a special kind of "merchandise" or as an impersonal "force" needed for production (the expression "work force" is in fact in common use) always exists, especially when the whole way of looking at the question of economics is marked by the premises of materialistic economism.

A systematic opportunity for thinking and evaluating in this way, and in a certain sense a stimulus for doing so, is provided by the quickening process of the development of a one-sidedly materialistic civilization, which gives prime importance to the objective dimension of work, while the subjective dimension — everything in direct or indirect relationship with the subject of work — remains on a secondary level. In all cases of this sort, in every social situation of this type, there is a confusion or even a reversal of the order laid down from the beginning by the words of the Book of Genesis: Man is treated as an instrument of production, whereas he — he alone, independent of the work he does — ought to be treated as the effective subject of work and its true maker and creator. Precisely this reversal of order, whatever the program or name under which it occurs, should rightly be called "capitalism" — in the sense more fully explained below. Everybody knows that capitalism has a definite historical meaning as a system, an economic and social system, opposed to "socialism" or "communism." But in the light of the analysis of the fundamental reality of the whole economic process — first and foremost of the production structure that work is — it should be recognized that the error of early capitalism can be repeated wherever man is in a way treated on the same level as the whole complex of the material means of production, as an instrument and not in accordance with the true dignity of his work—that is to say, where he is not treated as subject and maker, and for this very reason as the true purpose of the whole process of production.

. . . While one can say that, by reason of its subject, work is one single thing (one and unrepeatable every time), yet when one takes into consideration its objective directions, one is forced to admit that there exist many works, many different sorts of work. The development of human civilization brings continual enrichment in this field. But at the same time, one cannot fail to note that in the process of this development not only do new forms of work appear but also others disappear. Even if one accepts that on the whole this is a normal phenomenon, it must still be seen whether certain ethically and socially dangerous irregularities creep in and to what extent.

It was precisely one such wide-ranging anomaly that gave rise in the last century to what has been called "the worker question," sometimes described as "the proletariat question." This question and the problems connected with it gave rise to a just social reaction and caused the impetuous emergence of a great burst of solidarity between workers, first and foremost industrial workers. The call to solidarity and common action addressed to the workers—especially to those engaged in narrowly specialized, monotonous and depersonalized work in industrial plants, when the machine tends to dominate man—was important and eloquent from the point of view of social ethics. It was the reaction against the degradation of man as the subject of work and against the unheard-of accompanying exploitation in the field of wages, working conditions and social security for the worker. This reaction united the working world in a community marked by great solidarity.

Following the lines laid down by the encyclical *Rerum novarum* and many later documents of the church's magisterium, it must be frankly recognized that the reaction against the system of injustice and harm that cried to heaven for vengeance and that weighed heavily upon workers in that period of rapid industrialization was justified from the point of view of social morality. This state of affairs was favored by the liberal socio-political system, which in accordance with its "economistic" premises, strengthened and safeguarded economic initiative by the possessors of capital alone, but did not pay sufficient attention to the rights of the workers, on the grounds that human work is solely an instrument of production, and that capital is the basis, efficient factor and purpose of production.

From that time, worker solidarity, together with a clearer and more committed realization by others of workers' rights, has in many cases brought about profound changes. Various forms of neocapitalism or collectivism have developed. Various new systems have been thought out. Workers can often share in running businesses and in controlling their productivity, and in fact do so. Through appropriate associations they exercise influence over conditions of work and pay, and aslo over social legislation. But at the same time various ideological or power systems and new relationships which have arisen at various levels of society have allowed flagrant injustices to persist or have created new ones. On the world level, the development of civilization and of communications has made possible a more complete diagnosis of the living and working conditions of man globally, but it has also revealed other forms of injustice much more extensive than those which in the last century stimulated unity between workers for particular solidarity in the working world. This is true in countries which have completed a certain process of industrial revolution. It is also true in countries where the main working milieu continues to be agriculture or other similar occupations.

Movements of solidarity in the sphere of work — a solidarity that must never mean being closed to dialogue and collaboration with others — can be necessary also with reference to the condition of social groups that were not previously included in such movements, but which in changing social systems and conditions of living are undergoing what is in effect "proletarianization" or which actually already find themselves in a "proletariat" situation, one which, even if not yet given that name, in fact deserves it. . . .

For this reason there must be continued study of the subject of work and of the subject's living conditions. In order to achieve social justice in the various parts of the world, in the various countries and in the relationships between them, there is a need for ever new movements of solidarity of the workers and with the workers. This solidarity must be present whenever it is called for by the social degrading of the subject of work, by exploitation of the workers and by the growing areas of poverty and even hunger. The church is firmly committed to this cause for she considers it her mission, her service, a proof of her fidelity to Christ, so that she can truly be the "church of the poor." And the "poor" appear under various forms; they appear in various places and at various times; in many cases they appear as a result of the violation of the dignity of human work: either because the opportunities for human work are limited as a result of the scourge of unemployment or because a low value is put on work and the rights that flow from it, especially the right to a just wage and to the personal security of the worker and his or her family.

. . . Toil is something that is universally known, for it is universally experienced. It is familiar to those doing physical work under sometimes exceptionally laborious conditions. It is familiar not only to agricultural workers, who spend long days working the land, which sometimes "bears thorns and thistles," but also to those who work in mines and quarries, to steelworkers at their blast furnaces, to those who work in builders' yards and in construction work, often in danger of injury or death. It is also familiar to those at an intellectual workbench; to scientists; to those who bear the burden of grave responsibility for decisions that will have a vast impact on society. It is familiar to doctors and nurses, who spend days and nights at their patients' bedside. It is familiar to women, who sometimes without proper recognition on the part of society and even of their own families bear the daily burden and responsibility for their homes and the upbringing of their children. It is familiar to all workers and, since work is a universal calling, it is familiar to everyone.

And yet in spite of all this toil — perhaps, in a sense, because of it — work is a good thing for man. Even though it bears the mark of a "bonum arduum," in the terminology of St. Thomas, this does not take away the fact that, as such, it is a good thing for man. It is not only good in the sense that it is useful or something to enjoy; it is also good as being something worthy, that is to say, something that corresponds to man's dignity, that expresses this dignity and increases it. If one wishes to define more clearly the ethical meaning of work, it is this truth that one must particularly keep in mind. Work is a good thing for man — a good thing for his humanity — because through work man not only transforms nature, adapting it to his own needs, but he also achieves fulfillment as a human being and indeed in a sense becomes "more a human being."

Without this consideration it is impossible to understand the meaning of the virtue of industriousness, and more particularly it is impossible to understand why industriousness should be a virtue: For virtue, as a moral habit, is something whereby man becomes good as man. This fact in no way alters our justifiable anxiety that in work, whereby matter gains in nobility, man himself should not experience a lowering of his own dignity. Again, it is well known that it is possible to use work in various ways against man, that it is possible to punish man with the system of forced labor in concentration camps, that work can be made into a means for oppressing man, and that in various ways it is possible to exploit human labor, that is to say, the workers. All this pleads in favor of the moral obligation to link industriousness as a virtue with the social order of work, which will enable man to become in work "more a human being" and not be degraded by it not only because of the wearing out of his physical strength (which, at least up to a certain point, is inevitable), but especially through damage to the dignity and subjectivity that are proper to him.

Having thus confirmed the personal dimension of human work, we must go on to the second sphere of values which is necessarily linked to work. Work constitutes a foundation for the formation of family life, which is a natural right and something that man is called to. These two spheres of value—one linked to work and the other consequent on the family nature of human life—must be properly united and must properly permeate each other. In a way, work is a condition for making it possible to found a family, since the family requires the means of subsistence which man normally gains through work. Work and industriousness also influence the whole process of education in the family, for the very reason that everyone "becomes a human being" through, among other things, work, and becoming a human being is precisely the main purpose of the whole process of education. Obviously, two aspects of work in a sense come into play here: the one making family life and its upkeep possible, and the other making possible the achievement of the purposes of the family, especially education. Nevertheless, these two aspects of work are linked to one another and are mutually complementary in various points.

It must be remembered and affirmed that the family constitutes one of the most important terms of reference for shaping the social and ethical order of human work. The teaching of the church has always devoted special attention to this question, and in the present document we shall have to return to it. In fact, the family is simultaneously a community made possible by work and the first school of work, within the home, for every person.

The third sphere of values that emerges from this point of view—that of the subject of work—concerns the great society to which man belongs on the basis of particular cultural and historical links. This society—even when it has not yet taken on the mature form of a nation—is not only the great "educator" of every man, even though an indirect one (because each individual absorbs within the family the contents and values that go to make up the culture of a given nation); it is also a great historical and social incarnation of the work of all generations. All of this brings it about that man combines his deepest human identity with membership of a nation, and intends his work also to increase the common good developed together with his compatriots, thus realizing that in this way work serves to add to the heritage of the whole human family, of all the people living in the world.

These three spheres are always important for human work in its subjective dimension. And this dimension, that is to say, the concrete reality of the worker, takes precedence over the objective dimension. In the subjective dimension there is realized, first of all, that "dominion" over the world of nature to which man is called from the beginning according to the words of the Book of Genesis. The very process of "subduing the earth," that is to say work, is marked in the course of history and especially in recent centuries by an immense development of technological means. This is an advantageous and positive phenomenon, on condition that the objective dimension of work does not gain the upper hand over the subjective dimension, depriving man of his dignity and inalienable rights or reducing them.

. . . The key problem of social ethics in this case is that of just remuneration for work done. In the context of the present there is no more important way for securing a just relationship between the worker and the employer than that constituted by remuneration for work. Whether the work is done in a system of private ownership of the means of production or in a system where ownership has undergone a certain "socialization," the relationship between the employer (first and foremost the direct employer) and the worker is resolved on the basis of the wage, that is, through just remuneration of the work done.

It should also be noted that the justice of a socioeconomic system and, in each case, its just functioning, deserve in the final analysis to be evaluated by the way in which man's work is properly remunerated in the system. Here we return once more to the first principle of the whole ethical and social order, namely the principle of the common use of goods. In every system, regardless of the fundamental relationships within it between capital and labor, wages, that is to say remuneration for work, are still a practical means whereby the vast majority of people can have access to those goods which are intended for common use: both the goods of nature and manufactured goods. Both kinds of goods become accessible to the worker through the wage which he recieves as remuneration for his work. Hence in every case a just wage is the concrete means of verifying the justice of the whole socioeconomic system and, in any case, of checking that it is functioning justly. It is not the only means of checking, but it is a particularly important one and in a sense the key means.

This means of checking concerns above all the family. Just remuneration for the work of an adult who is responsible for a family means remuneration which will suffice for establishing and properly maintaining a family and for providing security for its future. Such remuneration can be given either through what is called a family wage — that is, a single salary given to the head of the family for his work, sufficient for the needs of the family without the spouse having to take up gainful employment outside the home — or through other social measures such as family allowances or grants to mothers devoting themselves exclusively to their families. These grants should correspond to the actual needs, that is, to the number of dependents for as long as they are not in a position to assume proper responsibility for their own lives.

Experience confirms that there must be a social re-evaluation of the mother's role, of the toil connected with it and of the need that children have for care, love and affection in order that they may develop into responsible, morally and religiously mature and psychologically stable persons. It will redound to the credit of society to make it possible for a mother — without inhibiting her freedom, without psychological or practical discrimination, and without penalizing her as compared with other women — to devote herself to taking care of her children and educating them in accordance with their needs, which vary with age. Having to abandon these tasks in order to take up paid work outside the home is wrong from the point of view of the good of society and of the family when it contradicts or hinders these primary goals of the mission of a mother.

In this context it should be emphasized that on a more general level the whole labor process must be organized and adapted in such a way as to respect the requirements of the person and his or her forms of life, above all life in the home, taking into account the individual's age and sex. It is a fact that in many societies women work in nearly every sector of life. But it is fitting that they should be able to fulfill their tasks in accordance with their own nature, without being discriminated against and without being excluded from jobs for which they are capable, but also without lack of respect for their family aspirations and for their specific role in contributing, together with men, to the good of society. The true advancement of women requires that labor should be structured in such a way that women do not have to pay for their advancement by abandoning what is specific to them and at the expense of the family, in which women as mothers have an irreplaceable role.

Besides wages, various social benefits intended to ensure the life and health of workers and their families play a part here. The expenses involved in health care, especially in the case of accidents at work, demand that medical assistance should be easily available for workers and that as far as possible it should be cheap or even free of charge. Another sector regarding benefits is the sector associated with the right to rest. In the first place this involves a regular weekly rest comprising at least Sunday and also a longer period of rest, namely the holiday or vacation taken once a year or possibly in several shorter periods during the year. A third sector concerns the right to a pension and to insurance for old age and in case of accidents at work. Within the sphere of these principal rights there develops a whole system of particular rights which, together with remuneration for work, determine the correct relationship between worker and employer. Among these rights there should never be overlooked the right to a working environment and to manufacturing processes which are not harmful to the workers' physical health or to their moral integrity.

All these rights, together with the need for the workers themselves to secure them, give rise to yet another right: the right of association, that is, to form associations for the purpose of defending the vital interests of those employed in the various professions. These associations are called labor or trade unions. The vital interests of the workers are to a certain extent common for all of them; at the same time, however, each type of work, each profession, has its own specific character which should find a particular reflection in these organizations.

. . . Their task is to defend the existential interests of workers in all sectors in which their rights are concerned. The experience of history teaches that organizations of this type are an indispensable element of social life, especially in modern industrialized societies. Obviously this does not mean that only industrial workers can set up associations of this type. Representatives of every profession can use them to ensure their own rights. Thus there are unions of agricultural workers and of white-collar workers; there are also employers' associations. All, as has been said above, are further divided into groups or subgroups according to particular professional specializations.

. . . In the final analysis, both those who work and those who manage the means of production or who own them must in some way be united in this community. In the light of this fundamental structure of all work—in the light of the fact that, in the final analysis, labor and capital are indispensable components of the process of production in any social system—it is clear that even if it is because of their work needs that people unite to secure their rights, their union remains a constructive factor of social order and solidarity, and it is impossible to ignore it.

Speaking of the protection of the just rights of workers according to their individual professions, we must of course always keep in mind that which determines the subjective character of work in each profession, but at the same time, indeed before all else, we must keep in mind that which conditions the specific dignity of the subject of the work. The activity of union organizations opens up many possibilities in this respect, including their efforts to instruct and educate the workers and to foster their self-education. Praise is due to the work of the schools, what are known as workers' or people's universities and the training programs and courses which have developed and are still developing this field of activity. It is always to be hoped that, thanks to the work of their unions, workers will not only have more, but above all be more: in other words that they will realize their humanity more fully in every respect.

In this connection workers should be assured the right to strike, without being subjected to personal penal sanctions for taking part in a strike. While admitting that it is a legitimate means, we must at the same time emphasize that a strike remains, in a sense, an extreme means. It must not be abused; it must not be abused especially for "political" purposes.

Furthermore, it must never be forgotten that, when essential community services are in question, they must in every case be ensured, if necessary by means of appropriate legislation. Abuse of the strike weapon can lead to the paralysis of the whole of socioeconomic life, and this is contrary to the requirements of the common good of society, which also corresponds to the properly understood nature of work itself.

The teachings of the apostle of the gentiles obviously have key importance for the morality and spirituality of human work. They are an important complement to the great though discreet gospel of work that we find in the life and parables of Christ, in what Jesus "did and taught."

On the basis of these illuminations emanating from the source himself, the church has always proclaimed what we find expressed in modern terms in the teaching of the Second Vatican Council: "Just as human activity proceeds from man, so it is ordered toward man. For when a man works he not only alters things and society, he develops himself as well. He learns much, he cultivates his resources, he goes outside of himself and beyond himself. Rightly understood, this kind of growth is of greater value than any external riches which can be garnered. . . . Hence, the norm of human activity is this: that in accord with the divine plan and will, it should harmonize with the genuine good of the human race, and allow people as individuals and as members of society to pursue their total vocation and fulfill it."

Such a vision of the values of human work, or in other words such a spirituality of work, fully explains what we read in the same section of the council's pastoral constitution with regard to the right meaning of progress: "A person is more precious for what he is than for what he has. Similarly, all that people do to obtain greater justice, wider brotherhood, and a more humane ordering of social relationships has greater worth than technical advances. For these advances can supply the material for human progress, but of themselves alone they can never actually bring it about."

This teaching on the question of progress and development — a subject that dominates present day thought — can be understood only as the fruit of a tested spirituality of human work; and it is only on the basis of such a spirituality that it can be realized and put into practice. This is the teaching, and also the program, that has its roots in "the gospel of work."

IIIA. Visions of Work from Other Cultures

At first thought beginning a discussion of the future of work in industrialized societies with a brief foray into cultures and times dramatically different from our own probably seems inappropriate, if not plainly irrelevant. What could we possibly learn from archaic ways that would help us deal with the dizzying changes of advanced industrial life? *That* cultures such as those of the traditional American Indian or South Pacific islanders are so very different is precisely their potential value to us: as we move into what Ron Howard calls "the brave new workplace,"* we should expect that the future of work will be as different from what we now have as our current lives differ from those of people in hunting-and-gathering societies. By facing such dramatic differences we might assist our imaginations and thinking to comprehend how life and work will be, and we might just manage to help create a world that resembles what we would wish it to be.

A very common picture of the history of human labor contains a fundamental contradiction which is based on two central elements in our modern view of work: the belief in *progress* and in the modern *work ethic*. Our belief in progress tells us that both in comparing modern with premodern societies and in comparing our lives with previous centuries of

---

*Ron Howard, *Brave New Workplace*. Howard is making the same point by linking the future of work with a piece of science fiction.

the modern era, work has gotten better: people today work less hard at less demeaning and physically taxing activities than our modern or pre-modern predecessors, our rewards are more bountiful as well as easier to come by, and, as a result of our easier and shorter workdays, we live longer and enjoy life more. Our modern myth about work tells us that the further back in human history we look, the more nasty, brutish, and short life will appear to be.

Yet while our belief in progress tells us that our predecessors, especially our so-called primitive ancestors, had to work dreadfully hard to scratch out an existence, our belief in the modern work ethic has us picture premoderns as lazy. Modern Europeans and Americans treated traditional people around the world as children in need of "discipline" and "salvation" because they viewed them as slothful and in need of "industry" (disciplined work). The colonizers "tamed the savages" by imposing on them the education necessary to make them "diligent workers" and "productive citizens."

How can we simultaneously believe that previous people both worked harder than we do *and* that they were lazy, lacking a proper respect for hard work? Can this paradox be resolved? Crucial to solving a paradox is self-understanding; before we can get unstuck from the horns of a dilemma, we must first understand how we got stuck. Historians know that every telling of a story, every historical account, is told from a point of view, with a set of beliefs, values, expectations. Consequently, every telling informs us as much about the teller as about the people and events being described. Perhaps we arrive at our paradox about premodern work because of *our* beliefs in progress and the work ethic: the contradiction might result from our perspective rather than from the history onto which we project those beliefs. *If* we see the history of work through the lenses of progress and the work ethic, then we create a contradiction.

Contemporary anthropologists and historians tell a far different story than the common one we just discussed. Humans, including women and children, worked long, dreadful hours under extremely harsh conditions for little recompense *during the first decades of the Industrial Revolution* (roughly the last part of the 1700s in England and the middle part of the 1800s in the United States and Europe). Since then workers in industrial societies have, through long years of struggle, won significant improvements in their working and living conditions. Working only eight hours per day rather than twelve or sixteen, having job safety standards, health and other benefits, and being able to retire ten to twenty years before you die *are* improvements over the conditions under which textile workers, miners, and farmworkers labored in 1820. But the history of industrialization should not be confused with the history of the West or of humanity in general. And whether or not humans are making progress depends very much on the yardstick we use.

Contemporary scholars paint a very different picture of working in the past, one which conflicts dramatically with the popular story we just described. They tell us that in many societies prior to the Industrial Revolution people worked a great deal less not only than workers in early industrial societies but also than most workers do today. Rural peasants during the Middle Ages probably worked an average of five to eight hours per day, and according to anthropologists, if we move back to preagricultural hunting-and-gathering societies, the evidence now shows that even people living in what we would consider extremely hostile environments (such as deserts or tundra) spent between one and three hours per day making a living. Furthermore, as anthropologist Marshall Sahlins argues in the first selection of this section, most work in hunting-and-gathering societies was done in a leisurely and highly sociable manner, leaving maximal time for other social and cultural activities. Sahlins contends that from the time of traditional hunters and gatherers through the medieval period people lacked our modern work ethic, but they did not experience this lack as a deprivation. For them life might have been shorter than ours, but it usually was not nasty or brutish.

Why is the popular story about work in premodern societies so different from the ones scholars are now telling us? Much of the difference results from the ideological function of history. History is not neutral. The stories we tell about the past determine how we think about ourselves and our contemporaries. If the Germans (Iranians, Japanese, Russians . . .) are viewed as barbaric people, and Nazism (etc.) is a natural outgrowth of this barbarism, we relate very differently to them in peace and in war than if they are seen as people very much like ourselves who are capable of evil as well as good depending on complex historical conditions. History is a powerful political/ideological tool. Beliefs like progress and the work ethic not only define windows through which to see the past, but they also justify our feelings about others and ourselves, and they can be used to spur us to action. If you want someone to accept the status quo and do the job expected of them (especially if the work is dull), a powerful tool to generate conformity and performance is the story that life today is as good as anyone has had it (progress) as long as people work hard at their assigned tasks (work ethic).

To continue the human saga as Sahlins sees it, during most of human history people spent most of their waking hours playing, socializing, dancing, and participating in numerous and complex ceremonies (what we would call leisure activities). They needed little time for meeting their material needs (what we would call work) because their material needs were few. Furthermore, hunting-and-gathering people would not even know what we meant by the word work. Why? First, every activity was tightly woven into the total fabric of society. Meeting one's material needs was never viewed or practiced as a distinct kind of activity from play or socializing or ritual. Our modern separations (dis-integrations) did not exist: a separation of time, place, and style did not set work apart from leisure. A second reason follows from the first: in societies where work is not distinct from leisure, meeting one's material needs is not viewed as an undesirable task. Contemporary activities like hunting and shopping often still carry some of the flavor which "work" more generally did in earlier societies. Hunting involves effort and danger, it requires skill, and for some, at least, it is still a way to meet a need for food. Yet it is also highly ritualized, it is play, and it is a very social activity.

Is hunting today work or play? Few people would have any difficulty categorizing it as work for only a few professional hunters and play for the majority — sports hunting. Why? What is the difference between the person for whom hunting is work and the majority for whom it is play? In a word, money. Work is what you do for pay; leisure is what you do when you are not working. This simple, and to us obvious, distinction marks a third reason why premoderns did not work: working is part of a conceptual system, a universe of thought and action, which modern humans invented and which we can enter through the door of *wages*.

In the Middle Ages working for wages was somewhat like welfare is for us: it is what people did if they could not make their livings in any other way. Most people made their way in the world through a very different system of meeting human needs and distributing wealth, a system which until its demise had little wage labor. Peasants toiled in the fields and craftspeople produced their wares, to be sure, but they mostly worked as part of a communal system using barter. For them there was very little incentive for hard work beyond meeting basic necessities. Why? To a great extent a medieval person's status was marked by birth, and no amount of hard work would change that; hard work would likely only ruin a person's health. Unless times were bad for an entire fiefdom or region, no one went without, even if by today's standards they did not have much materially. But as we saw in Section IIA, the life of a medieval person was not totally dull or meaningless — most of the material needs and wants of people were usually met adequately by this very different system, and they spent much of their time engaged in a rich and diverse cultural and social life.

Our first major idea in this subsection, then, is that work as we know it is part of a complex web of ideas, activities, traditions, beliefs, values, and social institutions developed over an extended period of time to meet human needs and desires. People have always had to extend effort to meet their material needs, but until quite recently (by historical standards) human material needs were few, and the actual notion of work, as opposed to leisure, is a fairly recent invention which only makes sense within a particular system. Furthermore, if effort to meet needs is the criterion for work, then traditional people and even to a great extent medievalists were very hard workers indeed . . . at leisure activities. Again, our ways of thinking about the world do not necessarily help us understand other people at other times.

Think about this contrast from a different angle—were premodern people not meeting their needs when they played and celebrated and socialized and ritualized? If humans for tens or perhaps hundreds of thousands of years spent most of their waking time engaged in complex and diverse cultural activities other than meeting their material needs, then perhaps humans have great need for the things which ceremony, socializing, play, craft, and other such endeavors provide. That this is obvious should not blind us to a crucial issue: by working so much are we ignoring crucial nonmaterial needs? Many students of human history and behavior have noted, in various ways, that modern humans are unique in the extent to which we try to meet our nonmaterial needs through material accumulation and consumption. From extreme behaviors like eating disorders or workaholism or conspicuous consumption to more ordinary modern patterns such as buying/consuming to soothe an anxiety or buying things for instead of spending time with a child, humans living in contemporary industrial systems meet many of their nonmaterial needs in very roundabout ways. Some thinkers, when reflecting on how different these patterns are and how ineffective material substitutes are for meeting needs like love, identity, security, and sociality, have suggested that modernism is not only unique but an aberration.

A major value of humanities study is the enhancement of our abilities to take an objective look at ourselves, to stand back and see through a long lens how we compare with others. Sometimes we can best understand ourselves by seeing through the eyes of strangers. This set of readings provides you with the opportunity to reflect on your own work experiences by contrasting them with people who were very different from yourself. Marshall Sahlins will help you think about how long and hard we work, but his writing will also raise the question of *why?* When most of us dislike much of what we do on our jobs, why do we work so hard and long? Dorothy Lee gives an illuminating description of the integration of work with other dimensions of life in a premodern society and thus helps us explore the ways in which our own separation of work and leisure might be harmful or beneficial to us as individuals and as communities. By bringing us ideas from past and distant peoples Sahlins and Lee offer the opportunity for dramatic reevaluation of what work is and could be in our lives. As you read these accounts of human life which are quite different from your own, open a path for thinking about your own life and work by imagining what it would be like to transfer to your own existence the pace, sociality, integrity, amount and kinds of work they describe.

Introduction
Marshall Sahlins, "The Original Affluent Society"

Marshall Sahlins is an American anthropologist and educator. He has been on the faculty at The University of Michigan and is currently professor of ethnology and Oceania at The University of Chicago. In the following excerpt called "The Original Affluent Society," from *Stone Age Economics,* the best-known of his several books, Sahlins challenges many of our assumptions about the nature of so-called primitive societies and about our own notion of progress.

Among the contradictions in our thinking about progress is that as we progress we have less work. Yet one of the ideas associated with progress is the Protestant work ethic. Why is it necessary to instill a work ethic if the amount of work and the need for work are declining? Sahlins goes even further to undermine our comfortable ideas about how "progressed" we are by arguing that we work much harder in modern industrial society than we did when we were stone-age people. He also suggests that if we understand the stone-age perspective, we might even come to believe that they are more affluent than we are! They have few possessions, but they have much time. Their goods are appropriate to their needs and desires and are easy to replace if lost. Thus they have a "psychology of affluence," whereas we, with our piles of material possessions, have a "psychology of scarcity."

Modern people have always assumed that primitive people had to work very hard to survive. Sahlins demonstrates this is not true and, in doing so, destroys one of the cornerstones of classical economics. He gives us a perspective from which to look at our own ideas about what we need, and he allows us to challenge the modern notion of "economic man." According to classical economists to desire more than you can have (the psychology of scarcity) is *natural*. Yet, as Sahlins shows, those who come closest to being "natural" humans are not economic "men." Sahlins contends that "economic man" is a bourgeois construction. We do not naturally want unlimited goods, but because we are part of an ideological system that has conditioned us to desire more than we can ever have we want ever more. There is little evidence that more and more makes us happier than stone-age people. In fact the evidence seems to point in the opposite direction.

Knowing this frees us. We can now begin to look at other ways of being that might make us happier workers and better caretakers of the earth. Remember, we are looking at stone-age society as a way of gaining perspective on our own age. Neither we nor Sahlins are suggesting a return to the past. We could not go back even if we wanted to. The value of Sahlins's study is to free us from false assumptions that have limited our ways of imagining the future. He shows us that we are not prisoners of a nature beyond our control, that we are free to shape our future in ways we might not have imagined. As you read E.F. Schumacher, Bob Black, and other visionaries in this last section, allow them to stretch your imagination about what kind of a work future might be most desirable. One of the great contributions of Sahlins's essay is to free our desires from the limits of material accumulation and to begin to exercise our desires in more imaginative ways. We are far advanced from the time when we could not easily meet our material needs; now we must learn to meet our more centrally human needs and desires in more intelligent ways.

Marshall Sahlins

The Original Affluent Society

If economics is the dismal science, the study of hunting and gathering economies must be its most advanced branch. Almost universally committed to the proposition that life was hard in the paleolithic, our textbooks compete to convey a sense of impending doom, leaving one to wonder not only how hunters managed to live, but whether, after all, this was living? The specter of starvation stalks the stalker through these pages. His technical incompetence is said to enjoin continuous work just

---

Reprinted with permission from: Marshall Sahlins: *Stone Age Economics* (New York: Aldine de Gruyter). Copyright © 1972 by Marshall Sahlins.

to survive, affording him neither respite nor surplus, hence not even the "leisure" to "build culture." Even so, for all his efforts, the hunter pulls the lowest grades in thermodynamics — less energy/capita/year than any other mode of production. And in treatises on economic development he is condemned to play the role of bad example: the so-called "subsistence economy."

The traditional wisdom is always refractory. One is forced to oppose it polemically, to phrase the necessary revisions dialectically: in fact, this was, when you come to examine it, the original affluent society. Paradoxical, that phrasing leads to another useful and unexpected conclusion. By the common understanding, an affluent society is one in which all the people's material wants are easily satisfied. To assert that the hunters are affluent is to deny then that the human condition is an ordained tragedy, with man the prisoner at hard labor of a perpetual disparity between his unlimited wants and his insufficient means.

For there are two possible courses to affluence. Wants may be "easily satisfied" either by producing much or desiring little. The familiar conception, the Galbraithean way, makes assumptions peculiarly appropriate to market economies: that man's wants are great, not to say infinite, whereas his means are limited, although improvable: thus, the gap between means and ends can be narrowed by industrial productivity, at least to the point that "urgent goods" become plentiful. But there is also a Zen road to affluence, departing from premises somewhat different from our own: that human material wants are finite and few, and technical means unchanging but on the whole adequate. Adopting the Zen strategy, a people can enjoy an unparalleled material plenty — with a low standard of living.

That, I think, describes the hunters. And it helps explain some of their more curious economic behavior: their "prodigality" for example — the inclination to consume at once all stocks on hand, as if they had it made. Free from market obsessions of scarcity, hunters' economic propensities may be more consistently predicated on abundance than our own. Destutt de Tracy, "fish-blooded bourgeois doctrinaire" though he might have been, at least compelled Marx's agreement on the observation that "in poor nations the people are comfortable," whereas in rich nations "they are generally poor."

This is not to deny that a preagricultural economy operates under serious constraints, but only to insist, on the evidence from modern hunters and gatherers, that a successful accommodation is usually made. After taking up the evidence, I shall return in the end to the real difficulties of hunting-gathering economy, none of which are correctly specified in current formulas of paleolithic poverty.

Sources of the Misconception

"Mere subsistence economy" "limited leisure save in exceptional circumstances," incessant quest for food," "meagre and relatively unreliable"
natural resources, "absence of an economic surplus," "maximum energy
from a maximum number of people"—so runs the fair average anthropological opinion of hunting and gathering.

> The aboriginal Australians are a classic example of a people whose
> economic resources are of the scantiest. In many places their habitat
> is even more severe than that of the Bushmen, although this is perhaps
> not quite true in the northern portion. . . . A tabulation of the food-
> stuffs which the aborigines of northwest central Queensland extract from
> the country they inhabit is instructive. . . . The variety in this list is
> impressive, but we must not be deceived into thinking that variety in-
> dicates plenty, for the available quantities of each element in it are so
> slight that only the most intense application makes survival possible
> (Herskovits, 1958, pp. 68–69).

Or again, in reference to South American hunters:

> The nomadic hunters and gatherers barely met minimum subsistence
> needs and often fell far short of them. Their population of 1 person
> to 10 or 20 square miles reflects this. Constantly on the move in search
> of food, they clearly lacked the leisure hours for nonsubsistence ac-
> tivities of any significance, and they could transport little of what they
> might manufacture in spare moments. To them, adequacy of produc-
> tion meant physical survival, and they rarely had surplus of either prod-
> ucts or time (Steward and Faron, 1959, p. 60; cf. Clark, 1953, p. 27 f;
> Haury, 1962, p. 113; Hoebel, 1958, p. 188; Redfield, 1953, p. 5; White,
> 1959).

But the traditional dismal view of the hunters' fix is also preanthro-
pological and extra-anthropological, at once historical and referable to
the larger economic context in which anthropology operates. It goes back
to the time Adam Smith was writing, and probably to a time before anyone was writing. Probably it was one of the first distinctly neolithic prejudices, an ideological appreciation of the hunter's capacity to exploit the
earth's resources most congenial to the historic task of depriving him of
the same. We must have inherited it with the seed of Jacob, which "spread
abroad to the west, and to the east, and to the north," to the disadvantage
of Esau who was the elder son and cunning hunter, but in a famous
scene deprived of his birthright.

Current low opinions of the hunting-gathering economy need not be laid to neolithic ethnocentrism, however. Bourgeois ethnocentrism will do as well. The existing business economy, at every turn an ideological trap from which anthropological economics must escape, will promote the same dim conclusions about the hunting life.

Is it so paradoxical to contend that hunters have affluent economies, their absolute poverty notwithstanding? Modern capitalist societies, however richly endowed, dedicate themselves to the proposition of scarcity. Inadequacy of economic means is the first principle of the world's wealthiest peoples. The apparent material status of the economy seems to be no clue to its accomplishments; something has to be said for the mode of economic organization (cf. Polanyi, 1947, 1957, 1959; Dalton, 1961).

The market-industrial system institutes scarcity, in a manner completely unparalleled and to a degree nowhere else approximated. Where production and distribution are arranged through the behavior of prices, and all livelihoods depend on getting and spending, insufficiency of material means becomes the explicit, calculable starting point of all economic activity. The entrepreneur is confronted with alternative investments of a finite capital, the worker (hopefully) with alternative choices of remunerative employ, and the consumer. . . . Consumption is a double tragedy: what begins in inadequacy will end in deprivation. Bringing together an international division of labor, the market makes available a dazzling array of products: all these Good Things within a man's reach — but never all within his grasp. Worse, in this game of consumer free choice, every acquisition is simultaneously a deprivation, for every purchase of something is a foregoing of something else, in general only marginally less desirable, and in some particulars more desirable, that could have been had instead. (The point is that if you buy one automobile, say a Plymouth, you cannot also have the Ford — and I judge from current television commercials that the deprivations entailed would be more than just material.)

That sentence of "life at hard labor" was passed uniquely upon us. Scarcity is the judgment decreed by our economy — so also the axiom of our Economics: the application of scarce means against alternative ends to derive the most satisfaction possible under the circumstances. And it is precisely from this anxious vantage that we look back upon hunters. But if modern man, with all his technological advantages, still hasn't got the wherewithal, what chance has this naked savage with his puny bow and arrow? Having equipped the hunter with bourgeois impulses and paleolithic tools, we judge his situation hopeless in advance.

Yet scarcity is not an intrinsic property of technical means. It is a relation between means and ends. We should entertain the empirical possibility that hunters are in business for their health, a finite objective, and that bow and arrow are adequate to that end.

But still other ideas, these endemic in anthropological theory and ethnographic practice, have conspired to preclude any such understanding.

"A Kind of Material Plenty"

Considering the poverty in which hunters and gatherers live in theory, it comes as a surprise that Bushmen who live in the Kalahari enjoy "a kind of material plenty," at least in the realm of everyday useful things, apart from food and water:

> As the /Kung come into more contact with Europeans—and this is already happening—they will feel sharply the lack of our things and will need and want more. It makes them feel inferior to be without clothes when they stand among strangers who are clothed. But in their own life and with their own artifacts *they were comparatively free from material pressures.* Except for food and water (important exceptions!) of which the Nyae Nyae / Kung have a sufficiency—but barely so, judging from the fact that all are thin though not emaciated—they all had what they needed or could make what they needed, for every man can and does make the things that men make and every woman the things that women make. . . . *They lived in a kind of material plenty* because they adapted the tools of their living to materials which lay in abundance around them and which were free for anyone to take (wood, reeds, bone for weapons and implements, fibers for cordage, grass for shelters), or to materials which were at least sufficient for the needs of the population. . . . The /Kung could always use more ostrich egg shells for beads to wear or trade with, but, as it is, enough are found for every woman to have a dozen or more shells for water containers—all she can carry— and a goodly number of bead ornaments. In their nomadic hunting-gathering life, travelling from one source of food to another through the seasons, always going back and forth between food and water, they carry their young children and their belongings. With plenty of most materials at hand to replace artifacts as required, the /Kung have not developed means of permanent storage and have not needed or wanted to encumber themselves with surpluses or duplicates. They do not even want to carry one of everything. They borrow what they do not own. With this ease, they have not hoarded, and the accumulation of objects has not become associated with status (Marshall, 1961, pp. 243–44, emphasis mine).

Analysis of hunter-gatherer production is usefully divided into two spheres, as Mrs. Marshall has done. Food and water are certainly "important exceptions," best reserved for separate and extended treatment. For the rest, the nonsubsistence sector, what is here said of the Bushmen applies in general and in detail to hunters from the Kalahari to Labrador — or to Tièrra del Fuego, where Gusinde reports of the Yahgan that their disinclination to own more than one copy of utensils frequently needed is "an indication of self-confidence." "Our Fuegians," he writes, "procure and make their implements with little effort" (1961, p. 213).

In the nonsubsistence sphere, the people's wants are generally easily satisfied. Such "material plenty" depends partly upon the ease of production, and that upon the simplicity of technology and democracy of property. Products are homespun: of stone, bone, wood, skin — materials such as "lay in abundance around them." As a rule, neither extraction of the raw material nor its working up take strenuous effort. Access to natural resources is typically direct — "free for anyone to take" — even as possession of the necessary tools is general and knowledge of the required skills common. The division of labor is likewise simple, predominantly a division of labor by sex. Add in the liberal customs of sharing, for which hunters are properly famous, and all the people can usually participate in the going prosperity, such as it is.

But, of course, "such as it is": this "prosperity" depends as well upon an objectively low standard of living. It is critical that the customary quota of consumables (as well as the number of consumers) be culturally set at a modest point. A few people are pleased to consider a few easily-made things their good fortune: some meagre pieces of clothing and rather fugitive housing in most climates; plus a few ornaments, spare flints and sundry other items such as the "pieces of quartz, which native doctors have extracted from their patients" (Grey, 1841, vol. 2, p. 266); and, finally, the skin bags in which the faithful wife carries all this, "the wealth of the Australian savage" (p. 266).

For most hunters, such affluence without abundance in the nonsubsistence sphere need not be long debated. A more interesting question is why they are content with so few possessions — for it is with them a policy, a "matter of principle" as Gusinde says (1961, p. 2), and not a misfortune.

Want not, lack not. But are hunters so undemanding of material goods because they are themselves enslaved by a food quest "demanding maximum energy from a maximum number of people," so that no time or effort remains for the provision of other comforts? Some ethnographers testify to the contrary that the food quest is so successful that half the time the people seem not to know what to do with themselves. On the other hand, *movement* is a condition of this success, more movement in some cases than others, but always enough to rapidly depreciate the satisfactions of property. Of the hunter it is truly said that his wealth is a burden. In his condition of life, goods can become "grievously oppressive" as Gusinde observes, and the more so the longer they are carried around. Certain food collecters do have canoes and a few have dog sleds, but most must carry themselves all the comforts they possess, and so only possess what they can comfortably carry themselves. Or perhaps only what the women can carry: the men are often left free to react to the sudden opportunity of the chase or the sudden necessity of defense.

A necessity so obvious to the casual visitor must be second nature to the people concerned. This modesty of material requirements is institutionalized: it becomes a positive cultural fact, expressed in a variety of economic arrangements. Lloyd Warner reports of the Murngin, for example, that portability is a decisive value in the local scheme of things. Small goods are in general better than big goods. In the final analysis "the relative ease of transportation of the article" will prevail, so far as determining its disposition, over its relative scarcity or labor cost. For the "ultimate value," Warner writes, "is freedom of movement." And to this "desire to be free from the burdens and responsibilities of objects which would interfere with the society's itinerant existence," Warner attributes the Murngin's "undeveloped sense of property," and their "lack of interest in developing their technological equipment" (1964, pp. 136–137).

The hunter, one is tempted to say, is "uneconomic man." At least as concerns nonsubsistence goods, he is the reverse of that standard caricature immortalized in any *General Principles of Economics,* page one. His wants are scarce and his means (in relation) plentiful. Consequently he is "comparatively free of material pressures," has "no sense of possession," shows "an undeveloped sense of property," is "completely indifferent to any material pressures," manifests a "lack of interest" in developing his technological equipment.

In this relation of hunters to worldly goods there is a neat and important point. From the internal perspective of the economy, it seems wrong to say that wants are "restricted," desires "restrained," or even that the notion of wealth is "limited." Such phrasings imply in advance an Economic Man and a struggle of the hunter against his own worse nature, which is finally then subdued by a cultural vow of poverty. The words imply the renunciation of an acquisitiveness that in reality was never developed, a suppression of desires that were never broached. Economic

Man is a bourgeois construction—as Marcel Mauss said, "not behind us, but before, like the moral man." It is not that hunters and gatherers have curbed their materialistic "impulses"; they simply never made an institution of them. "Moreover, if it is a great blessing to be free from a great evil, our [Montagnais] Savages are happy; for the two tyrants who provide hell and torture for many of our Europeans, do not reign in their great forests, — I mean ambition and avarice . . . as they are contented with a mere living, not one of them gives himself to the Devil to acquire wealth" (LeJeune, 1897, p. 231).

We are inclined to think of hunters and gatherers as *poor* because they don't have anything; perhaps better to think of them for that reason as *free*. "Their extremely limited material possessions relieve them of all cares with regard to daily necessities and permit them to enjoy life" (Gusinde, 1961, p. 1).

Hunting and gathering has all the strengths of its weaknesses. Periodic movement and restraint in wealth and population are at once imperatives of the economic practice and creative adaptations, the kinds of necessities of which virtues are made. Precisely in such a framework, affluence becomes possible. Mobility and moderation put hunters' ends within range of their technical means. An undeveloped mode of production is thus rendered highly effective. The hunter's life is not as difficult as it looks from the outside. In some ways the economy reflects dire ecology, but it is also a complete inversion.

Reports on hunters and gatherers of the ethnological present—specifically on those in marginal environments—suggest a mean of three to five hours per adult worker per day in food production. Hunters keep banker's hours, notably less than modern industrial workers (unionized), who would surely settle for a 21-35 hour week. An interesting comparison is also posed by recent studies of labor costs among agriculturalists of neolithic type. For example, the average adult Hanunoo, man or woman, spends 1,200 hours per year in swidden cultivation (Conklin, 1957, p. 151); which is to say, a mean of three hours twenty minutes per day. Yet this figure does not include food gathering, animal raising, cooking and other direct subsistence efforts of these Philippine tribesmen. Comparable data are beginning to appear in reports on other primitive agriculturalists from many parts of the world. The conclusion is put conservatively when put negatively: hunters and gatherers need not work longer getting food than do primitive cultivators. Extrapolating from ethnography to prehistory, one may say as much for the neolithic as John Stuart Mill said of all labor-saving devices, that never was one invented that saved anyone a minute's labor. The neolithic saw no particular improvement over the paleolithic in the amount of time required per capita for the production of subsistence; probably, with the advent of agriculture, people had to work harder.

There is nothing either to the convention that hunters and gatherers can enjoy little leisure from tasks of sheer survival. By this, the evolutionary inadequacies of the paleolithic are customarily explained, while for the provision of leisure the neolithic is roundly congratulated. But the traditional formulas might be truer if reversed: the amount of work (per capita) increases with the evolution of culture, and the amount of leisure decreases. Hunters' subsistence labors are characteristically intermittent, a day on and a day off, and modern hunters at least tend to employ their time off in such activities as daytime sleep. In the tropical habitats occupied by many of these existing hunters, plant collecting is more reliable than hunting itself. Therefore, the women, who do the collecting, work rather more regularly than the men, and provide the greater part of the food supply. Man's work is often done. On the other hand, it is likely to be highly erratic, unpredictably required; if men lack leisure, it is then in the Enlightenment sense rather than the literal. When Condorcet attributed the hunter's unprogressive condition to want of "the leisure in which he can indulge in thought and enrich his understanding with new combinations of ideas," he also recognized that the economy was a "necessary cycle of extreme activity and total idleness." Apparently what the hunter needed was the *assured* leisure of an aristocratic *philosophe.*

Hunters and gatherers maintain a sanguine view of their economic state despite the hardships they sometimes know. It may be that they sometimes know hardships because of the sanguine views they maintain of their economic state. Perhaps their confidence only encourages prodigality to the extent the camp falls casualty to the first untoward circumstance. In alleging this is an affluent economy, therefore, I do not deny that certain hunters have moments of difficulty. Some do find it "almost inconceivable" for a man to die of hunger, or even to fail to satisfy his hunger for more than a day or two (Woodburn, 1968, p. 52). But others, especially certain very peripheral hunters spread out in small groups across an environment of extremes, are exposed periodically to the kind of inclemency that interdicts travel or access to game. They suffer—although perhaps only fractionally, the shortage affecting particular immobilized families rather than the society as a whole (cf. Gusinde, 1961, pp. 306–307).

Still, granting this vulnerability, and allowing the most poorly situated modern hunters into comparison, it would be difficult to prove that privation is distinctly characteristic of the hunter-gatherers. Food shortage is not the indicative property of this mode of production as opposed to others; it does not mark off hunters and gatherers as a class or a general evolutionary stage. Lowie asks:

> But what of the herders on a simple plane whose maintenance is periodically jeopardized by plagues — who, like some Lapp bands of the nineteenth century were obliged to fall back on fishing? What of the primitive peasants who clear and till without compensation of the soil, exhaust one plot and pass on to the next, and are threatened with famine at every drought? Are they any more in control of misfortune caused by natural conditions than the hunter-gatherer? (1938, p. 286)

Above all, what about the world today? One-third to one-half of humanity are said to go to bed hungry every night. In the Old Stone Age the fraction must have been much smaller. *This* is the era of hunger unprecedented. Now, in the time of the greatest technical power, is starvation an institution. Reverse another venerable formula: the amount of hunger increases relatively and absolutely with the evolution of culture.

This paradox is my whole point. Hunters and gatherers have by force of circumstances an objectively low standard of living. But taken as their *objective,* and given their adequate means of production, all the people's material wants usually can be easily satisfied. The evolution of economy has known, then, two contradictory movements: enriching but at the same time impoverishing, appropriating in relation to nature but expropriating in relation to man. The progressive aspect is, of course, technological. It has been celebrated in many ways: as an increase in the amount of need-serving goods and services, an increase in the amount of energy harnessed to the service of culture, an increase in productivity, an increase in division of labor, and increased freedom from environmental control. Taken in a certain sense, the last is especially useful for understanding the earliest stages of technical advance. Agriculture not only raised society above the distribution of natural food resources, it allowed neolithic communities to maintain high degrees of social order where the requirements of human existence were absent from the natural order. Enough food could be harvested in some seasons to sustain the people while no food would grow at all; the consequent stability of social life was critical for its material enlargement. Culture went on then from triumph to triumph, in a kind of progressive contravention of the biological law of the minimum, until it proved it could support human life in outer space — where even gravity and oxygen were naturally lacking.

Other men were dying of hunger in the market places of Asia. It has been an evolution of structures as well as technologies, and in that respect like the mythical road where for every step the traveller advances his destination recedes by two. The structures have been political as well as economic, of power as well as property. They developed first within societies, increasingly now between societies. No doubt these structures have been functional, necessary organizations of the technical development, but within the communities they have thus helped to enrich they would discriminate in the distribution of wealth and differentiate in the style of life. The world's most primitive people have few possessions, *but they are not poor.* Poverty is not a certain small amount of goods, nor is it just a relation between means and ends; above all it is a relation between people. Poverty is a social status. As such it is the invention of civilization. It has grown with civilization, at once as an invidious distinction between classes and more importantly as a tributary relation — that can render agrarian peasants more susceptible to natural catastrophes than any winter camp of Alaskan Eskimo.

. . . Most hunters have no such concerns. Their existence is comparatively colorless, fixed singularly on eating with gusto and digesting at leisure. The cultural orientation is not Dionysian or Apollonian, but "gastric," as Julian Steward said of the Shoshoni. Then again it may be Dionysian, that is, Bacchanalian: "Eating among the Savages is like drinking among the drunkards of Europe. Those dry and ever-thirsty souls would willingly end their lives in a tub of malmsey, and the Savages in a pot full of meat; those over there talk only of drinking, and these here only of eating" (LeJeune, 1897, p. 249).

It is as if the superstructures of these societies had been eroded, leaving only the bare subsistence rock, and since production itself is readily accomplished, the people have plenty of time to perch there and talk about it. I must raise the possibility that the ethnography of hunters and gatherers is largely a record of incomplete cultures. Fragile cycles of ritual and exchange may have disappeared without trace, lost in the earliest stages of colonialism, when the intergroup relations they mediated were attacked and confounded. If so, the "original" affluent society will have to be rethought again for its originality, and the evolutionary schemes once more revised. Still this much history can always be rescued from existing hunters: the "economic problem" is easily solvable by paleolithic techniques. But then, it was not until culture neared the height of its material achievements that it erected a shrine to the Unattainable: *Infinite Needs.*

Introduction
Dorothy Lee, "The Joy of Work as Participation"

Dorothy Lee, like many modern professional women, combines a career as an anthropologist and writer with the role of wife and mother. In "The Joy of Work as Participation" she shares with us a personal insight into her own experience as career woman and mother that has allowed her better to reconcile the two worlds of her choosing. She was able to interpret her experience by drawing upon her knowledge of the Tikopia, a Melanesian society that, unlike modern Western cultures, stresses a communal context for work. Lee tells us that work can be joyful because it is a way in which we can experience ourselves as part of a community and thereby escape the loneliness and boredom of advanced industrial society.

Lee uses Tikopian society to challenge our assumptions that the separation of labor from other aspects of our lives is necessary and desirable. She does this, not by holding up an idyllic society where fruits and nuts are found on every tree, but by examining a society where hard work is necessary and yet where it is done without coercion and with genuine enjoyment. The Tikopians are a much-studied South Pacific island people who exemplify what we mean by working in a sociable manner. All that they do is done with, for, and through the group. The work is done and is done well, but, most importantly, the doing is communal, and work is not a distinct category of activity from social or cultural life.

Few modern people would prefer the kind of primitive life Lee describes in her article, but many would love to be part of a close community and experience working in a joyful manner. If Marshall Sahlins is correct, all humans once lived much like the Tikopians, who must come closer to representing what is natural for humankind than anything suggested by either John Locke or Adam Smith. The basic notion that Lee culls from her study of the Tikopians is that their work is social: through their work they transcend our ordinary boundaries of the individual. She claims that to work in this more satisfying way would require that we change our identities, that we alter our relations to other people, and that private property not be at the heart of our labor. This suggests fundamental changes in the undergirding of our economy, our social lives, and our identities, changes few of us would be inclined to risk. Still, the purpose in this section is to help us imagine the future. The risk we are asking you to take at this point is an intellectual risk. Try to use this new perspective to imagine what it would be like if most work was like knitting a Christmas gift rather than like working in a textile mill.

Dorothy Lee

The Joy of Work as Participation

It was in a domestic situation that I had that moment of discovery of which I want to write now. It was Christmas Eve; I was working late at night, listening to the desultory talk of my husband and my brother-in-law. I was exhausted after a day of housework, of coping with two small children, of Christmas preparations; but I had to finish making bedding for a doll crib, and I was working against time, wishing I were in bed.

I had been living a life of conflict since my marriage, since I had felt that I owed it to my profession to continue my work in anthropology. This meant that I had to organize my life so that my housewifely duties did not encroach unduly on my professional work; and I had to justify everything that I did as a housewife, as something imposed by the exigencies of my budget or by my role as wife and mother. In this way, I did not have to feel guilty toward my profession. The doll blanket I was making that night was amply justified; it would give happiness to my three-year-old daughter, and it had been necessary for me to take the time to make crib and bedding, for I could not afford to buy them.

As I sewed this Christmas Eve, I was suddenly astonished to discover that I had started to add an entirely unpremeditated and unnecessary edging of embroidery; and simultaneously, I was aware of a deep enjoyment in what I was doing. It was a feeling that had nothing to do with the pleasure the work would give to my daughter on the morrow; it had nothing to do with a sense of achievement, or of virtue in duty accomplished. And I knew that I had never liked to embroider. There was no justification for my work; yet it was the source of such a deep satisfaction, that the late hour and my fatigue had ceased to exist for me.

At this moment of discovery, I knew that I was experiencing what it meant to be a social being, not merely Dorothy Lee, an individual; I knew that I had truly become a mother, a wife, a neighbor, a teacher. I realized that some boundary had disappeared, so that I was working in a social medium; that I was not working for the future pleasure of a distant daughter, but rather within a relationship unaffected by tem-

From *The Hour of Insight: A Sequel to Moments of Personal Discovery,* edited by R.M. MacIver. Copyright 1954 by the Institute for Religious and Social Studies. Reprinted by permission of Harper Collins.

porality or physical absence. What gave meaning to my work was the medium in which I was working — the medium of love, in a broad sense. So far, my rationalization and justification of my work had obscured this meaning, had cut me off from my own social context. It suddenly became clear to me that it did not matter whether I was scrubbing the kitchen floor or darning stockings or zipping up snowsuits; these all had meaning, not in themselves, but in terms of the situation of which they were a part. They contained social value because they implemented the value of the social situation.

This was a tremendous discovery for me, illuminating in a flash my experience and my thinking. My mind went immediately to the Tikopia, about whom I had been reading, and I said to myself, "This is the way the Tikopia work." I had been puzzled about the motivating forces in the life of the Tikopia. These were people who were without organized leadership in work, yet who carried out large undertakings. And without any authority to impose legislation and mete out punishment, the business of the village was carried out, and law and order were maintained. Raymond Firth, the ethnographer, answering the unspoken questions of western readers, spoke of obligations, duty, fear of adverse opinion, as motivations. I did not like his choice of words, because he spoke of the obligation to perform unpleasant tasks, for example, and yet the situations he described brimmed with joy. Now I saw that the Tikopia did not need external incentives.

This was all very well, but when I came to examine my discovery, I could not explain it in any rational or acceptable way. My society did not structure working situations as occasions which contained their own satisfaction; and it assumed the existence of aggregates or collections of individuals, not of a social continuum. I had learned to believe in the existence of a distinct self, relating itself externally to work as a means to an end, with external incentives and external rewards. Yet it was obvious that if I got satisfaction from participating in a situation, there must be some medium, some continuum, within which this participation can take place. If my family and I were aspects of one whole, there must be some positive apprehension of a continuity which made me an aspect of my family, not a separate member; it was not enough to say that my physical being and my sensory experience did not in themselves prescribe the limits of the self.

And this is how I came to study the definition of the self among the Tikopia. It seemed to me that only on the basis of just such an assumption of continuity could their relations to man and nature and the divine, their words and phrasings and ceremonials be understood. I went back to Raymond Firth's books on the Tikopia, and read each detail with-

out placing it automatically against my own conception of the self. And
so I was able to see a conception of identity radically different from mine;
I found a social definition of the self. I found that here I could not speak
of man's relations with his universe, but rather of a universal interrelated-
ness, because man was not the focus from which relations flowed. I found
a named and recognized medium of social continuity, implemented in
social acts, not in words. And I found, for example, that an act of fon-
dling or an embrace was not phrased as a "demonstration" or an "expression" of affection — that is, starting from the ego and defined in terms
of the emotions of the ego, but rather as an act of moral support or of
comforting or of sharing, as a social act. I found a system of childrearing
which trained toward increasing interdependence and socialization, instead of toward personal self-reliance and individuation. And here I found
work whose motivation lay in the situation itself, a situation which included the worker and his society, the activity and its end, and whose
satisfaction lay in social value.

In Firth's presentation, the newborn Tikopia is not helped to recognize, discover, develop — or is it create? — his own separate identity; in fact,
he is not treated as if he had such a separate identity. In my own culture,
I had learned to speak of an infant as an "addition" to the family; and
my planning for the coming baby had been in terms of something added.
I found an additional room, additional furniture, and added implements;
I took out an additional insurance policy. But Firth spoke as if the child
were no such addition. He spoke of the "entrance" of the child into a
family circle, and everything he subsequently described conveyed the impression of a swelling of this circle, of an enhancement of social participation and social good.

From birth on, among the Tikopia, the infant is gradually and systematically introduced to a widening circle. At first, he is physically close
to his mother, held and suckled and comforted when awake, in immediate
tactile contact. Soon the female aunts and other older relatives share this
close care of, or involvement in, the infant. Then the father and the older
male relatives begin to nurse the child, seeking his companionship. More
and more distant relatives come, male and female; and the child is introduced to their society deliberately, so that his affection and dependence should be spread widely. At some point during this process, the
child is also introduced to the companionship of youths and maidens and
little children. The infant may be turned over to the care of a six-year-old
brother, who will be seen carrying him around, nuzzling and playing
with him, and otherwise showing his enjoyment of him. Adolescent boys

and girls, exchanging flirtatious talk in the shade, may choose to hold an infant in their arms.

This is not merely a recognition of the dependence of the infant. It is an expression of the interdependence within the social unit. Close and distant relatives leave their homes and their occupations to be with a little grandchild or niece or cousin several times removed; or to carry a young relative off for a visit, or down to the beach where the men sit together talking. It is not for lack of babysitters that babies are taken along by their parents when they go gardening. Firth speaks of how a man, called away from talk of men by his wife to stay with the baby, leaves the group with a sense of dignity, not of annoyance and interruption.

Many Tikopia parents go even further in widening the circle in which their children participate. They lend them out as "adhering" children to other households; then the children are parts of two family circles, sharing the intimate details of living with either, at their choice. Older children or adults may be invited to become adhering brothers or sisters or other relatives.

The structure of life within the family rests on the assumption that there is social continuity, and that this is good. In our own society, where we assume individual identity, we keep the physical entities strictly separate; only in sexual relations do we allow physical mingling. We do not like to breathe the breath of others, or feel the breath of others; and, evoking the sanction of sanitation, we even gave up for many years the most effective way of resuscitating the drowning, since it involved giving them our breath. We protect privacy with the sanction of health and sanitation; it is good to have a room of one's own and unhealthy to share it with five others. It used to be merely a question of enough fresh air; it has since been transformed into a question of mental health; whatever the sanction, it does ensure privacy.

———————

Work among the Tikopia is also socially conceived and structured; and if a man has to work alone, he will probably try to take a little child along. In our culture, the private office is a mark of status, an ideal; and a man has really arrived when he can even have a receptionist to guard him from any social intrusion without his private consent. Our kitchen planners, caught between ideals of privacy and efficiency on the one hand, and the new teachings of child specialists on the other, have not yet managed to introduce the child into the kitchen as anything much better than a necessary evil.

To the Tikopia, an American kitchen, with the mother mainly concerned with having everything within reach and no one under foot, would be an atrocity. When they prepare the meal, after they have returned from their gardening and other food-getting occupations, the whole Tikopia household works together. Nothing is within reach, and children fill this gap, fetching and carrying and running errands, forming a bridge between adult and adult. Father and mother, the unmarried aunt, the grandmother, the brother-in-law, all work together, firing the oven, scraping taro, grating coconut. One gets fiber for making a coconut strainer, another squeezes out the coconut cream, another is nursing the baby. While they wait for the food to bake, they carve cups out of coconut shell, or plait sinnet, or play. Jokes and anecdotes fly back and forth. No one apparently wants to be alone so as to concentrate or to work more efficiently.

The work situations which Raymond Firth presents always convey this joy and sheer satisfaction, at least to this reader. There seems to be no compulsion to work. When Firth speaks of "obligations," he probably does so to explain to his Western readers how it is that a man will work without external coercion of any sort. But we find the Tikopia often choosing these "obligations." For example, Firth tells how the husbands of women married out of a family group have the obligation to fire and tend the ovens when this family group performs a public celebration. He speaks too of the sons of widowed women, who are the guests of honor on such occasions, but who nevertheless choose to assume the role of their dead fathers and come instead as cooks; here is choice, not compulsion. People choose to make contributions to the donor during a great gift-giving occasion, even though they are to participate in the occasion as recipients, whether they have made a contribution or not. People manage to discover obscure avenues of relationship which will enable them to assume such "obligations"; this means that they will have to get and prepare and plait sinnet, or dig and scrape taro, or get pandannus and beat it into bark cloth; it also means a fuller participation and involvement in the social situation.

In our own culture, we do have what we call cooperative undertakings, and we urge parents to plan cooperative work for the family. But these are proposed ultimately for the benefit of the individual, so that the end is a collective end, not a common end. It would be a mistake to see the Tikopia situation as a cooperative one in this sense. Cooperation, like altruism, presupposes our own definition of a discrete self.

In the use they make of kinship terms, also, the Tikopia define the individual socially. Kinship terms, of course, always do define the individual on a social basis, and, to my knowledge, they are present in all societies. But not everywhere are they used as they are used among the Tikopia. Here the personal name is rarely used. Brothers and sisters call each other by kinship terms, and parents call their children "son" and "daughter" when they do not have to specify. In addressing or referring to older people, when specification is necessary, the name of the dwelling is used, such as "mother's brother from ————," not the personal name.

In the kind of terms which they choose to use, the Tikopia show the extent to which they view the individual as social. It seems to be a common practice, for example, to refer to, or address a relative, not in terms of his relation to oneself, but in terms of his relation to a common relative, thus widening the circle, and bringing in another relation by implication. A child, speaking to his mother's brother, will probably refer to his father as "your brother-in-law." A father may call out to his sons, "You brethren." A man may address his son-in-law as "You brother-in-law linked (that is, related as brother-in-law) to my son" thus evoking a fourth relative. A man may call his father-in-law *grandfather*-linked, thus introducing his own child into the term. And when non-kin speak of others who may be considered to be related to one another in however distant a manner, they often refer to them in terms of this mutual relationship, not in terms of who they are as individuals. For example, Firth tells of seeing two women going by, his asking who they were. The answer came: "They are father's-sister-linked" (they are a woman and her brother's daughter). Firth was asking for a definition of their identities; what he got was a completely social definition, and still did not know "who" they were. He adds that even when accepting the answer given he was left puzzled, because the relationship, when he finally worked it out, was so tenuous and obscure. Yet his informant chose this as the basis for his definition.

The individual is known also in terms of another definition. When he marries and is the head of a household, he and his wife are known by the name of their house plot. In fact, there is a continuity between *fenua* (land) and people which is evidenced in the use of the word. A man says, "My *fenua,* it is Tikopia," and he also says, "*Fenua* has made speech," and "*Fenua* is many" (many people are present). *Fenua* is also used to refer to the placenta.

This continuity with land-society has found expression, negatively and disastrously, in intense nostalgia during absence. Recruiting for plantation labor was prohibited in Tikopia when repeated experience showed that almost all the men died when away from home. On one occasion, the twenty men taken to Guadalcanal were absolved from all plantation work and allowed to fish all day by way of arousing in them an interest in life; but, in spite of this treatment, only one of the twenty survived to return to Tikopia. An attempt by the Melanesian Mission to send boys away to school in 1928 met with failure, and all three had to be sent back by the next boat.

The Tikopia are continuous with their dead society as well. Under the floor of their houses, or just outside beneath the eaves, dwell their dead relatives. The presence of the dead is taken for granted, and there is frequent communication with them. One long dead ancestor even became a Christian, as he happened to be inhabiting a living Tikopia at the time when this man was being baptized. A dead Tikopia who dwelt under the floor of Raymond Firth's house objected to the crowds who gathered when the ethnographer played the gramophone, and Firth had to give up this recreation. There may be merely a matter-of-fact awareness of the presence of the dead, or there may be specific contact in a dream, or through a medium.

The land "belongs" to the dead, and is under their care; so that their descendants walk carefully and in awareness on the land of their fathers. When a social offence is perpetrated, such as an incestuous marriage, it is the dead relatives who punish the living. At the beginning of a meal, some food is flung casually at the graves of the dead relatives; and, in fact, the relationship throughout has the casualness of an assured continuity. When the definite presence of a dead one is desired, a man will ask a medium to bring him for a visit. On one such occasion, Firth reports that the man who had issued the invitation had started on some occupation by the time his dead nephew arrived; so he simply asked the medium to offer the dead some betel nut and to tell him that his host was too busy to chew it with him.

The deities of the Tikopia are their early dead ancestors, so these also are eventually their relatives. They are addressed as grandparents, in terms implying a more relaxed relationship than the term for father or father's sister. They are treated with the same respect and concern accorded relatives. For example, Firth describes how an expert, repairing a canoe from which the three inhabiting deities had been removed lest they be disturbed by the disruption to their body, worked furiously against time and worried because the gods were being deprived of their body. It was a question of sympathy, not of currying favor. And with their gods, the Tikopia feel so comfortable that they play jokes on even the highest of them.

I have spoken of affection, sympathy, concern. The Tikopia have one word which covers these concepts and similar ones: *arofa*. Grief, gratitude, moral support, pride in, appreciation of another, all these are also included under this term. In fact, this is the term for social warmth, the social emotion, the continuity of which I have been speaking. *Arofa* and the acts of *arofa*, exist only among people who are socially continuous, kin and people who have shared living over a period of time. A man does not speak of feeling *arofa* for his sweetheart; in fact, the correct marriage is phrased as a violent and hostile abduction from the *arofa* group, separating an individual from it in the way a strand is removed from a cord.

Later, however, there is *arofa* between husband and wife. A man dividing his property, his clubs and spears, sinnet belts and ornaments, among his sons and grandsons, feels that he will now be "properly present" in his descendants; and such heirlooms are *tau-arofa* (bond-of-arofa).[1] Men and women wear *tau-arofa* of dead and living relatives: teeth, bored and suspended on a cord; hair made into a circlet, a waistcloth. Women in particular wear circlets made of the hair of sons or brothers or husbands or fathers. These are visible forms of *arofa*.

Arofa exists in the concrete act, as the Tikopia say; and such acts are many. Whenever an individual is in a position of strain or crisis, *arofa* is shown by his relatives through physical contact. If a small child wanders away from his father and is frightened or hurt, he runs back to be held in his father's arms. When he is older, this same physical contact gives him comfort and support under similar circumstances. When a boy or girl appears for the first time at the sacred dances of Marae, male relatives on the mother's side crowd around the novice, shielding the dancer from the eyes of the curious, holding up his arms, going with him through the motions of the dance. When a Tikopia is ill, the mother's brother will come and offer his back as a support to the sick one, or hold him in his arms. A more inclusive group of relatives, representing the complete social unit, assembles thickly at a time of birth, marriage, death.

———————

Society appears as the referent in other ways. The commonest curse, used casually and without offence, is a "social" one: "May your father eat filth." Even fathers use this to their children. Birth control and infanticide are carried on in the name of society, so that there should be enough for all. Gift exchanges are carried on in such a way that everyone in the unit participates in giving; gifts from a household are announced in the names of all, including those of the young children. If some giver's name is omitted by some oversight, some relative may whisper to have one of his gifts announced in the name of the slighted giver, so that this man, too, can have a share in the occasion.

With such a definition of the self within the medium of *arofa*, work can take place among the Tikopia without coercion, without the incentive or reward or the fear of punishment, without the spur of individual profit; because work as participation is meaningful.

———————

1. I have found no term in English which will convey the meaning of *tau*. Firth, faced with this predicament, uses the word "linked," which, I think, implies even more strongly a prior separation. Consanguine and affinal kin as well as certain forms of "property" are referred to with *tau*.

IIIB. Visions of Good Work in the Modern World

Work is a complex phenomenon. Every act of working takes place within an infinitely intricate web of beliefs, technologies, systems, relationships, skills, histories, and so on. Any serious attempt to alter and improve work must consider these many dimensions, but it must also set some priorities, if for no other reason than that we cannot do everything at once. Where do we begin? Humanists reflecting on the future of working typically start where humanists always begin — by looking at what they believe is fundamental to human experience. Most often this means trying to find the center from which people act, for without clarity on the nature of human motivation and action we will not be able to decide why we should work, what work to do, or how to do it. Discussion of this "center" comes under many rubrics — freedom, the self, human nature, the human condition, and motivation, for openers — but dialogue about crucial life-issues such as the why and how of work begin usually with explorations of whom we are.

The writers in this final part of *Working in America* do not agree in their assessments of who we are, nor would they all accept what Freud has to say about "civilization and its discontents" (the title of one of Freud's later works), but by beginning with Freud's perspective on work we can see a thread that weaves these pieces together. Freud believed that a natural and therefore inevitable tension exists between individual desires and the needs of civilization. Humans are pleasure-seekers who want to satisfy their basic desires for food and other material necessities, for security, for sexual satisfaction, and for aggression/destruction (his famous death wish: *thanatos*). These desires are not particularly compatible with a society's need for order and harmony and for material and cultural achievement: thus the inevitable tension. Freud believed that work is a primary locus where this conflict occurs and is resolved (*if* it is resolved . . . Freud was very pessimistic about this). As we have argued in contradistinction to this outlook, people want to meet their material and social needs, and they do so by working, by making products, and therein making themselves. Work, done properly, is a most crucial way in which societies can mesh individual needs and desires with the demands of civilization.

None of the writers in this subsection believe that people should not work or that society's demands for our labor are altogether unreasonable. Yet each of them, in his or her own way, would affirm the reality of worker discontent and the need for deep reform of what working too often means in late twentieth-century America. Freud believed that "civilizing" the destructive and antisocial tendencies of the individual requires strong and varied measures. While none of the reformers in this subsection would disagree with Freud's assessment that people need civilizing, none of them would agree that the scale tips toward individuals in the conflict between socially destructive tendencies in the individual and the order-creating forces of society. These writers would assert that society always has far more "firepower" on its side than does the individual and that conceiving of the situation in terms of embattlement overlooks the crucial point that society itself is the main force in shaping the self. Thus, if the selves in a society are socially destructive, society has no one to blame but itself. To do otherwise is a classic case of blaming the victim.

These thinkers would go beyond Freud's description of the basic conflict in two further ways. First, they would question the implicit assumptions that the push for order comes solely from outside the individual or that our society knows very well how to establish a truly humane order. They would argue that human individuals have what poet Wallace Stevens calls "a rage for order," and one need not look far to find multiple examples of social forms and institutions that spawn, rather than dissipate, the disorder which exists in any society.

The view of human nature which emerges from this discussion is crucial. Put somewhat crudely, most of the writers in this section would say that if people do not behave the way society wants them to, society needs to change the molds wherein people are made. If young people do not exit schools with the knowledge, skills, attitudes, and motivations society wants, then schools and homes need to change. To say that individual youths are to blame is more like cursing a defective machine than like holding a truly responsible person blameworthy for her actions. In the same vein, if workers become alienated, if they take advantage of the sick-leave system or vandalize the assembly line, or if they abuse themselves with drugs, attention should focus more on the nature of the work than on blaming the worker. People want and need to work, as evidenced by their willingness to take jobs which often are dangerous, harmful, or boring. Some American and many Japanese and European employers are beginning to understand the strength of this desire to work (thus affirming Freud's view), and they are seeing that they fare better if their workers are fulfilled rather than alienated. As a result these employers are bringing innovations such as "quality circles" and "flextime" to the shop floor. The message seems to be that conflicts between the interests of the individual and those of society need not to be a battle to the finish, with a winner and a loser. How to fashion work so that high-quality and low-cost products are made simultaneously with healthy and vibrant selves will require much thought, experimentation, and change. To this end the following selections are offered.

One way to deal with society's discontents is to remove (or at least reduce) that which causes the discontent. Bob Black, in an irreverent and iconoclastic essay, asks a simple, but radical, question: Why Work? If hunters and gatherers had to work very little to meet their real needs, surely with our immense wealth we could meet our own needs with plenty left over for research, high-powered education, and other pursuits, plus a lot of play, and all with little work. So why work? Many people do not like their jobs and, with a little liberation from the habits and mind-set of the work ethic, could find better ways to pass the hours.

Black does not believe, however, that people should simply sit around all day or only do "leisure activities." Leisure, he contends, is a pair with work—it is what we do when we are not working—and its main function is to help us recover from work so we can go back to work. He recommends *play*, but in the full-blown sense of creative, festive, convivial human activity which results in the most basic and important of human products—humans themselves. This definition does not preclude labor or material productivity. Rather, he opposes *forced* labor, work which is necessary and is controlled by someone else.

Many of the themes of this book come to a head in Black's essay. He asks us to take the question Why Work? very seriously, and he believes that for the first time in recent history, because of our great wealth and productive capacity, we can ask it. From this point on, he would say we should never again answer the question with the response of material necessity.

While he does not give us a blueprint for how to eliminate forced labor and to distribute our wealth so that everyone could play, Black sets the stage for thinking about the future of work. On the one hand, it has been a long time since Westerners took play seriously. He would agree with Huizinga or Schiller* that *only in play* can we attain our full humanity. On the other hand, Black challenges the necessity of humans ever again doing any work which is not chosen or enhancing of our humanity— what Frithjof Bergmann calls *good work*. Much of this subsection will focus on the issues of play and good work.

Albert Camus would agree with Black and Bergmann that changing the workplace is critical, but he would bring us back to another dimen-

---

*This is Friedrich Schiller's central idea in his *Letters on the Aesthetic Education of Mankind* and of Johan Huizinga's book *Homo Ludens*.

sion of Freud's analysis. While work can be better or worse, and it most certainly is a central location for our becoming human, we must not overlook the fact that living and working involve struggle. Using an ancient Greek myth about Sisyphus, the struggles of the most perfect human, Camus returns us to the Western tradition we discussed at the beginning of this book of seeing work as a curse. Unlike the Biblical tradition, though, Camus believes we have no god to fall back on, and therefore *we* must find whatever meaning there is in the process of living (working).

Sisyphus is condemned to spend eternity repeatedly rolling a rock up a hill, only to see it roll back down. For Camus this image captures the essential "absurdity" of life: no matter what we do, in any long-term or grand sense we are condemned to failure. What, then, are we to do? Camus recommends embracing life: digging in, with our eyes wide open, and pushing our "rocks" up the hill. Life, for Camus, is in the living, not in the end products: for him there are no ultimate rewards. We must do what we must do, but should we simply dig in to *any* work? Camus would answer yes . . . and no. Humans can dignify most any work. Think, for example, of Dolores Dante, the waitress whose testimony we heard at the beginnning of this book. Yet some working conditions deserve "resistance and rebellion" (these words are part of a title of one of Camus' books). Part of capturing whatever dignity we can in life is choosing how to work and what work to do.

Camus' Sisyphus embodies one version of Freud's "discontents," but he is not necessarily antisocial. His rock-moving could very well be a strongly community-building productivity, and Camus goes out of his way to tell us that this ideal man develops and expresses his magnificence in his life's work. E.F. Schumacher, drawing from a very different tradition, picks up this theme. From Buddhism Schumacher derives the view that the central goal of work is the enhancement of character. Schumacher quotes J.C. Kumarappa to explain the purpose of human labor:

> If the nature of work is properly appreciated and applied, it will stand in the same relation to the higher faculties as food is to the physical body. It nourishes and enlivens the higher man and urges him to produce the best he is capable of. It directs his free will along the proper course and disciplines the animal in him into progressive channels. It furnishes an excellent background for man to display his scale of values and develop his personality.

This is a summary of the famous Buddhist notion of "right livelihood," and Schumacher's essay spells out the implications of this important part of the "way" of Buddhism.

Schumacher, agreeing with Freud and the other writers in this subsection, says we should work to meet our material needs, but that is relatively easy to accomplish today, and our major focus should be on work which is "beyond toil." Economic activity should not be aimed primarily at the production of goods and services—that places truly human goals at the service of material goals. Rather, if we spend little time and effort producing things, we will have more time for the more important human work—the production of ourselves.

Schumacher shows that the general goals of Buddhist economics are much the same as those espoused by Bergmann or Black. His special contribution lies in his detailing the features of this alternative view of economics. While he agrees with Freud that humans tend to be ego-centered, he believes that if work is done with other people, this selfishness can be overcome. He further argues that we need to see work and leisure as parts of the same cloth: "work and leisure . . . cannot be separated without destroying the joy of work and the bliss of leisure." Most centrally, Schumacher argues that Buddhist economics stands mainstream economics on its head: "While the materialist is mainly interested in goods, the Buddhist is mainly interested in liberation," and the path to this liberation lies in "simplicity and non-violence." Schumacher would have us measure our standard of living by other than mere material means; in fact, simplicity implies that we should measure our success, not by how large is our total consumption, but by how small it is relative to meeting our needs. For Schumacher "small is beautiful" (the title of his famous book from which this essay is taken).

Henry Adams, in a famous chapter from his autobiography, shows that we must be very careful in choosing the proper images to guide our actions. Just as Freud might be wrong in his image that conflicts detract from our humanity (Hegel, Marx, and Bergmann argue, remember, that only *through* conflict do we become human), Adams believes that a major part of the socially destructive behavior Freud finds in modern humans may have to do with the images (stories) upon which our society is based. We have already referred to these images in several ways: atomic individualism in Locke's myth, "economic man" in Smith, and Social Darwinism in Carnegie. Adams not only gives us a contrast that shows the destructive nature of deep images in modernism, but he also gives us an alternative. Modern industrial societies are fashioned upon the image of the *dynamo;* most previous societies, and the society Adams recommends, are based on the *virgin.*

Like most powerful symbols, Adams' dynamo/virgin contrast is both simple and complex. The main thrust is simple enough: in the West (or now, across the globe) when we live by the dictates of modern scientific rationality as it is played out in industrialized societies, we live by the power of the dynamo, the *machine*. In most premodern societies, including a few which still exist today around the globe, the central image was the virgin, the creative energy of nature and of humans working through that nature. The virgin is the symbol of working with nature, of being powerful through harmony with nature. The dynamo, by contrast, has its own logic: it is invented to predict and control nature, and thus it often works against nature.

When a symbol resonates with people's experiences, it can be very powerful. The American flag and the bald eagle symbolize patriotism and love of country. To be so powerful the symbol must have elegant simplicity. But a powerful symbol is also a bottomless (fathomless) wellspring of inspiration and meaning. Various versions of the image of the dynamo and the virgin have spawned many reactions against the modernist tide. For example, many forms of contemporary feminism and of the environmental movement could be seen as visions of a world in which the virgin is the central image of how to live.

Some proponents of the movements to eliminate sexism, militarism, and environmental destruction have claimed that we must give up many of the material advances made through modern industrial life if we are to achieve worthy goals such as a healthy environment. Perhaps. But perhaps the truth lies elsewhere than in the dichotomy between the environment and our creature comforts: recently advocates of feminism, antimilitarism, and environmentalism have contended that a *sustainable* way of life requires living by the virgin rather than the dynamo: only if we treat workers (women and minorities as well as white men) and the environment well will our prosperity continue. To be out of harmony with social justice and the rhythms of nature (which is what the dynamo has come to mean) is a short-term solution which will bring long-term disaster.

Rosemary Radford Ruether is skeptical that we will very soon turn from the dynamo to the virgin. She contends that the systems we have created are so permeated with prejudice against "the virgin" that even though today we have a terrific opportunity to create economic equality and good work for women, we probably will continue to fail. Yet Ruether offers a vision that could provide hope. She believes that what ails us is nothing less than a fatal flaw deep within our most basic approach to the world. In a word, she finds that we have bifurcated the world into greater and lesser realms, casting nature, women, and everyday reality (including working-class people) into the lesser, and principles, men, and abstractions into the higher. We live in a dualistic world, and we will not find solutions to the many problems with work, sexism, racism, and environmental destruction until we adopt an alternative philosophy. Ruether, like many contemporary feminists, seeks a unified vision that simultaneously respects diversity without making invidious distinctions. This is a tall order in a world often organized around such distinctions, but the articulation of her viewpoint has helped many people advance one step closer to actualizing this vision.

Bergmann continues Ruether's iconoclasm by asserting that contemporary labor is rather odd: people continue to work very hard even though the relative value of their hard work diminishes in comparison with their actual needs and with the value of what they might do if they had more nonwork (or nonjob) time. Unlike many critics of bourgeois life, though, Bergmann does not conclude that people necessarily should quit working; rather, he sees that people get tremendous value from their work. Instead of recommending the end to work Bergmann argues for its improvement.

As we saw in his essay at the beginning of this book, Bergmann's story begins with the contention that the Industrial Revolution gave people a kind of promissory note: in giving up the relatively secure and stable lives of premodern societies to suffer the upheaval and dreadful labor necessary to start industrialism, people were promised unprecedented material abundance, an eventual diminishment of labor, and an overall enrichment of life. Despite some glaring deficiencies, modern market economies have delivered on the first two promises and in some ways on the third. Bergmann wonders, though, how much of human potential can be fulfilled given the nature of most people's work. He believes that we can greatly enrich ourselves and our communities if we take seriously the question of what work is for. His answer, as we have seen, is that work fundamentally is a place where human creation and creativity occur.

Bergmann's central goal, then, like that of most critics of modern societies, is similar to that of the liberal ideology he opposes: he envisions the flourishing of the human spirit. Because he has an alternative view of human nature, however, he has a different prescription for how to attain that goal. Calling on a long and rich tradition from Hegel through much of contemporary social science, Bergmann insists that the self is a social creation, thus squarely opposing the image of atomic individualism upon which the liberal story is based. For him our lives can as easily be enhanced as limited by social interactions and institutions because we are not humans without society. This is not to deny Freud's view of the inevitability of conflict, though. Bergmann agrees with Freud that life is replete with conflict; in fact, much of his image of human development comes from Hegel's famous master/slave model that says conflict is central to human growth and development. But from his perspective freedom is not a matter of *escaping* from society's influences or from the inevitable conflicts civilization brings; instead, to be free is a function of acting from one's identity, and that identity is socially formed. Thus, whether or not someone else's ("society's") action restricts or enhances my freedom (or my self) depends, not on my being uninfluenced (independent), but rather on my identification (socially formed) and on how *we* resolve the conflict.

The basic image which conditions and justifies liberal political economics comes from Locke's notion that the sphere of human rights and freedom is sacrosanct. If on the other hand the self and her rights are social creations, and furthermore if webs of relationships are fundamental to the self and its creation, then society has a right (and obligation) to condition an adult's economic activities in the same way as it does the character of a child. In the realm of work one of the central tenets of contemporary economics is that "no man (or woman) is an island," that the economic system is a complex ocean of currents in which we are but small eddies of activity. If that is true, then the issue is what kinds of eddies we (society) want and how to create them. Bergmann therefore has radicalized our capacity to question: with liberalism questions are limited to what kinds of encroachment (if any) can we make on human rights; with Bergmann we can inquire more deeply about the ideal society by thinking about what kinds of people we want to encourage (perhaps create is a better word).

Introduction
Bob Black, "The Abolition of Work"

Bob Black is an outsider. For years he has been decorating telephone poles, walls, and other locations of direct communication in Boston with his essays, posters, and pamphlets on topics ranging from politics to sex to work to hypocrisy and back to politics again. An advocate of an anarchist group called "The Last International," Black specializes in iconoclasm and laughter, with the intent of protesting and changing features of the modern world he finds objectionable. Black currently resides in Boston, and he writes for publications such as *Village Voice, CoEvolution Quarterly,* and a variety of small publications such as *To Apeiron, Troubled Times,* and *L.A. Reader.*

While sometimes outsiders are mere misfits who have little to offer except diatribe, they are also sometimes prophets. We believe Black fits into the latter category, but whether or not you agree, we think you will find him both interesting and stimulating. Black is not a scholar, but he does understand very well the poverty of spirit that afflicts modern workers. He understands its sources, and he suggests a solution. Like all serious critics of work, he understands that work is the hub of modern life. Consequently, like the best texts in this book, Black writes about the fundaments of human life when he writes about work.

While the title "Why Work?" and his iconoclastic persona may suggest a person who is out of touch with reality, Black does understand that work must get done. What he is against is, not work per se, but work that is *forced*. He understands that the necessity of work is used as a club by many to maintain dominance and social distinctions. Work is not just about getting things done; it is about who has power and prestige and who is victimized. Black's radicalism consists in his desire to reorganize the work system, or perhaps we should say unorganize the work system, to free workers from the tyranny of this dominance. As he points out, machines can do the majority of work, and, as we have seen in looking at other cultures, much work can be turned into non-enforced play.

While the lack of details in Black's plan leave many questions, particularly questions about how wealth gets distributed, we think you will find this essay suggestive. As you read, be critical. Raise questions that you think Black does not answer, but also be imaginative. Try to think of ways to use his ideas to begin reshaping our work future.

Bob Black

The Abolition of Work

No one should ever work.

Work is the source of nearly all the misery in the world. Almost any evil you'd care to name comes from working or from living in a world designed for work. In order to stop suffering, we have to stop working.

That doesn't mean we have to stop doing things. It does mean creating a new way of life based on play; in other words, a *ludic* revolution. By "play" I mean also festivity, creativity, conviviality, commensality, and maybe even art. There is more to play than child's play, as worthy as

Reprinted from *The Abolition of Work and Other Essays* by Bob Black. Published by Loompanics, Unltd.

that is. I call for a collective adventure in generalized joy and freely interdependent exuberance. Play isn't passive. Doubtless we all need a lot more time for sheer sloth and slack than we ever enjoy now, regardless of income or occupation, but once recovered from employment-induced exhaustion nearly all of us want to act. Oblomovism and Stakhanovism are two sides of the same debased coin.

The ludic life is totally incompatible with existing reality. So much the worse for "reality," the gravity hole that sucks the vitality from the little in life that still distinguishes it from mere survival. Curiously—or maybe not—all the old ideologies are conservative because they believe in work. Some of them, like Marxism and most brands of anarchism, believe in work all the more fiercely because they believe in so little else.

Liberals say we should end employment discrimination. I say we should end employment. Conservatives support right-to-work laws. Following Karl Marx's wayward son-in-law Paul Lafargue I support the right to be lazy. Leftists favor full employment. Like the surrealists—except that I'm not kidding—I favor full *un*employment. Trotskyists agitate for permanent revolution. I agitate for permanent revelry. But if all the ideologues (as they do) advocate work—and not only because they plan to make other people do theirs—they are strangely reluctant to say so. They will carry on endlessly about wages, hours, working conditions, exploitation, productivity, profitability. They'll gladly talk about anything but work itself. These experts who offer to do our thinking for us rarely share their conclusions about work, for all its saliency in the lives of all of us. Among themselves they quibble over the details. Unions and management agree that we ought to sell the time of our lives in exchange for survival, although they haggle over the price. Marxists think we should be bossed by bureaucrats. Libertarians think we should be bossed by businessmen. Feminists don't care which form bossing takes so long as the bosses are women. Clearly these ideology-mongers have serious differences over how to divvy up the spoils of power. Just as clearly, none of them have any objection to power as such and all of them want to keep us working.

You may be wondering if I'm joking or serious. I'm joking *and* serious. To be ludic is not to be ludicrous. Play doesn't have to be frivolous, although frivolity isn't triviality: very often we ought to take frivolity seriously. I'd like life to be a game—but a game with high stakes. I want to play *for keeps*.

The alternative to work isn't just idleness. To be ludic is not to be quaaludic. As much as I treasure the pleasure of torpor, it's never more rewarding than when it punctuates other pleasures and pastimes. Nor am I promoting the managed time-disciplined safety-valve called "leisure"; far from it. Leisure is nonwork for the sake of work. Leisure is the time spent recovering from work and in the frenzied but hopeless attempt to forget about work. Many people return from vacation so beat that they look forward to returning to work so they can rest up. The main difference between work and leisure is that at work at least you get paid for your alienation and enervation.

I am not playing definitional games with anybody. When I say I want to abolish work, I mean just what I say, but I want to say what I mean by defining my terms in non-idiosyncratic ways. My minimum definition of work is *forced labor,* that is, compulsory production. Both elements are essential. Work is production enforced by economic or political means, by the carrot or the stick. (The carrot is just the stick by other means.) But not all creation is work. Work is never done for its own sake, it's done on account of some product or output that the worker (or, more often, somebody else) gets out of it. This is what work necessarily is. To define it is to despise it. But work is usually even worse than its definition decrees. The dynamic of domination intrinsic to work tends over time toward elaboration. In advanced work-riddled societies, including all industrial societies whether capitalist or "Communist," work invariably acquires other attributes which accentuate its obnoxiousness.

Usually—and this is even more true in "Communist" than capitalist countries, where the state is almost the only employer and everyone is an employee—work is employment, *i.e.,* wage-labor, which means selling yourself on the installment plan. Thus 95% of Americans who work, work for somebody (or some*thing*) else. In the USSR or Cuba or Yugoslavia or any other alternative model which might be adduced, the corresponding figure approaches 100%. Only the embattled Third World peasant bastions—Mexico, India, Brazil, Turkey—temporarily shelter significant concentrations of agriculturists who perpetuate the traditional arrangement of most laborers in the last several millennia, the payment of taxes (= ransom) to the state or rent to parasitic landlords in return for being otherwise left alone. Even this raw deal is beginning to look good. *All* industrial (and office) workers are employees and under the sort of surveillance which ensures servility.

But modern work has worse implications. People don't just work, they have "jobs." One person does one productive task all the time on an or-else basis. Even if the task has a quantum of intrinsic interest (as increasingly many jobs don't) the monotony of its obligatory exclusivity drains its ludic potential. A "job" that might engage the energies of some people, for a reasonably limited time, for the fun of it, is just a burden on those who have to do it for forty hours a week with no say in how it should be done, for the profit of owners who contribute nothing to the project, and with no opportunity for sharing tasks or spreading the work among those who actually have to do it. This is the real world of work: a world of bureaucratic blundering, of sexual harassment and discrimination, of bonehead bosses exploiting and scapegoating their subordinates who—by any rational-technical criteria—should be calling the shots. But capitalism in the real world subordinates the rational maximization of productivity and profit to the exigencies of organizational control.

The degradation which most workers experience on the job is the sum of assorted indignities which can be denominated as "discipline." Foucault has complexified this phenomenon but it is simple enough. Discipline consists of the totality of totalitarian controls at the workplace —surveillance, rotework, imposed work tempos, production quotas, punching in- and out-, etc. Discipline is what the factory and the office and the store share with the prison and the school and the mental hospital. It is something historically original and horrible. It was beyond the capacities of such demonic dictators of yore as Nero and Genghis Khan and Ivan the Terrible. For all their bad intentions they just didn't have the machinery to control their subjects as thoroughly as modern despots do. Discipline is the distinctively diabolical modern mode of control, it is an innovative intrusion which must be interdicted at the earliest opportunity.

Such is "work." Play is just the opposite. Play is always voluntary. What might otherwise be play is work if it's forced. This is axiomatic. Bernie de Koven has defined play as the "suspension of consequences." This is unacceptable if it implies that play is inconsequential. The point is not that play is without consequences. This is to demean play. The point is that the consequences, if any, are gratuitous. Playing and giving are closely related, they are the behavioral and transactional facets of the same impulse, the play-instinct. They share an aristocratic disdain for results. The player gets something out of playing; that's why he plays. But the core reward is the experience of the activity itself (whatever it is). Some otherwise attentive students of play, like Johan Huizinga (*Homo Ludens*), define it as game-playing or following rules. I respect Huizinga's erudition but emphatically reject his constraints. There are many good games (chess, baseball, Monopoly, bridge) which are rule-governed but there is much more to play than game-playing. Conversation, sex, dancing, travel—these practices aren't rule-governed but they are surely play if anything is. And rules can be *played with* at least as readily as anything else.

Work makes a mockery of freedom. The official line is that we all have rights and live in a democracy. Other unfortunates who aren't free like we are have to live in police states. These victims obey orders or-else,

no matter how arbitrary. The authorities keep them under regular surveillance. State bureaucrats control even the smaller details of everyday
life. The officials who push them around are answerable only to higher-
ups, public or private. Either way, dissent and disobedience are punished.
Informers report regularly to the authorities. All this is supposed to be
a very bad thing.

And so it is, although it is nothing but a description of the modern
workplace. The liberals and conservatives and libertarians who lament
totalitarianism are phonies and hypocrites. There is more freedom in
any moderately de-Stalinized dictatorship than there is in the ordinary
American workplace. You find the same sort of hierarchy and discipline
in an office or factory as you do in a prison or monastery. In fact, as
Foucault and others have shown, prisons and factories came in at about
the same time, and their operators consciously borrowed from each other's
control techniques. A worker is a part-time slave. The boss says when
to show up, when to leave and what to do in the meantime. He tells you
how much work to do and how fast. He is free to carry his control to
humiliating extremes, regulating, if he feels like it, the clothes you wear
or how often you go the bathroom. With a few exceptions he can fire
you for any reason, or no reason. He has you spied on by snitches and
supervisors, he amasses a dossier on every employee. Talking back is called
"insubordination," just as if a worker is a naughty child, and it not only
gets you fired, it disqualifies you for unemployment compensation. Without necessarily endorsing it for them either, it is noteworthy that children at home and in school receive much the same treatment, justified
in their case by their supposed immaturity. What does this say about
their parents and teachers who work?

The demeaning system of domination I've described rules over half
the waking hours of a majority of women and the vast majority of men
for decades, for most of their lifespans. For certain purposes it's not too
misleading to call our system democracy or capitalism or — better still —
industrialism, but its real names are factory fascism and office oligarchy.
Anybody who says these people are "free" is lying or stupid. You are what
you do. If you do boring, stupid monotonous work, chances are you'll
end up boring, stupid and monotonous. Work is a much better explanation for the creeping cretinization all around us than even such significant moronizing mechanisms as television and education. People who
are regimented all their lives, handed off to work from school and bracketed
by the family in the beginning and the nursing home at the end, are
habituated to hierarchy and psychologically enslaved. Their aptitude for
autonomy is so atrophied that their fear of freedom is among their few
rationally grounded phobias. Their obedience training at work carries

over into the families *they* start, thus reproducing the system in more ways than one, and into politics, culture and everything else. Once you drain the vitality from people at work, they'll likely submit to hierarchy and expertise in everything. They're used to it.

We are so close to the world of work that we can't see what it does to us. We have to rely on outside observers from other times or other cultures to appreciate the extremity and the pathology of our present position. There was a time in our own past when the "work ethic" would have been incomprehensible, and perhaps Weber was on to something when he tied its appearance to a religion, Calvinism, which if it emerged today instead of four centuries ago would immediately and appropriately be labeled a cult. Be that as it may, we have only to draw upon the wisdom of antiquity to put work in perspective. The ancients saw work for what it is, and their view prevailed, the Calvinist cranks notwithstanding, until overthrown by industrialism — but not before receiving the endorsement of its prophets.

What I've said so far ought not to be controversial. Many workers are fed up with work. There are high and rising rates of absenteeism, turnover, employee theft and sabotage, wildcat strikes, and overall goldbricking on the job. There may be some movement toward a conscious and not just visceral rejection of work. And yet the prevalent feeling, universal among bosses and their agents and also widespread among workers themselves is that work itself is inevitable and necessary.

I disagree. It is now possible to abolish work and replace it, insofar as it serves useful purposes, with a multitude of new kinds of free activities. To abolish work requires going at it from two directions, quantitative and qualitative. On the one hand, on the quantitative side, we have to cut down massively on the amount of work being done. At present most work is useless or worse and we should simply get rid of it. On the other hand — and I think this is the crux of the matter and the revolutionary new departure — we have to take what useful work remains and transform it into a pleasing variety of game-like and craft-like pastimes, indistinguishable from other pleasurable pastimes, except that they happen to yield useful end-products. Surely that shouldn't make them *less* enticing to do. Then all the artificial barriers of power and property could come down. Creation could become recreation. And we could all stop being afraid of each other.

I don't suggest that most work is salvageable in this way. But then most work isn't worth trying to save. Only a small and diminishing fraction of work serves any useful purpose independent of the defense and reproduction of the work-system and its political and legal appendages. Twenty years ago, Paul and Percival Goodman estimated that just five percent of the work then being done — presumably the figure, if accurate, is lower now — would satisfy our minimal needs for food, clothing, and shelter. Theirs was only an educated guess but the main point is quite clear: directly or indirectly, most work serves the unproductive purposes of commerce or social control. Right off the bat we can liberate tens of millions of salesmen, soldiers, managers, cops, stockbrokers, clergymen, bankers, lawyers, teachers, landlords, security guards, ad-men and everyone who works for them. There is a snowball effect since every time you idle some bigshot you liberate his flunkeys and underlings also. Thus the economy *implodes.*

Forty percent of the workforce are white-collar workers, most of whom have some of the most tedious and idiotic jobs ever concocted. Entire industries, insurance and banking and real estate for instance, consist of nothing but useless paper-shuffling. It is no accident that the "tertiary sector," the service sector, is growing while the "secondary sector" (industry) stagnates and the "primary sector" (agriculture) nearly disappears. Because work is unnecessary except to those whose power it secures, workers are shifted from relatively useful to relatively useless occupations as a measure to assure public order. Anything is better than nothing. That's why you can't go home just because you finish early. They want your *time,* enough of it to make you theirs, even if they have no use for most of it. Otherwise why hasn't the average work week gone down by more than a few minutes in the last fifty years?

Next we can take a meat-cleaver to production work itself. No more war production, nuclear power, junk food, feminine hygiene deodorant — and above all, no more auto industry to speak of. An occasional Stanley Steamer or Model-T might be all right, but the auto-eroticism on which such pestholes as Detroit and Los Angeles depend is out of the question. Already, without even trying, we've virtually solved the energy crisis, the environmental crisis and assorted other insoluble social problems.

Finally, we must do away with far and away the largest occupation, the one with the longest hours, the lowest pay and some of the most tedious tasks around. I refer to *housewives* doing housework and child-rearing. By abolishing wage-labor and achieving full unemployment we undermine the sexual division of labor. The nuclear family as we know it is an inevitable adaptation to the division of labor imposed by modern wage-work. Like it or not, as things have been for the last century or two it is economically rational for the man to bring home the bacon, for the woman to do the shitwork to provide him with a haven in a heartless world, and for the children to be marched off to youth concentration camps called "schools," primarily to keep them out of Mom's hair but still under control, but incidentally to acquire the habits of obedience and punctuality so necessary for workers. If you would be rid of patriarchy, get rid of the nuclear family whose unpaid "shadow work," as Ivan Illich says, makes possible the work-system that makes *it* necessary. Bound up with this no-nukes strategy is the abolition of childhood and the closing of the schools. There are more full-time students than full-time workers in this country. We need children as teachers, not students. They have a lot to contribute to the ludic revolution because they're better at playing than grown-ups are. Adults and children are not identical but they will become equal through interdependence. Only play can bridge the generation gap.

What I really want to see is work turned into play. A first step is to discard the notions of a "job" and an "occupation." Even activities that already have some ludic content lose most of it by being reduced to jobs which certain people, and only those people are forced to do to the exclusion of all else. Is it not odd that farm workers toil painfully in the fields while their air-conditioned masters go home every weekend and putter about in their gardens? Under a system of permanent revelry, we will witness the Golden Age of the dilettante which will put the Renaissance to shame. There won't be any more jobs, just things to do and people to do them.

The secret of turning work into play, as Charles Fourier demonstrated, is to arrange useful activities to take advantage of whatever it is that various people at various times in fact enjoy doing. To make it possible for some people to do the things they could enjoy it will be enough just to eradicate the irrationalities and distortions which afflict these activities when they are reduced to work. I, for instance, would enjoy doing some (not too much) teaching, but I don't want coerced students and I don't care to suck up to pathetic pedants for tenure.

Second, there are some things that people like to do from time to time, but not for too long, and certainly not all the time. You might enjoy babysitting for a few hours in order to share the company of kids, but not as much as their parents do. The parents meanwhile, profoundly appreciate the time to themselves that you free up for them, although they'd get fretful if parted from their progeny for too long. These differences among individuals are what make a life of free play possible. The same principle applies to many other areas of activity, especially the primal ones. Thus many people enjoy cooking when they can practice it seriously at their leisure, but not when they're just fuelling up human bodies for work.

Third—other things being equal—some things that are unsatisfying if done by yourself or in unpleasant surroundings or at the orders of an overlord are enjoyable, at least for awhile, if these circumstances are changed. This is probably true, to some extent, of all work. People deploy their otherwise wasted ingenuity to make a game of the least inviting drudge-jobs as best they can. Activities that appeal to some people don't always appeal to all others, but everyone at least potentially has a variety of interests and an interest in variety. As the saying goes, "anything once." Fourier was the master at speculating how aberrant and perverse penchants could be put to use in post-civilized society, what he called Harmony. He thought the Emperor Nero would have turned out all right if as a child he could have indulged his taste for bloodshed by working in a slaughterhouse. Small children who notoriously relish wallowing in filth could be organized in "Little Hordes" to clean toilets and empty the garbage, with medals awarded to the outstanding. I am not arguing for these precise examples but for the underlying principle, which I think makes perfect sense as one dimension of an overall revolutionary transformation. Bear in mind that we don't have to take today's work just as we find it and match it up with the proper people, some of whom would have to be perverse indeed. If technology has a role in all this it is less to automate work out of existence than to open up new realms for re/creation. To some extent we may want to return to handicrafts, which William Morris considered a probable and desirable upshot of communist revolution. Art would be taken back from the snobs and collectors, abolished as a specialized department catering to an elite audience, and its qualities of beauty and creation restored to integral life from which they were stolen by work. It's a sobering thought that the Grecian urns we write odes about and showcase in museums were used in their own time to store olive oil. I doubt our everyday artifacts will fare as well in the future, if there is one. The point is that there's no such thing as progress in the world of work; if anything it's just the opposite. We shouldn't hesitate to pilfer the past for what it has to offer, the ancients lose nothing yet we are enriched.

The reinvention of daily life means marching off the edge of our maps. There is, it is true, more suggestive speculation than most people suspect. Besides Fourier and Morris—and even a hint, here and there, in Marx—there are the writings of Kropotkin, the syndicalists Pataud and Pouget, anarcho-communists old (Berkman) and new (Bookchin). The Goodman brothers' *Communitas* is exemplary for illustrating what forms follow from given functions (purposes), and there is something to be gleaned from the often hazy heralds of alternative/appropriate/intermediate/convivial technology, like Schumacher and especially Illich, once you disconnect their fog machines. The situationists—as represented by Vaneigem's *Revolution of Everyday Life* and in the *Situationist International Anthology*—are so ruthlessly lucid as to be exhilarating, even if they never did quite square the endorsement of the rule of the workers' councils with the abolition of work. Better their incongruity, though, than any extant version of leftism, whose devotees look to be the last champions of work, for if there were no work there would be no workers, and without workers, who would the left have to organize?

So the abolitionists would be largely on their own. No one can say what would result from unleashing the creative power stultified by work. Anything can happen. The tiresome debater's problem of freedom vs. necessity, with its theological overtones, resolves itself practically once the production of use-values is coextensive with the consumption of delightful play-activity.

Life will become a game, or rather many games, but not—as it is now—a zero/sum game. An optimal sexual encounter is the paradigm of productive play. The participants potentiate each other's pleasures, nobody keeps score, and everybody wins. The more you give, the more you get. In the ludic life, the best of sex will diffuse into the better part of daily life. Generalized play leads to the libidinization of life. Sex, in turn, can become less urgent and desperate, more playful. If we play our cards right, we can all get more out of life than we put into it; but only if we play for keeps.

No one should ever work. Workers of the world . . . *relax!*

Introduction
Albert Camus, "The Myth of Sisyphus"

Albert Camus was a French writer and philosopher famous for existentialist novels such as *The Stranger* and *The Plague*. Born in Algiers of a Spanish mother and a French father (who died in World War I), Camus during World War II participated in the French resistance, editing the resistance newspaper *Combat*. He died in an auto crash in the south of France in 1955, shortly after winning the Nobel prize for literature.

Camus came from that tough-minded branch of existential philosophy that was openly atheistic. In the "Myth of Sisyphus" Camus sets out to convince us that while life is both tragic and absurd, it is still our responsibility to live it. Because God is dead and we are alone in the universe, it is up to us to assume responsibility for our own lives and our own values.

Camus used Sisyphus to provide the central metaphor for the human condition. Sisyphus has been condemned by the gods to the worst of all fates: meaningless labor. If Camus is correct, we are like Sisyphus in that we are condemned to live in a mortal body and to work within a world with no intrinsic meaning.

While this is what Camus calls an absurd situation, he does not believe it is a hopeless situation. Instead he chooses to have hope. As Camus sees it, the nonexistence of God and the consequent lack of purpose in the design of the universe can be seen as an opportunity. For him this means that humans are free. Rather than live according to the rules of a god, we are free to shape our own meanings and purposes in life.

We are, of course, also like Sisyphus in being limited by nature, including our own mortal bodies, but like Sisyphus we are not limited in what we make of our existence. We have the freedom to choose values and to live according to them. The question is, can we overcome traditions that have denied the beauty of this world in exchange for a hoped-for eternal and otherworldly existence, and through our choices make this world a fit place for humanity for the brief time we are here? Can we achieve the adulthood of the human race and live a life without illusions? The critical issue is responsible use of our freedom. Can we accept our freedom? Can we use it to remake our world, including our work world, in such a way as to live the fullest human life in the time we have?

Albert Camus

The Myth of Sisyphus

The gods had condemned Sisyphus to ceaselessly rolling a rock to the top of a mountain, whence the stone would fall back of its own weight. They had thought with some reason that there is no more dreadful punishment than futile and hopeless labor.

If one believes Homer, Sisyphus was the wisest and most prudent of mortals. According to another tradition, however, he was disposed to practice the profession of highwayman. I see no contradiction in this. Opinions differ as to the reasons why he became the futile laborer of the underworld. To begin with, he is accused of a certain levity in regard to the gods. He stole their secrets. Ægina, the daughter of Æsopus, was carried off by Jupiter. The father was shocked by that disappearance and complained to Sisyphus. He, who knew of the abduction, offered to tell about it on condition that Æsopus would give water to the citadel of Corinth. To the celestial thunderbolts he preferred the benediction of water. He was punished for this in the underworld. Homer tells us also that Sisyphus had put Death in chains. Pluto could not endure the sight of his deserted, silent empire. He dispatched the god of war, who liberated Death from the hands of her conqueror.

It is said also that Sisyphus, being near to death, rashly wanted to test his wife's love. He ordered her to cast his unburied body into the middle of the public square. Sisyphus woke up in the underworld. And there, annoyed by an obedience so contrary to human love, he obtained from Pluto permission to return to earth in order to chastise his wife. But when he had seen again the face of this world, enjoyed water and sun, warm stones and the sea, he no longer wanted to go back to the infernal darkness. Recalls, signs of anger, warnings were of no avail. Many years more he lived facing the curve of the gulf, the sparkling sea, and the smiles of earth. A decree of the gods was necessary. Mercury came and seized the impudent man by the collar and, snatching him from his joys, led him forcibly back to the underworld, where his rock was ready for him.

You have already grasped that Sisyphus is the absurd hero. He *is*, as much through his passions as through his torture. His scorn of the gods, his hatred of death, and his passion for life won him that unspeakable penalty in which the whole being is exerted toward accomplishing nothing. This is the price that must be paid for the passions of this earth. Nothing is told us about Sisyphus in the underworld. Myths are made for the imagination to breathe life into them. As for this myth, one sees merely the whole effort of a body straining to raise the huge stone, to roll it and push it up a slope a hundred times over; one sees the face screwed up, the cheek tight against the stone, the shoulder bracing the clay-covered mass, the foot wedging it, the fresh start with arms outstretched, the wholly human security of two earth-clotted hands. At the very end of his long effort measured by skyless space and time without depth, the purpose is achieved. Then Sisyphus watches the stone rush down in a few moments toward that lower world whence he will have to push it up again toward the summit. He goes back down to the plain.

It is during that return, that pause, that Sisyphus interests me. A face that toils so close to stones is already stone itself! I see that man going back down with a heavy yet measured step toward the torment of which he will never know the end. That hour like a breathing-space which returns as surely as his suffering, that is the hour of consciousness. At each of those moments when he leaves the heights and gradually sinks toward the lairs of the gods, he is superior to his fate. He is stronger than his rock.

If this myth is tragic, that is because its hero is conscious. Where would his torture be, indeed, if at every step the hope of succeeding upheld him? The workman of today works every day in his life at the same tasks, and this fate is no less absurd. But it is tragic only at the rare moments when it becomes conscious. Sisyphus, proletarian of the gods, powerless and rebellious, knows the whole extent of his wretched condition: it is what he thinks of during his descent. The lucidity that was to constitute his torture at the same time crowns his victory. There is no fate that cannot be surmounted by scorn.

*   *   *

If the descent is thus sometimes performed in sorrow, it can also take place in joy. This word is not too much. Again I fancy Sisyphus returning toward his rock, and the sorrow was in the beginning. When the images of earth cling too tightly to memory, when the call of happiness becomes too insistent, it happens that melancholy rises in man's heart: this is the rock's victory, this is the rock itself. The boundless grief is too heavy to bear. These are our nights of Gethsemane. But crushing truths perish from being acknowledged. Thus, Œdipus at the outset obeys fate without knowing it. But from the moment he knows, his tragedy begins. Yet at the same moment, blind and desperate, he realizes that the only bond linking him to the world is the cool hand of a girl. Then a tremendous remark rings out: "Despite so many ordeals, my advanced age and the nobility of my soul make me conclude that all is well." Sophocles' Œdipus, like Dostoevsky's Kirilov, thus gives the recipe for the absurd victory. Ancient wisdom confirms modern heroism.

One does not discover the absurd without being tempted to write a manual of happiness. "What! by such narrow ways —?" There is but one world, however. Happiness and the absurd are two sons of the same earth. They are inseparable. It would be a mistake to say that happiness necessarily springs from the absurd discovery. It happens as well that the feeling of the absurd springs from happiness. "I conclude that all is well," says Œdipus, and that remark is sacred. It echoes in the wild and limited universe of man. It teaches that all is not, has not been, exhausted. It drives out of this world a god who had come into it with dissatisfaction and a preference for futile sufferings. It makes of fate a human matter, which must be settled among men.

All Sisyphus' silent joy is contained therein. His fate belongs to him. His rock is his thing. Likewise, the absurd man, when he contemplates his torment, silences all the idols. In the universe suddenly restored to its silence, the myriad wondering little voices of the earth rise up. Unconscious, secret calls, invitations from all the faces, they are the necessary reverse and price of victory. There is no sun without shadow, and it is essential to know the night. The absurd man says yes and his effort will henceforth be unceasing. If there is a personal fate, there is no higher destiny, or at least there is but one which he concludes is inevitable and despicable. For the rest, he knows himself to be the master of his days. At that subtle moment when man glances backward over his life, Sisyphus returning toward his rock, in that slight pivoting he contemplates that series of unrelated actions which becomes his fate, created by him, combined under his memory's eye and soon sealed by his death. Thus, convinced of the wholly human origin of all that is human, a blind man eager to see who knows that the night has no end, he is still on the go. The rock is still rolling.

I leave Sisyphus at the foot of the mountain! One always finds one's burden again. But Sisyphus teaches the higher fidelity that negates the gods and raises rocks. He too concludes that all is well. This universe henceforth without a master seems to him neither sterile nor futile. Each atom of that stone, each mineral flake of that night-filled mountain, in itself forms a world. The struggle itself toward the heights is enough to fill a man's heart. One must imagine Sisyphus happy.

Introduction
E.F. Schumacher, "Buddhist Economics"

E.F. Schumacher was born in Bonn, Germany, in 1911, became a British citizen, and was educated at Oxford and Columbia universities. He became famous as a counterculture hero during the 1970s with the publication of *Small Is Beautiful,* the best-selling book from which we have excerpted "Buddhist Economics." Although trained as an economist, Schumacher rejected much of classical economic thinking and became an advocate of limited growth and appropriate technology.

In the following excerpt he imagines what it means to be a Buddhist economist and by so doing helps us look critically at traditional Western economic assumptions and practices. This perspective, like Sahlins' essay on stone-age economics, makes us examine the seldom-questioned foundations upon which modern work is built. As Schumacher insists, economics is based upon certain value assumptions, values that he believes are flawed in at least two ways. First is the belief that the earth's resources are unlimited. He is writing during the 1970s, at a time when we first confront the finitude of the earth, and he is appalled by the waste inherent in the theory of progress.

Second, Schumacher believes, as we have insisted throughout this book, that work is about more than creating goods and services. While Buddhists are not antimaterialists, they are more concerned with people than with material goods. Therefore, Schumacher believes that good work should do three things: 1) allow us to develop our faculties, 2) allow us to overcome our ego centeredness, and 3) "bring forth the goods and services needed for a becoming existence."

Notice that the values upon which Schumacher bases Buddhist economics are more subtle than many of our traditional beliefs. Both traditional and Buddhist economists want what is best, but by comparison traditional economists make the crude assumption that more is always better. A "becoming" life takes more into account than the volume of consumption. Schumacher wants us to work in a manner that will allow us to live in harmony with our environment rather than ravage it, and he believes it will be better for us as humans in the long run if we do.

As we face the prospects of ever-increasing energy costs and the dangers of international confrontations over control of scarce resources, we should look carefully at this voice from the 1970s. He is one of the few economists offering alternatives to the seemingly inevitable conflict built into our present practices. It may be that he offers the only viable choice for human civilization if it is to survive and flourish.

E.F. Schumacher

Buddhist Economics

"Right Livelihood" is one of the requirements of the Buddha's Noble Eightfold Path. It is clear, therefore, that there must be such a thing as Buddhist economics.

Buddhist countries have often stated that they wish to remain faithful to their heritage. So Burma: "The New Burma sees no conflict between religious values and economic progress. Spiritual health and material well-being are not enemies: they are natural allies." Or: "We can blend successfully the religious and spiritual values of our heritage with the benefits of modern technology." Or: "We Burmans have a sacred duty to conform both our dreams and our acts to our faith. This we shall ever do."

All the same, such countries invariably assume that they can model their economic development plans in accordance with modern economics, and they call upon modern economists from so-called advanced countries to advise them, to formulate the policies to be pursued, and to construct the grand design for development, the Five-Year Plan or whatever it may be called. No one seems to think that a Buddhist way of life would call for Buddhist economics, just as the modern materialist way of life has brought forth modern economics.

Economists themselves, like most specialists, normally suffer from a kind of metaphysical blindness, assuming that theirs is a science of absolute and invariable truths, without any presuppositions. Some go as far as to claim that economic laws are as free from "metaphysics" or "values" as the law of gravitation. We need not, however, get involved in arguments of methodology. Instead, let us take some fundamentals and see what they look like when viewed by a modern economist and a Buddhist economist.

There is universal agreement that a fundamental source of wealth is human labour. Now, the modern economist has been brought up to consider "labour" or work as little more than a necessary evil. From the point of view of the employer, it is in any case simply an item of cost, to be reduced to a minimum if it cannot be eliminated altogether, say, by automation. From the point of view of the workman, it is a "disutility"; to work is to make a sacrifice of one's leisure and comfort, and wages are a kind of compensation for the sacrifice. Hence the ideal from the point of view of the employer is to have output without employees, and the ideal from the point of view of the employee is to have income without employment.

The consequences of these attitudes both in theory and in practice are, of course, extremely far-reaching. If the ideal with regard to work is to get rid of it, every method that "reduces the work load" is a good thing. The most potent method, short of automation, is the so-called "division of labour" and the classical example is the pin factory eulogised in Adam Smith's *Wealth of Nations*. Here it is not a matter of ordinary specialisation, which mankind has practised from time immemorial, but of dividing up every complete process of production into minute parts, so that the final product can be produced at great speed without anyone having had to contribute more than a totally insignificant and, in most cases, unskilled movement of his limbs.

The Buddhist point of view takes the function of work to be at least threefold: to give a man a chance of utilise and develop his faculties; to enable him to overcome his ego-centredness by joining with other people in a common task; and to bring forth the goods and services needed for a becoming existence. Again, the consequences that flow from this view are endless. To organise work in such a manner that it becomes meaningless, boring, stultifying, or nerve-racking for the worker would be little short of criminal; it would indicate a greater concern with goods than with people, an evil lack of compassion and a soul-destroying degree of attachment to the most primitive side of this worldly existence. Equally, to strive for leisure as an alternative to work would be considered a complete misunderstanding of one of the basic truths of human existence, namely that work and leisure are complementary parts of the same living process and cannot be separated without destroying the joy of work and the bliss of leisure.

From the Buddhist point of view, there are therefore two types of mechanisation which must be clearly distinguished: one that enhances a man's skill and power and one that turns the work of man over to a mechanical slave, leaving man in a position of having to serve the slave. How to tell the one from the other? "The craftsman himself," says Ananda Coomaraswamy, a man equally competent to talk about the modern West as the ancient East, "can always, if allowed to, draw the delicate distinction between the machine and the tool. The carpet loom is a tool, a contrivance for holding warp threads at a stretch for the pile to be woven round them by the craftsmen's fingers; but the power loom is a machine, and its significance as a destroyer of culture lies in the fact that it does the essentially human part of the work." It is clear, therefore, that Buddhist economics must be very different from the economics of modern materialism, since the Buddhist sees the essence of civilisation not in a multiplication of wants but in the purification of human character. Character, at the same time, is formed primarily by a man's work. And work, properly conducted in conditions of human dignity and freedom, blesses those who do it and equally their products. The Indian philosopher and economist J. C. Kumarappa sums the matter us as follows:

> If the nature of the work is properly appreciated and applied, it will stand in the same relation to the higher faculties as food is to the physical body. It nourishes and enlivens the higher man and urges him to produce the best he is capable of. It directs his free will along the proper course and disciplines the animal in him into progressive channels. It furnishes an excellent background for man to display his scale of values and develop his personality.

If a man has no chance of obtaining work he is in a desperate position, not simply because he lacks an income but because he lacks this nourishing and enlivening factor of disciplined work which nothing can replace. A modern economist may engage in highly sophisticated calculations on whether full employment "pays" or whether it might be more "economic" to run an economy at less than full employment so as to ensure a greater mobility of labour, a better stability of wages, and so forth. His fundamental criterion of success is simply the total quantity of goods produced during a given period of time. "If the marginal urgency of goods is low," says Professor Galbraith in *The Affluent Society*, "then so is the urgency of employing the last man or the last million men in the labour force." And again: "If . . . we can afford some unemployment in the interest of stability—a proposition, incidentally, of impeccably conservative antecedents—then we can afford to give those who are unemployed the goods that enable them to sustain their accustomed standard of living."

From a Buddhist point of view, this is standing the truth on its head by considering goods as more important than people and consumption as more important than creative activity. It means shifting the emphasis from the worker to the product of work, that is, from the human to the subhuman, a surrender to the forces of evil. The very start of Buddhist economic planning would be a planning for full employment, and the primary purpose of this would in fact be employment for everyone who needs an "outside" job: it would not be the maximisation of employment nor the maximisation of production. Women, on the whole, do not need an "outside" job, and the large-scale employment of women in offices or factories would be considered a sign of serious economic failure. In particular, to let mothers of young children work in factories while the children run wild would be as uneconomic in the eyes of a Buddhist economist as the employment of a skilled worker as a soldier in the eyes of a modern economist.

While the materialist is mainly interested in goods, the Buddhist is mainly interested in liberation. But Buddhism is "The Middle Way" and therefore in no way antagonistic to physical well-being. It is not wealth that stands in the way of liberation but the attachment to wealth; not the enjoyment of pleasurable things but the craving for them. The keynote of Buddhist economics, therefore, is simplicity and non-violence. From an economist's point of view, the marvel of the Buddhist way of life is the utter rationality of its pattern — amazingly small means leading to extraordinarily satisfactory results.

For the modern economist this is very difficult to understand. He is used to measuring the "standard of living" by the amount of annual consumption, assuming all the time that a man who consumes more is "better off" than a man who consumes less. A Buddhist economist would consider this approach excessively irrational: since consumption is merely a means to human well-being, the aim should be to obtain the maximum of well-being with the minimum of consumption. Thus, if the purpose of clothing is a certain amount of temperature comfort and an attractive appearance, the task is to attain this purpose with the smallest possible effort, that is, with the smallest annual destruction of cloth and with the help of designs that involve the smallest possible input of toil. The less toil there is, the more time and strength is left for artistic creativity. It would be highly uneconomic, for instance, to go in for complicated tailoring, like the modern West, when a much more beautiful effect can be achieved by the skilful draping of uncut material. It would be the height of folly to make material so that it should wear out quickly and the height of barbarity to make anything ugly, shabby or mean. What has just been said about clothing applies equally to all other human requirements. The ownership and the consumption of goods is a means to an end, and Buddhist economics is the systematic study of how to attain given ends with the minimum means.

Modern economics, on the other hand, considers consumption to be the sole end and purpose of all economic activity, taking the factors of production — land, labour, and capital — as the means. The former, in short, tries to maximise human satisfactions by the optimal pattern of consumption, while the latter tries to maximise consumption by the optimal pattern of productive effort. It is easy to see that the effort needed to sustain a way of life which seeks to attain the optimal pattern of consumption is likely to be much smaller than the effort needed to sustain a drive for maximum consumption. We need not be surprised, therefore, that the pressure and strain of living is very much less in, say, Burma than it is in the United States, in spite of the fact that the amount of labour-saving machinery used in the former country is only a minute fraction of the amount used in the latter.

Simplicity and non-violence are obviously closely related. The optimal pattern of consumption, producing a high degree of human satisfaction by means of a relatively low rate of consumption, allows people to live without great pressure and strain and to fulfil the primary injunction of Buddhist teaching: "Cease to do evil; try to do good." As physical resources are everywhere limited, people satisfying their needs by means of a modest use of resources are obviously less likely to be at each other's throats than people depending upon a high rate of use. Equally, people who live in highly self-sufficient local communities are less likely to get involved in large-scale violence than people whose existence depends on world-wide systems of trade.

From the point of view of Buddhist economics, therefore, production from local resources for local needs is the most rational way of economic life, while dependence on imports from afar and the consequent need to produce for export to unknown and distant peoples is highly uneconomic and justifiable only in exceptional cases and on a small scale. Just as the modern economist would admit that a high rate of consumption of transport services between a man's home and his place of work signifies a misfortune and not a high standard of life, so the Buddhist economist would hold that to satisfy human wants from faraway sources rather than from sources nearby signifies failure rather than success. The former tends to take statistics showing an increase in the number of ton/miles per head of the population carried by a country's transport system as proof of economic progress, while to the latter — the Buddhist economist — the same statistics would indicate a highly undesirable deterioration in the *pattern* of consumption.

Another striking difference between modern economics and Buddhist economics arises over the use of natural resources. Bertrand de Jouvenel, the eminent French political philosopher, has characterised "Western man" in words which may be taken as a fair description of the modern economist:

> He tends to count nothing as an expenditure, other than human effort; he does not seem to mind how much mineral matter he wastes and, far worse, how much living matter he destroys. He does not seem to realise at all that human life is a dependent part of an ecosystem of

many different forms of life. As the world is ruled from towns where
men are cut off from any form of life other than human, the feeling
of belonging to an ecosystem is not revived. This results in a harsh
and improvident treatment of things upon which we ultimately depend, such as water and trees.

The teaching of the Buddha, on the other hand, enjoins a reverent
and non-violent attitude not only to all sentient beings but also, with
great emphasis, to trees. Every follower of the Buddha ought to plant
a tree every few years and look after it until it is safely established, and
the Buddhist economist can demonstrate without difficulty that the universal observation of this rule would result in a high rate of genuine economic development independent of any foreign aid. Much of the economic decay of southeast Asia (as of many other parts of the world) is
undoubtedly due to a heedless and shameful neglect of trees.

Modern economics does not distinguish between renewable and non-
renewable materials, as its very method is to equalise and quantify everything by means of a money price. Thus, taking various alternative fuels,
like coal, oil, wood, or water-power: the only difference between them
recognised by modern economics is relative cost per equivalent unit. The
cheapest is automatically the one to be preferred, as to do otherwise
would be irrational and "uneconomic." From a Buddhist point of view, of
course, this will not do; the essential difference between non-renewable
fuels like coal and oil on the one hand and renewable fuels like wood and
water-power on the other cannot be simply overlooked. Non-renewable
goods must be used only if they are indispensable, and then only with
the greatest care and the most meticulous concern for conservation. To
use them heedlessly or extravagantly is an act of violence, and while complete non-violence may not be attainable on this earth, there is nonetheless an ineluctable duty on man to aim at the ideal of non-violence in
all he does.

Just as a modern European economist would not consider it a great
economic achievement if all European art treasures were sold to America at attractive prices, so the Buddhist economist would insist that a
population basing its economic life on non-renewable fuels is living para-
sitically, on capital instead of income. Such a way of life could have no
permanence and could therefore be justified only as a purely temporary
expedient. As the world's resources of non-renewable fuels — coal, oil and
natural gas — are exceedingly unevenly distributed over the globe and undoubtedly limited in quantity, it is clear that their exploitation at an ever-
increasing rate is an act of violence against nature which must almost
inevitably lead to violence between men.

This fact alone might give food for thought even to those people in Buddhist countries who care nothing for the religious and spiritual values of their heritage and ardently desire to embrace the materialism of modern economics at the fastest possible speed. Before they dismiss Buddhist economics as nothing better than a nostalgic dream, they might wish to consider whether the path of economic development outlined by modern economics is likely to lead them to places where they really want to be. Towards the end of his courageous book *The Challenge of Man's Future*, Professor Harrison Brown of the California Institute of Technology gives the following appraisal:

> Thus we see that, just as industrial society is fundamentally unstable and subject to reversion to agrarian existence, so within it the conditions which offer individual freedom are unstable in their ability to avoid the conditions which impose rigid organisation and totalitarian control. Indeed, when we examine all of the foreseeable difficulties which threaten the survival of industrial civilisation, it is difficult to see how the achievement of stability and the maintenance of individual liberty can be made compatible.

Even if this were dismissed as a long-term view there is the immediate question of whether "modernisation," as currently practised without regard to religious and spiritual values, is actually producing agreeable results. As far as the masses are concerned, the results appear to be disastrous — a collapse of the rural economy, a rising tide of unemployment in town and country, and the growth of a city proletariat without nourishment for either body or soul.

It is in the light of both immediate experience and long-term prospects that the study of Buddhist economics could be recommended even to those who believe that economic growth is more important than any spiritual or religious values. For it is not a question of choosing between "modern growth" and "traditional stagnation." It is a question of finding the right path of development, the Middle Way between materialist heedlessness and traditionalist immobility, in short, of finding "Right Livelihood."

Introduction
Henry Adams, "The Dynamo and the Virgin"

Henry Adams came from a long line or remarkable Americans. His great-grandfather John was the country's second president, his grandfather John Quincy was its sixth president, and his father Charles Francis was a distinguished political leader and diplomat. Adams himself became a leading historical scholar and made his contributions to America and the world through his writings. First published in 1907, his autobiographical *The Education of Henry Adams* was a virtual "who's who" of his times. But it was more than that. In the process of telling his own story Adams was also a visionary who anticipated what the future might bring for his culture. As a prophet, he was, as social analyst Daniel Bell observed, the first American writer who "caught a sense of the quickening change of pace that drives all our lives." As a historian of his own time he was also, as historian Richard Hofstadter noted, "singular not only for the quality of his prose and the sophistication of his mind, but also for the unparalleled mixture of his detachment and involvement." Adams, like many sages, was fascinated with the past, concerned about the present, and skeptical about the future.

In this excerpt from his biography, "The Dynamo and the Virgin," Adams gives us a powerful set of symbols for thinking about the changes taking place during the nineteenth century. He argues that ours is no longer a culture based upon the energy of the "virgin," the basic nurturing life-force of organisms and systems of nature. Instead, modern humans live by the forces of the machine, the "dynamo" that has an "unnatural" energy.

As you reflect on Adams' essay, ask yourself what these symbols mean and what their implications are for the way we work, for the way men and women relate to one another, and for the way we all relate to our environment. How is virginal power different from dynamo power? How are virginal societies different from dynamo societies? How is my own life different because I live in a dynamo society rather than a virginal society?

These are large and important questions being asked by many people today, such as feminists trying to find the basis for a nonsexist society, environmentalists looking for a way of living more harmoniously with nature, and those who are seeking a way of working that puts humans back at the center of the productive process. Our future may depend upon our ability to merge the best of these two worlds so as to tame the machine and subordinate it to truly human purposes.

Henry Adams

The Dynamo and the Virgin

Until the Great Exposition of 1900[1] closed its doors in November, Adams haunted it, aching to absorb knowledge, and helpless to find it. He would have liked to know how much of it could have been grasped by the best-informed man in the world. While he was thus meditating chaos, Langley[2] came by, and showed it to him. At Langley's behest, the Exhibition dropped its superfluous rags and stripped itself to the skin, for Langley knew what to study, and why, and how; while Adams might as well have stood outside in the night, staring at the Milky Way. Yet Langley said nothing new, and taught nothing that one might not have learned from Lord Bacon,[3] three hundred years before; but though one should have known the "Advancement of Science" as well as one knew the "Comedy of Errors,"[4] the literary knowledge counted for nothing until some teacher should show how to apply it. Bacon took a vast deal of trouble in teaching King James I[5] and his subjects, American or other, towards the year 1620, that true science was the development or economy of forces; yet an elderly American in 1900 knew neither the formula nor the forces; or even so much as to say to himself that his historical business in the Exposition concerned only the economies or developments of force since 1893, when he began the study of Chicago.[6]

Nothing in education is so astonishing as the amount of ignorance it accumulates in the form of inert facts. Adams had looked at most of the accumulations of art in the storehouses called Art Museums; yet he

"The Dynamo and the Virgin" from *The Education of Henry Adams* by Henry Adams. Copyright 1918 by the Massachusetts Historical Society. Copyright 1946 by Charles F. Adams. Reprinted by permission of Houghton Mifflin Company.

1. The World's Fair held in Paris from April through November.
2. Samuel P. Langley (1834–1906), American astronomer and inventor, in 1896, of the first airplane to fly successfully.
3. Sir Francis Bacon (1561–1626), English natural philosopher, author of *The Advancement of Learning* (1605).
4. Early Shakespearean comedy (1594).
5. King of England 1603–25.
6. The subject of Chapter XXII of the *Education*. The Chicago Exposition of 1893 first stimulated Adams's interest in the "economy of forces."

did not know how to look at the art exhibits of 1900. He had studied Karl Marx[7] and his doctrines of history with profound attention, yet he could not apply them at Paris. Langley, with the ease of a great master of experiment, threw out of the field every exhibit that did not reveal a new application of force, and naturally threw out, to begin with, almost the whole art exhibit. Equally, he ignored almost the whole industrial exhibit. He led his pupil directly to the forces. His chief interest was in new motors to make his airship feasible, and he taught Adams the astonishing complexities of the new Daimler[8] motor, and of the automobile, which, since 1893, had become a nightmare at a hundred kilometres an hour, almost as destructive as the electric tram which was only ten years older; and threatening to become as terrible as the locomotive steam-engine itself, which was almost exactly Adams's own age.

Then he showed his scholar the great hall of dynamos, and explained how little he knew about electricity or force of any kind, even of his own special sun, which spouted heat in inconceivable volume, but which, as far as he knew, might spout less or more, at any time, for all the certainty he felt in it. To him, the dynamo itself was but an ingenious channel for conveying somewhere the heat latent in a few tons of poor coal hidden in a dirty engine-house carefully kept out of sight; but to Adams the dynamo became a symbol of infinity. As he grew accustomed to the great gallery of machines, he began to feel the forty-foot dynamos as a moral force, much as the early Christians felt the Cross. The planet itself seemed less impressive, in its old-fashioned, deliberate, annual or daily revolution, than this huge wheel, revolving within arm's-length at some vertiginous speed, and barely murmuring—scarcely humming an audible warning to stand a hair's breadth further for respect of power—while it would not wake the baby lying close against it frame. Before the end, one began to pray to it; inherited instinct taught the natural expression of man before silent and infinite force. Among the thousand symbols of ultimate energy, the dynamo was not so human as some, but it was the most expressive.

Yet the dynamo, next to the steam-engine, was the most familiar of exhibits. For Adams's objects its value lay chiefly in its occult mechanism. Between the dynamo in the gallery of machines and the engine-house outside, the break of continuity amounted to abysmal fracture for a historian's objects. No more relation could he discover between the steam

---

7. Karl Marx (1818–83), German social philosopher, architect of modern socialism and communism; formulated his theories on the principle of "dialectical materialism."

8. Gottlieb Daimler (1834–1900), German engineer, inventor of the high-speed internal combustion engine and an early developer of the automobile.

and the electric current than between the Cross and the cathedral. The forces were interchangeable if not reversible, but he could see only an absolute *fiat* in electrictiy as in faith. Langley could not help him. Indeed, Langley seemed to be worried by the same trouble, for he constantly repeated that the new forces were anarchical, and especially that he was not responsible for the new rays, that were little short of parricidal in their wicked spirit towards science. His own rays,[9] with which he had doubled the solar spectrum, were altogether harmless and beneficent; but Radium denied its God[10] — or, what was to Langley the same thing, denied the truths of his Science. The force was wholly new.

A historian who asked only to learn enough to be as futile as Langley or Kelvin,[11] made rapid progress under this teaching, and mixed himself up in the tangle of ideas until he achieved a sort of Paradise of ignorance vastly consoling to his fatigued senses. He wrapped himself in vibrations and rays which were new, and he would have hugged Marconi[12] and Branly had he met them, as he hugged the dynamo; while he lost his arithmetic in trying to figure out the equation between the discoveries and the economies of force. The economies, like the discoveries, were absolute, supersensual, occult; incapable of expression in horse-power. What mathematical equivalent could he suggest as the value of a Branly coherer? Frozen air, or the electric furnace, had some scale of measurement, no doubt, if somebody could invent a thermometer adequate to the purpose; but X-rays[13] had played no part whatever in man's consciousness, and the atom itself had figured only as a fiction of thought. In these seven years man had translated himself into a new universe which had no common scale of measurement with the old. He had entered a supersensual world, in which he could measure nothing except by chance collisions of movements imperceptible to his senses, perhaps even imperceptible to his instruments, but perceptible to each other, and so to some known ray at the end of the scale. Langley seemed prepared for anything, even for an indeterminable number of universes interfused — physics stark mad in metaphysics.

---

9. Langley had invented the bolometer, with which he was able to measure intensities of invisible heat rays in the infrared spectrum.

10. Since radium, first isolated by the Curies in 1898, underwent spontaneous transformation through radioactive emission, it did not fit prevailing scientific distinctions between matter and energy.

11. William Thomson, Baron Kelvin (1824–1907), English mathematician and physicist known especially for his work in thermodynamics and electrodynamics.

12. Guglielmo Marconi (1874–1937), Italian inventor of radio telegraphy in 1895; Édouard Branly (1844–1940), French physicist and inventor in 1890 of the Branly "coherer" for detecting radio waves.

13. Wilhelm Roentgen (1845–1923) discovered X-rays in 1895.

Historians undertake to arrange sequences, — called stories, or histories — assuming in silence a relation of cause and effect. These assumptions, hidden in the depths of dusty libraries, have been astounding, but commonly unconscious and childlike; so much so, that if any captious critic were to drag them to light, historians would probably reply, with one voice, that they had never supposed themselves required to know what they were talking about. Adams, for one, had toiled in vain to find out what he meant. He had even published a dozen volumes of American history for no other purpose than to satisfy himself whether, by the severest process of stating, with the least possible comment, such facts as seemed sure, in such order as seemed rigorously consequent, he could fix for a familiar moment a necessary sequence of human movement. The result had satisfied him as little as at Harvard College. Where he saw sequence, other men saw something quite different, and no one saw the same unit of measure. He cared little about his experiments and less about his statesmen, who seemed to him quite as ignorant as himself and, as a rule, no more honest; but he insisted on a relation of sequence, and if he could not reach it by one method, he would try as many methods as science knew. Satisfied that the sequence of men led to nothing and that the sequence of their society could lead no further, while the mere sequence of time was artificial, and the sequence of thought was chaos, he turned at last to the sequence of force; and thus it happened that, after ten years' pursuit, he found himself lying in the Gallery of Machines at the Great Exposition of 1900, with his historical neck broken by the sudden irruption of forces totally new.

Since no one else showed much concern, an elderly person without other cares had no need to betray alarm. The year 1900 was not the first to upset schoolmasters. Copernicus and Galileo had broken many professorial necks about 1600;[14] Columbus had stood the world on its head towards 1500; but the nearest approach to the revolution of 1900 was that of 310, when Constantine set up the Cross.[15] The rays that Langley disowned, as well as those which he fathered, were occult, supersensual, irrational; they were a revelation of mysterious energy like that of the Cross; they were what, in terms of mediaeval science, were called immediate modes of the divine substance.

---

14. Copernicus (1473–1543), Polish astronomer, proved that the earth rotated around the sun and not vice versa; Galileo (1564–1642), Italian astronomer and developer of the refracting telescope, was condemned by the Inquisition for espousing Copernican heliocentric theory.

15. Constantine the Great (288?–337), Roman Emperor, issued the Edict of Milan in 313 proclaiming toleration of Christians, which paved the way for the ascendancy of Christianity.

The historian was thus reduced to his last resources. Clearly if he was bound to reduce all these forces to a common value, this common value could have no measure but that of their attraction on his own mind. He must treat them as they had been felt; as convertible, reversible, interchangeable attractions on thought. He made up his mind to venture it; he would risk translating rays into faith. Such a reversible process would vastly amuse a chemist, but the chemist could not deny that he, or some of his fellow physicists, could feel the force of both. When Adams was a boy in Boston, the best chemist in the place had probably never heard of Venus except by way of scandal, or of the Virgin except as idolatry;[16] neither had he heard of dynamos or automobiles or radium; yet his mind was ready to feel the force of all, though the rays were unborn and the women were dead.

Here opened another totally new education, which promised to be by far the most hazardous of all. The knife-edge along which he must crawl, like Sir Lancelot in the twelfth century,[17] divided two kingdoms of force which had nothing in common but attraction. They were as different as a magnet is from gravitation, supposing one knew what a magnet was, or gravitation, or love. The force of the Virgin was still felt at Lourdes,[18] and seemed to be as potent as X-rays; but in America neither Venus nor Virgin ever had value as force—at most as sentiment. No American had ever been truly afraid of either.

This problem in dynamics gravely perplexed an American historian. The Woman had once been supreme; in France she still seemed potent, not merely as a sentiment, but as a force. Why was she unknown in America? For evidently America was ashamed of her, and she was ashamed of herself, otherwise they would not have strewn fig-leaves so profusely all over her.[19] When she was a true force, she was ignorant of fig-leaves, but the monthly-magazine-made American female had not a feature that would have been recognized by Adam. The trait was notorious, and often humorous, but anyone brought up among Puritans knew that sex was sin. In any previous age, sex was strength. Neither art nor beauty was needed. Everyone, even among Puritans, knew that neither Diana of the Ephesians[20]

---

16. That is, the druggist knew of Venus only through selling medication for venereal disease; and since Boston was largely Protestant, he would only have heard of the Virgin as the object of idolatrous worship.

17. In Chrétien de Troyes's *Lancelot,* the hero was obliged to crawl across a bridge composed of a knife in order to enter a castle and rescue Guinevere.

18. A famous shrine in France known for its miraculous cures; the Virgin Mary was said to have appeared to a peasant girl there in 1858.

19. I.e., to conceal sexual organs and sensuality.

20. The shrine at Ephesus on the West Coast of Asia Minor was dedicated to Artemis, a virgin-goddess mother-figure.

nor any of the Oriental goddesses was worshipped for her beauty. She was goddess because of her force; she was the animated dynamo; she was re-production — the greatest and most mysterious of all energies; all she needed was to be fecund. Singularly enough, not one of Adams's many schools of education had ever drawn his attention to the opening lines of Lucre-tius,[21] though they were perhaps the finest in all Latin literature, where the poet invoked Venus exactly as Dante invoked the Virgin: —

"Quae quoniam rerum naturam *sola* gubernas."

The Venus of Epicurean philosophy survived in the Virgin of the Schools: —

"Donna, sei tanto grande, e tanto vali,
Che qual vuol grazia, e a te non ricorre,
Sua disianza vuol volar senz' ali."[22]

All this was to American thought as though it had never existed. The true American knew something of the facts, but nothing of the feelings; he read the letter, but he never felt the law. Before this historical chasm, a mind like that of Adams felt itself helpless; he turned from the Virgin to the Dynamo as though he were a Branly coherer. On one side, at the Louvre and at Chartres, as he knew by the record of work actually done and still before his eyes, was the highest energy ever known to man, the creator of four-fifths of his noblest art, exercising vastly more attraction over the human mind than all the steam-engines and dynamos ever dreamed of; and yet this energy was unknown to the American mind. An American Virgin would never dare command; an American Venus would never dare exist.

The question, which to any plain American of the nineteenth century seemed as remote as it did to Adams, drew him almost violently to study, once it was posed; and on this point Langleys were as useless as though they were Herbert Spencers[23] or dynamos. The idea survived only as

---

21. Lucretius (c. 99–55 B.C.), in *On the Nature of Things,* I.21: "And since 'tis *thou* / Venus alone / Guidest the Cosmos." Trans. William Ellery Leonard.

22. The Virgin of the Schools is a reference to medieval scholastic philosophers. The lines from Dante translate:

Lady, thou art so great and hath such worth, that if there be who would have grace yet betaketh not himself to thee, his longing seeketh to fly without wings.

(Dante, *Paradiso,* XXXIII, trans. Carlyle-Wicksteed)

23. Herbert Spencer (1820–93), English philosopher and popularizer of Darwinian evolutionary principles. Adams ironically suggests that Spencer's explanations were too general and abstract to explain this primal force.

art. There one turned as naturally as though the artist were himself a woman. Adams began to ponder, asking himself whether he knew of any American artist who had ever insisted on the power of sex, as every classic had always done; but he could think only of Walt Whitman; Bret Harte,[24] as far as the magazines would let him venture; and one or two painters, for the flesh-tones. All the rest had used sex for sentiment, never for force; to them, Eve was a tender flower, and Herodias[25] an unfeminine horror. American art, like the American language and American education, was as far as possible sexless.[26] Society regarded this victory over sex as its greatest triumph, and the historian readily admitted it, since the moral issue, for the moment, did not concern one who was studying the relations of unmoral force. He cared nothing for the sex of the dynamo until he could measure its energy.

Vaguely seeking a clue, he wandered through the art exhibit, and, in his stroll, stopped almost every day before St. Gaudens's[27] General Sherman, which had been given the central post of honor. St. Gaudens himself was in Paris, putting on the work his usual interminable last touches, and listening to the usual contradictory suggestions of brother sculptors. Of all the American artists who gave to American art whatever life it breathed in the seventies, St. Gaudens was perhaps the most sympathetic, but certainly the most inarticulate. General Grant or Don Cameron[28] had scarcely less instinct of rhetoric than he. All the others — the Hunts, Richardson, John La Farge, Stanford White[29] — were exuberant; only St. Gaudens could never discuss or dilate on an emotion, or suggest artistic arguments for giving to his work the forms that he felt. He never laid down the law, or affected the despot, or became brutalized like Whistler[30] by the brutalities of his world. He required no incense; he was no egoist;

---

24. Whitman's *Leaves of Grass* (1855) treated sex boldly and was much criticized on that account; Bret Harte (1836–1902) sympathetically portrayed prostitutes in such stories as *The Outcasts of Poker Flat*.

25. The wife of King Herod who collaborated with her daughter Salome in arranging the beheading of John the Baptist.

26. Just as the American language had no genders, American education was coeducational and in Adams's day entirely excluded sex as a subject from the curriculum.

27. Augustus Saint-Gaudens (1848–1907), American sculptor.

28. Senator James Donald Cameron (1833–1918), Secretary of War under President Grant, 1876.

29. William Morris Hunt (1824–79), noted painter, and his younger brother Richard Morris Hunt (1828–95), noted architect; Henry Hobson Richardson (1838–86), architect; John La Farge (1835–1910), muralist and maker of stained-glass windows; Stanford White (1853–1906), architect.

30. James Abbott McNeill Whistler (1834–1903), American painter and lithographer.

his simplicity of thought was excessive; he could not imitate, or give any form but his own to the creations of his hand. No one felt more strongly than he the strength of other men, but the idea that they could affect him never stirred an image in his mind.

This summer his health was poor and his spirits were low. For such a temper, Adams was not the best companion, since his own gaiety was not *folle;* [31] but he risked going now and then to the studio on Mont Parnasse to draw him out for a stroll in the Bois de Boulogne, [32] or dinner as pleased his moods, and in return St. Gaudens sometimes let Adams go about in his company.

Once St. Gaudens took him down to Amiens, with a party of Frenchmen, to see the cathedral. Not until they found themselves actually studying the sculpture of the western portal, did it dawn on Adams's mind that, for his purposes, St. Gaudens on that spot had more interest to him than the cathedral itself. Great men before great monuments express great truths, provided they are not taken too solemnly. Adams never tired of quoting the supreme phrase of his idol Gibbon, before the Gothic cathedrals: "I darted a contemptuous look on the stately monuments of superstition." [33] Even in the footnotes of his history, Gibbon had never inserted a bit of humor more human than this, and one would have paid largely for a photograph of the fat little historian, on the background of Notre Dame of Amiens, trying to persuade his readers — perhaps himself — that he was darting a contemptuous look on the stately monument, for which he felt in fact the respect which every man of his vast study and active mind always feels before objects worthy of it; but besides the humor, one felt also the relation. Gibbon ignored the Virgin, because in 1789 religious monuments were out of fashion. In 1900 his remark sounded fresh and simple as the green fields to ears that had heard a hundred years of other remarks, mostly no more fresh and certainly less simple. Without malice, one might find it more instructive than a whole lecture of Ruskin. [34] One sees what one brings, and at that moment Gibbon brought the French Revolution. Ruskin brought reaction against the Revolution. St. Gaudens had passed beyond all. He liked the stately monuments much more than he liked Gibbon or Ruskin; he loved their

---

31. Excessive.

32. A large wooded park on the outskirts of Paris; "Mont Parnasse": a Paris Left Bank district frequented by artists and writers.

33. Apparently Adams's adaptation of a passage in Gibbon's French journal for February 21, 1763.

34. John Ruskin (1819–1900), English art critic and social reformer, famous for his highly imaginative interpretations of great works of the Italian Renaissance.

dignity; their unity; their scale; their lines; their lights and shadows; their decorative sculpture; but he was even less conscious than they of the force that created it all—The Virgin, the Woman—by whose genius "the stately monuments of superstition" were built, through which she was expressed. He would have seen more meaning in Isis[35] with the cow's horns, at Edfoo, who expressed the same thought. The art remained, but the energy was lost even upon the artist.

Yet in mind and person St. Gaudens was a survival of the 1500's; he bore the stamp of the Renaissance, and should have carried an image of the Virgin round his neck, or stuck in his hat, like Louis XI.[36] In mere time he was a lost soul that had strayed by chance into the twentieth century, and forgotten where it came from. He writhed and cursed at his ignorance, much as Adams did at his own, but in the opposite sense. St. Gaudens was a child of Benvenuto Cellini,[37] smothered in an American cradle. Adams was a quintessence of Boston, devoured by curiosity to think like Benvenuto. St. Gaudens's art was starved from birth, and Adams's instinct was blighted from babyhood. Each had but half of a nature, and when they came together before the Virgin of Amiens they ought both to have felt in her the force that made them one; but it was not so. To Adams she became more than ever a channel of force; to St. Gaudens she remained as before a channel of taste.

For a symbol of power, St. Gaudens instinctively preferred the horse, as was plain in his horse and Victory of the Sherman monument. Doubtless Sherman also felt it so. The attitude was so American that, for at least forty years, Adams had never realized that any other could be in sound taste. How many years had he taken to admit a notion of what Michael Angelo and Rubens[38] were driving at? He could not say; but he knew that only since 1895 had he begun to feel the Virgin or Venus as force, and not everywhere even so. At Chartres—perhaps at Lourdes—possibly at Cnidos[39] if one could still find there the divinely naked

---

35. Egyptian earth-mother goddess; Adams visited Edfu, the site of the best-preserved temple in Egypt, in 1872–73 and in 1893.

36. A pious French King (1423–83) who often disguised himself as a pilgrim and wore an old felt hat decorated with the lead statuette of a saint.

37. Flamboyant Italian sculptor and goldsmith (1500–71), author of a famous autobiography.

38. Michelangelo Buonarroti (1475–1564), Italian sculptor, painter, architect, and poet of the High Renaissance. Peter Paul Rubens (1577–1640), 17th-century Flemish painter. Both are known for their exceptional renderings of the human body.

39. Cnidos or Cnidus is an ancient city in Asia Minor, site of the most famous of the statues of Aphrodite by Praxiteles (c. 370–330 B.C.); only a copy survives in the Vatican.

Aphrodite of Praxiteles — but otherwise one must look for force to the goddesses of Indian mythology. The idea died out long ago in the German and English stock. St. Gaudens at Amiens was hardly less sensitive to the force of the female energy than Matthew Arnold at the Grande Chartreuse.[40] Neither of them felt goddesses as power — only as reflected emotion, human expression, beauty, purity, taste, scarcely even as sympathy. They felt a railway train as power; yet they, and all other artists, constantly complained that the power embodied in a railway train could never be embodied in art. All the steam in the world could not, like the Virgin, build Chartres.

Yet in mechanics, whatever the mechanicians might think, both energies acted as interchangeable forces on man, and by action on man all known force may be measured. Indeed, few men of science measured force in any other way. After once admitting that a straight line was the shortest distance between two points, no serious mathematician cared to deny anything that suited his convenience, and rejected no symbol, unproved or unproveable, that helped him to accomplish work. The symbol was force, as a compass-needle or a triangle was force, as the mechanist might prove by losing it, and nothing could be gained by ignoring their value. Symbol or energy, the Virgin had acted as the greatest force the Western world ever felt, and had drawn man's activities to herself more strongly than any other power, natural or super-natural, had ever done; the historian's business was to follow the track of the energy; to find where it came from and where it went to; its complex source and shifting channels; its values, equivalents, conversions. It could scarcely be more complex than radium; it could hardly be deflected, diverted, polarized, absorbed more perplexingly than other radiant matter. Adams knew nothing about any of them, but as a mathematical problem of influence on human progress, though all were occult, all reacted on his mind, and he rather inclined to think the Virgin easiest to handle.

The pursuit turned out to be long and tortuous, leading at last into the vast forests of scholastic science. From Zeno to Descartes, hand in hand with Thomas Aquinas, Montaigne, and Pascal,[41] one stumbled as stupidly as though one were still a German student of 1860. Only with

---

40. Matthew Arnold's (1822–88) poem *Stanzas from the Grande Chartreuse* invokes the Virgin Mary in mourning the loss of faith formerly held by ascetic Carthusian monks.

41. Probably Zeno of Citium (c. 366–264 B.C.), Greek philosopher; René Descartes (1596–1650), French philosopher; Thomas Aquinas (1225?–1274), Italian philosopher and theologian who is the subject of the last chapter of Adams's *Mont-Saint-Michel and Chartres;* Michel Eyquem de Montaigne (1533–92), French essayist and skeptical philosopher; Blaise Pascal (1623–62), French philosopher.

the instinct of despair could one force one's self into this old thicket of
ignorance after having been repulsed at a score of entrances more promising and more popular. Thus far, no path had led anywhere, unless perhaps to an exceedingly modest living. Forty-five years of study had proved
to be quite futile for the pursuit of power; one controlled no more force
in 1900 than in 1850, although the amount of force controlled by society
had enormously increased. The secret of education still hid itself somewhere behind ignorance, and one fumbled over it as feebly as ever. In
such labyrinths, the staff is a force almost more necessary than the legs;
the pen becomes a sort of blind-man's dog, to keep him from falling into
the gutters. The pen works for itself, and acts like a hand, modelling
the plastic material over and over again to the form that suits it best.
The form is never arbitrary, but is a sort of growth like crystallization,
as any artist knows too well; for often the pencil or pen runs into side-
paths and shapelessness, loses its relations, stops or is bogged. Then it
has to return on its trail, and recover, if it can, its line of force. The result of a year's work depends more on what is struck out than on what
is left in; on the sequence of the main lines of thought, than on their
play or variety. Compelled once more to lean heavily on this support,
Adams covered more thousands of pages with figures as formal as though
they were algebra, laboriously striking out, altering, burning, experimenting, until the year had expired, the Exposition had long been closed,
and winter drawing to its end, before he sailed from Cherbourg, on January 19, 1901, for home.

Introduction
Rosemary Radford Ruether,
"Motherearth and the Megamachine"

Rosemary Radford Ruether received her doctorate from Claremont School of Theology and is currently Georgia Harkness Professor of Theology at Garrett Evangelical Seminary, Evanston, Illinois. She has been active in antiwar, feminist, and civil-rights groups and is author of many books, including *Religion and Sexism, Liberation Theology,* and *New Woman/ New Earth.*

The women's movement, like the civil-rights movement, began by trying to find a place within the existing system. Women asked for access to education, good jobs, and equal pay for equal work. Ruether is from the ranks of those feminists who have come to believe that women cannot find a place within the existing system and that the system is not good for even those males who *seem* to flourish within it. She calls for and provides a complete rethinking of the mythical foundations upon which our world is built.

Her critique begins with the foundations of our Christian heritage in the ancient world. Orthodox Christianity, she tells us, incorporated the classical Greek interpretation of life with Messianic Judaism at a time when both Greek and Roman civilizations were rejecting the embodied world (represented by women) for a transcendental otherworldly ideal. In other words, people from these formerly robust and practical societies were feeling alienated from this finite world and were seeking an escape in an otherworldly infinite existence. The result, as expressed so powerfully in St. Augustine's *City of God,* was to reject stewardship of this world and to diminish the status of women as representatives of this world. Philosophers like Plato conceived of the world in dualistic terms, and Christian interpreters of Plato added a gender dimension to this bifurcation: spiritual (male) and physical (female). Ruether describes this antibody, antifeminine, and antinature orientation as "a one-sided expression of the ego, claiming its transcendental autonomy by negating the finite matrix of existence."

Rather than continuing the male/female polarization, Ruether argues for saving the oppressor as well as the oppressed. She says we should not overthrow men but instead reintegrate the body and spirit through the reintroduction of traditional tribal celebrations of the cycles of life and the renewal of the earth. Believing that industrialization has been used to further our alienation, she concludes, "the new earth must be one where people are reconciled with their labor, abolishing the alienation of the megamachine while inheriting its productive power to free men for unalienated creativity."

Like many of the writers in this section, Ruether asks you to go beyond the surface and to rethink the very foundations of the world we live in. She gives us an important new way to imagine the future of work by connecting the de-alienation of work with changes in our social systems and personal behaviors and, most basically, with changes in our patterns and categories of imagining and thinking.

Rosemary Radford Ruether

Motherearth and the Megamachine:
A Theology of Liberation in a Feminine,
Somatic and Ecological Perspective

Christianity, as the heir of both classical Neo-Platonism and apocalyptic Judaism, combines the image of a male, warrior God with the exaltation of the intellect over the body. The classical doctrine of Christ, which fused the vision of the heavenly messianic king with the transcendent *logos* of immutable Being, was a synthesis of the religious impulses of late antique religious consciousness, but precisely in their alienated state of development. These world-negating religions carried a set of dualities that still profoundly condition the modern world view.

All the basic dualities — the alienation of the mind from the body; the alienation of the subjective self from the objective world; the subjective retreat of the individual, alienated from the social community; the domination or rejection of nature by spirit — these all have roots in the apocalyptic-Platonic religious heritage of classical Christianity. But the alienation of the masculine from the feminine is the primary sexual symbolism that sums up all these alienations. The psychic traits of intellectuality, transcendent spirit, and autonomous will that were identified with the

Reprinted with permission from *Christianity and Crisis*, April 12, 1972. Copyright © 1972 by Christianity and Crisis, Inc., 537 West 121st Street, New York, NY 10027.

male left the woman with the contrary traits of bodiliness, sensuality, and subjugation. Society, through the centuries, has in every way profoundly conditioned men and women to play out their lives and find their capacities within this basic antithesis.

This antithesis has also shaped the modern technological environment. The plan of our cities is made in this image: The sphere of domesticity, rest, and childrearing where women are segregated is clearly separated from those corridors down which men advance in assault upon the world of "work." The woman who tries to break out of the female sphere into the masculine finds not only psychic conditioning and social attitudes but the structure of social reality itself ranged against her.

The physical environment — access to basic institutions in terms of space and time — has been shaped for the fundamental purpose of freeing one half of the race for the work society calls "productive," while the other half of the race remains in a sphere that services this freedom for work. The woman who would try to occupy both spheres at once literally finds *reality itself* stacked against her, making the combination of maternal and masculine occupations all but impossible without extraordinary energy or enough wealth to hire domestic help.

Thus, in order to play out the roles shaped by this definition of the male life-style, the woman finds that she must either be childless or have someone else act as her "wife" (i.e., play the service role for her freedom to work). Women's liberation is therefore *impossible* within the present social system except for an elite few. Women simply cannot be persons within the present system of work and family, and they can only rise to liberated personhood by the most radical and fundamental reshaping of the entire human environment in a way that redefines the very nature of work, family, and the institutional expressions of social relations.

Although widespread hopes for liberty and equality among all humans rose with the *philosophes* of the Enlightenment, hardly any of these ideologies of the French Revolution and the liberal revolutions of the nineteenth century envisioned the liberation of women. The bourgeoisie, the workers, the peasants, even the Negro slaves were more obvious candidates for liberation, while the subjugation of women continued to be viewed as an unalterable necessity of nature. When the most radical of the French liberals, the Marquis de Condorcet, included women in the vision of equality, his colleagues thought he had lost his senses and breached the foundations of the new rationalism. The ascendency of Reason meant the ascendency of the intellect over the passions, and this must ever imply the subjugation of women.

The reaction against and suppression of the Woman's Liberation Movement has been closely tied to reactionary cultural and political movements, and the emanicipated woman has been the chief target of elitism, fascism, and neoconservatism of all kinds. The Romantic Movement traumatized Europe's reaction to the French Revolution, reinstated the traditional view of women in idealized form, while the more virulent blood-and-soil reactionaries of the nineteenth century expressed a more naked misogynism. Literary figures such as Strindberg and Nietzsche couldn't stress strongly enough their abhorrence of women. At the turn of the century, Freud codified all the traditional negative views of the female psychology, giving them scientific respectability for the new psychological and social sciences. The negative stereotypes have been a key element in the repression of the women's movement through the popular mass media.

This modern backlash against the libertarian tradition seeks to reinstate attitudes and social relations whose psychic roots run back through the Judeo-Christian and classical cultures into the very foundations of civilization building. The cry for liberty, equality, and fraternity challenged the roots of the psychology whereby the dominant class measured its status in terms of the conquest of classes, nations, races, and nature itself.

Lewis Mumford, in his monumental work on the foundations of ancient civilization, *The Myth of the Machine,* and its supplementary volume on modern technological society, *The Myth of the Machine: The Pentagon of Power,* has shown how civilization has been founded on a subjugation of man to machinery. A chauvinist, paranoid psychology has directed men's productive energies into destruction rather than the alleviation of the necessities of all, thus aborting the promise of civilization. The subjugation of the female by the male is the primary psychic model for this chauvinism and its parallel expressions in oppressor-oppressed relationships between social classes, races and nations. It is this most basic symbolism of power that has misdirected men's psychic energy into the building of the Pentagon of Power, from the pyramids of ancient Egypt to the North American puzzle-palace on the Potomac.

The psychosocial history of the domination of women has not been explored with any consistency, so the effort to trace its genesis and development here can only be very general. However, it appears that in agricultural societies sexist and class polarization did not immediately reshape the religious world view. For the first two millennia of recorded history, religious culture continued to reflect the more holistic view of society of the neolithic village, where the individual and the community, nature and society, male and female, earth Goddess and sky God were seen in a total perspective of world renewal. The salvation of the individual was not split off from that of the community; the salvation of society was one with the renewal of the earth: male and female played their complementary roles in the salvation of the world. This primitive democracy of the neolithic village persisted in the divine pantheons of Babylonia, despite the social class stratification that now appeared.

In these early civilizations, this holistic world view was expressed in the public celebration of the new year's festival, wherein the whole society of humanity and nature experienced the annual death of the cosmos and its resurrection from primordial chaos. In this cult, the king, as the personification of the community, played the role of the God who dies and is reborn from the netherworld. His counterpart was a powerful feminine figure who was at once virgin and mother, wife and sister, and who rescued the dying God from the power of the underworld. The king united with her at the end of the drama to create the divine child of the new year's vegetation. The crisis and rebirth encompassed both society and nature: The hymns of rejoicing celebrated the release of the captives, justice for the poor, and security against invasion, as well as the new rain, the new grain, the new lamb and the new child.

Somewhere in the first millennium B.C., however, this communal world view of humanity and nature, male and female, carried over from tribal society started to break down, and the alienations of civilization began to reshape the religious world picture. This change was partly aggravated by the history of imperial conquest that swept the people of the Mediterranean into larger and larger social conglomerates where they no longer felt the same unity with the king, the soil or the society.

The old religions of the earth became private cults for the individual, no longer anticipating the renewal of the earth and society but rather expecting an otherworldly salvation of the individual soul after death. Nature itself came to be seen as an alien reality, and men now visualized their own bodies as foreign to their true selves, longing for a heavenly home to release them from their enslavement within the physical cosmos. Finally, earth ceased to be seen as man's true home.

Hebrew religion is significant in this history as the faith of a people who clung with particular tenacity to their tribal identity over against the imperial powers of civilization. Hebrew society inherited kingship and the new year's festival of the temple from their Canaanite neighbors. But Yahwism repressed the feminine divine role integral to this cult and began to cut loose the festival itself from its natural base in the renewal of the earth.

This desert people claimed the land as a divine legacy, but they imagined a manner of acquiring it that set them against the traditional cult of the earth. They took over the old earth festivals but reinterpreted them to refer to historical events in the Sinai journey. The messianic hopes of the prophets still looked for a paradisal renewal of earth and society, but this renewal broke the bonds of natural possibility and was projected into history as a future event.

So the pattern of death and resurrection was cut loose from organic harmonies and became instead an historical pattern of wrath and redemption. The feminine imagery of the cult was repressed entirely, although it survived in a new form in the symbol of the community as the bride of Yahweh in the Covenant. But the bride was subordinate and dependent to the male Lord of Hosts, who reigned without consort in the heavens, confronting his sometimes rebellious, sometimes repentant people with punishment or promises of national victory.

The hopes for a renewal of nature and society, projected into a once and for all historical future, now came to be seen as less and less realizable within history itself. And so the prophetic drive to free man from nature ended in the apocalyptic negation of history itself: a cataclysmic world destruction and angelic new creation.

In this same period of the first millennium B.C., we find in classical philosophy a parallel development of the alienation of the individual from the world. Like the prophets, the philosophers repudiated the old nature Gods in their sexual forms of male and female divinities, and maleness was seen as bodiless and intellectual.

For Plato, the authentic soul is incarnated as a male, and only when it succumbs to the body is it reincarnated in the body of a female and then into the body of some beast resembling the evil character into which it has fallen. The salvation of the liberated consciousness repudiates heterosexual for masculine love and mounts to heaven in flight from the body and the visible world. The intellect is seen as an alien, lonely species that originates in a purely spiritual realm beyond time, space, and matter, and has been dropped, either as into a testing place or, through some fault, into this lower material world. But space and time, body and mutability are totally alien to its nature. The body drags the soul down, obscuring the clarity of its knowledge, debasing its moral integrity. Liberation is a flight from the earth to a changeless, infinite world beyond. Again we see the emergence of the liberated consciousness in a way that alienates it from nature in a body-fleeing, world-negating spirituality.

Christianity brought together both of these myths — the myth of world cataclysm and the myth of the flight of the soul to heaven. It also struggled to correct the more extreme implications of this body-negating spirituality with a more positive doctrine of creation and incarnation. It even reinstated, in covert form, the old myths of the year cult and the virgin-mother Goddess.

But the dominant spirituality of the Fathers of the Church finally accepted the antibody, antifeminine view of late antique religious culture. Recent proponents of ecology have, therefore, pointed the finger at Christianity as the originator of this debased view of nature, as the religious sanction for modern technological exploitation of the earth.

But Christianity did not originate this view. Rather, it appears to correspond to a stage of development of human consciousness that coincided with ripening classical civilization. Christianity took over this alienated world view of late classical civilization, but its oppressive dualities express the basic alienations at work in the psychosocial channelization of human energy since the breakup of the communal life of earlier tribal society.

What we see in this development is a one-sided expression of the ego, claiming its transcendental autonomy by negating the finite matrix of existence. This antithesis is projected socially by identifying woman as the incarnation of this debasing threat of bodily existence, while the same polarized model of the psyche is projected politically upon suppressed or conquered social groups.

The emphasis upon the transcendent consciousness has literally created the urban earth, and both abstract science and revolution are ultimate products of this will to transcend and dominate the natural and social world that gave birth to the rebellious spirit. The exclusively male God who creates out of nothing, transcending nature and dominating history, and upon whose all-powerful wrath and grace man hangs as a miserable, crestfallen sinner, is the theological self-image and guilty conscience of this self-infinitizing spirit.

Today we recognize that this theology of rebellion into infinity has its counterpart in a world-destroying spirituality that projects upon the female of the race all its abhorrence, hostility and fear of the bodily powers from which it has arisen and from which it wishes to be independent. One can feel this fear in the threatened, repressively hostile energy that is activated in the dominant male society at the mere suggestion of the emergence of the female on an equal plane—as though equality itself must inevitably mean *his* resubjugation to preconscious submersion in the womb.

This most basic duality characterizes much recent theology. Karl Barth, despite his model of cohumanity as the essence of the creational covenant, insists on the relation of super- and subordination between men and women as an ordained necessity of creation. "Crisis" and "secular" theologians such as Bultmann and Gogarten continually stress the transcendence of history over nature, defining the Gospel as the freedom of the liberated consciousness to depart endlessly from natural and historical foundations into the contentless desert of pure possibility. Such theologians are happy to baptize modern technology as the expression of the freedom mediated by the Gospel to transcend and dominate nature.

Today, both in the West and among insurgent Third World peoples, we are seeing a new intensification of this Western mode of abstractionism and revolution. Many are convinced that the problems created by man's ravaging of nature can be solved only by a great deal more technological manipulation. The oppressed peoples who have been the victims of the domination of the elite classes now seek to follow much the same path of pride, transcending wrath, separatism and power in order to share in the benefits of independence and technological power already won by the dominant classes.

Yet, at the same time, nature and society are giving clear warning signals that the usefulness of this spirituality is about to end. Two revolutions are running in contrapuntal directions. The alienated members of the dominant society are seeking new communal, egalitarian life-styles, ecological living patterns, and the redirection of psychic energy toward reconciliation with the body. But these human potential movements remain elitist, privatistic, esthetic and devoid of a profound covenant with the poor and oppressed of the earth.

On the other hand, the aspirations of insurgent peoples rise along the lines of the traditional rise of civilization through group pride, technological domination of nature and antagonistic, competitive relationships between peoples. Such tendencies might be deplored by those who have so far monopolized technology and now believe they have seen the end of its fruitfulness, but they must be recognized as still relevant to the liberation of the poor and oppressed from material necessity and psychological dependency.

We are now approaching the denouement of this dialectic. The ethic of competitiveness and technological mastery has created a world divided by penis-missiles and countermissiles that could destroy all humanity a hundred times over. Yet the ethic of reconciliation with the earth has yet to break out of its snug corners of affluence and find meaningful cohesion with the revolutions of insurgent peoples.

The significance of the women's revolution, then, may well be its unique location in the center of this clash between the contrapuntal directions of current liberation movements. Women are the first and oldest oppressed, subjugated people. They too must claim for themselves the human capacities of intellect, will, and autonomous creative consciousness that have been denied them through this psychosocial polarization in its most original form.

Women must be the spokesmen for a new humanity arising out of the reconciliation of spirit and body. This does not mean selling short our rights to the powers of independent personhood. Autonomy, world-transcending spirit, separatism as the power of consciousness raising, and liberation from an untamed nature and from subjugation to the rocket-ship male—all these revolutions are still vital to women's achievement of integral personhood. But we have to look beyond our own liberation from oppression to the liberation of the oppressor as well. Women should not buy into the masculine ethic of competitiveness that sees the triumph of the self as predicated upon the subjugation of the other. Unlike men, women have traditionally cultivated a communal personhood that could participate in the successes of others rather than seeing these as merely a threat to one's own success.

To seek the liberation of women without losing this sense of communal personhood is the great challenge and secret power of the women's revolution. Its only proper end must be the total abolition of the social pattern of domination and subjugation and the erection of a new communal social ethic. We need to build a new cooperative social order out beyond the principles of hierarchy, rule, and competitiveness. Starting in the grass roots local units of human society where psychosocial polarization first began, we must create a living pattern of mutuality between men and women, between parents and children, among people in their social, economic, and political relationships and, finally, between mankind and the organic harmonies of nature.

Such a revolution entails nothing less than a transformation of all the social structures of civilization, particularly the relationship between work and play. It entails literally a global struggle to overthrow and transform the character of power structures and points forward to a new messianic epiphany that will as far transcend the world-rejecting salvation myths of apocalypticism and Platonism as these myths transcended the old nature myths of the neolithic village. Combining the values of the world-transcending Yahweh with those of the world-renewing Ba'al in a post-technological religion of reconciliation with the body, the woman and the world, its salvation myth will not be one of divinization and flight from the body but of humanization and reconciliation with the earth.

Our model is neither the romanticized primitive jungle nor the modern technological wasteland. Rather it expresses itself in a new command to learn to cultivate the garden, for the cultivation of the garden is where the powers of rational consciousness come together with the harmonies of nature in partnership.

The new earth must be one where people are reconciled with their labor, abolishing the alienation of the megamachine while inheriting its productive power to free men for unalienated creativity. It will be a world where people are reconciled to their own finitude, where the last enemy, death, is conquered, not by a flight into eternity, but in that spirit of St. Francis that greets "Brother Death" as a friend that completes the proper cycle of the human soul.

Introduction
Frithjof Bergmann, "A Visit to Those Who Succeeded"

With this final selection in the book we come full circle: we began the book with Frithjof Bergmann's discussion of the need to rethink work in order to seize the historical moment when we can transform modern labor from bad to good; we are now ready to appreciate why he makes this claim and how this transformation might occur. Bergmann has engaged in a nearly two-decade uphill struggle to convince people that we will only manage to do this crucial historical change well if we begin by rethinking what work is for and if people comprehend how important work is in shaping human nature and society. Many people around the world, whether or not they have heard of Bergmann, have reached a similar point in their understandings. In our final reading we thus offer you the thoughts of a visionary who believes the practical must be philosophical and the philosophical practical.

Bergmann's career of thinking about and trying to alter contemporary work began with his work on freedom in the 1970s. He believes that the common American view of freedom as independence (being unhindered) and its underlying image of an individual constantly at war with society create people whose very attempts to gain freedom (escape from relationships, work, and responsibilities) render them weak and crippled. In its place Bergmann argues (in his book *On Being Free*) we should think of freedom as a matter of acting from one's self, with the self viewed as a social creation, as most contemporary social scientists contend. Thus what you do in relation to me may or may not limit my freedom depending on how I experience what you do; and how I experience your actions, in turn, is a function of the self having come to be through my social relations. Most centrally, your or my experience of freedom, from this standpoint, is a matter of acting in a way that is consistent with and grows out of our identities rather than being a function of being unhindered by others.

Work now enters the picture. If much of what we do is work, then it becomes clear why so many people contrast work and "living" (leisure, play, being alive, having time off, etc.): a major part of people's lives (work) is experienced as unfree, as contrary to their identities. Simultaneously, Bergmann's perspective helps make it clear why work is so important for human flourishing: if we do work that grows from the centers of our beings (as sometimes happens when we write or grow a garden or rear a child), such work is most liberating: it is among the times when we feel most free. Put another way, Bergmann believes that people feel free when they do what they desire, and, unfortunately, many people today do not truly desire to do the work they are "forced" to do.

One more ingredient in Bergmann's philosophy is needed to prepare you for the following story: once he links freedom to human identity and work to our experiences of freedom or unfreedom, he then uses the kinds of historical perspectives we explored earlier in the book to highlight the peculiar nature of our "job system." What Bergmann wants us to see is how we moderns have linked wealth and jobs: people in previous societies gained access to wealth (the means of material well-being) through effort, intrigue, and inheritance, but no society before modern ones ever had a system of jobs, of wage labor. For Bergmann this system has passed its golden days: increasing un- and underemployment with simultaneous labor shortages in various sectors of the economy indicate the breakdown of this system, and the service sector replacement of industrial jobs has reduced people's access not only to wealth but also to meaningful work—selling shirts not only is less lucrative than pouring steel, but it may not provide any more meaning either.

Frithjof Bergmann

A Visit to Those Who Succeeded

"Enough!" said the very old man. "No more lofty lectures, no more cunningly connected arguments. Enough racing from one workshop to another, presenting yet one more disquisition. It's too late for that! Things have deteriorated exactly as we knew they would: down from one level to the next, with ever greater wealth on one side and deeper destitution on the other.

"No more talking in the same old voice: noisy, pontifical, and shrill; instead a gentle tone, and only words that have no edges. Perhaps I should tell it as a story, fanciful and strange. I could perch myself upon a mound of trash, and from there recite a science fiction tale—in a city that is burning. How apt!

"For years and years I have shouted, but everyone sat immobile and smiled and agreed, without moving a thumb, or even an earlobe. Therefore, yes, a brand-new approach: a story in which all that I've envisioned and preached is not merely words and dreamed-up concepts but has already been achieved and is palpable and concrete. To have it real, not just imagined, would be an advantage. Still, even then only two or three are likely to understand. No matter, in that case my story will be a special present for those two!

"The story should be sparse and unembellished; just the account of a visit. Two people: one the visitor, the other his host. It will only be fantastic in that this is a visit to the land of those who succeeded; those who did not split into two hostile camps and sink into permanent terrorism and civil war. A land, therefore, that is immensely, unimaginably different from our own.

"Why did they fare so vastly better? This is the crucial question! In one sentence: the people of this distant culture decided that the entire architecture of institutions that structure how they worked—in other words, the totality of their entire 'work system'—had to be revamped from the ground up. To their own amazement and surprise they actually succeeded: through a gradual process they managed to stem and narrow the Niagara-fall of waste, until the level of their culture rose at an unprecedented rate. Fast and faster they spiraled upward until the gap in development between their culture and ours became as deep and wide as the gap between our current Western existence and that of a third-world peasant.

"The technological speed and the financial power created by their new, more efficient work organization resulted—ironically—in a condition of almost distressed abundance. The vastly increased capacity for production led to a satiation, a clogging up, and then a bursting of the pipes, a spilling over—of barns, warehouses, and silos. The excess was a surplus not merely of sausages or shampoos but of every product, in every corner. It was natural that this flood of merchandise and output could not continue to rush forever forward. The mounting of unused goods eventually created a resistance, and the energy was thus forced to find another outlet in a different direction. Indeed, this is how this culture was *coerced* to shift its awesome powers away from mere material production and turn them toward the loftier goals of striving for the improvement and further development of human beings.

"Many people found it distressing that 2,000 years of preaching should have been so glaringly ineffectual, that endless upbraiding about the sins of the flesh had made no noticeable difference, and that what actually succeeded, almost overnight, was as low and sleazy as a clutter of merchandise, achieved through the intelligent harnessing of labor. It was infuriating and deflating that a brief encounter with trite possessions, with satiation, with having enough, should produce the long wished-for conversion from the pig troughs of materialism. Immeasurable quantities of 'moral' and 'spiritual' aspiration could have been spent to better purpose if this ancient aim was so easy to achieve.

"Having turned a momentous corner in this surprising fashion, the members of this culture were now ready to apply the extraordinary storages of newly freed energy to the task of making people less crippled and maimed. To this end they invented all manner of political, social, and economic arrangements, and they did this systematically and in earnest — in profound contrast to the long past of merely paying lip service to change and reform. The advances they achieved were so unexpected, so novel and impressive, that describing them in a few words is utterly out of the question, especially with clichés, like they helped people to 'grow,' or become more 'centered,' or have 'closer contact with their deep emotions,' or become more 'intense,' or 'passionate,' or 'alive.' In fact, this is one of the most compelling reasons for spinning out this story: to give you even a hint of the fuller and riper human beings they achieved will take the full length of this meandering epic.

"If in our story there is to be a visit to this culture, then who should be the host? What qualities should he possess, and how should he have lived his life? Clearly, it would be an advantage if he were a 'novice,' someone who had arrived in this swiftly progressing land only a few years ago. He would then be slower, more sedate, and certainly less clownish than the average citizen. But that would be for the best, since the gap between the host and our visitor would in that case be less wide, and communication between them could be more nearly on even terms. If he were a novice who had still experienced some of the absurdities of our own 'job system,' then it would be even better, for this would provide some common ground, which given their profound differences would be most needed to facilitate some meeting of their minds.

"To achieve understanding would of course be difficult and require undauntable persistence, since our visitor's culture by then will be in a lamentably sick condition. For a new level of calamity is bound to occur.

If we continue on the downward turn of the last twenty years, then we will clearly be split in half: the terrorized remnants of the once proud middle class will be holed up in stainless steel towers, studded with surveillance and security equipment. Exhausted from the unending civil war, they will hide, surrounded by high walls and barbed wire, and large contingents of hired guards.

"To picture the deteriorated condition the poor would have reached, you only need to recall that for years now we have bulldozed down whole blocks in our cities that fell into decrepitude. We've done so with the justification that the half-abandoned houses are hazardous and unhygienic, but also for the more revealing reason that the clutter of open cellars, broken walls, and winding, narrow alleys is difficult to survey and even harder to control—a lesson we have learnt from warfare in the jungles. At the time of our visit not merely a few blocks but entire districts, and eventually whole inner cities, would have been bulldozed down and made into bare and level land. There would be no place to hide and nothing to see but for the wind stirring up vortices of dust. And the poor people would have done what they always did before—they moved, until there were ever fewer places to receive them, and at last none. This transformed the migration to the trash disposal areas, which had been a river, into a flood. For the majority of the poor, which reached three-quarters of the population, there was nothing else to do. Laws existed to keep them away from the garbage cans of those who still had houses, and the only remaining life-style was to scavenge in the public dumps.

"Myriads of improvised cardboard tents, lean-to's, and shanties sprang up out of the ground. But soon it was decreed that these shantytowns were also unhygienic and difficult to survey and control, and therefore these, too, were forbidden and then razed. As a consequence great masses of people, often hundreds of thousands in one group, would wander from hill to hill in the waste yards. But cold and rain and lack of clothes put an end even to this wandering. Now uncountable numbers of these poor gather into clumps so as to stay a little drier and give each other warmth. In the enormous refuse fields you can therefore now see whole mounds of human bodies, barely moving, yet shaking in the cold.

"If the chasm between another advanced culture and our own had indeed grown this wide, and if another group had outdone us with such finality and ease, then the most horrific prejudices about the members of this other culture would certainly spring up among us. In the earlier stages these fantasies would be very like those to which we have been long accustomed: they would be portrayed as inhuman and bestial: dirty, with a rancid, zoo-reminiscent smell; but they also would be pictured as inhuman, in the sense of being calculating and ice-cold, a mere machine that has no feelings. Later our media would portray them as Frank-ensteinian monsters whose arms ceaselessly whirl about them, like the wings of humming birds, but restlessly engaged in manufacturing.

"The first waves of genuinely warlike violence between the rich and the poor produced an exacerbation of these prejudices, so fierce that a pandemonium of incoherent, nightmarish notions was the result. Some at this juncture called it a carnival and clown show, and several analysts prognosticated that the entire structure would collapse of its own weight, but nothing of the kind occurred. On the contrary, close to the time of our visit the merest mention of 'Developmentalism'—a name sometimes used for this culture—produced hysteria in many crowds in our country. On several occasions the rage became so uncontrolled that 'sympathizers' were struck with stones and died of the effects.

"Knowing these outbursts, of course, played a role in the selection of the visitor. The search was painstaking, and the Developmentalists were fortunate in finding an almost legendary person. For fifteen years he had been a tireless mediator between the two parties of our, by then, appall-ingly divided country. Ceaselessly he had advanced suggestions, made proposals, presented lectures, given seminars, and written in the papers: he had talked until, as some people said, his lips were calloused and his throat a pipe of warts.

"Everyone agreed that his experience with people as wholly different from each other as our rich are from our poor would be invaluable for this attempt to initiate an exchange. More important, still, was the fact that he had waged a personal campaign to correct the worst malfunc-tions of the job system. This guaranteed that he would bring intense sym-pathy and also richly matured expert knowledge to the task at hand. He, if anyone, should be able to discover a bridge from our culture to one whose very birth abolished the job system and created a new and supe-rior work organization.

"One mild surprise for the visitor when he first met his host was the great watchfulness with which that courtly man deciphered even the most hidden discomforts and also interests of the new arrival. The advance briefing information had not mentioned that attunement to one's inter-locutor had been raised into an art form in this culture. On the other hand, it was no surprise when the host informed him, almost brusquely, that the inspection of technological marvels was not on the agenda. The host expressed this with whimsical exasperation: 'Whoever we invite al-ways wants to see a huge, chromed-steel contraption. Whether it is one of our bioenergy stations, where they are mesmerized by bacteria that produce electricity, or one of our ocean-wave machines, where they cannot get enough of the giant pistons moving up and down in their monster rhythm.'

"The visitor had long surmised that he would not have been invited if these were the things the Developmentalists wanted to explain. With a speed that later on struck the visitor also as characteristic, the host came directly to the point. 'Our first stop,' he said, 'will be a pharmaceutical research and production site. Among other things they produce a medication that makes it far safer for women to still have children even into the beginning of the menopause.'

"In a hurried and flat voice the host went on to say: 'I assume you know that the plant is almost entirely underground, as are most of our production centers, and that the usual access is of course by subway. That the "participants" who "perform" in this plant never stay there for more than three hours at a time should also not be news to you; surely, someone told you about our rules concerning boredom.'

"'It is likely that we will not go inside the plant. We shall fly there, principally because an "action" of the Work Transformation Movement (W.T.M.) is in progress at this very moment, and I thought that actually seeing this, and not merely hearing a description, might be useful.'

"Only very few more words were said before the host and his visitor climbed into the already waiting small helicopter-hovercraft, not gawkishly designed, as those we have at present, but round and smooth and sensuous, with the curves of a Porsche. After a few minutes flight they reached the valley in which the pharmaceuticals were made, and the visitor observed that both slopes were densely covered with a colorful mass of people. He explained that true to the host's request, he would not raise questions about the clowns, jugglers, and other circus performers, nor about the profusion of flowers, which for a moment made him think that they had reached a temple or a park. He said: 'We never have such entertainers at our demonstrations, but I have often thought that they would be a good idea, so there is no need to discuss them. Puzzling is that there does not seem to be a speaker and also, as far as I can see, a coherent crowd, but only numerous small groups, each apparently separate from the others. For a political demonstration this seems odd. Could you explain why it is so?'

"His host replied: 'Because the Work Transformation Movement does not need speeches any longer. The power they wield is so tremendous that even the largest and richest firms instantly remove their products from the shelves if the W.T.M. decides to call an action. Resistance would be corporate suicide. No one will touch a medicine, or a fruit, or a piece of furniture, or go to a bank, or even listen to a teacher if the W.T.M.

announces that one of their rules has been violated. They are far stronger than Environmentalism or Feminism were during their heydays; therefore, they also require no more organizational apparatus, nor uniforms, nor insignia, nor, thank God, advertising. They can afford entertainers and turn their demonstrations into picnic outings. They no longer need strategy or indoctrination: all that is behind them. It is their flamboyance which enfuriates their enemies. For nothing they do is ever effortful; nothing requires clenched teeth, or even concentration. If that is needed, then it is in their view already a mistake; then look for a sudden turn in their decision. Only if it can be done with superb ease, with the smile of a circus acrobat, is something worth doing.'

"To this the visitor responded that, despite all warnings he had received, this, so far, seemed plain enough. What he wanted to know next, however, and with a curiosity 'stretched to the bursting point,' was the reason for this demonstration. 'With only three hours of "participation" per day, and the best protection against boredom I have ever seen, and factories decked out in flowers—what could the W.T.M. still want? It is difficult to imagine that it would not be a frill?'

"The turn of that phrase had an effect on the host. He became suddenly far more intent, and with a voice vivid and compelling he launched into what quite obviously would be an extended answer. He said: 'Tossing off a brief explanation would be a disaster. You would hear it through the seven filters of your own assumptions, and make seven times your own sense of it, and the point of this visit would be forever lost. So, give me time, and muster some of your celebrated patience. Surely I will have difficulties, but I must give you some notion of what we fundamentally have tried to do. Otherwise you will be staring at one stone from a large mosaic.'

"'Let me start from something that for the first few minutes might seem irrelevant to you. In the last decades we have developed a new art form that does not consist in the making of pictures, or sculptures, or anything that you can physically perceive. Rather the works are made out of words and metaphors, but they are not for reading. They are mainly recited, but they are not poems. We think of them as serious intellectual tools, in some ways like buoys for a sailor: they help to orient one's thinking. We attach great significance to them because of their power, which far surpasses that of mere images. Some people here enjoy singular status and prestige just because they possess a famous collection of these works, which they sometimes, at festivals or parties, can be persuaded to recite.'

"'Unfortunately I can only give you a very flimsy notion of their quality and force, since I am untrained in this art. Still, there is one that is especially undemanding, and I could try to give you some suggestion of its shape.'

"'Start by asking yourself: What would be a precise description of the effects of work on the great majority of people? Should one say that it is "numbing"? Or should one use a phrase like it "cramps them" or "disfigures them" or "prevents their full development"? Do any of these phrases even come close to capturing the extremity and crispness of the actual facts, or are they all too vapid and worn down into clichés?'

"'We decided long ago that nothing will be gained by exchanging these tired words for others; others too will be pale and non-descript. Our dissatisfaction has deep, even philosophic, roots, and we developed the art of word images to improve this unhappy condition.'

"'Notice the contrast between such words and the image that I will now attempt to sketch: Try to picture a children's hospital and imagine that this hospital has a special ward for children with a quite unusual disease. Most of the children are no more than seven years old, yet they are wrinkled and shrunken, toothless and bald, and extremely frail. Their appearance is very like that of extraordinarily old people, but of course they have not actually lived a long life. They have only endured physiological changes at a frightening speed; that is their disease. Bewildering is the degree to which one feels that one is really talking to old people when one visits with them. Many nurses have also noted that they slip into the same condescension with these children that they use for the truly old.'

"'There are ever so many people who have lived for 60, 70, or even 80 years who are confusingly like these old children. It is as if they boarded a train when they were very young, and the landscapes and events of their entire lives only clattered past them at great speed. They never stopped to act in them and did not even experience them close up. They slumbered, as people do on trains, with the rhythmic monotony closing their eyes. Occasionally they woke with a start, looked about themselves, not quite knowing where they were, and then again fell back to sleep.'

"'Does this image not convey more accurately what work for many people is: the monotony, the passivity, above all, the sleep? But it would be too mild if you picture only the train. That is why we first visited the children in the hospital. Those who deboard this train, who have ridden it much of their life, are like the children in this ward: they are those whose lives were never lived, who return their unspent life, like a ticket never used, or a shirt not worn.'

"'We have countless such pictures, galleries of them! You should come to a recital where the best are performed; then you would see their force. That is why we prize them. Take the image which I just indicated for you: it was one of many we evolved to help us weaken the hold of old and silly platitudes: adages like work is always "noble" if only it is done "well" (meaning with no questions asked): that "bad" or horrible work simply does not exist, and that working always and everywhere deserves "respect."'

"'These inanities are absurd and unforgivable, but there are worse. One in particular we singled out as the epitomy of what we wanted to expunge. No part of the Work Transformation Movement can be understood if this is not explained. It was perhaps the most pervasive attitude of all regarding work: it was not masochistic; it was not work as a form of punishment or flagellation. Rather it was a mild and general greyness. On Sundays one "dressed up"; for weekdays one had "work clothes," and these were always drabber and less exciting. The same with work and holidays. Work stood for the grind, while holidays were festive and celebrated precisely because they were free from work! To us this was perverse, a sacrilege: to portray work that can be inspiring and glorious, the sweetest fruit of the gods, in such drab and unappealing overalls. How deep must footprints be until you recognize the tracks of an insidious prejudice, in this case against work, and presumably in favor of emptiness, of sheer water-treading leisure?'

"'We wanted to counter this destructive and erroneous stance. For many the holidays are most deadly and depressing (recall the suicides at Christmas!): those are the days when many suffer from boredom and lack the zest and gusto that comes with work. So we decided (naturally in a democratic fashion) to launch a campaign to usher people through a gradual change of opinion. We believe that in most people's lives, contrary to received opinion, it is mainly work that proves to be most exciting. Of course, in many people's whole existence the thrilling or adventurous, let alone the exalted, can simply not be found. But those who do receive some of this rain catch it only because some crisis, or rush of ambition, which arose inside their *work* pulls them out from under their domestic sleep roof.'

"'Many of our people found this idea thoroughly upsetting, but is it not a fact that for most people the moments of ecstasy do not occur in bed?'

"'Countless images were required to comfort people so that they could accept and live with this disturbing truth. Naturally, we did not rely on images alone but introduced an array of small and large institutions to assist people in this direction. Among much else we decorated our factories with an excess of flowers, making them look like gardens, to engrave in everybody's mind that places of work can be places of great pleasure!'

"'We have methodically tried to weaken the grip that the twaddle about work as "grayness" had on us—that a "job, of course, could only be a job"—and we systematically strive to live by a conception that has become central to our thinking, namely, the "polarity of work." In essence this is the idea that work, instead of being just "respectable" and "honorable," is for some people incomparably *more*: for *some* it is the source of drama and excitement, adding passion and substance to their lives. It has often filled the space left empty by lack of religion: it is work, instead of God, that gives them courage and endurance, and the most astounding power to prevail.'

"'None of this, however, has been true for "the mass of men." For them work has for the most part been degrading. The effects of their work, the ways they were maimed by it, are hard to describe and immeasurably more difficult to change. That is why we started to use images like the old children. The lies that made all work seem the same, all "honorable" but also "gray," built up a crust that has hardened for centuries. The images are our tools: they are the axe with which we chip away the plaster cast of lies.'

"'I have talked about the force of these images, and in the case of the hospital image many began to notice, slowly at first but then more frequently, on busses and on subways that people indeed were like the children in the ward. It seemed surprisingly patent, as if our vision had improved: we observed spots and wrinkles, pouches of dead skin, a resignation in the eye, a pallor of the spirit, where we had been blind before.'

"'Perhaps it is how physicians see the world: it is wonderful but also haunting. We now see that factories and offices, whole cities, are filled with people who are evidently ill. They look shrunken, caved in, and cold, and talking to them is like speaking to one of the old children: one sees a glimmer of life, exciting like a small animal, but then one looks closer and notices that the animal is dying under the weight of slabs of immobile, yellow meat.'

"'I have barely begun to sketch how we elaborated the idea of the "polarity of work," how we invented other pedagogical devices to bring home the recognition that some kinds of work—and not merely the rote or dull— are like the injections that were tested in concentration camps: by degrees and in precisely measured steps they kill a person. But also other kinds of work are just as potent in the reverse: they give life! This should not surprise you. Not all work tires; some is a recovery and the most invigorating recreation; even those cynical and drained, those catatonic from failure and despair, can be revived—can be resurrected—through the power of that work.'

"'Slowly we invented further images and other forms of art as well as new institutional arrangements with the goal not only of transforming our thinking about work but of changing our practice. We sought to devise a new work system, one which would embody the "polarity of work."'

"'But soon we realized that we could not advance two steps in this direction without first revamping our idea of technology as thoroughly as we had done this with our idea of work. So we started from the most basic elements and asked: What are our reflex associations? What are our quickest, most instinctive reactions at the mention of technology? We did years of research and eventually found that the distrust and hatred of technology is even deeper, and more virulent, than the prejudices connected to age and work.'

"'The degree to which these reflexes are imprinted reminds one of the response to the striking of a snake: particularly among young people a warding off and leaping back seem to have become part of the biological equipment. To reintroduce some measure of sense and thought in this domain proved far more difficult than we ever had supposed.'

"'The reasons for these prejudices stare one in the face. If technology turns rivers into sewage, and our air into one poison gas, if it devises ever more sumptuous instruments to tear one's enemies to shreds, then how could the reaction possibly be otherwise?'

"'At first we made no progress. In retrospect we see clearly that our sermonizing about technology being just a neutral tool, for good as well as evil, was an ineffectual flapping of a broken wing. Gradually the connections between technology and our discoveries about work dawned on us, and the shape of our task began to emerge.'

"'I will give you an image our artists devised to crack the misconceptions that had formed around the idea of machines, and tools, and the technological. Start with the picture of a huge field. Veils of fog are wafted across it by cold winds. It seems dotted with large stakes that men are driving down into the ground with mallets. The men are exceptionally muscular, half naked, with bare chests. Their number cannot be determined; fainter and still fainter they disappear into the fog. Once the stakes come into focus, you see that they are wooden pylons, the kind one drives into the earth to solidify a swampy ground or to build up a gridwork on which to lay a foundation. What happens then is very strange: there is an increase in your awareness, and your mind, not your eyes, recognizes that the mallets which the men use are very oddly shaped and that the sounds they make when they strike the pylons are also unexpected. Then, suddenly startled, you see that one man at some distance, half hidden by the fog, uses the naked body of a ten-year-old child to drive the stake into the ground. Your mind is reeling; your eyes dart from one man to the next. One by one you see that the whole army of men is using the bodies of children as mallets, swinging them through the air, raising them above, and bringing them down in a fall.'

"'The "polarity of work" is for us less an abstract idea and more a matter of perception. The crippledness of people that we have been discussing, the fact that the vast majority grew up like plants cramped into dark, small spaces and are, therefore, half withered and half rotten, and for the most part sadly disproportioned, became steadily more convincing and more detailed. In no way did it seem to be a way in which we chose to see the world. We could not help but recognize that they suffered and, indeed, were in this way misshapen. The damage done to them was as visible as that done on the enormous field of fog.'

"'There was no new insight, no unexpected or amazing element; only the connections to what we have been discussing became ever stronger and more clear. Ask once more: How are people shaped by their work? Now think of the coolie pushing his rickshaw and picture how that would change his back and thighs. Recall the peasants who pulled barges thousands of miles up the Yellow River, or read about the immigrants who built the railroad across the Donner Pass and find out how many of them died that winter? Visit an automobile assembly line where people perform the exact same set of motions for the duration of their employment—perhaps gunning four rivets into the muffler belt of each passing car. Try to imagine how going through exactly the same handful of gestures for 40 or 50 years—from age 20 till 65—would form one's muscles and one's mind? Has it occurred to you that there is incomparably more diversity and novelty to a life in prison than there is to serving such a sentence on an assembly line?'

"'Your job system has caused millions and millions to die—more than the world's concentration camps, more than the Gulags, and not only in coal mines, or sweatshops, or cotton fields. In our view the job system just as surely killed those dead from malnutrition or under the category of infant mortality rates, or those who could not defend themselves against the bacteria and the cold of an inner-city shelter.'

"'Earlier I described the attitude of many people toward technology. Certainly I could have been more qualified or more nuanced, but there is no doubt that many display a negative reflex reaction with a flourish. We maintain that they do this only because their bland and sentimental picture of work gets in the way. That picture hides the one decisive high step forward that technology has brought within our reach. If they saw how many kinds of work—that of salesclerks, of secretaries, of newspaper sellers, of ticket takers, of waiters—how many more?—use human bodies to drive stakes into the ground, they they would cry out that these kinds of work must be abolished! And that could transform technology: it could be turned into the means to this compelling and glorious goal. The fear and disgust it has inspired might then fade, for technology might turn into the clumsy giant on whose shoulders we could ride.'

"'It gives us comfort,' the host said with a smile, 'that this goal has already been translated into one of our comprehensive large-scale programs. The W.T.M. action which filled the valley with picnickers is part of it. But having technology take over ever-greater proportions of stupefying and debilitating work is only half. The other half is our hope that assisting people into work for which they have a passion, and which then becomes their pursuit, will transfigure them and will fulfill the ancient promise to make humans more complete and glorious and ripe.'"